NERUDA

An Intimate Biography

The Texas Pan American Series

VOLODIA TEITELBOIM

NERUDA

AN INTIMATE BIOGRAPHY

Translated by Beverly J. DeLong-Tonelli

University of Texas Press, Austin

Copyright © 1991 by the University of Texas Press
All rights reserved
Printed in the United States of America

Translation of *Neruda,* 2d ed. (Madrid: Ediciones Michay, 1985). Copyright © 1984 by Ediciones Michay, S.A.

First Edition, 1991

Requests for permission to reproduce material from this work should be sent to Permissions, University of Texas Press, Box 7819, Austin, Texas 78713-7819.

∞ The paper used in this publication meets the minimum requirements of American National Standard for Information Sciences—Permanence of Paper for Printed Library Materials, ANSI Z39.48-1984.

The Texas Pan American Series is published with the assistance of a revolving publication fund established by the Pan American Sulphur Company.

Library of Congress Cataloging-in-Publication Data

Teitelboim, Volodia, 1916–
    [Neruda. English]
    Neruda : an intimate biography / by Volodia Teitelboim ; translated by
Beverly J. DeLong-Tonelli. — 1st ed.
        p.   cm. — (The Texas Pan American series)
    Translation of: Neruda.
    Includes index.
    ISBN 0-292-75548-1 (alk. paper)
    1. Neruda, Pablo, 1904–1973—Biography.   2. Poets, Chilean—20th century—
Biography.   I. Title.   II. Series.
PQ8097N4Z8713   1991
861—dc20
    [B]   90-27605
                                                                                      CIP

Contents

Translator's Foreword   xi

Preliminary Note   xv

Part One. FROM RAIN TO WAR

I. *Frontier Boy*

1. Visiting His Mother   3
2. Farewell to Parral   6
3. Return   9
4. A Camp City   14
5. His "Momother"   17
6. The Brusque Father   19
7. I Don't Know How or When . . .   20
8. A Dream?   23
9. Childhood Friends   25
10. The First Poet   26
11. The Ostrich   28
12. A Boy Knocks on Gabriela's Door   29
13. Stammering Poet   31
14. Boy and Pianos   32
15. His Brother's Birthday   33
16. Beginnings   35
17. Prose Writer of Necessity?   38

II. *Twilight Youth*

18. The Crazy Twenties   41
19. Unamuno and Patriotism's Stockholders   43
20. Boardinghouses and Tenements   45
21. Maruri and Twilights   47
22. Why "Neruda"?   49
23. The Student   50
24. Friendship and Bohemia   53
25. Flown Away   55
26. Pablo de Rokha   58
27. The Girl from Temuco   62
28. Women and Their Poems   66
29. Incandescent Pollen   69
30. A Tomb for Birds   73
31. The Girl from Santiago   75
32. A Strange Violator of Secrets   79
33. Love and Poetry   84
34. The Verse Changes: The Woman Remains the Same   89
35. Letters as Confession and Anguish   92
36. The Period of the Sturgeon-thin Poet   96
37. Farewell   100
38. Crisis in Bohemia   104
39. The Lazy Man Who Works Like a Factory   106
40. Writers and Elephants   108
41. To the Islands   110
42. Departure   112

III. *Anguish and Creation in the Orient*

43. Pressures from Afar   116
44. Responsibilities in Batavia   119
45. Family Letters   122
46. Vigils and Dreams on the Crossing   124
47. Solitude in Burma   126
48. Ambitions and Desires   129
49. Messages from a Castaway   133
50. Doubts in Rangoon   138
51. Realism in *Residence*   141
52. Letters from the Orient   144
53. Solemn Communique   147
54. Return to "Maligna"   150

IV. *Writing in the School of Hard Knocks*

55.	The Poet and the Mask	154
56.	Song of Songs?	156
57.	Two-man Bullfight	158
58.	Arrival at the Main Office	163
59.	Two Unique Consuls	166
60.	Misfortunes	168
61.	"Ant" or "Neighbor"?	172
62.	Dogs and Poets	177
63.	A Warm Welcome	178
64.	Affinities	181
65.	Controversies	184
66.	Rectification	187
67.	The Polemic over the *Anthology* and Tagore's *Gardener*	190
68.	A Heavyweight Fighter	194
69.	On the Eve . . .	197
70.	Execution in Viznar	200
71.	Why the Change?	203
72.	The Book on Spain	207
73.	The Poet in the Street and a Femme Fatale	210
74.	Literary Passions	216
75.	President of Intellectuals	219
76.	Water of Life and Death	221

Part Two. PASSION AND DEATH

V. *His Discovery of America*

77.	Accursed Cities	227
78.	Elections in Chile	230
79.	Houses	231
80.	Operation "Salvage"	233
81.	The *Winnipeg* Adventure Continues	236
82.	Reflection of the Spanish Experience	240
83.	Repentance	243
84.	Magical and Violent Country	243
85.	Mexican Miscellany	247
86.	Battles, Serenades, and Slashes	252
87.	Ascent to Origins	256
88.	Personal and Extrapersonal Meaning of Machu Picchu	259

89. Four Journeys   263
90. An Unusual Speech   266
91. Congressional Debut   270
92. The Problem of Time   275
93. The Honorable Mr. Reyes Praises Lucila Godoy Alcayaga   277
94. Pro Memoria   278
95. Strange Waltz   281
96. The Great Somersault   285
97. The Poet Accuses   289
98. Clandestine Life   292
99. Looking for a Way Out   296
100. Preparations in the Forest   299
101. Toward the Ends of the Earth   301

VI. *The World Voyage*

102. Saint Martin of Free Men   305
103. The Charge to Publish the *General Song*   306
104. Parisian Debut   308
105. Europe Makes a Discovery   311
106. The Wind of the Old New World   313
107. Farewell to the Senate   314
108. Encounter with Pushkin   316
109. The Verse Underlined by a Young Suicide   321
110. Love and Phlebitis   325
111. Conversation with Exiles   328
112. Italian Interlude   331
113. The Two-headed Woman   336
114. Polygamy and Disinformation   338
115. Welcome at Home   341
116. The Intellectuals Gather   343
117. Joy and Sadness of Sofré the Bird   347
118. Tales and Tallies   348
119. The Prize Adventure   350
120. Donations, Foundations, and Equivocations   351

VII. *Narrator of Himself*

121. Fifty Hurrahs and Two Condemnations   355
122. Houses and Women   358
123. The Breakup   360
124. The Invisible Man Makes an Appearance   362

125. The War of Less Than a Hundred Years   **364**
126. Exchanging Titles   **367**
127. Neruda Yes, Neruda No   **369**
128. Clear Days and Cloudy Ones   **372**
129. Sebastiana and Wine Pitchers   **375**
130. The Party Man   **377**
131. Epistles   **378**
132. A Forgotten Heroine   **381**
133. Earthquake in His Childhood Land   **381**
134. History's Bearded Men   **382**
135. The Joking Bird   **384**
136. Outlines   **386**
137. Airy and Earthly Poetry   **387**
138. Mysterious Simultaneity of Ideas   **388**
139. Three-dimensional Man   **390**
140. With the Turk and the Spaniard   **391**
141. Civil Registry Official   **393**
142. The Burden of Fame   **394**
143. Summing Up and Self-analysis   **395**
144. His Companion William Shakespeare   **398**
145. Feet Blue with Cold   **399**
146. The Book of the Bountiful Table   **400**
147. Kites   **401**
148. The Impersonator   **402**
149. Paparazzi Ire at the Nuptial Hour   **403**
150. The Mythical Bandit   **404**
151. Jorge Sanhueza   **407**
152. Real Birds and Riddle Birds   **408**
153. The House with the Blue Flag   **409**
154. The Lilt of the Barcarole   **410**
155. The Mapuche *Trutruca* Horn and the Troubadour   **411**
156. The Shell Collector   **412**
157. A Bit of Philosophy   **413**
158. Standard Bearer   **415**
159. An Unusual Campaign   **418**
160. A Deaf Old Man with an Accordion   **420**
161. The Poet and His Century   **421**
162. Interdisciplinary Madmen   **422**
163. The City of the Caesars   **423**
164. Stones, Wait for Me!   **424**
165. Midnight Speech and Morning Conversation   **425**

VIII. *The Song of the Ancient Mariner*

166. Upsetting News   **433**
167. The Swedish Decision   **435**
168. Flashbulb Time   **438**
169. Jubilation at Home   **439**
170. Red Corpuscles   **440**
171. Revelation   **442**
172. A Castle in the Air   **443**
173. Futurism's Sister   **446**
174. The Albatross Country   **446**
175. Projects and Relapses   **447**
176. Araucanian Stone   **451**
177. The Cantalao Dream   **455**
178. Tapestries of the Poor   **456**
179. Revised Dedications   **457**
180. On Alert   **458**
181. The Overcoat   **459**
182. Posthumous Work   **461**
183. Memoirs and Manuscripts   **465**
184. Farewell   **466**
185. Death in the Midst of Death   **467**
186. The Errant Coffin   **470**
187. Unwelcome Visitors   **472**
188. The Cortege   **475**
189. Until We Meet Again!   **478**
190. It So Happens I Will Live On   **479**
191. Postscript of 12 July 1984   **482**
192. Six Months Later   **483**

Notes   **487**

Index of Names   **493**

Translator's Foreword

The interface between artistic and socio-political activity is a pronounced feature of contemporary Latin American culture, hence it should come as no surprise that both the author and the subject of this book have been fervent participants in the literature and politics of twentieth-century Chile. It was poetry that brought Volodia Teitelboim and Pablo Neruda together as young men in Santiago, and it was as writers and political activists that they remained comrades and confidants for forty years, until Neruda's death in 1973, just two years after he received the Nobel Prize for literature and less than two weeks after the violent overthrow of Salvador Allende's Popular Unity government.

Teitelboim, who was a senator in that Allende government, never had any intention of writing a biography of Neruda, although he had published numerous articles and essays about the poet. Nonetheless, at the insistence of a Madrid publisher, he accepted the challenge of doing a book about the author whose own *Memoirs* had already been published. "My book," he says, "offers the perspective of someone who was very near to Neruda, but at the same time is capable of a historical distance denied to the individual who is talking about his own life." That perspective is apparent in Teitelboim's attempt to rescue Neruda from the pedestal of myth and allow him to again walk the streets of the world he loved so much.

Drawing on his own talents as an acclaimed novelist, Teitelboim has given us a biography that reads like a novel, presenting an intimate look at the poet and his work, from his humble childhood in what was then a frontier land in the south of Chile, through his bohemian youth as an impoverished university student in Santiago, his lonely existence in Southeast Asian consular outposts, his joyous discovery of Spain and his lifelong devotion to poetry, love, Chile and politics, ending with his unquiet death in 1973.

Volodia Teitelboim was born in 1916 in Chillán, in the Chilean province of Ñuble. His university studies took him to Santiago, where he studied law, wrote poetry, read voraciously in several languages, and became active in journalism and politics. His first book, a historical study of the dawn of capitalism and the conquest of America, was published in 1943.

From 1947 to 1952, repressive measures by the González Videla government against leftist political figures forced Teitelboim and others, including Neruda, to go into hiding, and ultimately he was imprisoned in the Pisagua concentration camp. This same period saw the publication of two of his novels, *Hijo del salitre* (Nitrate's Child) in 1952, deemed a masterpiece among historical novels, and *La semilla en la arena* (Seed in the Sand) in 1957 (titled simply *Pisagua* in later editions). Both novels have been translated to more than six European languages.

In the following decades, Teitelboim gained prominence as one of the left's leading theoreticians and also served as Valparaíso's representative in congress and as Santiago's senator, a post he held until the military junta which masterminded the 1973 coup d'état stripped him of his Chilean citizenship and forced him into an exile that lasted for sixteen years. During that exile, he published his third novel, *La guerra interna* (Internal War) in 1979, critically hailed as an extraordinarily ambitious work which demonstrates the forces of continuity at work over a forty-year period of Chilean history, culminating in the violence unleashed in 1973. It has also been published in German, Bulgarian, and Russian translations.

During his exile, which ended only in 1989 with a popular vote rebuffing General Augusto Pinochet's efforts to remain in power for an additional ten years, Teitelboim served as executive editor of the cultural journal *Araucaria de Chile* (Madrid) and wrote extensively on literary, historical and political themes, not only in scores of articles, collections of essays, and his biography of Neruda, first published in 1984, but also in an account of a secret trip he made to Chile in 1987 (*En el país prohibido: Sin el permiso de Pinochet,* In the Forbidden Country: Without Pinochet's Permission), as well as in a comparative study of Latin American and Russian/

Soviet literature (*El corazón escrito,* The Written Heart), published in 1986 in Moscow. His biography of Chile's first Nobel Prize poet, Gabriela Mistral, has just been published in Chile.

I should like to express my appreciation here to my friend and colleague Jack Schmitt, who first called my attention to this book and has generously offered his support and suggestions throughout.

In addition, it is a privilege to express my gratitude to Volodia Teitelboim for his constant collaboration and encouragement, not only from the outset of this project but most especially during my visit with him in Santiago in March 1989, shortly after he had finally been granted permission to return to his own country—a return still fraught with anxiety and insecurity in that precarious period, which only intensifies my appreciation for his generous availability.

I should also like to express my thanks to Inés Moreno in Santiago, Carlos Orellana in Madrid, and Claudio Teitelboim in Princeton; and to gratefully acknowledge support for this project from California State University, Long Beach, with special thanks to Karl W. E. Anatol, Dean of Humanities and now University Provost, and to the University's Scholarly and Creative Activity Committee.

And ultimately, my thanks to Franco Tonelli for tolerating and encouraging my sometimes frustrated but always optimistic attempts to stroke two languages and two cultures into an implausible but necessary coupling.

Beverly J. DeLong-Tonelli
Laguna Beach, California

Preliminary Note

This manuscript includes two types of end notes: those which appear in the Spanish edition and are almost without exception of a strictly bibliographical nature, and those termed "Translator's Notes." The first group are signaled in the manuscript text with conventional superscript numbers. The second group are signaled in the text with superscripted lowercase letters.

All translations of quotations within the text are my own.

Beverly J. DeLong-Tonelli

Part One
FROM RAIN TO WAR

I.

Frontier Boy

1. Visiting His Mother

As we enter the house, almost in ruins, there's a certain emotional tension. I prepare myself to observe the observer. Neruda has come in search of the unknown story of his mother, who died a few weeks after giving birth to him. I want to see and somehow feel his experience. I'm aware of the distance between the "I" and the third person. The first person touches; the third person is at the other extreme or hovers around a neutral point. I sense the contradiction between the trembling interior of the man who inquires about his mother and his restrained exterior, that appearance of calm in the heavyset mature man who has just arrived by car, the orphaned infant from the past, now transformed into a celebrity.

An old neighbor who had known the dead woman soon appeared. She doesn't quite know how to address this famous man who is coming to look for memories, descriptions, sayings, anecdotes—in short, anything to do with his mother, of whom he has no recollection at all. She goes off and returns in a few minutes, carrying in her hand a sepia-colored picture, more accurately a daguerreotype. There she is, Rosa Neftalí Basoalto. She hands it to the expectant man.

For the first time he is faced with a photograph of his mother. Later, in answer to a question from a professor, he will explain that this is the only known picture of her. It was reproduced years later, in 1980, to illustrate a book entitled *El río invisible* (The Invisible River), which includes the poetry and prose written in his adolescence and early youth.

In that book, he dedicates two poems to the mother he never knew. The first is titled simply "Moon":

When I was born my mother was dying
with the sanctity of a spirit.
Her body was transparent. Beneath
her flesh was an orb of stars.
She died. And I was born.
And so I bear
an unseen river in my veins,
an invincible song of twilight
that kindles my laughter and chills it.[1]

The second one he calls "Humble Verses to Put My Mother at Rest":

Dear mother, I've come too late to kiss you
and have your pure hands bless me;
your lighted passage was already fading
and had begun to return to earth.
You asked for little in this world, dear mother.
Perhaps this bunch of misty violets
is too much for your sweet hand
that never asked for even one.

Ingenuous poetry of a beginner, yes, but not devoid of sincerity. It's not the first conversation he has envisaged with his mother. The novelty is in the fact that here the imaginary dialogue is put into print.

The photo shows her in almost full figure. He thinks of the devastating illness that killed her so soon, plunging her into oblivion. For a long time he studies that likeness in silence, then hands the photograph to Matilde. After several minutes, she gives it to me. I look at it eagerly. On the back, someone had written a now-faded inscription in old-fashioned, careful penmanship, "Neftalí Basoalto Opazo de Reyes, mother of Pablo Neruda." She gave her baby the baptismal name Neftalí at birth. I study her features and look at her son out of the corner of my eye. It's not hard to see the resemblance. Similar facial lines. Uneven eyebrows arched over heavily lidded eyes with small pupils, suggesting a bit of a questioning look or a hint of apprehension. The nose is prominent, with that curved line of country people accustomed to smelling the change of seasons and discovering—as her son would say—secluded birds' nests. Is there anything to suggest that this woman might be looking at the abyss or that she might suspect she was about to fall into its darkness? We don't know. In appearance, her expression gives off radiance, with nothing to suggest any falseness that would hide what she might be feeling. But there's something in her look of the dreamer or the sickly. In that face you can see a struggle. The mouth is large, with lips that reveal at the least an attachment to life, if not sensuality. The chin is strong, without being exaggerated. Long earrings, dark and round like ripe cherries, hang from her earlobes. A sculpted, meticulous hairdo, typical of the period, with waves that fall lightly over the wide forehead. The silver-worked brooch stands out against the dark background of the dress, which might seem to be a fore-boding of mourning if it weren't for the coquettish lace on the sleeves. Her large hand is curved over the straight back of the embossed leather chair. Looking into the enigmatic camera is a tall, thin woman attempting in this one second to freeze her image forever. It's conceivable that she suspects or fears that her life is a question of days or hours. Perhaps this will be the only message that she leaves to the world and to her son, pos-sibly bringing to mind a sentence of St. Augustine that he read and under-lined in the book loaned to him by the church: "Eternity is only the total possession of oneself in a single, unique moment."

That face in the portrait, with its alert expression, seems to be that of a human being who is eager to cling to life. But in that duel between light and shadow, which is etched on the yellowing cardboard, a fearful spark flickers.

Neruda took the photograph again. He needed to engrave her image within himself. He wanted to know if she had an expression of peace or of anguish. He doubtless saw both.

The picture was apparently taken in this very house and in this very room where we are now. Even then, in 1904, it shows the sweating walls, the spots of humidity, and the poorly made plaster. It reveals no furniture other than the little bit of the chair back.

We go out to the small patio where she used to spend hours reading, sometimes looking at the sky to see if rain was coming, and watering the plants that still grow there in disorder. His mother's friend, who serves as the poet's guide to lead him through his small tour of acquaintance with Rosa Neftalí, expressly informs him, almost underlining the fact, that his mother used to read books. She emphasizes that "She adored poetry, and she would bury herself in reading, like someone who's on a ship being borne to a faraway place!"

Neruda spent a long time trying to reconstruct the intimate features of that woman. He asked several times about her character and her tastes. About any phrases she used to repeat, about words she liked. What other person might be able to tell him something else about her? He needs that photograph. The lady gives it to him as a gift. Isn't he the one who should have it? Moved, he looks around the humble dwelling. He surveys the abandoned and unfurnished dusty provincial house where he was born. It's all a rusty key that opens his beginnings. This man who collected antique keys all his life will put this one in the pocket of his memory, since he can't take it away with him. All that remains of the maternal fountain is in this house, and though it isn't much, he is pleased to learn that she assiduously kept in touch with the printed word.

That neighbor offers him details that he partially knows. At the outset of his mother's career, she was a country school teacher. In 1900, she began work as a primary teacher in the Parral Girls' School No. 2. She wasn't so very young when she married; according to the ideas of those times, when Rosa Neftalí Basoalto married José del Carmen Reyes in 1903, she was already prepared to spend her life dressing religious statues in the church. The marriage train had left her behind. She was almost without hope . . . until the moment when she unexpectedly caught the last car. But she paid dearly for it. She was thirty-eight years old, born in 1865, daughter of Buenaventura Basoalto and Tomasa Opazo. The newlyweds, so soon to be parted by death, went to live in the house that we are visiting now, on San Diego Street between Unión and Urrutia.

She had her son when she was already thirty-nine years old. Her death certificate, No. 1454, records an almost immediate date: 14 September 1904, two months and two days after the boy's birth.

Matilde says almost nothing. I walk around the patio, which I think must be almost the same as on that long-ago 12 July 1904, birthdate of the baby whose arrival in the world cost his consumptive mother her life. The crowning blow was probably delivered by puerperal fever, which in those days used to kill as many women as tuberculosis. Women died and men were born. The death-birth linkage was a common event in that period and that environment.

2. Farewell to Parral

When the baby's mother dies, his paternal grandfather, José Angel Reyes Hermosilla, takes him into his home. He is cared for by his step-grandmother, Encarnación Parada, the grandfather's second wife. The baby's father was from his first marriage. Doña "Encarna" searched among the estate's farm wives for a young woman still nursing her own child. As wet nurse she picked María Luisa Leiva, wife of Estanislao León, who had plenty of milk for her own child and another. The motherless child grew strong, although he was somewhat spindly.

Not only the earth was fertile, for Neruda's paternal grandfather has fourteen recognized children. How many "orphans" is not known, nor even if he exercised his *droit du seigneur* as owner of the "Belén" estate, which wasn't all that impressive. With his first wife, Natalia Morales Hermosilla, he had just one offspring, José del Carmen, father of the child who was left motherless. He had the other thirteen with Encarnación Parada. Several were baptized with biblical names: Abdías, Amós, Oseas, Joel. . . .

During Belén's long days the grandfather used to talk expansively and affectionately with the boy, but he was also given to reading out loud with a sermonizing voice. The boy would listen without understanding what he was hearing.

"Abdías got his name because I didn't want him to be haughty or gloat over the misfortunes and sorrows of his brothers and sisters.

"I named your uncle Amós because I didn't want him to be a city man but rather a shepherd and a sensible man, one of those who know that horses can't gallop on rocks and you can't plow the sea with oxen."

With Oseas, God was more severe: "Go and take to yourself a fornicating woman," the grandfather would say, reading the "Book" with a stern expression and pointing ahead with his index finger—*fornicating woman*. "I don't understand, Grandfather." A woman who misbehaves, who goes with men who are not her husband. And the command is that the sons fight with their mother, be angry with her for the things she does. God threatened her with making her like the day she was born, in other words, naked, and leaving her like a desert, like dry land, and you know that dry land dies of thirst.

"And Uncle Joel, Grandpa, why is that his name?"

"To wake up the drunks, and there are a lot of drunks on this earth. Let the drunks awake and weep. Let all who drink wine like fishes mourn. Because I will take the grape juice from their mouth. I have a vineyard, but its purpose is not to make men crazy. Joel talks that way in the 'Book.'"

His grandfather read with enthusiasm, as if reciting: "Animals of the field, fear not; for the pastures of the desert will turn green again. . . ." He even survived to a biblical age, dying in 1939, after outliving his son José del Carmen.

The young widower was far from being a businessman. Some plots of grapes, with which the region's esteemed juices were made, weren't sufficient to get him out of financial straits. Nonetheless, he was a hard-working man. During the year that he was able to have with his wife, he didn't live as a "schoolmarm's husband," in spite of being married to a delicate teacher. Between the two of them they managed to meet their expenses. But in Chile, teaching was among the worst paid of professions. Sometimes her salary was held up for months before being paid.

The twentieth century had not brought happiness to the nation nor well-being to people without wealth. That year of 1904 was uneventful except for earthquakes and repressive actions against workers in the big northern cities.

Don José del Carmen belongs to a family of proud impoverished noblemen, in a country where "Don" precedes the name even of those who don't have money but who merit respect. He was left with a newborn son whom he would entrust to the care of his better-situated father. And he would join the army of wandering Chileans in search of work. He crossed the cordillera of the Andes trying to find economic relief in Argentina. He returned empty-handed, turned into a Chilean migrant. Should he move north, like so many from this area, taken in by the preachings of labor recruiters who sign up workers in the town squares by talking of nitrate as if it were the new Golden Fleece? He is a man of green fields, from the central part. Rather than looking toward the North he turns his eyes to the South. The desert isn't for him—he prefers the forests and the rain. In those days, a trip of 60 miles was a long one. He relocates between 120 and 180 miles to the south. He will change from being a broke, small farmer to being a simple paid laborer, which is a sign of moral courage and a challenge to prejudice, a laborer on the Talcahuano Dam project.

There, he bears his sorrow without tears, telling no one his pain. But he feels like getting away, going—going far away. They again insist that the promised land is in the nitrate fields, but he looks toward the opposite horizon, toward old Araucanía, that region where the Spanish conquistadors and Mapuche Indians fought a war that lasted more than three centuries. Now they call it New Araucanía, the conquered land. Just as they speak of the Far West in the United States, here they speak of "The Frontier," because in both, civil conflict is resolved in favor of whoever has the most up-to-date rifle. And so the dam worker pulls up stakes to become a traveler who arrives in Temuco in a horse-drawn coach, similar to the stagecoaches that would begin to appear in Western movies. One day, he packs up his young son and takes him with him to this recently settled town. There's not much luggage, but it holds a photograph with a notation on the back: Neftalí Reyes Basoalto. Villa Prat. October 13, 1906.

The boy in the picture is delicate-looking, two years old, with a sad expression. A sort of white cape or long bib hangs over his shoulders, covering his chest. A pleated light-gray robe, with little starched cuffs, covers him to the knees. Below, black trousers and shoes buttoned on the sides. Like his mother in her photo, his left hand rests on the shiny black chair with its carved legs. His outfit indicates that, in spite of the springtime photo, the child is carefully wrapped up, so that what happened to his mother won't happen to him.

The other photo, the one of her, stayed in Parral. His late wife may have written poetry, but none of her verses have been found. If she wrote any, they are doubtless lost forever, which doesn't matter to her widower. Poetry is for daydreaming women.

What the father does take along is an official document from the Linares diocese: "I certify that the following declaration of baptism number 1033 is recorded on page 269 of baptismal book 39. In the Parral parish of San José on the twenty-sixth of September nineteen hundred four, holy oil was administered to Ricardo Elisier [*sic*], two months and twelve days of age, legitimate son of José del Carmen Reyes and Rosa Neftalí Basoalto; baptized by Father San Martín; godparents in attendance, Manuel Ijido Basoalto and Beatriz Basoalto; sworn by me. José Manuel Ortega." There is a signature of the parish priest and the seal. Even earlier, the first of August 1904, the baby had been registered in the Civil Registry with the name of Ricardo Eliecer Neftalí Reyes Basoalto.

That was his farewell to Parral.

3. Return

I accompany him on his return to his birthplace, with his shoulders mantled in fame. Nonetheless, I see no glorification of him. No stupefied crowds come out to cheer the hero. Except for relatives, a few friends, and the inevitable regional poets who invite him to a clubhouse with sagging armchairs and a grayish atmosphere, nobody seems excited by the arrival of that Parralian who had conquered the world (in the words of one purple prose journalist). Near indifference. And something more definite:

the irritation of the old estate owners, the unenlightened aristocracy of rural winemakers. We should add one fact that explains the half-disdainful, half-hostile reception extended to the poet. Not only are they not interested in poetry and could care less about literature, but they also despise the political affiliation of their countryman.

Pablo's comment to me: "I've never seen so many pests in one place." But he is grateful for the poor people's recognition of him as one of their own, who makes them feel proud.

That night in the social club some bottles are uncorked, probably filled with some variation of those juices that his father had cultivated.

We're staying in the house that belongs to his uncle, José Angel Reyes Parada, a man with fine Latin American features, a thick mustache and an air of country dignity. He and his wife wait on their nephew and his wife and the politician who is with them, demonstrating that friendly, loving hospitality still maintained in small towns and old villages in this country, a kind of heart-felt courtesy. Don José Angel is proud of the soil. "I'm a Los Alamos farmer," he offers as his calling card. His second joy is his own fertility. "I have nine children and thirteen grandchildren." His wife, a beautiful woman, Matilde Mora, gives a proud nod. "Pablo's father," he continues, "was the last Reyes Morales in the family. The rest of us are Reyes Parada. When the boy's mother died," he refers to Neruda, "we brought him to my house. My mother raised him. We were living on Libertad Street. As I've told you, we were playmates until he was six. He used to spend days with his paternal grandfather in a place called Belén, near Parral, which reminds me of Christ in Bethlehem." Pablo listens to him in surprise. That uncle, José Angel Reyes Parada, only four or five years older than himself, is revealing new things to him. Now he can perhaps conclude that he was six years old when he went to live in Temuco. His uncle is a man who works with animals. The nephew, when he was barely twenty, had written a short novel, *El habitante y su esperanza* (The Inhabitant and His Hope), with Russian influences, in which galloping horse thieves engaged in violent love affairs and quarrels. Now he is reminded of those rustlers and suspects that his uncle, who travels so easily through the narrow passes of the cordillera, perhaps on occasion uses some tricks of the smuggling trade. He looks at his childhood playmate, scrutinizing him so closely as to be examining his veins. Maybe he found something he had been looking for.

Only the youngest son of the family, a cousin of Pablo who's around twenty years old and resembles the poet as he looked in the days of *Crepusculario* (Book of Twilights) or *Veinte poemas de amor y una canción deses-*

perada (Twenty Love Poems and a Song of Despair), seems to be pleasantly confused by the presence of such a famous yet simple relative, whom he doesn't quite know how to treat but whose self-effacing expressions make him laugh and ask questions about that unknown world in which his cousin has moved about.

The next morning, there's a rather challenging visit to the Parral Girls' School. All the students are lined up in the patio, and then they go into the gymnasium to listen to this half-bald man, who was born in the same region and writes poems about love and other things.

I always admired Neruda's gift for feeling at home anywhere. He takes a little book out of his pocket and for twenty minutes reads poems that everybody can understand and that go right to the heart of young people.

It's true that Dante was persecuted in his lifetime and exiled from his home town, forbidden ever to return to Florence; but once he was dead, that city claimed for itself the glory of having been the birthplace of the author of *The Divine Comedy*, while other cities in Italy challenged that claim. In Neruda's case, Parral didn't seem concerned by the fact that a man who divided people politically had been born there. Matilde was smiling, and I was learning a little about applied political science.

Years later, I saw the vindication of the poet, who was declared a prophet in his own land. For that to happen, Parral had to have a change in political parties and a Socialist mayor—Enrique Astorga, owner of "La Florida" estate. That day, a Sunday, 26 November 1967, oil mixed with vinegar and day joined night, as the people all joined together in two celebrations: the Official Rodeo and the proclamation of Pablo Neruda as "Illustrious Son of Parral," the first time the city government had ever given such an honor. Everybody joined in. The holiday had really started the day before, Saturday, with *huaso* cowboys on Chilean saddles and wearing authentic ponchos, firemen in scarlet uniforms and shiny helmets, boy scouts, schools, the Red Cross, teachers, journalists, labor unions, priests, attorneys. *Campesinos* without horses were there, too. A procession, so to speak, of the lowly and the mighty, of pawns and knights. The day was warm, and the poet, wearing a clear eyeshade and dark sunglasses, headed it all up, with Matilde at his side, chatting with Jimena Pereira, the mayor's wife.

"How much agreement did you have in naming him 'Illustrious Son?'" I ask. "Unanimous," the mayor answers.

The Parral Municipal Theater is packed. Enrique Astorga, a rare Socialist landowner, slender as wheat, prematurely gray, not only adores beautiful women but also is apparently capable of feeling passion for poetry. Parral's history encompasses two hundred years, he says, and the book of homage remained empty all that time, waiting until finally the name of Pablo Neruda could be inscribed in it. It's not easy, he adds, for a plain man to talk about a man from the mountain top, but emotion can't be measured for elevation, and the people are here, from city districts, from towns, from fields, as well as the children and our Chilean cowboys.[2] Neruda always refused to be alone on occasions of public recognition. He used to celebrate his birthdays *en masse,* and for his ten-year birthdays he would invite friends from all over the world. On that occasion, as well, he organized the gathering on a large scale. I always marveled at the expansiveness by telephone, telegram, and correspondence with which he invited people from 3,000 or 6,000 or 12,000 miles away, to conferences, lunches, celebrations, all as if he were inviting a neighbor or someone from across town to dinner. The most surprising thing is that those invited from faraway places usually came. This time, the celebrations were attended by rich and poor from Parral, local people and foreigners, some from quite distant countries, including a member of the Soviet Union's Central Committee of the Communist Party, Anatoli Tchernigov; the Moscow Latin American Institute's scientific collaborator, Igor Ribalkin; and a minister from the Supreme Soviet, Georgui Sheeko. At the lunch on Sunday the 26th at the Catillo hot springs, several Rumanian guests also took part, including Stefan Andrei who would later become his country's foreign minister, and Mijail Florescu. Everything is combined in a kind of whirlwind where the world and the village, the sounds of many languages and clinking glasses still can't drown out the shy request from a Boys' School teacher, who is also treasurer of the Rodeo committee, as he asks that the distinguished visitors write greetings for the children. Neruda clears off a bit of space on the table, puts on his glasses, takes out his pen, and in green ink writes, "Parral, 25 November 1967. To the boys of the school. Good morning!! The important things in life are the 'Good Mornings.' They are the unit with which human beings communicate hope. The hope of our little lives, and of our neighbors' lives, which ARE MORE IMPORTANT, which are all-important. We live in order to be ourselves and then to understand others, the others who are more important than us! GOOD MORNING!"

Francisco Coloane is nearly six feet tall. He stands up with his fleshy gigantic body, his lionlike head, and his startled child's eyes. He has already been named National Prizewinner for Literature, and he is speaking in his capacity as president of the Chilean Writers Society. His voice is somewhat thunderous, but softened by a benevolence you could almost touch. Poetry and spontaneity are hidden within his prose and his speeches, to which he devotes himself with the enthusiasm of the self-taught. He is overwhelmed by a Nerudian image—the one that refers to the "electric hazel tree." He can no longer look at the southern forests without being struck by the tree's magnetic brilliance, by that spark that it never had before. The poet's eye captures virgin materials and gives off sparks and splendor. The "electric hazel tree" has already dropped its leaves on music, ballet, song, and theater, he says, a bit overcome in his oratory. But there is something else that is super-dazzling for him—the lady of the house. He invents a dream image to tell her about it. "When I was a boy, I dreamed of a woman, and it was you." Listening to him, one of the guests, Miguel Otero Silva, exclaims, "You devil, you've copied my dream!"

Otero, novelist and old comrade of Neruda, came from Caracas for that day when the poet's home town, after half a century, smiled on him apologetically, following several rebuffs and dirty looks. Otero was presented on the stage of the theater as a Venezuelan senator and publisher of *El Nacional* newspaper, but his most important credential on that occasion was his friendship with the poet, about whom he recounted several unpublished anecdotes.

That night there was a Chilean-style party at the mayor's estate. María Maluenda offered a reading. Parral seemed to have changed: the new judge, Alberto Rubio, is a poet, and a good one. The director of public works reads an acrostic, "To Parral's Neruda," and he, too, is no spur-of-the-moment writer, having published biographical articles about Neruda in the regional newspapers.

Neruda took philosophically and in good humor this "Parralization." He granted that this time the city was receiving him affectionately, but without knowing him very well. After all, he had spent his life in other places, but in Parral, he recalled, his mother is buried and the Reyes family goes on growing. "So far," he winks, "no other Reyes poet has come forth."

The house we visited was later destroyed by an earthquake. I don't know whether it was ever rebuilt.

When Neruda is asked about Parral, his modest reply has the feel of a poem from *Residencia en la tierra* (Residence on Earth): "I remember very little. I was taken away from here as a very small boy." He says it next to the crackling bonfire of the native barbecue. This recollection of his infancy, along with that of his early boyhood astonishment at seeing the Malleco Viaduct, has as a backdrop the Chilean *cueca* folk dance. "You have once again accepted me like an itinerant offspring."

4. A Camp City

Two years after the death of Neruda's mother, José del Carmen Reyes will marry Trinidad Candia Marverde. Her second family name is poetic. Though others claim its correct form is Malverde, it's obvious that she had nothing to do with "mal" ("bad"). She is the poet's good *mamadre* ("momother") seven times over. She is in fact a Marverde ("green sea") from Parral, but she's also linked to Temuco, where she has dozens of relatives.

How do those destinies come to be joined? At this point, the son of a North American couple living in Chile comes in—Carlos Masson, a businessman in Parral who was a friend and companion of José del Carmen Reyes. In Parral, Masson had met and married Micaela Candia Marverde. Since Parral didn't offer a great business future to an enterprising young man, he moved, probably in 1903, to Temuco, that burgeoning town where everything seemed open to the future—people were coming to settle in that empty space offered by the recently cleared rain forest and the dispossessed Indians. The main line of the railroad had already been built when he opened first a bakery and then a hotel near the station. Micaela brought her sister, Trinidad, to Temuco. Masson didn't forget his Parral companion, and when he learned that Reyes had been widowed and, even worse, that he had no steady job, he proposed that he move to Temuco to work with him in the bakery. Thus, the depressed and penniless José del Carmen went to Temuco. Once there, it was not at all surprising that he would marry Masson's sister-in-law. Ricardo Neftalí (later Neruda) continued living with his grandparents, in Parral or in Belén. Exactly when his father brought him to Temuco to live isn't completely clear, but everything seems to indicate that it was not any later than 1910, though the boy would still return to his grandparents' home to spend some summers. Carlos Masson sold the bakery on the corner of Matta and Lautaro to his old comrade, and later its owner became Raúl Reyes Toledo, the poet's nephew.

Is Temuco a city or a military camp transformed into a town? As recently as 1887, the two provinces of Malleco and Cautín had been created, to oversee the white domination of the last aboriginal strongholds.

Later, in the period that follows the colonization of Cautín province, the little boy will be taken there. The central government in Santiago still hasn't forgotten certain dangers—not only the Indians but also the attempt by Orélie-Antoine I, that crazy-looking Frenchman who had himself crowned king of Araucanía, possibly suggesting something more than just a picturesque inoffensive madness. After all, Napoleon III put Maximilian on the throne of Mexico! It's the period of conquest and railroads. Francisco Kindermann orders the manager of his hacienda in Santo Tomás to buy from the Mapuches all the fields that he thinks are promising. In those days, a future colleague of Neruda, Vicente Pérez Rosales, consumed and exhausted by the California gold fever, but still moved by an adventuresome spirit that now gets on track, acts as agent for European colonization, bringing German workers and craftsmen. But one intermediate zone between Concepción and the Gulf of Reloncaví still hasn't been subjugated—Araucanía. Politicians of the Independence period will exalt the Mapuches as symbols of emancipation. Neruda will do the same thing by singing of Caupolicán and Lautaro.

The slaughter has been extensive. A Chilean Custer, Colonel Cornelio Saavedra Rodríguez, is a military expert in clearing territory by violent means. This didn't stop him from claiming that he hadn't spilled one drop of blood and that good treatment had been shown to all, both "Indians and civilized Chileans." The conquest was taken up again in 1868, after the conflict with Spain. Halted again in 1870, it had penetrated into indigenous lands with blood and fire, grabbing 1,160,000 hectares of fertile land. Like a Spanish conquistador, the Chilean emulator established forts that were transformed into towns, like Mulchén, Negrete, Angol, Collipulli, Lebu, Cañete, Toltén. Several came back again as forts. They had had their first incarnation in the times of the Spanish Conquest. The fires of war were still burning on the frontier, and the white army knew defeat and disaster. In the battles of Coipue, Traiguén, Centinela, Muraco, Collipulli, commanders got their practical training for the 1879–1883 Pacific War against Perú and Bolivia.

Before and right after the Pacific War, total war was launched against the Araucanians. It had already lasted, sporadically, for more than three centuries.

Back in the sixteenth century, when someone in the court in Madrid was looked on with disfavor or was about to fall on misfortune, they would tell him, "Look out or you'll be sent to Chile." Chile was the most remote place in the world; Lope de Vega called it "Ultima Thule." That Indian field of Flanders inspired *La Araucana*, published in 1569. Juan de

Guzmán, an oracle of the period, proclaimed its author, Ercilla, a new Homer. And Vicente Espinel in his *Casa de la memoria* said:

> Fort Arauco's courage is released
> by Alonso de Ercilla's hand,
> torn down and raised up again,
> defeated and honored in defeat.

Ercilla, in the prologue to the second edition, explains that "the Araucanos deserve every honor, because for more than thirty years they have maintained their position without ever having put down their weapons."

The young boy arrives in this area when the long struggle has just come to an end, and Temuco is still just a village. Neruda remembers that the first houses were beginning to be built and the land was being distributed to people as they arrived. On the outskirts were the forests and fields where the Mapuche Indians (the Araucanos of yore) lived.

When he was awarded the Nobel Prize, a French journal, *L'Express,* asked him about his first school, among other things. His answer contains a picture of the ambiance. Yes, he went to public school, where his classmates' names were German, English, French, Norwegian, Sephardic, and of course Chilean, or rather Spanish. Nevertheless, that infant society had its own particularities: in that first period, it was a world without classes. We were all equal, Neruda affirms. The stratification into classes came later, when some began to get rich. In that early phase, in his opinion, Temuco was sort of a great popular democracy, where everyone had work. Landlords and big landowners didn't exist. When they ask him about the Indians, Neruda responds that they lived entirely separate. Driven from their lands at the end of the last century, the Mapuches didn't live in Temuco proper, but in the surrounding fields. A hut here and there another, several miles away. They used to go to the city to sell their goods: wool, eggs, textiles, lambs. In the evening, they would go back to their huts, men on horseback, women on foot. There was no communication with them. "We didn't know their language, outside of a few words. Nor did they speak Spanish; even today, they speak it poorly."

In the face of such explanations, the obviously surprised journalist persists and reminds him that despite all that, his poetry has been characterized by the presence of the Indians. "That's true," answers Neruda. "I have kept the feeling for history which is a bit like the conscience of the people. The biggest battle of the Araucanía was at Temuco. The Spanish conquistadors were searching for gold, gold, gold. But they couldn't succeed with the Araucanian Indians, not only because they were poor but also because no other Indian people in America fought the Spanish with such ferocity. It's a fact too often forgotten," he adds.

In my final conversation with Neruda, I heard him speak of the Indians. To his mind, the governments of Chile have always hidden the truth with respect to the Indian question. They even try to minimize their number, saying that fifty or sixty thousand remain, while in reality there are half a million or more, forming an ethnic minority with their own language—in his opinion one of the most beautiful in the world—their own traditions, their own culture.

5. His "Momother"

He often said that the principal personage in his early childhood was the rain. In the South, it's common to hear that cities have two stations—one for trains and one for winter.[a]

Mud personified the dark enemy, the ogre that made it hard to walk in the unpaved streets. The fundamental material was wood. The forest was everywhere, in castlelike stacks of planks, sawmills, carpenters working the handsaw and the plane. Clouds of sawdust spread the smell of freshly cut trees through the air. The wooden houses were spacious and primitive, but their galvanized roofs didn't entirely prevent the rain from entering. And if the sound of rain was the piano of Neruda's infancy, its maddening notes were the drips that filtered through the roof, falling into pails, wash basins, pans, chamber pots, spittoons. There wasn't enough in the way of receptacles to catch all the raindrops. The most unimaginable containers were put to use. The monochord artillery of the drip-drip that fell incessantly had to hit the mark, otherwise the whole house would be flooded.

Another specter, a crimson one, threatened the town and almost always attacked in darkness: fire. At night everybody would awake terrified by a single cry: "Fire!" The town of planks was almost as combustible as fuel oil, and entire city blocks were often devoured in the blink of an eye. Improvised firemen, along with the entire town, would try to contain the hungry flames. Unceasing rain and frequent fires painted the landscape of his childhood. The boy observed everything. More than anything else, he was afraid of fire when they were at home alone without his father, who had got work on the railroad, thanks to the Masson Candia Hotel, we might say, for that establishment was a gathering place for railroad personnel. There José del Carmen Reyes became friends with several company officials who helped him get the job.

He usually slept on the train. Toward the end of his life, he was a conductor, not on passenger trains but on ballast trains, those that carried rocks, sand, and other materials to hold fast the wooden ties of the rail bed, constantly under attack from torrential rains. His shifts would last for days, thus the train was his father's second, or first, home, where he had a coach to sleep in. The greatest joy of Neruda's childhood was to go out with his father on the ballast train and spend a few days surrounded by the forest, discovering flowers, beetles, the life of the woods.

We were like nomads with nothing to do, he remembers. And so he would explore nature, her rivers and mountains. He didn't know then that on those trips on the ballast train with his father he was gathering material for his poetry. On those outings, when he would bed down at night in the rail car, he used to miss his mother, for he needed hugs that his father didn't give him but were lavished on him by his mother, rather his "momother." He never liked the word for "stepmother," *madrastra*. For him, she was tenderness itself, a truly marvelous woman. Perhaps in order to do away with the cruel stepmother of children's stories, out of love for this loving woman, he invented the word *"mamadre."* He dedicated his first attempt at poetry to her, when he was seven or eight years old, and when he read it to his parents, unmindful that they were busy, his father asked, "Where did you copy that from?" He would later recall, "And that's when I received my first inattentive demonstration of literary criticism." Doña Trinidad didn't act as a critic; she didn't have the heart for that, and the boy realized it. That's why he always refused to use the term "step-mother" to refer to that woman he considered the guiding angel of his early years. Diligent and sweet, with a country sense of humor, active and untiring goodness—those are the characteristics attributed to her by her grateful stepson.

Later, when he was ten, on Doña Trinidad's birthday, he wrote her a message in which the poet was struggling to come forth: "For you, beloved mama, I chose this humble card / so you could see / a landscape of golden scenes / Neftalí," rhyming "Neftalí" with "see." And for the moment, that was sufficient for the budding poet. In later years, he improved. "Sweet *mamadre*—I never could call you 'stepmother'"—he says to her in the poem dedicated to her. For him she was "goodness dressed in poor, dark cloth, the most useful saintliness—that of water and flour." She was synonymous with the bread he ate, the struggle against winter, against the leaks that flooded the house. She was the good soul who portioned out their scarcity, their poverty, so that all those who depended on her humble mothering could be kept afloat. And it was all done with an expression that made it seem "as if you had been / distributing / a river of gems." He sees her shod in noisy wood-soled shoes, like those worn by the unassuming women of that period in those regions, yet trying not to make too much noise, organizing everything to deal with the damage from the wind, the collapse of the roof, the toppling of walls. The wind would howl like a puma, and there was Doña Trinidad Candia Marverde, "sweet like the shy coolness / of the sun in stormy lands, / like a shining lantern," showing them the way. The Nerudian symbol is obvious: the mother became bread for the children, bread which is parceled out by the same hands that cut up flour sacks to make his underwear in his boyhood. She did what mothers have done for centuries: cook, wash, iron, cool the fever of a sick child. Sow a plot of land, and sow life and an approach to life in her children. She did it all in silence. It came from inside her, her duty, her maternal vocation. And when the children were grown and making their own way in the world, then his "momother" went off "to the little coffin / where suddenly she had nothing to do / under the cruel rains of Temuco."[3]

6. The Brusque Father

Neruda scholars have established the contrast between the images of his "momother" and his father. Some go even further, carrying the interpretation into history and psychoanalysis. When they talk about Diego de Almagro and about the rapacious conquistadors who plunge into physical possession of unknown lands, someone will always liken this attitude of the former Spanish swineherd with rape of the mother, transforming it into a tellurian symbol. And they manage to deduce that somehow Neruda unconsciously likens the image of the father to the vision of the violent conquistador.

These interpretations are based on isolated expressions that might bring a certain appearance of probability to the picture, but they are carried to an extreme that destroys their veracity. His relationship with his father was more complex: a mixture of fear and tenderness, of distance and compassion. In fact, he talks about his brusque father, especially in *Memorial de Isla Negra* (Notes from Isla Negra). The man's way of announcing his presence was appropriate to his profession: the piercing whistle of the locomotive. Shortly afterward, the door would shudder, and when his father entered, "the house / would shake; / the startled doors / would rattle with a sharp / crack like gunshots; / the stairs would moan, / and a loud hostile voice / would start to scold." This is the gruff side of his father, his nocturnal face.

In the next stanza, the poet openly says, "nevertheless, he was a man of daylight," to be seen in his entirety, as captain of his train, in motion at the crack of dawn. The sun barely up, one makes out his beard, the railroad signal flags, the station lanterns, the engine coal. His father was working at his job—a railroad man. "The railroad man is a dryland sailor, / and in the little fleetless ports / —towns in the forest—, the train races on / setting wilderness free, / steady ahead on its terrestrial course."[4]

This hard man was cordial, fond of being at a table full of friends. There, fraternity won out, as thick glasses sparkling with wine rang against each other in toasts. They say that when he didn't have anyone to share lunch or dinner with, he used to stand in his doorway and invite the first passerby to chat over bread and wine. His son inherited this custom, which perhaps came from many generations back. He couldn't conceive of an empty table. He wanted it to be a meeting place for masculine camaraderie and full glasses.

We spoke earlier of compassion. Neruda felt admiration and sympathy for his father's difficult job. His whole life, like that of many men, was a chain of coming home in order to leave in a hurry, getting up at dawn and wearing himself out in a kind of perpetual serving, until "one day with more rain than usual / José del Carmen Reyes, conductor / boarded the train of death and so far hasn't returned."

7. I Don't Know How or When . . .

Naturally, the man was already present in the boy. Aunts proverbially recall with authority the infancy of their nieces and nephews. This boy—they said—looked weak, but he had a will of iron. His first poems earned him some blows, but the whippings didn't stop him from getting where he wanted to go.

In 1910, he enters the Temuco Boys' Lyceum. The boy who sits next to him, Gilberto Concha Riffo, is four years older, which is a lot at that age. This feeling of being the littlest guy in school—in a period when the minimum age for enrollment wasn't strictly enforced—later turned into the sensation of being the youngest. "I was always the youngest, and now I'm sixty years old," he told me ruefully on his sixtieth birthday.

But the bigger boy doesn't bother the smallest nor anybody else.

Gilberto is a quiet one, not like a stone but like a tree, perhaps a *coihue* beech. He's from Almagro, a little town near Nueva Imperial, where his family owns a mill. During classes, talking isn't allowed, which is fine for Gilberto, but little Ricardo Reyes is simply inattentive. His mind is on the ballast train, on the forest beetles, the tiny partridge eggs, the "snake mother" insect, and the tough-guy Monje, a scar-faced railroader who works with his father and takes the boy to learn the secrets of birds' nests and the mysteries of the forest. As it happens, in arithmetic class, he has a graph-paper notebook and instead of numbers he doodles whatever comes to his mind. He draws a fine, black line and says to his neighbor, "Gilberto, take away that little hair that's fallen on this page." The boy tries to clean off the page, and Ricardo laughs. They leave the school and amble slowly through the muddy streets, observing everything. When they get to the Reyes house, frozen and often soaked, Doña Trinidad towels them off and gives them dry clothes. She gives them a snack, gently apologizing to Gilberto, who will get his coffee black because Ricardo is supposed to have his with milk, and "there's not enough for both of you," she explains. Little Ricardo's health is more delicate.

In time, Gilberto will be known as Juvencio Valle, and Ricardo Eliecer Reyes will be known as Pablo Neruda, both of them poets from the south of Chile, both of them winners of the National Prize for Literature. It can be said they were friends from the beginning. Juvencio is a quiet man, but not taciturn. He speaks out especially when justice must be defended. Then his voice thunders and he turns into a giant. It's his way—whenever he's had to fight for truth, for decency, never for himself but for the rights of all, Juvencio—that almost speechless Gilberto who sat next to Ricardo in school—has been one of the most honorable. He's the one who fell for the joke about the hair in the notebook that belonged to the boy who was drawing in class and dreaming of adventures on the ballast train. When they were both great men, Neruda renamed his friend with a slight twist on his literary pseudonym, calling him "Juvencio the Silent" or "Silent Valley."

Neruda, when he was older, in response to an inevitable question, said he didn't know how it was that poetry came looking for him. "I don't know where it came from. I don't even know when." Juvencio Valle, the poet who was his companion in childhood games and shenanigans, perhaps didn't know that he himself was or would be a poet, but on the other hand he knew for a fact that the younger boy definitely was one. He immediately detected clues in the quiet slender child, with his melancholy reserve and yet something in his eye that was the opposite of inertia and indifference. He noticed the intensity with which the boy experienced his surroundings. He was astounded by the small, unashamedly wide-open eyes. I, too, have noticed this wide-eyed phenomenon, which is important. Once I asked him in all candor, "How could you discover so many secrets in the trees, the birds, the stones, in all the world of nature?" He was sixty years old when he gave me this answer, "It's a way of seeing." Is one born with that way of seeing? No doubt about it, according to Juvencio Valle's observation about the child Neftalí Ricardo Reyes. But it's also a training of the eye, a kind of respect for the subject, an unabiding profound interest in things, their texture, their shape, the interpretation of their inner world. I remember that Vicente Huidobro always said that stones have guts. Neruda discovered in things their faces and their guts.

That capacity to observe things' interiors, which was also a tendency to explore the inner human being, must surely be accompanied by an external sign that reveals the messenger. What is a poet for a little boy like him? Maybe a man with a cape and wide-brimmed hat, worn by European artists in the nineteenth century. Juvencio recalls that one day as they were walking together in Temuco after school, ahead of them he saw an eccentric fellow who was dressed like someone out of *La Bohème* and he commented, "What a weird guy!" Pablo looked with seriousness at the man and pointed out, with an unforgettable certainty, that the man in front of them was an individual who had a wonderful profession, "He's a poet!" It should probably be added that he wasn't seeing visions of any halo, but was rather talking about someone known to him. It was his uncle, Orlando Masson, editor of the *La Mañana* newspaper.

Neruda's self-awareness of being a poet comes to him at an early age and a bit later in Juvencio, who explains that:

> Poetry unquestionably is born with the man. This unexplainable fervor comes lodged in us within our human glands. My acquaintance with Neruda goes back to a very young age, and from that early period, when no visible sign could possibly have foretold the future powerful poet, I already felt he had a special uniqueness, an imperceptible vibrancy, a style that belonged only to him and made him different. A feeling which didn't exist for the ordinary observer, but for me, yes, as an actual, real potentiality. I believe that all of that was poetry. I passed over a lot of other kids and gravitated toward him to become his friend. That mysterious inner halo of his pulled me toward him and made me feel good in his company. While our classmates ran around together in groups, jumping about and shouting, we would spend the day looking at the world's little things, a leaf, an

insect, any old track at all. Poetry was silently working away in that beautiful friendship.[5]

Both Neruda and Juvencio, without attempting to, will later suggest a psychological study of the child-poet as one who comes to literature and art as compensation for a childhood feeling of physical inferiority in a world of physical competition. Juvencio reacts against the idea of anything of the abnormal in the child-poet, as he discusses childhood games and acts of violence. He clearly points out, "We were not serious or deep kids. Our childhood was a natural one. We were excitable and enthusiastic." But they never won in any shouting matches, and in a race, "Even the lame boys would beat us. So we could only take refuge in our own private corner, that marvelous world of dreams, where we were always first and therefore unchallenged champions."

Neruda confirms this vision of his childhood. In the acorn-throwing battles, in which he always took part, he also always lost, because he would stand there looking at the lovely flight of acorns in a green, polished arc, like a marvel of nature. And in the midst of this stupefied ponderation, the acorn would come down on his head not at all like a work of art but like a bullet. And nobody who hasn't felt that blow can know how much an acorn barrage can hurt.

8. A Dream?

He thought he had dreamed it. A childhood dream? He didn't know exactly how old he could have been. This time it wasn't a trip on the ballast train, but on the night train. A special event. He ate chicken and rolled meat, like many other passengers. All the trainmen—the engineer, the conductor—knew his father. He heard them talking. A bottle of wine made its appearance. They asked him questions. No, they weren't going to Santiago. Nor to Concepción. To tell the truth, he didn't know where they were going. But his dad had urgent business. He liked the train, even if third class didn't have green velvet, or red, or any other color velvet. He enjoyed the clickety-clack, the restful monotony of the rails, the train that said over and over, "Eliecer Ricardo, Eliecer Ricardo, Eliecer Ricardo. . . ." His father's friends were smoking Joutards. He saw twilight fall and swallow up the countryside. When night erased all outside images, he concentrated on what was happening in the coach. Someone, a blind man, began to sing a tango. One of his father's friends whistled along. He got sleepy. "It's the strangeness of traveling," the whistler explains. "No," the child proudly says, "I'm always traveling." His father assents, "He's my ballast train partner. A railroader's son. A chip off the old block." The boy knows his Sunday suit is wrinkled, but he's a seasoned traveler. He'll have to stay awake. He blows his breath on the windowpane and then runs his finger over the steamed glass to write his initials. He has just learned to read and write, ahead of other children. He blows his breath again, as his father says, "We're pulling in."

His nostrils flare; his mouth feels wet. Is it nerves? He's anxious to get off the train. "Who's waiting for us at the station?" he asks. "Nobody," answers his father. He peers through the lights toward the platform. Not true; an old acquaintance is waiting—the rain. It's pouring cats and dogs in San Rosendo. A crowd in that cold station, run-down but busy, where one catches the train to Santiago. You can take refuge in a little restaurant where they sell fast foods and potato sandwiches for a snack. But his father doesn't take him to the restaurant. Besides, he's not hungry. He's just sleepy, sleepy in this dream of the nighttime trip from rain to rain. They get drenched walking a couple of blocks, which seems like a long way to him. But why, when he's walked all his life in the rain? Maybe because he's sleepy and cold, and his shoes are soaked. His father stops at a door. A flickering lamp lights a sign with white letters on a black background: *Pensión*. He notices that his father takes a key from his pocket and opens that door, like somebody going into his own house or some piece of property that belongs to him. A tall blue-eyed woman with a shawl around her neck appears. She's younger than his mother. Instead of greeting the boy, she runs her hand over his shirt and says, "He's soaked." "Like a mud hen," murmurs his father, who has merely nodded to the tall woman. She strokes the boy's neck, rubs his wet head. She looks him up and down. "Come on, I'm going to change your clothes," she says, taking him by the hand. She sits him down, undressed, on a chair and wraps him in a sheet. She comes back with a nightgown which he doesn't want to put on. "It's for a woman," he objects. "Don't be silly," she reproaches. She speaks a language that to him is strangely defined, harsh and loud. But if I'm naked, why do I notice the way the lady talks, he wonders, as she struggles to pull the nightgown over his head. The hardest part is to put on the sleeves. She gets it on him by force, as if she were dragging him by the ear. He puts up a terrific fight, but in retreat. He ceases all opposition when he hears her say that male youngsters as well as female youngsters use those gowns for sleeping. "Male youngsters and female youngsters." Why doesn't she say "boys and girls?"

Then she takes him by the hand and leads him to a bedroom nearby. His dad follows. There are two beds. In one, a little girl, much younger than he, is asleep. She's wearing a nightgown just like the one the strange-talking lady has just forced onto him. The girl has long eyelashes. In the big bed she looks like a tiny black-headed bird in a white cage. Only her head and the top of her shoulders are visible. She chews on the sheet in her sleep, one hand uncovered. The rain patters on the window. Someone is knocking insistently on the door. The lady goes to answer. The girl's fingernails are bitten down. He doesn't want to get in bed. The lady is slow in returning.

The boy takes advantage of her absence to tell his father, "She doesn't talk like a Chilean." He answers, "She's Catalunyan." Catalunyan? What can "Catalunyan" mean?

When the woman returns to the warm bedroom, she says, "Tonight you will sleep in the same room with your little sister. Take good care of her."

He looks at his father, who says nothing. But next day, the three of them, including his little sister, set out for Temuco. He would always wonder, was it a dream? But he never asked his father, nor his *mamadre*, nor even Laurita, his only sister.

9. *Childhood Friends*

On his sixtieth birthday, he recounted that a week before he had invited some old classmates from the Temuco Boys' Lyceum to have lunch at his home in Santiago—Alejandro Serani, Vicente Cid and Alberto Aracena. They weren't the three musketeers, but they grew up together in the South and entered the University of Chile together. "If it weren't for Serani," confesses the poet, "I never would have graduated, because he always did my algebra problems for me, since I could never learn the multiplication tables." This fact finds some reflection in his work, where abstract logic doesn't fit in with his physical, earthy poetry, which doesn't mesh with the world of numbers.

After half a century, when he meets up with these Temuco companions, Neruda inevitably notices the effects of time, which has written a different biography for each one. But it was a joyful reunion, almost as happy as the day way back then in 1918 when they formed a football club in Temuco, a club so small that they called it the "Little Club."

Another of his Temuco friends, the writer Diego Muñoz, recalls that they first met when both were first-year students in the Lyceum. Diego, a live-in student, was in First Year B; Neruda, a day student, was in First Year A. The latter is pictured as very thin, very serious, with an absent-minded expression, arriving late for classes. That skinny faraway semblance leads Diego to deduce that Pablo was already a poet. Maybe he had other written clues. The frail poet was fascinated by adventure. They would hide away in the "Little Stairway," where the beardless students would cleanse their honor with bare fists. They were visitors to the Cautín River, robbers of fruit from the Lyceum acreage, travelers of the whole length of the traintracks, frequenters of the neighboring fields, and experts on every detail of Ñielol Hill. They would say that there they did their homework, gathering from the earth material for their collections of herbs and insects.

This land, with the rain and the mud as its central characters, nurtured in his generation several poets who were Neruda's schoolmates. He used to play football with them. Even worse than he at sports was Norberto Pinilla, who would be a teacher of Spanish who worked in the University of Chile's Pedagogical Institute and wrote on Chilean literature and poetry. The other classmate-poet was a boy with a long angular face, Gerardo Seguel. The son of an evangelical preacher, he received his normal-school teaching credential and later, in Santiago, wrote poems recalling the Toltén River. He was one of the first Communist intellectuals in the country. While a member of the Party's Central Committee, he published several works investigating the roots of Chilean literature in the old colonial chroniclers: one about Ercilla, another about Pineda y Bascuñán. He published a book of poetry, *Horizonte despierto*. During the González Videla dictatorship, he was killed by a truck. Once the three boyhood horsemen had ridden to Pillanlelbún.

10. The First Poet

It has been said that Neruda was a precocious reader and at the same time slow and poor at numbers. Possibly the legend has distorted the facts. González Vera swears that when they used to hand a book upside-down to young Neruda, he would read it straight through. He adds that he used to do sums with all kinds of figures, very rapidly, without bothering about exactness. Adding, perhaps; multiplying, no. They say that when he was going over some papers in Isla Negra, with his spectacles riding on the end of his nose, he asks his sister, "Hey, Laurita, how much is five times eight?" Laura Reyes looks at him with pity, as if he were a dull pupil in the Technical School where she's an examiner. She shakes her head, faced with someone who has asked her the same question many times before, and answers with saintly resignation, "Good heavens, Pablo! Forty." This anecdote demonstrates that if Neruda didn't know how to multiply and lacked any kind of mathematical ability, there was always someone nearby who could fill that gap. Pocket calculators were not yet in use. The poet might have solved the problem if he had had a musical one. Because the music in his poetry eventually turned out to be extremely profitable, multiplying loaves and pesos.

A mythical character already mentioned, his uncle Orlando Masson, the first poet that he knew in his life, was also the first social combatant that he came across. In his childhood he admired him as a complete man. He was a rebel. He had a newspaper where he battled for justice and denounced abuses, mentioning by name those who were unjust. The response was the last fire that Neruda saw in Temuco, when that clarion of justice burned down. Fires in the city were usually intentional. Either some bankrupt debtor would hope to escape his debts by setting fire to the business, or the flames would spring forth from the vengeance of the powerful who felt injured, as was the case with the fire that reduced *La Mañana* to ashes. The flames erupted under the protection of darkness to hide the face of the arsonist.

The young boy took that fire like a personal affront, for it had been in that newspaper that he published his first essay and his beginner's poems. There he imitated the typesetters, his fingers got stained with ink, and he came to know the acid smell of antimony. He was also sorrowed by the death of that press whose rebellious owner had edited the first book of poetry published in all the southern territory. Its theme was the same one that later would stir the publisher's nephew. The book was called *Flores de Arauco*. Direct rebellious poetry. Afterwards, in India, he heard similar works by poets who would recite melopoeias or monologues in the streets. He also saw it years later in the Soviet Union, where recitation is a passion and an art, in which the poet also participates as actor. His uncle's own public readings used to have a devoted following. In the boy's house they would help the performer prepare for his recital of a particularly moving poem, "The Beggar," by ripping up his clothing in spectacular fashion. Then they'd sew it up again, darning it if necessary, for him to recite another very successful poem, "The Artist," which didn't require that the mending be perfect. And if they didn't have enough time it didn't matter, since it was all covered up by the big poetic cape. His uncle en-

courages the inclinations of that thin pale nephew who has a special aptitude for writing, and the day of his thirteenth birthday, the boy gives the
editor an article titled "Enthusiasm and Perseverance," whose tone and
positive direction could very well justify its being the newspaper's editorial
column. His uncle proudly publishes it. In order to "persevere in enthusiasm it becomes necessary to use the experience of humanity and its great
historical figures."

Aside from his poet-uncle, nobody seems to attach any importance
to what the young apprentice writes. Among the family he goes on being
Neftalí Ricardo Eliecer Reyes. He is nicknamed "Shinbone," perhaps because in those days he was as thin as a leg of that starved, pale, and other-
worldly Gandhi. That was his most lasting nickname. And of the three
baptismal names that he had, they chose to call him by the biblical one,
Neftalí, taken from the Book of Books, like those of his paternal uncles
Amós, Oseas, Joel, and Abdías.

11. *The Ostrich*

Neruda says he doesn't like Buffalo Bill because he kills Indians, but
he admires him as a good horse racer. He consumes books by the hundred,
as he would do later as a young man in the solitude of the Orient. In
Temuco he jumps unsystematically from adventure books to Vargas Vila,
and to carry the chaos to extremes, his eyes go from Strindberg to Felipe
Trigo, from the tormented Scandinavian to the at-that-time pornographic
Spaniard; from the intellectual Encyclopedist Diderot to Maxim Gorky,
the nomadic traveler of Russia's steppes among downtrodden men and
revolutionaries. He trembles at the misfortunes of Jean Valjean, the sorrows of Cosette and the loves of Marius in *Les Misérables*. A thirteen-year-
old romantic, he sighs over the pages of Bernardin de Saint-Pierre. It was
a truly dazzling banquet: "The sack of human wisdom had broken open
and was being gleaned in the night of Temuco. Reading, I didn't sleep
or eat."

He was an ostrich that swallowed books. He devoured all the
printed words that were put in front of him. Naturally, Salgari and Jules
Verne. Then, all the books that his uncle Orlando Masson had in his
house. Next, those in the Lyceum library. He read the *Quixote* in an edition
given him by Juvencio Valle. His reading was somewhat guided by his
French teacher, the poet Ernesto Torrealba, a fan of Russian literature who
loaned him several books by Gorky. He gave him a warning, or rather a

bit of advice: "If you want to write, don't study 'Spanish,' because you won't be able to get away from the lessons." He gave him works by Rimbaud and Baudelaire. The boy read not only French literature, but also English. He liked to translate poems from both languages. He translated some lines from English and showed them to his teacher, who looked at him in silence and somewhat taken aback. Neruda tore the paper to pieces, but the teacher began to put the sheet back together. Before he could complete that puzzle, the boy had rewritten the poem. He also had a rubber stamp made with the name Neftalí Reyes, and with it he stamped the sheets on which he would copy and sometimes translate poems by Verlaine, Sully-Prudhomme (he used to recite from memory in French "La Vase Brisée"), Paul Fort. It was a way to learn. Thus he began to take classes in school on European poetry.

12. *A Boy Knocks on Gabriela's Door*

Among the finest and sweetest friends I have known is Laurita Rodig. She was always a militant revolutionary as well as a painter and sculptor. One day when I was a young man, she determined to do a portrait of me and even attempted a sculpted head. Skeptical about the project, I thought that nothing of all that would come to fruition, but I used to willingly go to her studio on Monjitas Street when I finished work, for long sessions of stupendous conversation. She was a very good friend of Gabriela Mistral, and had at one time lived with her in Magallanes and in Temuco. She accompanied her once on a trip to Mexico, and the poet dedicates to her the poem "To the Thinker of Rodin" in the book *Desolación* ("With chin resting on his rough hand, / the Thinker remembers that he is / flesh for the bone pit").

Back from Mexico where she made contact with the muralists, with Rivera, Orozco, Siqueiros, having fallen under the influence of that experience and convinced that that was the kind of painting that should be done at that time, Laura Rodig painted a large mural in a bookstore on Moneda Street. In it were represented the Chilean writers she considered most significant from the past and from the present. Naturally, Neruda stood out. He was shown in the foreground, just as he was at that time, a thirty-year-old man. Much later, in our sessions, while she did sketches I would ask her about certain events that she was personally acquainted with. She spoke beautifully and properly, with great discretion, and nothing seemed more alien to her than showy stories. When she was living with Gabriela Mistral in Temuco, she told me, among her duties was that of screening visitors for that lady, who was the Lyceum director. After 1914, when *Los sonetos de la muerte* (Sonnets on Death) received a prize in a Santiago literary competition, the poet-director was (to her misfortune) invested as high priestess and dispenser of literary grace. Handfuls or bands of male and female poets would come to her house, almost all of them quite young, with poems in their hands, to receive the Teacher's blessing. Since almost all were Lyceum pupils, she would receive them like a mother. She would listen to them, ask them questions, and look at their poems. One day a boy with olive skin arrived and asked Laurita for the director. She told him the *Maestra* wasn't in. He waited three hours without saying another word to the cool secretary, who in those days must have been just a bit over twenty years old and was a timid receptionist. The poet and his poetry went away very sad. But, since that boy didn't belong to the flock of sheep who give up easily, he came back the next day, timorously, with the notebook in his hand. Yes, Gabriela was home, but she couldn't receive him because she was ill with a splitting headache. The sallow-faced adolescent, in spite of his inhibition, couldn't hide the look of sorrow on his face. Laurita kindly asked him, "But what do you want, young man? Please tell me." "I've brought some poems," the small boy murmured, stammering. Laura Rodig thought to herself, "The same old thing. I've seen this before." But because she was courteous and perceived that that skinny boy was distressed, she said to him softly, "Can't you leave them with me? She will look at them when she has time." "Yes, I can leave them," answered the boy. "But I need to talk to her in any case. I want to know her opinion." "Okay, be patient, then. Come back in a few hours. Maybe . . ."

When the time had passed, the boy again banged on the door. He saw in front of him the woman who personified poetry. He bent over in a deep bow, something he wasn't accustomed to. She descended from her invisible throne and behaved like a loving mother, telling him, "I have fixed myself up to rèceive you. I was sick, but I began to read your poems and I've gotten better, because I am sure that here there is indeed a true poet." Then she added, "I have never made a statement like that ever before."

That friendship was never broken.

Long decades later, when Gabriela Mistral was already dead, on a visit to the University of the North, in Antofagasta, the little girls of the schools and the lycea were singing as Neruda passed by. His friend, Andrés Sabella, also known as the poet of Antofagasta, asked one of the girls, whom Neruda had patted on the head, "Are you singing for the greatest poet of Chile?" "No," the little girl answered, "for Mr. Neruda . . . ; the greatest poet of Chile is Gabriela Mistral." Neruda burst out in laughter, and patting the little child again, he said to Sabella, "I'll tell 'the old lady' that in the valley of Josafat . . . How much she'll enjoy it!"

13. *Stammering Poet*

He was filling up notebooks with copies of his poems written in his neat penmanship. The child poet Neftalí Reyes contributes to the Santiago journal *Corre Vuela,* which wasn't a literary publication but rather a widely circulated magazine with information and sections accessible to the masses. There was also a corner where provincial poetry found refuge, titled "Chilean Muse." Neruda begins to send in his poems, and sixteen are published there. He is a beginner who is determined not to remain unpublished. He sends contributions to several publications, and persists in taking part in literary competitions, from his earliest days. His poems appear in little student journals: *Cultural* in Valdivia, *Siempre* in Valparaíso, *Los Ratos Ilustrados,* published by the students of the Boys' Lyceum of Chillán, whenever they can manage it.

But what was he writing about? What was his idea of poetry? What was he reading in those days?

José Santos González Vera, in his book *When I Was a Boy,* recounts that when he saw Neruda for the first time, in Temuco, he was carrying a book by Jean Grave, *Dying Society and Anarchy.* The skinny poet believed that the world in which he lived was poorly constructed and it was necessary to change it by first enunciating a loud "NO." He felt himself to be an anarchist at sixteen years of age. He was so enthused by this book that he translated Jean Grave.

Early on, another facet of his personality reveals itself. He will never willfully be a poet who turns his back on the world. There is in him an unquenchable thirst for fellowship, which is manifested from his earliest boyhood. While his participation as a child is directed toward the formation of one of the smallest football clubs, later it tends toward the organization of groups of poets, like the Ateneo Literario of Temuco. When Gabriela Mistral, in 1920, is named director of the Girls' Lyceum in that city, the slender president of the Ateneo, poorly dressed in a dark suit and still half-twisted up in the "awful pronunciation" that is characteristic of the region's inhabitants, goes to offer her the title of "Honorary Member" of the Ateneo that he heads. The boy is timid, barely able to address that tall woman, wearing a long, severe dress, who not only came from snow-covered Punta Arenas but also came covered by the halo of poetry. He discovers that her face is like that of Monje the brakeman, minus the scars. She is a simple, big Chilean woman who looks at him with welcome in her greenish eyes; talks to him about Tolstoy, Dostoievski, and Chekhov, thus widening the furrow opened by his teacher, Torrealba; and loans him books by Russian authors who stamped upon him an indelible mark.

The Russians speak to him not only of literature; they give him lessons about how to write and also how to see the society in which he is living. They teach him to hear the call of everything that surrounds him. The result—at fourteen years of age he will be a social poet. At fifteen, he acts as a promoter and correspondent for the journal *Claridad* in the Temuco Lyceum. In him is reproduced an experience which is repeated in the collective sensibility of his own generation and in those which came later: baptism by the fire of politics is the essence of student unrest for each successive period. The poet, who publishes revealing poetry in *Claridad,* the journal of that period's revolutionary youth, also becomes very soon the editor of burning issues and is the author of the resounding "Challenges" published on the first page.

14. Boy and Pianos

When World War I breaks out, the boy is reading newspapers and is interested in what is happening in the world. In the Lyceum, two groups form: "allies" and "Germans." In the growing little city, full of Germanic, French, English, and other colonists, divisions are deep. Several young men go off to fight for the countries of their foreign parents.

At ten years of age, he was already a combatant in the war against dripping water leaks. He felt that the rain was an accomplice in his act of writing, and totally so. Once he said that "in order to write I needed the sweep of rain on the roof." He also needed the sound of the leaks, that poor, water-soaked piano of his infancy. He would tremble at the sound of his father's mournful train when it reached the Temuco station, but he also dreamed of a real piano. He hoped for one in the house, not only because of the status that came with saying "they have a piano," but also in order to listen to his aunts play a favorite waltz, "Over the Waves," to the beat of the rain. No Steinway or any other kind of piano ever came. The one that always came, punctually, with no need to buy it, was the piano of water leaks that played the same music for months at a time. The boy learned to discern that while the rain was falling into the pandemonium of containers distributed in various critical points of the house, each container responded with a different melody. No, the rain didn't have just one note; it was a background music that accompanied the poet as he wrote his first poems and went on forever saturating and giving rhythm to his poetry.

One Neruda scholar maintains that in his first poems the poet was cursing the rain and her child, the mud, which covered the streets like a swamp. Just as a skeptical and disillusioned Eça de Queiroz used to say about his own Portugal that it had one good thing, the fast train from the south that went to Paris, the only charm that Neruda found in Temuco was that the Rain lived there, the Rain that he was in love with. Let's compromise by saying that he had a contradictory love-hate relationship with the rain.

One professor, talking about the conflict between Neruda and the rain, illustrates it with an image in which he sees the teenager huddled on a bench by a door, scowling at the falling rain. Doubtless that's how it was. But at the same time, his poetry is full of references to that inevitable companion, without whom the muddy earth of his infancy would be inconceivable.

15. His Brother's Birthday

Is the gift of poetry written into the genetic code? If so, then the code is very peculiar. His father was suspicious of poetry and never became resigned to having a poet for a son. He wanted him to study a serious profession. He didn't like bohemians, clowns even if they were sad; he didn't like those who were crazy nor those who were lazy. And possibly he didn't want his son to be a railroader either, not seeing in the boy any inclination for it. He wanted him to be a doctor or dentist, an engineer or lawyer or teacher, but never a poet. That wasn't a profession. He could imagine somebody from the union, some machinist or fireman, introducing him— with a chuckle—as the father of a poet. It would be enough to die from shame. He reproached the boy more than once for dedicating himself to the ugly and lonely vice of writing poetry, which he called "little verses." He punished him severely. That is the origin of the pseudonym Pablo Neruda, which he adopted later, mainly in order to spare his father the dishonor of having a poet for a son.

Perhaps it was from Doña Rosa Neftalí Basoalto that he inherited his interest in reading and a certain delicateness of spirit. There are signs of this, although the fact isn't totally established. And the genetic code isn't quite so simplistic.

His sister Laura had nothing to do with poetry nor with literature. But Pablo was her brother and she adored him, just as she adored her younger brother, Rodolfo. Laurita's love for her brothers wasn't in the least related to any false reverence. She was a small woman of delicate physique, with an aquiline nose, fiercely independent, who could react with sharp claws to any attack against her brother, but who also told him, face-to-face, the truth, like a person incapable of speaking flattery. No, he was just her brother. She wasn't impressed by fame or the glories of this world. She loved him as much as Rodolfo. As representative of the family group, she dreamed of uniting her separated brothers. Why that distance? Life dug a trench between them, carrying them along very different roads. For Laurita, Pablo was her big brother, and that was enough, just as Rodolfo was her little brother, and that was also enough for her to love them equally, according to the law of the Reyes tribe.

The brothers almost never saw each other. Neruda loved Rodolfo; he saw in him a natural product of his family line, with many jobs and no success but a fondness for women, a trait that made Pablo proud. Rodolfo finally succeeded in settling down as a city employee. Years later, in retirement, he set up a small store in La Granja, where I used to see him when I was visiting the district on parliamentary business. Pablo used to talk to me with a certain admiration about his brother Rodolfo's several marriages. "Almost like Rudolph Valentino," I told him. "No, this Rudolph is much simpler," he answered me with a raised eyebrow. The younger brother, enormously proud, resisted paying homage to the older.

I had first met him one morning, in the poet's home in Santiago's Los Guindos neighborhood. Neruda introduced me to a man with a Spanish-Chilean air about him, calm, nice looking, unaffected. "This is my brother Rodolfo," he told me. I understood that the scene must not be disturbed by any exclamation. I just shook hands with him, murmuring the obligatory "pleased to meet you," and left them alone. They talked a little while standing in the garden, and soon Rodolfo left.

Some time later, Laurita, who was radiant because of her brothers' having come together—in which she was doubtless the prime mover—announced to me with a hand hiding her lips, like someone revealing a state secret, that Rodolfo's birthday would be celebrated at Los Guindos.

I've never seen the poet more worried about the details and the over-all festivities than in that announced party. It wouldn't be at night, but at lunchtime, as expressly requested by Rodolfo, according to Laurita. The expansive Nerudian table was set up at the entrance to the park next to the house, like in a scene from a Chekhov play. They say that as a child Neruda liked to drink water from a multicolored glass. On this occasion, they brought out Mexican glasses in blue, red, and green hues, not to drink water but wine. Neruda himself placed them on the table. He fidgeted about the china. He walked through the park picking flowers to put by each plate on the table, creating a contrast between the metal of the knives and the delicacy of the pansies and roses. Spring had come and it was a glorious day, because of the beauty of the day and because it would be the day of the great reconciliation. The birthday party was to begin at one o'clock. Among Pablo's friends, who were in the majority among the guests, there was a certain sympathetic expectation, a legitimate eagerness to witness that reunion of the two brothers. The clock struck one. Long minutes went by, and we all attributed the slight lack of punctuality to the classical Chilean custom of discrete tardiness. At 1:30, he still didn't arrive. We saw Laurita's tense face, her large nervous eyes. Some of us went out to stroll in the park and talk about something else to kill the waiting time. Two in the afternoon. Neruda went on finalizing a few details in his role as perfect host for his brother. At three, he gave up, without proclaiming his defeat. He clapped his hands and invited people to the table to celebrate *in absentia* his brother's birthday. Inside, he was certainly filled with sadness. He had failed in his invitation. The only thing he said, with a shrug, was "That Rodolfo . . ." Laurita jumped like a tigress and shouted sharply, "Why 'that Rodolfo'? He was always brighter than you. When you were a child, you were a dunce. . . ."

The Mexican glasses were quickly emptied. The mood seemed normal. The poet was chatting naturally. Only Laurita could not hide her disconsolation.

16. Beginnings

I have recounted on various occasions my own discovery of two thick unsealed envelopes on the long table in Neruda's Isla Negra home. The house was quiet. It was the favored time for siesta, one Sunday in winter. Intrigued, I began to look over the envelopes' contents. Handwritten notebooks of Laurita, where she used to prepare her school work. But on the back of the pages, poems written in a different handwriting, in the poet's penmanship, which had hardly changed at all, despite the passage of more than four decades. It was the poetry of the child, the adolescent. He himself says that his first poem was about four semirhymed words long. In these school pages there was an inevitable "Nocturno," published before he was fourteen years old. Naturally, the incipient poet is feeling his way.

In his uncle Orlando Masson's newspaper, which had "wild and violent people" as readers, the boy Neftalí Reyes rhymes "canciones" with "corazones," "ilusiones" with "rincones," "amor" with "rumor." It's not great poetry, although it does carry within itself a certain daring for such a pragmatic city.

The poems published in the journal *Corre Vuela* in Santiago, on 20 October and 25 December 1918, and on 5 and 12 February 1919, are not works of art, but they have the virtue of constituting the prenatal period of the poet.

Once, precisely in the prologue to *The Inhabitant and His Hope,* he maintained that he had a dramatic concept of life.

At fifteen, the poet writes "Simple Minutes" in free verse. When someone speculates that he has just read the Uruguayan poet Carlos Sabat Ercasty, he returns to rhyme.

He is satisfied that his first literary prize was just barely an extremely modest third place in the Floral Games of Cauquenes, very near his native Parral, awarded for the poem "Ideal Communion." The jury was composed of Aníbal Jara, Domingo Melfi, and Alberto Méndez Bravo. The first two, in time, will be famous journalists, Melfi becoming an introspective and philosophical scholar on Chile. Soon after comes a period of small prizes in succession, until in 1920 he wins First Prize in the Poetry Competition of the Spring Games in Temuco.

It has been said, quite rightly, that the foundation of all Nerudian poetry is autobiographical. The poem called "About My Life as a Student" shows in a precocious way this characteristic. In class, distracted, he hears feminine voices and drafts social rebellions. For the moment they are premonitions. "Lament of Sad Men" is a description of himself. His reiterative theme appears in "I Dreamed of You One Afternoon . . ."

The poet is aware that poetry can be made of his own life. Neruda, since he was a child, is inclined to celebrating in verse his own birthdays and those of relatives and friends. In his "Autobiographical Sensation," he writes "I was born sixteen years ago / in a faraway dusty white town that I still don't know." It's one of the first references to Parral in his poetry. The sense of personal affirmation of self appears very early: "Ah, I remember when I was ten / I mapped my path against all the dangers / that might conquer me along the way." And what were his goals in that period? To love a woman and write a book. He confesses his defeat with oblique self-irony: "I have not prevailed because the book / is handwritten and I loved not one but five or six."

In his sister's notebooks there are two book projects, with titles: *Strange Islands* and *Useless Exhaustions*. They were never published, but some of their poems were included in *Book of Twilights*, his first published work, in August 1923.

The year 1920 in Chile is not only a date of violent political and social upheaval, with the election of a formidable demagogue as President of the Republic, Arturo Alessandri Palma; nor is it simply the year of baptism for the stormy university generation to which Neruda belongs. It is also the year in which the name "Pablo Neruda" is born for the poet. It happens in October. As has been said, he needed to escape from the control of that dragon who hated poetry, that ballast-train conductor who kept an eye on his studies with mistrust and annoyance. Nothing more must be published with the name Neftalí Reyes. The first poem that he signs with the name of Pablo Neruda is "Lost Love": "My desires follow my beloved / in peaceful or violent riverbeds / and they tremble in the face of her glance / like the woodland in the face of the wind."

The boy is still living in Temuco, but his cousin Rudecindo Ortega Masson, then a university student in Santiago, has taken some of his poems to the capital and informs him that a selection of them will be published in *Claridad*. It is urgent, therefore, to become if not an incognito poet then at least a pseudonymous poet.

Raúl Silva Castro arranged their publication, with an introductory note signed by Fernando Ossorio, taken from a Pío Baroja character in *Camino de perfección:* "From Temuco comes a promise of significance, stroked by perhaps ancestral sorrows; soon to visit our city."

In the struggle against the father, which is the battle of a vocation defending itself against those who try to deny it, he lifts up a cry of rebellion in the poem called "Lyceum" in his sister's notebooks: "My whole pitiful life in a sad cage, my youth lost . . . But it matters not—Come on!— tomorrow or the next / I shall be middle-class like any little lawyer, / like any little doc wearing glasses and frock, / with all roads to the new moon blocked . . . / What the hell, in life, like in a magazine, / a poet has to graduate in dentistry!" The next poem carries a title along the same lines, "Norm for Rebellion": "Be a tree with wings, . . . with wings spread wide send them into flight."

Besides writing in his sister's notebooks, he also used paper with the letterhead of his uncle Orlando's *La Mañana* newspaper. From then on, without variation, he signs himself as Pablo Neruda.

His sister Laura Reyes Candia saved another of the handwritten notebooks signed by Pablo Neruda, with the title of the projected book, *Helios,* which shows that, since childhood, he liked to link poetry with drawing and then with painting. He himself used to sketch out roughs of bookcovers.

"A Farmer's Hands," published in the journal *Selva Austral,* in Temuco in 1920, contrary to what has been said, is not the first poem in which one sees the poet's social purpose, but it is the first where that purpose is clearly stated.

The theme is linked with another essential preoccupation: love, fleeting love: "Every time I hold you—love—in my hands / I know not how you come and know not how you go."

In the poem that he openly calls "Pleasure," the poet will record a young male's new experiences with naked frankness: "Like a relaxing furrow I felt your body open up / to receive my being's greatest tribute . . . /- To feel, . . . to tremble. And, oh flesh, to sink, to sink, to sink, / just like the sun into evening."

17. Prose Writer of Necessity?

Although he never spoke enthusiastically about it, nonetheless he wrote prose from his first moment to his last. Looking at death, he dictates the last pages of his *Memoirs, Confieso que he vivido* (I Confess to Having Lived). He wrote newspaper prose, propaganda prose, and divine prose.

It isn't possible to follow his career without traveling along the parallel lines of his poetry and also his prose.

A *leitmotif* of early Nerudian prose is antiprovincialism, rebellion against a mediocre atmosphere. The boy of fifteen reads Azorín with a contradictory point of view, for he detests Azorín's gray towns, which he finds too sad. He furthermore reprimands banal literature, empty metaphors that circulate like coins; he makes fun of *the glory of the heroic race, the copihue trees as red as blood, the impenetrable forests.*

He criticizes *the distinguished people, those who stroll in the evening through the square,* describing them with such epithets as "frivolous, vulgar, fops, more or less common." For him, the truly distinguished people are those who work, write, read; those who maintain their dignity in the solitude of their dreams. This article is incisive, with the flavor of a melodrama or a pamphlet. A personal and concrete event has been its motive: he refuses to be excluded because his father has been a laborer, is a train conductor, does not belong to society. Like a challenge to officialdom, he openly proclaims himself a poet. He dresses like one, with a flowing black cape. He is also in love with a girl . . . from society. Her family rejects him because he is "poor trash." They ridicule him with a nickname, "Vulture." If it were the poetical "Raven" of Edgar Allan Poe, perhaps he might accept the comparison, but "Vulture" is an insult, to which he replies with the forcefulness that will always be one of his characteristics. The theme returns in subsequent articles: "How much we hate, how much you hate, you young and strong reader who is reading these lines, how much you hate those indifferent and egotistical people who don't see the suffering of anyone, who venomously slide along under their mournful umbrellas, while winter's rage evaporates in water. . . ." He is not ashamed to proclaim that "the burning flush of sex, pleasure" has been discovered and attracts him like a perfectly simple and marvelous phenomenon. But he rejects the libidinous philistine, the sanctimonious hypocrite who doesn't go to the ballet to see the dance but only to look at the Russian ballerinas' legs.

He is around fifteen or sixteen years old, and he stridently proclaims himself a rebel. In his "Glosses of the City," in one titled "Employee," he postulates the class struggle without beating around the bush: "We," he says, "we call it exploitation, capital, abuse. The newspapers that, exhausted, you read on the trolley, call it order, rights, fatherland, etc. Perhaps you feel weak. No. We are here, we who no longer are alone, who are like you, and like you are exploited and suffering, but rebellious."[6] In other words, from the time of his adolescence, that poet of love was tempted by the demon of politics and, what is even worse, revolutionary politics.

Sometimes his language has a whiff of both anarchy and poetry, mixed together. He speaks on behalf of *the exploited in all the factories of the universe*. He considers ridiculous the idol of the warring fatherland, and he issues an invitation to daily rebellion. He is the author of several proclamations published in *Claridad,* which were edited almost always by young anarcho-sindicalists of the university, who greeted the October Revolution as the beginning of the new era. In his *Memoirs,* Neruda remembers that as soon as he arrived in Santiago he immediately enlisted in the anarcho-sindicalist ideology of the students. He signs his prose pieces with several kinds of pseudonyms, such as "Lorenzo Rivas." For his piece called "Miserables," he signs himself as "Sachka," taken from the Leonidas Andreiev character, Sachka Yegulev.

The youthful prose writer Neruda begins with inflamed pronouncements, for he is a student journalist very much in tune with his time, who will demonstrate from his first article his polemical fervor.

II.

Twilight Youth

18. The Crazy Twenties

Neruda is still living in Temuco, where he's enrolled in the sixth year of humanities in the lyceum. He is beginning to be shocked by certain events.

Persecuted young political figures of that period are taking refuge in the most distant provinces, among them, the writer José Santos González Vera, a moderate anarchist of the time, who reaches Temuco in July 1920, a few days after the attack on the Student Federation in Santiago. The fugitive, curious to meet that novice Temucan writer who publishes poems and incendiary prose in *Claridad,* went to wait for him at the door of the lyceum as soon as he arrived in the town. He saw something like two little dark sparks in the boy's eyes, and a face sharply honed like a sword. He gave an impression of extreme physical weakness, but a determined spirit could be detected. He spoke little and his smile revealed sorrow and cordiality. They took afternoon walks, conversing as they visited the little neighboring town of Padre Las Casas.

Later, González Vera worked as a journalist on the Valdivia newspaper, and subsequently he again came in contact with his sharp-faced friend in the *Claridad* discussions at the Student Federation.

The students would have to reorganize after the tremendous attack, which was the topic of many meetings where fires were struck in the generation of 1920, whose most exalted poet would be Neruda. Boyhood readers of the Encyclopedists and of Prudhon, devotees of the Russian Revolution and enemies of war, they discovered that their marginal nation, located on a slender edge of the world, had nothing to do with justice nor with respect for the human dignity of workers. His was a generation of assemblies in constant debate, where political discussion was mixed with literary fervor and the vague desire for a new culture. In the long evenings that usually lasted until dawn, controversy gave way to the passion for exchanging ideas. As typically happens in student meetings, the speaker didn't always blend reality with his romantic argument. When Pablo Neruda arrived in Santiago, he was sixteen years old and he went almost immediately to the Student Federation, where he was electrified. The most imposing speakers were Juan Gandulfo, to whom he dedicates his first published book, *Book of Twilights;* Pedro León Ugalde, Santiago Labarca, Eugenio González Rojas, González Vera, Rubén Azócar, and so many others.

Also present were Oscar Schnake, Daniel Schweitzer, the poet Roberto Meza Fuentes, all sharing the obligatory bohemian days when they smoked cheap tobacco, played billiards with a passion, drank "milk with wood alcohol," lived on credit by pawning their watches or clothing in the "rich aunt" (the Chilean version of the pawn shop) or eating and drinking with IOU's in the down-and-out café or bar found on every street corner.

In our conversations about that period, when I ask Pablo why he dedicated his first book to Juan Gandulfo, he shakes his head, as if in doubt. "He had the makings of a fiery politician," he says. "I've never seen a pamphleteer like him. If he had lived longer, I don't know, perhaps he might have developed politically, but that's a mystery." The electrifying orator died on 27 December 1931 in a car accident on his way to Viña del Mar. He was thirty-six years old. Neruda got the news in the Orient. The charismatic university leader of the generation of 1920 had died on Zapata Hill, about 600 feet from the turnoff to Casablanca.

Beginning in 1920, the next three years, all of Neruda's university life, are spent under the shadow of the crisis that paralyzed the nitrate fields, multiplied unemployment, increased worker unrest—a climate that completely engages the students at the University of Chile. They didn't like to use the term "politics," but preferred another which dominated their rambling discussions and firmly established itself as the topic of all controversies. That was "The Social Question," the fate of the working class, which the established powers saw only as an ignorant mass, born to be exploited. Thus, just as Gómez Rojas and then Neruda were the poets of that generation, Juan Gandulfo embodied their politician. For correct-thinking people he was the enemy of everything that should be respected: order, country, property, religion, morality. He was the treacherous anar-

chist who sold out to "Peruvian gold." They always need some kind of
"gold" so that whoever questions the legitimacy of the system can "sell
out." When Ladislao Errázuriz, a big vineyard owner, realized that the
crisis was about to boil over, he invented an act of war on the border with
Perú and Bolivia and called up several military contingents to move the
army to the north, whereupon Juan Gandulfo reacted with one stony
word, "Lies!," which earned him several months in jail. Neruda, as we
know, used to write the "Proclamations" in *Claridad,* but their most frequent editor was Gandulfo, under the pseudonym of Juan Guerra. He had
the rhetoric that was in fashion, and a certain lively eloquence inflamed
him. "Steadfast young generation! The world is ripe, the moment is now!"
he said in *Claridad* number 14. A small man, weak in appearance, he was
nine years older than Neruda, and in this situation that's a big difference.
The writer Manuel Rojas, an itinerant worker who was tied to that generation, believed that audacity was Gandulfo's dominant characteristic.

Not all of them were orators, but all shared the principle that had
been born in 1918, inspired by the movement for university reform in Córdoba, whose motto was "Coming together with the worker, hand in hand,
heart in heart, to carry out social justice." All of this was criticized as
revolutionary and unpatriotic activity. Those young people also committed other crimes: they founded the Lastarria Popular University, and
the Pedagogical Center opened the first night lyceum. In June 1920 they
added other illegal acts: the Student Convention debated "The Social
Question" and "International Movements" and proclaimed that "the interest of the individual, the family, and the nation must be subordinate to the
highest ideals of justice and human brotherhood." All of this constituted
heresy and obscenity. In the Senate, an honorable father who had been
drafted into the military maintained that those who supported such ideas
"should be put in jail to grow old and die there."

19. Unamuno and Patriotism's Stockholders

Events came to a head, to the great joy of the upper classes, who are
pursuing hell-bent-for-leather the musical comedy performance of "Don
Ladislao's War," which was linked to election manipulations designed to
avoid victory by the indecisive Liberal Alliance candidate, Arturo Alessandri, who had also been branded by conservative propaganda in quite novel
fashion as being bought by not just one kind of gold but two—the gold
of Peru and the gold of Moscow, in addition to being an emulator of the

drastic, mysterious, and distant Ivan the Terrible. President Juan Luis Sanfuentes, along with his war minister, Ladislao Errázuriz, declare military
mobilization. On 18 July 1920, the Student Federation has a special meeting to discuss the danger implied by preparations for war. The next day, a
group of cowardly right-wing "White Guard" vigilantes shouting "Long
live war" and "On to Lima" march by the student headquarters at 73 Ahu-
mada Street. They attack Santiago Labarca and Juan Gandulfo, then they
destroy the Numen printshop and ruin the original copy of a novel by José
Santos González Vera, *El conventillo*. Julio Valente, one of the pressmen,
was imprisoned for six months in the penitentiary. Since the newspapers
refused to publish anything about all this, the Student Federation had
their positions and denunciations printed in flyers that the students and
workers distributed by hand to passersby, an initiative which provided an
excuse for beatings and arrests. The next day, 21 July, at about 1:30 in the
afternoon, the attack on the Student Club took place. The attackers enjoyed themselves: they threw the furniture into the street and burned everything they found inside.

As in the case of García Lorca, sixteen years later, poetry had to pay
a special price. The student chairman and poet José Domingo Gómez Rojas, along with some workers and students, was taken to the penitentiary,
where he was beaten and tortured so badly that he went mad. Having
been transferred to the mental hospital, he died on 25 September, in effect
a murder victim. He was an enormously talented poet, killed just when his
work was beginning.

Don Miguel de Unamuno, on 26 July, wrote from Salamanca in
Spain with a message of protest and solidarity, which has not lost its force:

> Order! Order! shout the stockholders of patriotism, the pharisees
> like those who had Christ crucified as antipatriotic. They will resort to a
> principle of authority so that nobody will see that civilization is based on
> the end purpose of authority, and that this purpose is justice. Over there,
> just as over here. Over there, in that generous and noble Chile where the
> blood of Valdivia and Caupolicán are mixed, and no little bit of my own
> Basque blood, it has been a plutocratic and pseudo-aristocratic oligarchy,
> with its treasure near the altar and protected by the military, that has given
> rise to your black legend, the legend of an imperialistic and Prussian Chile
> that wallows in guano and nitrate.
>
> And they talk about the fatherland! Those stockholders in patrio-
> tism! For them the nation is a business or a mortgage held by creditors.
> And the landless are the nationless: those who work under the earth, in

dark tunnels, without sharing in the sunlight that shines on all. I have seen that you are accused of selling out for Peruvian wealth. They couldn't resort to any other specious argument. It's the same everywhere. These stockholders in patriotism don't understand any point of view except in terms of money, which is their only god.

Professional patriots! Patriotic professionals! Officers who attack a printing press. I have read the list of individuals who took part in the attack and sacking, and I see that they say one was a "pilot and sportsman." I don't know about over there, but "sportsman" means a loafer and somebody without much between his ears. And I see that the majority of those attackers were students. Obviously not studious ones. Students of false patriotism!

I know those pitiful students, whelped by an oligarchy which is both plutocratic and stockholder in patriotism. I know those students. They're the same ones who acted as "honorary policemen" over here and someday will act as "honorary hangmen" to establish the principle of authority and order, by strangling its final purpose, which is justice. These times are supremely trying and full of agony and labor pains, in the birth of universal and human activity, of justice between peoples. Militaristic and plutocratic imperialism fights back from on its last frontiers and attacks printing presses. Intelligence is the object of its hatred. In sacristies and flag rooms the attribution of "intelligent person" is pronounced with a feigned disdain between clenched teeth. With a disdain that contains within itself the envy and rage of impotence.

With their deck of cards or roulette wheel, kings and stockholders in patriotism and professional bullies. Here at least (Spain) this is the kind of despotism that remains in Europe; the only things that are left with free rein are gambling, the vilest of pornography, subservience to the authorities, and crooked business deals.

From across the ocean, from the tomb of so many hopes and the cradle of many more, a trembling and warm hand stretches out to you.

20. *Boardinghouses and Tenements*

To the poet who dies, fame flies. Gómez Rojas had a dramatic talent, we might even say tragic. And immense energy. He was the poet for an anarchistic and romantic young generation. His death brought with it a cold shivering sensation, and a question as to whether youth was to remain without a voice to enthusiastically sing its song. Who would come forth with the spiritual greatness which was needed in order to take a deep breath and speak with a clarity and beauty that wouldn't be mere prettiness?

As if generations and peoples in need of saying what they feel were able to bring forth out of their heart those personalities capable of speaking for them, it was very quickly revealed that the new poet who would be their voice was making his appearance. In the 1921 competition sponsored by the Student Federation, the jury announced its decision on 14 October. The winning poem appeared in print the next day in the journal *Claridad,* and thousands of young people learned by heart "The Festival Song":

> Today when the old earth is shaking
> with a dusty and violent quaking,
> our young and full hearts go forth
> like the wind-driven sails of a boat.

In that autobiographical Pentateuch, *Notes from Isla Negra,* many years later, under "1921," Neruda talks about the event: "The festival song . . . October, / prize, / of Springtime: / A Pierrot with broad tones who releases / my poetry into madness / and I, thin edge / of a black sword between jasmine and masks / still traveling stubbornly alone, / slicing the crowd with the melancholy / of the southern wind, beneath the bells / and unrolling of paper streamers."

The younger generation had its poet. The poems that would come forth immediately, in profusion, like a constant waterfall, would say more clearly than ever that the country could count on a poet the equal of his old provider of books in Temuco, Gabriela Mistral.

Everywhere he went they wanted the poet to recite "The Festival Song." Just as it later happened with his "Farewell." Neruda got bored with it; he only likes to read aloud whatever he has just finished writing. And even less does he like to repeat himself.

Just as once we made a pilgrimage to the poet's birthplace, in our peripatetic conversations there was always a background of rediscoveries, distant moments, persons, dwellings, boardinghouses, plazas. We would talk about everything and anything. Sometimes, about literature; habitually, about politics, and although I didn't plan then to write anything very biographical about the poet, inevitably, in some way or another, a question would come forth about episodes I had heard about or had seen in the extensive literature that had been produced about Neruda. Suddenly he would say to me, "Look, this is the house on Padura Street." "But this street is called Riding Club Street." "Before it was Padura. Prettier. I lived here in 1922." I think that's when he was writing *Book of Twilights*. He lived almost like a character out of Gorky. Actually, the house was a tenement. His friends would appear in his room, where he had just an iron cot, an Indian blanket, a nightstand with a candlestick whose candle was lit for poetry and blown out for conversation. Of course, they were eighteen, twenty years old. They didn't even mind sleeping on the brick floor. One, the closest one to being a gentleman, Orlando Oyarzún, wanted to be a businessman in order to get his friends out of poverty, away from those badly plastered walls. He would become a capitalist, a dream shared by nobody else in Neruda's group. Orlando in those days could sleep peacefully under the editorial page of *El Mercurio*. The house was near Manuel Rodríguez Plaza, in the old nineteenth-century section of Santiago, already declining and therefore endowed with a certain cozy feeling, frequently interrupted by the scandalous nocturnal shouts of these revelers.

21. *Maruri and Twilights*

Neruda used to say that he might forget numbers, of his house, of his telephone, but he would never forget one particular address: 513 Maruri. The house in "The Twilights of Maruri." When I arrived from the province to study in the Law School at the University of Chile, I also lived on the inevitable Maruri Street—the street of poor people and penniless students. I lived there ten years after Neruda. And doubtless the street hadn't changed in the least during that period. Parallel to Independence, on the north side of the Mapocho River, it is near the rough neighborhood that was then called Las Hornillas, where lowlife and houses of prostitution predominated. And one wondered: There's poetry here? (*Book of Twilights* was a book of poetry.) Yes, there, in the most antipoetic place in the world, poetry is brought forth by the poet. That's how, very slowly, this came forth: "Over the rooftops the evening settles down, down . . . Who gave it wings so that it might come?" There he wrote a poem that I still hear in many voices: "That autumnal butterfly that flutters all about and disappears." And the mysterious suggestion of the word *saudade* (melancholy), "this sweet word of ambiguous perfumes." He perceives it in Eça de Queiroz. "Listen, friend, do you know the meaning of this white word that slips away like a fish?"

One of those hand-to-mouth boardinghouses was on Maruri, a gray street that really had a smell of gas, of old brick and coffee made of figs, which the poet sniffed immediately in March of 1921, when he got off the night train and went to live in Santiago in order to study at the university. He himself speaks of the uniformly ugly houses, inhabited by strangers and bedbugs. The world would get dirtier, darker, and drearier when autumn and winter extinguished the leaves and left the trees naked and desolate.

But the poet sees what others cannot. He feels things in a particular way. He discovered what nobody, before or after, discovered: that that humble street was visited by the most extraordinary twilights. Visionaries see apparitions of the Virgin or the Lord; there in his room on that sad street, Neruda marveled at the brilliant sunsets that came with their rapidly changing effects, their plays of light, only to die away in just a few minutes. Did he, like the impressionists, consider light a poetic substance? Or were those the illuminations of a magician? In that student pensión on Maruri Street, he recalls that he lived a life of "complete hunger, writing much more than at any point up to then, but eating much less," almost supporting the "hunger theory" that starving poets write more and better.

When, later, it was my turn to live on Maruri Street, every morning at eight, I used to see a beautiful student in a beret climbing aboard the "gondola." She was studying history in the Pedagogical Institute, and in time she would marry Salvador Allende. We used to travel as best we could, almost doing acrobatics, in broken-down buses that made the trip toward España Avenue, where the Pedagogical students were unloaded. Everybody called these dilapidated vehicles "gondolas." An illegitimate triumph of poetry, because Santiago has never been nor ever will be Venice, nor was the Alameda the Grand Canal. But just as Byron, a century before, discovered the beauty of the Rialto in Venice, Neruda would reveal the hidden charm of the twilights of Maruri.

Later we returned with him to the area that was between the Pedagogical Institute and the Main Station, to the house at 25 García Reyes Street. Down below, there used to be the fruit stand of Doña Delmira, a good friend, and up above, the then inseparable pair, Tomás Lago and Neruda, who began to work on the translation of *Nigger of the Narcissus*, by one of the period's admired writers, Joseph Conrad. That venture never reached port.

The small band was so poor that Neruda, one day at dawn, let loose in the middle of the street, like François de Villon, a tremendous curse against the deprivations, miseries, and bad luck that made poets howl with poverty. Tomás Lago added his voice to the curse. But Orlando, the hopeful financier who always read the stockmarket page in *El Mercurio* (although he didn't have a penny), raised his deep voice, more stentorian than the others, in an encouraging harangue: "Fellows, don't worry. This is all going to change. I've got a hunch." The others didn't believe in his hunch. But the wizard Orlando had faith in witchcraft and in business. He read the future in a crystal ball or on the market page.

22. Why "Neruda"?

In a letter to his sister Laura, he writes, "I haven't lost my habit of eating every day." There was no guarantee that the habit would be fed, however, and in his crowd the themes of poetry and hunger were equally in vogue.

When he arrived in Santiago he was an ambitious but starving poet. His 1921 prizewinning poem, "The Festival Song," was not read by him personally but by Roberto Meza Fuentes, who was at that time sort of a dictator of literary contests and winner of almost all like competitions. In addition, he really wanted to read the poem. The winning author's pseudonym was Sachka Yegulev. When they opened his envelope they were met by another pseudonym, Pablo Neruda. The question of why he adopted that name was put to him a thousand times, pursuing him to the point of tedium. The poet remembered that a great Czechoslovakian writer and masterful journalist, Erwin Kisch, doubtless moved by patriotic curiosity about the puzzling adoption of a Czech name, repeated the question to him wherever they met, in cities throughout the world—during the war in Spain, during exile in Mexico in the Nazi period, after the liberation of Prague. In the latter city, he took the poet to Jan Neruda's house on Mala Strana Street and begged him, "Tell me the truth once and for all. I am old and I've followed you about for a long time."

One day, when the fourteen-year-old Neruda, like the Praguian Kafka, feared his father more than usual, he decided to change his name, adopting a *nom de plume,* precisely out of fear of his progenitor, not because his father was just a butcher, as was the case with the pseudonymous Kafka. But poems were to blame for the bad grades Neftalí received in mathematics, and the railroader, according to his son, smouldered with an infernal phobia against poets, unable to understand what they were good for. And he had the bad luck to be cursed with a son who belonged to that dreadful breed! Almost worse than if he were a delinquent. What he wanted was for the boy to be a practical member of society. He reasoned like people of the poorest middle class, who—coming out of peasant stock—wanted to see their children climb in society. Since he had neither land nor money, the only way for his son to make his way in life was to study in the university for a profession and earn a profitable and respectable degree. For that reason, he even burned the books and the notebooks in which his son used to write poetry. One day, fearful that his father might discover that he had not abandoned his ill-fated and shameful vocation, when he had to send a poem off for publication, knowing that the name Neftalí Reyes as "author" would unleash all the fury of the irate "author" of his birth, the boy chanced upon the pages of a journal in which there was a short story signed by Jan Neruda. The word "Neruda" had a nice sound, and he liked the name "Pablo." He thought it would be an expedient that would only last a few months. Thirty-five years later, having become totally accustomed to his new identity and having eliminated his original name even from his subconscious memory and instinctive reactions, he was to legalize this "Pablo Neruda," which displaced and erased "Neftalí Reyes" on his birth certificate. Back in his youth, though, he simply took a fictitious name which would allow him to hide from his father his persistence in the vile practice of poetry, because, among other things, he couldn't do without the needed paternal allowance.

Among families in the provinces, a poor student would do everything he could to find an aunt or some relative who might have a rooming house in Santiago. They were cheap. In general, those residences had two characteristics: they were full of fleas and the food was bad. The poet later came to the conclusion that a whole generation of university comrades lived in those houses, faint with hunger and nearly dying of starvation.

23. The Student

Since he had to study a profession and he wanted it to be of some use in establishing contact with poetry, he enrolled as a French major. At that time in Latin America, English had not yet become the principal foreign language, and French carried the prestige of being the language of culture—the prestige of being able to read Baudelaire, Rimbaud, Mallarmé, Apollinaire, in the original. His studies enabled him to devour these writers with voracious frenzy. He completed the required four years of study, but he never received the degree. According to him, he was swallowed up not only by the student political movement, which was intense and unceasing, as we have seen, but also by the literary life of the period.

In the wild bohemian nights, there was drinking but there were also exchanges of poetic discoveries and readings by new poets. The world was
just beginning for the nineteen-year-old youth.

His university years were decisive. Here in my own exile, I have one
of Pablo Neruda's signed typescripts, saved from the burning of his books
and his "dangerous" papers, in which he sketches some recollections of his
youthful days as a student politician. Perhaps it might be useful to reproduce here that text, which was written on paper imprinted with Neruda's
ex libris in the form of a fish:

Isla Negra, April 1973.

One day in 1923, the president of the Republic, Don Arturo Alessandri
Palma, walked past the door of the old Pedagogical Institute. We students
who were standing around in little groups, did not respectfully greet him
but simply looked curiously at him, in silence. The truth was that we didn't
consider him our friend.

That old Lion of Tarapacá shook his symbolic mane and his cane,
accusing us of being disrespectful and insolent. We still didn't respond, and
he soon walked away with his indignation and his cane.

Half a century has gone by and now a comrade president comes before you to present a masterful opening class, involving himself in the
knowledge, the intelligence, the life of both students and teachers.

Our president, our students, our lives have all changed.

Nonetheless, my memories linger tenderly on the old university
school where I knew friendship, love, the meaning of popular struggle;
in other words, my apprenticeship in consciousness and life.

Out of that school and my successive poor-student lodgings, came
my first published books: *Book of Twilights* in 1923, and *Twenty Poems* which
will celebrate its fiftieth anniversary next year in 1974.

Poetry, delirious curiosity, the ferment of all the books, the youthful
rapture of finding other creatures who dream the same dreams we do; the
streets of Echaurren, República, España Avenue, all full of student boardinghouses; the poets Cifuentes Sepúlveda, Romeo Murga, Eusebio Ibar,
Víctor Barberis, gone from this life but not from poetry; the busy streets
where twilight struck you with a sudden gust and was perfumed by honeysuckle and lilac. Those long-ago love affairs, pleasurable, lancing, ephemeral. All of this shaped my existence.

Our most serious steps led to the Student Federation on Agustinas
Street. A few doors from there, on the doorstep of the Workers Federation,

I often saw, in vest and shirt sleeves, the most important working-class man of this century, Don Luis Emilio Recabarren.

Let these recollections serve as a greeting on this inauguration of the 1973 academic year, which you are celebrating this morning.

And naturally, because everything has changed and because the revolutionary transformation headed by President Allende is also an accomplishment of the people and the university, I think that those years are a necessary antecedent of what we have achieved and what we shall achieve: above all, the sense of responsibility, of struggle, of commitment to our obligations and to cultural benevolence, which is now opening onto its greatest possibilities in history, here in our country.

A brotherly greeting to Vice-rector Ruiz and to the masterful teacher Allende, as well as to all of you, who are my old and new companions at the same time.

Pablo Neruda

The document is significant in its own right, as a reencounter with his youth as a student, during the last year of his life. It is all framed within the panorama of that period, at whose opposite corners two men stand out: Arturo Alessandri Palma, the bourgeois political boss, and Luis Emilio Recabarren, Chile's most important worker-leader of the twentieth century. The contemporary period is politically and socially represented by a man who was transformed from just a man of his time into a permanent figure—Salvador Allende.

But that document also brings to life his student days, the streets near the old Pedagogical Institute, the shadow of smoky boarding houses, the names of his generation's poets. It evokes love affairs and also social passion. A few doors beyond the Student Federation is the Workers Federation. In the twentieth-century history of Chile, that proximity provides a useful symbolism.

Neruda used to go almost every afternoon to that Student Federation on Agustinas Street, where he would work on its journal, *Claridad* (without pay, of course). That was the building they attacked. In Chile, popular organizations have often been the object of assault, destruction, arson, like that fire which did away with his uncle Orlando's newspaper in just a few minutes one night in Temuco. But among the saddest of history's noteworthy attacks, besides the 1907 slaughter in Iquique's Santa María School, two are especially remembered by our people: the burning of the Workers Federation in Punta Arenas, where many Patagonian sheepmen were burned alive, and the attack on the Chilean Student Federation, on 21 July 1920. The dates of both conflagrations are not far apart. They belong to one and the same tide of regression. And they are faint signs of the destruction that would engulf Chile in a sea of blood, less than half a year after the day on which the poet wrote his lines in Isla Negra.

24. Friendship and Bohemia

He used to claim that friendship is a good locale for poets. "I have a southern sense of friendship. I've never lost friends. Only death has taken them away from me." In truth, death did deprive him of many friends. He had their names carved into the beams that supported the "Alberto Rojas Giménez bar" in his house in Isla Negra. One day, I heard him reading the names out slowly to Camilo José Cela. Neruda thought it was an appropriate place to commemorate them, next to the colored bottles, the juices and liquors of the country, next to the mulled wines, so that the living, seated at small, round cafélike tables, could drink and chat and perhaps from time to time look at the names inscribed in the hardwood, and perchance fleetingly evoke their memory.

Nonetheless, it wasn't only death that took friends from him, but also life's complications. He lost some very violently to the war of passions. For example, his second divorce, the end of his union with Delia del Carril, which split Neruda's world in two and estranged him from longstanding friends. Shortly before he had said, "Here I walk the streets of Santiago with Tomás Lago, never talking about books, just as we were thirty-four years ago. Together we published that book, *Anillos* (Rings), which contains some remarkable poetry of his." He broke with Tomás Lago. The Neruda clan was shattered by the civil war occasioned by the domestic separation.

But his southern sense of friendship was genuine. I met Alejandro Serani many years afterward, in Santiago, when he was a democratic politician and lawyer. Neruda once said, "I never would have got through the humanities program if it hadn't been for Sacha." That was his name for Alejandro. In the lyceum, they translated English poets together, and Sacha helped him with mathematics, which was Neftalí's nightmare and mortal enemy. They chose a pleasant spot in which to do their lessons—the shores of the Cautín River. Serani suggested they follow the same schedule as in the lyceum, forty-five minutes for class and fifteen for recess. Neftalí thought it would be better the other way around, but Sacha wouldn't compromise. Neftalí simply had to learn algebra and geometry. The study period was intolerable, and Neftalí's eyes would wander to the water and the flowers on the shore. When recess came, they would play at skipping rocks across the water, choosing smooth flat stones to skim over the surface in such a way as to raise little splashes with each skip.

The friendly duo performed well. In the fifth year of humanities, Neftalí was elected president and Sacha secretary of the Athenian Club. In the Student Association, Sacha was president and Neftalí secretary. In the sixth year final examinations, required for entering the university, they were confronted with the impassable Great Wall of China, and the dragon which guarded it, determined that it not be passed, was mathematics. Though Sacha helped him, he also could count on a certain complicity from the rector, Marco Aurelio Letelier, who perhaps saw that the boy, although clumsy with theorems and equations, had a kind of invisible halo which might not precisely light up the world of numbers but could certainly illuminate the world of letters.

The poet shared his first room in Santiago with his friend Sacha, on España Avenue. It was relatively dignified, but expensive. In addition, the landlady had a policeman's soul. She used to spy on their friends, especially the females. She would stick her nose into their activities and their comings and goings. Dissatisfied, Pablo went to live in a tenement house, laxer and cheaper, together with Rubén Azócar and Tomás Lago. But, given the theatricality of life, it so happened that Don José del Carmen Reyes came to Santiago to be operated on. So they had to resort to a little one-act play: the honorable Sacha went to spend a few days in the tenement house, and the poet moved back to the less unsavory house on España Avenue for as long as his father would remain in the capital.

Friendships multiplied, recruited from university companions, writers, and artists. Soon, certain pubs became their meeting places, like the Hercules, the Jote, the Venice, along with more exalted spots like the German Clubs on Esmeralda Street and San Pablo, as well as the Posada del Corregidor. They all frequented the cabaret belonging to the pug-nosed Inés, and later, the Zeppelin. During those times, the group included the poets Alberto Rojas Giménez, Angel Cruchaga, Rosamel del Valle, Gerardo Seguel, Homero Arce, Rubén Azócar; the painters Armando Lira, Julio Ortiz de Zárate, Isaías Cabezón, Israel Roa, Paschin; the caricaturist Víctor Bianchi, who would help Neruda more than twenty years later to cross the Andes in the days of persecution by González Videla. There were other group members, like his great friends Orlando Oyarzún and the incorrigible bohemian journalists, Antonio Rocco del Campo and Renato Monestier. They used to sing in all the languages they knew and in some they didn't know, and in the midst of drinks and out-of-tune choruses, there was poetry. Someone would take out a book and say something about the author. In those meetings, the names of Marcel Proust and James Joyce were spoken for the first time in Chile. Later, when Neruda was asked about who had influenced him, he answered, "There is one that nobody talks about, and yet he has been a very important influence on me—Proust." During that period, he also translated some poems by Joyce into Spanish.

That sense of male camaraderie never left him. On Maruri Street and on García Reyes, his roommate was Tomás. But there was always a respectful relationship between them, obvious in the fact that they never used the informal *tú* form of address with each other. Many times we heard them saying, "*Usted*, Pablo," "*Usted*, Tomás." That Chilean *usted* is peculiar. It used to be that spouses always used the formal *usted* with each other, and many couples still do. Children, of course, used *usted* with their parents, a custom which has almost completely disappeared now. Back then, even parents would address their children as *usted*.

Diego Muñoz tells about a time when he was put in charge of decorating the walls of what was to be the Zeppelin Cabaret. In the contract, a form of payment was stipulated which was partly eccentric and partly alcoholic: 5,000 pesos in cash and 5,000 pesos in drinks at half price. The muralist and his friends had to drink 25,000 bottles of beer or their equivalent in other libations in order to get paid. The young fellows in the group suffered no thirst for many, many months. That same Diego Muñoz recalls that the pug-nosed Inés, owner of the cabaret, was very fond of what she called her young gang and used to give them credit. On stage, the singer was a one-eyed young woman who covered up her empty eyesocket with a lock of hair. They were all fans of the *clery* pitcher of white wine flavored with pieces of fruit. And of dancing. Neruda didn't dance.

25. Flown Away

Rojas Giménez came up to me one noonday in the packed entry hall of the University of Chile's main building, which was always filled to overflowing, but at that hour there wasn't room for even a pin. The students were getting ready for a picnic outside the city, which of course would not be ruled by any Dry Laws. Rojas Giménez asked me for some money to pay his share. "Unfortunately," I told him, "I don't have a cent." I wanted to go along and couldn't. He wanted to go along and went. He would always go along, especially where he thought that happiness would pop up like the cork in a bottle. He was a fine, delicate poet. For years, I couldn't get out of my head a little jewel of his, which I quote without the text, doubtless inaccurately, "Your words are small ones, yet I love your words. In them there's so much of you that there's no need of deep meaning for me to be filled with joy." It ended by saying that the words fluttered about him like butterflies around the lamp. That's how he fluttered through life and that's how he was consumed, dazzled by the light he couldn't control and by the most devouring thirst. In a certain sense, he belonged to a tragic generation. Along with the poet Aliro Oyarzún, Orlando's brother and author of *El barco amarillo* (The Yellow Ship).

The most bohemian among those bohemians was Alberto Rojas Giménez, whom I met in the thirties. He was the magician of madness, of frenetic ideas and little paper birds. He wrote unfailingly beautiful poems, which are usually republished as the sign of a talent destroyed by bohemianism, too early, just as it killed him. I remember him coming in at student functions in the Palace of Fine Arts. Somebody would ask him to say a few words, or to get something started, or talk about his life in Paris or his friend Neruda. He would sit down at the table and accept on one condition—that they first bring him a bottle.

Rojas Giménez was very different from the supremely relaxed Pablo; the former was a hedonist, a follower of Pan, a worshipper of wine, an epicurean every day and a bohemian every night and dawn. He had something that was missing in the group: barroom charm, theatrical grace, the ability to turn everything into an entertaining show, the gift of communication and effervescent congeniality. For the melancholy Neruda of those days, he was like the opposite image. And doubtless that happily demonic side of Rojas Giménez attracted him and made him a bit afraid. If we read his poetry of that period, *Book of Twilights, Twenty Love Poems, The Ardent Slingsman,* we are confronted by a sad man who is also attracted by dionysian excess. Perhaps he brought from Temuco his habit for eating, along with one for wine. In that sense, Rojas Giménez was the temptor who suggested to him the pleasures of heaven and hell, who invited him not to fear giving the green light to pleasure. Orlando Oyarzún wonders if Rojas Giménez had much influence in Neruda's decision to abandon his studies of pedagogy and devote himself totally to literature. Perhaps that was one of the factors that moved him to that decision, but by no means was it the only one nor certainly the most important.

Another member of the jovial bunch was the painter Paschin, artistic pseudonym of Abelardo Bustamante, who used to dream about Paris. One day, in one of those strange twists of fate, a first class ticket fell to him by chance, for passage on an English ship that was going to London. He proposed to his friend Orlando Oyarzún that they exchange the first class ticket for two in third class and travel together to Europe. Orlando's approval brought him a visit from Rojas Giménez, who used all his charmer's tricks to plead that the second ticket be given to him. After hearing a hundred plaintive reasons, the kind-hearted Orlando agreed. Everybody, including Neruda and Tomás Lago, went to Valparaíso to bid farewell to their two friends. Zoilo Escobar acted as guide so they could penetrate the nocturnal secrets of the port city. They had no place to sleep, but the journalist Novoa put them up with newspaper mattresses and blankets. The next morning, the group met at the shipping company to divide the one ticket into two. The British agent lost his composure when he heard such a preposterous idea. In the midst of despair, they appealed to the highest provincial executive in his big third-floor office above the Sotomayor Plaza. After taking in the scene with a couple of glances, Rojas Giménez confronted the official with a persuasive ultimatum, "If you deny me this favor, I shall not go back to Santiago alive, and I swear to you that I will jump from this balcony." At 1:30 in the afternoon, the two travelers waved good-bye to their friends from the ship's deck

Rojas Giménez was small, a pretty-boy as Neruda used to say, with a profile rather like Rudolph Valentino. At the time, the myth of the Latin lover was all the rage and on its way to becoming a prototype. The little Chilean was always besieged by women, and he showed them handsome indifference. He wrote noteworthy poems, like "Carta océano" (Ocean Chart). A product of that voyage which he received from Paschin out of the generous withdrawal of Orlando was the very short ingenious book, *Chilenos en París*. Maybe that's where he found the little paper birds of Unamuno, which he fashioned and flew with unerring accuracy in all the bars he used to frequent. He often went from his nocturnal splurges straight to jail, from there sending out illustrated messages requesting money, assistance, and freedom.

But on one occasion he went to the Posada del Corregidor without any money, ate his fill, and had to leave his coat and jacket as a guaranty. It was winter, and he went out into a torrential rain, catching pneumonia, which his weakened condition could not fight off. A few days afterward, his friends attended his wake in the Quinta Normal home of his sister. Shortly before going to the cemetery, a stranger arrived and looked for a long time at the deceased's face. Then, to the stupefaction of all, he leaped over the coffin to the other side, like a circus acrobat, and went away without saying a word. He may have been paying off a bet or obeying an order.[b] The funeral had the same kind of flavor. Seldom had Santiago seen so much rain, and the Mapucho River was nearly overflowing its banks as the cortege crossed above it, on foot. Vicente Huidobro was pale beneath a dripping umbrella. On the way back, several of the friends went on to a "drown your sorrows" bar, where some of them wrote the news to Pablo, who was then serving as consul in Spain. Neruda got the letter in Barcelona and went into the Santa María del Mar Cathedral to light candles in memory of his friend. He answered the letter by sending his poem, "Alberto Rojas Giménez Comes Flying."

That religious attempt to save the lost soul of a great sinner condemned to deepest hell reveals Neruda's vocation as *postmortem* redeemer of his friends. In 1964, he spoke about those candles he lit in the cathedral to a co-worker, María de la Luz Uribe, whose brother Armando Uribe, a conscientious poet and knowledgeable Catholic, had not lit candles of any kind but had stayed for a long time by Neruda's side, just as he continued doing in exile.

26. Pablo de Rokha

The days of hunger, when they didn't have enough to get a blind beggar's blessing, grew longer than the map of Chile. When his father found out that he had abandoned his studies, he was infuriated and cut off the monthly allowance. His "momother" used to send him a little money on the sly, as much as she could, by way of Laurita, to whom Neruda used to write letters addressed to all sorts of variants of his "Rabbit" nickname for her: *Coneja, Koneka, Conekita, Laura coneja,* telling her, "I'm too young not to eat every day." The thin postal orders were enough for breathing space, and they would eat every other day. They became characters out of Quevedo or Cervantes, picaresque starving students who went to a restaurant on the first block of San Antonio Street, called "The Chinamen from Tokyo" through some Latin American quirk of geography. If the waiter wasn't in sight, they'd gobble down the bread from a table, covering it with salt, pepper, and olive oil from the cruet. The blessed waiter almost never appeared, and they repeated the operation on several days. Finally, one day he paid attention to them. He was Chinese and told them, with all the expected distortions of pronunciation, "You will not be served." "Why not?" "Because you eat up all the olive oil."

They used to spend a good part of the day figuring out how to calm their stomachs. One day, Neruda raised an eyebrow and emphasized his directing role as financier. "If it weren't for this head," he said, pointing to his own, "we wouldn't eat at all. I'm the one who thinks it all out and provides it all. And you, Tomás, are not at all cooperative." Tomás Lago was a proud fellow, and he answered, "What the devil head are you talking about? Why, the only thing you know how to do is send me every day to ask for five pesos from Rudecindo Ortega or ask poor Orlando to go out and sell a couple of secondhand books."

Given this condition of ravenous poverty, the young poets easily mingled with panderer and cardshark. Sometimes they seemed to be beggars and were spongers. At night they linked up with charitable streetwalkers. With their feeling of being idlers and vagabonds, they had to satisfy their hunger every day and figure out how to do so without any money. They exemplified the not unheard-of type that joins together the student and the rogue, often out of necessity and without the natural capacity to carry out that ancient profession. If Don Quixote says that there is no greater victory than to conquer oneself, the truth is that it's not all that easy to triumph against hunger every day. The fictional Lazarillo de Tormes and Guzmán de Alfarache were real colleagues for them. But then, someone came along who was older by ten years, with an authoritarian nature and more experience in the difficult art of living and eating without resources. Without asking their opinion and without any democratic election, this Pablo de Rokha set himself up as leader of the group. He was a poet who had published an enormous book (in terms of its physical dimensions), which overnight became a scandal and a target of critical derision. The contradiction between poetry and money was constantly posed in his pitifully austere life, interrupted whenever possible by wild binges and feasts. He had to scheme every morning how to stave off the day's hunger. He used to go from door to door selling his books. He tried to sell plows and agricultural machinery. He would travel through the countryside trying to pique the vanity of landowners who were rolling in money, in order to palm off paintings by famous artists, all forgeries. Hero and anti-hero in the daily battle, he becomes an adventurer who lives in many different situations and conditions. This thirty-year-old poet relates to the twenty-year-olds because they are all drawn together by poetry, deprivation, and the need to find some way of surviving.

This broad-shouldered man with sideburns worthy of the opera *Car-*

men, looking like a Spanish conquistador, has a swaying walk like a bear or an orangutan. With an imperious not-to-be-questioned voice, he issues orders to the youths to get going on their mission of asking for loans, of selling books, of committing little swindles. There are some specific points at which one can see a lover of literature, a naïve human being, or a supportive spirit. Events thus become more organized, shaded by digressions against bourgeois morality and by literary miscellanea. They're poor, but they're not fools. The geographic frame of their vicissitude is the city of Santiago. Every day holds a trip, many trips along different streets and social surroundings, to silence the growling of empty stomachs. Real success is rare, and there are many refusals and embarrassments, which Neruda and his companions feel deeply. This business of living off charity and groveling for bread is cruel, like not respecting themselves, like denying their value as men. Although they try to assume their leader's more naturalistic and unjudgmental approach to life, they come to consider him repulsive. That life of theirs stinks like rotten eggs, and they would like to break away from it. To do so, however, they had to rebel against the dictatorship of the boss, and they were afraid and beaten down. His booming voice and threats made them tremble. To break the chains, they plotted an uprising which would take place in the prearranged meeting spot, the Hercules Restaurant. "The Man" arrives at the usual time, and they return empty-handed, offering ineffectual excuses. They will be reprimanded, but the plotters are determined to face him down, to break the ignominious yoke, once and for all. When he asks them for an accounting of the activities they had been charged with, they reply that they've not collected a cent. He insults them, crushing them with a flood of abuse. Contrary to what they had pledged to do, they couldn't utter a word. Exasperated and angry with themselves, they later take action and follow him into the urinals. There, surrounded by the typical odors of the location, they raise the flag of liberty with shouts. The first to wave it is Tomás Lago, followed by Diego. They attempt to attack their bewildered boss; the devil yells but doesn't spit fire; and the air smells not of sulphur but of piss. The uprising spreads to all the group, including Neruda, who always would remember the scene. Naturally, with the passage of time, he would view it with laughing amusement, but emphasizing that it was a liberating event.

That leader of starvelings, that immensely insolent man of extremes, is a very complicated figure in Chilean literature, for Pablo de Rokha dreamed of making the young group his literary disciples and acting as their teacher in poetry. His own work was a shapeless mass, unruly, intense, cursing, heretical, and baroque. His published book, *Los gemidos* (Wailings), was measured by some in kilos. It was without proportion, but its imbalance had some grandeur. It conveys his dejection, his vision devoid of illusion. He was a pre-revolutionary with the virtue of never becoming a post-revolutionary. He wasn't born to be an ascetic, and he loved life in a terrible way, but for him it always turned into anxiety and tension, leading him to insolently oppose it. He was not without a caustic sense of "black humor," which he dispensed in great quantity. He was incapable of refuting with the contented man's serenity either the accursed need for daily bread to feed his debilitated wife and the horde of children which grew larger every year, or his own pitiless existence. He was the opposite of the flatterer, yet he had to make an effort to be uncharacteristically amiable toward the potential purchaser of his self-published book or an unauthentic painting, toward the unwilling lender.

His whole life was hazardous, dealing him blows that he returned as best he could by saying awful things about it in his books and loving it to death. This failed organizer of impoverished poets never pardoned them for the uprising in the Hercules, not only for economic reasons but also, above all, for literary ones. He always attacked that group, and he wrote scathing and biting pages and even entire books against Neruda. His *Neruda y yo* (Neruda and I) is the crowning blow in that literary battle, carried to the point of obscenity as its evangelical doctrine, full of endless sarcasms. Sometimes he could be a festive, comic writer, but at heart he was an immensely tragic poet—so tragic that he committed suicide one day when it seemed to him there was no place in the world for him.

But he wasn't an emulator of Master Cabra,ᶜ fighting for the depreciation of man. Nor was he endowed by birth to be leader of a fraternity of ruffians. He was a victim of the delusion that in that country, in that world, he could live off poetry, eating by means of medieval tricks or traps worthy of a shabby penny-ante financier. Sometimes he posed as a troublemaker, but the time for bullies had passed. Life obliged him to become a crank politician, an inventor of tall tales, but he was never a genuine wit like those who are amoral by nature and insensitive by temperament. No, when his empty stomach growled, this man responded to hunger with exaggerated gestures, becoming at one moment an impressive or lamentable malcontent, at another a fabulous creature.

He was the most constant and annoying enemy that Neruda had in his whole life, a great Quevedo-like poet with that capacity to convert enormous onslaughts and rage into ugly words and dark, ripping caricature. He was the hyperbolic insultor, the man who fervently hoped for a great revolution, perhaps to put an end to his own despair. Meanwhile, he dealt out his slashing blows however he could, avenging authentic and imagined ingratitudes, and attacking Pablo Neruda, his favorite target, in the very heart of his poetry. Except that he didn't know that Neruda's poetry had an armored heart.

27. The Girl from Temuco

Neruda has recounted some moments of his love life, in his *Memoirs* and especially in his poetry. Like spotlights, those brief references illuminate a much greater secret area of semihidden nocturnal regions beneath the thicket of the poet's personal life.

One time, he experiences a precocious erotic revelation when two little girls are poking around under the frightened child's clothing, trying to decipher a puzzle. Later as an adolescent, as evening falls over the harvested field, a night-shrouded woman slips down next to him on the seeded earth, to depart under cover of the darkness when it's finished. And he still doesn't know the identity of his accomplice in the marvelous adventure. The poet—the man, that is—enjoys the instant shock of physical attraction so many times he loses count. There are intense brief relationships, and love affairs that seem to be the real thing when they begin, and finally there are the great loves of his life that in some cases end as great enemies.

An unfaithful husband will try to placate his jealous wife by telling her, "Sweetie, don't worry. You're the cathedral, and the others are little chapels." Neruda had many chapels and several cathedrals. Cathedrals submerged in the waters of his poetry, they slowly come floating to the surface.

Several meteorites timidly pass through the sky of the budding poet, with the name of "Blanca" crossing like a streak. The poet assumed the role of his noble colleague, Cyrano de Bergerac, whose "Roxanne" was Blanca Wilson, daughter of a Temuco blacksmith. One of Pablo's friends was in love with her and wanted to tell her so but didn't dare say it out loud. Nor did he have at hand a copy of the "Lover's Secretary" with its sample letter to be sent, but he did have a friend reputed to be a poet who could therefore write convincing love letters. Neruda was not only a good friend to his friends, but he also loved to snoop about in others' hearts. He wrote the letters, emptying out his own feelings in the other's name. He became a substitute, feeling that the ardent confessions he was writing to Blanca Wilson were his own. She was half-astonished, and whether by hunch or because she was acquainted with her supposed admirer, she doubted that he was the true author of that correspondence, in which she sensed something special.

Neruda recounts that, one day, she asked him if he were the one who was writing the letters. "I didn't dare disown my own work and I nervously answered yes. Then she gave me a quince apple, which of course I refused to eat and kept as a treasure. With my chum now out of the girl's heart, I went on writing love letters and receiving quince apples."

The boy used to fall in love without the girls' even knowing it. The poet kept locked up inside for many, many years his memory of one platonic love. One day, now mature, he recalled it quite innocently, since it refers to a childhood emotion:

> When my sister invited you over
> and I went to answer the door
> it was the sun and stars that came in
> it was two braids of grain
> and two interminable eyes.

That childhood fixation moved him to many homages, unbeknownst to the woman who was the source of such distinction. In the great hall of his home in Isla Negra, the poet installed a ship's carved figurehead, which he baptizes in the name of that fifteen-year-old offspring of German parents. The poem that evokes her has a question for its title, "¿Dónde estará la Guillermina?" (Where Can Guillermina Be?).

Some journalists, when they read the poem, attempt to clear up the mystery by means of appropriate searching. They find a surprised grandmother, a widow with two grown sons, who can't hide her astonishment at the news that a poem had been dedicated to her. Her reply includes a delightful picture of the period, "There are so many Guillerminas! I only saw him a few times outside my house, but we never talked." Then, a charming conclusion, "That's how they courted in those days."

Platonic love won't last long. His heart will sometimes be unfaithful to the young girls in flower, and he will take up with women in full bloom or those who have already given fruit. He fell in love with "the widow," Amalia Alviso Escalona, who was left alone with two small children at the death of her husband. The daughter of a North American father and a Chilean mother, she was a beautifully physical woman according to those who knew her. Neruda's heart seems to have a good memory, for his sister Laura in Temuco used to receive Pablo's letters from Santiago, Java, Colombo, Rangoon, Buenos Aires, Madrid, Paris, asking about "the widow," the lovely widow who was the daughter of rich business people and unattainable for him. All indications are that she never responded to the open admiration from the young man in the dark railroader's cloak and old-fashioned, wide-brimmed hat.

There is some evidence that the poet, from earliest youth, was not impeccably monogamous. His eyes would wander, and—though melancholy—he used to play around. Is the book *Twenty Love Poems* dedicated to only two girls? Usually, it's believed that Terusa and Albertina are the only ones. But many years later, in a flight of reminiscence, the poet lets the cat out of the bag. "Puerto Saavedra smelled like the sea and honeysuckle. In back of every house there were bowered gardens, and morning glories perfumed the solitude of those transparent days. There I also met the dark, flashing eyes of María Parodi. We used to exchange little pieces of paper folded so many times that they would disappear in your hand. Later, it was for her that I wrote Poem 19 of *Twenty Poems*. Puerto Saavedra is also in all the rest of that book, with its piers, its pine trees and its endless flight of gulls." And then, "I realize now that I've been talking about unimportant things. Those cellars, and those books, and those black eyes perhaps carried off on the wind."[7]

And then the three Bombal girls appeared—María Luisa and her twin sisters. During summer vacation, they used to descend on Temuco, shocking the town. They were pretty, with bobbed hair like French pageboys, and they dressed in the fashion of Paris or Santiago. They loved to pass themselves off as foreigners and crazy ones to boot, and to behave like harebrains. They had met Pablo in Santiago and used to come knocking at the door of his home in Temuco. Doña Trinidad would open the door, looking very virtuous and scared of these outsiders of ill repute, and she would always answer bluntly, "He's not here." She wanted to protect him from the she-devils.

So the three girls would depart, dying with laughter, and go sit in the Temuco Square. They'd begin to do outlandish things to attract the attention of the provincials—eat ice cream, dance the Charleston, recite things out loud—until suddenly the sought-after Neruda would appear, maybe a bit in love with one of them, Loreto. Many years later, he went to Viña del Mar with Matilde (his last wife) to visit Loreto, who had a brain tumor. Pablo went in alone to see her, trying to cheer her up by reminding her of the scenes in the Temuco Square. He came out destroyed, and she died shortly afterward.

Nonetheless, his great love from the province is Terusa, as he calls her in *Notes from Isla Negra.* The poet remembers her as happy and full of light. And another detail—What a beauty! She had that special something that lovers discover. And all the others, in this particular case—or were they all in love with her? In 1920, she was elected queen of Temuco's Spring Festival, and Neruda was the author of the prizewinning verses in honor of the sovereign. Poetry brought them together and she became his muse, whose effect was like that of a force pump, drawing up poetic inspiration and sometimes amorous prose. "Woman, in those moments I love you without loving you, . . . but your love resides beyond and deeper than my own self. Enchanted glass that carried to my lips the sweetest wine—a glass of love," he tells her in "Aquel bote salvavidas" (That Lifeboat).[8]

Adolescent love in a period when they still used chastity belts, still a long way from the sexual revolution. Girls are supposed to remain virgins, and the fear of pregnancy is paralyzing. The young man refers to it in his prose piece, "Pudo esta página" (This Page Could . . .), "Desire rises like a wave on the horizon of our life, and dies like a wave. That's the drama . . . that then there is never a corolla for my heart of a bee, never a nest for my heart of a bird in flight, and never do I find the flute that my mouth of a shepherd requires."

An urge to hide something, a need for secrecy? He calls himself "Paolo" to hide the relationship. This beginning of his voyage to the final pseudonym is taken from the Italian, and D'Annunzio is the intermediary, "And as I departed, I left your name and mine written in the wet sand, in a big wide sign:

PAOLO

TERESA

He offers one observation—the sign on the beach of Puerto Saavedra "was prettier than this one."

This "Paolo" which becomes the Spanish "Pablo" is inspired by a pair of lovers who were carried away by amorous frenzy. I once walked on the stage of those passions as I strolled through a modernday Rimini in Italy. Earlier, a native of the city, through the magical dream-vision of an adolescent Federico Fellini, situated the tale in the Mussolini period. Like our poet, he expresses the tremendously desperate stirrings and joyful awakening of erotic dreams. But Neruda in that period tends to identify himself with classical characters. In "Ivresse," he is "Paolo" and she "Francesca":

> Now that the passion of Paolo dances in me
> and my inebriated heart throbs with a joyful dream;
> now that I know the joy of being alone and free
> like the pistle of an infinite marguerite.
> Oh woman—flesh and dream—come charm me a while,
> come spill on my road your cup of sunshine;
> and let my yellow ship feel your trembling breasts,
> wild and drunk with youth, of all wine the best.

The pair incarnates the literary transformation that the youngster attempts to carry over from prototype to life. It was a time in which he was imitating books, copying them into his existence, trying to experience love as his tragic models did. Nonetheless, it was not simply literary exaltation; it was also to satisfy a requirement of his body, the flame in his veins where he discerned the flow of a fire that was his, not borrowed. In reality, it was impossible for the relationship between the thirteenth-century Italian lovers to be equivalent or similar to the link between these two young people. In addition, although they were the same age as Romeo and Juliet, Verona was not exactly like their shabby and damp Temuco. Even though the poet dreamed great dreams, he still couldn't quite swallow the Shakespearean passion in all its details. For him, the two stories were complementary and legitimate.

He didn't take the image of Paolo Malatesta and Francesca de Polentani from *The Divine Comedy,* where the cousins are consumed by guilty love and therefore condemned to punishment in hell, but rather from Gabriele D'Annunzio's *Song of Blood and Passion.* This exhibitionist author also interested Gabriela Mistral in her early years, so much so that she took his name for the first half of her pseudonym, adding the last name of the French poet, Frédéric Mistral. Neruda, in his day, was equally dazzled by the great Italian farceur.

28. Women and Their Poems

An army of critics, scholars, professors from learned and unlearned universities, dilettantes, exegetes, structuralists and impressionists, mapmakers and geographers of poetry, divers who explore the depths of his underwater secrets, those who work with their own rosetta stones like Champollions in Egypt—they all decipher Neruda's alphabet, creating a kind of navigational chart or aerial photograph in order to describe point by point the enigmas of his atlas and language. Something has been accomplished by these dedicated intruders and rummagers in regions of the abyss, and although much of the subsoil of his poetry is still unknown territory, the truth is that heretofore unknown origins have been discovered, removing the shadows from around some female inspirations, outlining their faces and names, and determining which one is the muse of this or that composition.

Terusa, in *Twenty Love Poems and a Song of Despair*, is the inspiration for eight of them: Poem 3 ("Ah, your mysterious voice . . ."), Poem 4 ("The clouds move like white kerchiefs of farewell"), Poem 7 ("Bowing at evening I throw my sad nets / into the ocean of your eyes"), Poem 8 ("In my soul there's still the buzzing of an absent white bee"), Poem 11 ("It's time to take a new path where she will smile no more"), Poem 12 ("You plow the horizon with your absence"), Poem 14 ("Ah, let me remember you as you were"), and Poem 17 ("You, too, are far away, farther than any").

Her name is neither Vásquez León nor León Vázquez. (Some critics and even Neruda himself have identified her with these names.) She used to spend summers with her family in Puerto Saavedra, with its wide melancholy beach enveloped in an infinitely lonely atmosphere. The Reyes family also spent the summer there, principally in the Pacheco house. The boy lavished names on her (he was always an expert at dispensing new names): Terusa, Marisol. Let's focus on "Marisol." For the somber-hearted youth, she held the fascination of the unfamiliar, joyous creature. She was "the brown butterfly as sweet and definitive as the wheat and the sun, the poppy and the water."

But careful! He will call his other youthful love not Marisol but Marisombra (contrasting the sun and the shadow), with his name-giving art which was never devoid of significance.

He writes to Terusa some verses that for many years remained unpublished and others which went into *Book of Twilights* and *The Ardent Slingsman,* as well as those several in *Twenty Love Poems.* She is also the woman of that book's "Song of Despair" ("Love is so brief and forgetting so long").

Of her he says, "She was the earth of the road, . . . at the time of kissing we were both the mouth and the grape . . . God alone can say how much I love her." To her he even dedicates the poem called "The Story of the Mad Prince" in which "The prince was mad from loving and not being loved." In the *Album Teresa 1923* he includes "Puerto fluvial" (River Port) and "Cuando recuerdo que tienes que morirte":

> When I remember that you must die
> I feel like never leaving
> like staying forever.
> Why must you die? And how?
> They'll close your eyes and join your hands
> as they did for my mother when she died,
> and then the voyage unknown to you,
> unknown to me because you loved me.

The preoccupation with the mother, linked with death, is transposed to Terusa, possibly in an attempt to deceive or conquer death by totally giving in to it. "Let me possess you so you'll endure in me, . . . consume yourself in flames and give me light." She is the woman in "Amiga, no te mueras" (Beloved, do not die), "Playa del Sur" (Southern Beach), and several poems in *Book of Twilights*. He is still thinking of her in *The Ardent Slingsman,* where the poet confronts the night and desire, "She is like the tide, when she fixes on me / her mourning eyes." He has carved her name on the trees of the forest, and she becomes a breeze that stirs, ready to hand over everything, and he to hold her, desire her, receive her. "Fill yourself with me. / Desire me, tire me, empty me, slay me. / Ask me. Hold me, contain me, hide me." This is followed by "Canción del macho y de la hembra" (Song of the Male and the Female), "You receive me / like the sail receives the wind. / I receive you / like the furrow receives the seed."

The last poem in the collection sings of the cosmic proliferation of desire throughout all species and all ages:

> It's true, my love, my sister, it's true!
> Like the gray beasts that graze in the meadow
> and in the meadow make love, like the gray beasts!
> Like drunken tribes that peopled the earth
> killing and loving one another, like drunken tribes.

When he was fifty years old, Neruda told an eager audience:

> I promised you an explanation for each one of my love poems, but I forgot that years have gone by. It's not that I've forgotten anyone, but rather that,

now that I think about it, what would you get out of the names I'd give you? What would you get out of some black tresses at a certain twilight? What would you get out of wide eyes in the August rain? What can I tell you of my heart that you don't already know? Let's be frank. I never said a single word of love that wasn't sincere, nor could I have ever written a single line that wasn't true.[9]

In *Twenty Love Poems,* there are two loves who are fundamental in the poet: the one from his adolescence in the province and the one he later discovers in the labyrinth of the capital. The girl from Temuco and the girl from Santiago.

29. *Incandescent Pollen*

The girl from Temuco is given an unoriginal designation—doll. In her, rivers sing, and her waist is of clouds. He evokes her enveloped in the marine landscape, "Ah, the vastness of pine trees, the sound of breaking waves . . ." In Poem 4 of *Twenty Poems* "The morning is beset by storms / in the heart of summer." The poet, in Poem 10, has a personal notion about "Lost Time," which is not exactly like Proust's: "We have even lost this twilight. / Nobody saw us hand in hand at eventide / while the blue night fell over the world." She is associated in Poem 12 with the nature-setting of the South, with the sensation of the sea and the feel of departure:

I've said you sang in the wind
like the pines and like the masts.
Like them, you are tall and silent,
and suddenly sad, like a voyage.

Terusa is linked, in all innocence, with a poem that stirred up a literary scandal, Poem 16, but we'll talk about that later (in Chapter IV), because it concerns a situation in which I was personally involved.

The girl from Temuco is dark and lithe, the opposite of the poet who had nothing at all of the gymnast and was introspective, yet pursued a girl who played with the sun. He slips along in shadow, and in Poem 19 is conscious of the contrast:

Dark, lithe girl, there's nothing to draw me to you.
There's all to turn me away as from the day.

You're the dazzling youth of the bee,
the wave's giddiness, the strength of wheat.

However, opposites are attracted to each other, and "Yet my somber heart is searching for you, / and I love your bright body, your free clear voice."

Also dedicated to Terusa is Poem 20, which is on the "hit parade" of a thousand reciters: "I could write the saddest verses tonight. / For example, I'd write 'It is a starry night / and the heavens from afar sparkle with blue.'" The end of the poem, the farewell, became a classic text:

I no longer love her, it's true, but still perhaps I do.
Love is so brief, and forgetting so long.
Because on nights like this she was in my arms
my soul won't rest for having lost her.
Even though now she can do me no harm,
and these may be the last lines that I send her.

He was living in Santiago and still couldn't forget Terusa, who also inspired another poem from the same book which was recited with great frequency, the "Song of Despair." In his fifties, the poet recalled that "The piers in the 'Song of Despair' are the piers of Carahue and Baja Imperial. They're the broken planks, and timbers like stumps beaten by the wide river . . . Love and memory closed in on me as I was stretched out on the deck of one of those little steamers that used to cross between Carahue and Puerto Saavedra. From somewhere on the boat an accordion was playing. I'm not including these accordions out of literary considerations—I heard them for the first time on the Imperial River."[10]

From Santiago, between 1922 and 1924, he writes many letters to Terusa, which throw light on the beginning of the relationship as well as on its difficulties. "Do you remember back there in the 'biographs' when we used to cast long looks at each other? We still hadn't spoken with each other, but already you made me happy." Those pleasant days, when we used to call the movies "biographs." A few days later he writes, "Autumn, and you still beautiful and bright, like that spring when I first loved you."

The following year, the letters specialize in describing his attacks of loneliness. In black times, "How sweet and lovely it is to receive letters from one's faraway beloved, from you, and to again love life and to again feel happiness!" Two solid days of rain in Santiago fill him with nostalgia for the endless rain of Temuco, "Love me, little one." As if proud of his somber mood, he tells her, "My kingdom is greater than yours. You are Queen of the Spring, whereas I am King of the Autumn and Winter." He sends her a photograph of himself and his room, his favorite corner, where "It's night and I've just arrived. How much I'd give to be with you on this starry night. What are you doing? I'm working. I'm sending you a very bad picture—do you like it? It's grotesque. Will you write to me? Will you love me? Good-bye, until tomorrow. A kiss. Two. Three. Four. Another."

He draws pictures for her, one of a running monkey, "Pepe," which he puts in charge of delivering a package of love to her. He sends the monkey as his slave, of whom he's jealous, telling her that Pepe is an outstanding dancer. "He can very well replace any young brute who might want to embrace you under pretext of dancing the shimmy in the Sunday dances at the International Tennis Club."

Besides geographical distance, there is something else that separates them—social distance. He's twenty years old, and he asks his "sweet little thing" to "Tell me—haven't you ever thought about these things that hammer at my heart? Haven't you ever put aside your *ladylike mentality* to feel a little bit sorry for the abandonment of this boy who loves you?"

Ladylike mentality. In another letter, in 1924, he goes on, "We're so far apart, aren't we, Terusa? We're growing apart, aren't we? Or is it my impression?"

One of the last letters overflows with as much disconsolation as Poem 20 of the *Twenty Poems* or of the "Song of Despair," "No, I can't write you any more. Sorrow is tightening around my throat or my heart. My Andalusian girl, is it all over? Say no, no, no."

Perhaps the Andalusian girl (so called because she once wore such a costume at a party) doesn't say "no," but she doesn't say "yes" either, which is one way of saying "no" or at least showing that she's fearful. Soon, we'll see why. Many years later, in "The Moon in the Labyrinth" section of *Notes from Isla Negra,* under the heading "Amores: Terusa I" he wonders:

> And now where lies
> that
> old love of mine?
> Is she now
> a tomb for a bird, a drop
> of black quartz,
> a chunk
> of wood pocked by the rain?

The question is developed in an aura of desolation. What may remain of that body that used to shine like the moon, of that hand that held clarity itself, the eyes frozen like night minerals? He asks about the death of love and the girl of his dreams, "Love, where does love go to die?" To faraway fields, to the foot of dead rosebushes. There is such agitated delicacy in that search for the emotion that had broken the young man's solitude! She has disintegrated like a great violet's scattered petals, but he can't forget the kisses that crept over his flesh. She was also the dark streak of his first heartbreak, the dark bird of his first descent into the abyss—strangely and suggestively without walls, perhaps because that love ripened among the almond trees, the incandescent pollen, the wild genista, in the region of mysterious mosses, as the poet muses.

He evokes her as a woman born of the landscape, springing up from the forest and the rooted kingdom, with the splendor of mint, hair of ferns, pubic moistness. He was born with her love, and he felt the petals of her love touch his parched skin. Rarely have I read a poem dedicated to vanished love that is so full of fidelity—"Terusa, unquenchable even in oblivion."

They used to see each other in Temuco and Puerto Saavedra during their vacations, and she probably took an occasional trip to Santiago. She seemed changed to him, and in "Amores: Terusa II" he would beg her to sit once more on the grass, "Now your face / seems changed to me. / Where are your eyes gazing? / Why do you have that severe look / on your face when I'm the same person as always? / Where did you lose your golden body? / What became of your half-open hands and your jasmine-shine?"

He pleads with her to go back, but it's impossible. He asks her to be again as she used to be, next to the honeysuckle on the balcony, next to her amber throne on the Moon—impossible. He begs her to be the shining portrait that looks motionless at him until the boy who loved her can once again see her and discover himself as he was, back then, in her beloved heart.

The portraits he refers to did play a role. We can see a snapshot of her taken by a photographer in the Temuco Square, where she is seated next to her mother and stepfather precisely in the period of her romance with Neruda. In truth, Terusa had hair the color of shining coal, huge magnetic eyes, and something about her that danced and shone forth from a heart geared for happiness.

The poet talks about "pure reclining bodies," and he doubtless felt as if a primeval charge emanated from her. Among the winter trains, she was motionless beauty. On a lonely map, she signified the main station of wonderment, his first great love.

30. *A Tomb for Birds*

More than sixty years have gone by since that tempestuous idyll, enough time for prohibitions against revelations to lapse, and for archives to be opened. Almost all the protagonists are dead. Younger generations heard about that love as part of their family history, which gradually became more visible and detailed as the reputation of the latter-day bachelor increased. It was they who broke the silence, beginning to talk about Aunt Teresa's love as a natural thing, not without some pride nor devoid of a certain condemnation of the earlier period's social prejudices.

In 1971, when I was staying at the Chilean embassy in Paris, Neruda—with a smiling expression that seemed to be recalling old unspoken tales—introduced me to a pleasant man in his forties, a well-known economist and Central Bank official who was part of the finance mission sent by President Allende to the Paris Club to renegotiate our foreign debt. As ambassador, Neruda headed up the delegation, a responsibility he fulfilled with some amusement and some resignation, given his well-known incompatibility with figures. Suffice it to say that though he may have understood nothing of the technical details of the matter, he was fully cognizant of it in political terms.

Among those who were able to navigate the reefs of those astronomical sums was this economist, whom Neruda introduced very briefly as Teresa Vásquez's nephew. The fellow smiled as he heard the distant connection referred to, and from the little he said I understood that that old love affair had become a legend which the family no longer had to keep hidden.

Later, a niece was more explicit. She wrote a letter to the newspaper supplement, *Buen Domingo,* dated 15 August 1982, about Pablo Neruda's first sweetheart.

I referred earlier, in passing, to the fact that, just as Pablo Neruda was not the legal name of the poet until he was quite a bit older, his first love's legal name was not Teresa Vásquez but Teresa León Bettiens. The reason for the fiction was not literary but had to do with the second marriage of her mother. It was appropriate that her children should bear the name of the mother's new husband. Her family belonged to "society" in Temuco, a town which apparently lost very quickly its quality of being the

"popular democracy" where all were equal, as Neruda described the somewhat uncivilized city of his boyhood.

The settlement town rashly began stratifying into classes, and the
Reyes family was low-class, outside of "society," whereas the León family
was high-class, in "society." The niece who writes the letter to *Buen Domingo,* Rosa León Muller, is assistant director of the Noel School of San
Miguel in Santiago, and she clarifies the role which social pressure played
in the rupture between Pablo and Teresa.

> My aunt often told me the reason for the split, and it was also discussed a
> lot in the family. It was due to the open opposition of her parents, because
> they considered him a young man of dubious background, whose family
> wasn't known and who himself wasn't known to anybody in society there.
> And that's why they didn't allow her to have any contact with that boy.
> What's more, they had a nickname for him—"Vulture," because he used to
> wear a cape and a wide-brimmed hat.

"Vulture" was an insulting nickname, a put-down applied to railroaders, poets, and artists. Some people who were freethinking followers
of Voltaire also used it for priests. But in the case of Neruda, they ostra-
cized him for being a poet and poor. Without a doubt, Teresa was influenced by the prejudice, but apparently the image of her first love never
vanished from her life and endured beyond the reaches of "the treachery
of immense oblivion." And just as Teresa would shine in the poet's
memory of the region between pale childhood and worldliness, so too
Pablo was an integral part of Teresa's life, the love that she perhaps regretted having lost. Was it a late regret that came as she saw his star on the
rise? We don't know, but she did hold on to any paper or picture that
would allow her to relive that orange-blossomed past. With those huge
eyes that had been stressed so often by the poet, she used to look again
and again at the albums full of photographs and letters, signed with various pseudonyms, from that boy who not only had to hide his identity
from a father who didn't want poet-sons, but also from the relatives of his
beloved who wouldn't put up with "vulture-suitors." The niece remembers
the album, covered in leather with pink, yellow, and green pages of thick
cardboard. Somewhere in it there's an ink-framed inscription that was
scratched on the beach of Puerto Saavedra, "I walked in the sand and
wrote your name and mine—Paolo and Teresa."

If the truth be known, though, she was neither all that docile nor
that much restricted by tribal law, as revealed by a photograph which

shows her disguised as a Mapuche Indian girl. Her Andalusian disguise was within the bounds of a Mérimée-style exoticism, but the Mapuche whim showed more than bad taste; it contained a betrayal of the white race. To dress up like the Indian enemy, to put on her forehead the Araucanian tiara, was to go over to the enemy camp. It was a characteristic defiance, just as her love with the poet also contained a challenge. Was the latter perhaps too daring, much more serious than the one-day Mapuche disguise? Most certainly.

She was possibly hurt by that love which the poet carried into the world's literature and which was set in that land where "water dripped unceasingly." How else to explain the fact that for many years she remained unmarried, in spite of being a delightful and happy woman, for whom "the bells of Cautín used to ring" and suitors were too numerous to count?

Not until twenty-five years after the end of her relationship with Neruda was she married, to a man twenty years younger than she, an expert typewriter repairman. At the age of forty-five, her regal splendor was undiminished, and she was still very lovely. The beautiful Teresa died in 1972, very shortly before Neruda, in the house of her niece on San Nicolás street in Santiago.

Those lines from "The Moon in the Labyrinth," which follow even more dramatically the tradition of Ronsard's nostalgia for lovely Helen's lost beauty, do not constitute an elegy for love that has vanished or been made ugly by age—they are an elegy for truncated love, a song to the suffering ashes of yesteryear's heart. Those passions are not buried in a cemetery, but in a bird's tomb, in a drop of black quartz, in a chunk of wood pocked by rain. There they will defy the passage of time.

31. *The Girl from Santiago*

I've spent forty years looking at her out of the corner of my eye and face-on, asking myself the absurd question whose answer is the old truth that reason never understands the reasons of the heart. Besides, why should I judge certain tastes of the poet?

The period of Marisombra began, the love from Santiago, personified in Albertina Rosa Azócar.

I met her when the relationship had ended. Neruda was just back from the Orient, with his first wife, María Antonieta Agenaar, and Albertina used to be present at gatherings, with her silent presence, which was more like an absence, and her eyes that seemed to be asleep. I suppose she was watching everything. Later, during the long reign of "The Ant" (Delia del Carril), she was a quiet and faithful member of the court that surrounded the then-splendid Delia. Nobody in the 1930s and 1940s used to talk about the deep ties of love that bound Albertina to the man of the house. I had become part of Neruda's circle of friends a bit late, and in an atmosphere where everything was discussed and passions were a favorite topic, that silence kept me unaware for a long time of the famous love which united that woman of long silences with the poet whose verses in *Twenty Poems* I knew by heart, not knowing that one of their inspirations was right next to me, talking in a low and friendly voice in a perfectly ordinary manner.

Afterwards the researchers came, the spies, the trespassers of long-closed rooms, the policemen of past love. And I learned that my taciturn acquaintance had been the girl in the gray beret known in poems quoted by millions—including myself—without being identified by anyone.

She was a year older than Pablo, but at the time of the affair neither was yet twenty when they met as students of French in the Pedagogical Institute.

When I found out about it, I began to see her in a different way. So she was the one! What at first seemed unbelievable, I later came to consider plausible. I proceeded to study her, to unworthily estimate the damage done by Time, that great enemy. For a Neruda anguished by the physical and social adversities of his relationship with Marisol-Teresa, who perhaps considered love a complicated game and was always fleeing like the waves, his love in Santiago did imply fulfillment, though it was also troublesome. Yes, there at my side is the one who seems to be a calm and assuaging Albertina. I can still recite from memory Poem 1, where she is:

> Woman's body, white mounds, white thighs,
> you are the world ready to succumb.
> In you my untamed peasant body will plunge
> and from the earth turn up the son.

Albertina Azócar Soto has a face of twilight. Neruda used to love not only the Maruri twilights. In the midst of the group's garrulous conversation, where Pablo has his back turned to the past and doesn't noticeably look at Albertina, she would exchange some words with me, and I could confirm that the poet's unfettered imagination is strictly realistic. Now that I'm sure of it, I compare one by one the verses dedicated to her with the model who inspired them. Yes, "silent, my dear . . . absorbed," because psychologically Albertina is like that One of the most beautiful songs to silence and also a portrait of laconic love is the much-examined Poem 15, "Me gustas cuando callas" ("I like you when you're still"):

> Because all things are full of my soul
> you emerge from things, full of my soul.
> You are like my soul, dreamy butterfly,
> and like the word spelled "melancholy."

Almost an interior photograph. The poet is the one who speaks, who has to take that initiative, but he speaks for her in Poems 5 and 11, "And I see my words far away. / They are yours rather than mine."

She has white hands, soft as grapes. And in Poem 13, she is the timid one, the thirsty one, who gives herself over to his fiery crosses that mark the "white atlas of your body." He spins stories for her so she won't be sad, and talks of a swan. She gives herself, and he wants to venerate her, "to sing, to burn, to fly, like a campanile played by a madman."

Albertina Rosa Azócar, along with her brother Rubén, is always present in the Neruda gatherings. Another familiar face, quite beloved by all, is an older poet, affable and really gentle, who breaks his silence only in bacchanalian parties or to eulogize a friend, and then, with his half-closed, near-sighted eyes cast downward, he explodes with a pantheistic, religious, and profane eloquence. Angel Cruchaga Santa María is a great Chilean poet who at one time writes in a certain mystic vein, perhaps because he converted into unattainable goddesses all the women he fell in love with. As his contemporary, I listened more than once as Vicente Huidobro, whose "palace" was a customary gathering place for young poets of the generation of 1910, used to say that Angelito (his name for Cruchaga) was mystically in love with the proud Manuelita Portales, at that time Huidobro's wife. And now, with a more than eucharistic passion no doubt, he loved Albertina, the woman who had once been the love of another great poet. Angel and Albertina were wed some years later. In short, Marisombra, like Marisol, entered into marriage considerably after the relationship with Neruda had ended. Was there some hope, some impression, some residue that made them wait a good while before taking that step? Pablo was apparently happy about the marriage of Angel and Albertina, two mature individuals who had been so dear to him. When he receives the National Prize for Literature (1945) he dedicates part of it to Angel Cruchaga.

Cruchaga was from an aristocratic family, devoutly Catholic, and fallen on hard times. People without wealth but from "society" usually have recourse to positions in the bureaucracy, and Angel served long and with meager return in administrative positions that had nothing at all to do with his true vocation. In time, he was able to combine bureaucracy with taste when he was put in charge of the Nuñoa Cultural Center. He looked like a good-hearted bishop and was a romantic equipped to live in the previous century. His first book, *Las manos juntas* (Folded Hands), is basically an elegy, inspired by the death of a girl he used to love who had a sad air that disturbed him. He is also a forebearing man, capable of finding beauty even in the sufferings of man. Although Lucifer also attracts him, the theme of his next book is *Job,* "Saint of the dung heap, terrible saint, your stony howl against the Eternal is a tower that quakes with terror. Hell was perfumed with your hairshirt." He wrote a poem that is a premonition: "Make me like the blind man, Lord. He sees not the breadth of the world, but within his kingdom he reconstitutes You." God punished him as he did Job, for he suffered from retinitis, which was aggravated by diabetes and left him with progressive blindness. His intensified interior life is evident in *Los mástiles de oro* (Golden Masts), *La ciudad invisible* (The Invisible City), and *La hoguera abandonada* (Abandoned Bonfire). When Neruda, in an article sent from Madras in November 1927, alludes to shadowy fish covered with velvet, singing fish, he is speaking of our poet and of a fish that, in his opinion, was swallowed by Angel Cruchaga—a fish from the most ancient of deluges. After his own relationship with Albertina was over but before she had given her heart to another, Neruda sends from Batavia, Java, in February 1931, an "Introduction to the Poetics of Angel Cruchaga," which serves as prologue to the collection *Afán del corazón* (Anxiety of the Heart). These two pages of prose are essential, twins of Neruda's poetry in the first two books of *Residence on Earth*. They begin with a declaration, that Neruda will later leave behind, "Neither he who heartily curses like an outcast nor he who weeps with great emotion are banned from the house of poetry's muses, but he who laughs—that one is banned." No, not always are the muses personified by those ladies adorned in painful organdy, and later, Neruda himself sometimes laughed in his verses. *Estravagario* is evidence that the one who laughs is not always doomed to remain outside the house of the muses. But in any case, that short introductory text is a penetrating illumination of Angel's ambience. "Cruchaga's women—living and dead—have had a titanic predisposition toward death; they have existed in such a pure state, with their hands so solemnly crossed over their breast, with such an aptitude for twilight behind an abundance of stained glass, in such a motionless physical passage, that they seem to be more like water plants, dark and immobile flowerings."

He notes a sign which foresees something that will come to pass, reestablishing a kind of connection between their two stories, for that apparently cryptic text ends with a mysterious paragraph that later events make clearer: "And among the repeated mystical manifestations in his work—so desolate—I feel his low-frequency presence around me, behaving with infinite control." [11]

The reason for that low-frequency presence was Albertina. The two seemed very different, but something brought them together. The husband was, as Neruda says, "extraterrestrial and sublunar" sometimes. He was in contact with comets and celestial phenomena, and he smelled of heaven but couldn't live without the earth. And it is woman, this feminine warm woman, who provides him with the earth and "the worn-out decorations, thick carpets, yellowed roses, old addresses." For her former lover, she was sometimes a magnificent and tender treasure chest, and now she is the same thing for her husband, another poet. Considering the illustriousness of her experience, she always maintained an invincible reserve, until a moment came when that reserve was thunderously destroyed.

32. A Strange Violator of Secrets

In 1974, Sergio Fernández Larraín publishes in Spain a volume containing the letters that Pablo Neruda wrote to Albertina during the period of their love affair.[d] The event unleashed a storm, not only because it represented a backdoor entry into the secrets of a private life which had been kept out of public view for fifty years but also because the individual who forced that entry was the one least likely to do so. This Fernández Larraín had put together in 1954 a kind of intelligence report in which he accused Neruda of being an extremely dangerous agent of that diabolical web that attempts to spread its evil over the world—communism.

Neruda was never a man of halfway measures, and his habit was to respond to a rash enemy with no pretensions of diplomacy. On this occasion, he gave what was due, publishing on the first page of the 12 October 1954 issue of *El Siglo* a diatribe titled "Mr. Fernández Larraín Will Not Change History."

It's a text quite distinct from the one devoted to Angel Cruchaga

Santa María. Written in a prose that is direct, basic, denunciatory, and active, the piece has been lost for a long time. Let us reproduce at least a few representative paragraphs:

> To judge by the summaries that have appeared, (the report) is a long novel, poorly written and in Fernández Larraín's typically cruel and monarchical-fascist poor taste.
>
> But I wouldn't be concerned if it were only a question of his predilections for creating fables. With this lie, there is a continuation of the threat, the slander, the war against Chilean freedoms and against the dignity of Chileans.
>
> North American monopolies have temporarily swallowed up Guatemala in a bloody operation that was preceded by a tenacious anticommunist campaign. The Fernández Larraíns of Central America armed themselves with pamphlets and then with aircraft, which unleashed their artillery, bloodying the face of America.
>
> They have selected Mr. Fernández Larraín not only because he represents the catacombs and the shadows of the Middle Ages, but also because he represents a specific antecedent in history.
>
> In point of fact, there exists in our national history a proclamation by traitors to our country, signed on 9 February 1817 by a troup of renegades, which "recognizes as sole monarch Fernando VII, in whose obedient service these subjects lived happily (and) offered to defend the rights of the king with their lives, their property, and with no reservation of any kind," asking that "the audacity and pride of the other side's insurgents be punished appropriately."
>
> These insurgents were O'Higgins, the Carreras, Manuel Rodríguez, Camilo Henríquez, Juan Egaña, the Fathers of our Chilean nation. They went off to prisons, to the terrible Cordillera, to Mendoza.
>
> One of the traitors was the Marquis of Larraín. After 137 years, it is a Larraín, Fernández Larraín, who requests prison, Cordillera, concentration camp, starvation, whip for the patriots. Not unusual.
>
> Mr. Fernández Larraín used to be a fan of Hitler, he is a disciple of the Caudillo Francisco Franco, he admires that little provisional jackal (in Guatemala) called Castillo Armas. Is it unusual that he opposes the University of Chile and its rector, opposes university institutes, opposes poetry foundations, and opposes humble Chileans, professors, workers, opposes all those who want more dignity, more freedom, fewer rags for our country?

An aggravating circumstance, that of 1974, when Fernández Larraín got possession of the letters by dishonest means. Albertina herself, eighty years old and appearing to be in robust health, in contrast with her illnesses at twenty which worried Neruda so much in the letters of that period, recounts with the same imperturbable expression as always, what happened with those letters. She kept them for more than half a century, more accurately she virtually kept them buried, hiding them from everyone but especially from her husband. It required cleverness and imagination to find secret nooks and crannies that wouldn't be discovered for a long time. It was to her credit and due to her sense of the value of those dangerous papers that she didn't destroy them, which is so often the way compromising papers are handled. She saved them like a holy relic. Beneath her cloak of silence lay a capacity for being discrete and for protecting buried treasure.

When the bruhaha breaks out about the letters' publication by Fernández Larraín, and Albertina brings a lawsuit against him, she is besieged by journalists. Her answers are impassive, her face crisscrossed with wrinkles that make her resemble very much her brother Rubén's "Face of a Man." "I was living with my husband Angel on a plot of land in the La Reina section of Santiago, where I had all my belongings. When Angel died, I couldn't stay on there."

She was left with her widow's pension and a small stipend from her husband's National Prize for Literature, and she went back to the city to live, naturally taking all her possessions with her. A nephew of her husband's, Fernando de la Lastra, between one visit and another, made her some deceptive suggestions: Why not sell me some of those books—what are you going to do with them? He poked and pried, sniffed and snooped like a bloodhound, as if he were looking for something which he never mentioned. He bought a few books from her, and then one day— Eureka!—he found the box where Albertina kept Neruda's letters. With much concern and attentiveness, he deplored the poor condition of the box which was ravaged by time. He offered to put the letters in order and keep them in a sturdy container that could resist the attack of paper-eating moths. With the find under his arm, off he went, to return only once to show her how they were being ordered and catalogued, and then he again departed with his precious burden. His aunt never saw him after that. Around that time, she went to work in a florist shop that belonged to the lovely white-haired Delia Solimano, who was the sister of one of Neruda's friends, Manuel, the great *cacciatore* (hunter), as the poet called him. Delia and Manuel had been born in Portofino and Santa Margherita in Italy's Ligurian region, and had come to Chile as children, by way of Ecuador. Manuel was an automobile dealer, with Neruda on occasion his customer. Later, Delia Solimano married her first husband, an Italian businessman who owned a soda fountain on Agustinas Street, where she also worked, as cashier. Around 1933, Vicente Huidobro used to invite me to go there every evening to have a little something, so that he could pay the cashier and tell her for the thousandth time that she was the loveliest woman in Santiago. She would keep her head down, like someone listening to the rain, and take the money in a businesslike and distant way. She had a daughter, and later, after annulling her marriage, she wed Tomás Lago and set up a florist shop. It was there that the widowed Albertina went to work. One day, between orders for rose bouquets and a sale of carnations, a friend entered and asked her, "Do you have some letters that they say Pablo wrote to you?" She answered in the affirmative and called her nephew Fernando in alarm to ask him what was going on. "Nothing," he replied. "I've shown them only to my boss." Her nephew was not to be seen, but Sergio Fernández Larraín did show up in Delia Solimano's flower garden, telling Albertina in a very amiable way that he wanted to talk to her about something important. She invited him to her house, thinking that he wanted to talk to her about Angel. To her surprise, he arrived carrying Neruda's letters, and she asked him where he had got them. "Your nephew traded them to me for some candelabras," was his response. "He refused to discuss it," adds Albertina, "and he told me he would publish them in any case and would write a very nice prologue." He was quite insistent and went to the house two or three times with the same proposal, until finally Albertina authorized him to publish them.

In Madrid in 1983, in an interview with the *ABC* journalist Mónica Guzmán on 23 September, the tenth anniversary of Neruda's death, Albertina is asked whether she was given any part of the royalties. "Absolutely nothing—he gave me just one copy of the book."

Eight or ten months after its appearance, with two lawyers she initiates a lawsuit against Sergio Fernández Larraín, who was ordered to return the letters to her, . . . but when he had already published them.

Why did Albertina authorize their publication? Maybe because she didn't want to carry the secret with her when she died? Maybe because as an old woman she wanted to enjoy while still alive that happiness of being remembered as the girl in the gray beret who at twenty years of age inspired poems that would project into posterity an image of her surrounded by a romantic halo?

The publisher of those letters, that terribly irate political enemy of Neruda and his ideas, many years before as a rich landowner in Mclipilla had been involved in a failed uprising against the Popular Front. On 25 August 1939, he took part in the "Ariosto coup," a conspiracy headed by General Ariosto Herrera. Three years after Francisco Franco's uprising in Africa against the government of Spain, this general tried to become the Chilean Franco who would overthrow the constitutional government of the radical Pedro Aguirre Cerda. Fernández Larraín had a fondness for all the Francos of the world, and he participated in all the anti-Communist leagues that could be found. He served as a belligerent deputy and later as senator from the Conservative Party, and was ambassador to Spain during the Franco period, which was like the culmination of his dreams. The day the *caudillo* died, he mourned him as one of the greatest men of the twentieth century.

So what explanation is there for that interest in getting hold of letters that aren't his —an interest that goes beyond the law and against every code and standard? How do you explain that interest in publishing the letters, thereby creating a sensational scandal? Letters that were expressly from an adversary whom he denounced as undesirable and who, in his turn, censured him politically and morally with his most outspoken prose?

There is probably not one but several factors that might explain the purpose, the psychological motivation, the combination of interests and passions and ambitions that pulled his personality in such apparently contradictory directions.

A type of bedazzlement in the face of men he paints as agents from hell? There are individuals who are attracted by those whom they seem to be publicly hating; individuals who are irresistibly driven to discover a secret life in the existence of persons they themselves accuse of the most terrible crimes. Is it the tribute rendered by the enemy to someone who possesses what they, monetarily rich, don't have and would like to have?

Yes, what they would like to have, because that little feudal lord from Melipilla always dreamed of being considered an intellectual, a writer. Lacking any talent of his own, he decided to lay his hand on the talent of others. To do so, he sometimes made use of money, sometimes of deceit. If there is one personality that is distinct from his in the Spain of this century, it is Miguel de Unamuno, yet Fernández Larraín got hold of some letters from the author of *The Agony of Christianity* and published them with his own prologue, which earned him a ticket into the world of literature, even though he had to wear borrowed clothes to get in.

Just as in 1974 Fernández Larraín publishes a book with the letters from Pablo Neruda to Albertina Rosa, in 1978 in Santiago we have the *Love Letters of Gabriela Mistral* published by the Andrés Bello Publishing House, with "Introduction, Compilation, Commentary and Notes by Sergio Fernández Larraín." It's like a mania. Included are letters from Gabriela Mistral to Alfredo Videla Pineda, and then thirty-eight letters to the poet Manuel Magallanes Moure. That correspondence has an intrinsic value, and the letters to Magallanes are a hidden gold mine that changes the perspective we used to have on Gabriela's emotional life.

Those letters of other people, which enabled the compiler to become a member of the Chilean Academy of the Language, are worth more in literary and biographical value than would be their weight in gold. They are precious materials for knowing about the personal world of their authors, filling out portraits and correcting impressions.

Albertina Rosa finally ended up selling her letters. After their rescue from the hands of Fernández Larraín, she deposited them in the vault of the Banco Exterior de España in Santiago. When the bank's president, Francisco Fernández Ordóñez, traveled to Chile to preside over a meeting of stockholders, Albertina Rosa agreed to sell the 115 letters and 17 poems, in addition to some photographs from those days.[c]

33. Love and Poetry

The letters from Neruda to Albertina Rosa constitute a unique complement to his literary work of that period. They are indivisibly linked to his poetry in *Book of Twilights, The Ardent Slingsman, Twenty Poems,* and the first phase of *Residence on Earth*. They are a painting of his emotions, almost a personal diary of his tribulations and problems, an index of his intentions, and a portrait of his times and surroundings.

The relationship between Pablo and Albertina begins when they were together in the same classroom and walked through the same corridors of the old Pedagogical Institute, located on the corner of Alameda and Cumming. Just as Neruda came from Cautín province, Albertina was also from the South, born in Arauco to a family connected with education in Lota Alto, near the coal mines that inspired Baldomero Lillo's *Subterra*. She, therefore, also came from a land of rainfall and Mapuches. There was something in her face, and even more in that of her brother Rubén, that suggested indigenous blood.

Classes in the morning and the afternoon, French literature and grammar, Latin, psychology. Misfortune strikes a year later when they open a French course of study in the University of Concepción and Albertina's father sends her there to study, close to their home in Lota. A very painful separation for the poet.

What impression does she have of her sweetheart sixty years after the romance? "Pablo was one year younger than I. He used to recite poetry in a monotonous singsong voice. He was very thin and taciturn, and he used to walk me to the boardinghouse where I lived with my brother."

How long were they together? "I think it was a year, maybe a bit longer. When we used to go on vacation, we took the train together. We separated at San Rosendo, and I would go on to Concepción and he to Temuco. In those days we had vacations in September, a month, and in December."

She spent two years in the Pedagogical in Santiago, and Pablo finished four years, that is to say the full course of study. For Neruda, the distance between Santiago and Concepción, 300 miles, was immense, and he filled it with a desperate correspondence. Was the distance greater or lesser for her? She answered his letters late, poorly, and never.

A tyrannical sense of family was imposed on her. Her father, Ambrosio Azócar Peña, and her mother, Juana Soto Rodríguez, were teachers, and she too will be one. In one of his letters, Neruda blames her brief letters on her professor complex. Everybody in her family is in education, the three males and the three females. The oldest brother is Víctor, then comes Rubén, author of *La puerta* (The Door) and *Gente en la isla* (People of the Island). The youngest boy, Augusto, dies early. Among the girls, first comes Etelvina, then Adelina, and third Albertina. The same diminutive ending for all the girls' names. Once in Rubén's home, on a Sunday afternoon, I saw all the surviving siblings together, and they gave an impression of being of hardy stock.

In Chile, classes used to begin in March, the end of summer. That's when all of us youngsters from the provinces who ever went to Santiago to study, trying to get into the university, would take a third-class seat in a train whose wheels on the rails cut the umbilical cord that tied us to our family and our adolescence.

The day of Cupid's arrow is marked down as 18 April 1921. Can one be so exact? Is the *coup de foudre,* the bolt from the blue, determined by a cosmic calendar or by a mathematical law of the heavens? It's probable that the precise dates for love are part of the *a posteriori* legend and fables that will later surround the poet. If it's a question of dates, let us refer to the letters, although many show neither date nor place of their composition.

Although the Banco Exterior de España mentions 115 letters, Fernández Larraín refers to 111.[f] Neruda wrote them from all the places in which he found himself during that period: Temuco, Puerto Saavedra, Santiago, Valparaíso, Ancud, Colombo, etc. The correspondence goes on much longer than the direct relationship, and the first letter is dated in 1921, with the last one eleven years later, 11 June 1932. Usually handwritten, the one written on 11 April 1925 on the poet Augusto Winter's typewriter is a rare exception. A good part of Neruda's correspondence contains drawings, including self-portraits, floor plans of the houses where he's living, sketches of his rooms. He likes paper of a great variety of colors, and he tries out inks of red, blue, lavender, with a preference for green in his mature years. It has been said that he would have liked to have the rainbow for his inkwell.

The boy tends toward introspection and self-analysis, and doesn't seem to admire himself. During the vacation periods, he carries on a correspondence with almost no reply.

With the passage of time, the poet confuses the poems dedicated to his love from Temuco and the one from Santiago. When he was fifty years old, he maintained that in *Twenty Poems,* those numbered 3, 4, 6, 8, 9, 10, 12, 16, 19, and 20 were for Marisol (Terusa), and the other ten (with an evenhandedness almost worthy of Solomon) were for Marisombra (Albertina). He attributes the "gray beret" to Marisol, and then, in the letters, puts it on the head of Marisombra. Emir Rodríguez Monegal, in *El viajero inmóvil* (The Stationary Wanderer), talks about an era of berets—perhaps both girls wore one, or could it be that the poet combines his two heroines in one?

But, as has been pointed out, Poem 15 is unalterably Albertinesque. Neruda had published it in La Serena in the journal *Vendimia* in November 1923, calling it "Poesía de su silencio" (Poetry of Her Silence). It contains a variation that the poet later eliminates:

I'll not interrupt, so that you'll be quite still,
and all will be mine, your silence all yours.
What was your stillness like when you were small?
Were your hands always at rest on your breast?
If you will not tell, then I shall have to ask
your brother, the poet, who went off to Mexico.

In January 1924, the poem is published in the Santiago journal *Zig-Zag* with some changes. I also have the impression that Poem 2, "In her mortal flame," is a later composition that replaced the first version, which was published in the book's first edition. Its construction is different, although the personage is identified, "Silent, my girl . . ." In Poem 5, he feels that he is speaking on her behalf, "And I see my words far away. / More than mine, they are yours."

Poem 7 shows fear at the mystery in her eyes, where he suspects the presence of misfortune, "I see only darkness, faraway woman of mine, / a hint of the edge of fright in your eyes."

And in Poem 11, "Anguish that cut my heart like a knife, / it's time to find a new path where she will not smile."

In Poem 13 he creates a variation on Poem 1, the woman's body, which he sings of with joy, but "when I reach the coldest most daring of heights / my heart folds up like the flowers at night."

He tells her in Poem 14, "You're like none other now that I have loved you," exhibiting his gift for transforming into uniqueness the ordinary, common woman of flesh and blood, changing her into one who plays "every day with the light of the universe."

He could never decipher the unknown woman of Poem 17, "Who are you, who?", and the lament in Poem 18 is "I love what I don't have. You are so far away."

The poems were written in student boardinghouses, principally located between Brasil Street and the Main Station, on rare occasion near the Mapocho Station, in the confusion of a difficult passion, to which he contributes love but which brings him almost nothing but words, written and spoken words.

Twenty Love Poems has been Latin America's most used and abused book for lovers. It became a kind of helper for those who needed to declare their love and, often without giving credit to the author, resorted to these lines by Neruda for their wooing. This seemed marvelous to the poet, like a justification of his poetry. When Albertina is asked which ones she thinks are the best of those dedicated to her, she replies simply and evasively, "The one that became the most popular is the poem 'Silencio.' He wrote several for me, but I don't remember which ones. It's so long ago now."

Neruda loved her for all the reasons and hopes that go into loving a woman, but also because she was the motivating excuse and springboard for the poetic leap. He is not only the man who has to express the whole world, but in addition he is also a young man, a vigorous male. He will have to express those two integral qualities by reaching for the stars with a poetry that also speaks on behalf of the defiant young man's passion. "On a night all full of cold errant stars, / like two crazy vanes I spin my arms."

Such is the atmosphere of *The Ardent Slingsman* Part I, which was not published until ten years later, in January 1933, with the poet's apology for its quality of "a document from my obsessive and feverish youth." Behind one and another of its pages Albertina hovers as the image of woman.

He conceived the project of developing the slingsman theme as a cycle comprising several volumes, as he later did with *Residence on Earth.* He goes on to say that the first volume will be called *The Ardent Slingsman,* and later would be followed by *The Wife of the Slingsman, The Slingsman's City, The Trumpet in the Woods.* At one point, he calls it *The Ardent Archer,* proclaiming it to be grandiose poetry "but small compared to what is planned." Albertina is the ocean tide, with her mournful eyes fixed on him and her body of white moving marl. It is she who has torn from him the exclamation "Beloved, do not die," written on a couple pages of letterhead from the Chilean Student Federation, which will appear somewhat modified as Part II: 5 of *The Ardent Slingsman,* whose original manuscripts were sent in part to Albertina and in part to Terusa.

It is true that those two loves exist side by side for a while, with the Santiago relationship the more intense for being more complete. The encounter between the man and the woman is fully realized, and *The Slingsman* is the testimony of that raging passion. There are even moments when he feels some response, "You are here, you exist, and I love you! I call to you and you answer!" The book's emotion is ambitiously framed by the youth who wishes to embody the universe, making Nature take part in his own nature, and wishes to be, along with his beloved, the vastest sunset in the heavens.

Many were the poems written immediately after *Book of Twilights,* with the majority doubtless lost "forever," as the poet said in his prologue to *The Ardent Slingsman.* When the book was published it included twelve poems: 1) "Like two crazy vanes I spin my arms," 2) "She's like a high tide," 3) "You are made of light and gentle foam," 4) "I feel your tenderness cling to my flesh," 5) "Beloved, do not die," 6) "Leave my hands free," 7) "My soul! My soul! Source of my wandering thirst," 8) "Fill yourself with me," 9) "Song of the male and the female," 10) "My slave, fear me. Love me. My slave!" 11) "Thirst for you that hounds me on hungry nights," 12) "It's true, my love, my sister, it's true." Of those originals, Albertina saved seven. Unfortunately, the others were lost. Neruda recalled that he had written them in a frenzy, seized by a starry inebriation. "I was in love, and rivers and floods of love poems pursued the slingsman."

34. *The Verse Changes: The Woman Remains the Same*

He later recalled that the *Twenty Poems* are "the romance of Santiago, with its student streets, the university, and the honeysuckle smell of shared love." Earlier, he had said that he was helped a lot in his writing by the Imperial River and its mouth, and the landscape, just as he was also helped by being in love, even though it was not always a "shared love." Organically, from his very innards, he felt the impulse to convert his passions and his geographical surroundings into poetry. That is a characteristic of this particular creator. He loved because he loved, and because he wanted to reveal it and needed to talk about it. Like the man that he is, he will take pleasure in his life experience, his emotional anguish, his erotic adventure; but like the poet that he is, he will immediately transform all that into poetry. Usually, he will not put any temporal distance between feeling and writing; they will be consecutive acts, and the paper will absorb almost immediately the still warm sensation of the bed. He has come into the world to tell what he experiences and what others experience, and he will do so with unusual quickness. This continuous movement from life to word will enable the word to always reflect, in immediate fashion, the changes produced in his life, his body, his spirit.

His love for Albertina will pass through several books, although each of his books is different from the previous one and from the next one, despite the fact that they may share a common name, as is the case with the various volumes of *Residence on Earth*.

Neruda is a poet of constant breaks with himself, from book to book. The greatest break occurs between the poetry of his first three books (*Book of Twilights, The Ardent Slingsman, Twenty Poems*) and *Endeavor of the Infinite Man*. The poetry of his first phase (keeping in mind that each book is different) is still relatively indebted to a renewed modernism and to European poetry prior to the aesthetic revolution. He used to consider *Endeavor* to be the ugly duckling of his work, his least understood book. When he was sixty years old, I heard him say in the National Library of Chile that he viewed it as a real nucleus of his poetry. In spite of its being the least read and least studied of his works, it is totally distinct from the others and one of his most important. He explained this affirmation by saying that while he was working on the book, he gradually experienced an awareness that he had not felt before. (It's one of the few times that he talks of his poetry as "work," not because it wasn't but because he took pleasure in passing himself off as a great loafer.) "If there is any place where the expressions and the clarity or mystery are measured and weighed," he said, "it is in this extraordinarily intimate book." [12]

Prior to that occasion, in 1961 when he joined the faculty of Philosophy and Education in the University of Chile, he reminisced that in those days, influenced by Stéphane Mallarmé and Guillaume Apollinaire to do away with grammar and established norms, he eliminated punctuation and uppercase letters from his books. "You can still see my old book, *Endeavor of the Infinite Man*, devoid of commas and periods."

Endeavor is a bridge in flames, where not only are uppercase letters, commas and periods burned, but also the then-prevalent literary forms and concepts come tumbling down, consumed in the fire of his own poetic metamorphosis, rapidly opening the way to a new phase, the *Residence* phase.

The poetry changes, the woman remains the same—Albertina. In one letter, he asks her to tell him in detail what she has done and what she is doing, whether she feels pain and what she's thinking about. He imagines her steps as he writes to her, that Tuesday morning. Then he copies a poem for her that later will form part of *Endeavor of the Infinite Man*, "At my side, lady in love, / who but you like the drunken bells / of an untitled song?" Here there are uppercase letters, commas, question marks, but they will all disappear in the book, after the poem's initial publication as "Canción para su destino" (Song for Her Destiny) in 1925, in the journal *Dínamo*.

The recipient responded to the poems that were dedicated to her with an aloof, or timid, silence. Does the poet write for his beloved, for himself, for the world? If it were only for his beloved, the result would not be an overwhelming success, and he knows it. But at some point he needs for her to know the lines that somehow she inspires in him, and he especially wants to hear from Albertina a word about his work, in essence a word about his life, about himself. Although he's aware that the result won't be impressive and perhaps no response at all will be elicited, he sends her a letter saying, "I have taken the incredible trouble to copy for you this poem from my next book, in order to find out if you're at all interested in what I write for you. You give me a feeling of indifference that makes me curious." [13]

If *Endeavor* is a crossroads on the journey, *Residence on Earth* is the arrival in a new country. But first the growth crisis will become an earthquake that does away with the prose region of his so-called novel, *The Inhabitant and His Hope*, and the texts of *Rings*.

The first, dated 1926, is preceded by a meaty prologue where the

twenty-two-year-old author defines himself: "I have a dramatic and romantic concept of life; anything that doesn't deeply touch my feelings
doesn't suit me . . . As a citizen, I am a peaceful man, an enemy of established laws, governments, and institutions. I am revolted by the bourgeois
and fond of the life of people who are unsatisfied and agitated, whether
they be artists or criminals." It's also the self-portrait of a transition which
features another trait of that young man who "was always inclined toward
grand ideas" and is now haunted by doubts and vacillation. He is searching for an expression which will be more or less his own, and he believes
that in *Twenty Poems* there was "some fruitful work," which provokes in
him an aggressive joy "unknown to those well-balanced fools who form
part of our literary life." *The Inhabitant and His Hope* is both a story and
poetry, although he underscores that he isn't interested in narrating anything. In contrast to Albertina, "Irene is heavy, blond, loquacious," and
she hurriedly drags him inside the house to tell her his tales. Rivas and the
narrator are horse thieves. She's fond of these rustlers, like Diego Coper,
a haughty proud man, imprisoned by the Cantalao police "on account of
some trouble with animals." When the narrator is freed, he receives her in
his room as he eats an apple, eager to tell her everything about his childhood and his lonely days at school. Last night, Florencio Rivas killed his
wife Irene. The two men ride off together. The narrator found her dead
on the bed "like a great sea mullet, cast there into the nocturnal foam."
The ending brings us up against the melancholy Neruda of that period,
"Oh, pity the man who is alone with his ghosts. . . . Now I'm sitting at
the window, and a great sadness moistens the glass. What is happening?
Where was I? Behold how this silent house also exudes the smell of the
sea, like a huge oceanic mollusk where I am motionless. It is time, because
the solitude begins to fill up with monsters; the night twinkles on a prom-
ontory with faded dying colors, and dawn lifts its weeping eyes from the
water."

Nobody needs to feel concern or sympathy for Neruda as a prose
writer, although he always said he was a poet who wrote prose out of
error or out of necessity. But *The Inhabitant and His Hope* reveals a writer
open to all literary genre. Once I heard him say, in reference to a talented
young writer, that you can write poetry, stories, novels, and essays, but
you have to stake out a preference.

The difference between the prose of *The Inhabitant* and *Rings* is
apparent, even though both books are published in the same year, 1926.
The latter is poetic prose, while the first is a tale written by a poet. In
Rings, "Morning Glory Autumn" has the feel of poetry with a distinctive

typographical arrangement. The same thing occurs with "South Imperial River": "Mysterious willpower, the sea's insistent multitude, beasts condemned to the planet, there is something in you that's darker than night and deeper than time." All of this is like a return to the South and the piers of Carahue, the springtime of August, the reminiscence of "Childhood's Province":

> From this romantic balcony I unfold you like a fan . . . Oh fearful winter of floods, when my mother and I used to tremble in the frenzied wind. Rain falling everywhere in sad unending extravagance. Lost in the forest, the trains howled and mourned. Cornered by night, the frame house creaked, and the wind leaped over windows and toppled fences . . . I was the lover who led the wide-eyed girl along leisurely paths, at twilight, on unforgettable mornings. . . . Province of a childhood that slipped away into secret times unknown to anyone. Resting now on platforms soaked by new rain, I propose you to my destiny as the sanctuary of return.

Always the rain, as in "Solitude of Towns": "Rain, friend to those who dream and those who despair, companion of those who do not act and those who sit and wait."

Some texts, like "Sadness" and "The Lieutenant's Lady," are perfumed by the Scandinavian and Russian literature of those times.

35. Letters as Confession and Anguish

Neruda began to write *Residence on Earth* between 1925 and 1927, prior to his first trip abroad, during a period in which his life had become extremely difficult. He keeps at the book in the Orient, where Albertina Rosa continues to bring him long days of sorrow. On 18 September 1929, he announces to her in a letter that a new book of his will soon come out in Spain, amplifying that it contains many things written for her. He copies down for her the first four lines of his "Madrigal Written in Winter":

> At the bottom of the deep deep sea,
> in the long roll calls of night
> your silent, silent name
> passes like a horse in flight.

Silent, silent name. Rafael Alberti recalls the episode when plans for the publication of *Residence on Earth* in Spain fell through. It was ultimately published for the first time by Nascimento in Santiago on 10 April 1933, in an edition of only one hundred numbered and signed copies.

From Ceylon, Neruda also sends "Slow Lament" to Albertina. On top of the anguish and exhaustion he experienced late in his youth in Chile, now in the Orient an unknown and overwhelming solitude has been added, in the form of Asia before the conclusion of the colonial period.

Neruda's letters to Albertina begin when he is a boy of sixteen, and when he writes the last one from Java, he is twenty-six, although some will still be sent after his return to Chile. They hold the intimate story of a passion that went largely unanswered, or which involved two such distinct temperaments, two such dissimilar people, that the one who totally gave himself up to it will inevitably feel despair at the response or lack thereof. But, in addition, those letters contain a compendium of clues for deciphering the young Neruda, for they are like a record of his spiritual heartbeat as well as a full chronicle of his mode of existence.

Letter 1 is accompanied by a full-length self-portrait of the poet in Puerto Saavedra, standing on the beach, without his cloak but wearing a wide-brimmed hat and dark suit, with his angular face and eyes looking off in the distance, hands in his pockets. A small adventure is noted: "I've stolen a very beautiful little Roman cat; I'll bring it to Santiago."[g]

As in a Mallarmé poem, the poet has read all the books, he has seen all the stars in the southern skies, he has spoken with all his friends. He knows by heart the "yellow sad town," sadder because she is not there. They are separated by the distance between Temuco and Concepción, and his crisis with his family is growing deeper. "All my plans to write, study, think, are falling apart. I feel bad in the town, bad in my house, everywhere. Today at noon, I had a violent desire to go back to Santiago and happily bury myself in my tenement house." The following Monday, he plans to go to the country, riding six miles on horseback. In the midst of this whole hostile tableau, he misses her. The letter is written in the summer, possibly January. He's not studying, but he'll do so in February, and in March he will see "the tea-eyes of the little girl, the Naughty Little Brat who writes me ten lines in eleven days and forgets my address."

In the third letter, his account of a train trip is a *costumbrista* folkloric picture of the period. To avoid paying for their ticket, stowaways (they call them "turkeys" in Chile) had to hide in the most unlikely places. "At midnight they hid me under a cot, where I spent five hours freezing." Then, a third-class coach, where his letter invites her to share the pan of coals for a little warmth. He wants her to bring along two or three of the attributes which constantly show up from beginning to end of his poetry of that period—her beautiful sad eyes, her silence that he likes so much, and to cap it all off, "your mouth, which needs my kisses." In the letters, he celebrates something which is inherent in a writer, the discovery or rediscovery of words. "Nowadays I like the word apple . . . If I have a daughter her name will be Manzana . . . If she were to be your daughter, then she would be tall and very pale, like those long yellow apples they store wrapped in tissue paper during winter."

Back again in Santiago, in his room at 758 Manuel Rodríguez Street, he claims that his principal hardship is poverty. "Every day I have to find money to eat on. I've suffered my share, my little one, and I have felt like killing myself out of boredom and despair."

In summertime, the youth goes from the tenement house to mother nature. On the small rural estate of Miramar, a few miles from Temuco, he describes a real countryside, with wheat fields, sunsets, *maqui* bushes, pennyroyal, virgin mountain with lions. In the evenings, he stretches out under a *peumo* tree and thinks about her. All of this is written on a piece of paper that is really a notecard sent by Juana de Ibarbourou. By some miracle, he has found some ink. He's not studying his university texts, but he's happy with his rifle. He wants to be a sportsman, an equestrian jumping champion. He has futilely wasted shells shooting at the eagles that frequently perch in the oaks. In the morning, he calls himself the terror of wild birds.

One individual comes and goes in the letters, very much at home—Rubén Azócar, Albertina's brother. In letter II, she's told he will write to her brother with instructions, and "with Rubén you will come by hook or by crook; what you tell me about your health requires the trip at once. You are to take the train, even if all hell breaks loose. Today I had it out very seriously with Rubén and criticized him severely for his ill will, and to push him to make up his mind I told him that your trip was mandatory for reasons I couldn't tell him about." The paragraph reveals the writer's imperious character, evident even without any analysis of handwriting. He gives orders (you'll come by hook or by crook, you're to take the train even if all hell breaks loose). The poet was not weak-willed, and with an inborn tendency to dominate, he possessed what is called a gift for command, planning actions and movements. That personality trait, in time, became a powerful resource in his literary career. Seemingly disorganized, he had an unusual capacity for doing things, for putting together individual and group efforts. He was always planning something, not only in the realm of literary creation, but also in that of personal and social activity. He was a great dynamo of undertakings, and this characteristic, though fruitful for him, nonetheless clashed with the passive resistance of Albertina, who did not obey instructions and was capable of ignoring hook and crook and didn't relish all hell breaking loose. She was like stone, imperturbable and unyielding in her frequent silences and her determination to do only what she considered necessary.

The poet is almost her opposite. He writes her virtually every day and sends her newspapers where there's a poem about the absent girl: "(You're the absent girl.) On the other hand, you—in ten days, one letter. While I'm stretched out on the damp grass in the evenings, I think about your gray beret . . . I've quarreled with many sweethearts I used to have, so I'm more alone than ever, and I would be happier than ever if you were with me. . . . Besides, tomorrow I'll send up a four-colored kite in your honor and I'll let it fly clear to the sky of Lota Alto. One of these nights, darling, you will receive a long message, at the moment the Southern Cross passes in front of my window. Tomorrow I'll send you a nice book by Chekhov."

In another letter, he calls her Arabella. He gives her a hundred names. Neruda is the greatest name-giver we've known. Perhaps this mania for inventing names and nicknames and aliases comes from both the force of his imagination and from the fact that he grew up in a world that had only recently become part of the so-called civilization of the white man—a still unnamed world where it was necessary to bestow the cross and holy oil of names in order to differentiate human beings, places, and things.

We don't really know whether the origin of what is claimed to be the poet's earliest memory comes from legend or from a false memory stimulated by the stories of his elders, but it describes a scene in which he is very small and is seated on some blankets spread out on the grass, in front of his house, which is burning down in one of the voracious fires that in Temuco were their daily—or nightly—fare. The scene is repeated in July 1923. "The other night, yesterday," he writes in a letter to Albertina, "there was a fire here, in front of my house. We almost burned up. Beautiful high flames, water, my mother's wailing. I enjoyed it a lot. Then it rained . . ." The violent crackling commonplace of fires, the torrential commonplace of rain. "It's almost always raining. I spend the time half-asleep. Huddled in a big armchair as old as my grandmother, beside a pan of coals, I think that in hell it must rain just like in this damned town."

Later, he sends Albertina a picture of Pola Negri with some verses and reproaches her for abandoning her *Paul*. In the next letter he calls her Netocha, from the Dostoievsky character, Netocha Nezvanova.

He is seventeen or eighteen years old and full of doubts and torments. He finds life in Temuco, without her, intolerable. "These days have been bitter, my little Albertina. Nervous crises or shitty gatherings, I can't take it alone any longer. At night, long and painful insomnia. I become desperate and feverish. Last night I read two long novels. Day was already breaking and I was still tossing and turning in my bed like a sick man. Here they don't even let me sleep late in the morning. My family—stupid, bad people. My God, what solitude! Why was I born among these stones? And worn out like this, I'm not strong enough to take the train. I still have four days here. Isn't it true, Miss Albertina, that I'm moaning and groaning like a woman?"

In addition, the poet complains because he has no reply from the woman he writes to. He notes the absence of her words and says he understands the sad truth. "Who are you? And I, who am I? What do you care what I'm doing or suffering? What am I to you? Perhaps nothing, deep down, in the most hidden truth. Something alien to you, next to you a man who gestures, talks, goes away, comes near." His passion doesn't kill his sense of reality, and while he is feeling with his whole being, out of one corner of his eye he sees her as she is, without deceiving himself.

Did Neruda, who was a long time in making the final break, perhaps assume the role of the poet who sang the object of his dreams not only because he dreamed of her but also because of the overwhelming need to express himself, to turn into poetry what was happening to him on the inside, even though the source of his inspiration might cause him suffering and might frequently be as indifferent as a stone? He would strike sparks from that stone. He would transform it into poetry. But he cannot avoid letting out a howl as he bids her farewell with a sad irony. He will mail the letter, "With the hope that it gets lost, and that it maybe will get lost, if you receive it. I am honored to kiss you."

This love will swing back and forth for a long time.

36. The Period of the Sturgeon-thin Poet

During the period of *Book of Twilights*, in that poem dedicated to his sister's birthday, he regrets that he has nothing to give her. He is poor and living in supreme penury. "Everything I have I get from afar. / Sometimes even my soul seems distant from me." He has no money for a gift, but he will celebrate the 18th of April, the anniversary of his love for Albertina, by giving her that name that is precious to him, one that he repeats the most. In order to get her to come from Concepción, he desperately tries to find 500 pesos to pay for her trip and temporary lodging.

He has the impression that what he writes isn't very important to "Netocha," but he still can't keep from telling her, so toward the end of January, he informs her that he's pleased because, "Yesterday and the night before last, I wrote something with enthusiasm, and for such a long time I had been concerned about my inactivity. . . . I'm going to write like crazy this whole time. You don't care about all this."

In spite of the poet's name for her, "Netocha" is apparently not interested in Russian literature, maybe in no literature at all: "You're a loafer, and you never read Sachka Yegulev, the story of a bandit very much like me. *Bandit!*"

In our wanderings together one sunny morning, while walking through the old neighborhoods of his youth, Neruda and I stopped in front of 330 Echaurren Street. He had sent a letter to Albertina with a sketch of that house between the signs *Lavance* (Laundry) and *Dulcería* (Sweet Shop). He's pleased with his bright, happy room, he tells her, but he's still sad. In any case, he's beginning to feel the need to go abroad. One day his letter is bitter, the next day it's optimistic. "Your beautiful lilac-colored letter deserves this ink the color of a parakeet's wing . . . Are you studying? I am putting into shape the originals of a book, *Twenty Love Poems and a Song of Despair.* There are a lot of things there for my faraway Little Girl." Afterwards, he threatens and gives in, only to again demand. He accepts the idea of going to study in Concepción, because she is there, although "for me the province is tough. If we don't spend this year of 1924 together, it is unlikely that our paths will cross again in this long life. But if we don't manage it, we will go away with Rubén, later this year."

Bohemia snares him. One day at three o'clock in the morning, he goes into *El Mercurio* and at the counter where they edit the financial news, he makes use of paper, pen, and ink to write her, confessing that he is on a binge, like every night.

In that man, so impassioned by being and existing, nothing was more extraneous than the idea of suicide, yet the notion did once momentarily visit him during his tormented youth, although he received the visit with some skepticism, if the truth be known. "All day yesterday, in a deathly mood. I thought furiously about killing myself. I wonder if it's worth the trouble. Isn't it probably useless, besides? . . . Here comes my sister, curious about what I'm writing. As she eats apples she is trying to open the talcum can, she's talking to me about wild pigeons and about how she doesn't like wine. Now she's gone."

He wants to travel, though the destination changes frequently. Rubén is in Mexico at the time. Neruda suggests to Albertina a trip there. "Naturally if the revolution ends, both of us will go to Mexico, to love each other in freedom, even if we live in poverty." Later, he makes plans to go to Germany, but the trip on board the *Adriana* fell through. He now refers to Albertina as "my little brat" and "little rotter."

There is a passing allusion to a friend who will soon become an enemy, "I'm enchanted that you tell me you don't like that de Rokha; I, too, think he's unpleasant. . . . I'm horribly jealous, shameless one! The three-legged table tells me you have loved no less than three men. I include myself there, and I think I know another name, but who is the third one?"

Neruda's letters are known, whereas Albertina's are not, which leaves gaps and opens up mysteries. What does he mean when he tells her, "I'm not a total cad, my dear little lady, and I understand the good and the bad—all the good and all the bad—that I have done to you; but a large part of that pain you have had from me was inflicted because of my wish to not drive you away, to not be able to do so, to make you more beloved to me." What is the background of this paragraph? An enigma! The problems of an epistolary monologue!

Just ahead, staring at him with a terrible gaze, the examinations. "I haven't studied, almost not at all; I'm overcome with deadly laziness, total nihilism," he writes on 17 March, and in the next sentence the mood is the opposite, "I am so happy that we will spend another year of our lives together."

That happiness is soon clouded. He discovers in his "beloved little girl" what in others gives him the most despair—a cold heart. At that point, he feels like knocking her head against the wall. Wicked one, frog, snake, spider—all of them delicate forms of address for her. Apparently she is not well, for an injury is mentioned. He is drinking like a fish. "Last night, back at home, I wrote to you—I was very drunk. I don't want to open the letter so I send it to you not knowing what it says—you tell me."

The relationship goes from one storm to another. Pablo sends Albertina Rosa a strange New Year's greeting, "You will be forgotten forever, exiled from my heart, even if that doesn't mean much to you. Verdict: because you have been a bad companion, and because I have made a mistake—a painful one—in believing in your intelligence and your goodness. May the new year bring you happiness, if by chance you have none now."

Shortly afterward, a complete somersault in letters where he orders her to claim her mail in the name of Albertina Neruda and then Netocha Neruda. The "solitary earthworm" doesn't react.

He writes from Valparaíso asking her to come at once because he has many confidential things to tell her that she doesn't know about and that only right now will she ever be able to hear from him. Then he announces that he intends to write her name in the sand that afternoon. He doesn't overlook the effect of surprise, and one day, he tells her he has been blind since ten o'clock in the morning. Another time he displays more names for her than usual: my earthworm, toy, little heart, bitterness, poppy, bee, snail, ugly brat, "Why do you quarrel with me? . . . You write me letters as tiny as flies."

In Temuco, Neruda writes letter number 75 (according to the enumeration assigned later by scholars) on letterhead of the daily *La Mañana*, where he informs her that he is tutoring two pupils in order to earn a few pesos. He complains of poverty and asks her not to simply tell him she feels sick. She must inform him immediately and in detail about her leg pains, for he knows some remedies—intramuscular and intravenous injections. He likes her last photograph and admires the parasol above her precious face. "I don't much recognize the leg, which is swollen and an irresistible temptation for me. For you, no working and no standing on your feet, even if your grandmother has to do the cooking for lady Amanda and your family."

Suddenly a letter comes for him from far away that makes him happy, but he will again criticize her lack of response. He is confused and bothered. "It's as if you were thinking about something else while I'm talking to you, or as if I were talking to you from behind a wall without hearing your voice. Since I am vain, I'm very sensitive to all that."

Suddenly up pops the name of a book that reveals some of his reading material of the period, which he thinks might interest his laconic correspondent. "Did they bring you *Juan Cristóbal*? If you have time for reading, tell me what you think of it."

On Monday the fifth, summertime, he writes her from Temuco, demonstrating the persistence with which they both construct a beautiful chain of impediments to their happiness. "If there weren't fondness, the chain would be enough to hang either one of us." His relationship with his family is dreadful, "I've stayed upstairs in my room and I haven't even come downstairs to eat. Here I've earned a reputation in my family of being a wild man with a bad personality, which maybe I don't deserve . . . They are always comparing me with a cousin Carlota, a very somber young widow who lives off by herself and never associates with anybody. The truth is that as soon as I set foot in this town, I'm beset by overwhelming crises of bitterness and boredom." Then he jokes, "Is my little one by chance a lost case? Don't lose weight. Eat, laugh, take walks. Do you have a sweetheart? Oh, that is completely indispensable! You see how I am thin as a sturgeon, without a sweetheart. Are you reading? Shall I send you some books, beetle?"

37. *Farewell*

"Yesterday in the country I saw a marvelous rainbow. Soon I'll go to a nearby town, to revise a book. Are you studying? Do. Don't forget. Write to me, today."

He is obsessed by the exams. "In reality," he recognizes, "I'm not a whiz at political economics." He has with him several thick tomes that he plans to review starting in mid-February.

In those days, especially with the arrival of summer, an exciting notice used to spread through the provinces, "The Hungarians are here." This meant that the gypsies had set up their tents in a nearby clearing. Neruda would wander around their camps, half-amused and half-fascinated, flirting with the girls and giving them his hand so they would read his fortune. Signs, as might be expected, of a long happy trip, which he was yearning for, and of a woman. "You, no doubt," he points out to Albertina, to whom he recounts his visit to the camp, where they gave him a charm that he should keep out of sight on his right side. It's a mysterious yellow root, and the poet is convinced of its magical power, saying that in his whole life he won't ever be without it, "because just yesterday I received a check that I had been expecting in vain for a long time."

The cajoling earthworm, who lacked all cajolery, seems to be concerned with only two unspecified things—a headache and thinking of him. He doesn't have much faith in that description. "Is it possible that you don't eat, go out, converse, quarrel, read, recover a little from that trouble; that you haven't gone to the movies, don't go to the post office, don't smoke, haven't met any interesting girls; that your friend with the motorcycle hasn't written you; that somebody hasn't gossiped about me; that you haven't read the newspapers, haven't visited with anybody? Secretive girl!"

Doesn't he possibly see Marisol in Temuco? Sometimes he doesn't seem quite so sad. On clear days he can see the island of Mocha. Black sea lions and nostalgic tuna raise their heads. Later, he announces that he won't take the exams. Nonetheless, he discovers someone more unfortunate than himself—Albertina's brother. "He has more misfortune than a bad penny." To his way of thinking, "He is weak of will and excessively timid." Actually, Neruda wants to influence Rubén to help in his relationship with Albertina, which is smashing up against the stubborn opposition of the rest of her family.

Almost in passing, as if it were something unimportant, on 9 January he writes her from 733 Amunátegui in Santiago, informing her that his latest book has come out. "Tomorrow I'll send it off to you—we'll see if it reaches you." All very offhanded, and he's talking about nothing less than *Twenty Love Poems and a Song of Despair*. Once again in Temuco, on 6 February, he complains about not having stamps and having to delay the posting of several letters. He adds a few lines which illuminate a very different angle, alluding to the "outlandish excursion by de Rokha and Rubén who end up pawning their leggings as a last resort." I heard once that the first one left the other one in hock in a Temuco boardinghouse as payment for the bill.

Money, money, that Great Dictator is the eternal worry. He tries to earn a little bit, somehow. By now he is a well-known poet within the limited confines of the nation, but to publish his first book he had to go into debt and pawn his watch. Royalties are virtually nonexistent. He asks Albertina to speak plainly to Rubén "so he'll do everything he can to get money." His plan (Neruda was always planning) is for the three of them to go abroad. Pipe dreams that go up in smoke from one day to the next, but he will persist so that one day the trip may come about. She maintains a standoffishness that he scolds her for. He reminds her of the occasion on which she went off to a student-festival parade when he was supposed to visit her, and he sarcastically reproaches her for "prancing around sick and unmindful of her old friend, accompanied by her housemates among the paper streamers." He suggests they travel together to the South and tries to build up her enthusiasm by saying that he will tell her all about his life, morsel by morsel, "the first night that we sleep together beneath the stars of Ancud."

Meanwhile, the break with his family, especially with his father, takes place. "My sister was here with my family until a short while ago. I barely saw them the whole time, and I didn't go to tell them good-bye when they left—you can see that the thing was completely cut. Fortunately, my mother bought me a suit, otherwise you would probably have found me turned into a dishrag. My suit is beautiful, striped like a zebra." He is drinking considerably. "Now I'm out on *binges* every night." Next to the Chilean expression *curaeras* (pickling cures) he sketches two bottles and a glass. His sousings give flight to emotion, and when he reached his room he was overcome by tenderness and sank into bed, planting "a huge firm kiss on the portrait of the indifferent faraway girl." In all these letters, there is a literary feeling that, amidst the joking, prefigures the magic realism or capacity for whimsical invention that will later characterize one period of Latin American literature. "It's now more than twenty days later, but wonder of wonders, as witness to that miracle, the kiss is still stuck to the glass."

His little student room contains several photos of her, which he calls "indispensable." He sends her drawings, which he describes as "snapshots of my room." Each one bears an explanation, as if they might not be sufficiently recognizable: bed and corner with your portrait, pitcher and wash basin. In the mirror he draws his silhouette. At one side, he sketches the gypsy talisman. The clothes brush. The inkwell, empty from so much writing. His pipe. A child's wooden horse. Main door with curtains.

Complaints, many complaints. "You have a right to think about forgetting me—this way, my companion is no use to me. . . . This whole thing is very bad, worse than you think. I, also, wrote you for New Year's, but it was a bitter letter, breaking off with you. In reality, you are the only thing I have to lean on during this dreadful time. . . . For my torn-up existence it is hard to reject love, to forget what is loved, and I specifically wanted you to remain outside of the miseries and absurdities that I am acquainted with."

A new and rare typewritten letter. "I think I'm a great typist, therefore I'm writing on the typewriter. . . . I find that with a typewriter one lies with greater ease. Every afternoon I write, I aswer [sic] one letter or another on this machine that belongs to Don Augusto Winter. Now I see that up there I put 'aswer' and that fills me with sadness." The same letter begins by saying, "Albertina, you're a naughty woman. You never write me." He sends her postcards covered with poems. He tries to get Nature to assist him, galloping over the hills and filling his pockets with hazelnuts, *chupón* nuts, *copihue, boldo,* myrtle berries. He doesn't have any such luck with the sea, the Pacific doubtless being too rough. "Don't tell anything to the sea," he writes her, "The sea is my enemy. When I go swimming, I shout great insults at it, and it tries to drown me and pummel me, full of fury."

In those days, he is writing *Endeavor of the Infinite Man* and preparing for his trip to Chiloé to meet Rubén, who has found a teaching job there. He intends to go to Ancud at the end of October. Occasionally, she writes more expressive letters to him, and he pressures her to give up everything and come to live with him. "I don't want them to go on killing you in that obscene school; I want to keep you young and pretty like when I first loved you, and you keep that in mind so that I'll be happier." To carry out these plans, he needs money, and he informs her that he intends to embark on a movie venture.

He is finishing his book for delivery to the publisher and prides himself on being the editor of a little soon-to-appear journal, *Caballo de Bastos.* He is an unrepentant night owl, and there are some days when he doesn't get up and is still in bed at eight at night when he writes letters to her. Finally, he received some money from his publisher and spent it all at once. Now he has a beautiful desk. "The lack of a desk was the main reason I couldn't write you." When she says she has written letters that he never receives, he answers sarcastically that he receives all his letters but especially those that are written. He exaggerates to her the beauty of the room that awaits her: new cushions, a thick floor mat, a real tortoise that answers to the name of "Luca," with whom the poet converses entire afternoons. It may be a chat in which he gets as many responses as in his conversations with Albertina. The tortoise likes the aluminum foil from his cigarettes. Albertina had sent him a picture of a dog, and the tortoise is insanely jealous and is furiously eating Tótila Albert's book on sculpture. He asks her to inform a mutual friend, Yolando Pino, who is studying in Germany, that he has three books in press, *Endeavor of the Infinite Man, House of Cards,* and *Book of Twilights.* He asks also that Pino send him some of his own verses and of his favorite German poets, for his journal *Caballo de Bastos,* which will appear in ten days. He signs off with a kiss from himself and a grunt from the tortoise.

On 22 February 1926, he announces that he is going to Ancud. The news item is that, besides "ugly Rubén," de Rokha has been in Santiago for two days. "I've just left them in the dumpy hotel where they're staying."

The next letter is explosive. He acidly demands of her why his letters have been returned unclaimed to Santiago, opened according to the new postal laws. In Chile a military dictatorship has virtually enthroned itself, and opened letters are a common occurrence. "You haven't even taken the trouble to see that those secret things in my heart and yours do not fall into outsiders' hands. Fine, now I believe many things about you. I suppose the same thing must have happened to my letters from Temuco, Osorno, Puerto Montt. To tell the truth, Albertina, time has gone by, and you're not the same person."

A few days later, the tone changes completely as he radiantly informs her that just that day the decree was signed in the Ministry of Public Education which authorizes him to perfect his study of French ("laugh, will you") in France. There's one problem—he still doesn't know whether he will get passage. He asks her for a portrait in profile, in sharp profile, and explains what he means with a line drawing of his own silhouette.

38. Crisis in Bohemia

It was the era of collective readings by the poets in the Pedagogical Institute, which took place in the central hall of the University of Chile. The main participants were Pablo Neruda, Julio Benavides, and Víctor Barberis, who would later be my French teacher in the Curicó Lyceum. He would also be the first one to introduce me to the verses of his fellow student and literary soul mate, the young author of a precious little book, *Book of Twilights*. Another reader was Romeo Murga, a tall ungainly boy who would soon succumb to tuberculosis.

The poet Neruda was much sought after. Delegations of girls used to arrive at the tenement house at 330 Echaurren Street to request a reading at their school. More than once, they found him on his cot in a room where a sugar crate served as the night table. The poet was always gallant. Among those petitioners was Laura Arrué, at that time a resident student at the Normal School No. 1, whom young Neruda would visit at the house on Peñaflor, taking a train at eight in the morning and transferring at Malloco to a four-horse carriage. In 1924, when Neruda gives her a copy of the recently published *Twenty Poems,* he offers her a piece of advice, "Hide it under your mattress so your aunts don't take it away from you, because they'll tear it up." Before going to the Orient, he gives her the manuscript of *Endeavor of the Infinite Man* for safekeeping.

Later, Laura Arrué married Homero Arce, a short, robust little dark-complexioned man with huge dark eyes and a gentle personality, who worked for the post office. After he retired, Homero was Neruda's secretary until the poet died. He typed the majority of the books Neruda wrote during the last twenty years of his life.

In his hour of acknowledgments (*Notes from Isla Negra*), Neruda wrote the poem "Arce":

> Here once more, because you have lived
> my life as if it were your own,
> I thank you, and for your gifts
> of friendship and frankness,

and for that money you gave me
when I had no food, and for your
hand when mine didn't exist,
and for every task
in which my poetry came to life
thanks to your painstaking gentleness.

Girls seek him out, but he is not happy. The point comes when it seems to him that his whole life is in crisis. Bohemia was a confusion and not a solution. This muddled kingdom of night crowned by wine, that panting dance of male and female in the midst of tobacco smoke and strident or whispered conversations, "the drunkard's green cackling," had to come to an end, along with the fleeting alliances with the prostitutes who frequented the bars where this adolescent sits among the bottles, searching for something more, even though he is initially seduced by the "conversations of empty audacity." No, he would definitely not be like his venerated Rojas Giménez of those "Crazy Friends" (*Notes from Isla Negra*):

. . . strictly
mad, raising
smoke in one glass
and rambling tenderness
in another,
until he went from bad to worse
as if wine had carried him away
to an ever more distant place!

When he receives the news of Rojas Giménez's death, he is convinced that he himself has escaped a similar fate. He evokes him in "Rojas Giménez Comes Flying":

Among bitter-colored bottles
among anis rings and mishaps,
raising your hands and crying,
here you come flying.

Nor can he be like another of his beloved compatriots in poetry, Joaquín Cifuentes Sepúlveda, who killed for love.[h] Neruda pictures him with the look of an 1810 patriot, elegant and pale with "a commanding face in the rain . . . a Hussar of Death."

Another reason he has for leaving Chile is to get out of that suicidal sort of life. He is aware that his friends are killing themselves. As soon as he escapes, he will feel compelled to write elegies about them. "Absence of Joaquín" appears in the first *Residence*, "Here and now I see him plunging into death, / and behind him I hear the days of time being closed." He must flee from what Joaquín did not flee from, his dissolute nights, his constant pallor, and his habits of "a soul that disobeys" the laws of survival.

That's not for Neruda, who is astonished by the "Clever Mouse," a master of canteens and king of blasphemy who, like an apostle of wine, instructs his followers in the so-called teachings of Latin American manliness: Man was born to drink, fornicate, and challenge the establishment. He was something of a primitive anarchist, who didn't draw any clear distinction between himself and low life. He preached a terrible all-encompassing brotherhood, and with his skill in fiery language he was the bard of insults and the successor of all the bad mouths of history, an outlaw who wielded lightning-fast knives and words, a semiliterate who possessed that earthy wisdom that comes from a singleminded and unfocused primitive negativism.

Neruda was endowed with a highly developed constructive determination. He would not allow his existence to be consumed in vain like that. In the midst of hunger and disorderly nights, he aspired to creative order. He knew he possessed a powerful birthright in poetry, which sprang from his very being and which he must respect, in order for it to reach its greatest potential. He felt that he had received it as an inheritance from the earth's species, like a secret treasure that he could not sell cheaply.

Besides, the affair with Albertina was so difficult. The Temuco romance had evaporated, and he turned his face and his soul away from several women. He had friends, he was interested in socializing, but he felt alone in the midst of a crowd, almost lost in the streets where he wandered in hunger. He bent over his books and wanted to write, above all else, to extract "the mineral from the soul / until you, Poetry, are the one who is reading, / until the water sings with your mouth."

39. The Lazy Man Who Works Like a Factory

He felt that writing poetry was like constantly being born, a strange activity without any closure, but one that he pursued with pleasure. His life had "a leaky roof but stars shine through the holes." No, he is not inclined to ruin himself. He will not do that. He will exist, in spite of everything.

Notwithstanding all the sorrow he experiences with Albertina, what is most important to him are his books. The problem is to find a publisher. It will turn out to be Carlos George Nascimento, who was once asked about his first meeting with Neruda. "In those days," he responded, "I was still more or less new at publishing. I had done *El hermano asno* (Brother Ass) by Eduardo Barrios, who told me that I would have a visit from a very quiet, modest boy who used the pen name Pablo Neruda and was going to be a great poet who would attract a lot of attention some day, and I shouldn't let him get away. And I didn't. There was something about him—I can't put my finger on it. He was very skinny and pale, he barely spoke, but he was always so calm and certain that, without my realizing it, he convinced me so much that I even had to design the book's size according to his specifications—large and square, which wasn't economical, because a lot of paper was wasted. But you can see that even as a skinny, quiet man he got his own way."[14]

Ever since his early youth, the poet doesn't conceive of literary activity as a closed-off compartment. Literature is a house of many connected rooms, and he goes from one chamber to another leaving in each one more than an occasional inspiring message. Before the age of twenty, he produces an abundant body of book commentaries, if not literary criticism. He uses the pseudonym "Sachka" in *Claridad* to sign his article on "The Romantic Story of Sacha Pagodin as Told by Leonidas Andreiev," doubtless the source of his customary pen name as author of notes about new books, which always express the admiration and the sense of discovery experienced by a youth who keeps his eye open and pays attention to the literature of all nations and all types. He reviews the work of an author who influences him, Carlos Sabat Ercasty: *Poemas del hombre: Libros del corazón, de la voluntad, del tiempo y del mar* (Poems about Man: Books of the Heart, the Will, Time, and the Sea). He expresses wonderment at the first book by Gabriela Mistral, *Desolación* (Desolation). Early on, in August 1921, in *Juventud* (No. 15) he extols the poems of Manuel Rojas. He warmly analyzes *La Torre* (The Tower) by Joaquín Cifuentes Sepúlveda. In point of fact, every issue of *Claridad* in those days contains several notes written by Neruda on works that have just come out. In No. 95 in July 1923, he reviews the poetry collections of Rubén Azócar (*La puerta*, The Door), Salvador Reyes (*Barco ebrio*, Drunken Boat), Fernando Mirto (*Se-*

renamente, With Serenity), and Manuel Chávez (*El silbar del payaso,* The Whistle of the Clown). Later, he critiques one of his fellow provincials, Gerardo Seguel, and in 1924 writes about Aliro Oyarzún and Tomás Lago.

Before he is twenty-two years old, he has published 108 items in *Claridad,* and also writes for the literary sections of *El Mercurio* and *La Nación,* as well as for journals like *Zig-Zag, Atenea, Juventud, Educación, Dínamo, Alí Babá, Renovación, Panorama, Abanico* (in Quillota), and *Quimera* (in Ancud).

Translation is another room visited by this man who believes in the law of adjoining spaces. He is extremely interested in the translation into Spanish of the great books. In May 1923, he hails a version of his always venerated Walt Whitman done by a Chilean professor in the United States, Arturo Torres-Rioseco. Enthused by Rainer Maria Rilke's *The Notebook of Malte Laurids Brigge,* Neruda himself translates fragments of it for publication in *Claridad* in October and November 1926. By the same token, he does Spanish versions of Marcel Schwob's *The Sleeping City* and *Earthly Fire.*

Another corner in which he labors and continues to freely do so throughout his life is that of selections and prologues. In 1924, Nascimento publishes *Páginas escogidas de Anatole France* (Selections from Anatole France), with an introduction by Neruda.

This self-proclaimed lazy beast was a tireless worker.

40. *Writers and Elephants*

His principal duty was to write, and the most important thing was to build his work. Neruda felt that, in spite of all the romantic theories to the contrary, that way of living and not being sure of eating on any given day was not the most propitious climate in which to develop his creativity. Furthermore, in his mind, he had to be concerned not only about himself but also about the drama and fate of the Chilean writer, beaten down by poverty, by general lack of understanding, and by official suspicion. But at the same time it was necesary to demand a sense of responsibility and solidarity on the part of the author. He would demonstrate that notion, in print.

Back on 8 October 1921, he publishes an article in *Claridad* called "On Intellectual Life in Chile," in which he tartly criticizes a Chilean writer who won't defend Professor Carlos Vicuña Fuentes, who had been fired on account of his political ideas.

Neruda was the antithesis of those writers who detested other writers. He tended toward encouragement and praise, although he also had a sharp eye. In September 1921, his call "To the Poets of Chile" appeared in *Juventud,* asking poets to fight for the release of Joaquín Cifuentes Sepúlveda from imprisonment in Talca, "Comrades, the authorities keep him locked up without sunshine, without light, without fresh air, for a crime he did not commit. And what if he had committed it? He was a poet . . ." At seventeen, he was naïvely propagating a special right, beyond the legal code—for him, to be a poet was sufficient cause for not being liable to punishment.

His tendency to encourage the efforts of his colleagues was so extensive that he will praise writers who later repay his acclaim with vitriole.

On 16 December 1922, in that same *Juventud,* Neruda publishes a very laudatory review of *Wailings,* a huge book by Pablo de Rokha, the very same wild Barrabas who in time will unleash drumfire against him, including an entire book devoted to insulting Neruda. Again, in June 1924, he publishes an article titled "In Defense of Vicente Huidobro," who will attack him ten years later in resounding campaigns.

When he returned from Spain (in the 1930s), I had a long conversation with him in which he talked about the need to abandon the egocentric tendencies of those writers who based their own greatness in the extermination of their competitors, turning the field of literature into something worse than the Darwinian jungle. No, literary life must not be a battle between dinosaurs and glyptodonts, between giraffes and canaries; it must be neither a dog fight nor a horse race. Down with literary egotism and the hostile monopolists of poetry! Just as all men have a right to live on this earth, let us respect the universal peaceful coexistence of poets. Let's be like the elephants!, he proposed. They're so big, and there's room for all of them in the forest! Hearing these declarations that called for the solidarity of writers, someone jokingly remarked that Neruda had an elephant complex. With great seriousness, he again explained his idea. "The writer who is not heard and is up against the wall because of economic conditions in a cruel period, often has gone out to the marketplace with his own product, releasing his doves in the midst of the noisy crowd." Trapped in desperation by a dying light, somewhere between nocturnal twilight and bleeding dawn, that writer tried somehow to break the menacing silence. "I am the best," he shouted. "I am the only one," he went on repeating with unceasing egomania. And so he was left alone, and people got tired of listening to him.

41. To the Islands

After an early youth of turbulence and sinfulness, it was time to come to his senses. He was pursued by specters of disintegration: Alberto Rojas Giménez, Joaquín Cifuentes, the "Clever Mouse." But Rubén Azócar was very different; though just as sparkling and charming as they were (he once made a guitar out of a plate), he had a responsible notion of life. In 1922, he passed the last exams for his degree as professor of Spanish and philosophy.

He was named to a position in the lyceum in Ancud and took Neruda to Chiloé. "To the islands, we said." In March 1923, Rubén went to Mexico, at the invitation of José Vasconcelos, who had also signed up Gabriela Mistral. A big farewell in a cheap eatery that smelled of deep-frying, on General Mackenna Street. Since they had no money to pay for what they consumed, they left their jackets in hock. Rubén Azócar returned to Chile in May 1925, after having been detained at the Callao oasis by Peruvian police, who suspected him of being a leftist. He was locked up for twenty-one days in the Panóptico Prison in Lima, before finally reaching Valparaíso on a Japanese ship, the *Seju-Maru,* whose passengers took up a healthy collection for him when they found out about his recent adventure. It was almost midnight when he reached Santiago, and from the Mapocho Station he headed for the Venecia bar at the corner of Bandera and San Pablo, looking for his friends. He didn't find them there, so he went to El Jote, then on to all their customary bars and restaurants. The nocturnal expedition to celebrate his return was beginning to look like a complete failure, and in crestfallen sadness at such an unwarm welcome, he trudged along Bandera Street. Suddenly, on the corner of Catedral he saw Neruda coming along all alone. They returned to the Venecia and there had a great party, just the two of them, reunited after two years. Then they went to the Forestal Park to look for four-leaf clovers, and at nine in the morning, quite cool, they headed for the Pedagogical Institute.

Neruda was just managing to keep body and soul together, even though the publication of *Twenty Love Poems* had just met with astounding success. In spite of the clamor, the poet was suffering under the anguishing burden of knowing that his whole way of life was in crisis. Either his life would change, or he would perish. He saw that one phase of his existence was ending, and he needed to begin another, more serious in all aspects. Affairs of the heart were not going well. And notwithstanding the success of his just-published book, he judged that there must also be a turnaround in his poetry.

At that moment, he got the invitation to go to Ancud to spend some time with Rubén, newly designated as Spanish professor there. They made a stop in Concepción, where Rubén visited his family and Pablo saw Albertina. Also in Concepción, they saw the poet of *La torre,* Joaquín Cifuentes Sepúlveda, who wined and dined them as if they were Pantagruel and Gargantua. Next stop, Temuco. A shouted clearing of the air between Neruda and his father. Why did you abandon your studies? The sincere reply was incomprehensible to Don José del Carmen. It was very difficult to understand a man who wanted to be a poet, and that idea simply couldn't penetrate his head.

Later, Neruda joined his friend in the Nilsson Hotel in Ancud. A change of fortune, and the beggars had changed into Cresos, eating the very best and recalling the wretched crowd in Santiago, to whom they send sacks of shellfish. "We fired / fresh oysters in all directions." It was there that Neruda wrote *The Inhabitant and His Hope,* and helped Rubén correct his students' exams and homework. For a few days, he became a careful secretary. At night, one was the captain and the other the young student who recited some chivalric verses with tremendous shouts from opposite ends of Ancud's Plaza de Armas:

> The captain Don Gabriel of
> the Moon
> and the student Don Gabriel of
> the Bloom
> dueled each other one night
> 'neath the moon
> by the light of two eyes
> in full bloom.

Rubén recalls that a certain Alicia, a dark-skinned girl with big eyes, fell in love with Pablo. One day, Neruda told his friend, "I must go back to Santiago with some Oxford trousers." They were popular then, but this latest fashion hadn't reached Chiloé yet, so Neruda had to sketch the tailor a pattern, showing him the wide bell-bottoms.

About 150 people, including the most illustrious of the town, showed up at the hotel for his farewell celebration, where something happened that shows the breakdown in communication that can occur between the poet and the stars. A hairdresser named Ojeda, who was also the lottery agent for Concepción, insisted annoyingly that Rubén Azócar buy his last lottery ticket. Knowing the too acquiescent nature of his friend, Pablo urged him with hand signals not to make that useless purchase. After several offerings, the seller insisted for the last time. As Rubén was preparing to put his hand in his pocket to take out his wallet, Pablo convinced him not to throw away his money, whereupon two other partygoers bought the ticket half-and-half.

The next day, at eight in the morning, Pablo departed on a little boat, the *Caupolicán,* that took him back to terra firma. At noon, Rubén received a telegram from Neruda from Puerto Montt, telling him that the last ticket, sold about midnight by Ojeda, had won the jackpot in the lottery, a fortune that, if administered judiciously, would have solved the winner's economic problems for his entire lifetime. The news was accompanied by the most virulent self-insult that the honorable telegraph office could transmit. For forty years, the two friends' conversation would periodically turn toward imagining the changes that their lives would have had if they had bought the ticket that Rubén wanted and Neruda made him forego. They would give free rein to all the possibilities, fantasizing and creating various scenarios. The question was: Would our lives have been different, would we have stopped being what we are, would we have become millionaires, would we have kicked poetry out of the house, what would you be like as a satisfied bourgeois? The fantastic speculations went on and on about the ticket that was not bought. Since both were optimists, they soon gave themselves over to consolation and self-justification. No, it would have been repugnant and fatal to have won the jackpot, like renouncing themselves and their concept of life, poetry, revolution, love. And, in addition, they were resigned because they know beyond doubt the true story of the two persons who bought the ticket that night of Neruda's farewell in the Nilsson Hotel in Ancud. One committed suicide shortly afterwards, and the other one landed in jail on account of debts stemming from poor investments, which the friends figured he wouldn't have gotten mixed up in without that unlucky jackpot.

42. Departure

Before, he had had fleeting moments of self-satisfaction. At twenty, he felt a passing sensation of having done a good job. And he said it with an unpopular word that he defended: "Sincerity. In such a modest word as this one," he says, "so old-fashioned, so abused and despised by the glittering entourage that erotically tags after aesthetics, perhaps in that word is defined my constant activity."

In the daily *La Nación* he publishes "Exegesis and Solitude," where he explains to the clerks and pedants who personally dislike him that he may be an indifferent student in the area of French but that he has undertaken his creative venture to illuminate words. He has dedicated exactly half his life, ten years, to this solitary task of searching for a means of expression. Out of it came *Twenty Poems,* and he has suffered while writing the poems, which are songs taken from his life and his love for a few women. He affirms, without vanity, that with those poems he achieved something like a victory, by dint of sincerity and determination. He won't boast about any discipline, which he has not had, but he calls himself "a good thinker," who writes about what concerns him. Yet now, such triumphant self-knowledge has abandoned him, and he feels it necessary to burn bridges and cut ties. He will never repeat any of his published books and will break with his previous poetry. He will strike out in search of other continents, not only on the map but also in his own creation.

Everything pushes him to leave. One period of his life was coming to an end, and he had to take distance and get far away. At this point, another of the great friends from his youth appears, Alvaro Hinojosa, who was already infected with the traveling bug. In 1924, he had returned from the United States but was already dreaming only of departing once more. Through him, his sister Silvia Thayer met this poet barely twenty years old, who seemed to her to be languid and imperturbable, almost indifferent, and very quiet. She heard him say once, "Who do you suppose invented this business of talking?" A quiet and somewhat flighty woman, she innocently attributes the well-known fact that the poet ate very little, to his sober almost ascetic habits and not to his lack of money.

The Hinojosa family lived in Valparaíso, on the corner of Deformes and Victoria. Between 1925 and 1927, Neruda frequently visited their home. He liked to look at the sea, and with Alvaro he visited the markets and piers, climbed the hills of the port city, and after dark steeped himself in its nightlife. The first time he went to that house, Alvaro (who was more than met the eye) warned all the family not to pursue conversations with the young visitor because he didn't like to talk. Shortly thereafter, Pablo struck up a two-hour chat with the mother. Full of curiosity, the daughter asked her what they had talked about for so long, and she answered, "About business affairs. He's a charming boy." And it was true. During that period, Pablo and Alvaro had their heads full of business projects, plotting to escape from poverty and become Rockefellers, though underdeveloped ones. As soon as they would have a guaranteed living, they could peacefully dedicate themselves to writing poetry.

In June 1927, both friends departed from that house at 2810 Deformes in Valparaíso to take the train that links up with the trans-Andean railway. They would go to Buenos Aires where they would board the ship *Baden* and head for Rangoon, by way of Europe. After their departure, there was a period during which many letters and telegrams arrived at that house, from girls who despairingly asked about Pablo, who had told almost nobody of his departure. Silvia would open the communiques and answer the most moving ones "almost out of pity."

Alvaro didn't stay long in the Orient, but returned to the United States. I met him there in 1938, when he was married to a North American dancer. Seeing him, I remembered all of Neruda's stories about his friend's being by vocation the most consistent and unremitting Don Juan he knew. I had asked him to explain to me how this Don Juan operated. Apparently, he would get straight to the point. They would be walking along a street in Paris, where they had stopped briefly before going on to Burma, and Hinojosa would see a woman who pleased him and would go up to her, and in his horrible French, would propose making love to her. Ninety-nine would reject him, some with slaps, but (according to unofficial statistics) one would accept the request. And ten years after those forays, I found him installed there in a New York apartment, thin-nosed and pale-eyed beneath thick, heavy eyebrows, having become a freelance writer who from time to time managed to publish a short story in some magazine, but earning his principal living from giving Spanish lessons.

I observed him with some perplexity, trying to detect his Casanova image. He said nothing about his European and Asian adventures, and he had a certain prudence that contributed to his mystery and legend.

When Neruda returned after the war in Spain, I went to see him in an apartment on the second block of Vicuña Mackenna Avenue, to do an interview that appeared a few days later in *Qué Hubo en la Semana*, edited at the time by his great good friend, Luis Enrique Délano. That apartment, where he and Delia del Carril, his second wife, were staying as guests, belonged to Silvia Thayer, from whose home he had departed years prior for his journey to the Orient.

Thirty years after Pablo and Alvaro had said good-bye to each other in the Orient, they met again in the home of the painter, Nemesio Antúnez, in Santiago. They embraced each other and stood there a long time without saying a word.

That same year, 1958, Silvia Thayer introduced Neruda to the Puerto Rican Antonio Santaella Blanco, who was on a tour promoting his country's freedom. Neruda then conceived the idea of writing a book advocating the independence of Puerto Rico, which he would call *Puerto Pobre* (Poor Port). The initial poems formed the embryo of *Heroic Song,* published in Havana in 1960. In the prologue Neruda wrote, "I first envisioned this as a book about Puerto Rico, her martyred condition as a colony and the current struggle of her insurgent patriots. Afterwards, with the unselfish events in Cuba, the book grew and was developed within the entire Caribbean sphere."

Alvaro Hinojosa, after trying a thousand different jobs, became a short-story merchant, disguised with a pseudonym that combined enigma and ingenuity worthy of an Alexander Dumas character. Thus he was able to return to Paris, intending to live the rest of his days in the city of his dreams, the Paris of 1927 and those wild years of amorous conquests. There was one small problem. More than forty years had passed, and Paris was older but kept herself young. He was younger than Paris, but he seemed older. He arrived at a categorical conclusion: Paris was no longer Paris, it was declining, and he left.

III.

Anguish and Creation in the Orient

43. *Pressures from Afar*

The poet finally manages to get appointed as honorary consul in Rangoon. Later, he was to occupy the same post in Colombo (Ceylon, later Sri Lanka), Batavia (Java), and Singapore (Malaysia).

He wrote to Albertina from all these spots, but the letters which have been preserved are those from Ceylon. On 17 December 1929, from Colombo, he again addresses her as his "Netocha Girl," and the same old story seems to be repeating itself, "I didn't intend to write you until you answered my earlier letters, but it's night and it's hot, and I can't sleep." Just as in that room on Echaurren Street, here, too, her picture is on the night table. He has a sense of artistry and has put it in a frame of tamarind, because he is so fond of precious woods. Thus, he arranges for those eyes, which he thought he might never see again, to gaze at him day and night.

The letter has an aura of finality. He doesn't wish to lose her companionship now that she has her own project, "because this may be the last time in our lives that we try to get together. I'm getting tired of solitude, and if you don't come, I shall try to marry someone else. Does this sound cruel to you? No, what would be cruel would be for you not to come. You are aware that I have a certain small social position connected to my 'Honorable Consul,' and it's obvious that this creates certain hopes on the part of mamas (whose daughters are sometimes lovely). But listen! I have never loved anyone but you."

When she finished her studies in the University of Concepción, Albertina went to work in an experimental school. One day, the director called her in and suggested she go to Brussels to study the audio-visual teaching methods being expounded by Professor Decroly, and shortly thereafter Albertina Rosa left for Belgium, where Pablo's letters reach her.

The anxious consul gives her precise instructions about the ship she should take to the Orient—go to the Branch Service company, with offices in Paris and Marseilles, passage costing about a thousand Chilean pesos. "Every day and every hour I wonder, will she come? You can imagine how I don't have any news at all from Chile."

The next day, he sends her an airmail letter, telling her that no airplane has ever carried so many kisses. His tone is determined: he doesn't think they should sacrifice or postpone or put stumbling blocks in the way of their possible happiness. He would not allow her to return to Chile. His idea is for her to come join him however she can, even using the return ticket to Chile, which she could exchange at the shipping company. Is he suggesting something that she might consider dishonest? Never fear, he tells her, he knows exactly what it means, but after they are married he will write to the rector of the University of Concepción, Enrique Molina, and try to pay for her ticket and expenses down to the last penny. Still and all, he proceeds with bureaucratic caution and requests that, if she agrees to what he is asking, she should do it as a surprise, without anyone knowing that he has suggested it, since it could hurt his career. He hopes that his sweetheart will come to join him; he commands her over and over again, but she does not obey.

After sending her some poems he is writing for *Residence,* he tells her, "You've probably noticed that my verses were still about you." Then he qualifies it, "Except for a few," and finally amends further, "The best ones are about you."

The enamoured young consul resorts to a fortuneteller, who boasts of divining the name of the woman whom he loves and who loves him, and writes the name on a piece of paper.

More letters on consecutive days, demanding replies. That of 19 December, following one sent by surface mail and another by air, takes a new tack. "I'm writing you because at this time I think it is possibly improper to put you in conflict with your 'duties.' Truly, pardon me if I have upset a little bit your *autrement* peaceful sojourn. This means that, with great pleasure, I leave you free to do whatever you think is wisest and most convenient for you. In no way do I want to force you to come with me. I can't put myself in your place, and after reading your only letter for the hundredth time, I see that perhaps you wish to return to Chile. You would also have to accept, along with your trip, your share of suffering and misery, which exist in my life in greater quantity than in that of other men. Do as you please."

The correspondence of that period reveals hints of a solitary life. For weeks on end, he talks with no one except a servant. There is nobody to whom he can unburden himself. "You know," he tells her, "I don't have a very good disposition." His outburst is worse when a registered letter is returned to him from Belgium, stamped: *Left with no forwarding address*. Cruel irresponsibility! The young lady doesn't deign to reply. He thinks he'll go mad with rage and disappointment. His tone is final, "Forget any plan that will require a lot of time. It is now or never."

When she is back at the University of Concepción, he sends her a letter breaking it off. One can imagine his mood. "I wanted to make you my wife as a token of our love . . . Furthermore, I wish you to destroy the originals of my letters and everything of mine that you still have, and to send me the pictures I have given you. I do not want them to end up in the hands of your Concepción friends (I'm informed). In particular, I need for you to send me by return mail the picture I sent you twice in registered letters to Brussels. It's a picture of me, in a Bengali outfit, that I urgently need, and I beg of you, as a last and great favor, to return it to me immediately. Farewell forever, Albertina. Forget me, and be assured that I have only wanted your happiness."

It is definitely the end. Nonetheless, he will write her a few more letters from Santiago in 1932. In one of them, he informs her of what she already knows, "You probably know that I have been married since December 1931.[i] The solitude that you refused to alleviate for me became more and more intolerable. You must understand that, if you think about so many years as an expatriate." The next paragraph almost shows a return to the past and indicates that his passion has not completely died, "I would so much like to kiss your forehead a little, to stroke your hands that I have loved so much, to give you a bit of the friendship and affection that my heart still holds for you."

The third paragraph is characterized by prudence, "Don't show anybody this letter. Nor will anyone know if you write to me."

The fourth paragraph contains an invitation in the form of a question, "Can you come to Santiago for a day?"

On 15 May 1932, a letter written, like the others, on letterhead of the Ministry of Foreign Affairs, where he is working, attempts to again set forth the poet's point of view and the events that led to the break, "I don't wish to hurt you, but I think you made a big mistake. My telegrams, my letters told you that I was going to marry you when you got to Colombo. Albertina, I had already taken out the marriage license and made the request for the needed money . . . Now my sister tells me that I asked you to go live with me without marrying you, and that you said this. Never! Why do you lie? Besides the horrible bitterness of your not having understood me, now I have this one of your defaming me . . . But enough, let's forget the bad we have done to each other, and hopefully let's be friends."

There is one final letter, dated 11 July 1932 in Santiago. The heart of a man in love is puzzling, and sometimes it takes a long time for a break to come about, thus, "I remember you every day. . . . But you are as stubborn as always. I still cannot understand what happened to you in Europe; I still don't understand why you didn't come to me."

Half a century later, she recalls such long-ago events with tranquility and concision. "Pablo wrote me from Rangoon. He wanted me to join him and for us to get married. Then I went to Paris and to London to spend Christmas with my girlfriend. I received some of Pablo's letters after a delay, and some were returned to him, and he got very angry."

When she returned to Concepción, she began to use the Decroly system in her classes at the university, where the poet's letters to her were sent. "One day, the director, who was a prudish man, very different from what he preached, opened one of Pablo's letters and reprimanded me for what it said. Then I asked him how he could have allowed himself to open a letter of mine, and I left the university. I went back to Santiago to the home of my brother Rubén, who was married, and there I met Angel Cruchaga."

44. Responsibilities in Batavia

In 1983, a journalist asks Albertina whether she would have married Pablo Neruda. Her reply, as so many of her statements always do, leaves an unexplained void, "Yes, I loved him very much, but times were different. I couldn't." Why couldn't she?

In 1935, some time after meeting him, she married Angel Cruchaga. When she is asked to describe her husband, she says simply, "He was ten years older than I. Very different from Pablo. A bachelor, a very fine person," (repeating) "very different from Pablo, very tranquil." His father was Basque, tall, good-looking and blue-eyed, with a long mustache.

Of all the names bestowed on her by Neruda, "Netocha" was the one she liked best.

Neruda corresponded with Angel Cruchaga from Jabanq', Sumatra and from Batavia. There's a touch of ironic coincidence in the fact that the letter of 26 January 1931 from Batavia charges Angel with a strange mission. "I've gotten married. Please have this picture of my wife printed in a nice layout in *Zig-Zag*. They already have a photographic plate of me. No need to tell you that this is a favor to her. She already knows you well; you're a familiar face in this house. I beg you to send two copies of the *Zig-Zag* it appears in. But don't forget, because you could destroy a home's peace and quiet!"

Twenty days later, he sends a new letter asking if that photo of his wife has been sent yet to *Zig-Zag*, repeating the request for two copies of the corresponding issue. He encloses a text about the latest book by Angel Cruchaga and asks him to send a copy of *Atenea*, where his poem "Colección nocturna" was published.

The wedding of Angel Cruchaga and Albertina Azócar took place in his absence. He congratulated them, and they later formed part of his faithful circle for several years, until the public appearance of Matilde broke up the sisterhood of Neruda's former sweethearts and girlfriends, who were comfortable being around the throne of the ex-queen (Delia) but couldn't tolerate the triumphal arrival of a younger outsider. But prior to that breakup, on 6 July 1944 from his "Michoacán" home in Los Guindos on Lynch Street in Santiago, Neruda sent Angel Cruchaga a sonnet and a Muzo butterfly:

> Accept these two dawnlike wings
> that yearn, Angel, to see you again
> on city streets and in the spring
> wrapped in albertine flags.

Years later he evoked Albertina-"Rosaura" in *Notes from Isla Negra:* "Love is like a marsh / . . . / there we fell, trapped by deep pleasure / . . . / Oh love of body on body, / without words, / and the moist loam kneaded / by throbbing frenzy."

That love and its reverberation remained as part of his life, at the level of emotional memory, "The torn sheets remained." Rosaura's life is contained in water and in time, just as for the poet the city is contained in the river. He spells out, number by number, the precise year of that love—1923. All those numbers fall into the water, and "Rosaura" forgot those days "on the corner / of Sazié Street, or in the little Padura / Plaza, in the pungent rose / of the tenement house that shared us."

It is a love affair between impoverished students. A room that looks onto a "tiny patio / full of stray cats' droppings." Both naked on the hard bed of slums, not sleeping as "we prepared ourselves for love."

Then the poet, after so many years, tells her something rather serious:

> And maybe never again
> was there fire in your life,
> maybe you existed only then.
> We set fire to the world and quenched it;
> you remained in darkness,
> I went on traveling my roads.

The same river lies between them, separating them, "an invitation to oblivion / like time."

Viewing his relationship with "Rosaura" in retrospect, he insists, "Love gave us our only significance." Then, something that he sees as lack of resolve on her part, "Amidst institutions sullied / by prostitution and deceit / you knew not what to do." They used each other in love until it hurt, living and confronting each other in their essence as man and woman, inventing fire. That fire died slowly, but without a doubt it left them scarred forever by its flames.

How much time has passed since that evening in October 1921 at the amateurish event in the Municipal Theater when fame came to the "Festival Song" written by the thin sentimental poet dressed in black and with a plaintive voice that many years later would be trained in phonetics classes given by the Wagnerian singer, Blanca Hauser, who was also from Temuco!

Once, Neruda told me he was unable to resist love or feminine innuendo, especially if he liked the woman. An attitude very typical of one concept of masculinity, which says that a real man has to answer the call. He had major love affairs and he had flings, which for him were never simply adventures. That was his way of reacting even during his university days in the time of Santiago's squeaking trolleys, when he was twenty years old and the city was as full of girls as the river was of water. He views them like honeysuckle blossoms falling on the bed, signs of spring, "one-time loves, quick and eager," but he attributes a profound significance to these contacts:

> I think my poetry was founded
> not just on solitude but also on one flesh

next to another flesh under a bare moon
with all the world's verses around.

45. Family Letters

Among Neruda's letters are twenty-eight that he sent to his sister
during various periods. They were published in 1978 in Madrid, and are
written in a family tone. Laurita, as we have seen, was a simple woman
with a great sense of family. She specialized in maintaining links with near
and distant relatives and was a meticulous keeper of her brother's papers,
beginning with his school days. She preserved many texts of the early
Neruda, guarding them under her inviolate protection. Her manner of
speaking was short and direct; she either liked a person or she didn't. She
thought that Pablo had inherited something from their paternal grandfather, who was fond not of writing verses but of reciting them. Besides
reading the Bible out loud, he used to recite a long poem by Victor Hugo,
translated by Andrés Bello, "La oración por todos" (Prayer for All Men).
In addition, she was convinced that from his father he got his bent for
having many friends. Laura Reyes remembers that in their kitchen the tea
kettle used to be on all morning long, so that railroaders who came by
could breakfast at any time. Her brother was devoted to Laurita; once
when he found her scared to death because she had broken a china vase,
he took the blame.

She didn't care one whit about fame, and she showed no greater
admiration for Pablo than for their brother Rodolfo, whom she used to
praise for his imposing tenor voice and his taste for opera, especially *La
Traviata* whose arias he used to sing. Rodolfo dreamed of being a singer
and even enrolled in the National Conservatory of Music, but just as their
father opposed his older son's being a poet, he didn't want the other one
to become a singer. Imagine, two idlers, as if one weren't enough!

So far as men were concerned, I always saw Laurita alone. "She's a
widow," Pablo explained to me. She was married to a relative, Ramón
Candia Quevedo, a farmer in Parral, who died of a heart attack in 1941
when they had been married less than two years. Their only child had died
at birth. "You can see we've produced very few offspring," the poet sighed.
In 1938, Laura moved to Santiago, where she was a supervisor in the Girls'
Technical School No. 2, where she worked for twenty-four years. When
she retired, she took a trip to Europe and spent six months with Pablo in
Paris, when he was ambassador there. She wanted to have a look at the

nightlife, and she did—after all, nobody knew her there. She went with a friend, María Maluenda, to the Folies Bergère and had a night on the town in La Coupole, and that was enough for her!

Laurita had a vivid recollection of their early childhood. "When Pablo was a little boy, whenever he was sick he liked for me to go over to the window, and he would ask me to tell him everything that was going on outside, without leaving anything out, not even the tiniest detail. And I would tell him, for example, there comes a little Indian woman selling ponchos, with four little kids playing at her side. I would get bored, but he was tireless in all this business of what was happening outside, and I would have to go be the lookout again, and talk and talk." It's not an insignificant piece of testimony. He needed to feed on stories and know everything that was going on. Like an ant, he was stocking up for winter.

A man who was not at all sticky-sweet, Neruda always treated Laurita with great gentleness. I've never seen two siblings with such different interests, but she always respected her brother's ways. Sometimes she couldn't hold back a comment about his choice of certain friends, though. "I don't like that man," she would mutter under her breath, without explaining why. At bottom, she felt obliged to somehow look out for her brother, as his mother had done. But she had to carry out that duty without his noticing it and without forgetting the imperial authority claimed by official wives in the matter of being supervigilant about the poet's mistakes or follies.

Pablo called her only Laurita, never Laura. In his letters, he bestowed on her all possible alterations of the word "Coneja" (Rabbit) or "Conejita" (Bunny), with unimaginable variations in spelling.

When he goes off to study in Santiago, she will act as the eyes of Argos for the poet, watching everything that happens in Temuco in order to transmit it to the absent one. Using a secret code, he inquires about individuals by using just one initial. He presses her to tell him everything, because she is the one sitting at the window in Temuco. His deprivations in the capital shine through in the letters: he looks for a job and doesn't find one, but Segundo (Rudecindo Ortega) "has behaved in the best possible manner. . . . I don't want anyone to worry—I'm sure they'll give me something. Note down the address: Mr. Ricardo Reyes, 736 Santo Domingo, Santiago."

By letter, he rails against the "stupid tailors who need a letter that guarantees cash payment . . . I can't pay so much money all at once."

The abject vicissitude that forces him to move from one boardinghouse to another becomes an extremely frequent item in the letters. On

27 October 1926, he writes his dear beloved Bunny, "As of yesterday I'm without a boardinghouse." He asks about a woman called Amalia, to whom he wasn't going to send his latest book because he thinks she won't like it. (He refers to *Endeavor*.) "Nevertheless, if you insist, okay. Listen, isn't she ever going to come to Santiago? It seems so hard for me to get back to the south. I'm even thinking about heading off to Europe in a little while. It's a pity not to see her."[15]

His dream is to leave. He writes his sister that he's quite fed up with quarreling with his father and that he will leave within a month. The problem is, he only has money for the ticket and nothing more. "What will I eat in Genoa—air? Let's see if you can manage something." He writes this letter in mid-December 1926, while he's living at 25 García Reyes.

The next letter to Laurita is sent a half-year later, 15 June 1927, from Mendoza, Argentina. It's a delayed farewell, but an indispensable one: "Bunny, give my regrets to my father [not his "papa," a more intimate word] and to my mama for not having been able to tell them good-bye with a hug, because I had my reservations made and the trans-Andean was going to leave any time, but only yesterday was it able to run. I was truly sorry and miserable, but I think this separation won't last long. I will again pull your ears. Ricardo."

46. Vigils and Dreams on the Crossing

Ricardo-Pablo is like a dog in a new territory the first time he goes abroad, sniffing and looking at everything with the gusto of someone who adores what he has not yet met in the world.

In July 1927, he boards the *Baden* in Buenos Aires—final destination, Rangoon. The dispatches he sends to *La Nación* constitute his travel diary. Is he a born feature writer? It might seem so to judge by the eye that penetrates not only nature but also the hiding places of man. With a touch of the humorist, he knows how to laugh, how to find the hidden angle, how to show self-irony.

The Atlantic is big, but Brazil is immense, and one day the spirit of that country descends upon the boat in the port of Santos, with its smell of coffee and oranges and with the chatter of macaco monkeys and royal parrots. Suddenly, the light that was missing—a woman shines forth, a passenger whose face is all eyes. A beautiful Latin American, old buddy! Slowly, the boat draws away from the coast, and his friend, Marinech, "speaks in melifluous Portuguese and gives enchantment to her playful language. She is surrounded by a circle of fifteen suitors."

Lisbon, Madrid, Paris.

Paris in 1927, the zenith of Montparnasse. Four or five days and four or five nights in the Domme and in La Coupole, like his little sister almost half a century later. The cafés are full of Argentines. Those were the days when the tango was the rage, as he evokes in "Paris 1927" from *Notes from Isla Negra:*

> Tangos still remained on the floor,
> ecclesiastical brooches from Colombia,
> spectacles and teeth from Japan,
> tomatoes from Uruguay,
> a thin cadaver from Chile,
> all to be swept away,
> washed away by huge scrubwomen,
> it would all end forever:
> powdery ash for the drowned ones
> who were swaying incredibly
> in the natural oblivion of the Seine.[16]

Marseilles, and from there across the Mediterranean to Port Said. African palms, narrow alleys, and brilliant extravagant bazaars, smelling markets full of rancid odors, full of greens and reds. The inevitable literary association with an author who was read then but no more, Pierre Loti, and the resurrection of his *Disenchanted*. Arab women behind the veil, showing only flashing eyes, who seem alien to the bustling atmosphere, "as if they were fatigued by that task of maintaining their literary prestige." But in the view of the young observer, although they suggest the hidden harem, they spark little curiosity in him, which causes the poet a sort of melancholy shock. He was born with a passion for meeting book characters on every corner, and right there are flesh and blood narghile-pipe smokers, with the introspective look of people who are obviously unaware of the halo bestowed on them in those days by European authors devoted to a cultish oriental exoticism. A general proof that the sun is adorned with misery.

In Djibouti the sun is so overwhelming that he has to write his dispatch with his left hand (he claims), while the right one shades his eyes. In the bay, Somali boys retrieve coins with their teeth. The poet feels as if that port belongs to him, because his colleague Arthur Rimbaud wrecked his life there. But there's also a scene worthy of *Salambó,* when he enters the dancers' street. Yet, this twenty-three-year-old Chilean is not as sad as Flaubert when he tried to reconstruct Carthage. Here he is, all of a sudden, reclining on a carpet, as two naked women dance with slow movements, like silent shadows. Then the music of their bracelets is heard, and he speaks to one of them in Spanish, without any shyness and with such power of persuasion that the little dancer throws her arms around his neck, and then he realizes that she understands his Spanish—"a wonderful language!"

The ship sleeps during the crossing. Soon they will reach Sumatra. His friend, Alvaro Rafael Hinojosa, "dozes without sleeping and dreams of seamstresses in Holland, teachers in Charlesville, Erika Pola in Dresden." Surrounded by the snoring of Annamese, Chinese, Mediterranean sailors, Martinique blacks, the wide-awake travel writer is afraid of waking them and thus will try not to dream of phonographs or bells or Montmartre. In that situation, it's best to dream about silent women, Lulú, or preferably, Laura, "whose voice was more like reading, more like dreaming."

As appropriate for a sleepy crew and a sleepy trip, the Colombo they reach is completely dead—nocturnal, priestly, without drinking and without singing. In the morning, the city comes to life. He rides a ricksha pulled by a Singhalese whose movements resemble those of a running ostrich. Pablo meets a betel-nut vendor who looks just like his friend Homero Arce. Life is like that; we find familiar faces in strangers we meet as we wander the world.

When he left his third-class berth in Singapore, he didn't have enough money to continue the trip to his post in Rangoon, so he went to the Chilean consul to get help in buying the ticket. His request was denied until "I threatened to give a lecture on Chile in Singapore," he relates half-smiling. "He got so edgy that he loaned me the money in an instant," and he boarded the ship for Burma.

47. Solitude in Burma

Once settled in Burma, he has entered the realm of mosquito nets and musty smells. In this region, the mosquito net is as necessary as food. He experiences an oppressive need to rest. The water in the lavatory is warm, and mosquitos buzz around by the thousands. This is the beginning of a period in his life that will be characterized by loneliness and abandonment. I stopped off once in Burma, and I discovered that the

Neruda of *Residence,* considered by some to be obscure, is painfully and clearly realistic. The poet who wanted so desperately to get away from his own country landed in a hole, in a deep pit, but he did not drown in its waters. He was too strong.

When his sponsor in the Foreign Affairs office, after countless negotiations, had listed several cities spread around the world where there was a possibility of a Chilean consular vacancy, the stunned poet could only grasp the name of one, which he had never heard before—Rangoon. Now, he was in Rangoon as consul, and he regretted it from the first moment. Every four months a ship would arrive from Calcutta, loaded with solid paraffin and crates of tea destined for Chile. For a couple days there was work for the consul to do, stamping and signing documents related to the shipments of tea and oil for candles. Then, four more months of waiting. No Burmese wanted to go to Chile, and no Chilean ever came through Burma.

The poet used to talk about the inertia of those days, which were spent, in part, observing markets and temples.

He notices something that amazes him—a country where women are dominant. They were everywhere, elegant ladies of the local aristocracy, wearing their quickly wrapped saris of flashing colors, especially bright gold or blue with white flowers. Some smoked long cigars. The English colonizers had given them the right to vote at a time when British suffragettes were fighting for that very same privilege in the streets of London and behaving scandalously in Trafalgar Square. A poor country that lived under the domination of the yellow gold brilliance of the great main pagoda, with its dangling vines, whose purpose was to show off the temple where three hairs from the Buddha are kept in a kind of amphora covered with rubies and emeralds. This man from a gloomy region ruled by the gray of cold rain was fascinated by the orange-colored river that flowed through the city when the buddhist monks emerged to beg for food in the streets.

Such is the multihued technicolor vision of Rangoon. The hot city extends beyond the white man's hotel and the golden pagoda, down to the lepers' streets, just as the river comes down from the jungle to wind alongside the dirty roadway, covered with betel spit and peppered with market dancers. There, beside the waters of the Martaban River, the consul found transitory girls:

> a woman to love, to bed,
> silvery or black, virgin or whore,

heavenly orange-colored carnivore,
it mattered not . . .[17]

He liked to watch the "Carriage of Love" passing slowly through the outer neighborhoods. A Burmese donkey set the pace for the strange brightly colored cart. Inside, behind drawn curtains, was an exotic-eyed courtesan with her hair piled high and wearing cheap necklaces and bracelets, offering a trip to love. He used to see young men and old, dressed in white and carrying black umbrellas, closing a deal while running alongside. The propositioned poet would board the cart of passion that traveled over streets and roads, and then in a flash the curtains would hide the playing-out of the intimate scene. The act was carried out accompanied by the philosophical steps of a donkey whose long gray ears and watery eyes could understand it all. The poet who observed the erotic traffic approached the amorous vehicle more than once, throwing himself into its fires.

He visited not only market places but also temples, where he reacts with total negativity to those serpentine gods, twisted like the Aztecs' Quetzalcoatl, inviting man into nothingness.

His most radiant and painful page in Burma is reserved for Josie Bliss. I read "El tango del viudo" (Widower's Tango) in a Chilean journal before it appeared in *Residence,* and I've already said somewhere that it is the most moving tango I've ever read, a shocking heresy of course for true tango fans. Later, more than once, I asked Neruda about Josie Bliss, the English pseudonym of that Burmese woman who in privacy abandoned her western clothing and Anglo-Saxon name to return to what she truly was. He had to stealthily flee from her, from that knife-wielding apparition of enraged beauty, dressed all in white, behind the mosquito net, who was ready to kill him out of jealousy. The ship had barely begun to cut through the Gulf of Bengal when the fugitive poet wrote that "Widower's Tango," in 1928, and in Ceylon he still feels her absence:

And just to hear you urinating in the dark, at the back of our home,
pouring out fine honey, tremulous, shining, stubborn,
how often would I give up this shadowy chorus I own,
and the sound of futile swords that beat in my soul.

What does being alone mean for Neruda? What does being alone mean for a man who was always surrounded by women and was always seeking them out? It means lack of communication with his surroundings, absence of contact with a strange world, isolation. It's a period when those countries in which he lives are still under British and Dutch domination. The poet detests the masters of the haughty cities and has some contact with national liberation movements, but he is still an outsider. In order to understand his solitude, it is worthwhile to take a cruise in the waters of *Residence* and also to look at the letters he wrote in those days, especially those addressed to the Argentine short-story writer, Héctor Eandi, most of which (twenty-two in all) are sent from the Orient. The collection is indispensable for knowing the reasons for his anguish. "I must tell you," he writes to Eandi on 16 January 1928 from Merkara in the Bay of Bengal:

> I am fleeing from Burma and I hope it will be forever. I'm not going far—Ceylon, far for you, for me the same latitude, the same climate, the same fate. Inside of three hours now, the ship will reach Colombo. I'm coming from Calcutta, two months out of my life. And now, to prepare ourselves for the horror of these abandoned colonies and drink the first whiskey and soda, or "chota pegg," in honor of your friendship, Eandi. Furious drinking, heat, fever. Sick people and alcoholics everywhere. In the cabin next door, fever and delirium. . . . Three years in Assam. It's enough to see the eyes of the poor young Greek to want to throw yourself into the sea every five minutes. *Les femmes soignent ces horribles malades de retour des pays chauds.*[18]

With obvious changes in personality, the picture could have come from the pen of his venerated sinner-saint Rimbaud. He is starving for newspapers from Latin America. He feels overcome by the sickness of sleep, consumed by the heat. "I write no letters, no verses, my heart is full of smoke." He feels as if he's in a withdrawn cataleptic state and is mystified by the eternal movement of the world. But in his judgment, what is missing are notes of grandeur, superhuman tones, what he calls "solemn and selfless choirs." He is not interested in that world where religious feeling becomes a passive and inert contemplation. He doesn't even see it as a pure enough cause to move him to activity. Submission to a foreign master horrifies him.

48. Ambitions and Desires

Four months later, from Rangoon, he writes a letter to his friend which contains a kernel of self-criticism in regard to the desperation of the previous letter. He realizes that he must conquer that feeling, but it will be very difficult. The first *Residence* spells out that depressed condition of his soul; Neruda is struggling with himself. Accordingly, he thanks Eandi for his words from Argentina, "uplifted spirits," but at the same time he explains the source of the personal crisis he's going through. The letter from Rangoon on 11 May 1928 is chillingly eloquent:

> Now I want to get out of a really miserable state of mind by writing you in answer to your valuable and noble letter, which I have read so many times with great pleasure. I have spent my life making my literary work more and more difficult, rejecting and burying things that were very dear to me, so that now I waste my work on petty worries and empty thoughts, influenced by those sudden outbursts that I am very slowly beginning to overcome. I thought about your letter, about its very valuable and very kind implications, and I felt useless, cruelly incapable.
>
> Sometimes, for long periods, I am so empty, unable to express anything or to fulfill anything deep within me, and a violent poetic urgency that never leaves me leads me along a more and more inaccessible path, so that a great part of my effort is accomplished with suffering, owing to the need to take possession of a somewhat remote domain with forces that are doubtless too weak. I am not talking to you about doubt or confused thoughts, no, but rather about an unsatisfied aspiration, a frustrated awareness. My books are that accumulation of unrelieved anxieties. You, Eandi, in expressing your concern with so much intelligence, you come close to me and touch me in the most profound and personal way, above and beyond any literary implications. I must embrace you, Eandi, and be very grateful to you.

Let it be noted that his problem derives somehow from a great ambition to express with maximum literary profundity all that surrounds him, and to go even beyond. Through his poetry he must reach what is most personal and deep, in a word, what is most human. And it is a twenty-four-year-old man who will have to do this, by turning a "dreadful, solitary and motionless life" into a launching pad that obliges him to write, perhaps as never before in western poetry, a body of work that emerges from the humus left by destructions and from the annihilation left by a terrible domination founded on poverty.

This foreign youth, this unsalaried consul, feels himself destined to reflect that floating and dispersed world in his poetry. To reflect is not in this case to explain or share. The Orient sometimes seems to him the essence of what is human-inhuman. He doesn't fall on his knees in front of the holy men and gurus, even though the West about that time tends to be enchanted by them. A short while after that, Krishnamurti undertakes long lecture tours through country after country in Europe and America. I hear him in the Caupolicán Theater in Santiago. He fills theaters with curious people who are missing something, and come to see if he reveals the "Word" to them. Literary exaltation follows. Neruda is living in the belly of Asia, and he can testify (as Martí did about the United States) that:

> It strikes me as strange that "exotic" writers speak in glowing terms about Eastern tropical regions. There is no land less appropriate for panegirical or allegorical effusiveness. These regions need only *constant acquaintance and unswerving attention.* A great wind of fire and dazzling plant life have reduced man to a minuscule status. In India, the human being is part of the landscape, and *there is no discontinuity between him and nature,* such as occurs in the contemporary West. The great cultural periods of the Brahminic Orient do not destroy man's roots nor supplant his flourishing, as Christianity did; rather, they are built like huge monumental walls, without great connection to the pains of being human but certainly with a powerful tribute to the mystery surrounding him . . .[19]

For this "resident on earth," there's something else he disagrees with. His whole being rejects any principle which leaves man, in his earthly existence, lying defenseless and, in the caste system, even condemned to a fatalism that the poet cannot accept.

> Yes, time can construct only idols, and what is remote is directly divine. Origin and Perpetuity are antagonistic virtues; the original being is still submerged in the spontaneous, in that which creates and that which destroys, whereas everlasting lives survive in abandonment, without potential for beginning or ending. Without losing itself and by losing itself, the being returns to its creative origin, "like a drop of sea water returns to the sea," the *Katha Upanishad* says. To participate in that which is divine, to return to that unbreakable activity, isn't this a seed for impossible and fatal doctrinal obscurity?

The solitary poet doesn't claim that he has penetrated the mystery. He knows that much of the enigma is beyond him, and he does not possess the sibyls' art. In those oriental regions, the sphynx continues to guard its secret under seven seals. But he knows one thing—that particular civilization is not his, and something about it violates his consciousness as a man who wants man to make of his residence on earth a passage that is not marked by predetermined acceptance of his own annihilation. "I'm in no hurry to write about India and Burma and Ceylon, because many foundations and origins seem hidden, and many phenomena are still unexplainable. It all appears to be in ruins and falling down, but the truth is that strong and viable basic ties link these appearances with bonds which are somehow secret and indestructible."

The alternatives were clear: either he would be swallowed up by the sultry environment, or he would find strength in weakness and, spurred on by the danger around him, would convert his own apathy into creative energy. And he believes he can succeed if he makes up his mind to the struggle. He will transfigure what depresses him, transforming ominous and dark elements into the basic material of his poetry. That is the battle he undertakes in the work he is writing.

"I have almost finished a book of poems, *Residence on Earth*," he confides to Eandi, "and you will see how I succeed in isolating my expression, making it constantly hover around danger, and what solid and uniform substance I insistently give to one and the same force . . ." His book reflects his surroundings, but it plays a life-saving role. With that *Residence* he will pay for his right to live, and he will survive. Stylistically, a specialist's eye can probably detect a clear similarity between the poetry and the letters he writes in that period.

He asks for help in getting some news of America for nourishment, some of her essence to gulp in like air, and he thanks Eandi for having sent a copy of *Don Segundo Sombra*, recently published in Buenos Aires. "I read it thirstily," he declares, "as if I could once again lie down in the clover fields of my country and listen to my grandfather and uncles. The book is truly something grandiose and natural, isn't it, something very moving. A smell of distances, horses, human lives, all so clearly mirrored and so completely conveyed."

It is after this letter that he flees from the feline "Maligna," Josie Bliss, and he immediately feels the lash of nostalgia in that "Tango" in her memory:

> How much darkness I'd give from my soul to have you back,
> and how menacing I find the names of the months,
> and how much the word "winter" sounds like a sad drum.

The next letter is sent from Wellawatta, 5 June 1928, just after his move to Ceylon. He tells his friend that he's calmed down now and can write him with tranquility. . . . Not too much tranquility, though, because Lord knows there are still problems. In spite of the invocation to divinity, this time his tribulations are strictly material ones.

Consuls of my rank—appointed and honorary consuls—have a miserable income, the lowest of all the personnel. Lack of money has made me suffer immensely up to now, and still in this period my life is full of ignoble conflicts. I get 166 American dollars a month, which over here is the salary of a third-class shop clerk. Even worse, this salary depends on the income the consulate receives; in other words, if in any given month there are no exports to Chile, there's no salary for me either. All this is such hardship and humiliation for me—in Burma, I went five months without any income, without anything. And what's even worse is that I have to pay all the necessary expenses: desk, furniture, postage, lease. And to boot, I don't have transportation privileges, so if I hadn't spelled out what I wanted in my cable to you, I would have been in despair thinking of a sudden transfer with no means to pay for my journey. Thank you a thousand times, Eandi, and excuse these mournful details, which are the truth and torment of every day. Maybe if my income were commensurate and fixed, I mean if I could be sure of receiving it at the end of every month, maybe I wouldn't care about living my life in any old corner of the world, hot or cold.

While I used to be one who continually held to a doctrine of irresponsibility and being on the move, for my own life and for others, now I feel an eager desire to settle down, to become secure, to live or die in peace. I also want to get married, but soon—tomorrow—and live in a big city. Those are my only consistent wishes; perhaps I'll never be able to fulfill them.

49. *Messages from a Castaway*

In Asia, he is beset by wishes to get away, just as he was in his last days in Chile, yet he's not made for escapism, and he clings to life. He's tied to it by women—still not "The Woman." But this business of going from bed to bed, from girl to girl, whether it be native or mulatta or English, hurts him inside and fills him with boredom. His great passion is literary creation. For the first time since he began to write, poetry comes more slowly, as if it were meeting an interior obstacle that probably derives from something exterior. In addition, tortured by his difficult economic situation and in need of money to get away from the Orient, he is thinking of poetry as an activity that might provide him with some monetary return. He wants to go to Europe in 1931, but to do so he needs money. His dream is to publish not in Buenos Aires but in Spain. "Argentina still seems like a province," he writes Eandi. Since his youth, Neruda has mapped out a dream of conquering the capital cities of the Spanish-speaking world, as a form of establishing recognition for his poetry in the principal centers of the language. And it should be noted that on the map of his consular assignments, once he returns from the Orient, the main Spanish-speaking cities are marked with little red flags: Buenos Aires, Madrid, Mexico City. But there he is, consumed by the torrid heat, pondering how to work out his destiny.

It's all very difficult for him. He has written to Spain and has marked time looking at the calendar and despairing of receiving an answer. He won't give up, and in the absence of recognition, perhaps he himself will discretely praise his book, breaking that modesty that keeps him from talking about the merits of his work. But he goes on seeking the agreement of the world. "Somehow," he writes to Eandi, "it seems possible to have a drop of success over there in Madrid, a little bit of approval, which would be enough. I've been writing these poems for nearly five years. You already know that they aren't numerous, only nineteen; however, I think I've achieved that necessary essential, which is a style of my own. It seems to me that every one of my lines is saturated and dripping with *me*."

The last resort for him is to publish in Chile. If he should end up doing that, it might constitute a confession of defeat and of following the path of least resistance. But he doesn't discount it. If the poems don't get published anywhere else, he'll have to resign himself. After all, he has a faithful publisher in Santiago who accepts from him the good and the bad (according to his own expression) and pays him, although those royalties are quite meager. Besides, maybe a new book of his will be noted on his résumé in officialdom as a point in his favor, and will perhaps one day be of influence in a decision to move him out of an Oriental hole to some country where it's easier to breathe. Like Gabriela Mistral, though never as abundantly and intensely, he feels that there are people in his own country who get their kicks by insulting him. "Look, Eandi, do you remember my verses in 'Juntos nosotros' (Together We Two)? They were also published in Chile, and immediately there were three or four critical pieces in the newspapers, full of the worst insults and talking about my 'imbecility' as a foregone conclusion, in that tone."

For many enthusiastic readers of *Book of Twilights* and *Twenty Poems,* the first poems from *Residence* were surprising. They missed the melodious clarity of the love theme which had been expressed in sweet postmodernist modulations of tenderness and nostalgia. Now they were met by obscurity, and their eyes couldn't get used to the deep shadow. And many readers simple-mindedly concluded that the poet Neruda was finished. It was possible that the twenty-year-old was no longer the same at twenty-five. They didn't understand that the poet who used to write in Chile was different from the one who now was writing in Rangoon or in Colombo. His reality had changed, his awareness had grown, and therefore his poetry is different, conditioned by his new surroundings and by the metamorphosis in his life and creative process.

In addition, those dreams of poetic greatness (frustrated dreams, in his judgment) that had tried to find an outlet in *The Slingsman* now were coming back in a different shape. He wanted to revolutionize all Spanish-language poetry, which he judged at that moment to be weak and without vigor. "You can see," he writes to Eandi, "what poverty there is in poetry written in Spanish; groups have lost all intensity and devote themselves to intellectual exercises, out of pleasure, as if it were a sport, and even in that category they all seem to me quite mediocre players. Lugones, who is so scorned, truly seems richly endowed, and his poetry almost always seems poetic, that is to say legitimate, even if it's a baroque anachronism." This paragraph underscores a philosophy of poetry which García Lorca would call a poetry *closer to blood than to ink* in referring to Neruda, which is a basic key to understanding him. Mistral also underlines that same quality when she calls her fellow countryman's work poetry in a major key.

The next letter, dated 21 November 1928, delves deeper into his concept. The poet should not make a gymnastic exercise out of poetry, "There is one commandment for him, and that is to penetrate life and make it prophetic." The poet doesn't conceive of poetry except in relation to man and the world. He should not be a heavenly fool but a human being loaded down with all the weight of universal dreams and passions. His correspondence with the Argentine writer during that period is a photographic plate on which are engraved his most intimate and demanding thoughts, his creative intentions, and his philosophy as a man and as an artist, not as a disengaged being but one integrated into his environment and into nature and society. He is critical of the predominant poetry around him:

For some time now, the intelligence of poets has separated out all human relationship from what they say, and insofar as the poetic message is concerned, all cordiality and friendship have fled from the world, when in reality, what other purpose is there for poetry than that of consoling and helping us to dream? I'm talking like a society girl, but she's right on this point—poetry should be filled with universal content, with emotions and things. That's what I want to create, a poetic poetry. When I sit down to write at night, alone with a piece of paper, very little is left of my scientific curiosity, my admiration for automobiles, my attraction to this exotic nature. Then, only I myself exist, and my afflictions, my joys, my private passions . . .

He is obsessed by his anxiety to be published in Spain. He carefully copies out his new book, *Residence on Earth,* and sends it to the peninsula, to a friend whom he still knows only through correspondence, Rafael Alberti. He isn't sure that it will be published, and his doubts were justified, because that first *Residence* did not go to press on that occasion in Spain. But he was happy to have finished the book, feeling the same joy that mothers do upon giving birth and that writers feel upon putting the last word to a work they have written with all the pain of childbirth. A happiness that is soon dimmed by uncertainty—he doesn't feel sure about the book, doesn't know what to think of it, not in regard to its truth, which seems to him indubitable, and he alone knows how very much sincerity there is in it. But neither moral goodness nor honesty are sufficient to make books worthy. His uneasiness comes because of its deep tone, its darkness, perhaps a lack of internal contrast in the work, "Is it perhaps too gloomy? Maybe monotonous?" He justifies himself: if the book were to suffer from a somberness and be boring, he would have to attribute it to his disagreement with the ideas that predominated at the time. From that point, his allegation carries him to an arbitrary conclusion, "The old books are all monotonous, a fact that does not deny them other qualities."

He receives no reply about publication of the book. His state of mind becomes anguished in that waiting period. Since he can't speak Spanish with anybody, he uses his own language only by himself, when he is writing or talking to himself. He lives for years carrying on a conversation without any other speaker. Neruda said once he came from a part of the earth where they spoke very little or very poorly, and on 24 April 1929 he writes from Colombo, "I have grown up handicapped in communicable expression." His life is suspended, just as his words are—a time of soliloquy. He's frightened when he discovers that he wants to have a conversation, even with himself, and he can't find the right words. "All my phrases seem banal, with nothing of *me* in them." He lives in silence and empty hours, and it is then that he drinks that "terrible tropical whiskey." He feels alone. His servant, Ratnaigh, comes to refill his glass every ten minutes. He has a sensation of being exiled and about to die, in a full-fledged Graham Greene atmosphere, but it is Joseph Conrad that he refers to, asking his correspondent-friend if he remembers the books about hopeless expatriates, "How many objective or unobjective novels you would create out of this word 'perhaps' if you heard it in this part of the planet, Eandi." But if Eandi is too far away to write those novels, then Neruda can reduce them to poetry, because he is living in that hot region of the earth and because he has the gift. And he will write that way because he is alone, so alone that he collects dogs from the streets to be able to talk to them. And then they leave, the ingrates. Nonetheless, he is aware that he is not a Conrad character, because the sense of existence is too strong in him. So, in spite of everything, "I sense some virtues in this life." He is not inclined to renounce it, and life is not only everyday living but also poetry. Life is at the foundation of his literary philosophy. His Argentine correspondent mentions Jorge Luis Borges, and Neruda immediately establishes the differences that separate the two of them. Borges seems to him to be more preoccupied with cultural problems, which don't attract Neruda because, in his opinion, they are not human (or at least, let *us* say it, not as human). With a slightly savage sharpness and youthful irreverence, as well as inborn exaggeration, this not yet twenty-five-year-old Neruda defines his likes and dislikes: "I like good wine, love, suffering, and books as consolation for inevitable solitude. I feel a certain disdain for culture as a way to interpret things; I think it's better to have an acquaintance without antecedents, a physical absorption of the world, which exists in spite of and in opposition to us." He thinks that the exegetes, the explainers, the entomologists of literature, and the enigmas of knowledge are all vast and complex speculations, not without emptiness. His eyes have a certain peculiarity, which may lead him to a sort of color blindness. He understands bodies, sun, and sweat more than he does the endless commentary on ideas; he's fed up with wordiness.

   Residence on Earth reveals, on the other hand, the impact of ancient Eastern poetry. I have seen poets in India reciting their long singsong verses for hours in the streets, accompanied by musical instruments. Those extended poems were punctuated by sounds from long serpentine horns and dull gongs, giving them the feel of liturgy or asiatic opera or sacred invocation. If westerners are unaware of this influence in his work, it's not through any fault of Neruda, who told Eandi in writing that *"Residence on Earth* is a mass of almost ritualistic verses of great monotony . . . with mystery and suffering, like those created by the poets of old."

50. *Doubts in Rangoon*

Long interruptions occur, producing silent periods, which do not indicate that nothing is happening, but do reveal that something is taking place deep within him. He comes to doubt himself and to doubt literature. He feels superfluous, believing that things have found expression on their own and that he has no part in them and doesn't have the capacity to comprehend them. These moments of crisis come to him after finishing his book, when he struggles to free himself from it even while still feeling nervous about its uncertain publication. Neruda questions the sense and reason for being of still unwritten books and berates himself. He wishes to get out of the literary cage where the main objective is to change form, "a surface problem that seems senseless to me." Is he possibly suffering from that illness where form is sought just for the sake of form? Can that virus have soaked into his bones? Such an ailment would mean, in terms of literature, a mortal illness that would lead him to sterility. In those early days after composing the first volume of *Residence* he feels empty. Nothing moves him to write, not because the things around him seem empty, but because they have so much interior meaning that their very existence is sufficient for them to express themselves.

Although he doesn't feel like writing, "how good it is to read, to listen to music, and to swim in the sea." He reads all day and claims it to be the only pleasure left to him. He's reading almost exclusively in English. Every month, a friend of his, Leonel Wendt, sends him bags of the latest books published in London, especially detective novels. Fascinated, he becomes interested in some other authors who were in vogue during those years, including T. S. Eliot and D. H. Lawrence. He reads at one sitting *The Seven Pillars of Wisdom* by Lawrence of Arabia. Since the native milieu was culturally more and more impenetrable, he took refuge in English literature, to such an extent that he learned the names of London's streets and taverns by reading Stevenson and Dickens. All of that doubtless influenced his poetry in that period.

Eminently changeable, he experiences a radical change in his poetry. This does not mean he is wrong when, in response to a question about whether he is an evolutionary poet of distinct books or whether there is a common core in them all, he answers that he feels his poetry to be just one solitary book that he writes and creates every day. Anyone who is attentive to his work will without great difficulty see the recurrence of great topics that concerned him, the same themes in differing forms. Not an unusual situation nor one without precedent, for one of his recognized masters, that man with a beard like branches of snow, Walt Whitman, in *Leaves of Grass* did nothing but write the constantly expanded edition of one and the same book. Perhaps in the same sense of "The Book of Books," for, like the Bible, Neruda attempted to name everything he had seen and known, to embrace with his own words as much of the world as he could, as if he were discovering it and had to name it all anew. Sometimes that gave him the feeling that he was always beginning new variations of the same poem.

But there are certain breaks, ruptures, and profound differences in the manner of seeing and recounting things, sensations, and feelings. That manner in *Residence* is abundantly different from his earlier poetry. This need for transfiguration was in him even before his departure for the Orient. The beginning of the book is Chilean, and the first poem in *Residence*, "Galope muerto" (Dead Gallop) was published in mid-1925 in Santiago. It is born of a growth crisis in his poetry, which now looks at the world through a different lens, enabling his eyes to explore beneath the surface of all things—water, air, creatures:

> And so, in the stillness, stopping, to see,
> then, like immense flapping, up above,
> something like dead bees or numbers,
> ah, so much my pale heart cannot feel . . .

Between 1925 and 1927 in Santiago he writes "Débil del alba" (Weak From Dawn) where "The pale day comes forth, the day of the timid, / with a piercing cold smell and gray-clad spirits." These are days of discouragement, of long hesitations and confusion, of "obvious destitution." Unlike the Orient, light does not come forth "like a clanging, but rather like tears." The day's fabric is not brilliant; it is a flimsy cloth that "serves as a bandage, serves to wave / farewell, in back of absence." He is bidding farewell, preparing himself for absence in order to "cover, swallow, conquer, lay down distances." His "Diurno doliente" (Mourner by Day) is written in Chile, and its cryptic lines become clear when one knows the concrete situation of their author, "a mortal servant dressed in hunger."

When he reaches the Orient, he feels the absence of Chile in all the four corners of his room, where he immediately begins to miss what he left behind. From afar, Albertina appears in "Fantasma":

> How you do emerge from yesteryear
> tall and pale-faced student
> whose voice is still needed
> to console months that drag and halt.
> . . . .
> From a place far away, where
> the smell of earth is not the same
> and eventide arrives with tears
> in the shape of darkened poppies.

She is present in "Lamento lento" (Slow Lament), where in dreams he is pursued by what he left behind. His "Colección nocturna" (Nocturnal Collection) brings "the wind that shakes the months, the whistle of a train." He hears the dream of "old companions and beloved women . . . comrades who rest their heads on casks," casks on a fugitive ship.

And once again nostalgia for the distant woman in "Together We Two," where "My exiled mouth bites flesh and grape." She is also the "heartless lady" of "Tiranía" (Tyranny) with "your sharp indifference like a knife and your cold sense of oblivion." But in "Angela Adónica" (Adonic Angel) it is perhaps Marisol-Terusa who is remembered, "Today I laid beside a young virgin / as if next to a pure white sea."

Some poems of that period, written while he was still in Chile, are not included in the *Residences*, yet they presuppose a way of seeing nature and things in his country with an apparently deconstructed interior vision. Nonetheless, that vision is also universal, and "Alianza" could have been written anywhere on earth, while at the same time it corresponds to a problematic spirit that is debating the sensation of emptiness and slow death in an atmosphere where it is growing late, and metals reflect no light. That boy with his hard life attempts to ride off on poetry, as in "Caballo de los sueños" (Horse of Dreams), where he feels unnecessary, "I uproot hell's captain from my heart . . . I wander from place to place, absorbing illusions."

In "Unidad" (Unity) he declares, "I work in deafness, circling above myself / like the crow above death, dressed in black."

But this tendency toward allegorical inquiries into solitude becomes more profound when he reaches the Orient, which is a different world and a dreadful otherness.

51. *Realism in* Residence

While Neruda is living in Rangoon, he hears a refined acquaintance say proudly that the Strand Hotel is the most *chic* place in the whole of Britain's Indies empire. Neruda is repulsed by the irresistible charm and old-fashioned pomp of the Strand, where British gentlemen smile professionally at Burmese aristocracy. And he detests those native Burmese who are happy because their country in 1886 became a province headed by the unreachable symbol of the distant and severe Queen Victoria. The Burmese, nonetheless, are not puritanical. They drink scotch at any hour; they challenge each other with luxury; they compete to see who can give the most extravagant parties. It's a way of gaining a social reputation—maybe the report will reach the columns of London newspapers. That would guarantee prestige.

The poet has only to go outside to realize the abyss separating splendor from a deathly poverty that is even more horrifying because it is unaware of its misfortune. In spite of the fact that he soon learns that the word "Rangoon" means "end of the war," he walks through the streets of the teeming city with a feeling that the war between rich and poor has not yet begun. He stops in front of the Schwegadon pagoda, covered with stories told in gold. In the street, people are dying of hunger. A country full of monasteries, almost like Tibet. Monks and young novices flow through the roadways like hundreds of piraguas in the Irrawady River. The rainy season has begun and the river is up.

In the evenings, the consul from Chile likes to go see the dancers and contemplate their undulating necks, pivoting hips, and rolling eyes. He begins to count up the positions and movements but never even comes close to the 2,000 they talk about. The nocturnal spectacle is quite different from the daylight vision of monks with shaven heads and bare feet, robed in purple or red or bright yellow. They move with difficulty among the giraffelike women whose necks are imprisoned in high neckbands that they can't ever remove. Street vendors offer the poet little statues of Prince Siddharta. By his side is Josie Bliss, her head covered with jasmine blossoms.

Here, poverty is holy. Indigence goes on and 5,000 temples and pagodas go on. Neruda travels to Pagan, where one-third of Burma's capital was swallowed by the Irrawady between the eleventh and thirteenth centuries. He goes to Mandalay because they say it's the seat of arts and letters. The panorama is not much different—pagodas and monasteries, and on a hill the royal palace. And surrounding it all, carts pulled by donkeys and carriages pulled by humans, and children and adults holding out an open hand. This is the environment that surrounds him as he writes the major part of the first *Residence*. Its tone is not one of joy.

But the ancient new land where he is now established seeps into the cracks of his writing, bringing the seasonal green wind, the May monsoon, that blows over the recently arrived traveler with the confused soul, "What tranquility for beginning, what little hope for loving . . ."

In the midst of chaotic shadows and dreams, of feverish days and nights, the writer attunes his ear to all that happens. He will be like a mirror, "like a slightly hoarse bell," but he must tell what happens and reply to "objects that call out and are not answered." This is his poetic creed of that period.

On a trip to the Orient in December of 1976, I had physical and spiritual proof of the solid realistic re-creation in Neruda's Asian residences. I was taken by the almost mathematical precision with which such a subtle spirit and atmosphere are reproduced in the poetry. Crossing India between Hyderabad and Kakinada, I was greeted by a red and blue dawn over the Indian Ocean that becomes both sea and day as it plows the Bay of Bengal. When I deplaned in Rangoon, I was astonished to see an undulating serpent not far from the airplane. This place has "a coloration put together like a snake," Neruda said in "Aura," written right here in Rangoon fifty years ago, and now I am breathing the same smells and colors and atmosphere of *Residence*. It's after the monsoon season, when the poet lived "in mourning like a widower enraged by each day of life," when "unadorable and with my ordinary face, I go among Mohammedan merchants and people who adore the cow and the snake." To the north is Mandalay, "and beside me my wife, at my side a sound from far away, my Burmese wife, a king's daughter." Here is all the scenery of the "Widower's Tango" with its tropical vegetation: "Later, buried near the coconut palm you will find / the knife I hid for fear you would kill me." In front, the river. Not long after that, Josie was buried in the waters of the Irrawady to the sound of "copper chains and flutes." Feeling the Orient and seeing its workers and its women, beauties dressed in violent purple and "scarlet muslin," the idea is confirmed that Neruda always relied freely on reality. He felt the elements of nature and perceived their hidden truth and their visible appearance, the true perfume of creatures and things. He viscerally lived those countries, this continent which is as different as it is gigantic, and which we are just now beginning to discern behind the monotonous rhythm of tom-toms and shadowy dancers, and the funeral pyres. My trip was proof of the verism of *Residence*.

The prose pieces in the first *Residence* are one more personification of the poetry, where he is observing the world he has fallen into, so to speak, from another universe. Observation of nature, memories of ostracism, eagerness for a new planet, and then, typical for a man in his twenties, astonishment at the wide-eyed girls with budding hips and "lightning-yellow flowers" in their hair, rings on their toes, rigid chokers around their necks, who are statuesque in demeanor.

He is also seized by suspicion in the face of the unknown, a feeling of being spied upon, which begins with that love-deranged woman who tries to envelop him every waking moment.

"Caballero solo" (A Man Alone) is like a film with many sequences, plots and characters worthy of development: young homosexuals, amorous girls, countless widows, wives just thirty hours pregnant, hoarse cats, uniformed lovers, fat couples and thin ones, happy ones and sad ones; the life of trousers and skirts, the sound of silk stockings, female breasts that shine like eyes, the seduction consummated at last by the little clerk, the seducer's evenings and the spouses' nights, the animals' open fornication, the strange game played by cousins, the adulterers' love—all are present in the hallucinations of "A Man Alone."

A man alone, autobiographical, who in "El ritual de mis piernas" (Ritual of My Legs) slowly investigates his body's mysteries, the how and why of his limbs, in the conviction that beyond his legs is where "the names of the world (begin), foreignness and remoteness."

Surrounded by all this hustle and bustle in which he has fallen and where he lifts himself up, where so many elements seem to encompass him in a desolate and deadly aura, the poet closes his book with "Significa sombras" (The Meaning Is Shadows), ambitiously affirming himself, "Let not the tremor of deaths and births disturb / the innermost space I wish forever to keep for my own."

Thirty years later, he went back. I receive his letter from Rangoon, with the lion coat of arms on the letterhead of the detested Strand Hotel, dated 4 July 1957, "Dear Vol, After Colombo we will go with the two Amados to China, and here we are still waiting for some baggage we lost in Madras. We are worn out by this horrible city—how could I have lived in it? (miracles of youth). It's the season when the rain falls without cease on accumulated filth." His opinion about the place has not changed.

52. Letters from the Orient

He reads with the hunger of a horse that's traveled a long way alone. He translates Joyce, but he isn't dazzled by the search for novelty of form, preferring flesh and blood stories, direct and active with a feeling of movement, even at the price of exterior untidiness. That apparent untidiness becomes something attractive and unusual for our poet, who confesses that his first law of literature up to now was always the dictatorship of form.

On 9 June 1930 he leaves Ceylon "forever." His heart beats with new-found emotions. He has said good-bye to his house by the sea, his dogs and cats who were his close confidants and companions in nocturnal dialogues, and his friend Andrew. But in that letter to Eandi announcing his consular transfer, a few lines at the end refer to a tormenting worry—he hasn't heard anything about the book he had sent to Madrid in October 1929.

What's going on with that book? It has been sent twice to Spain, but the publishing house of Editora Iberoamericana, which was supposed to publish it, has folded. The poet sends several urgent letters, with no reply. This doesn't mean that there is absolute silence about Neruda, though, for José Bergamín refers to him in the prologue to a classic book of twentieth-century Latin American poetry, César Vallejo's *Trilce*, and several articles appear in Spain. In view of the fact that Madrid is not the propitious market, the originals of Neruda's book are in Paris, where a Miss Alvear has undertaken to publish a few poems in the journal *Imán*. She will send him the check (important!) and then the contract to publish *Residence*. The poet is very skeptical; he has never heard of that journal nor that lady, nor does he know whether the book is to be published in Argentina. "It's enough to drive one to whiskey for three months. I feel my book should appear, for God's sake; unpublished, it's going stale and growing old."

The crisis about the value of literature and the uncertainty about his own usefulness as a poet has been fleeting. "It's wrong to talk about dropping literature," he writes to Eandi on 5 September 1931 from his new post in Batavia, Java. "One thinks he's finished, but there is something gathering together inside him, drop by drop. I would die if I couldn't write more."

The heartrending correspondence to his friend Eandi is quite distinct from that which he sends to his sister Laura, so much so that they seem to be written by different individuals. They are written by the same man in the same place, but to two very different readers. Neruda was always able to make his language conform to his listener and to speak to each one in his own idiom. He knows that he could confide to Eandi his most complicated anxieties and his most torturous doubts about literature and his own role in it, because he would find in him perfect understanding. And this fact shaped the form and content of those letters. At the same time, he knew that the letters he sent to his family had to be understood by them, which explains their basically simple, direct, strictly informational quality, designed to elicit news that he needed to know or to convey reassurance so that they wouldn't worry about him. Nevertheless, beneath their apparently banal surface, there is a synopsis of movements, events, trips, warm weather, fear of illnesses, eagerness to go to Europe, and a sensation of exile. In those letters to Laura one sees sort of a Temucan sense of clan that never leaves him. Out of that exchange of letters, extremely lacking in details, he also hopes that some news about his country will come forth and that back there they will press negotiations to enable him to leave the Orient, with a transfer to more amenable climes.

The letter to Laura of 28 October 1927 from Rangoon is written on letterhead of the Consulate of Chile in Burma and conveys greetings to Rodolfo and his wife, Teresa, and their son Raulillo. "Tell me about the folks who ask about me." He specifically asks if Amalia, widow of Alviso de Springfell, has remarried. And he assures his sister that he, Neftalí Ricardo, will not marry, don't worry.

The next letter, dated 28 February 1928, is written from Shanghai during the period of political events which, to locate them in literature, will be used by André Malraux as the background for *The Human Condition*. Neruda has been away from Rangoon for a month, visiting other countries in Asia.

He goes to India and to Indochina, where he unexpectedly discovers the fraternity of heart and the greatness of her artisan people, who organize a festival of music and dance in honor of this poor stranger lost in the jungle, this unknown guest. They can't exchange a single word with him in a common language, but there Neruda perceives intuitively that all peoples are brothers. On that occasion, there in the Vietnamese jungle, he did not feel lonely.

He writes to Laurita from on board the ship returning from Japan, a very beautiful country where he would have liked to stay; however, he's fearful about pneumonia and sneezing, and it's hellishly cold, and there are innumerable strange things. Rangoon, which bores him to death, is just the opposite, "Like living in an oven day and night. Life in Rangoon is a terrible exile. I was not born to spend my life in a hell like that." He's afraid of getting malaria. He wants to go to Europe to finish his studies, and he thinks that any day now he will pack up his bags and go, even at the risk of starving to death.

He always asks about "the veterans," his parents, but he doesn't expect to have any personal communication with them, because that was cut off some time ago, with his father in particular, and with his mother it is scanty and strictly about everyday matters. But his concern for her throbs with the sincerity of a good son from times past, "Tell my sainted mother that I think of her often, and that I believe the eye problem is probably caused by nerves more than anything else; tell her to take a mental tonic and not to think too much about her illness."

All those letters appear to be without substance. A great wall separates him from the family circle. It is the difference between two off-center worlds which follow separate tangents and really never touch each other or coincide in any way. It is that which gives rise to the thinness of the correspondence, even though it's affectionate and shows a certain joking humor and some wordplay, but nothing more. "I'm going to have lunch; say hello to everyone, and to you—too-to-you joy and love . . . And so, be happy with these few words, since the rest of what is happening to me wouldn't interest you nor would you understand it."

A letter dated 12 December 1928 reveals that he has been transferred to Colombo, with the same salary, and he has accepted the move with pleasure, because Rangoon was becoming intolerable for him. He sees the only news item about Chile that is published in those years—the earthquake in Talca. He doesn't seem to be so alone now, as he flutters around women and they around him, "Here, all the chicks try to marry me; I heroically resist them. They are too intelligent, they know too much, which is a drawback for me. In any case, if anything stirs my heart, I'll let you know. Give a hug to the beloved veterans and everybody, and don't forget your brother 'Shinbone.' Neftalí Ricardo."

On one rare occasion he sends a long letter to his "most dear and unforgotten mama Mrs. Trinidad C. de Reyes," in response to one from her. It provides some concrete details about the atmosphere in Colombo. "I'm renting a bungalow or chalet at the seashore, and I live completely alone in the house, which is large . . . It's frowned upon for white people to do anything for themselves. Of course this seems completely wrong to me, but it so happens that my well-known laziness has increased in the heat of these countries, and if you, my dear Mama, should pass by my house in Colombo you would hear how I yell at the servant boy from morning to night to bring me cigarettes, paper, lemonade, and to take care of my trousers, my shirts, and all the other items I need in order to exist."

The town where he lives, Wellawatta, reminds him of the never forgotten Puerto Saavedra. Very early in the mornings he walks along the beach, dressed in a swimming suit, taking advantage of the only time of day when it's cool. That's how he is photographed by his friend Salzberd, in a tee shirt, under a palm tree, with an expression of infinite boredom. He tries to swim; other days there's nothing to do but sleep. "What I need is a wife, but you can see that apparently nobody wants your ugly son." He asks about all his relatives, all the Reyes family, the biblical uncles, Amos and Oseas; about the young uncle José Angelito, and his saintly cousin who is an ordained priest. He adds one of those ironic comments that frequently slip in below the surface in his correspondence, "Truth to tell, he didn't look like a saint, or else I don't know my saints." In distant lands, it often happens that one feels more strongly the ties with relatives, "What's become of Don Manuel Basoalto, and Aunt Rosa? . . . Soon it will be two years since I left Chile, and I don't know when I'll be able to return."

From so far away, he sends cables and letters to the cousin who had helped him since early childhood, Rudecindo Ortega Masson, asking to be moved from there as soon as possible. Rudecindo is the influential man who doesn't forget his poet-relative who was so inept at mathematics. He's a lawyer and a caring professor, such a meticulous dresser that the jokers call him "Dude Ortega."

Neruda is very much alone, swimming in the sea and playing with cats and dogs—all to become a part of his life from then on.

53. Solemn Communique

He dispatches a letter with a touch of solemnity from the "Consulate of Chile for Singapore and Batavia," written on letterhead with a Dutch name, Weltevreden, and dated 15 December 1930. It is one of the few he addressed to his father, and it complies with a filial obligation.

> I must inform you of something of great importance—I have gotten married. My marriage took place in this city on the sixth of this month. My wife is of Dutch nationality, and she comes from a distinguished family who settled in Java many years ago. My wish was to inform you of my decision to marry and await your consent, but owing to several circum

stances, our union took place well before the date we intended. I believe that even so, if you and Mama had had the good fortune to meet the woman who is now my wife, you would be proud of her, as I am, and you would love her, as I do. For me, she is perfect in every way, and we are completely happy. . . . From now on, you will not have the worry of knowing that your son is alone and far away, now that I have someone who will be with me forever. I am sending you and Mama some photographs of our wedding. My wife is a bit taller than I am, blond with blue eyes. Since I don't yet speak Dutch and she doesn't speak Spanish, we get along with English, a language we both speak perfectly. She does not have wealth of her own; her father was ruined by some risky investments. In any case, we are poor but happy. María has a good character, and we get along marvellously with each other.

The single consul, who was then twenty-six years old, was an exotic character in Batavia in 1930. For some mamas in a matchmaking mood who were inclined to be guided by appearances, he might even have seemed a good catch. Furthermore, they say he writes poetry, which does not of necessity imply that he's a depraved or mad man. He's seen in the evenings in certain *soirées* talking with marriageable girls. He is charming and doesn't say idiotic things; he gives the impression of being a bright young man with a future. Toward the beginning of the year, he meets María Antonieta Agenaar Vogelzanz, a girl almost five feet nine inches tall, a typical, well-endowed Dutch girl. The abandoned consul thinks she may be the woman he needs. He has made so many efforts to get Albertina to come join him, to no avail. He begins by shortening the Euro-Javanese girl's name. He will call her Maruca. Neruda is a man fond of deadlines, and he has set 1930 as the year he will get married. He does so just before the calendar runs out, in December.

On 28 July 1931 from Batavia he alludes to an important event in Chile, "I have just yesterday had news of the resignation of Ibáñez (which took place on the 26th), and I'm glad there was no need of a revolution to get rid of the *pig*. I'm also glad for my exiled friends, who will be able to return to Chile (Carlos Vicuña Fuentes, Pedro León Ugalde, Enrique Matta Figueroa, Don Eliodoro Yáñez's son, and many others are friends of mine)." This is one of the few references to politics in the letters to his family. It leaves no room for doubt about young Neruda's satisfaction with the fall of the military dictatorship. He shows particular sensitivity toward the situation of his exiled friends, perhaps because he also feels like an exile. None of the people he mentions is an intimate friend, except Alvaro, nicknamed Pilo, who is the son of Eliodoro Yáñez and later will be considered somewhat of a cryptic writer of rather brief works under the pseudonym of Juan Emar. His father, a well-known liberal leader and founder of the then influential daily *La Nación,* put his son in charge of the literary supplement, and it is Pilo who asks Neruda to send articles from the Orient, which the poet does with several dispatches that are now included in his *Complete Works.*

He had had a thrilling and happy experience, related to politics, in December 1929 when he went to Calcutta where the All-India Congress was being held, bringing together in one of the suburbs more than 20,000 delegates gathered around Mahatma Gandhi and Jawaharlal Nehru. There were gathered the dreams and hardships and hopes of a continent's people who were not resigning themselves to foreign domination. Neruda saw a physically exhausted Gandhi as he lay on a cot, either sleeping or resting, in the sight of everybody. He would lie down for a few minutes and then return to the fight against what was then the greatest empire on earth. The poet began to think about the political differences between the areas of what today is called the Third World. It was a period defined by relative stability, which would be broken by the great crisis already precipitating from the United States. Chile and Latin America, dominated in large part by military dictatorships, knew the crushing invasion of the North American companies that were replacing the old British lion's supremacy. In India, its mane had not yet been clipped, although it was getting ruffled by winds of rebellion. The mystic element was not a predominant factor in Latin American politics, and in his judgment this absence of mysticism constituted something positive.

The economic crisis unleashed by the New York stockmarket crash in 1929 spreads throughout the world contained in the United States' financial sphere and counts Neruda among its victims. The fall of Ibáñez was provoked in part by the collapse of the Chilean economy, which in turn was a sequel to the plummet on Wall Street. The government that replaces the dictator declares bankruptcy and notifies the poor consul, Ricardo Reyes, whose salary checks are as scarce as hen's teeth in any case, that there is no money to continue paying for his services. The Neruda couple then return to Chile. "I'm writing you from a Dutch ship," he tells his sister Laura. They are traveling on the *Pieter Corneliszoon Hooft,* and in Ceylon they will take an English cargo ship, the *Forafric,* to travel by way of South Africa and the Straits of Magellan to finally dock in Chile at Puerto Montt—a crossing of sixty days. He liked slow ocean trips, which invariably were productive.

54. Return to "Maligna"

This Neruda who bade farewell to Ceylon forever returned there twenty-six years later, in June 1957, for a Peace Meeting. When he goes into the street, some people eye him curiously as if wondering who is this man, don't I know him? Afterwards come the greetings with characters from *Residence,* in the midst of its landscape and atmosphere in the Wellawatta neighborhood, where crows hop about in the coconut palms, the brilliant shoeflower is in bloom, and the huge leaves of the temple bower are shining. He strides along in a cloud of beggar children, near a narrow-gauge train that announces its presence with whistle blasts at the crowd making its way along the edge of the sea.

He stops near the rails with a kind of apprehension, and shows a big scar on his right leg. He had tripped one night on the railway and had fallen unconscious on the rails just as the locomotive was approaching. His dog Kuthaka saved him with his barking, which was like a howling siren that told the engineer he should stop because someone had fallen on the tracks. In homage to the one who saved his life, various dogs that Neruda had in Chile and elsewhere were named Kuthaka. Neruda has told how long after hearing that word every day he finally learned that in Hindi it means "I bring food to the dogs." That Kuthaka who was his inseparable friend during his time in Colombo used to go with him morning and evening to the mouth of the river to see the elephants bathing. Possibly he envied those strange competing giants that spewed forth from their trunks such strong spouts of water. Kuthaka also announced the appearance of great sailboats that turned the dawn almost white near the garden of the house.

Now in 1957 he again suffers with the heat that used to bother him so much. He feels languid and has no energy. His pace slows, but he reaches the side street, number 42, and a house with a marble plaque that says Muhm. Alex S. Lamabadusuriya. He knocks, and a man tells him with a smile that he's mistaken, pointing to the house next door. Not that one either. He goes from door to door. "I don't remember very well," he murmurs. "That part of the street that leads to the sea has changed a lot. Before, there were no houses, just trees and an occasional hut." He doesn't find it. Neruda searches his memory for a piece of information to guide him. He is accompanied by a Chilean friend, Juan Lenín Araya, as they head for the home of Boya Pieres, where there's a small sign at the entrance—Coral Strand. They are received by a dark man with skinny, bare legs and wearing a huge, white hat. He studies them in puzzlement and invites them inside. He sits down in a wicker chair, and then suddenly gets to his feet with a shout, "Ricardo Reyes, the Chilean consul!"

In those bygone days, their relations were not neighborly. Boya Pieres tries to pin down the dates, "When was it? In 1928–1929? Oh yes, I remember Brampy, the boy who used to be your servant. I never heard of him again; when you left, he went away and we never saw him again."

There is one person he doesn't mention, who is there almost separating them in spite of time's passage. It is Josie Bliss. He mentally reconstructs the situation in those days. Boya Pieres was not his friend. It was he who gave asylum in his home to that "Maligna" from the poem, and from there she would fire daily letters and insults at the poet. "She said she would poison me, that I couldn't get away alive. I couldn't explain anything to Pieres; those were personal matters. It's logical that he would be inclined to protect her. Later, it all came to an end when she got bored and went off to her own country." The memory of both men is stalked by "Maligna." Neruda walks through the house and senses her hidden there, weeping with rage, threatening, drinking her afternoon tea alone, frequently remembering him. She stops cursing him aloud while he is still complaining of the tropics, but she goes on watching him in jealous silence.

As he leaves, he pronounces the meteorological forecast that he learned there—the coming of the monsoon, which joins together thunder, downpour, and whistling wind. Afterwards, the light of Ceylon will come again, within which he learned his "lonely lesson of burial." It was an excessive light that dried up his brain and tore through his clothing. Perhaps that light, he wrote in his poetry, illuminated with cruel clarity his destiny. But in despair and disinherited of everything that belonged to him, in the midst of that brightness like a permanent noontime, he reached the conclusion that there was nothing to do but live. After having submerged his eyes, his flesh and his soul in that flood of constant sunlight, his subconscious idea of color changed. After his return to Chile, the sunlight of his country seemed opaque to him, containing something of a shadow.

"Let's get out of here," he urges, but he stops in front of a rusty rundown shanty. "Here's where a fishing couple used to live," he says. "Every Saturday, I don't know whether it was because of a strange superstition or out of alcoholic wrath, the fisherman used to punctually turn loose his weekly rage on his wife. She would run to my house, the consulate, in desperation, demanding international protection. I would let her in, and the old woman would stay there until the next day, when the man would arrive in embarrassment to fetch his wife, who went off thankful and happy to return to her energetic and now repentant husand. That was the only consular asylum and the only refugee," he comments, "the only occasion on which I extended extra-territoriality, to free an old woman from periodic conjugal beatings. She stopped suffering them and she cried a lot when her husband succumbed to a poisonous snakebite while he was cutting wood."

They finally find the guide they need, the writer-lawyer S. P. Amarasingan. He serves them a shot of gin and recalls the city's occupation during the Second World War, when all the residents of the neighborhood had left, except for him.

"The house where you lived," he tells Neruda, "was converted into a barracks. I held on to a letter from you until a few years ago. I remember your handwriting was very elongated. I regret very much having destroyed it. I also remember your trained mongoose." (Pablo explains to him that he could never bring it to his friend's home because his dogs would chew it up.)

The host and his visitors cross the steaming sidewalk and enter what used to be the poet's old house, now unoccupied and about to be torn down. It's surrounded by a dense unkempt garden, and there's a patio with two thick coconut palms. "I caught a squirrel once in that tree," he points out. "This was my office, where I used to go crazy doing customs permits for shipments of tea to Chile, which is how I made my living. It's a pity that nowadays we don't drink Ceylon tea, which is the best in the world."

Going from one old unfurnished corner to another, suddenly something significant comes back to him, sparked by some unknown association of ideas. He almost shouts, as if not to forget it and so that it can be heard and taken note of, "Once the government informed the consulate that some political prisoners had escaped from Easter Island. It was the only time I ever had that kind of cable. They told me they might land on this island, since they had escaped on a barge. . . . For days I sat here waiting for them, to have somebody to talk to. Naturally I had no intention of turning them in. But they never came."

They never came. Does he mean Cástor Vilarín, a Communist exiled to the middle of the Polynesian Pacific, a resolute man with an adventurous spirit who so thirsted for freedom that one day, with some other comrades, he fled in a boat and was lost at sea? Or does he mean the storybook escape of Carlos Vicuña Fuentes and other political prisoners who were exiled to that island during the dictatorship of Ibáñez?

On that return trip in 1957 he was accompanied by Matilde. He was searching for not only the mental trace of a woman whose body had been burned on a bonfire but also for the house he lived in, because this poet married his houses and was widowed by them. "I have been left a widower by so many houses in my life, and I remember them all with tenderness. I wouldn't be able to count them and I wouldn't be able to live in them again, because I don't like resurrections . . . Only once did I try to go back to a house I'd lived in. That was after many long years, on the island of Ceylon." [20] But that house had gotten lost. He remembered the name of the neighborhood, a suburb between Colombo and Mount Lavinia. Never in any other house did he have so much time to become acquainted with himself. His days, then, were full of questions. In the midst of so much torrid leisure, the man came to realize that he was still a stranger to himself. Out of that absorption in thought came what he calls a "little book, *Residence on Earth,* a tormented dictionary of my self-examination."

Another symbol. He found the lost house after almost thirty years on the eve of its demolition. It had made an appointment with him and without knowing it he "arrived punctually on its last day of life." When he went into the little living room and then into the tiny bedroom where "I had only an army cot during so many years of my residence on earth," he felt the shadow of Brampy, his servant, and of Kiria, his mongoose. Thus he bade farewell to his house in Ceylon, one day before it fell under the ax or the bulldozer. The poet believes that coincidences like this "will be a mystery so long as houses and men exist."

IV.

Writing in the School of Hard Knocks

55. The Poet and the Mask

In 1932, after the government did away with his consular post in the crisis that left the Chilean economy in ruins worthy of a nine- or ten-point earthquake, Neruda returns through the Straits of Magellan. Amazing events have taken place in his country: toward the end of 1931 the Navy rebelled; in mid-1932 a Socialist Republic held power for two weeks; and on the main campus of the University of Chile, governing council soviets were set up for workers, peasants, soldiers, and sailors. Neruda, for the moment, views these events simply with curiosity and sympathy.

Laurita recalls that the telegram announcing his arrival in Temuco wasn't delivered on time, and she was at the window of the house when she suddenly saw suitcases being unloaded from a car. Then she spotted Pablo and Maruca, who were received with coldness by her father. They spent only a week in Temuco.

In Santiago, he has to work at two jobs, one in the Ministry of Affairs and the other, for a time, in the bureaucracy of the Ministry of Labor's Department of Culture. In the latter, his superior is an attentive old white-haired gentleman who is connected with journalism, Tomás Gatica Martínez, a man who recruits into his employ not only beautiful women and the poet, but also several of Neruda's youthful literary companions from 1920 and such significant Chilean writers as Joaquín Edwards Bello. Although Neruda is constantly in jeopardy of being laid off ("I run the risk that they may eliminate the department where I work"), the family begins to think that he has enough influence to find a job for his brother Rodolfo.

Yesterday compared with now—he is far from Probolingo Street and his house in Batavia; he has returned from the Orient, which impressed him as a "huge unlucky human family whose rituals and gods found no place in my consciousness"; and he and Maruca live in a modest rooming house near the National Congress. He is not contented. But he meets up with old friends again and returns to the bars of yesteryear.

It's a different man who returns. Although in a given moment he tries to renew a hidden relationship with Albertina, and at night he frequents the Hercules, the Jote, and the Alemán on Esmeralda Street, his spirit has been imbued with the Oriental experience of a gradual maturation in times and spaces so different from these that he can't find what he wants in these surroundings. A lot has changed. Even all that which he wrote to his father from Batavia about his wonderful wife. That love is fading, and he feels removed from her. He spends the night talking in taverns, and when he goes back home at three or four in the morning he sees her on the balcony waiting for him since who knows when.

Officialdom didn't welcome him with joy, but rather with indifference. He began to think that maybe he hadn't spent enough time away and perhaps he should leave the country again. But he cannot permit interruptions or pauses in his work, and he begins the second *Residence*. He will also have to show his compatriots something of what he has written during that five-year absence, for when he returns that first time there's a sort of unstated expectation in the literary world.

One day, a reading by Neruda is announced for the Miraflores Theater in Santiago. I was an adolescent who had just arrived in the city to begin my university studies. I was very interested in poetry, and for me Neruda was a legend, although I had never seen him. So I wanted to see him, though I wasn't daring enough to introduce myself to him or try to shake hands, much less strike up a shy conversation. No, it was just to look at him and listen to him from my seat in the dark balcony of the run-down theater. I arrived early and timidly settled down in the peanut gallery where I would barely be able to make out the poet's face. The curtain opened, and on the stage there were painted oriental masks serving as screens or strange curtains, which produced a feeling of Chinese opera and gave off an aura of remoteness and mystery. Suddenly, from behind those enormous larger-than-life masks came a nasal twangy voice, dragging like a lament, that began to say these verses from "Together We Two":

> How pure you are by sun or dark of night,
> what triumphant rarity in your halo of white,
> and your breast white as bread, from lofty climes,
> your beloved crown of dark trees . . .[21]

He went on principally with poems from the first *Residence,* the voice unchanging, almost mumbling in a monotonous wailing tone without inflection, as if it were disbursing sleeping pills. That was the impression I had for several minutes, and although the melodic curve of his voice didn't show the slightest modification in more than an hour that the reading lasted, after a while it became like the sound of slow-moving water or a special kind of wind, not because the message coming from that throat was clear and refreshing but because what those words conveyed was like some kind of libation for a thirsty spirit. The words created a warm climate and generated an atmosphere where you could see the struggle of a stormy soul, speaking from an interior world inhabited by many phantoms. Those words communicated to us the adventures of a man, his solitary life and his travels, his awareness and his language, in such a way that we could not remain as we were when we had settled down to listen to him in that corner of the Miraflores balcony.

That afternoon, we came to know the poet's recital voice, and it seemed to be related to the Araucanian *trutruca* wooden horn. But why didn't he show his face? At the end of the reading would he appear to accept the applause or the indifference of the listeners, at least half of whom were vacillating between amazement, stupor, and bewilderment? Neruda did not appear, and we were left with our unfulfilled wish to see him.

In 1982, on 24 and 25 September in the Patrizi Palace in Siena (Italy), there was a symposium on the work of Neruda, in which experts from several countries participated. One of them, Professor Alain Sicard from the University of Poitiers (France) gave a lecture that created a stir and lit polemical fires, "The Face as Mask: Autobiography and History in Neruda's Poetry." I took part in the animated discussion which followed the presentations, offering a recollection of that long-ago reading from fifty years before in Santiago's Miraflores Theater with the poet completely hidden behind gigantic Oriental masks, and I concluded that Sicard was not far off the mark.

56. Song of Songs?

He wasn't born to be a bureaucrat, but I've watched him bending over official papers with a pencil in hand, performing his office tasks. That year of 1932 in Santiago he lives the martyrdom of the sedentary employee. He needs two salaries to live. From his work in the Library of the Ministry of Affairs he earns 400 pesos a month, barely enough to cover the rent for the mediocre rooming house on Santo Domingo Street. He earns a bit more from his job in the Cultural Department of the Ministry of Labor. The galley slave is still suffering at his oar, but his thoughts are on poetry. He gives another reading in the shadows of the Posada del Corregidor, and that year the second edition of *Twenty Love Poems* comes out, eight years after the first edition, an indication that the poet was not yet a big discovery. Later, when he went from being an unknown poet to being a public poet, that book broke the sound barrier of one million copies. Someone called it the "Song of Songs" for Spanish-language poetry. However, Neruda was no King Solomon, even though both were poets.

The Bible says that Solomon composed 3,000 proverbs and that his songs numbered 5,000, and our poet did turn out to be as prolific as the Wise King, but whereas Solomon wrote about trees and spoke of the cedar of Lebanon and the hyssop that springs from the wall, and whereas he did mention animals, birds, reptiles, and fish, our poet devoted entire books to birds, to the house on the sand, to food, to the barren terrain, to sky stones, to the flaming sword, and a new version of the couple who survive the deluge. While Neruda tried to be architect and poet all at the same time, that sensible and sensual king of the Bible built the temple and then sang of woman. Yet, his woman is more expressive than Albertina, or at least Solomon gives her verses that are born of a woman in love: "My spikenard sendeth forth the smell thereof. A bundle of myrrh is my well-beloved unto me; he shall lie all night betwixt my breasts. My beloved is unto me as a cluster of camphire in the vineyards of Engedi. He brought me to the banqueting house, and his banner over me was love. The time of the singing of birds is come, and the voice of the turtle is heard in our land." While Rubén Darío says somewhere that there is no longer a Shulamite to sing praises to, as King Solomon did with "Thy navel is like a round goblet, which wanteth not liquor; thy belly is like an heap of wheat set about with lilies," Neruda never stopped singing her praises, and though none was called Shulamite, in effect all women were she. This poet was never visited by the Queen of Sheba, but in a purely imaginary expression he says he has married the daughter of the king of Mandalay. Though, unlike his colleague in the *Song of Songs*, he never married the Pharaoh's daughter, he did treat all his women like queens, with no importance given to the fact that they all were common folk and the vast majority were daughters of poor people. His colleague of the *Song of Songs* garnered an amorous reputation and much experience, although the Bible is somewhat contradictory in this regard, saying on the one hand that he has 60 queens, 80 concubines, and countless maidens, although only one is the perfect dove Shulamite, and affirming elsewhere that he had 700 wives and 300 concubines. That word "concubine" used to make Neruda break out in uproarious laughter. A lady friend of his who became the common-law wife of one of the funniest men in Neruda's group, Vicente Naranjo, a merchant from Valparaíso, used to tell the poet that in legal terms she was called a "concubine," and the two of them would explode in laughter, because such a ridiculous outmoded word seemed so comical to them, as if all of antiquity and the prejudices of millennia were telling them that the world had not changed.

When Neruda wrote his own "Song of Songs" he was dreadfully poor, and when Solomon wrote his, he was fabulously rich, with an annual income of 666 gold talents. Neruda had a golden talent, but not one penny. One reigned over all the kingdoms from the Euphrates to the land of the Philistines and the Egyptian border, and the other reigned over only his dreams.

57. Two-man Bullfight

Neruda was now eating every day, but his economic situation was precarious and his future cloudy.

In the summer, he goes back to the South, to Puerto Saavedra. He is writing *Residence on Earth II*. He views the sea of his childhood with more mature eyes, and his poem is closely related to the "Song of Despair," speaking of his interior processes. His marriage is becoming dismal and is falling apart. This return to the South brings him nostalgic reminiscences of the state of his heart ten years earlier, and now it seems to be full of dust. If "she" should breathe life into it, "it would beat with a dark sound, like the sleepy noise of train wheels. . . . If you should breathe on my heart, close to the sea . . ." In the end, that love is a ghost.

There, he also writes "El sur del océano" (Southern Sea), a poem full of the most concentrated solitude:

> It's a lonely place; I've spoken before
> of this place that's so very lonely,
> where the earth is full of ocean,
> and there's no one but the tracks of a horse,
> there's no one but the wind, there's no one
> but the rain falling on the waters of the sea,
> no one but the rain spreading over the sea.

When he returns to Santiago, after a rather sad summer, he has one consolation—the first publication of *The Ardent Slingsman,* a book that he deliberately kept out of print for ten years. This delay is his prescription for a time lapse that will excuse its weaknesses in terms of influence and emotional excess, to which he confesses in the prologue. He also experiences an even greater joy—*Residence on Earth* is published for the first time. After having fought so bitterly for its publication from his desolate consular posts, until it became almost an obsession, as seen in his letters to Eandi, the book has not come out in Spain, as both he and Rafael Alberti had hoped it would, nor in Argentina. It is brought out in Santiago by his faithful and up to now exclusive publisher, Carlos Nascimento. So, for Neruda, April is not the cruel month of Eliot's *Wasteland,* but rather the jubilant month of a golden autumn, when the presses bring forth a book born of solitary periods in Chile and in the British and Dutch East Indies of the Far East. The edition is almost deluxe, considering the poor quality of Chile's publishing industry at that time.

He soon rejoins the Ministry of Foreign Affairs, and on 25 August 1933 informs his father that he has been named to a post in the Buenos Aires consulate. For the first time he calls his father "my dear Papa," which would lead one to think that his sire is changing his mind, perhaps beginning to suspect that such a useless son who has turned out to be a poet can earn his own living and take care of himself. Neruda has to leave again, and there's no time to say good-bye. The disorganized government approved his appointment but gave him no travel money. Here Amalia Alviso, the desirable widow, cedes not to his amorous entreaties but to economic ones and loans him a thousand pesos to pay for the trip.

Then the largest Spanish-speaking city in the world, Buenos Aires is a magnet for an ambitious poet, and he establishes contact with Argentine literary life. During the few months he was in Buenos Aires he had to put up with a bureaucratic job that clashed with his spirit, but all was soothed by his good relationship with the consul general, Sócrates Aguirre, who had a dark-complexioned, bright-eyed little daughter who becomes a good friend of Uncle Pablo, who used to dress up in costumes for her parties. Later, Margarita Aguirre will be one of his most authoritative biographers. The boredom of his functionary position is acidly reflected in the poetry he writes in that great city, "It so happens I'm tired of being a man . . ." He's like a wild creature lost among tailor shops, smells of beauty shops, merchandise, eyeglasses, elevators. He tires even of himself, his hair, his shadow. And he would like to create a scandal, "to go through the streets with a green knife." He is tired of being a subterranean root in darkness; he wants no more misfortunes; he's bored with his prisoner-face. "Walking Around" delineates his state of mind, and "Inexpedient" leads to a cursing of his life buried in "the pile of papers, in the darkness of offices," loathing the examination of certificates and decrees. He is horrified by offices, the smell of ministries, tombs, and rubber stamps.

He does a translation of *Chamber Music* by James Joyce, which is published that year, 1933, by the *Revista Internacional de Poesía* in Buenos Aires.

His relationship with his wife is one of indifference. For a while, that crazy little coquette who used to create a scandal in the Temuco Plaza, María Luisa Bombal, lives in his house, where she writes *La última niebla* (*House of Mist*) and *La amortajada* (*The Shrouded One*). That same year, Neruda falls in love with her sister, Loreto. María Luisa, whose life was filled with tragic periods, was for Neruda "an adored bee of fire," and he was always attracted to her—as a writer. Fifty years later he visited her in the United States and found her drinking in bed, victim of a great disappointment. He was saddened by that meeting.

All this happened under the sad gaze of a good wife, a woman as remote as the moon, Maruja-Maruca Agenaar. The general feminine opinion was that she was not for him, and his lady friends used to good-naturedly call her "The Policewoman."

Neruda was always looking for his long-dead natural mother in all his women. María Luisa Bombal declined the honor, "Not all of us are made to be mamas."

The high point of delight during his stay in Buenos Aires was his meeting and the beginning of his friendship with Federico García Lorca, who had recently arrived for the premiere of his play *Blood Wedding*. Neruda shared in the joy of the group around Lorca, which included Oliverio Girondo and Norah Lange, Alfonsina Storni, Jorge Luis Borges and his mother Leonor, Pablo Rojas and his wife "The Blonde," Amparo Mon and Raúl González Tuñón. Their gatherings were brazen and liberally irreverent, which counteracted Neruda's boredom with the office and tension at home.

Federico used to outshine Pablo in the gatherings, with his sparkle, his joy, his laughter, his songs and dances, and Pablo gladly faded into the background. Lorca used to interpret his friends' personalities on the piano, and Neruda's was done with slow notes. When Lorca had to return to Spain, he told his friends, "I don't want to leave. I'm going to die. I feel very strange."

Neruda's custom of celebrating his birthday with friends went with him everywhere, and in Buenos Aires, besides Lorca, Ramón Gómez de la Serna and Arturo Capdevilla also took part. That birthday night in Buenos Aires they went out for a swaggering tour of the city, with an empty taxi following them—Federico's idea. When they asked what sense that taxi made, he answered, "It's out of respect." They ended up in the Pescadito restaurant in the La Boca neighborhood.

In 1956, on 19 October in the lecture hall of the University of Chile, Neruda described Federico García Lorca as the most joyful man he had ever seen. He recalled that he had met him in the home of Rojas Paz, an Argentine prose writer who coincidentally had just died that same year when Neruda was talking of him. Neruda recalled that he had almost caused Federico's death once in Argentina. It all happened in one of those big ranch houses in the pampa, with its typical lake and a huge tower. Neruda and an exquisite young woman dressed in white climbed to the top of the tower, and Lorca acted as protective "madam." Under cover of the night and drunk with the pampa's perfume, Neruda began the amorous siege. Federico took it into his head that the event should be celebrated with shouts of "Long live poetry! Long live those who are anti-Ortega y Gasset!" In his enthusiasm, he began to call out to people and to run down the stairway. He fell and almost broke his leg. "'You're a fool,' I told him." That fool was the greatest poet in Spain and his most charming friend. The two were united by poetry, which at the same time established the bridge between Spain and Spanish America.

They believed that one of the supreme builders of that bridge had been wrongly forgotten—Rubén Darío, the poet who had written a "Song to the Glories of Chile" and also a "Song to Argentina." The PEN Club of Buenos Aires invited Lorca and Neruda to a banquet in 1933, where the organizers and other guests were puzzled when Neruda sat at one end of the table and Lorca at the other. When Neruda was given the floor, he stood up and said the word "Ladies" whereupon Lorca got to his feet at the other end of the table and continued with "and gentlemen." Imitating a pass from the bullfight called *al alimón*, in which two bullfighters hold the same cape as they elude the charging bull, Neruda announced that Federico and he were going to team up, but with the intent of issuing an invitation to a dead man, "a guest hidden in the shadows and widowed by a death greater than any other, widowed by life, which was for him in his time a brilliant mate . . . We are going to repeat his name until his power springs forth from oblivion." Lorca is sure that when his name is spoken, "Glasses will shatter and forks will leap . . . We are going to name the poet of America and of Spain." Then Lorca says "Rubén" and Neruda completes it, "Darío," continuing with a question, "Where in Buenos Aires is Rubén Darío's plaza, his park, his statue?" Federico asks, "Where do they sell Rubén Darío roses?" And he adds that Darío "sleeps in his native Nicaragua under a dreadful plaster lion . . . He conveyed the sound of the jungle with one adjective . . . and put his hand on the Corinthian column with a sad and ironic doubt about all ages." Then the Spanish poet delivers a glowing vision of what Darío contributed to his country, Spain:

> As a poet in Spanish he taught the old masters and the young in Spain, with a sense of universality and generosity that is lacking in today's poets. He taught Valle-Inclán and Juan Ramón Jiménez, and the Machado brothers, with his voice of water and nitrate plowing through our venerable language. From Rodrigo Caro to the Argensolas to Don Juan Arguijo, nobody had given to Spanish the festival of words and the collision of consonants, light and form, as Rubén Darío did. From the landscape of Veláz-quez and the bonfire of Goya, and from the melancholy of Quevedo to the refined apple-redness of Mallorcan peasants, Darío traveled over the land of Spain as if it were his own.

Neruda said of Darío in Chile that "In our country the great poet began to be seen." And in the absence of material statues, Neruda proposed making him a statue in the air, and Lorca decides that on that statue of air should be put "his blood like a branch of coral, his nerves like an X-ray . . . his vague and absent eyes like a millionaire of tears, and also his flaws . . . his dramatic inebriation, his charming bad taste, and his daring verbosity that fills his crowd of verses with human qualities."

In Neruda's *El fin del viaje* (Journey's End), published by Seix Barral in 1982, another Neruda-Lorca collaborative work is published for the first time, "Interior Dove, or the Glass Hand, an Interrogation in Several Stanzas Composed in Buenos Aires by the College Graduate Don Pablo Neruda and Illustrated by Don Federico García." The original work had been done in honor of Doña Sara Tornú de Rojas Paz, and its only copy was bound in burlap with the drawing of a dove embroidered in green thread on the front cover. It is quite a bit more than a bibliographical curiosity, where one great poet writes the verses and another no less great provides the illustrations. The poetry is not festive, and it begins with a foreboding poem, "Sólo la muerte" (Only Death), which presaged the death of the artist-poet García Lorca only two years after its composition, the same death that would surprise Neruda, the author of the poem, as he was "sailing to a port where (Death) is waiting dressed as an admiral." Or as a general. At the end of the little book, the premonition shows up in the hands of the unique illustrator, who closes with a drawing identified in Lorca's handwriting as "Truncated heads of Federico García Lorca and Pablo Neruda, creators of this book of poems."

Federico leaves for his country, and Neruda soon follows him. On 28 March 1934 he writes to his sister Laura from Buenos Aires, "I didn't want to tell you that the government has transferred me to Spain, to Barcelona, where I must go shortly. When I know the exact date, I'll let you know." In those southern regions, international telephone calls are still in the early days of discovery. "In any case, before leaving I will telephone you . . . You can hear very clearly, and I want my mama, my papa, you and Raúl [his nephew] to be there."

58. Arrival at the Main Office

In May 1934 he disembarks in Spain, where his name had arrived years before on board a book. Rafael Alberti tells about it with an angelic talent straight out of his own book *Sobre los ángeles* (About Angels). That surprising manuscript came into his hands on a rainy winter night. (Here follows the story of Neruda's book told from the third angle of the triangle, whose first angle was Neruda's desolate account in letters from the Orient to the second angle, Héctor Eandi, who received it in Buenos Aires.) Alberti found it at the Nacional Hotel on a table full of bottles, mostly empty except for some sherry which was destined for immediate consumption. The book's title—*Residence on Earth;* its author—a poet almost unknown in Spain. It had been brought to him by a secretary from the Chilean embassy, Alfredo Condon, who later wrote an article about Neruda that the poet liked. But he in his turn was only a conduit, since the manuscript had been sent by Carlos Morla Lynch, ministry advisor and a very good friend of Federico García Lorca. Alberti, on his first reading, was stunned. The poems were fascinating and quite unlike what was being written in Spain. He asked for information about the author and was told that he was the Chilean consul in Java, where he not only wrote poems heavy with solitude but also letters asking the world for help and for news, and especially for anything in Spanish. Months went by without his being able to speak it with anyone. Rafael was moved as much by the book as by the poet's rough luck in being virtually buried alive in such a remote exotic place. Excited by his discovery, Alberti for some time carried the book everywhere he went in the city, to cafés, bars, literary gatherings, where he would read some of the poems aloud. He gathered young poets of that period into a fraternity of admirers of the author who was shouting for help from that unheard-of Java: Arturo Serrano Plaja, José Herrera Petere, Luis Felipe Vivanco, and others who were just beginning their acquaintance with the muses. They went out in broad daylight like Diogenes with his lantern searching for a publisher, but to no avail. Rafael approached the poet Pedro Salinas, translator of Proust, hoping he might arrange something with the *Revista de Occidente*. He had to resort to this prestigious intermediary because, just as Lorca had done in Buenos Aires, here in Madrid Rafael Alberti had given a lecture in which he insulted the pope of that journal, the philosopher José Ortega y Gasset. The only thing they accomplished was that the *Revista* published a few of the poems, which even so was something, for it introduced a name that was destined to attract readers' attention. Rafael from time to time wrote to his distant anguished friend, receiving in reply urgent supplications to send a good Spanish dictionary to the poet who was always fearful of making errors in grammar and spelling.

In 1931, Alberti transferred his efforts on Neruda's behalf to Paris, where he contacted that young Argentine woman, Elvira de Alvear, about whom Neruda expressed lack of confidence when he wrote to Eandi, despite her promise to publish *Residence*. She must have been someone of importance, or at least someone with money, because her secretary, a young Cuban writer named Alejo Carpentier, sent a cable to Neruda informing him of a very welcome advance of 5,000 francs. As we know, the book was not published, and Neruda received only the cable and not the advance. Then and there, Alberti swore to himself that he would never again fight to get others' books published, "A promise I've never kept," he adds.

Many years later, I witnessed at first hand Neruda's own efforts to publish in Chile a book by his "brother, " his *confrère* as he called Alberti. Neruda wrote a prologue for the book, *El poeta en la calle* (Poet in the Streets), in which he poured out all his appreciation for the Spanish poet's marvelous life and work. In Chile's totally wretched publishing climate, the project met with difficulties very similar to those encountered by Alberti in his efforts of twenty years before to publish a book by Neruda, buried far away in remote islands of the Orient. Neruda then compared the two situations and concluded that even though poets may be out in the streets, they don't control publishers and they are helpless to overcome political prejudice.

After the failed attempt to publish *Residence,* Alberti didn't hear from his friend for a long while, but one day somebody runs panting up the stairs to his home in Madrid and introduces himself, "I am Pablo Neruda. I have just arrived and I came to say hello. My wife is downstairs, but don't be afraid because she's almost a giant." This happened one morning in 1933. The warning about the very large wife struck him as a rather innocent joke, but she truly was imposing, and as promised he held back any sign of surprise when he saw her. Rafael Alberti and his wife, María Teresa León, set about looking for a house for Pablo and his wife and found what was called "The House of Flowers." It was destroyed during the Spanish civil war, but I have made a pilgrimage in Madrid to the place where it used to be, only to find an ordinary apartment complex there today.

Rafael was one of Neruda's first professors of politics. The Spaniard recalls that soon after his arrival Neruda told him, "I don't know anything about politics, I'm a little bit 'anarchoid'—I want to do whatever I like." His journal, *Caballo Verde de la Poesía,* to which the best young poets of that time contributed, postulates an impure poetry, open to all subjects, but he still considered himself politically pure and aseptic.

Gerardo Diego, compiler of an anthology of Spanish poetry from the first third of the twentieth century, which introduced the so-called Generation of 1927 to audiences on the American continent, admits that he and Neruda didn't always see eye to eye, but he is nonetheless proud that he was one of the first in Spain to know his work. He claims that Neruda reached Spain and Europe by what was then the typical route, through France. In October 1926, a fragment of *Endeavor of the Infinite Man* had appeared in *Favorables Paris Poema,* a short-lived journal of only two issues. Perhaps an irony of literary history is the fact that the individual who discovered that text in France and then published it in Spain should be another poet who was always on bad terms with Neruda, so bad that Neruda chided him in verse as "Juan Tarrea." It was this Juan Larrea who chanced to find a copy of the French journal, tossed away in an editorial room, and came upon that selection from *Endeavor.* When he published it later, he sent a copy to Neruda, who responded that it was his first poem published in Europe. Strictly speaking, Larrea and his friend, the Peruvian poet César Vallejo, knew *Book of Twilights* and *Twenty Poems,* which they judged to be nice books but easily dispensed with because of their decidedly romantic flavor, which constituted a defect, according to their philosophy of poetry. However, they did take notice of *Endeavor,* which may or may not validate its author's repeated claim that it is his most overlooked book even though it marks his transition to a new aesthetic. Outside Madrid, in the Spanish provinces, there was more than just an occasional Neruda fan. In Oviedo, Fernando de la Presa, who had traveled throughout the Caribbean and South America, including Chile, opened a bookstore in 1927 and proposed to Gerardo Diego that he help introduce Neruda in Spain. Several years after that, one day when Diego was visiting the home of Carlos Morla Lynch, the latter showed him the first edition of *Residence,* that large-format edition by Nascimento, too big to fit in the bookcases. Federico García Lorca was also supposed to come that night, but he stood them up, not for the first time. Several nights later, he showed up and in that house this young poet, recognized by Manuel de Falla to be a formidable musician himself, listened in wonder as a compatriot of Neruda, Claudio Arrau, played the piano. Gerardo Diego, who saw Neruda as soon as he arrived in Spain, unexpectedly had to leave soon for the Philippines, so Neruda gave him expert advice on how to travel in those hot regions and presented him with a white linen suit that fit Diego better than it did Neruda, since he had gained forty-five pounds. As a guide to the Orient, he also gave him a nineteenth-century French travel book about the Indian and Pacific Oceans.

Neruda arrives in Barcelona on 5 May 1934 and is captivated by the metallic sound of the Catalán language and by the intelligence of so many people who speak Catalán with steel-like crispness and also Spanish with liquid fluidity. He associates with writers and poets. It's the time of the Asturian repression, the Black Biennium, which spreads through all of Spain like a stratum of lead covering up a turbulent flood of agitation. He meets people from the Catalán left—Socialists, Communists, and more than one Anarchist—all of whom are noticeable influences in that period. He also makes an effort to read Catalán poetry.

59. Two Unique Consuls

He is obliged to spend some time at his consular duties. He frequently picks up the phone, which is becoming a popular instrument in Europe, and talks with the Chilean consul in Madrid. Their conversation may deal with detailed office matters, but most of the time it veers off to the delicious exchange of news, tidbits or digressions about individuals or books, much to Neruda's great delight. This is no ordinary professional consul who is talking on the other end of the line, but rather it is Gabriela Mistral. What has brought these two great Chilean poets into stellar alignment in the consular firmament of Spain is not destiny but an invisible mentoring hand that sometimes guides certain appointments in very concrete affairs. They fulfill their bureaucratic obligations, but they allow themselves many breaks and liberties to deal with their shared spiritual business in juicy conversations by phone or face-to-face, enjoying each other's company with zestful amazement at being able to chat at will about poetry and other specialties of the house. They are very good friends, and there is no pettiness in that relationship between the great woman and the great man. For them, the Nerudian theory of the elephants is the rule; they can coexist in two consulates in one and the same country, and in one and the same room they can carry on pleasant or meaty dialogues, because in the jungle of good friendship, peace and fraternity between two poets is what reigns.

As it happens in adventure movies, the sky seemed calm until one day it was split by lightning. Thunder and sparks, intrigues and imprecations rain down on the head of Gabriela Mistral. *El Mercurio* runs a story that sets it all off, accusing her of running off at the mouth with independent opinions which are incompatible with her consular responsibilities. By nature, she is frank and sharp-tongued, and it is whispered or shouted about that her love for speaking the truth out loud has surely hurt the country she is serving in. The sentence is not appealable: she must leave Spain.

The episode serves to increase her natural mistrust. It involves an injustice, and it means a complete lack of understanding of her visceral closeness to Spain, which her *Recados* (Messages) makes clear. Her book *Materias* (Topics) begins by saying, "On the night train from Barcelona to Madrid I wake to the welcome exclamation of 'We're crossing Castile.'" Her eyes are full of the Catalán Mediterranean, with its indigo and sun colors, and she finds it hard to get used to that Castillian landscape which is sometimes ashen and sometimes "coppery like an old helmet." There she says you cannot base yourself in being condescending to people and controlling your impulses. She refused until her death to write a colorless work, which is of use "neither to God nor the Devil." This trait also explains the incident when she had to leave under a shadow, abandoning Madrid and Spain. She, who goes so happily to Avila in loving pursuit of Santa Teresa and talks in secret with her because they are temperamentally and poetically alike. She is captivated by Segovia and the towns of Spain. She loved Barcelona, but it frightened her a little. "Latin American travelers," she affirms, "are very comfortable in Barcelona, which is a real city in the terrible sense that New York has given to that word. But I walk on the Ramblas with nostalgia for old cities, and as soon as the sea leaps out at me at the end of the avenues, I say 'Let's go to Mallorca today.' My Barcelona friends tell me, 'A quick look at Palma and then off to relax in Valdemosa.' Fill your eyes with plenty of blue from the Mediterranean, because Castile is going to set them on fire."

Castile fascinates her more because of its dry inhabitants than for its dry earth. Here there is none of Seville's sensuality. She is reminded of the bald-pated north of Chile, and she associates it with the pastureland she missed in "unfortunate Antofagasta." Nevertheless, she points out, it would be simplistic to blame Castile's desolation only on the Castillian personality. "The existence of latifundia anywhere causes destruction of forest land," she explains, "and this Spanish phenomenon of huge land estates is the forefather of our own latifundia. The fact that in America it didn't kill the earth's beauty as it did here is because over there the earth restores itself and is rich in spite of its disastrous landlords." She confesses with almost a blush that her feeling for Spain is closer to tenderness than to passion. A woman who talks like that truly loved what she calls "that Spain of ours," but by evil means she was forced to leave it practically overnight.

60. Misfortunes

She goes to serve in the consulate in Lisbon, and Neruda goes to the Madrid office on 3 February 1935. There, in a happy reunion, he is received by a good-hearted Chilean writer, Luis Enrique Délano, who had been very close to Gabriela Mistral. Pablo was happy with his friends, but he was unlucky in his marriage, and doubtless Maruca was even more unlucky. Yet, disagreements are not always indicative of a total break in conjugal relations, and shortly before this a potentially happy event had occurred, one that he has long hoped for. It will put the lie to his poem "Farewell":

> From deep within you, on his knees,
> a child, sad like me, is watching us.
> For the sake of the life that burns in those veins,
> our lives would have to be intertwined.
> . . . .
> I don't want him, Beloved.
> So that nothing entwines us,
> so that nothing will tie us.
> . . . .

. . . From your heart a child bids me farewell.
And I say farewell to him.

Now this situation is reversed, and although his wife is possibly no longer the "Beloved," nevertheless he does want a child. A daughter is born on 18 August 1934, and he proudly and euphorically announces the event to the whole world with printed cards that he sends off to three continents. She will be named Malva Marina, because it combines the precious mallow flower with the oceanic sign of her father.

His friends are excited by the longed-for event. Malva Marina Trinidad has been born! The most joyous was García Lorca, joyous, yet heartbroken and silent. So silent that he goes home and writes a poem which will only be known fifty years later, "Verses on the Birth of Malva Marina Neruda." Black and white poetry, sorrowful because death was a spy at her birth and rocked her cradle. She was born prematurely and almost died at birth. Federico offers an incantation so that she may live, white-magic verses, an invocation for the salvation of the newborn's body and soul:

Malva Marina, if I could only see you
on the ancient waves like a dolphin of love,
while the waltz of your America distills
venom from the mortal dove's blood!

If I could only shatter the dark feet
of the night that howls through the stones,
and could halt the immense awful wind
that takes away dahlias and leaves shadows behind.

The poet died sooner than the child did, perhaps believing that the entreaties he offered as a benign magician had been heard. For him she was Chilean by her father, Javanese by her mother, and Spanish by her birth:

The White Elephant is wondering
if he'll give you a sword or a rose;
Java—steel flames and green hand,
Chile's ocean—waltzes and crowns.

Little child from Madrid, Malva Marina,
I'll not give you flowers or shells;

thinking of you, I place on your lips
a branch of grace and love, heaven's breath.

He couldn't save himself, and he couldn't save her. Those verses in manuscript, which were half a century in coming to light, were never known by Neruda. Probably nobody knew of their existence until Lorca's family sorted out his unpublished papers and uncovered that unknown poetry. On 12 July 1984, *ABC* in Madrid commemorated the eightieth anniversary of Neruda's birth by publishing the poem for the first time. Luis Enrique Délano, in Mexico during the final days of his long, second exile (the first one had been shared with Neruda), commented on the discovery by recalling Malva Marina, "I remember her as a pale child with dark hair and dark eyes, like Neruda's. Weren't there any of her mother's Nordic features in her? Thinking back, maybe the shape of her face was Maruca's. I remember her in her cradle and in the little carriage in which her mother used to take her to the park, the Parque del Oeste, which was the one closest to the House of Flowers where the Nerudas lived, a kind of writer's complex like Mexico City's Condesa where the poet would also live. The child didn't talk, she just watched with her big, sweet, almost frightened eyes. And she sang! Her mother, who was very musical, had taught her to sing, and the little girl followed the melody of songs with a very good ear."

As said, there were problems from the very moment of birth. A few days later, they notice with alarm that something isn't normal in the baby—strange symptoms. Later he writes to Don José del Carmen Reyes a letter in which his spirit wavers between sadness and hope, "I have not rushed to tell you the news because it hasn't gone too well. The thing is that the child was born early and she's had a hard time of it to live . . . The baby is very, very small, weighing only five pounds at birth, but she is very pretty, like a little doll, with blue eyes like her grandfather, Maruca's nose, fortunately, and my mouth . . . Of course, the struggle isn't over yet, but I think the biggest battle has been won and that from now on she'll gain weight and will soon be chubby."

He tries to feel hope, but the doctors don't confirm it. The diagnosis cannot fail to be reflected in his poetry, which frequently takes on the character of a recurring autobiography where he will indirectly reveal the sad situation that is troubling him. It's true that the references are cryptic and related to his environment, perhaps requiring at times a code to translate them, but in some moments the truth comes out in all its tragic clarity. Some poems from the second book of *Residence* contain the poetic crystallization of the drama that is shaking his home: "Melancholy in the Family," "Maternity," "Illnesses in My Home," "Ode With a Lament."

There's a pervasive smell of camphor, a broken glass, an empty dining room. He comes in from outside covered with mud and death. But the most awful thing is the empty dining room, and the man who sits down to write is sad in this house of misfortunes and sobs. He asks the dark mother to strike him with ten knives in the heart, and he begs for a time of clarity, a springtime without ashes.

He was anxious to be a father, and he accepted paternity like a sought-after inexpressible feeling. Now he is covered by a cloud and "from whom do you beg mercy for a grain of wheat?" he asks in "Illnesses in My Home," where he calls upon all that is most dear to him to come to his assistance in this crisis:

> Help me, leaves that my heart has silently adored,
> harsh winds, southern winters, women's
> tresses damp with my earthly sweat,
> southern moon in a leafless sky,
> bring me one day without sorrow,
> one minute when I can see my veins.
> I'm tired out by just one drop,
> I'm injured in just one petal
> and a pinprick opens a hopeless river of blood,
> and I drown in the dew that stagnates in shadows,
> and because of a smile that won't grow, and a sweet mouth,
> and some fingers that the roses would love,
> I'm writing this poem which is just a lament,
> simply a lament.[22]

A poem of love for his daughter. He asks her pardon for her misfortunes, "I can only love you with kisses and poppies." He underlines a sign of doom painted on his forehead, "There's much of death, of funereal events / in my forsaken passions and desolate kisses." He tells the child:

> Come into my soul all dressed in white, with a branch
> of blood-stained roses and goblets of ashes,
> come with an apple and a horse,
> for inside there's only a dark room, a broken candleholder,
> some twisted chairs that wait for winter,
> and a dead dove, wearing a number.

The child suffered from hydrocephaly. She couldn't stand light and lived closed up in a dark room. She was a little baby with Down's Syndrome, fated to be an invalid and to die young.

The disaster did not strengthen a crumbling marriage, but rather shattered it forever.

After pouring out his sorrow in his poetry with a terrible nameless eloquence where all was lucidly intelligible, the poet went from lament to silence, which is not necessarily the same thing as forgetting. Neruda went on carrying that sorrow within himself as long as he lived, but it was not something to be discussed. It became a silent sorrow which the passage of time would assuage but not erase.

Perhaps his whole marriage was a mistake. He will only hint at this in his poetry, but there is one revealing fact: although this man in one sense generously immortalized in verse women both insignificant and outstanding, giving to Cinderella the queen's slipper, returning over and over again in different periods and new forms to evocation of his loves, he apparently devoted not one poem to his first wife, which seems strange. He probably wrote some, but none are known. Many years later, in the autumn years of his poetry, with obliquely self-critical disenchantment, he wonders:

Why did I marry in Batavia?
I was a knight with no castle
an unprepared voyager
someone without clothing or gold
a pure and errant idiot . . .[23]

61. "Ant" or "Neighbor"?

One night in Rome, in the gallery of the Spanish painter José Ortega, near the Piazza del Popolo, there was one of those gatherings that Rafael Alberti can turn into a magical session, and on that occasion he told me something that left me dumbfounded. "I met 'The Ant' before Pablo did," he announced, referring to Delia del Carril. "It was in Paris, in a beautiful neighborhood where Victoria Ocampo lived, the editor of the journal *Sur* and Argentine writer and literary hostess. I took along some poems, because she had asked me for them. There was a garden between the gate and the luxurious house, and I rang the bell for a while until finally someone came to let me in. It wasn't a liveried servant, nor the chauffeur, nor the gardener, nor the cook; it was a radiantly mature young-looking woman, with a dancing walk and the confidence of a born world conquerer. And a conquerer of men, I thought to myself. I asked for Victoria Ocampo. 'She's not here,' she told me. Maybe she saw a surprised look on my face, for she consoled me with a gracious smile and a very short statement, 'But I am.' She invited me in. I told myself that this woman should live in Spain, and I suggested so to her. She answered, 'Right now I don't have any money.' I insisted, 'That's exactly why. Spain is cheaper than France.' I tried to enthuse her, 'You'll have very good friends there.' A short time after that, she was knocking on my door in Madrid and taking part in the work of Republican intellectuals for a time."

When Gabriela Mistral was caught in the web of intrigues that forced her to leave her post as consul in Madrid and Neruda replaced her, he was received wholeheartedly by the circle of poets and artists in which Delia del Carril was active. They met each other in the home of Carlos Morla Lynch and it was love at first sight.

At the time, this irresistible woman is fifty years old and has lived a unique life. I once heard her recount how, when she was a child in the last decade of the nineteenth century, during the Argentine winters her whole family would take the steamship, as they called it then, and travel to Europe: the father, a wealthy cattleman; the mother, a member of the Buenos Aires cultural circle; and their thirteen children. Scenes straight out of Fellini's *E la nave va*. The Carril family traveled with their own cow in the ship's hold, so the children would be sure to have fresh milk on the crossing. They used to go to an enormous hotel in Paris, which that bunch of youngsters turned into pandemonium until the parents enrolled them in an exclusive school. Delia would never forget the French nuns, but she dreamed of getting back to their ranch on the pampa. As a child, her passion was horses, trotting and galloping kings of the pampa, free, speedy, friendly, noble, and beautiful. She would dedicate herself to painting them, for she is also an artist with solid technical training from Fernand Léger. Years later, she would become the top equestrian painter in contemporary Latin American art, and her only subjects are the horses of her childhood, which she even turned into humans.

Before the First World War, the girl married a sophisticated Argentine playboy, and they became a pair of beautiful creatures who cultivated extravagance. Although honeymoons are usually designed for making love, theirs had to be marked by an amazing originality that would make it unique and would provide a topic for Buenos Aires gossip, so they chose Alaska as their destination, during gold-fever times.

The young husband was an artist at mental torture, a follower of Machiavelli and the Marquis de Sade, who used his diabolical knowledge to destroy his wife's will power and to exercise his evil talent for setting friends at each others' throats. The couple bought a castle in the Balearic Isles, and between Paris and the island they consumed themselves in a life full of parties and scandals, interspersed with constant fights. She felt deathly ill with the nineteenth century's "sickness of the spirit," but she wasn't strong enough to break the bond. She was a wreck when, one day, Ricardo Güiraldes, her sister Adelina's husband, arrived in Paris and saw the whole picture. Her brother-in-law took her by the arm and gave her an order, "You are going back to Argentina with me." Once back in her own country, among her family, she gradually recovered. Inactivity was her nemesis. She used to sing like an angel and began to study with Ninon Valin and Madame Batori. Her first concert drew a packed house, but when she appeared on the stage, she lost her voice—one more catastrophe and trauma. In hundreds of gatherings here and there and at parties at home, when she was living with Pablo, everybody used to sing—those who could along with those who couldn't—but Delia never joined in on those out-of-tune choruses.

When she returned to Paris it was to continue her study of painting, to reestablish her contacts with the familiar world of the aesthetic revolution—Picasso, Juan Gris, Aragon and the surrealists. That was where she had that conversation with Alberti when he proposed that she go to Spain to live the life of the Republic. This aristocrat by birth had joined the Communist Party and from then on she was always a militant, politically aware of everything, endowed with vision and shrewdness. These facts have a special significance, for she will soon become teacher and mentor to a Neruda who is enormously sensitive to social problems but in those days was somewhat naïve. To Rafael Alberti's political teachings will now be added those of Delia del Carril. Thus, the poet's civic definition will come about through friendship and love.

Delia used to do translations for the Party press and also studied in Madrid's Academy of San Fernando. The trauma of that first concert failure, which would forever prevent her from singing alone in public, seemed to be somewhat soothed in Spain in that bustling inspired atmosphere that soon led her to the Workers' Choir. (Neruda had no ear for music, but he was captivated by singers, whether they sang or not. His lifelong friend was Blanca Hauser, from Temuco, who sang Wagner's "Dream of Elsa" like nobody else in Chile; then came Delia "The Ant," a silenced singer;

and later, Matilde, who had earned her livelihood from singing until she met him.)

Delia was everywhere doing good works. She was so active that they nicknamed her "The Ant," a name she felt flattered by. "I was like the ants," she would recall, "because I carried a burden that weighed more than I did." Later, Neruda gave her another nickname, both funny and appropriate—"The Neighbor." By character and sensibility, she was in her element dealing with anything related to sociability, human contact, art, politics, diplomacy; but she was unfit for the minuscule demanding tasks of daily life. She reigned outside the kitchen, which was a world she neither understood nor was interested in. She, like Pablo, had inherited from her father a fondness for a dinner table crowded with guests. She, too, would invite half the world, but she couldn't conceive of worrying about the meal. Many times Neruda had to see to the empty pots and pans, sending friends to buy food at the last minute, and devising quick maneuvers to meet the emergency while taking care of the guests. He saw in her "The Neighbor," who spends all day next door in delicious and sometimes deep conversation, without taking into account the trifling little problems. Carried away by her revolutionary ardor, by her political and intellectual passion, her realm was that of great problems and the salvation of the world. Maybe that's what fascinated him about her, that nobility of spirit and the vigor of her intelligence, that interior strength and fervor for higher values. She was a different kind of woman from all he had known. Unmistakably attractive, she had a radiance like a fine strong light and an appeal that turned him head over heels.

The sad wary eyes of Maruca observed the romance. Delia knew how to sting, and she repaid the vigilance with sharp cruel nicknames. Her love for Pablo immediately took control of her, and she saw in him the poet she could push on to greater heights. She gave in to her feelings without any consideration of the fact that she was twenty years older than he. She might have served in a given moment as the mother he lost as an infant, thinking maybe she could refine this thirty-year-old man who had learned bad habits in taverns in a marginal corner of the globe where he was brought up, then had suffered onslaughts of solitude in far-off islands of Southeast Asia, and had a habit of saying bad words. He could well stand for her to sand down that rough wood and give it a little polish, somehow clean up his speech and behavior, and make him more worldly; but especially he needed her to make him truly conscious of his responsibility, not to poetry, for he had apparently always felt that obligation, but to human beings and people. Nonetheless, this pedagogical plan was secondary to the hurricane force of her love for the poet, a force she gave in to without hesitation and without false scruples. She immediately went to live in Neruda's home, and even though Pablo might seem shocked, she entered his bed and created impossible situations in front of a trembling and distrustful wife who saw her already lost domain so shamelessly invaded.

So obviously did Delia take the offensive that the marriage came to an end, and Pablo and Delia began to live together openly. They were married in Mexico in 1943 in a ceremony not recognized by Chilean law.

At heart, she felt herself to be "The Protector." Many years after they had separated, she repeated for the hundredth time that Pablo was a child. "His health greatly improved," she would say, "because I took care of him. He was born to a mother who died of tuberculosis only months after his birth. The baby had developed in a sick body." She had to take care of that child of thirty years, who used to play games and liked the circus and disguises and loved his friends who pretended to be aerialists risking their lives by walking an imaginary line on the floor. Their gatherings were full of jokes. In a Madrid café, he dressed up like a waiter with a mustache and little beard and white apron, and burst into a high-class party laden down with dishes that tottered precariously. Delia was quaking but at the same time dying with laughter. She didn't take part in these hijinks; she could applaud their daring, but she was also there to put a limit on the foolishness.

In that union, Delia considered herself to be the one who was both serious and happy at the same time. Pablo, on the other hand, could suddenly become disagreeable and icy, and she would have to melt him down and turn him again into a pleasant man. When she is ninety-five years old, she is asked what it was in him that had attracted her attention. "He never attracted my attention—I felt compassion for him. Poor Pablo had such a restricted life." Perhaps for her he never stopped being a child, "a little boy just out of Temuco."

He was the little boy who would come home and begin to write like a dutiful schoolboy, and she was his teacher. Then he would show her his homework, for he used to say that Delia was his harshest critic. And, in fact, she did give him critical comments, but on one occasion she suggested a dishonorable deal, that she rewrite a line of poetry. He asked her if she was crazy—how could she change what he wrote!

Neruda once saw a toy sailboat in a Madrid shopwindow and, like a small boy asking his mama for a specific gift, he insisted she buy it for him. She went to the toy store accompanied by León Felipe, who went wild when he found out what the purpose of the trip was, wild like any good

Spanish Quijote and serious poet, hooting "Those are for little kids!" Delia used to call Neruda the *arriveé mental,* which he pretended not to understand, and then she would translate it to Spanish—"mentally retarded. . . ." When Louis Aragon and Elsa Triolet heard the expression, they chided her for it, but afterwards when they were kidding around, they began to use it, too. For "The Ant," a proof of the ingenuousness and childish innocence that never left him was his weakness for certain objects, his passion for snails, butterflies, masks, old hand-organs, enormous shoes, Hindu dancers, papier-mâché horses. Nonetheless, in the matter of knowing human beings and judging situations, I never knew a man who was less naïve than the poet.

From the distance provided by separation and time, when Delia is asked whether she liked that boyish trait of Neruda's, she answers that everybody likes for a big grown man to still have that childlike quality. All men have it, she adds.

She had to educate this big boy. Her conversation was mainly political, and she opened his eyes. "Delia is the light from the window that opens onto truth." But more than Delia's teaching, it was the atmosphere and the events in Spain in those days that gave the poet daily lessons in politics, for he was passionately interested in all that surrounded him.

Sometimes, in front of Delia and with an air of mystery, Neruda would come up to us and ask a kind of riddle: "Where was 'The Ant' born?" The standard answer was, "In Argentina," but no, "She wasn't born in Argentina." Then the group of friends, with feigned curiosity, would follow the game's routine and ask, "Then where?" He would answer, "Ask her," so "Where were you born, Ant?" "In Brazil." "But in which city?" "In a city in the south." "What's it called?" "I don't know." "How can you not know?" "I don't remember." "How can you forget such a thing?" The clownish questioning went on and on, to be ended by Pablo's saying, "The Ant won't say it because she was born in Pelotas." Delia would look very severe when he pronounced this metaphor for "stark naked" and shake her finger at him, speaking to him with the formal form of address like a mama, "Pablo, if you could see your face when you say bad words, you would never say them again."

62. Dogs and Poets

Neruda and Alberti were joined together by dog stories, which the latter recalls. One foggy night in Madrid when you couldn't see anything,

Pablo found an injured dog in the street and took it home. But he didn't have a balcony, and Alberti did, so he telephoned his *confrère*. "Bring it to me," Alberti answered. The dog was like a silver crysanthemum. "Leave it here with me," he said. "What shall we call it?" "Let's call it Fog."

According to Alberti, Fog was with him throughout the civil war and behaved like a perfect soldier. He put up with the bombings, and one time a piece of glass fell on him and drew blood. When Franco's army was about to enter Madrid, the dog, along with the family and many other people, were evacuated to the Levant coast. When the front at Castellón de la Plana was surrounded, the dog couldn't get back to Rafael's mother-in-law, and he firmly believes that it was taken prisoner and shot.

The two poets shared a real passion for dogs. Ten years later, in Neruda's home in Santiago, he would talk to Alberti about "Calbuco," the big dog he had brought back from the volcanic shores of Lake Esmeralda; about "Chuflai," who had the very distinct characteristic, according to Neruda, of biting every Englishman he found in his path. Once again he had a dog named "Kuthaka," in honor of that four-legged companion who had saved him from being run over by the train in Ceylon. The tender recollection of their dogs also occupied them one day in 1936, 7 November, when the two poets went to the Intellectuals' Alliance to get *El Mono Azul* to publish Neruda's "Song to the Mothers of Dead Soldiers," the most solemn of the poems produced by the Spanish civil war. Later, as they recalled that day, they again took off their hats to all their "dogs of war and peace from those wonderful and terrible years."

63. A Warm Welcome

Neruda fits into Spain like a fish in water. He is bosom friends with the new poets, from Lorca and Alberti to the youngest, the shepherd Miguel Hernández.

But neither life nor literary movements flow in just one direction. Literary Spain, like political Spain during the turbulent 1930s had its generation of patricidal poets, those inclined to murder their fathers, although the young poets, along with hostilities against some of their elders, also recognize others as worthy precursors. Some great older writers are still active in that period: Miguel de Unamuno, Antonio Machado, Juan Ramón Jiménez. Soon the milestones of the newest poetry are inscribed with the names of Jorge Guillén, Gerardo Diego, Pedro Salinas, Federico García Lorca, Rafael Alberti, Vicente Aleixandre. They are each distinct, with some affinities in taste and treatment, and with some polemical differences among a few.

Neruda lands in the motherland of Spanish at a critical and controversial moment. The political agenda was changing, while in many poetic spheres they still stuck to the old schedule and in others were moving the clock ahead.

He sees clear signs of literary renewal and of poetry's flourishing. From a Paris which was both very near and very far away, new inspirations are projected onto Spanish letters, including surrealist ruptures. Yet, the majority are still cultivating poetry as if it were a garden, respecting the stanza, observing rhyme, aspiring to precision.

The letter of introduction that Neruda carries with him on his arrival in Spain is a *Residence* which is like a dark tide expressed frequently as an ambivalent and elusive enigma.

He knows that the Spanish milieu will teach him something, and when the defeat of the Republic closes that episode of his life, he gives a lecture on 24 March 1939 in Montevideo's Mitre Theater, where he recognizes what he owes to Spain and what Latin Americans can learn from her literature: "I understood then that what was needed in our American romanticism and in our flowing volcanic construction was that essential alliance that I saw coming about in Spain before this terrible war, that joining together of mystery and exactitude, classicism and passion, past with hope."

Neruda's access to the Spanish audience was provided by the most generous and qualified presenter and the most popular of poets. Federico García Lorca introduces him at a lecture-recital in the University of Madrid on 6 December 1934 with words which applied not only to Neruda, but which also constitute the perfect future vision of the best of Latin American poetry and prophetically herald the most penetrating aspect of the Latin American novel, which will gain the readership of Spain and Europe with the brilliant authors of the 1950s:

> And I urge you to get ready to listen to an authentic representative of poets whose ears are attuned to a world that is not ours and one that few people see. A poet closer to death than to philosophy, closer to pain than to intellect, closer to blood than to ink. A poet full of mysterious voices that fortunately he himself doesn't know how to decipher; a real man who already knows that the reed and the swallow are more eternal than the face of statues. . . . But not all these poets have the sound of America. Many seem peninsular and others have a voice accented by strange, especially

French, gusts. But not the great ones. In the great ones, the broad light of America crackles: romantic, cruel, disproportionate, mysterious. Blocks about to sink, poems sustained above the abyss by a spider's thread, a smile with a subtle hint of jaguar, a great hairy hand that delicately plays with a lace hanky. These poems have the sound of the great Spanish language spoken by Latin Americans, so linked to the sources of our classical writers, poetry which is not ashamed to break molds, which doesn't fear ridicule, and which suddenly begins to weep in the middle of the street.[24]

Neruda had spent a few days in Madrid in 1927 on his way to the Orient, but nobody seemed to notice his presence then. Seven years later, he is received in triumph. He himself recounts that *Residence* was acclaimed in extraordinary fashion. In Spain he regained confidence in himself. He became convinced that his work was a living organism, created by a man who had worked hard, pushing himself and making interior demands on himself, just as the coal miners in Chile do, thousands and thousands of feet below sea level, to emerge at the surface with a product in hand. In his case, the product was his poetry, as much a part of him as his tears.

He points out that a generation of poets is emerging that he considers to be as brilliant as the generation of the Golden Age. He emphasizes that he arrived in a uniquely propitious moment, as an eager American who saw the birth of the Republic in a nation that for three centuries had held a great part of his own continent as a colony. When he got off the train, there was only one person waiting in the station, Federico García Lorca with a bunch of flowers in his hand. That was more than enough.

He compares the reception that he was given by the young poets of Spain with the difficulties he had had to suffer in Chile and with his lethargic isolation in Rangoon, Colombo, and Java. And without embarrassment, he confesses that he felt happiness in Spain, where the Spanish poets treated him unselfishly and even decided that he should be the editor of the journal *El Caballo Verde de la Poesía* when it was published by Manolo Altolaguirre.

Their welcome to him was printed in the Cantos Materiales edition of *Residence on Earth* as a dedication in praise of Pablo Neruda. This text, which is replete with tributes signed by individuals who are inscribed in the historic annals of Hispanic poetry, constitutes an exceptional example of unselfish generosity in the world of literature. "Chile has sent to Spain the great poet Pablo Neruda, whose obvious creative force and total control of his poetic destiny are producing extremely personal works that bring honor to the Spanish language. In publishing these new poems, which are the latest example of his magnificent creation, we who are poets and admirers of this outstanding young American writer are simply emphasizing his extraordinary personality and his unquestionable literary superiority. By here repeating a cordial welcome to him, this group of Spanish poets is pleased to once more declare publicly our admiration for a work which indisputably constitutes one of the most authentic realities of Spanish poetry.—Rafael Alberti, Vicente Aleixandre, Manuel Altolaguirre, Luis Cernuda, Gerardo Diego, León Felipe, Federico García Lorca, Jorge Guillén, Pedro Salinas, Miguel Hernández, José A. Muñoz Rojas, Leopoldo and Juan Pancro, Luis Rosales, Arturo Serrano Plaja, Luis Felipe Vivanco."

64. Affinities

Many agree that Neruda's arrival in Spain is comparable to Rubén Darío's of forty years earlier. Did he influence Spanish poetry? Yes, certainly; not in the sense of making it Nerudian, but by showing it new directions. Everybody was his friend, but almost nobody was a disciple. In the case of one novice, the thirty-year old poet treats him like a mature colleague. His name is Miguel Hernández, and Neruda is moved by this innocent youth with a face "like a freshly dug potato," who approached him with "an air of Fray Luis, of orange blossoms, of manure burning in the hills," and had "a nightingale in his mouth."

Miguel Hernández came from Orihuela and the circle around Ramón Sijé, editor of the neo-Catholic journal *El Gallo Crisis*. Neruda gives him his frank opinion, "Dear Miguel, I am sorry to tell you that I don't like *El Gallo Crisis*. It smells too much of church and is smothered in incense. . . . Soon we'll do a journal here, dear shepherd, and great things."

Miguel changes, breaking with Sijé and *El Gallo Crisis*. In a letter to his Chilean friend, he shows his friendship, his affection, and his concern for Neruda's family problems. He confides in Juan Guerrero, to whom he sends a copy of "that homage we Spanish poets have paid to the great Chilean poet," saying that "Pablo has a little ten-month-old daughter who is sick, and I will be grateful if you will tell me whether there are some good doctors who specialize in childhood illnesses." He also wants to take Neruda to see his homeland, "our 'palestine' towns, Cabo de Palos [in Murcia] . . . I want to know if you could live on the island of Tabarca or on one of the islands in the Mar Menor [inland salt lake in Murcia]." He anticipates that the Chilean would prefer a broader sea, which would give him the feeling of that ocean at Puerto Saavedra.

Nobody was more dazzled by Neruda's latest book than the young poet from the fields. He says so straight out in an article in *El Sol* on 2 January 1936, "I must speak of the enthusiasm that has held me in its grip since I read *Residence on Earth*. It makes me want to throw handfuls of sand in my eyes, smash my fingers in doors, climb the highest and most difficult pine tree. That would be the best way to express the tumultuous admiration that I feel for such a gigantic poet. It's dangerous for me to write about this book, and I think I won't express almost anything of how much I feel. I write, but I am fearful." [25]

It is said that Neruda and Aleixandre influenced Miguel Hernández's break with classical forms which allowed his potential to come forth unfettered. If that is so, it is fortuitous, because the Miguel Hernández who gives the green light to all that was locked up inside becomes a great poet of Spain and of the Spanish language. From *Residence on Earth* he can see quite clearly that meter in and of itself is not poetry. He rebels against the so-called *arte menor* and proposes to write an impure poetry, in the Nerudian sense of a poetry that flows like a torrent and sweeps up everything in its path that can be converted into a poetic element. Overwhelmed by his admiration, he composes an "Ode Mixed With Wine and Blood for Pablo Neruda."

Politics entered into impure poetry on its own right, just like sadness, moonlight, and "I love you." Neruda's formula for defining the dangers of cold marble ran thusly, "He who flees from bad taste falls into ice." More than ink, blood. "In the house of poetry, nothing is permanent except that which has been written in blood to be heard by blood."

In those days, another resident of Madrid was the impassioned Argentine poet Raúl González Tuñón, a self-confessed and convicted Communist, who plays on all of poetry's piano keys and is not afraid of the big bad wolf of politics. They get together in Neruda's home or in the Cervecería de Correos bar, where they talk until dawn about the role of poetry in times of crisis.

In his prologue to *Viento del pueblo* (Wind of the People), dedicated to Vicente Aleixandre, Miguel Hernández tells the latter, "You and Pablo Neruda have given me indelible examples of poetry." He will dedicate *El hombre acecha* (Man Lies in Wait) to Neruda.

For Neruda, Miguel never stopped being a poet of the earth, and it is through the earth that he comes to political statement:

In all his poetry
there is porous earth,
seeds of grain, sand,
mud and wind,
there's the shape
of a Levantine vase,

. . . .

it's a red shaft of wheat,
a guiding star,
sickle and hammer written with diamonds
on the darkness of Spain.

In terms of his own indebtedness, Neruda publicly recognized Alberti's role in his ideological evolution, "The valiant attitude of Rafael Alberti, already a popular revolutionary poet, had a profound influence on my political ideas."[26]

Now he himself is exercising a visible tutelage over young Hernández, who begins to view life and the world in a different way, obvious in his poetry, his theater, and his articles. But all his writing during the war and after, more than anything responds not to influences but to his own genuine ability, his undeniable authenticity, his own terrible situation. Given a temperament as rich and gifted as his, the circumstances of history convert him into not only a poet of the people and a poet of the war, but into simply no less than a great Spanish poet.

When his old friend and teacher Ramón Sijé believes the battle for Miguel's soul has been lost, he points the finger at the guilty ones: "Neruda-ism (what a horror—Pablo and jungle, subhuman narcissistic ritual of the crotch, of hairy forbidden parts and forbidden horses!), Aleixandre-ism, Alberti-ism."

The Alberti-Neruda relationship was one of *confrères* where one, Rafael, was politically well advanced when Pablo reached Spain. The Lorca-Neruda relationship was one of two brothers, where the former opened the door of his home with a radiant smile and welcomed him to the Spanish solarium where the host was the prototype of the acclaimed poet. The Neruda-Hernández relationship was the fondness for a younger brother or a grown son, in whom the Chilean sensed the perfume of "clover in the rain, / crimson ash, / burning dung, evening / in the hills."

In truth, Neruda felt strangely moved by that poetry which was "a bunch of corn on a golden stalk." Miguel's imprisonment, his long incarcerations under Franco, his death, all saddened Neruda like a personal loss.

He moved heaven and earth to save him, and he didn't succeed. He always considered this to be one of his most painful failures. In the face of Miguel's death, Neruda may have been consoled by his total confidence in the unbreakable permanence of the younger man's poetry, "He spoke from the earth, / from the earth / he will speak forever."

65. Controversies

For some, Neruda arrived with the credentials of the devil's consul. He was the demon personified, dedicated to corrupting and ruining Spanish poetry. In the forefront, naturally, was the delicate knight of pure poetry, Juan Ramón Jiménez, who saw in him the face of Mephistopheles. The quarrel was serious and it struck sparks, for the clash was almost inevitable.

Two opposing philosophies of poetry confronted each other: pure poetry versus impure poetry; silence and withdrawal as a natural habitat versus turbulence and confrontation with the world, even contact with the antilyrical masses. On the one hand, order and equilibrium as the poem's subtle and crystalline condition; on the other, acceptance of expressive chaos, introduction of the flood and the marketplace. Aspiration to perfect form in one; piled-up collection of objects and sensations in a huge storehouse of castoffs in the other.

That's how Juan Ramón Jiménez viewed *Residence on Earth*. For his taste, *Twenty Poems* showed more respect for poetry, perhaps because he thought he saw his own influence in that melodious book. Among Juan Ramón's private papers, the critic Ricardo Gullón found a sheet of paper with notes, perhaps jotted down for an article he planned to write or perhaps to point out his disagreements by means of a memo:

> Criticisms Pablo Neruda / My influence on him / *20 songs of love* / My poems in *Laberinto y Estío* / My poems in *Poesía y Belleza* / His poem Tagor-JRJ / Affair I don't sign / Telephone / His note in *El Sol* / Banquet for Cernuda / Bergamín / My profile in *Españoles* / My letter correcting / Letters / America the somber by J. Revueltas / My response / Second song to Stalingrad / Communist tribute / as Chilean consul[27]

As a matter of fact, it was more serious than a question of disagreement between the two. Some time before, Jiménez's differences with the youngest Spanish poets had burst into the open—those same poets who received Neruda with open arms. Something that happened far away served as the match that lit the fire—an accusation of plagiarism against Neruda in the journal *Pro* in Chile, based on the similarity between his Poem 16 in *Twenty Poems* and Tagore's Poem 30 in *El jardinero* (The Gardener) as translated to Spanish by Zenobia Camprubí, wife of Juan Ramón Jiménez.

Furthermore, the editorial in the first issue of Neruda's journal *Caballo Verde* strikes Juan Ramón Jiménez as an acid attack. He is not mentioned, but he believes it to be patently directed at him, and he is scandalized and enraged by what he believes are horrible allusions to him in that gospel or pretended *ars poetica* that talks about the poetic appropriateness of coal sacks, used surfaces, foot and hand prints; sweat and smoke that smell of urine and lily; a suit of clothes, like a body, spotted with food and shameful behavior, sexual desire; allusions to the frenzied bookworm—all of it horrible verses directed at him, and he is appalled and dreadfully upset.

He's not the only one who is scandalized. In Barcelona, *La Hoja Literaria* publishes an irate article against the *Caballo Verde,* calling it a strange example of American fauna, this green horse, a young beast that "chases around through Spanish letters as if it were in a corral full of moist warm droppings."

Juan Ramón Jiménez won't remain silent either. He regularly publishes aphorisms in *El Sol* in a column whose title is a description of himself, "With the Immense Minority." There he loftily responds from on high, describing two kinds of poetry and poets, "Fans and poets of delirium and of precision. A green horse can gallop with precision, and a diamond can shine with madness."

But his unadorned frontal reply is published on 23 February 1936 in *El Sol*. It is a defense of the idea of pure poetry as synonymous with authentic and original poetry, sharp and rare and direct—living poetry, in short. He calls the supporters of so-called impure poetry "little pale yellow poetic chickens." It is final—there is nothing but pure poetry, and it must be responsible. Its conscious side must always answer for what its subconscious side writes.

The literary guerrilla warfare continues with exchanges of blows, like a boxing match.

In a lecture written in 1936–1937, during Juan Ramón's trips to Puerto Rico and Cuba after the outbreak of the civil war, the father of *Platero y yo* renews his attacks. But now it's a charge unloaded not only against Neruda, his main target and supreme temptation, but also against those Latin American or Spanish poets who don't follow his own direction, as he accuses them of cosmopolitan intention.

Victims of this thunderous attack are Vicente Huidobro and especially Neruda, who is accused of deforming Herrera y Reissig, Sabat Ercasty, and Parra del Riego, as well as borrowing from Spain. But the fatal epidemic has also spread to writers Jiménez calls the "Spanish Huidobristas," like Juan Larrea and Gerardo Diego, and to the retarded "subrealist" Nerudians, although in his diatribe he says that Neruda is "a traveler without a language." Moving then to an attempt to explain himself, he claims that Neruda's approximating and fluctuating language is more understandable to inexperienced America than to "our age-old Spain." The polemic will do an about face, and now it isn't Neruda who influences Spain's poets, but rather Spain that influences Neruda and Huidobro, given the fact that Spanish poets like Moreno Villa and then Alberti, Lorca and Aleixandre had already gone the same road with "more style and consciousness." Juan Ramón says all of this in a lecture suggestively titled "The Spiritual Crisis of Contemporary Spanish Poetry."

The heavy artillery is fired in all directions, and the barrage doesn't miss those he calls the "professor poets": Jorge Guillén, Pedro Salinas, Gerardo Diego, and Dámaso Alonso.

The event was not unique and the conflict was longstanding. The story of his contacts, which soon became converted into rifts and attacks on several of the younger Spanish poets, makes for entertaining reading in Rafael Alberti's delightful, still unfinished, memoirs, *The Lost Grove*. After an initial friendship that turned sour, Jiménez says, "I've learned that Alberti runs around with gypsies, bullfight *banderilleros* and other no-accounts. As you can see, he's ruined." Something worse was the judgment he reserved for Federico García Lorca as a dramatist. After the opening of *Mariana Pineda,* when the press was calling him "a young author with a great future," Juan Ramón was saying, "Lorca, poor Lorca! He's ruined." For him, *Blood Wedding,* which he certainly never saw, "was nothing more than an operetta."

This author of *Arias tristes* (Sad Arias), who conceived of poetry as something "pure, clothed in innocence, [which] I loved like a child," suddenly saw it prostituted by bums.

In a sketch of Pablo Neruda in 1939, Juan Ramón Jiménez focused his attacks a bit, calling him "A great bad poet, a great poet of disorganization . . . an unskilled translator of himself and others, a pitiful exploiter of his own and others' mines, who sometimes confuses the original with the translation . . . A prolific and careless realistic writer full of unbridled romanticism." One might say that the pure poet is capable of impure accusations, and this won't be the last double-edged blow.

66. Rectification

The clash of two kinds of poetry, two philosophies, two generations, two personalities, and in a way, the clash of two continents. This last aspect takes on more significance than might be apparent. It holds the nucleus of Juan Ramón's later revision of his judgment of Neruda's poetry, which we'll call a sensational shift in the quarrel which Neruda's enemies made great use of. Now the author of *Jardines lejanos* (Distant Gardens) changes his opinion in his "Letter to Pablo Neruda" from Coral Gables, Florida, published in *Repertorio Americano* on 17 January 1942. The document is extremely important:

> My present long stay on the American continent has made me see many things about America and Spain in a different light (as I have already said in the journal *Universidad de la Habana*), including your poetry. Now, it is obvious to me that you express with exuberant probing an authentic and universal Hispanoamerican poetry, with all of this continent's natural revolution and metamorphosis of life and death. I regret that in a great part of Hispanoamerica, poetry shows these qualities; and I don't know how to experience it, just as you say that you don't know how to experience Europe, but it exists. And chaotic accumulation precedes a necessary and definitive lucidity; the prehistoric is prior to the posthistoric; the heavy, turbulent shadows come before the more desirable clarity. You are prior, prehistoric, and turbulent, heavy and dark. In my opinion, Spain used to be the "heads" and America the "tails" of my coin. Whenever I would reach the middle of the Atlantic, that coin would split. I won't say that now America is my "heads" and Spain my "tails," but rather that they are now two "tails" or two "heads" totally different from before and different from each other. But truth, especially poetic truth—where is it, what is it, what is it like, and whose is it? In my book *Modernismo*, which I've been working on for some time, I will attempt to present my own view on this important question.

As can be seen, Juan Ramón understands Neruda to be a man from an imperfect Hispanoamerica, a faithful exponent of prehistoric turbulence. If in the past he was Neruda's opposite, now he recognizes that they are two opposites, both entitled to exist. He says so because he has under-stood and touched the Chilean as something legitimate within his own torrential environment, which made Neruda a telluric poet appropriate to the third day of Creation, at the latest, if not to the period before Genesis. Neruda was not unaware of this change in Juan Ramón's attitude, and he responded to it, trying to express himself without directly addressing the change but recognizing it in an unstated way. The letter's overt statement makes clear his sorrow at the death of Miguel Hernández:

> Mexico City, 15 October 1942
>
> Mr. Juan Ramón Jiménez
> Miami
>
> My respected friend:
>   I have not answered until now your open letter, because of the inter-ference of a thousand things in my daily work, but before going into it at length I want to tell you, in advance, of the deep emotion I felt as I read your lines, whose sincerity increases the admiration I have felt for your work throughout my life.
>   Today I write you for a painful reason. I am sending you a copy of a confidential letter from my embassy in Madrid, telling me of the death of our Miguel Hernández: one more assassination is added to many terrible others. But perhaps I've never felt a greater wound, and I think you may feel the same way.
>   I am planning a book in his memory, which I'd like to begin with some words from you, hopefully extensive. I will also write something, and I'll ask Rafael Alberti to contribute to this memoriam.
>   I hope you will rush your reply to me, and whatever you decide to send can come later.
>   I regret that my first letter brings you this sorrow, but that's how we are living every day during this period.
>   Greetings and admiration from your friend,
>
> Pablo Neruda

The confidential document which he enclosed contained the report of the death of Neruda's young poet-friend.

One day, I decided to make a midnight pilgrimage in memory of that poet from Orihuela, contemplating from the outside a grim and sordid monument, the Ocaña prison. We sat in the square where the Classical Theater had presented the figure of the Comendador of Ocaña in that long-ago Golden Age, and we saw it all as if it were an enormous setting or a huge theater from another period where each house was a viewer's box looking onto the stage where the plot was developed. We moved from Lope de Vega's message to the ultimate picture of a poet who loved his fellow-writers from that Golden Age, but who was also a man of his own time. My thoughts go back and forth from the report that Neruda sent to Jiménez with his letter, to the martyrdom of the poet who looked on him as his "big brother from Chile." Neruda remembered having first seen Miguel in Madrid before the civil war, one summer day. When the younger man told him that he liked to listen to the sound of milk in the belly of mother ewes, Neruda saw in his face the face of Spain, "crossed by light and creased like a plowed field," and he judged him to be a man who joined together tradition and revolution into one and the same thing. The official document says that after several prison transfers, the young poet was stricken by typhoid fever in the Ocaña prison, which severely weakened him. The Chilean embassy, constantly pressured by Neruda, requested and obtained his transfer to the jail-sanatorium in Alicante, where he contracted a bad case of tuberculosis. That body, which had suffered the hardships of the civil war, followed by years in prison, survived for two months before succumbing on 28 March 1942 in a prison hospital, because they had not acceded to the Chilean embassy request that he be transferred to a nonprison sanatorium.

When Neruda wrote to Juan Ramón Jiménez asking for his collaboration on the memorial book for the poet-victim, he recalled that when Miguel first appeared as a writer, Juan Ramón had greeted him as the "extraordinary boy from Orihuela." Miguel Hernández had admired the older poet, especially his *Sad Arias,* and when he was just starting out as a poet, the boy wrote to his idol, expressing his worshipful adulation: "Like so many dreamers, I plan to go to Madrid. I shall leave the sheep behind— ah, their bells at eventide—and with the little money that my parents can give me, I will take the train in a couple weeks and head for the capital. Would you, dear kind Don Juan Ramón, be able to see me at your home and read what I bring you? Could you send me a few words telling me what you think best? Please do it for this shepherd, who's a tiny bit of a poet and will be eternally grateful to you."

In a 1946 article titled "Poetic Modernism in Spain and Spanish America," Juan Ramón Jiménez calls Pablo Neruda "the most powerful poet in Spanish America after Rubén Darío." He speaks of his enormous influence and of a poetry unlike his own, but one in which he recognizes "extraordinary and clear origins."

In the lecture he gives in 1953 in the University of Puerto Rico, he includes Neruda among the most representative poets of the twentieth century, along with Rubén Darío, Unamuno, Machado and Lugones in Spanish, and Yeats, Pound, Eliot, Rilke, Ungaretti, and Montale in other languages.

In Neruda's *General Song* the Spanish poet sees an expression of the indigenous, and compares Neruda with Diego Rivera. All of that was quite alien to Juan Ramón, who was its total opposite, but he came to understand that it had a right to literary expression.

The episode shows how Neruda entered the waters of Hispanic poetry by cleaving them with his keel. He contributed to their separation, to a delineation of poetic tendencies and philosophies. In this sense, there is probably no foreign poet in the twentieth century who has opened such a wide division within Spain.

67. The Polemic over the Anthology and Tagore's Gardener

In Chile, literary polemic was burning on three sides: Neruda, Huidobro, and de Rokha. Some time earlier, someone had thrown the apple of discord into the midst of Poetry, the lovely Helen, and her suitors.

It first took the shape of agitated and frightful political ferment.

In the first months after my arrival in Santiago, events are played out which would convulse our year of 1932. I feel irresistibly drawn toward what is taking place around me. I'm not made to be an aloof spectator, and so I dream of taking part and letting myself be carried along by the great tide of that feverish, romantic moment. I believe that revolution is the poetry of the world, and that poetry is so tied to revolution that the latter can't exist without the former. But poetry will therefore have to be revolutionary and break with all that is established, reducing to ashes the old cathedrals of words and putting to the test everything that we used to intuitively call "Truth."

Gabriela Mistral had captured us from within, with her tremendous net, but her moving *Desolation* was no longer enough for us. We knew by heart all of Neruda's *Twenty Love Poems* and many poems from *Book of Twilights*. About that time, the first edition of *The Ardent Slingsman* is published, with its raging instinct and naked sexuality, all of which is okay, very fine. But . . . Is there something more? Is that all there is? The world is shifting, and it must be totally altered.

At that moment, a magician with some miraculous doves comes on stage, brought back to his native country from Europe by the economic crisis. He opens his bags and in front of our amazed eyes out come rabbits, airplanes, images . . . the literary movement called Creationism. He gives it to us as *El espejo de agua* (Water Mirror), *Horizón Carré, Tour Eiffel, Hallali, Ecuatorial.* He speaks ill of Marinetti, but in *Pasando y pasando* (On and On) he repeats the Italian's own words: "I detest routine, clichés, and rhetoric. I detest mummies and museum basements. I detest literary fossils." Vicente Huidobro had gone to Paris the year I was born, in 1916. There, his poetry experiences a complete turnabout. One must "create a poem the way nature creates a tree." He begins to write in French. Huidobro is playing, playing beautifully:

> I invented water games
> in the tree tops,
> I made you the loveliest of women,
> so lovely you turned red at evening . . .
> I made rivers to run
> that have never been,
> with a shout I made a mountain.

Huidobro hopes to create a new aesthetic. He signs our copies of *Automne regulier* and *Tout a coup.* Here is the new poetry, not in Neruda. We bury ourselves in *Altazor* and *Temblor de cielo* (Heavenly Earthquake). He talks about Maldoror and the songs written by Lautréaumont, whose influence is evident in his theatrical work, *Gilles de Raiz,* published that year, 1932. Huidobro makes himself out to be perverse, proclaiming himself a member of the satanic school and plenipotentiary ambassador of the aesthetic revolution in Paris. He wanted to form a literary school in Chile, have followers. Eduardo Anguita and I were his first converts.

It was all very complicated, but we were obliged to be new poets in order to be total revolutionaries, or so I thought. Anguita had other ideas, never abandoning a certain religious principle. In the evenings I became a bookworm in the general knowledge section of the National Library. I gulped down everything that came from France. In there, almost always, I used to find another reader who was no less voracious, but a bit mysterious, an expert in making discoveries which were both authentic and apocryphal Eduardo Molina Ventura. But I went on reading all the poetry that I could get my hands on. One day, in Rabindranath Tagore's *The Gardener,* I heard the echo of Poem 16 of Neruda's *Twenty Love Poems.* I compared the texts and they were almost the same, except that, as the Mexican poet, Efraín Huerta, said years later, "I'll take the paraphrase, a thousand times over. To plagiarize the Latins or the Italians, you had to be and have the name Garcilaso de la Vega; to paraphrase Tagore, you had to be Pablo Neruda." I discussed the matter with a poet friend. Soon, the coincidence was published as an accusation in the journal *Pro,* which was edited by Vicente Huidobro. The affair got a lot of mileage in those days. Neruda's friends explained that it wasn't plagiarism but a paraphrase. Several recall having recommended to him, before the appearance of the first edition of *Twenty Love Poems,* that he include a note pointing out that Poem 16 was a paraphrase of Tagore's *The Gardener.* Neruda himself recollects that on one of the period's typically wild nights, as he was walking through the streets of Santiago at dawn, out of the blue he asks Joaquín Cifuentes Sepúlveda, "Don't let me forget that I have to include a notation about the Tagore paraphrase in the book that's in press." Joaquín told him, "Don't be silly, Pablo. Don't do it. They'll accuse you of plagiarism, and that will be sensational publicity—the book will sell like hotcakes!"

Later, in December 1937, in an afterword to the fifth edition of *Twenty Love Poems,* published in Santiago, Neruda wrote:

> Having been wholeheartedly involved in the Spanish Civil War, I am astounded by the fact that this is the fifth time this book goes to press without my having had time to review it. Just one last word: Poem 16 is, in great part, a paraphrase of a poem by Rabindranath Tagore in *The Gardener.* That fact has always been publicly known. Those resentful individuals who tried to make hay out of this detail during my absence, have appropriately fallen into oblivion, in contrast to the concrete vitality of this youthful book. This edition is dedicated to my beloved friends, the great writer Diego Muñoz, the sparkling intelligence and nobility of Tomás Lago, and the bright splendid heart of Antonio Rocco del Campo, who witnessed the book's birth as an invincible plant or a primitive metal taking shape.

> Pablo Neruda, Santiago de Chile, December 1937.

That *Gardener* by Tagore was a favorite poem of Terusa. And he had been trying to please her by doing a paraphrase.

That poem is just one of the thousands that Neruda published. His originality is more than verified in his titanic lifework, but the *affaire* was rekindled on several occasions, and naturally the victim felt wounded.

In April 1935, we committed another sacrilege. The *Anthology of New Chilean Poetry* was published and quickly became a source of scandal. Anguita and I, as the compilers, took advantage of our position and included ourselves among the ten poets selected for inclusion. Mistral was not represented, but Neruda was, with some of his most recent poems, still unpublished, which would later appear in the second book of *Residence on Earth.* Also represented was de Rokha, justifiably so in our judgment, even when seen from today's perspective. He condemned the compilation as being colonized by Huidobro, an accusation not without some foundation.

Is this a selection by pretentious clowns? That was the question that "Alone" thundered out one Sunday in *La Nación.* He managed to immediately inform Neruda, at that time still in Spain, of his role as bombardier in razing the *Anthology* and its authors, sending a triumphant letter to him at the consulate in Madrid. No stone of the *Anthology* would be left standing, aside from a few snickers. "Alone" had vented his fury in a propitious moment; our insurrection was a sign of the times in all fields, and it would have to be controlled with an iron hand.

Jenaro Prieto, author of *El socio* and a biting journalist with the ultramontane *Ilustrado,* a politician by nature and rightist deputy (four times as a Conservative), split his sides laughing at the comic opera revolving around the *Anthology,* its compilers and Neruda. In his article, "Vanguard Poetry," he claims that "It is a proven fact that serious people are tired of vanguard poets." He takes aim at me, talking about euphuism and alludes to Quevedo's criticism of gibberish. We represented the new gibberish. Quevedo absurdities were brought up to date. In my case, he wasn't mistaken, for I was fond of involved obscurities. In regard to Neruda, he said that he had gathered together three doctor friends and asked them "Why are hospitals painted blue?" The unanimous reply was, "Because of flies." He corrected them with "You're wrong. It's because of García Lorca," and read them the poem Neruda had dedicated to Federico, "Because they paint hospitals blue on account of you. . . ." This appeared in *El Ilustrado* on 30 November 1935. Four days later, the same column carries a "Vanguardist Letter" attributed to a furious reader, Onías Pérez P. de Lota, written of course by Jenaro himself, who is fond of this kind of pastiche, which ridicules Neruda and sends a few parallel kicks in the direction of Huidobro.

68. A Heavyweight Fighter

As could be expected, de Rokha was much more caustic. Two months later, a quartet was published on successive days, beginning on 10 June, in *La Opinión*. Like a Katinsha cannon on the Russian front, de Rokha's rapid-fire assault left nobody unscathed. First, some lines for us: "These anthologies only exist so that a few unknown young whipper-snappers can come forth and make themselves prominent at the expense of others." Then, he gives it to "Alone" with, "so that a certain cave-dwelling intellectual can dance on the high wire." He also has some phrases for Helfmann, at that time the owner of the Zig-Zag Publishers who brought out the anthology "so that a certain businessman who is more or less Chilean or more or less stingy and obscure can make money off writers." His "Notes on the Anthology" proclaimed its unjust and arbitrary selections. The worst injustice was the exclusion of Winett de Rokha, in addition to "twelve more who are excluded," though with unusual sweetness he added that "I find some of them despicable and repugnant." Then he turned to Neruda, "the poet of bourgeois decadence, the poet of spiritual ferment and dung heaps." He charged into Eduardo Anguita, "sexton, altar boy, and minion of the pontiff." (Huidobro was the "Supreme Instigator.") Strangely enough, he didn't touch me, at least not by name, but he saved some special epithets for Angel Cruchaga Santa María "and his little angels and his little virgin, and that blond celestial jelly." He offered a less-trimmed slice to Rosamel del Valle, "a snail with a wigmaker's baby face; a shark who writes in several languages at once and speaks an English that sounds more French than even his German does." The main target, of course, was Huidobro, "a small high-bourgeois, a *metèque* alien who has contact and close ties with imperialist Europe and its dying beast-of-burden art filled with tricks, mischief and weakness, . . . a vanguard literary man who comes back telling us news that we already knew."

Huidobro jumped as if he'd been stung by a hornet and responded in characteristic fashion. First, he did an introductory round with footwork, warmup and punching bag: "I haven't had a thing to do with that book . . . De Rokha has played more of a role than I have, since he tried to force inclusion of some of his wife's poems."

Then Vicente went on to a psychoanalytical interpretation, very fashionable in those days: "Many people wonder, why that aggression against everybody? But now, Freud is known, and it is understood that those displays and boasts only reflect an inferiority complex. The *Anthology* bothers him because he thinks it gives me superiority. He talks about fifty-six pages being devoted to me and thirty to him. What kind of flame is this that fears being extinguished with the first puff of air?"

The battle was just beginning, but with a vengeance. De Rokha published a three-column letter in response, chastising the "little literary lord."

Huidobro returned the attack, lining up his soldiers in three columns. He called his antagonist a specialist and professional in slander, a rabid rifleman, a Marxist-Leninist-Stalinist-Grovist card-carrying revolutionary, and a street bully, among other niceties:

> Your amusing letter is somewhat like a public confession, in the way you show the world your wounds and your weaknesses . . . You haven't responded to anything . . . you go on at the level of empty howls . . . I called you a fibber several times. You lie, and you know you're lying, when you say that I have imitated poets who, except for Apollinaire and Lautréaumont, come after I do and with whom my poetry has no connection. The truth is that you don't understand any of those authors whose names you rattle off . . . I have no reason to talk of your poems about childhood, written up until last month . . . And your *Jesucristo*, in spite of the padding that has added some pseudorevolutionary sprinklings to it, continues to be a pious little devil's scrawl of a poem. . . . You claim you don't read me, and every minute you make references to my works . . . ; it's obvious you have read them too much, which doesn't mean that you understand them . . . It's apparent that you are obsessed with the fact that I come from a well-off family. That is not my fault, and I may be completely pardoned for it if we remember that Engels made his living as the owner of a textile factory in Manchester. . . . My works are judged by authorities higher than you . . . Scholars have many serious documents to consult . . .

Then he cited several books and a dedication from Max Jacob, "To Vicente Huidobro, who invented the new poetry," and ended up with a request to, please, don't tell us you earn your living by hard work, because that doesn't prove anything.

Santiago was enjoying this cross fire of insults. *La Opinión* was sold out. A few days later, a new epistolary tank attack was received with certain despair by the newspaper's editor, Juan Luis Mery, announcing de Rokha's withdrawal from the battle. "I'm not going to go on beating up on you," the heavyweight fighter said. "It tires and sickens me, poor little Vicente. You harangue and bellow so much that your buffoonish claims fall apart, and you're left naked with no dignity, stamping your foot, fat, pink, stupid, indescribable like a rich man's baby. I'm bored now with the story of poor little Vicente. Besides, I'm not such a coward as to knock down a hen that clucks because she says she has produced an egg in Europe . . . ; your swindling counterfeiter's saddle bags squeak with moral poverty, little Vicente."

Huidobro countered three days later with another set of delicacies:

> You end your polemic as expected, with a big mess of green drivel . . . You retreat without having proved anything. . . . I demanded proof from you, and the public also demanded the same. Respectable people are laughing at you. And the sudden weakness that has come over your laughable body is quite sad. Backed into a corner, you spin around like a puffed-up seal and head off in another direction. Poor little Pablo, you're accustomed to shrieking and falsifying. . . . You thought you were going to continue your trade with nothing ever happening to you and without ever getting knocked down. . . . This lesson may teach you something. In addition, it was necessary to clean the environment of a poisonous scorpion. You are such a fool that in forty-two years you've still not realized that you're a fool. You've finally set a record at something. You should be pleased.

> Vicente Huidobro

The polemic was not a model of profundity, but rather a document of its time and a picture of the belligerent ardor of two very different contenders. They were both of more value than what they said in rage, but that was an inevitable component of their wounded egos and their violent exhibitionism.

Far away in Spain, Neruda was not publicly participating in the bitter dispute. Someone later discovered several pages of unsigned typed verses in his style, though, which recalled the war among Spain's Golden Age poets, Góngora, Lope, and then Quevedo. The verses were sometimes vulgar, but he had the good taste not to ever publish or recognize them as his.

Neruda took no part in the dispute, although he was intrigued by literary guerrilla warfare and held to the principle that one should never ignore an attack but respond to it immediately. His literary adversaries continued the hostilities, and de Rokha never lowered his battle flags. Neruda, who was not, I repeat, a man to turn the other cheek, didn't take up the role of an enemy power against whom war has been declared, perhaps because he already had victory in his hand. He had won it some time ago,

with his work and with public and critical recognition, international renown, and an ever-increasing flood of translations of his poetry to more
and more languages. And perhaps, at heart, he took no pleasure from this
squandering of energy, this spectacle where poets undressed in public and
went at each other tooth and nail to claim a "number one" position. He
again recalled his theory of the elephants. Poets should be like those giant
pachyderms, with their ivory tusks and water-spouting trunks, that he had
watched in the mornings in Ceylon—not like wild beasts who fight to the
death over a piece of some animal, because in the last analysis, it would be
they themselves who were devouring their own sense of dignity. Besides,
there were more important things to do, like writing poetry.

On the other hand, he couldn't divorce his spirit, which had just
lived through the literary polemic in Spain, from what was happening in
other fields in the peninsula, where society was demonstrating many signs
of a volcanic eruption.

69. *On the Eve . . .*

He was being looked at out of the critical corner of an eye named
Rafael Alberti, who was not at all enthusiastic about the *Caballo Verde
Para la Poesía,* edited by Neruda. The Spanish poet preferred *Octubre,*
published by revolutionary writers, intellectuals, and artists. In a sense,
blood had begun to run in the streets, for there was almost never a day
when some worker wasn't killed. People who sold leftist newspapers were
in danger of being murdered. Every week, burials had to be arranged for
those sacrificed to a fascism which was on the march. Alberti felt that what
should be done was what he was doing with the journal that carried the
date of the Russian revolution as a kind of challenge. The situation was
too dangerous, and it demanded very clear statements. That's why he
didn't like Neruda's journal. The struggle was raging, and the horse in the
title of *Caballo Verde* wasn't even trotting through the streets pulling a cart
of bread or weapons, nor was it carrying on its back a rider who had any
precise destination. This withdrawal by Alberti couldn't escape Neruda's
sharp eye, and one day he met the Spaniard in a bar near the House of
Flowers and told him:

"Dear *confrère,* what's the matter? You seem very stern with me."

"Nothing is wrong with me. I just think you are a little out of
touch . . . We want to do something else."

"But you know that I'm a diplomat; I don't understand politics at all, and I'm not interested in it. I understand and I see that Spain is like it is, and I support you all, but I think the journal can still be done."

"Fine, go on doing it . . ."

Neruda's life as a poet in love with poetry continues to evolve, with translations of poetry and resurrections of great half-forgotten fellow poets. The Madrid journal *Cruz y Raya,* edited by his friend José Bergamín, carries his translations of "Visions of the Daughters of Albion" and "The Mental Traveller" by William Blake, a poet who fascinates him and whose *Marriage of Heaven and Hell* was often on his lips as having impressed him deeply. He moves to another poet who increasingly affects him to the end of his life, Quevedo, for whose *Sonnets of Death* he writes an introduction. Then, *Poems* by Villamediana, a man who had lived through court intrigues and about whose love and misfortune I often heard Neruda speak. Finally, his own *Residence on Earth (1925–1935)* is published in Spain, in *Cruz y Raya*'s Arbol editions. In the early months of 1936, *First Love Poems,* including the *Twenty Love Poems,* is published in Madrid.

He was constantly with Federico García Lorca, in his own home or in that of Carlos and Bebé Morla. There, the two wizards of merry imagination were Federico and the Chilean composer, Acario Cotapos. They would ask Federico to sing, and he would say, "No, I've got a cold and I'm tormented by at least six personal tragedies." But he would sing.

Pablo often goes to see the productions of La Barraca, directed by García Lorca. He attends their presentation of *Fuenteovejuna* (*The Sheep Well*), with scenery and costumes by Alberto Sánchez, a baker from Toledo who was as silent and strong as the stone he sculpts. After the defeat of the Republic, he lived and worked in the Soviet Union, where he did the scenery for Kozintsev's film of *Don Quixote,* among other activities. Every time Neruda went to the Soviet Union he would visit his dear friend Alberto and his wife Clarita.

During Neruda's stay in Spain, he was very impressed by La Barraca's presentation of *El burlador de Sevilla* (The Deceiver from Seville), and made a special trip to Zamora, where Federico, Rafael Rodríguez Rapún and Luis Sáenz met him at the station. Unamuno, who is also in the audience, said "Culture is one thing, and enlightenment is another; enlightenment is what is needed."

After the tours of La Barraca through the towns and villages of Spain, whenever the young theater company was back in Madrid, they used to descend on the House of Flowers, where many would arrive bearing food, because sometimes it was a veritable regiment that showed up.

They would all have a good time under the watchful eyes of a bearded man in a wall poster who advertised Dr. Winter's poultices. Here and there, someone would fall asleep, to wake up thirsty. There were times when someone would stay at Neruda's house for three days and nights, talking and partying, sleeping and then talking some more.

Federico would reminisce with Neruda about his eight months in Uruguay and Argentina. For Federico, the pampa was "the most melancholy place in the world, with the most piercing silence." They sometimes talked politics. Neruda, like Lorca, was disturbed by what was happening in Spain. Federico was fond of predictions, and he used to deliver them like a gypsy reading the future. "Awful things are going to happen."

On 31 March 1934, in the Torlonia Villa in Italy, Mussolini received several generals and politicians from the Spanish far right. He signed the Pact of Rome with them and ordered delivery of the first cash installment for purchase of weapons, in preparation for Franco's rebellion.

"In this world, I am and always will be on the side of the poor," Lorca used to say. "I will always be on the side of those who have nothing, who are even denied the tranquility of nothingness."

The atmosphere was not at all serene. Generals Franco and Godet had already sent Moorish troops and the Foreign Legion from Morocco, to crush the Asturian miners. Someone said, "In Spain, they kill and don't count the dead." That is the climate in which stage productions are mounted for *Yerma* and *Doña Rosita la soltera, o el lenguaje de las flores* (Doña Rosita the Spinster, or the Language of Flowers), the latter in its premier performance on 12 December 1935 in Barcelona, with Margarita Xirgu. But Federico had also been summoned to court to explain his "Ballad of the Spanish Civil Guard," which had been denounced by a virtuous citizen of Tarragona for "insulting the meritorious institution" of the Civil Guard.

Federico sends a telegram to Alberti's wife, María Teresa León: "I fondly greet all the workers of Spain, united on this First of May by the intense desire for a more just society." He announces that he is working on a new play, and on 7 April predicted to a reporter from *La Voz* that on the day when hunger disappears, "the greatest spiritual explosion that humanity has ever known will take place throughout the world. Men won't ever be able to imagine the happiness that will burst forth on the day of the Great Revolution. . . ."

On 11 July 1936, Federico was eating Andalusian *gazpacho* in Pablo Neruda's house. As Rafael Alberti was expressing his pleasure at the meal, the parliamentary deputy Fulgencio Díez Pastor arrived to announce that the uprising was set for the 15th. Mussolini had invaded Ethiopia, and Hitler was occupying the Rhineland. In the Anfistora Theater Club, another of Lorca's works was in rehearsal, *Así que pasen cinco años* (*When Five Years Pass*). There were some people who were waiting to hear a coded sentence transmitted by Radio Ceuta from the African coast: "Throughout Spain, the sky is clear."

Federico was a man given to disappearances and silences. He even used to hide away from his friends, vanishing like smoke. He would disappear as if swallowed up by the earth, and then he would show up looking like a guilty child. One time after a typical vanishing act, he reappeared in the tavern on Luna Street, took out a white handkerchief from his pocket, spread it out on the floor and kneeled down in front of Neruda, begging his pardon with all the clever impishness that is typical of gypsies the world over.

To get Neruda's attention, Federico gave him a new collection of about twenty poems, titled *Sonetos del amor sombrío* (Sonnets of Dark Love). What happened to them, Neruda used to wonder. Had they been shot, too?

Neruda had arranged to meet Lorca on the night of 18 July 1936 to take in the wrestling show that a Chilean, Bobby Deglané, was presenting in Madrid. But then Neruda learned that Federico had gone to Granada. His own car, on the way to the Price Circus, was stopped by the Militia, which was already in action.

When Federico decides to go to Granada, Díez Pastor tells him, "Stay here. You'll be safer in Madrid than anywhere else." He recounted that a friend had shouted to him to "Go away, Federico!" Afterwards, it was discovered that it had been one of the leaders of the fifth column. Federico arrived in Granada on the morning of 17 July. Radio Ceuta broadcast the innocent statement, "Throughout Spain, the sky is clear," and the rebellion broke out. That day, the garrison at Melilla rose up in arms, setting off the civil war that would leave a million dead. July 18 was the Day of Saint Federico. Death had marked a cross on the poet who once wrote, "How strange that Federico is my name!"

70. *Execution in Viznar*

On the night of 17 July, Granada learned of the fall of Melilla when the military governor, General Campíns, received a telegrammed communique from the government: "A military uprising has broken out in Africa.

Distribute the weapons." He was sure there wouldn't be a single rebellious soldier, but, on the contrary, the fifth column was in charge of the army. The people were asking for weapons, and in response, the plotters took command of the military and apprehended the mayor of Granada, Doctor Fernández Montesinos, Federico's brother-in-law, on 20 July. Up until then, Lorca had gone about openly, but from that day on, he confined himself to the family's Huerta de San Vicente rural home. He had intended to write a new play, *Los sueños de mi prima Aurelia* (The Dreams of My Cousin Aurelia), in which Federico as a child would be the main character. The Huerta de Tamarit, where his uncle Francisco lived, was searched. Federico would be captured by the Falangist deputy, Ruiz Alonso, in the Granada home of the Rosales family, where he had taken refuge. He departed from his friends with "Until we meet again! Try to do something to help me!" He asked for blankets and cigarettes to be brought to him. Out of all those who tried to see him, only Manuel de Falla could even get inside the prison, where he pleaded, "I come as an artist and as a Christian." The reply they gave him was that "It's completely useless." For his own safety, they urged him not to get mixed up in this matter, and besides, "García Lorca was shot tonight." It was a lie.

In 1935, Federico had said to Carlos Morla, "Death fills me with panic, not because of what may happen afterwards, which doesn't concern me, but because of the horror that comes over me to think that I may 'feel myself going,' that I may be departing from myself." Strangely enough, Laura Reyes would later reveal that her brother Pablo Neruda's last words were, "I'm going, I'm going."

García Lorca used to gleefully confess, "I'm very fond of myself." He also had a great horror of blood. I heard Pablo recall that Federico believed with all his heart in bad-luck signs and certain gypsy superstitions. For example, you shouldn't cross the ocean because you'll urinate blood.

When Federico was born in Fuente Vaqueros, the town was called Asquerosa, which means "loathsome." They say that when he was confined to his loathsome cell, he was visited by the same priest from his childhood, Father Enrique Palacios, a distant relative, but this has never been documented.

In the middle of the night, they requisitioned a car from a well-to-do youth from Granada, and from the Government Building they brought out Federico García Lorca and a crippled city hall employee. They were escorted by two Falangists and two uniformed guards. Federico thought they were just going to a different jail, and he tried to calm down the crippled man, telling him, "We'll make a puppet stage and put

on plays." They arrived at the little square in Viznar, then went on to
Alfacar. They made the crippled worker get out of the car, and Federico
heard shots. Then it was his turn, and he began to scream, "You can't kill
me! I haven't done anything! I am not a Communist—I'm Catholic!"
They claim he asked for a priest to hear his confession, but was refused,
with insults. In his fright, he couldn't remember the "My Lord Jesus
Christ" prayer and so he said the "Our Father . . ." He was executed in
Viznar, a stone's throw from the well they call Fuente Grande. There are
two rocky slopes there which form a ravine, with a pine forest on one side.
They dug a hole in the middle of a pine grove, exactly where a solitary
olive tree stands, abandoned by its fellows, the only one of its kind in that
forest in Andalusia.

The news of Lorca's death reaches Madrid on 9 September. Neruda
learns it from the newsboys' shouts of "Federico García Lorca, shot in
Granada!" *El Sol* was unsure, with a front page headline "On the Supposed
Assassination of García Lorca." What was presented as a proven fact was
the execution of Granada's Socialist mayor, who was married to Lorca's
older sister. The next day, they publish a telegram from Herbert George
Wells, president of the International PEN Club in London, to the authorities in Granada, saying that he "anxiously wishes to have news of his distinguished colleague Federico García Lorca and would greatly appreciate
the courtesy of a reply." The courtesy was expressed thusly: "Do not know
whereabouts of Don Federico García Lorca. Signed, Colonel Espinosa."
The colonel was perhaps not only unaware of the final destination of
Don Federico García Lorca, but also of the fact that a poet by that name existed or might have existed, and had been assassinated by Ramón Ruiz
Alonso's gang.

Later, they couldn't any longer deny the fact of the murder. In November 1937, the correspondent from the Buenos Aires newspaper *La
Prensa*, according to the *Complete Works of the Generalissimo*, asked Francisco Franco, "Have world-famous Spanish writers been shot?" The generalissimo's reply was, "There has been a lot of talk in other countries
about a Granada writer; there's been a lot of talk because the reds have
waved this name like a propagandistic decoy. The truth is that in the early
moments of the revolution in Granada, this writer died while mixed up
with the agitators. Those are natural accidents of war. Granada was isolated for many days, and the insanity of the Republican authorities in
giving weapons to the people gave rise to flareups inside the city, and in
one of them the Granada poet lost his life."

Neruda would not accept either chance or fate in that death, much less any responsibility on the part of the Republican authorities. In his mind:

> (Federico García Lorca) belonged to the people like a guitar does; he was happy, melancholy, profound and pure like a child, like the people. If they had painstakingly searched, inch by inch, in all corners, for someone to sacrifice as a symbol, they wouldn't have been able to find in anyone or in anything the quickness and profundity of the popular spirit of Spain, to the degree that it existed in this chosen creature. Those who wanted to strike at the heart of his people have chosen well in shooting him. They have selected him in order to bring down and martyrize Spain, to consume her keenest perfume, to cut off her strongest breath, to silence her most indestructible laughter. The two most irreconcilable Spains have experienced each other in that death: the Spain turned black and green by the horrible hoof of the devil, the subterranean and accursed Spain, the crucifying and poisonous Spain of great dynastic and ecclesiastical crimes; face to face with the Spain that shines with vital and spiritual pride, the meteoric Spain of intuition and continuity and discovery, the Spain of Federico García Lorca.[28]

That event left Neruda perfectly clear. It changed the world for him, and it changed his poetry. A bomb had fallen on it, a drop of blood from the poet who was sacrificed in the little forest of Viznar. Undoubtedly, that drop of blood filled to overflowing a container that was already brimming with many drops of blood and many reasons for his poetry's evolution, or revolution.

71. *Why the Change?*

As a man, he had to speak out, and he did so with his poetry, above all else. He sat down at his desk and wrote the poem, "Explico algunas cosas" (I Explain Some Things):

> You all may ask: And where are the lilacs?
> And the metaphysics covered with poppies?
> And the rain which often struck
> upon his words
> leaving them pocked
> and full of birds?

I'll tell you now what's happening to me.

I used to live in a part
of Madrid that had bells,
and trees and clocks.

From there could be seen
the parched face of Castile
like a leathery sea.

My house was called
the house of flowers, for everywhere
geraniums blazed; it used to be
a lovely house
full of dogs and children.

      Raúl, do you recall?
Do you recall, Rafael?
      Federico, do you recall,
deep there in the earth,
do you recall the balconies of my house
where June's light filled your lips with flowers?
      Oh, my dear brother!

And further on in the poem, he spells out the reasons for his shift:

And one morning it was all ablaze,
and one morning firestorms
erupted from the earth
consuming creatures,
and from then on, flames,
gunpowder from then on,
and from then on, blood.

Outlaws with planes and Moors,
outlaws with rings and titles,
outlaws blessed by black monks
came through the heavens to kill children,
and in the streets the blood of children
flowed simply, like blood from children.

   . . . .

You all may ask why his poetry
doesn't speak to us of the dream, the leaves,
the great volcanoes of his native land?

Come and see the blood in the streets,
come and see
the blood in the streets,
come and see the blood
in the streets!

Could any other statement be more explicit and enlightening about the reason for the turnabout that affects the whole sense of Neruda's life and work? In effect, the Second World War had begun. Not only did the Moors arrive in Spain along with the self-proclaimed nationalists, but also Hitler's Nazis and Mussolini's Fascists. Like good writers, Neruda and his colleagues frequently discussed whether the first chapter or the prologue of the new worldwide conflagration was being written in Spain.

Alberti and other writers and artists immediately formed the group called the Alliance of Anti-Fascist Intellectuals. They took over the palace of a fugitive aristocrat, the Marquis Heredia Spínola, where the organization began its operations. They published a newspaper for the soldiers, which went straight to the trenches and was read aloud at the front—*El Mono Azul,* a title taken from the blue coveralls worn by Spanish laborers. The bombardments of Madrid had begun, and the people attacked and took the Montaña barracks without any support, by dint of sheer courage. Neruda was amazed to see such heroism. Barely ten days had passed since the uprising when he went to Alberti and told him, "Dear *confrère,* I'm giving you a poem, my first poetry for this war. I ask that you publish it, but without my name—I'm still in the diplomatic service."

In Santiago, we were overwhelmed when we read that first poem, which had also stunned Alberti when he received it, the "Song to the Mothers of Dead Soldiers":

They have not died! They still stand
amidst the gunpowder,
upright, like blazing torches.
Their pure shadows come together
in the copper-hued meadow

like a curtain of armored wind,
like a barrier colored with fury,
like the very sky's invisible breast.

The House of Flowers had been bombed and almost entirely destroyed, so he went to live near the embassy.

His commitment seemingly came about all of a sudden, instantaneously, but that impression is somewhat deceptive. It did not come to pass in a vacuum, nor should it seem unusual, for it was actually the culmination of a gradual process. A sometimes interrupted line of social responsibility runs throughout long periods of his life, beginning with the child in Temuco who rebels against bourgeois existence and injustice and says so in his earliest poetry and apprentice articles. It follows its course in the poet of the generation of 1920, who writes incendiary columns for *Claridad*. As a young man, he realized his heart was on the left. The long process moves toward a full-fledged definition in the man who has just turned thirty-two. Now it's not only his heart that's on the left, but also his social consciousness, which had been so deeply wounded by the annihilation of the friend and poet in whom Neruda saw the culmination of life's grace and unceasing creative brilliance. It is not a primitive desire for revenge that inspires him, but something greater. In his view, all this holds a tragic lesson—the definitive proof that fascism is incompatible with intelligence. That is his thinking, and in consequence he concludes that fascism is also his personal enemy, an enemy of poetry, of art, of humankind. And he will fight it with all his strength, *wherever he can and however he can,* joining together with all those who are determined to resist it. The where and how are, in his case, rooted principally in the works he writes. He sets himself to the task, and in a few months, as if his hand were a medium receiving messages dictated by the historical events that are all around him, he completes a cathartic book which expresses in synthesis the violent spiritual change he has suffered as a result of, first, Lorca's assassination and then, the war. This book, called *España en el corazón* (Spain in My Heart), is hailed by Louis Aragon as "the most stupendous introduction to our age's modern literature."

Shortly thereafter, in a Paris lecture in February 1937, Neruda explains in prose what he had expressed in poetry:

Many people perhaps expected from me tranquil poetic words unconnected with the world and the war . . . I am not a politician, nor have I ever taken part in political conflict, yet my words, which many might have wished to be neutral, are colored by passion. Please understand me, and please understand that we poets from Spanish America and from Spain will never forget and will never pardon the assassination of someone we consider to be the greatest among us, the angel of our language in these times . . . We will never be able to forget this crime, nor forgive it. We will never put it out of our minds, never will we excuse it. Never.[29]

Notice that Neruda says, "I am not a politician, nor have I ever taken part in political conflict." He still feels a certain distrust for the word "political," left over from the anarchist ideology of his early youth. But the above paragraph is a practical demonstration of how a man can be pushed by life into politics. It should be noted that his statement is made at a time when his actions already have him participating in *political* conflict. At about the same time, he adds that he is neither Communist nor Socialist, and it is not a pretense, yet neither is he neutral. In his own political definition, he is anti-Fascist. Years later, in the light of a perspective made clearer by time, he will say, "I believe I was acting as a Communist in Spain." There is only a seeming contradiction in his statements, for the process leading to a stand was already at work in his consciousness. And one day he will have to realize that Federico's death was but one catalyst and not the only factor in determining his attitude. Deep down, he was defining an over-all position in regard to society, based not only on what happened to one man, however dear that man might have been to him, but also on what happens to billions on this earth.

72. *The Book on Spain*

Initially published as separate poems, the work originally was to have appeared in Madrid with a prologue written by Rafael Alberti, but that project didn't come about. Instead, it came out in a Catalán edition which was printed as a war operation, with the collaboration of soldiers on the eastern front.

Spain in My Heart suffered publishing ups and downs appropriate to its content and the circumstances surrounding its birth. The poet Manuel Altolaguirre recounted in a 1941 letter how the book was put together in 1938, not far from the thunder of artillery. "It was printed in the Montserrat monastery, where the monks had one of the best presses in Catalunya. . . . We found out that near the front, in Orpi, there was an abandoned paper mill, and we decided to put it to work . . . The day that the paper was manufactured for Pablo's book, the mill was worked by soldiers. Not only did they use raw materials furnished by the commissary (paper and rags), but the soldiers also threw in clothing and bandages, as well as trophies of war like an enemy flag and a Moorish prisoner's shirt. The book . . . was set in type by soldiers and printed by soldiers."

Alberti thinks that that work by Neruda is the greatest book to be generated by the Spanish civil war, but careful! *It was generated by the war acting through an anguished man;* it was written by a poet who turned the dramatic event into a work of art. It is also the work that signals his move from introverted poetry to public poetry.

Alberti mentions another equally emotional book that comes out of the horrible event, *España aleja de mí este cáliz* (Spain, Take This Cup from Me) by the Peruvian César Vallejo, whom he recalls as a very silent and mysterious man.

Third Residence is the general title of a collection of five dissimilar parts: 1) "The Woman Drowned in the Sky"; 2) "Furies and Sorrows"; 3) "Reunion under New Flags"; 4) "Spain in My Heart"; and 5) "Song to Stalingrad." In other words, the *Third Residence* is a voyage between two worlds, two situations, two periods, undertaken by a traveler who changes because of the suffering he experienced. This passage through time and events lasts for ten years, from 1935 to 1945.

In the first part, the poet of the *Caballo Verde* rides from Asian despair to a different landscape, still dominated by a feeling of uselessness. "I don't exist, I'm of no use, I don't know anyone." The lonely man continues in his inclination to go on being a lonely man:

> Don't call me anything: that is my function.
> Don't ask my name nor my condition.
> Leave me alone on my private moon,
> in my own mutilated terrain.[30]

He travels through Europe, but his poem "Brussels" describes him as still "dying by night, . . . like a vegetable, alone." A similar atmosphere is seen in "Abandoned." Both are written just before the illumination that the catastrophe will bring him. In 1934, taking inspiration from a line by his idolized bitter Quevedo, "There are furies and sorrows inside my heart," he writes an especially strong poem, "Furies and Sorrows," which is almost an older brother of *The Ardent Slingsman,* with its culmination of his erotic poetry, where love is confused with hate.

I remember just one day
that maybe was never meant for me,
a day without cease,
a Thursday without origin.
I was a man led into happenstance
with a woman discovered by chance,
we removed our clothes
as if to die or swim or grow old
and we entered each into the other,
she, enveloping me like a hideout,
I, heaving at her like one
striking a bell,
for she was the deafening sound
and the firm cupola ready to shudder.[31]

"Setting aside the syllables of fear and tenderness, / forevermore exterminated," the poet moves on in "Reunion under New Flags," passing through the tunnel of his journey's middle ground, where he has a dream of joining his lone wolf's steps with those of man. He will no more take pleasure in his sadness. He will banish the cultivation of voluptuous sorrows, and will put an end to tears as an answer or as relief. He will no more search for "asylum in the sobbing void."

Within one and the same book, we can see a sudden change, rupture, and break, which deep down embody his own essence as it functions under new conditions, whose abruptness derives from the tragic moment he is experiencing.

Spain in My Heart, Hymn to the Glories of a People at War (1936–1937) is both dreadful reality and splendid poetry. Its structure is like that of an ancient poem: invocation, curse, story, analysis of causes, explanation, exaltation, picture of the past, report on the war, Dantesque condemnation of General Franco to hell, song of some ruins, landscape after a battle. Its heroic spirit gives it a flavor of epic poetry.

But the poet who still says he's not a politician, in his poem called "Spain, Poor Because of the Rich" damns "those who offered the solemn motherland / not bread but tears." He criticizes tradition, "full of dead snot." In short, he utters a judgment that falls headlong into the political arena.

He immediately gives himself over to the suggestively sensual or austere musicality of pronouncing the placenames of the nation now consumed in flames. Almost all of his lengthy "How Spain Used to Be" is an enumeration of villages on the peninsular map. He adds not one adjective, simply names them. And what could have seemed a tourist or onomastic guide takes on the quality of an intimate portrait of the geography and soul of Spain, thanks to the poet's selection of suggestive words. Its resonance is fed by Iberian, Roman, Jewish, Gothic, and Arabic springs, which charm the ear of the poet who is discovering in those names the intricate message of many centuries of history.

After the three-minute pause for naming the towns, he returns at once to the epic which he has been privileged to witness in the "Arrival in Madrid of the International Brigade":

> Then, breaking the frost of Madrid's cold month, at misty dawn
> I saw with these eyes, with the gaze of this soul,
> I saw them come, the proud upright combatants
> of the slender and firm, mature and ardent brigade of stone.

Neruda explained his turnaround several times. The man and the poet emerged from Spain transfigured. Like the legendary salamander, he went through the fire and survived, but he came out changed. In March 1939, in the note that precedes *Furies and Sorrows,* he recalls an illuminating and definitive conclusion: "This poem was written in 1934. How much has happened since then! Spain, where I wrote it, is a string of ruins. Oh, if only we could calm the rage of the world with just a drop of poetry, but that can be done only by struggle and a resolute heart."

The struggle and the resolute heart are the secret to the metamorphosis that *Spain in My Heart* represents in Neruda's work. As he himself said, he had changed, his poetry had changed. In one sense, we come face-to-face with another Neruda.

73. *The Poet in the Street and a Femme Fatale*

Mr. Consul had lost his composure, abandoning all the discretion that he had maintained in the beginning. At the same time, the Chilean ambassador in Spain, Aurelio Núñez Morgado, lost his patience, which wasn't too hard for him to do, since he was an old-time petty politician. A member of a ghostly Radical Socialist Party and a follower of President Arturo Alessandri Palma, he had moved from Parliament to diplomacy, where he was ready to interpret to the letter the rightist character of Chile's ruling government. The embassy had been turned into a house of refuge for the fifth column. Naturally, he didn't do this on his own, but in obedience to instructions from the chancellery in Santiago. His government was sympathetic to the rebels, and when the Spanish Republic's semipermanent seat in the League of Nations was voted on in Geneva, the representative from Chile's La Moneda government house, Agustín Edwards MacClure, who was the owner of *El Mercurio,* voted to exclude the Republic.

Luis Enrique Délano used to work afternoons in the Madrid consulate while he studied literature at the university during the mornings. Only three years younger than Neruda, he shared not only official duties with his old friend but also, and especially, his anguish about the fate of Spain. The drama they were experiencing had the same effect on both—it changed their life. They made no mystery about their position. In addition, Neruda had become a public figure and poet of the Spanish war. He did so without hesitation—he had crossed the Rubicon. The ambassador assiduously reported the poet's every move to Santiago, which wasn't necessary, since the wire service transmitted all the consul's openly committed activities, which violated the theoretical neutrality of the government he represented.

It was no surprise, then, that he was dismissed. When Pablo Neruda was thrown out of his position, he became the second poet to be turned out of the Madrid consulate within a very brief period. He was out on the street in a bombarded city that continued to resist the attack; out on the street but not alone, and among very good company, in his judgment.

Nor was his reaction very surprising. He was not at all apprehensive—perhaps it was all for the best. This way he could fight without his hands being tied. So far as eating was concerned, that would take care of itself.

He had to contribute to the struggle in whatever way he could, and in 1936 he and the English writer Nancy Cunard inaugurated the journal called *Los Poetas del Mundo Defienden al Pueblo Español* (Poets of the World in Defense of the Spanish People). Each issue contained poems in English, French, and Spanish. It was sold in London and Paris, with proceeds going to the Republican cause. Original texts were contributed by several old friends of Nancy Cunard, including Tristan Tzara, Louis Aragon, Langston Hughes, Brian Howard, and other well-known figures. Poets in Spanish included Pablo Neruda, Federico García Lorca, Rafael Alberti, Vicente Aleixandre, Raúl González Tuñón and Nicolás Guillén.

Neruda and his Spanish friends decided that he would be most useful in France, so he went to Reanville to help Nancy with the printing chores. Five issues were published in Paris, and several publications in other countries were patterned after the Neruda-Cunard issues, including a noteworthy anthology of Chilean poets published in Santiago and dedicated to the Spanish people.

Nancy Cunard had been born in 1896 in Nevil Holt, Leicestershire, in a gleaming majestic gray-stone mansion with a castlelike façade, 13,000 hectares of family grounds and seven centuries of famous ghosts. She felt lonelier there than the man in the moon, estranged from her father, Sir Bache Cunard, and from an early age detesting her mother, Maud Alice Burke, a rich heiress from the United States who used to seek out distinguished companionship, preferably among musicians and writers. When she was fifteen years old, Nancy left the ancestral house of her birth, never again to have a fixed home.

Nancy Cunard was one of the myths of that period, a femme fatale. I met her through Neruda, when I went with him to visit her in a fifth-class hotel in Santiago, where she had gone after the fall of the Spanish Republic. The wicked halo of a literary super-character surrounded her. Aldous Huxley pictured her as Lucía Tantamount in *Point Counter Point*, his spiteful vengeance for unrequited love. She became an obsession for him, and he turned her into the anti-heroine of several of his novels. She is the disintegrated woman in *Vicious Circle*, the dangerous aristocrat who plays for a bit with the clever mouse and sends him away without eating him because she doesn't find him tasty. As an exorcism, Huxley tries to free himself of his ruinous passion by setting it down on paper. She is the anti-Queen Victoria, here called Myra Viveash. With the eyes of a Siamese cat, she moves as if she were floating or walking on the edge of a knife. Evelyn Waugh put her in a novel where he called her Virginia Troy. She is the image of the novelistic romantic ghost who has roamed about between the two wars, the last of those exquisite faint-voiced women who were purveyors of damnation and the cause of men's agony. She had gone from being an admirer of Meredith to Proust, and she liked absinthe because Baudelaire and Oscar Wilde drank it. At one time, she was excited about Bernard Shaw; she argued about T. S. Eliot; and she became impassioned about D. H. Lawrence. She was mad about the cubist explosion, Epstein's sculptures, Stravinsky's music, the Russian ballets of Diaghilev and Fokine in Paris, and American jazz. She was drawn to surrealism, and Louis Aragon puts her at the center of his novel, *Blanche or Oblivion,* and he falls in love with her with a passion that demands exclusivity. "In my life there was one woman, who was very beautiful, with whom I lived several years and with whom I was really not meant to live." In Venice, when Aragon threatens to commit suicide, Nancy encourages him to kill himself at once, adding that she would be quite astonished if he had the courage to do so, whereupon he goes to a hotel and takes a strong dose of barbiturates. His emotion is poured into the "Poem for Screaming in the Ruins," published as part of the paradoxically titled book, *The Great Happiness*.

One of Aragon's friends, André Thirion, witnessed that stormy relationship and provides a sketch of Nancy in those days. He recalls her as a lovely woman about the same age as Louis, a thin fake of medium height with the eyes of a snake, an imperious walk and an extravagant way of dressing, which she exaggerated after nightfall, the time for hunting. Her voice was like a siren, and at night she habitually became a drunken aggressive siren who used to strike men with her metal and ivory bracelets. Sometimes she received bruising responses, whose marks would be hidden by day under heavy purple veils attached to the brim of the stunning hats then in fashion.

When she was sober she could be sweet, but life with her very quickly became impossible and destructive, especially because, if she wanted a man—and this happened with extraordinary frequency—she had to satisfy her desire at once. She would openly go on the offensive, which would drive to distraction her on-duty lovers (who were always temporary).

In "The Black Man and My Lady" she proclaims in print that "I have a black friend, an intimate friend." He had gone to Spain as a reporter for the Associated Negro Press.

She rebelled with all her being against her family and her environment, particularly against her mother, who was for many years the lover of the famous orchestra conductor, Sir Thomas Beecham. Lady Cunard belonged to the intimate circle around Edward VIII and Wallis Simpson, and when the king abdicated she, too, was banished from the Court of St. James. Nancy detested social and sexual conventions and would pay a cruel price for her explosive rebellion.

On her first trip to Spain in the summer and autumn of 1936, during the Spanish civil war, she met two men who would remain her friends for many years. One was Angel Goded, doorman at the Hotel Majestic in Barcelona, and the other was Pablo Neruda, whom she met in Madrid.

At about the same time, her contentious countryman, George Orwell, arrived in Barcelona, where he remarked on the social atmosphere that allowed waiters and store clerks to look straight into the eyes of their customers and treat them as equals. Nancy, whose taste for gondoliers, taxi drivers and hotel employees was rumored to stem from her depraved nymphomania, was in her element.

She found the plebeian consul from Chile infinitely more likable than the one from Great Britain. He struck her as a warm human being who loved friendship, good food, wine, and women. He was fascinated by Nancy and immediately introduced her to his Spanish poet-friends. At forty years of age, she had the same effect on them that she had had on the surrealists at thirty.

Pablo tried to become a typographer at her house in the south of France, but he was a mediocre typesetter. Once he transformed the word *párpados* into the nonsensical *dárdapos*, leading her to later write him from London as "My dear *Dárdapo*."

She arrived in Chile in January 1940 after a five-week sea voyage, traveling on a visa that Neruda had helped her obtain. She was accompanied by a young Spanish bullfighter, and in the course of her twenty-month stay in Chile she took as a lover a toothless bohemian poet from the provinces, who used to administer nocturnal punishments that obliged the British lady to wear huge dark glasses in broad daylight to hide the damage.

Well in decline, during the years that followed she continued to vacillate between euphoria and depression, struggling against her ever-increasing physical and mental deterioration. In 1960, Neruda was disturbed to learn that Nancy had been expelled from Spain after spending several days in jail, first in Valencia and then in Mallorca. She would quarrel with the police wherever she could, inciting fistfights, creating scandals, and receiving gentle or vicious kicks in return. Her tendency toward paranoia thus accentuated, she would drink like a fish and rave deliriously about political persecution. Her cold exhibitionist sexuality was accompanied by public drunkenness that frequently turned into sidewalk spectacles. "Mental imbalance aggravated by alcohol" was the diagnosis of a doctor who examined her. In his judgment, she was an alcoholic who should be put under guardianship. Alcoholism made her speech incoherent, and her verbal attacks became uncontrollable and frightening. There was a confinement in St. Clement's Hospital in London's East End, where she wrote inflamed accusations characterized by ideological phrasing and content, to be sent to heads of government, including Khrushchev, demanding that she be set free. She did get out, but only to land again in a mental institution, this time for four months in the Holloway Asylum. Her friend Charles Burkhardt explained her condition thusly, "She is out of her mind, but she is not an insane person." Her former lover, Louis Aragon, took pen in hand and came out in defense of the woman who had driven him to attempt suicide. Georges Sadoul denounced her confinement in the insane asylum. The North American poet Walter Lowenfels also interceded in her behalf, calling her a victim of herself but also a victim of the Cold War. Neruda, in 1960, was in Chile, far away from what Nancy herself termed her "administrative insanity."

She left the asylum, but in time the crises became more serious. Sometimes she would become irrational and delirious. She was literally becoming just skin and bones, and in the last year of her life she weighed only fifty-seven pounds. She looked like a survivor of Buchenwald or a very peculiar "Lady," with African necklaces around her throat and bracelets up to her elbows, resembling the starving people of Biafra. She had a broken thigh and talked without stopping. She would turn to reminiscing about her love affairs, which she never kept count of. When drunk, she would fire off hot-headed insults against the thousand-times-over abominable Fascists, whose number increased with each night.

On one especially tiring and nightmarish day, she told her exhausted friends Sadoul and Michelet that she had reserved a room in one of Paris's lowest-class hotels. It was on the third floor and there was no elevator. They supported her on the climb, although she wanted to go it alone in spite of her broken leg. She had to frequently sit down on the steps to gather strength. The unreal journey to her room took about two hours.

Other occupants going up to their rooms were astonished and frightened when they saw this skeleton of a woman seated on the stairway asking them bizarre questions: "Do you know Pablo Neruda? Do you think he'll get the Nobel Prize for Literature this year?" Then she asked her escorts to find out if Samuel Beckett, a friend who held her in high esteem, was in Paris. She wanted him to come visit her. "Give him this message—This woman (she used to refer to herself in the third person) has just celebrated her sixty-ninth birthday today and has entered her seventieth year." She was a little mistaken about the date, or she was fibbing with coquettish solemnity.

The next morning, when they went to see her, they learned that she had fled the hotel. Three days later, the woman who had been the heretical image of English intellectuals in the period between the two world wars, lay dying in the very same Cochin Hospital where Neruda, six years later, would be operated on for a disease that would cause his death in 1973. And so, on 16 March 1965, left with nothing but eyes and bones, Nancy Cunard died alone in an oxygen chamber in a hospital ward. The *Evening Standard* bade a "Sorrowful Farewell to a Queen of the Twenties." Georges Sadoul filled in her portrait in *Les Lettres Françaises:* "She was more than just an eccentric figure from those crazy years. Hovering in her shadow are Afro-American blues and spirituals, Spanish Republican ballads, and modern French poetry's immoral hymns."[32]

Great-granddaughter of the founder of the Cunard Line, the first transatlantic steamship company, Nancy would be sunk like the *Titanic*. She collided with an immense unmovable iceberg—life, and we would also add, her social class. In her case, her personal decline was so visible that the ostensible shipwreck merely sank a pitiful little boat already stripped of its mast, which had been off course for a long time, although she thought she had lost neither compass nor tiller. Proud of her ideas and her tragic rebellion right to the end, Nancy Cunard disappeared in the ocean with flags raised, defiantly waging her last battle.

How can I forget her? She's right there in front of our eyes, in a dirty run-down hotel in Santiago, once again in the presence of her friend Pablo, with whom she spent unforgettable days working on that poetry collection that she considered one of the really meaningful things she had done in her life.

74. Literary Passions

The out-of-work poet will now demonstrate his organizational spirit. Together with César Vallejo he founds in Paris the Spanish American Group for Assistance to Spain. French writers ask Neruda to help line up men of letters from the American continent to participate in the congress that was supposed to take place in Spain. He gladly accepts and is assigned a tiny salary. It is intense and time-consuming work. Selections must be made about who would be invited, and he knows better than anyone who is who in Latin American literature. Many letters must be written. At that point, virtually all the well-known authors sympathized with the embattled Spanish Republic. The Second International Congress of Writers took place in July 1937 in Madrid and Valencia. Among those present were André Malraux, Louis Aragon, Ilya Ehrenburg, Waldo Frank, Ernest Hemingway, and many from Latin America, including Nicolás Guillén and Juan Marinello from Cuba, Octavio Paz from Mexico, Alberto Romero and Vicente Huidobro from Chile.

Before departing, Huidobro had said very precisely that beneath the electric sky of Spain, the bomb exploded, and a horde of traitors and bas-tards rose up in arms to close off the road to triumphant democracy and stifle the logical development of the people, putting up a wall of rifles before the great destiny of mankind on the move. His words were impas-sioned. "We follow with an anxious heart the ups and downs of the strug-gle," he had said, "and our greatest sorrow is not to be there among those heroic people who are defending the future of the world." Early on, his prediction was optimistic, as he added, "The Spanish people cannot lose. The hidden course of history cannot be stopped. Time belongs to them, or rather to all of us." He had delivered this article to the press expressly for publication on a twelfth of October, "on the anniversary of the master-piece written by the Spanish people on oceans and continents," he said, ending on a personal and solemn note: "As a child of your race and of these lands you pulled up from the unknown, my emotions greet you, sorrowful and sublime Spain, upright and never on your knees."

He departed for Spain as soon as he received the invitation. He would return to Paris, his second—or first—motherland. He would an-swer "Present!" in the midst of gunfire in Spain. But things didn't turn out as he expected them to.

The bilingual poet, who wrote in French and Spanish, realized that in Paris he was now considered a foreigner, and that in Spain there was another concern—the war had become a raging beast that was devouring everything and vomiting out corpses at every turn.

Was the Spain of the Cid—his "My Cid"—really an accursed Spain? His own blood came from there, even his title of nobility that he didn't use, Marquis of Casa Real. He had written a poem, unknown in the pen-insula, about the epic hero, an incarnation of Huidobro himself. He sus-pected that Franco was winning. And something much worse—he real-ized that on the Republican side, other writers were more highly thought of than he. The Congress in Valencia turned out to be an affront to his feelings and his pride as self-proclaimed "Father of New Poetry." His po-etic lineage, unlike any other, received almost no attention. In his view, the hierarchies which were taken for granted at the meeting struck him as obscene, as the names of Rimbaud, Mallarmé, Apollinaire, Huidobro were overshadowed by the gurus from India, the Antonio Machados, the André Malrauxs, and—a million times more unseemly—the Nerudas. The true poets were forgotten. Poetry about cooking was being deified, while those who wrote authentic books about the Discovery were ignored.

Was Spain's spirit at this point still upright or on its knees? If he earlier was a prophet of victory, wasn't he now foreseeing defeat? Was he moving from hope to demoralization? He still didn't know with certainty, and even less could he admit it.

Vicente Huidobro was aware that in France and in Spain, Neruda had acquired a prestige that to him was a scandal, a deceit. He was presented as the most outstanding intellectual in Latin America.

Several incidents took place on the train from Paris to Madrid, on solid ground, and in the congress itself. He was very disappointed when he returned to Chile, and I thought he seemed evasive. At first he said something appropriate to the magnitude of the tragedy. "What is happening in Spain is tremendous, noble and atrocious." But he returned in defeat as the top poet of our continent. I wondered why he had gone to Spain, but he had gone just because one had to go to Spain. He couldn't remain stuck in the farthest province in the world when the great ones, the semigreat ones, the "who's who" of literature were heading for Spain, as the Tibetan wise men head for Katmandu.

He became very sad. The master found no laurels in Europe. He viewed the Valencia Congress of Writers as a perfidious assembly, an anti-Huidobro microcosm where momentary talents foamed up like bad smells. False pearls were being sold, and his own greatness went unrecognized there, in that tiny closed-off, hypocritical preserve, where plaster gods rubbed elbows with the prostitutes and thieves of literature. He preferred the street, except that in the street bombs were falling, and something might happen to him. Night and day, his fantasy worked like a machine that manufactured disillusionment.

Neruda took on a demonic connotation for him. The author of tangos became a nightmare, and the "Widower's Tango" wasn't just an accident but the one robin that does signify spring. A simple poetaster from the provinces, an audacious vampire, an infernal low-brow.

One dark Sunday evening, Eduardo Anguita and I sat down at our usual table in the Fuente Iris, and I began to read *El Imparcial*, a gloomy evening paper that symbolized the Middle Ages in print journalism with its daily demand that the Left be crucified. We were the only customers there. Suddenly I said to Anguita, "Listen to this article, 'Spain in Neruda's Heart.'" I read him a few paragraphs.

"Who's it by?" he asked.

"The Just One."

"Who's The Just One?"

"I recognize him from the tone. Vicente," I answered with dismay.

It was a poorly disguised attack. The author passed himself off as a follower of Franco, inflamed by anti-Republican frenzy. Thanks be to God, Neruda's Spain will one day be able to fit in his heart, because it is growing smaller and smaller, thanks to the Caudillo's victories. The camouflaged intricacy of its style revealed the unmistakable paternity of this *brulote*. It smelled of his very characteristic expressions and his unequivocal twists—somewhat like poetry with naphthalene—Neruda-tangoist, Lorca-dittyist. By putting on that disguise, he was destroying all that I used to adore. A bitter truth was revealed to me: Vicente believed only in himself.

75. *President of Intellectuals*

The Valencia Congress resolved to organize Alliances of Anti-Fascist Intellectuals in as many nations as possible. Neruda takes charge of this endeavor in Chile. He leaves the dubious rat-trap hotel in Paris where he's living with Delia, and they take a French cargo ship bound for Chile, along with the Argentine poet Raúl González Tuñón and his wife Amparo Mon. Looking at the sea from on deck, he mentally weighs the situation: the Congress of Intellectuals has been an accomplishment, but the Republic is on the verge of collapse. He looks about, and the prospect is disturbing. National Socialism is at its height, and there will be no respite.

In Chile, they feel the war in Spain as their war, too. Not long before, the Popular Front had been organized, comprised of Radicals, Democrats, Socialists, Communists, and the Chilean Workers Confederation. There are frequent confrontations in the streets with Nazis, headed by González von Marées. The atmosphere is heated, and the day's first news always concerns Spain. Neruda is received in his country as the Chilean most directly tied to the embattled people of Spain.

An explosive theatrical event takes place that in a way recalls the Buenos Aires lecture presentation *al alimón* with García Lorca, but Federico can no longer present lectures anywhere on earth. He has been sacrificed to that fascism that Neruda is here to decry and to alert Chile as part of the world that lives under threat.

This isn't a bullfight *al alimón*, but it is a dual lecture pronounced one Sunday morning in Santiago's Municipal Theater, which is full to overflowing and trembling with emotion at what was heard. The presenters are the Chilean poet Pablo Neruda and the Argentine poet González Tuñón, and the topic is an original report on the Spanish situation, the most throbbingly convincing and emotionally fiery picture that audience has ever listened to. The magic of truth-poetry, reported by individuals who come straight from the frontlines. That day, the Municipal Theater is filled with the smoke from battles and the sound of spilled blood is in the air.

Not only the transmittors of that message but also its recipients understand that wherever the word "Spain" appears, it could easily be "Chile." There is also the risk that fascism may one day slither into our country.

That morning, Neruda revealed himself to an overwhelmed audience as a personality who fused the disquieting and penetrating greatness of poetry with the intensity of socio-political definition. He showed himself to be capable of touching the heart and of stirring the mind with his clear analysis of the tragedy that was taking place over there and of the similar danger for his own country tomorrow or the next day.

On the seventh of November in 1937, a date deliberately selected to correspond with the twentieth anniversary of the Julian calendar date of the October Revolution, Pablo Neruda convened the Alliance of Chilean Intellectuals in the university's Hall of Honor. At that same session he was elected president of the alliance, which has been the most extensive and active cultural movement in the history of Chile. In it were joined together people from all fields of the arts and sciences. Its membership also represented all ranges of aesthetic approaches, political ideologies and beliefs, except Fascists and reactionaries. Hundreds of intellectuals worked in the alliance, including Alberto Romero, Juvencio Valle, Angel Cruchaga, Antonio Quintana, Humberto Díaz Casanueva, Judith Weiner, Francisco Coloane, Carlos Vicuña Fuentes, Roberto Aldunate, Acario Cotapos, Luis David Cruz Ocampo, Gabriel Amunátegui, Guillermo Labarca, Rubén Azócar, Oscar Castro, Gerardo Seguel, Bernardo Leighton, Sergio Larraín, etc.

Among the specific methods employed by the alliance, the principal tool was one neither widely disseminated in the country nor greatly respected in official circles—the printed word. On 24 December 1937, the first Book Fair opens on the Alameda. It becomes a tradition that later unenlightened regimes would do away with as if it were an offspring of Satan.

The alliance was a beehive of activity that operated not only in the capital, but also in centers which were organized in Iquique, Antofagasta, Valparaíso, San Felipe, Rancagua, Concepción, Temuco, and other cities. Neruda's very personal involvement is seen in his formulation of ownership laws for his fellow-writers and his campaign in defense of literary property rights.

A new period in his life is beginning. He is at the center of cultural activity and a driving force in solidarity with Spain. He takes part in Chilean politics as a unique figure in the Popular Front, doing public relations work for its presidential candidate, Pedro Aguirre Cerda.

It's possible that all that activity ameliorates somewhat his painfully vivid memory of the widespread death he has just come from in Spain. He feels a need to rejoin his country and rejoin life, and to take part in organized struggle.

76. *Water of Life and Death*

At that point, he is dealt several blows in rapid succession by the death of people who were close to him. He receives the news of the Paris death of a poet he considered to be as towering as the Peruvian Andes, a poet who worked side by side with him on behalf of the Spanish Republic during his last period in Europe. His "Ode to César Vallejo" will evoke the stone of a countenance chiseled with deep creases like the arid mountain ranges of his country.

Their lives followed separate paths. Neruda had streaked through Paris on his way to the Orient, fleeing her charms, her truths, and her lies. Vallejo had stayed, "in the run-down hotels of the poor." Later, when they were called by the blood in Spain, both responded simultaneously. His Peruvian friend was a two-time exile, whom he calls "My Brother," despite the fact that the literary life of the times had its own good samaritan who tried to turn their relationship into a cockfight.

When he receives the unhappy news, Neruda writes the article "César Vallejo Has Died" for the first issue of the Intellectual Alliance's journal, *Aurora de Chile*. "Old soldier of hope, old beloved one. Is it possible?" He calls him "our dearly admired one." He imagines him yearning for Latin American soil, but Spain kept him on in France, where nobody was more a foreigner than he. He was a man of our America, and in Neruda's eyes, he was like a mine, a lunar cave. He quotes a letter from Juan Larrea, who says of Vallejo that "He paid his dues to many hungers." Neruda goes on, "The situation in Spain has been the auger of your immense quality. You were a great man, Vallejo. You were a private man and a great man, like a great palace of subterranean stone . . ."

But death also comes to cut down his family in that same feverish and difficult year. His father was very ill and died on 7 May 1938. Neruda must go to Temuco to bury him. His journey, by rail, is filled with memories of the ballast-train conductor who now will become one with the earth of Araucanía. The poet's view is interrupted every so often by castlelike stacks of wood, as he again enters the never forgotten realm of rain and living botany that his father had showed him as a child. So many journeys on the night train! This one is the saddest of all. At dawn, he feels once more like a prodded schoolboy as he watches the children from poor towns walking through the mud and water, carrying their book bags, on their way to the unfurnished schoolroom. Dressed in black, he is met at the station by his uncles. In the house, he sits silently for a while beside his father's body. Then his uncles call to him from behind the patio as they cut open the breast of a lamb to fill a glass with its blood, which they give him to sip.

Now he will bury his father, and once again comes the sensation of his early years, when that gruff voice would cut him like a knife. Funeral rites always have a religious aura, even though the poet insists on pointing out their "strictly secular" nature. He will stay in the home of his friend, Dr. Manuel Marín, who had treated his father. There he spent a long time writing some lines that would appear in the *General Song*. He couldn't help but bid farewell to his father immediately, and though he didn't leave these verses beside the grave, he did compose them as soon as he left the cemetery:

> From far to the North came Almagro with his withered spark . . .
> When he ends, the night is dark . . .
> All the foam departs from his oceanic beard,
> filling him with coal's mysterious kisses.

He returns to Santiago, where in a few weeks he receives another terrible telegram, telling him that his "momother," unable to bear her husband's passing, died on 18 August. Again in mourning, he goes back to the southern rain. Now his father's resting place would have to be changed, so that the couple could sleep side by side in their longest night. "At noon," he said, "my brother and I went with some railroad friends of the deceased, and we opened the vault, which had already been sealed and cemented, and took out the coffin, already covered with toadstools growing on a wreath of dead, black flowers. The region's humidity had cracked open the coffin, and as we took it out I couldn't believe what we saw— great quantities of water poured out from it, like unending liters of his body substance pouring out from inside him."[33]

However, it was all quite simple—the same element that had encompassed him in life also encompassed him in death. But why be surprised? He was just returning to his own element. "So everything is explained— this tragic water was rainwater, perhaps just one day's rain or maybe the rain of a single hour of our southern winter, and this rainwater had crossed over roofs and balustrades, over bricks and other materials, and over other mortal remains to reach my father's grave. I was reminded once more by this special and frightful water of my unending connection with one specific life, one region and one death; reminded by this terrible water that comes from an extraordinarily unfathomable and impossible hiding place to show me its torrential secret."[34]

He belonged to the rainy region. He always met up with rain, and always would, both in life and in death.

But with sunshine, too. It's appropriate to say that he probably kept his mind on the rainbow.

Part Two

PASSION AND DEATH

V.

His Discovery of America

77. *Accursed Cities*

The poet was in Temuco, where he had gone to bury his father, when he received a request from certain provincial officials whose plea won him over: "You're the only one who can help us! You're the only one who can convince her!" Who was it he had to convince? None other than that lady in the long tan dress and low heels who used to loan him books by Russian writers when he was a boy and who one day, after his several failed attempts to see her, had assured him that he had the makings of a poet.

The headquarters representatives from the Education Department were apparently on the verge of a nervous breakdown. Gabriela Mistral was scheduled to travel by train through the Temuco station, but from the mountain resort of Bariloche in southern Argentina she had refused all requests to stop for a few days or even a few hours in Temuco, where a possibly guilty conscience wanted to offer her an apology in the form of an homage in front of the entire population and accompanied by singing school children. She had firmly refused. She would not accept such glorification, especially in Temuco, for she had old scores to settle with that city. In her typically strong manner, she had written about it in a footnote to a poem in *Desolation*, whose publication elicited from someone in that city a comment that she considered despicable and filthy. She never forgave it. As Neruda told me many years later, she included Temuco among the accursed biblical cities. She felt she shared the blood of prophets and in her veins burned the fire of a vengeful god in the face of whoever was blasphemous and perverse. She admired that purifying divinity that was capable of ordering the destruction of Sodom and Gomorrah by fire and bloodshed.

Neruda was quite aware of all this, and he realized he was being offered an extremely difficult mission, but he was their last resort. They implored him to ask her, as one poet to another and as a friend, to spend a couple hours in the city which was so anxious to honor her.

In those days there was no telephone connection between Temuco and the Argentine mountain resort. He was offered the only means of talking personally with Gabriela Mistral—Mr. Mayo's radio, still a fledgling operation in that province. Contact was established, and Neruda spoke to Gabriela with all the warmth of his heart, not so much because of the request but because that's how he felt about her. After a few objections and jokes, she agreed to the slightest of gestures—she would issue a greeting from the train's boarding steps or even from the station platform, during the ten- or twenty-minute stop in Temuco. It wasn't a big victory, but half a loaf is better than none.

On the appointed day, even before the established time, the station was packed by a crowd eager to see the legendary woman and to hear a few words from her mouth. Children were there to sing her some of her own verses and to bid her a moving choral farewell when the locomotive started up.

But she did not come to the platform, nor did she show herself on the steps or look out the window. The curtains were closed in her sleeping-car compartment. Nobody saw her, and she saw nobody. She never did remove Temuco from her list of accursed cities. Not for her to look back as fire and sulphur rained down on Sodom and Gomorrah! Not for her to turn into a pillar of salt as "smoke and fire come from the earth like smoke from an oven."

Naturally, when Neruda is telling me all this, he doesn't reproach Gabriela in the least. She didn't limit her mistrust to Temuco, but also levied many criticisms against the entire country. She once said in a letter that if she were to go back there to live permanently, with the itch that some people have to devalue, be indifferent to or beat down others, she would end up within three months being "old Gaby" instead of "Gabriela."

That woman, who came from peasant stock, maintained that "all culture has begun with the earth . . . In Chile they think that culture begins with the college degree." She used to complain that every day she would receive anonymous messages which were "incredibly aggressive and cruel." As for a certain type of mentality that exists in Chile and also in other Latin American countries, which brags of racial superiority, she was always on the alert, calling them "the unfortunate Latin Americans . . . who proclaim at the top of their lungs their European purity, whereas their high cheekbones and olive skin and slanted eyes reveal to me the mystery of their drop of Asiatic blood, which so nobly reveals in them the Indian that they try so hard to deny. . . . They're almost always sick people, because of their lack of authenticity." Neruda agrees with that view, as his work shows. She used to offer a piece of advice, which he followed: "Guard against, strangle, and eliminate the slightest outbreak of xenophobia that appears in our people." She was horrified by overbearing and aggressive militarism, and also by weakness and inconsistency in so many frightened advocates of democracy. "The fate of our Hispanic peoples makes me shudder. It all strikes me as waves of upheaval and lethargy alternating between dictatorships, which are swollen with what most corrodes both soul and conscience—swollen with power—and democratic governments, which are devoid of energy, vision, necessary political action, and effective social direction." She wasn't happy with what she considered her own country's limited awareness of her work. "Chile is the country where I am least known . . . where I am read the least."

She had a long memory for the disdain and cruelty she suffered. When she was awarded the Nobel Prize, she recalled that when she was a child they used to throw stones at her until her head was bloodied, just because a teacher got the foolish notion to accuse her of theft. In that La Serena school when they first introduced tests to measure children's intelligence, she is twelve years old, and the result of that terribly scientific evaluation is the pronouncement that she has "absolutely no aptitude for any kind of schooling." She never forgot that. Included in the basket of insults is one inflicted by a man who took over the *Sucesos* journal in 1917 and systematically insulted her for six months. Nor did she forget the fact that when the Mexican government issued her an invitation in 1922, the parliamentary deputy who had just founded the Chilean Communist Party, Luis Emilio Recabarren, proposed that the legislature allocate to her 5,000 pesos since she didn't have the funds to make the trip, and the proposal was turned down amid laughter and quips, in a period when all the armed forces officers used to have lavish travel allowances to go off to Europe with their families.

Her notion of the "accursed cities" is joined with that of the country ruled by sinister gods who are capable of devouring their own offspring.

78. Elections in Chile

In 1938, for the first time, Neruda found himself involved in the details of a presidential campaign, which in Chile used to go on for a long time and necessitated trips from one end of the country to the other in a contest for every single vote. The poet worked doubletime on public relations for the Popular Front candidate, Pedro Aguirre Cerda, a lawyer and radical politician. For Chileans on the left it seemed to be a titanic struggle, encompassing perhaps a too ambitious effort to defeat the incumbent party's candidate, a multimillionaire international speculator who was finance minister in Arturo Alessandri Palma's second presidential term. Gustavo Ross Santa María had quickly won for himself several popular nicknames, including "Minister of Hunger" and "The Last Pacific Pirate." He could count on money, in a period when bribery still paid off and often determined the outcome of elections.

Later, Neruda will depict the dark marvels of that systematic buying of consciences or inconsciences in a poem in the *General Song* called "Elections in Chimbarongo (1947)." There he reveals how "the mainstays of the nation were elected." The morning of election day, the creaking wagons arrived full of dirty, hungry, barefooted sharecroppers, the serfs of a still thriving Middle Ages. Holding a ballot in their hand, they were unloaded like a herd of animals. "Later / they were thrown meat and wine / until they were left like / vilified forgotten beasts." Then he listened to the speech by the senator whose election had been thusly bought—a patriotic declaration in defense of law and order from a virtuous son of spirituality risen up in opposition to Marxist materialism. Neruda viewed him as a mammoth that emerged hissing from prehistoric times, but such cave dwellers with juicy bank accounts had always considered the country to be their rightful personal property. They were the only ones who counted; the rest were a salable commodity. Neruda participated in politics with a moral sense, but in order to make politics ethical it was first necessary to change the economic and national reality of the country.

When elections were held on 25 October 1938, he had seen several voter roundups, organized in particular by Guillermo Francke, an energetic lieutenant of Gustavo Ross, that opportunistic public works contractor who played havoc with the public treasury. In large uncultivated areas, where he was erecting treasury buildings at great expense, thousands of citizens suddenly became prisoners, watched by police so they wouldn't violate their orders. They received one shoe before the election and the other one after voting to the satisfaction of the bribery agent. The same system followed with half a mattress, which was made complete only when the bought-off voter showed proof of compliance in casting his ballot. But the poet also witnessed a kind of antidote against the evil, when masses of workers entered the roundups by force, scattering those who had been bribed. This resulted in violent encounters where the police would guarantee the intangible sanctity of the buyer-seller contract, the right of the right-wing candidate to get votes by making a modest contribution either in money or in kind.

The motto of the Popular Front was "Against Reaction and Fascism," a simple expression, but it reminded Neruda of Spain, from where he had just returned with a heavy heart. His obligation to that country was not yet finished, and he was adding up his options in consideration of that fact: if the Popular Front was victorious in Chile, it would be possible to help Spanish Republicans who were in mortal danger.

At ten o'clock on election night, the whole country was on pins and needles, for official results should have already been announced. A suspicious delay! People flooded into the streets demanding respect for the will of the voters and renouncing any kind of manipulation of the count, a skill that the right wing historically was accustomed to using with a dexterity that bordered on sublime cynicism.

Neruda was on the Alameda, along with thousands of others, when the results were announced. The Popular Front candidate had been elected president by a margin of slightly more than 2,000 votes. The temptation to falsify the results was strengthened by the closeness of the vote, but the crowd's massive presence in the streets squelched the plan by some right-wing hot-heads to alter the outcome.

At midnight, Neruda was celebrating the victory in his house on Irarrázabal Avenue, near Pedro de Valdivia Street. His friends were inside, singing and dancing with great abandon, and he was making plans. He would not forget his Spanish brothers.

79. *Houses*

He wanted to settle down again in Chile, with a house in the city, but more urgently, one near the sea, where he could concentrate on his work, far from the noisy hustle and bustle of urban life.

He had begun to collect more substantial royalties, which he uses to acquire a modest stone house in a still almost undeveloped area, Las Gaviotas, on the Pacific coast where Valparaíso province begins, northwards from San Antonio and Cartagena on the road to Algarrobo. He pays the first installment to the owner, a Spanish gentleman named Sobrino, who feels very honored that the buyer is a man whose actions in Spain he approves of. The stone house has only a dining room, a bathroom, a kitchen, and two bedrooms. That's enough, for now. The place was found through a newspaper advertisement. Mr. Sobrino had had more than one adventure in his lifetime. Delia, "The Ant," remembers him as a sea captain who disembarked with his guitar and lost his ship. Out of nostalgia for the ocean, he bought a piece of land near the sea, which at that time was worth very little. When he learned that it was Pablo who wanted to buy it, he said, "For Neruda, whatever he wants, considering what he did for Spain!" Later, with the years, the house will grow like a child who becomes a giant. The poet will add a tower, transforming the house into a Latin American castle, which nevertheless can't hide its original stamp, so similar to that leaky wooden house in Temuco. The poet, incorrigible and obdurate bestower of names, changes the designation of the tiny three-family hamlet, calling it Isla Negra, a name that reveals his daring imagination, because it is not an island but is solidly secured on terra firma. And its color is not black but actually combines the shades of the cliffs and the sandy earth with the pure green of coastal vegetation.

A friend who is an expert in pension rights suggests to him that he can buy a house in Santiago through the Public Employees and Journalists Pension Fund. He looks around in a neighborhood he likes, which stretches from the Los Guindos square toward the end of Nuñoa Street, in the direction of the Andes. It's not an elegant residential zone, but there are still large lots for sale there which would give him a property 300 feet deep and about 90 to 120 feet wide. He prefers two building materials—stone and wood. Finally he finds a simple old house, covered with vines and not at all spectacular. It's on Lynch Street, which in those days was the very picture of calmness. He will put his builder's imagination to work. Remembering his friend García Lorca, he creates a theater stage at the point where a tree divides the patio's long perspective. A garden grows near the bedrooms, and the tile floor and colored glasses shine in the dining room. In time, the house is transfigured by Neruda's touch. Shortly after the Second World War, I witnessed the visit of Count Sforza, then Italy's minister of foreign affairs. He entered the house, looked around and proclaimed it "a Chinese palace."

Houses, like people, have a destiny. They live through changes; they grow, especially this one; they become old; they have adventures. When Neruda goes to Europe, his house is secretly occupied by a band of gypsies, who decided to warm themselves during the winter's cold by ripping up the floor boards.

80. Operation "Salvage"

After the fall of the Spanish Republic, his friends who left the peninsula face a tragic fate. We're at the beginning of 1939, and the Second World War will break out in September of that year. The Republican refugees in France are not extended a cordial welcome by the Socialist government of Leon Blum. Under pressure from the right wing, caught in the Non-Intervention Committee's trap, and fearful of Hitler, they dump the Spanish exiles in concentration camps in the South.

There, in Colliure, in a scene out of the Exodus, two days after his arrival in France, death comes to the man whom Neruda considered the most important poet of Spain's Generation of 1898, Antonio Machado. When he learned of it, Neruda recalled the Spaniard's poem "At the Burial of a Friend" where Machado wrote that "The sound of a coffin striking the earth is a perfectly serious thing." He had heard Machado tell the Unified Socialist Youth:

> Perhaps the best advice that can be given to someone who is young is that he be truly young. . . . From a theoretical point of view, I am not a Marxist, I have never been one, and I may very possibly never be one. . . . Nevertheless, I see quite clearly that socialism, insofar as it supposes a way for humans to live together, based on work, on the equitability of means given to all in order to have work, and on the abolition of class privileges, is an inevitable stage on the road to justice. I see clearly that this is the great human experience of our time, to which we all must contribute in some way.

Neruda heard him say this on the first of May in 1937 in Madrid, and he agreed with the older poet's reasoning, but he himself chose to be a Marxist, because that seemed to him to be a way of making access to the road to justice more possible.

In addition, during the closing session of the International Congress of Writers in Valencia, he had heard Machado make a statement which later became classic with him: "To write for the people—my teacher used to say—what more could I wish for!" Just as Neruda sang of the militiamen of 1936, Don Antonio put them under the protection of Jorge Manrique's verse: "After putting one's life on the line so many times in another's cause," those bearing arms are betting their life "on a cause they profoundly care about." Juan de Mairena (Machado's alterego) has descended into the tomb, and on it have fallen "heavy clods of dirt." Neruda hasn't been able to do a thing for his friend, dead on the sand in exile. He will have to save Spaniards still living.

He talks to the Chilean Communist Party, which gets in touch with the Popular Front's minister of government affairs, Abraham Ortega, and with the president of Chile, proposing to them the operation to save the lives of thousands of Spanish Republicans who are struggling in the coastal dunes of southern France, under humiliating conditions, subjected to all kinds of misfortune and deprivation, and in danger of soon being trapped in Hitler's claws. They will have to work fast or it will be too late.

Neruda is given a mission of extreme urgency, with the title of Special Consul for Spanish Immigration, headquartered in Paris. He takes a deep breath of relief mixed with happiness and apprehension. It's a race against the clock, against death. He is in agreement—no need to be like the foolish virgins in the parable who arrive when their lamps are already out of oil.ⁱ He departs at once for his destination.

Actually, Neruda had sought this charge in every possible way. At a dinner they gave him in Santiago to celebrate his participation in the campaign, one of the guests had been the new president of Chile, who had been Gabriela Mistral's sponsor three decades earlier, clearing a path for her through the tangled bureaucratic jungle so that she could enter the secondary teaching profession and become a lyceum director. This poet wasn't asking for a teaching position, but was making a request that struck the president as quite unusual—that he be sent to Europe to organize Spanish immigration. He looked at him in surprise. He didn't know the poet very well and probably thought that, like many who sought positions in France, he just wanted to have a good time in Paris. But Neruda, president of the Alliance of Intellectuals and quite a personality, had worked hard in the campaign, and so his request was granted.

When he reached Paris, Neruda realized the enormity of the task he had undertaken. He made immediate contact with the Spanish Republic's government in exile and explained why he was there. He wanted to help those who were in concentration camps in France. They looked at him with a mixture of sarcasm and hope. This was a question of half a million people. Chile couldn't absorb all of them. A half-million good Spaniards: people who had risked everything, workers who knew their jobs, outstanding intellectuals, including the poets who had survived, but not that poet who reached France with his mother only to succumb within two days.

The mother was ninety years old, and Antonio Machado was sixty-five. When he dies, his mother will live only two more hours. Neruda associated all that with the successive deaths of his father and Doña Trinidad Candia Marverde. But the Machados died as two fugitive émigrés, weighed down by all the sadness and misfortune that can be borne by a body and a spirit imprisoned in the painful awareness of having landed in a concentration camp, like falling into a trap or into a tomb.

Neruda settles down in Paris to mount that effort, which he calls "the noblest responsibility I have ever had in my life." He lives in the Quai de l'Horloge, with "The Ant." Soon, Rafael Alberti and his wife, María Teresa León, will come to share that same roof.

He puts all hands to work. The plan was to fill every nook and cranny of a huge ship with 3,000 to 5,000 Spaniards from among those crowded into camps in southern France. The Spanish government in exile, headed by Dr. Juan Negrín, got hold of a ship, the *Winnipeg*. Neruda works full time with a practicality that is almost unbelievable, given the reputation of poets for being daft. He paid a lot of attention to the refugees' professions, because he was also thinking about their usefulness to his own country. He selected groups of builders, skilled fishermen, experts in paper manufacturing, agronomists; in short, all the fields of work and knowledge that Chile needed.

Among a thousand problems, one stood out as particularly serious: everybody wanted to leave on that ship, which was understandable. For many, it was their only chance to escape from hell, to flee from death. The difficulty was that no ship in the world could hold half a million people. The vessel of hope seemed large, and it turned out in the end to be very small, considering all those who wanted to go aboard. The situation in the camps was worsening, and every day people were dying in epidemics. One can imagine how many letters Neruda was receiving, begging him for space, even if it were only on the deck. One letter said, "Great poet Neruda: I know that your wife is like a little bird that sings in the morning." "The Ant" was bombarded with jokes about being changed into a flying soprano, but the letter touched Neruda and, in the end, the man who considered Delia to be a nightingale got on board.

Alberti witnessed it all and collaborated in everything. Whereas he was a lunatic in his own right, he felt like a sensible man who detected in Neruda qualities of a terrible capricious child, as well as a captivating personality. Be careful not to fall under his spell! One of Pablo's manias in France, mecca of good wine, was to look for Chilean drinks, something that for Alberti was a misguided act of childish patriotism or something worse than betting on which national anthem sounds better. In the middle of the herculean tasks of organizing the voyage of the *Winnipeg,* Neruda would do strange and wondrous things, according to Alberti. Example: They were walking one day along a typical Parisian side street that figures in the novels of past centuries, the *Rue du Chat qui Pêche,* when they spotted an enormous iron key affixed by two supports to the wall above a shoemaker's door.

"Dear *confrère,* have you seen what a marvelous key? I want to take it to Chile for my key collection."

"But that's absurd—a key that's fastened to the wall!"

He went inside to the shoemaker and, spreading his arms wide, asked in French, "Sir, do you have a key this big?"

The shoemaker didn't remember having a key of that size, and he said, "Pardon, sir, a key?"

"Yes, yes, come here. I want to buy that key."

"What do you mean, you want to buy that key? What madness!"

He went back two, three times. The fifth time, he went with a stone-mason from the Communist Party, carrying a ladder. The workman chisled into the wall, and they carried away the key, in exchange for 2,000 francs paid to the shoemaker, who remained convinced that life is full of strange happenings.

81. *The* Winnipeg *Adventure Continues*

The Chilean ambassador in France at the time was Gabriel González Videla, who did not view with sympathy this insane task of saving Republicans, although in his country he had been president of the Committee for Solidarity with Spain. He was put off by the popularity of Neruda, at whose side the ambassador was becoming a shadow. He began to report back to the government in a way that caused problems for the special consul.

Here is where a certain individual puts his nose or his hands into things, by acting as a close advisor in the affair. Neruda used to talk to me about this fellow at every turn, because he was really a character out of a Hitchcock movie, who would become a personage in one of Elsa Triolet's novels. His name was Manuel Arellano Marín, and in the early 1930s he had been a boy wonder at the Catholic University in Santiago. Several of his plays were performed in the city's theaters, and he used to spend his nights in long card games with the rector, Monsignor Carlos Casanueva.

He was sort of a bespectacled snake with a sharp face, evasive watery eyes, long sweaty hands that were never quiet. His sponsors got him a job in the Chilean consulate in New York, which was directed by Alfonso Grez, a man in the export business and personal friend of President Alessandri.

I met Arellano Marín in mid-1938 in New York, when I was there as a member of a large Chilean delegation to the Congress of Youth for Peace, which took place at Vassar College in Poughkeepsie. The presidential election in Chile was approaching, and Arellano Marín's bloodhound instinct told him that the Popular Front might win. He thought he could earn some points with me by announcing his unexpected leftist sympathies, using all his theatrical experience as both author and actor to lay out scenes of almost tearjerking revolutionary sincerity and to declare his readiness to sacrifice everything in order to embrace the cause of the people. I recall that as we were crossing Brooklyn Bridge once, he spoke vaguely about his love for an inaccessible older woman, whom I knew but who had never struck me that way. Besides, he seemed quite attached to his mother.

The night of the Popular Front's victory, he took the first plane out of New York and landed in Santiago the next day. He came straight to see us and announced his irrevocable decision to give up diplomacy and devote his life to communism and the revolution. He wore sandals and no necktie, and declared that he wanted to do people's theater in the streets and stadiums, and to organize choral groups with thousands of workers. He was an impassioned convert, and with the light of Damascus still sparkling in his ever-shifting eyes, he brought gifts for his new comrades.

Two weeks later he was ensconced in the Ministry of Affairs, as an advance man for the Popular Government, turned into advisor to the man chosen by Pedro Aguirre Cerda to be minister of affairs. He received me in what I'll call the map room, because an entire wall was covered by the image of mother earth, on which tiny flags of various colors indicated the location of Chilean embassies and consulates. What happened next brought to mind that scene Neruda had experienced twelve years earlier in his pilgrimage in search of a post abroad, for Manuel Arellano was pointing out various assignments around the world. He looked at me with what seemed to be a good-natured smile and said, "Pick the consulate you want."

"What?" I answered, stupefied.

"Yes, the consulate you want, since you're too young for an embassy."

"I want to work here," I replied. "Besides, it's not my decision alone.

The Party should make the assignments. I'm not asking for anything, nor do I want to leave the country."

Later, I found out that he repeated that scene with several young intellectuals of the period.

This man, who had sworn to give up diplomacy forever and to dedicate himself to developing a revolutionary art for the masses, reached the Chilean embassy in France before Neruda got there. When the poet appeared in Paris, Arellano as principal advisor received him warmly. Neruda introduced him to the leftist literary world, and he became a friend of Louis Aragon and Elsa Triolet. He participated in the negotiations with the Republican government in exile and seemed to be a trustworthy man whose actions appeared to be those of a militant ready to carry out any task.

When the World War begins on the first of September in 1939, Neruda, with Arellano's agreement, gives asylum in the embassy to Aragon and his wife, for the police were looking for the author of *Les beaux quartiers* during that period of "the phoney war." The Spanish Republican Government, which at that moment was between the devil and the deep blue sea, entrusted a good part of its funds to the secure hands of Manuel Arellano Marín, who disappeared shortly afterward, taking the treasury with him. He had gone off on a honeymoon with a Turkish lover, and the money which had been earmarked for saving Spanish lives slipped through his fingers like water.

Years later, after the end of the Second World War, a couple of Republicans finally track him down in a New York hotel and ask him for an accounting. Arellano Marín breaks out in a cold sweat and, on his knees, tearfully begs for forgiveness. The Spaniards leave without a penny and without laying a hand on him.

Several times during his tenure as special consul, Neruda called Arellano's attention to his frenetic and questionable spending sprees and asked him where so much money was coming from. This was in the desperate period just before and after the Nazis took Paris, when fortunes were being paid for life-saving passports, and hoards of gold and jewels were being offered in exchange for a chance to flee to the American continent. Naturally, Neruda's skeptical comments about his squandering of millions got Arellano Marín's hackles up, and with his characteristically visceral cunning he helped to discredit the special consul in the eyes of Santiago officialdom.

Later, after more than one adventure in Hollywood, where he was involved in the journal *Cinelandia,* when he had already used up or lost the riches of this world and was "in a downhill rut" as the tango says, he published a movingly virtuous announcement in *El Diario Ilustrado* describing himself as the living example of an innocent angel who had once been deceived by communism, but now, having cast off his innocent sin, was finally returning in repentance to the Holy Mother's breast.

Many years later, I unexpectedly saw him inside the train from Santiago to Puerto Montt. His gaze was even shiftier, and he had the look of a declining *pícaro*. He had bamboozled the Austral University of Valdivia, where he was once general secretary, no less, but now was turned into a swindler who continued to play his games with overdrawn checks. He fell lower and lower, and was in and out of jail, but he always snared some gullible soul with his con game, at which he was an almost unequalled expert. In her novel, Elsa Triolet doesn't give a complete picture of the irresistible rise and fall of Manuel Arellano Marín, which is a pity, because the fellow's life followed the lines of a perfect parabolic curve, which still cries out for a novelist to describe it from beginning to end.

Neruda's task of selecting the refugees was finished. The passengers were impatient to set sail, and the special consul couldn't wait for the *Winnipeg* to be under way with its cargo, which would find salvation on the other side of the ocean. The poet is assisted by a short fair-haired Spanish youth with a thin face, who speaks with a strong peninsular accent and is perpetual motion personified. Darío Carmona acts occasionally as Neruda's secretary and later settled in Chile, where he worked for many years as an outstanding journalist and captivated women of diverse nationalities with his green eyes and charming talk. After the Pinochet coup he returned to Spain, greatly saddened, but he didn't feel at home in the country of his birth and decided to return to his Spanish-Indian America. He died in an equatorial country dreaming the impossible dreams of the eternal exile.

Due to the unfavorable secret reports from the ambassador and his principal advisor, Neruda's standing at La Moneda government house had fallen, and one day they sent him a curt message: "Newspaper reports say you are administering massive Spanish immigration. I ask you to deny report or to cancel voyage of immigrants." When he read the unexpected ultimatum, he thought of two solutions. First, to call in the press, show them the ship loaded to the gills with 2,000 Spaniards, "read the telegram with a solemn tone and immediately shoot myself in the head." Second solution, to depart on the ship with his immigrants and "disembark in Chile by logic or by poetry."

The Chilean Communist Party intervenes with the government, defining the problem as a matter of life and death. We have already mentioned the difficulty and spottiness of long distance telephone communication in those days, but Neruda picked up the receiver and talked loudly enough to be heard in Chile, where the minister of foreign affairs backs him up, but Chancellor Ortega joins in denouncing Neruda, creating a cabinet crisis which forces the government to give in and authorize the voyage of the *Winnipeg*.

The French authorities congratulated Neruda for what they called "perfect organization." There wasn't a single note of discord among those who were going to depart, people from all over Spain, whose country had fallen apart on them. The world seemed about to cave in, with only a few days left before the outbreak of the Second World War. Later, Neruda would receive a letter from President Aguirre Cerda thanking him for the magnificent Spanish people he had sent to Chile.

The *Winnipeg*—a word he liked from the beginning because "it has wings"—finally raised anchor and set off for Valparaíso, with passengers who both laughed and cried. He maintained afterwards in his *Memoirs* that it was the best poem he had ever written. "Let critics do away with all my poetry, if they like. But this poem, which I evoke today, can't be done away with by anybody."[35]

82. *Reflection of the Spanish Experience*

We went to the port in Valparaíso to wait for the ship. Everybody was there. It was a reception in which the first words of welcome heard by those cramped passengers were songs of the Spanish war, which Chileans sang as if they were their own melodies—"The Fifth Regiment," "Where are You Going, Girl?" and "The Drummer Boy." The newcomers had traveled over several oceans, passing through the Panama Canal to then maneuver in the Pacific Ocean, which was infested by something worse than sharks—Nazi submarines. They were coming to the farthest country on the map and there they saw the port that from on deck looked like a huge multileveled horseshoe, drawing them in with their own hymns and songs that they had sung on the battlefields. They felt a sense of family.

The welcome in Santiago's packed Mapocho station was equally warm. Chileans realized they were greeting people who had suffered deeply and had lost everything. They wanted to somehow show them that here they could begin their life anew. It was a complicated undertaking to find lodging for the refugees in a city that at that time had very limited hotel space. Many people were temporarily put up in private homes.

After completing his work in France, Neruda also returned to Chile by way of the Panama Canal and met again with the *Winnipeg* passengers. He had taken seriously the verse from our national anthem which calls Chile an "asylum from repression."

His dream was for his friends, especially the poets, to come and live in his southern nation, except perhaps Vicente Aleixandre who was ill and never left his house "in a neighborhood full of flowers, between Cuatro Caminos and the budding University City, on Wellington Street." He repeatedly tried to get Rafael Alberti to settle in Chile, but the latter preferred Argentina, a larger and more populous country with publishing opportunities. He spent nineteen years there without a passport, unable to go anywhere. In all, he lived twenty-four years in exile in Argentina and sixteen in Italy.

Neruda didn't lose hope. He used to tell Arturo Serrano Plaja and Vicente Salas Viú, "You're the only friends from my literary life in Spain who have come to my country. I had wanted to bring everybody, and I've not given up. I'll try to bring those who are in Mexico, Buenos Aires, Santo Domingo, Spain."[36]

Yes, he wanted to bring them all. . . . Oh, if only he could have saved those who died! He imagined Lorca in Santiago . . . He missed Miguel Hernández. He had been on the point of bringing him when Miguel had been freed from his earlier imprisonment by Cardinal Baudrillart's direct request to Franco. The prelate is almost blind and after listening to poems dedicated to the Holy Sacrament, which were written by Miguel as a boy, he is moved to make the request. The poet takes refuge in the Chilean embassy in Madrid, and from there he writes to Neruda, "I will come to Chile. I'm going to Orihuela to get my wife . . ." A fatal trip, for they incarcerate him again, and he will leave prison only as a corpse. In an article Neruda publishes on 20 April 1940 in the Santiago journal *Qué Hubo,* he talks about what his contact with Spain has meant to him. Recently returned to his own country, with the *Winnipeg*'s odyssey completed, he concludes that Spain clarified his thinking and that he, in turn, helped Spaniards with what he terms "profound problems, before, during, and after the war."

> You have helped me more. You have shown me a happy and nurtured friendship, and your intellectual decorum surprised me at first, for I was coming from the cruel envy of my own country, from its torment. After

you accepted me as your own, you gave such certainty to my reason for being and to my poetry that I could peacefully go on to struggle in the ranks of the people. Your friendship and your nobility helped me more than treaties.

And up till now, this simple road is the only one that I can see for all intellectuals.[37]

I went to visit him on 2 January 1940, when he got off the ship. As I interviewed him for *Qué Hubo,* he gave me a new poem for publication, "Hymn and Return." It was the last page he would devote to the *Winnipeg,* a leaf now being turned over in order that he could dedicate himself more completely to his own country. He had gone out to search the earth for children for Chile and to lift up the fallen in her name. Now, at least for a while, he wants to look deeply at what he judges at that time to be the enigma of his country, transformed into a spot of light that shines in the dark sky of the American continent. Affirmation and uneasiness. He wonders whether his country will be able to protect that light, which he calls difficult, "this destiny of human beings / that calls on you to defend a strange flower / all alone, in the immensity of slumbering America."

Like any good poet, he had a prophetic vision, an alert and watchful conscience that knew what an arduous task it is to defend that light in these regions.

That year of 1940 brings the publication in Buenos Aires of what is considered to be the first in-depth critical study of his work, *Poetry and Style in Pablo Neruda* by the Spaniard Amado Alonso. More than forty years have gone by since its appearance, and the stylistic method therein raises many arguments, but in its day it was a milestone. Since then, Nerudian studies has become a critical area with authorities in almost all European and American countries, not to mention several in Asia. It regularly finds expression in seminars and roundtable discussions and is a mandatory topic for symposia and publications.

Amado Alonso's interpretation covers Neruda up to the *Residence,* which for him represents a point of increasing introspection, anguish and disintegration, "an apocalypse without God." Prior to *Residence,* he sees in the poet a sadness which takes comfort from its own beauty, a melancholy that will become "truly infinite" sorrow only in the *Residence.* Alonso's subtitle is decisive—*Interpretation of a Hermetic Poetry.* When his book is published, Neruda is turning over a new leaf; he comes out of seclusion into a clarity which marks the transformation his life and his work experienced as a result of his catalytic experience in the Spanish war.

83. Repentance

His friends gather round him almost every night in Los Guindos, where they eat and drink to their heart's content and to the extent of the provisions of the house. The time invariably comes when Neruda goes off to bed, but this doesn't mean the discussions come to an end. Everybody feels at home, and each one will leave whenever he pleases. As a general rule, Pablo sleeps well, without insomnia, on his back to begin with, and maybe snoring, though he's not sure nor does he care. One night, as he sleeps, he has the feeling that his faithful Chilean Kuthaka is licking his hands, a habit the dog has just to show his fond attachment to his master. But suddenly the master awakes with a sensation of extremely wet hands under a great tangle of hair that isn't quite like Kuthaka but more like a lion, a lion that is weeping, sobbing and talking like a man. To be exact, a man asking forgiveness.

"Pablo, Pablito, I'm a coward and a traitor. I want you to forgive me. I'm a traitor," the kneeling giant repeats, his shoulders shuddering in lamentation.

Neruda comes fully awake. In the darkness, he makes out the owner of the leonine head, but he has already identified him by his trembling supplicant voice.

"I can't hide it from you, Pablito. I've been to Pablo de Rokha's house. We began to drink and he said ugly things about you. I didn't stick up for you, just kept quiet like a louse. And now I have to confess it."

Pablo decided his friend was a Latin-Americanized character out of Dostoievsky, and he quickly gave absolution to the pathetic fellow, partly so that he'd let him sleep in peace.

84. Magical and Violent Country

Neruda was always going away and always coming back, but never haphazardly. He knew where he was going and what he was looking for. Now his telescopic gaze was fixed on a country that fascinated him, the most populous of Spanish-speaking countries, the most colorful, and endowed with such an indigenous presence. Like Gabriela Mistral, Neruda felt in the marrow of his bones the hypnotic spell of "flowery and thorny" Mexico.

The Popular Front government names him consul general in Mexico. He travels on the Japanese ship *Rácuyo Maru*, along with his friend and comrade Luis Enrique Délano, who has also been named a consul in Mexico City. They disembark in Manzanillo in August 1940, and after one day in Guadalajara, they go by train to the capital. From his room in the Montejo Hotel on the Paseo de la Reforma, he summons his friends, the Spanish intellectuals who had landed in that land of generous asylum: the poets José Herrera Petere, Juan Rejano, Pedro Garfias, Lorenzo Varela; the cinematographer Eduardo Ugarte, and the painter Miguel Prieto.

He soon rents an apartment on Revillagigedo Street, where he plays host to the anti-Fascist German writers Ludwig Renn and Bodo Uhse. Anna Seghers, who will become his very dear friend, along with her husband Johann Lorenz Schmidt (Laszlo Radvanyi), arrives later, following adventurous sea voyages and round-about journeys. They have had to escape from the Vichy regime in France and then travel on the French ship *Paul Lemerle* headed for Martinique. The ocean crossing had to originate in the Algerian port of Oran, passing by Casablanca and the Strait of Gibraltar to land in Santo Domingo, where Trujillo rules in glory and cruelty. They had to suffer through the drama of visas, in that period of nervous telegrams and anxiety about ever reaching the dreamed-of Mexican port of Veracruz.

Through their conversations and thoughts, the image of the *Winnipeg,* the ship of life, still sails. It makes other crossings, but now as a ghost ship so that the Third Reich's submarines don't find it bearing more anti-Fascists to American soil. Neruda hears about the new feats of the now legendary ship, how it transports political refugees, stopping in Port of Spain, going on by way of Barbados. There the passengers hear a news item—Hitler has invaded the Soviet Union and expects to conquer it in six weeks, according to the confident announcement over German radio.

The *Winnipeg* had a relative, the Portuguese ship *Serpa Pinto,* which was the last one to head for Mexico with German anti-Fascists on board. Their journey from Casablanca to Veracruz began in November 1941 and lasted twenty-nine days, through the Azores, Bermuda, Santo Domingo, Cuba, and Mexico. When they were passing by Santo Domingo, they learned of the outbreak of war between Japan and the United States.

Neruda has left ample proof of Mexico's seductive hold on him. It's an endless country if one travels it lengthways, and from night to day it is brilliant in color. He went everywhere, sniffing out the pre-Columbian element, returning to the pyramids, buying figs, stopping in colonial houses. He observed nature with a gaze that delighted in volcanoes, mountains, deserts, birds, and butterflies bigger than he had ever seen anywhere. He was fascinated by Yucatán, Nayarit, Baja California. He always searched out marketplaces, but especially there, "because Mexico is present in the marketplaces." There he graduated as a specialist in sea shells, putting together a collection of 15,000 different examples.

He moves to a larger house, the Rosa María villa. Close by, near an old free-form swimming pool, was where the Chilean boxer Raúl Carabantes trained for his unsuccessful bout with Kid Azteca. There where the fighter used to make the punching bag resound with rat-a-tat-tats, the poet Ramón López Velarde used to live, and when the boxer left, he was replaced by Neruda's Spanish friends, who never struck anybody: the poet León Felipe, Marx's Spanish translator Wenceslao Roces, the essayist Sánchez Vásquez, the poet-painter Moreno Villa, the former director of *Cruz y Raya* José Bergamín, the writer Constancia de la Mora, the air force general Ignacio Hidalgo de Cisneros, the Mexicans Carlos Pellicer and Octavio Paz, the Guatemalan Cardoza y Aragón, and often the German novelist Anna Seghers. He always had company for dinner, and went often to visit Alfonso Reyes, Enrique González Martínez, General Heriberto Jara, and the writer José Mancisidor.

Shortly after the Popular Front victory in Chile, when the Chillán earthquake struck in January 1939, the Mexican government put forth a request for a visa to Chile from the painter David Alfaro Siqueiros, who had recently been released from imprisonment, along with his wife Angélica Arenal. The idea was to demonstrate solidarity by building a school in Chillán with murals by Siqueiros and Xavier Guerrero.

Luis Enrique Délano gives an eyewitness account in his essay "Pablo Neruda in Mexico"[38] of how Neruda granted the visa without formally asking for authorization from the ministry of foreign affairs. The response was to accuse him of a "lack of discipline" and suspend him without pay for one month. Thanks to this lack of discipline, Chillán's Mexico School acquired the mural *Death to the Invader*.

Some time later, early one morning in Santiago's Alameda Station, we boarded a coach on the presidential train to go to Chillán for the public opening of the Mexico School and its murals. Pedro Aguirre Cerda had died, and the president who traveled in the entourage was the tall aquiline-nosed Juan Antonio Ríos. Siqueiros was enthusiastically received, and someone reminisced that the poet had done well to grant the visa that earned him a ministerial reprimand and sanction.

In Mexico, Neruda published *Araucanía,* a stimulating journal whose cover pictured an indigenous woman. Sinfully bad taste! Another slap on the hands from the ministry—in Mexico they would think that Chile was a country of Indians! And that's how *Araucanía* was born and died, in only one issue, thanks to the authorities' white complex.

Neruda was in Mexico during the period of Lázaro Cárdenas and during the Nazi invasion of the Soviet Union. He joined the Committee to Aid the Russian War Effort, headed by Antonio Castro Leal. In reality, the Soviet Union was all alone in resisting the attack. Support for opening the second front was becoming more clamorous, and Neruda turned that feeling into poetry which gave rise to arguments. He writes in the "Song to Stalingrad" the accusatory lines, "Are you leaving them alone? Soon they'll come after you! . . . You want more dead men on the Eastern Front / until the dead fill your sky completely." The poem was read in the theater of the electricians' union and posted on the walls of Mexico City. The *Novedades* magazine expressed indignation at such desecration of the streets, which are not appropriate for poetry and even less for political poetry. Since the poet's call went unheeded, he stubbornly repeated it in his "New Love Song for Stalingrad," in which he responds to the first poem's detractors. He read it at a big banquet of intellectuals in honor of the Soviet Union, where Anna Seghers also spoke movingly. Her novel, *The Seventh Cross,* had been made into a Hollywood film and was seen around the world, portraying the sacrifice and selflessness of anti-Fascist Germans in the struggle against Hitler. The banquet also marked the novel's publication in a Spanish translation by Wenceslao Roces. The "New Love Song for Stalingrad," which quickly became famous, is an acme of rhymed quartet and epic poetry, with a personal reference in which the poet emphasizes the change his work has undergone:

> I once wrote about time and water,
> I learned of mourning and its metallic purple,
> I once wrote of the sky and the apple,
>   now I write of Stalingrad.

He will pay dearly for those poems plastered on walls. In Cuernavaca's Amatlán Park, so reminiscent of a Mexican eclogue, one placid Sunday afternoon Neruda and Delia are there with Délano and his wife Lola Falcón, their son Poli, who will later be a penetrating short-story writer, and their friend Clara Porset. They're talking about the main topic of those days, the war that rages in the distance and still reverberates behind them all. Their conversation is quite audible and full of constant aversions to fascists. The euphoric moment came when they raised their glasses to toast

President Roosevelt and Avila Camacho. Suddenly an avalanche falls on them, unleashed by a bunch of German Nazis who were drinking beer at a private table and attacked them without warning and without any regard for the women nor the child. The fray intensified, going from fisticuffs to blows with chairs and bottles. Blood started flowing from a wound on Neruda's head, struck by either a rock or a pistol, whereupon the aggressors fled in an automobile. The assistant prosecutor brought charges, but the police never found the perpetrators. Pablo was taken to the emergency room in Cuernavaca with a wound nearly four inches long on the upper part of his head. After he was taken to Mexico City, the doctors ordered a long period of absolute immobility in case he might have suffered a brain concussion. He would offer an immediate reply to the attackers with his prologue to Ilya Ehrenburg's book, *Death to the Invader*.

85. Mexican Miscellany

Neruda gave prophetic support in 1941 to two Mexican students who were returning from a summer session at the University of Chile. These two friends were Luis Echeverría and José López Portillo, who in time would be elected successive presidents of Mexico. His speech was delivered in the National Preparatory School's Bolívar Auditorium and was published in the journal *Tierra Nueva*. It can be seen that the poet wasn't just tossing out words like flowers at a parade nor like diplomatic sweets:

> A new oratorical mythology leads us to easy flattery. We think we're mutually elevating each other when we point out the similarities between our two countries. As for me, I assure you that two sister nations as different from each other as Mexico and Chile do not exist. Between blue Acapulco and polar Punta Arenas there's a whole world of difference in climate, race, and geography . . . As Mexicans and Chileans, we meet only in our roots, and that's where we should look for each other: in our roots' hunger and unsatisfaction, in the search for bread and truth, in our same needs, our same anxieties; yes, in the earth, in our origins, and in our earthly struggle is where we mix with all our brothers, with all the slaves of hunger, with all the poor of the world.[39]

Neruda's consular office and houses, including those he occupied later on Elba and Varsovia Streets, were beehives of activity, full of the comings and goings of Mexican intellectuals and exiled European anti-

Fascists. The air was filled with the impassioned conversation of Vittorio Vidali, the Fifth Regiment's legendary Commander Carlos, and his wife, the Italian photographer Tina Modotti, who had been the companion of the Cuban revolutionary Julio Antonio Mella. The two had been walking together on a Mexico City street when Gerardo Machado's assassins riddled Mella with bullets. Tina would also soon depart this world, evoking a farewell poem from Neruda, "Tina Modotti Has Died," both a song to a valiant-hearted sister and a message to the Italian people who soon will be liberated from fascism. The poet perceives the signs that are floating in the air:

> In your country's old kitchens, on the roads
> covered with dust, something is said, something stirs,
> something again calls to your shining people,
> something awakens and sings.

Another participant in those discussions was Mario Montagnana, Italian anti-Fascist and brother-in-law of Palmiro Togliatti. All of intellectual and artistic Mexico felt at home there, including the then-young writer Fernando Benítez, and a fascinating woman, María Asúnsolo, along with the actress Rosario Revueltas and her brother Silvestre, the composer who let his music speak for him.

One of the first things Neruda did was to give a party for the Mexicans who had been in Spain. Guests included Elena Garro, Juan de la Cabada, Octavio Paz, and Silvestre Revueltas. Three days later, at a concert at the Bellas Artes, the audience gave a standing ovation to a piece by Revueltas, demanding that he take a bow, but he could not accept, for he had just died. The viewing of the remains took place in that very hall. Later, near the open crypt, Neruda read the minor oration, "To Silvestre Revueltas of Mexico, at His Death," saying "From this day forth your music-filled name will soar / as from a bell whenever your country is tolled."

Those whom Mexicans call *gachupines* (Spaniards) are always coming into Neruda's house through its constantly open door. Some day someone should study a bit the power the poet had for attracting people to him. On occasion, there was the risk of creating a kind of court, for unrestrained admirers discovered in him a sort of king of poetry, who had to be paid appropriate homage. But he was a plebeian at heart, or rather a man of the people, and this was recognized most perceptively by his wife,

"The Ant." A democratic spirit prevailed in most of their acquaintances, who were friends rather than courtesans.

In Mexico, this curious child enjoyed a perpetual Sunday, especially when he could go to the Lagunilla market to discover secondhand items, old picture postcards, music boxes, irregular-shaped glasses, brilliantly colored bottles, and always more shells and more butterflies, along with paintings by unschooled romantic artists. He writes to Juan de la Cabada requesting him to ask the fishermen in Yucatán and Campeche to find him some deep-water shells, and although Neruda received no response, the poet took Juan into his house for four or five months in 1943, his house that was full of loquacious *gachupines*. During the lengthy visit, at five or six in the morning, while Delia was still asleep, Neruda and his friend used to go out to eat maguey grubs in a cantina on 16 de Septiembre and Colima Streets, and then they would stroll leisurely through the city.

Neruda had his first falling-out with Octavio Paz and José Bergamín over a disagreement about the poets included in their anthology of Spanish American poetry, *Laurel,* published by Séneca in 1940. They had excluded three poets whom he considered essential: Herrera y Reissig, Nicolás Guillén, and León Felipe.

Thus, in Mexico just as in Spain, Neruda provoked literary tempests. The break with Octavio Paz occurred at a banquet in the Chilean's honor. Divided in two camps, Neruda-ists and anti-Neruda-ists, the poets matched the Mexican painters in their ability to openly declare their guerrilla war. The Chilean not only broke piñatas in his patio at home but also in literature's patio, planting not peace but the sword, which was not at all to the liking of Paz (whose name means "peace") and other poets who, despite the stridency of one Maples Arce, had been discrete up until then and did not cultivate noisy quarrels. In a seemingly diplomatic interview, Neruda made a statement infused with both literary criticism and paradox: "In Mexico you have some great poets; I would like for Chile's poets to have that special quality that is rooted in form, like poets here . . . I can't tell poets in Chile anything about this, because I have purposely attempted to do away with form, that form which is appropriate to Mexico."[40] In one way, he drew a line of demarcation, which was not purely literary, but was also defined by the notion of a suffering poetry, which would become greater as it became more human, greater as it became a vessel for a content that embraced an obligation capable of being translated into the transformation of society. He said as much in Morelia's San Nicolás de Hidalgo University, when he was given an honorary master's degree. In his address to the students, he offered them an unmistakable message, which was wildly received:

> As of today, I take on your existence as an acquired characteristic, young brothers and sisters, and I know that from now on, in my thoughts, neither the forests nor the beautiful monumental stones will be empty, but they will be inhabited by fire, by youth, by hope, by what you are and will be, by the spirit that you protect with your presence in this hall, surrounding a man who searches for no other way to be great than the way of being human. . . . Let my passage among you, young and fraternal hearts, help you to journey from Morelia's noble stones along the path of knowledge, of culture, toward ultimate brotherhood among all men.[41]

War was raging in Europe and inflaming emotions, beginning with those of the poet. He was in no way neutral, but rather he spoke up everywhere about his sympathies and antipathies. In his "New Love Song for Stalingrad" he answers impugning poets directly, without any kid gloves. He refers pointedly to the old beautifully plumed swan, whose neck had to be twisted, according to the poetic battle cry of González Martínez:

> I know that the old young man of changing
> plumage, like a leather-bound swan,
> unbinds his noteworthy sorrow
>   for my love cry for Stalingrad.

> I put my soul where I want,
> and I don't feed on worn-out paper
> flavored by ink and printing.
>   I was born to sing of Stalingrad.

As a result, political attacks were added to the literary polemic, and they again reached the point of physical aggression. Once again, in the Bolívar Theater and precisely during an homage to the liberator of that name, after a speech on "Bolívar, a Spanish Patriot" by the philosopher Joaquín Xirau, Neruda's "Song for Bolívar" was heard for the first time in public. The audience was caught unawares when a group of falangists interrupted Neruda, shouting "Death to the Spanish Republic!" and "Long live the Generalíssimo!" The listeners reacted and within minutes the elegant room became a battlefield of Agramante. The university took great pains to make up for it and published the "Song for Bolívar" in a beautiful monographic edition with illustrations by Julio Prieto.

In 1943, he attempted to publish a journal in which poetry and politics would go hand in hand. There were long deliberations about what to call it, before they decided on *La Sangre y la Letra* (Blood and Writing). Neruda would be the publisher, with José Iturriaga, Andrés Henestroza, and Juan Rejano as editors, and Wilberto Cantón as secretary. Neruda was also the treasurer, and the money which would be used to finance the journal was kept in an illustrated edition of Walt Whitman. One day, he went to get the money and it had disappeared. He turned the house upside down, pulling up the rug and ranting all the while. Cantón picked up the copy of *Leaves of Grass* and examined it closely. In a corner of the cover there was a message, "Refer to Bernal Díaz del Castillo, Vol. II, page 309." On page 309 of that book there was another note, "See Santa Teresa, page 120." And from Santa Teresa they went to Milocz, and then to César Vallejo, and to Elizabeth Barrett Browning, and from her to Aeschylus, Dante, Rainer Maria Rilke, Plato, Rabindranath Tagore, Alonso de Ercilla, Goethe, Dostoievsky . . . After a trip through all of world literature, they found the money in a treasury of children's literature, at page 213 of Andersen's stories. The practical joker's identity was never discovered, and the journal never came to fruition. Délano claims that the perpetrator of the dirty trick was Jaled Mujacs, a geologist and antiquarian whose principal activity was as an expert fabricator of such puzzles.

It is common knowledge that Neruda liked to marry off his friends and name their children. In his Los Guindos house in Santiago, they held the wedding of Margarita Aguirre, who was his secretary and would be his biographer, and his Argentine comrade Rodolfo Araoz Alfaro, a gentleman with the look of an old-time gaucho, who served as lawyer for victims of political persecution. In Neruda's home in Mexico City, the daughter of Andrés Henestroza was baptized Cibeles. That was the day the property owner evicted his tenant Pablo Neruda, not so much because he had 500 guests but because many of them, with hundreds of liters of mezcal and tequila in their system, went wild and turned into monkeys, climbing trees and breaking branches in an attempt to better contemplate from on high the primitive and classical Greek plays being acted out by José Revueltas and Neruda himself.

Henestroza tells of the poet's taking any gathering as an excuse to dress up as a general, a fireman, or a ticket collector. His interpretation was that Neruda wore disguises because he was horrified by his ugliness, a rather questionable supposition that makes no sense to me.

He used to give his friends special presents, like that of early 1943—a hundred printed copies of his *General Song of Chile,* which is the embryo of what will be the epic *General Song.*

86. Battles, Serenades, and Slashes

As in Spain, so too in Mexico, Neruda is recognized as the poet who never declares a truce, convinced as he is that he must serve poetry as history's recording secretary, with a certain right to recreate and recount history in his own voice. Whereas *Spain in My Heart* is designated as Part IV of the *Third Residence,* Part V corresponds in great part to poems conceived in Mexico. In addition to the first two "Love Songs for Stalingrad," there he also writes his "Seventh of November. Ode to a Victorious Day." Hitler had sent out invitations for a 7 November 1941 celebration of his capture of Leningrad, to be held in the Hotel Astoria across from St. Isaac Cathedral on the Neva River. Hitler was equally confident he would ultimately celebrate in the Kremlin after the fall of Moscow. In the poet's heart, as he followed every minute of the back-and-forth battles, he praises the heroes and hopes that that "army made of the people and steel" will plant "a rose as big as the moon" on the field of victory. He says it from a personal autobiographical point of view, knowing that in his respect for the combatants he speaks for millions:

> On this day I greet you, Soviet Union,
> with humility: I am a writer and a poet.
> My father was a railroad man; we were always poor.
> Yesterday I was with you, far off in my tiny
> country of great rains. There your name grew
> warm, burning in the breast of the people
> until it reached clear to my homeland's sky!

He will never paint all Germans with the same Fascist brush. Proof of the old historical truth about the day and night sides of nations comes to him in his very deep and friendly relationship with the German exiles in Mexico, several of whom he had met during the Spanish war where they served in the International Brigades. Furthermore, he knows the names of Marx and Engels very well, and he has loved Heine since he was a boy. The wartime attribution of the poem "The Lorelei" to "an unknown author" strikes him as an affront to all poets, a declaration of war against beauty. "Free Germany, who says you don't fight? Your dead speak across the earth . . . Brigades / of German brothers: / you crossed the whole world's silence / to put your great heart / at our side." He invokes forbidden names: Einstein, "a voice full of rivers," Heine, Mendelssohn, . . . "Thaelmann's voice like an underground river."

There in Mexico, surrounded by his Catalunyan friends, he writes his "Song to the Death and Resurrection of Luis Companys."

His poetry has inspired many revolutionaries. In his days in the Bolivian jungles, Ché Guevara always carried a copy of the *General Song,* in which he underlined a significant and almost autobiographical verse in the "Song for Bolívar," which says "You, tiny corpse of a valiant captain." A premonition of his own fate.

In March 1942, Neruda visits Cuba for the first time, at the invitation of José María Chacón y Calvo, cultural director for the ministry of education. He gave several lectures, including two on Quevedo, in the National Academy of Arts and Letters. There he evoked for the first time in America His Majesty's royal courier Don Juan de Tarsis, count of Villamediana and impassioned admirer of Queen Isabel, who one day set fire to the curtains in the palace theater in order to have an excuse to flee with the beloved but forbidden royal personage in his arms. In Havana, he looks back on the Araucanians, and he recalls a young Cuban who had fallen in defense of the Spanish Republic and lies forever in the Brunete cemetery "This is Alberto Sánchez, Cuban, taciturn, strong and small of stature, a captain at twenty."

He adds some verses that back in 1942 foretold the Cuban revolution:

> Praise another of Cuba's heroes, strong and fragrant Cuba,
> remember the one who sleeps in Spain,
> sleeps so that you may wake, so that earth does not sleep,
> and so that above his laurels which rot in a distant grave,
> may one day be heard your march, your song, my song,
> our song, the only one, the song of Freedom and Victory.[42]

During that month of suspension from his consular duties because of the "Siqueiros affair," he traveled to Guatemala, where he began a friendship with Miguel Angel Asturias that lasts for the remainder of their lives. In a way, these two resembled each other in the chest and midsection that jutted forward like those of turkeys. Someone once saw them walking together and nicknamed them "the two turkey-gobblers." But Neruda always gave a man the honor due him, and he used to call Miguel Angel "The Great Turkey-gobbler."

On 18 June 1943 in Mexico, death came to Doña Leocadia Felizardo de Prestes, mother of the Brazilian Communist leader Luis Carlos Prestes. Brazil's president Getúlio Vargas denied Mexico's request to allow the woman's son to leave his triangular prison cell in Rio de Janeiro in order to attend his mother's funeral.

Neruda, at the grave, said, "The petty tyrant wants to hide the flame / with his little cold bat wings." Apparently the reference to bats hit a sore spot in Getúlio Vargas, and the Brazilian ambassador made some bitter comments, giving rise to the suggestion that the Chilean consul would be withdrawn from Mexico because of Itamaraty's protest in La Moneda government house in Chile. Neruda responded:

> As Chile's general consul (and not a diplomatic representative) my duty is to work for intensified trade relations between Mexico and my country. But as a writer, my duty is to defend liberty as an absolute norm of the human and civic condition, and neither complaints nor incidents of any sort will change my behavior or my poetry . . . I am a man who is not in the habit of recanting my actions, and even less so when it is a question of living up to my obligations as a free man. . . . We Chilean writers have a tradition: in accepting a public responsibility or a government position, however exalted or modest it may be, we are not in the habit of mortgaging our liberty nor our dignity as free men, much less changing our fidelity to the ideological or social principles that each one of us represents in his own right . . . In regard to the legal situation of Luis Carlos Prestes, official claims are not enough. We all know how certain legal actions are manufactured on the basis of common crimes, in order to annihilate political adversaries.[43]

Then comes the melancholy linkage between journeys and mourning, the distant memory of a two-story house penetrated by the smell of camphor, the empty dining room, the repeated "because I'm sad and I travel, / and I know the world and I'm sad." Memories of a fatally marked maternity. He wants only for the little child "to be able to talk and not die," but the time comes when "there is nothing but tears, nothing but tears, / because there's only suffering, just suffering, / and nothing but tears." It is 1942, and he has just received word that his daughter Malva Marina has died in Holland. He is disconsolate and very anxious to return to Chile. Overwhelming nostalgia and an irresistible urge to go back lead him to make concrete plans.

He made a mental inventory of his stay in Mexico, then pronounced it aloud: He is fondest of the agronomists and the painters rather than many of the poets, whom he reproaches for their "lack of civic morals," once more eliciting extremely virulent attacks from Octavio Paz and José Luis Martínez.

The reply to their furious charges is announced on posters affixed to the city's walls, inviting people to a farewell homage to Neruda. Despite its sports setting, the organizers weren't Basque jai alai players, boxers, football players, or wrestling champions, but rather writers, musicians, ceramists, professors, diplomats, political and trade union leaders, congressmen.

On 27 August 1943, Mexicans would bid farewell to Neruda. All his acquaintances and connections want to attend the event not to say "farewell" but "until we meet again." There was a flood of gatherings and fond toasts in private homes and restaurants, and the University of Morelia very solemnly awarded him an honorary doctorate. Everything was to culminate in a huge public farewell. Since no place was large enough, they had to resort to a sports stadium, the Mexico Frontón, where the field was turned into an immense dining room for more than 2,000 people to send off a foreign poet, a completely unheard-of occurrence.

He wrote a poem for the occasion, first calling it "On Mexico's Lips" but then changing it to "On Mexico's Walls." In it he gave testimony of events he had experienced, heartfelt acknowledgments, and openly expressed gratitude: "I sing of Cárdenas. I was there, / I lived the Castillian torment . . . / Then only the red star of Russia and the gaze / of Cárdenas glowed in mankind's night. / General, president of America, in this song I give you / a bit of the light that I gathered in Spain."

Thus he said farewell, for the moment, to Mexico, which always intrigued him as an American millenary country, a land with germinating powers. In that autobiography in verse that he called *Notes from Isla Negra,* he harmonizes his "Serenade for Mexico." He had set his southern foot in the soil of the most northern of sister countries, and as he traveled it he felt as if the earth were saturated with himself. There he was astounded a thousand times by the fantasy of her people and her natural environment. He was moved by "the violin of nocturnal / sawmills, the universal / cantata / of a secret / village of cicadas."

He was awed by that subterranean, prehistoric world which was more alive in Mexico than anywhere else. He felt that the syllables of the past were in his veins, in his breath, and he had a duty to give expression to them.

As soon as he gets back to Chile, whenever he sits down and rests his chin on his hand in front of the picture window of his Isla Negra house, he will imagine that the birds plunging down in search of something in the sea will some day land "on the shores of indomitable Mexico, . . . the last of the magical countries," as if following "a mysterious path." He commends those birds to the earth, to her brother the sea, "so they will descend / on the phosphorescent aniline / of crackling indigo / and spread the map of their flight / over the Mexican Californias."

On September first in 1943, the Balbuena airport was filled with mariachi groups singing farewell to their poet colleague, whose own verses had also become songs. They hadn't forgotten that he had written a "Minor Oratory" for a Mexican musician who, though he was not a mariachi nor had he sung in Garibaldi Square, nonetheless was esteemed as a member of the same guild as those who sang folksongs. They sent the traveler on his way with "Las Golondrinas."

87. Ascent to Origins

When the plane lands in Bogotá, it is boarded by a protocol officer from the ministry of affairs, dressed in proper black and wearing a beribboned hat, which he removes as he greets him with Napoleonic rhetoric: "Four hundred poets await you."

Neruda didn't so much associate the statement with millenary Egyptian pyramids and realms, as with Rubén Darío's four hundred elephants.

"Four hundred! And what am I going to do in the midst of so many poets?"

His seemingly sleepy eyes were always watching, gathering material. In his mind he was incubating a plan for a symphonic poem about America. He had observed that pinched waist where the continent narrows and then spreads out, and will one day memorialize Vasco Núñez de Balboa with a reference to the wound of the Panama Canal, his first stop on the trip back to Chile.

Now he will make his second stop in Bogotá, known as the "Athens of America." The man in black wasn't mistaken; the Techo airport had never seen such a noisy mixture of propellers and poets, with all generations waiting to receive the sacred creature, a fabled lion. That same afternoon, in the reception room of the house belonging to the Chilean consul, poet Juan Guzmán Cruchaga, they all gathered together again: Jorge Zalamea, León de Greiff, Jorge Rojas, Gerardo Valencia, José Umaña Bernal, Carlos Martín, Darío Samper, Jaime Posada, Fernando Charry Lara . . . The emotional moment is floridly described by Eduardo Carranza: "There among us was our immense poet, our great brother, our new father and magical teacher!" He takes his cue from Darío's reference to Verlaine as a "celestial *liróforo*," a bearer of lyric. Nevertheless, this *liróforo* who had come down from the sky belonged to the earth rather than to the heavens.

So much was he a part of the earth that the discussion soon divided along ideological lines. The traveler's head became the target for the Jovian political rages of Colombian conservatism's boss, Laureano Gómez, who fired at him with murderous passion from his *El Siglo* newspaper. Deep within himself Neruda felt the roar of the old volcano that always spewed forth his sulfuric responses to venomous attacks. He learned that a month prior to his arrival in Colombia, *El Siglo* had begun to publish anti-Neruda editorials in which the insults contained more noise than truth. They were rudimentary assaults, but possibly Neruda was just a pretext, because at bottom what Gómez was attempting to do, with his usual harshness, was to attack the sitting Colombian President Alfonso López. Considering the two overt antagonists, it was only natural that the battles would sometimes take on a literary shape: the ultramontane leader repeatedly criticized the "Stone and Sky" group of poets, who replied with more stone than sky. Neruda didn't remain silent and unsheathed his pen to respond in his favorite green ink with a series of "Punitive Sonnets."

The return trip was filled with detours in which just about everything happened. It took two months and four days for him to reach Chile. Since he was flying, it's obvious that the stops turned into lengthy stays to allow him to absorb the countries he was visiting—and with good reason, for he believed that he didn't know South America at all. He felt that the time had come to become more profoundly and precisely acquainted at first hand with his continent and with what that world was made of. Up to that time, he had been just a Chilean who fell headlong into the Orient, then awoke in the violent splendor of Spain after spending a brief time in Buenos Aires. It was Mexico that really gave him the disturbing sense of an almost unknown America, to which he owed something, for he had never penetrated his own subsoil. Therefore, when he reached this other pre-Columbian empire, he realized that he must visit Cuzco and Machu Picchu. It was a meeting he had anticipated for a long time. Greatly stimulated by his Mexican experience, he had a growing notion that beneath his feet there was a buried universe on which he was treading almost unaware of its existence. His roots were there, not individual roots but the origins of all those peoples that he belonged to.

That apparently ordinary journey later took on a unique outline. Just as Bolívar had called Alexander Humboldt the second discoverer of America, there are some who consider Pablo Neruda to be the second discoverer of Machu Picchu. He didn't have to work as hard at it as Hiram Bingham, granted, and Neruda's discovery was intellectual in nature.

There are photographs of "The Ant" and Neruda walking about the fortress city in shirt sleeves with his jacket over his arm, showing no evidence of any special solemnity. In addition, an old anecdote will be repeated over and over again about an unserious reply to a serious question: "What do you feel, honored poet, in the presence of this centuries-old sight?" "I feel that it's the most ideal place to have a barbeque," he's supposed to have replied. Some time later, when he is asked about the accuracy of the quip, he dubiously explains, "I don't know whether I said it. But perhaps when one is struck dumb by a colossal and mysterious phenomenon and he's asked a transcendental question, the first psychological defense of someone who is face-to-face with a moment out of eternity is to grab hold of the most obvious everyday phenomenon in order to affirm his earthly existence."

Many events had an immediate poetic reaction in Neruda. He would experience something and within minutes or a few hours he would write the poem that had been suddenly awakened in him by the suggestion of a face, a conversation, a whispering poplar, a friend's death. His poetic reaction seemed to be instantaneous. That is not the case with Machu Picchu, which entered into him like a seed that germinates slowly and deeply, and was two years in sending its flower to the surface. He visited Machu Picchu in October 1943, wrote the poem in Isla Negra in August and September of 1945, and published it for the first time in 1946.

Those two years of maturation should be understood as the time needed for him to develop the evolving idea that had been born as he contemplated the lost city, an idea which was also associated with events in his own personal and political life that serve to define more clearly his position in regard to society and history.

When he writes the poem, he is already a senator from the Chilean Communist Party, representing a region that until 1879 had been part of Peru and Bolivia. Not very far from Machu Picchu, it had been sort of a province of the Inca empire. Many of the field workers who elected him to congress are direct descendants of his poem's Juan Comefrío, Juan Cortapiedras, Juan Piesdescalzos. Offspring of Wiracocha and Estrella Verde, grandsons of the Turquesa, today are voters in Tarapacá and Antofagasta, and yesterday were creators of Machu Picchu's "granite lamp, petrified bread." He will help tell the story of those who were and still are forgotten, so that it will be known, which is the first step in changing that story: "Come into my veins and my mouth. / Speak through my words and my song." He will be their spokesman. This is not a political oration, but it corresponds to the same (heretical!) idea that he expounds in political meetings in the nitrate fields, in sight of the sprouting roots of those anonymous creators of the "elevated city of ascending stones." His speeches are often poetry, literally, because they usually consist of reading his poems to those workers in the desert, who today prepare the dynamite charge to blow up the earth and expose the deposits from which nitrate is extracted. Yesterday, they sowed grains of maize, they spun the wool of vicuñas, they obeyed the warriors. Here and there, some still live the same way, "dead in one single abyss, shadows in a profound cavern."

There is another date that helps explain the poem's meaning. On 8 July 1945 Neruda officially and publicly joined the Communist Party, and the next month he began to write *Heights of Machu Picchu*. The two events correspond not only as temporal simultaneities but also as activities which are mutually evolved and interwoven.

88. *Personal and Extrapersonal Meaning of Machu Picchu*

His poetry was never spectral, nor does it lend itself in this case to mythic interpretations. He was not an archaeologist; he was a poet looking at history, with a new perspective. Now he listens to the voice of the past with a different ear. In a way that he would never have done in Spain, he now sniffs the mysterious perfume that emanates from the ruins. If he had gone to Machu Picchu when he was twenty, he would probably have written a poem, but a very different one.

Nor is this nostalgic literature, in spite of some scholarly opinions. What he wants to do is reshape himself and reinsert himself in the context of a world which he was part of. He isn't trying to narrate the story of the governing elite, in the fashion of ancient bards or even Inca sages, whose secret initiation bestowed cultural privilege on them. The poet embraces the idea that only revolutions, only great social change, will produce the transformation that recognizes the indivisible human condition of Juan Cortapiedras and his brothers of those times and especially of today.

His poem is not travel literature nor a hymn in praise of ancient gods. For him, it is principally a passage across a long ancient frontier that separated him from pre-Columbian history, where he is convinced that at least a part of his own history comes from.

Sometimes the poem seems to be written beyond the bounds of any possible question and, in fact, it contains a coherent body of affirmations. It goes beyond magical thinking to point out the fracture line between two civilizations, between possessors and possessed.

He will break with the traditional sense of understanding history and poetry, and will conceive the poem as a child of experience. In Machu Picchu, he will answer his own questions by carefully observing the stones and other materials in all their detail. He fixes his attention on the marginal man who built the hidden fortress, buried for centuries. For him this is the symbol of the downtrodden class of all times. He imagines the expressions of the man who is exploited, probably without being conscious of it.

Since that was an oral culture, Neruda discovers in Machu Picchu's silence the word that was spoken and not recorded by anyone. He struggles to reconstruct the lost expression, written on the stones' message. The poet sees himself as the spokesman and rescuer of collective memory and speech.

That city hid silently in the forest for twenty human generations. The poet will be its voice and will give new life to the choked-off throat of those who were neither seen nor heard. He will reinvent Machu Picchu, assimilating the Indian city into his own being and himself into it. He will convert it into a revived image, an image of himself in part, putting it into current expression, into a page of literature and history. He will create from silence a word that is reborn. The enigmatic city will again come forth by means of what it says to the poet, seeing with his eyes, walking with his feet, and breathing with all his life force.

Those two years which intervene between his climb to the mountain city and the poem's composition are a period of mental activity whose ingredients and seams reveal themselves bit by bit and result from a fertile mixture of an unconscious effort, a collective imagination, and a revolutionary concept of society.

Neruda returns in this poem to an old acquaintance, Death, which he views not as inertia and intemporality but as change and succession, where the weight of centuries mounts up. The entire indigenous city died a long time ago, and nevertheless its message still lives. He feels the rhythm and the breath of history, which he knows is never motionless.

That hidden city is not a monolith toppled by some remote collapse. He arrives there and immediately detects the same irreversible rupture that splits all divided societies: the great war, either silent or spoken, between the powerful and the weak, rich and poor.

His journey to Machu Picchu was not ingenuous. He was also searching in the past for a way to justify the contemporary revolution which he deemed to be necessary. In time, the city provides him with slowly matured justifications. He sensed the dialectic that links the working of millions of hours, of days, centuries, and millennia, with that decisive leap to sudden rupture, which takes on the features of mutation. A mutation that he also feels within himself.

Machu Picchu is a revolutionary event in his work. It proposes a new destiny and a new road for Latin American poetry. Machu Picchu rejects the idyllic sacredness of the "Cities of the Sun." The exploration of the past must become a helper of the present but also a reformer of the view of what has happened. Machu Picchu reflects the change in his way of thinking. It is an act of social consciousness. Machu Picchu is the poet at forty.

The poem occupies a privileged position in Neruda studies, with many different aspects receiving attention, as a reflection on death, on ancient man and modern man, as the connection between Neruda and the Inca Garcilaso in their centuries-long attempt to salvage the validity of the Indian.

A North American scholar declares that this book constituted his own simultaneous introduction to a continent and a poet.[44]

Without a doubt, the poem transcends a personal invention, even though it begins with the speaker-poet describing himself as he walks through the streets "from wind to wind, like an empty net." But someone waited for him "among the violins," someone who helped him "find a world that was like a buried tower." In short, he is led to discover the genesis of America, thus beginning his descent not into the depths of Hades but into the secret of History. He will go down to the soul of its peoples, he will go down a thousand years. He wants to enter "the eternal unfathomable lode." His question is, "What was man," in what part of him lives that which is "indestructible, imperishable, alive," despite the fact that each one will have his death, "a tiny death with heavy wings." Death has often winked invitingly at him during his lifetime. He has seen it everywhere, and in some way he has died in the death of others, in that of the men who once populated that eagles' nest.

Then he climbs upward, "through the awful tangle of lost jungles /

toward you, Machu Picchu," where he finds "the lightning's cradle." Manuel Scorza, stirring up these same roots, called one of his novels about rebellion in the Peruvian Andes *The Lightning's Tomb*.

The city perished, and perhaps that's why now nobody weeps there. It would seem that now only oblivion and mist reign. There where the sky and earth are crowned by fog, one has the feeling that time has devoured it all.

The poet finds there "the elevated site of human dawn," and he will not remain silent nor bow low in front of universal death. For him, the discovery of that lost city is a command to live and to love. "Climb with me, love of America. / Kiss the secret stones with me." In a long interrogative section, he questions what is the city's message, what do these remains want to convey, what became of their gods? Machu Picchu is an American poetic manifesto, something greater than indigenism.

Then after the questions come the defining images: "astral eagle, misty vineyard . . . " He may ask about the light, the serpent, the lunar horse, but the essential question is about man, "Man, where was he?" Because Machu Picchu is not a stone created by stone, he asks for the return of the poor mortal, his brother who worked the stone and piled it up. He wants to know how his brother lived, what were his dreams, how he built the wall, because that man is ancient America, his own ancestor, the sower of maize. The poet asks that the forgotten man be remembered, "because man is broader than the sea and its islands, / and we must descend into man as into a well in order to emerge from the depths / with a handful of secret waters and submerged truths."

These lines contain a fundamental key to Neruda's thinking of that period. They define the man, but also the task and obligation of the poet—to descend into the deep well-springs in order to again come to the surface with a revelation of truths hidden in the depths.

He rejects elegiac tones and proposes resurrection, submersion in order to return to life. "Rise up to be born with me, my brother." The poet opens his arms to that brother, asks for his hand so that he may free him. He commands him to "Look at me from the depths of the earth; / worker, weaver, silent shepherd: / tamer of protective guanacos. / Mason of the daring scaffold . . . " He asks all the workers to come pour their lives into the chalice of a new life. He will reveal their sorrows. "I come to speak with your dead mouth, . . . you shall speak through my words and my blood."

Reference has been made to the metaphoric comment about the poem producing Machu Picchu's second discovery, but on the practical level it really did stimulate the construction of a series of accessways and conveniences for the waves of tourists who began to progressively increase with publication of the poem. Strange power of poetry!

89. Four Journeys

On 3 November 1943, Neruda arrives in Santiago, as war rages in Europe and the Orient. His journey along the Pacific coast and his climb into the Andes have brought him more than geography lessons, for he has also searched more deeply within himself, becoming more conscious of his own identity, which he sees not only as a telluric emanation of his own being but also as a total definition of mankind in which the poet inscribes his political position.

The man who returns to Chile as he approaches his fortieth year had begun to change in Spain, as we know. He later said he had made his decision during the civil war. "Over there, the Communists seemed to me to be the great revolutionary force of this century, capable of transforming the capitalistic Old World and building a just and shining society. Since that time, I consider myself to be a militant."[45] Those words date from his fifty-fifth birthday, and when he turned sixty he declared, "For me, being a Communist is a natural thing. What is strange is that it took me so long to become one."[46]

His invitation in *Heights of Machu Picchu* to "Rise up to be born with me, my brother" is not only a poetic declaration but will be a way of life. Upon his arrival in Chile in 1943, though, it's not yet related to a membership card.

One month after his return, on 8 December in the University of Chile's Hall of Honor, he delivers his lecture on "A Journey Through My Poetry." To hear it was to witness several revelations, clearly presented and permeated with what Goethe called a crucial element in poetry—its tremor. But there was something else in that speech: a profound outpouring about the life of a boy and a man, about their secrets, about the path that led him over time to certain crucial definitions.

That wasn't the only journey he recounted. There were four in that period which cast light into the shadowy corners of his voyage and explained its trajectory. The second lecture was his "Journey to Quevedo's Heart," followed by "Journey Along the World's Shores" and "Journey to the North." All are intertwined as explications of investigations into himself and the heart of mother nature. He had undertaken the last trip with an eagerness to discover a region of his own country, the great Tamarugal Desert, a land of sand and solitude that was almost totally new to him, a native of the central part of the nation who had grown up in the South, dominated by greenness. That trip from South to North has many ramifications: it's a trip from rain to sunshine, from solitude to companionship, and it is a political trip to integration that melds both poetry and society in his inner self.

Anyone who attempts to investigate the transformation of the man and the poet as he enters middleage should not overlook these trips, for they contain many significant clues.

As he reaches middleage, he turns his eyes more than ever toward history. He finds links that, if not totally new, are seen in a clearer light. "Earth, people, and poetry are one and the same entity tied together by mysterious subterranean passages. When the earth blooms, the people breathe freedom, the poets sing and show the way. When tyranny darkens the earth and punishes the people, the loudest voice is sought out and the head of a poet falls into history's deep well. Tyranny cuts off the head that sings, but the voice at the bottom of the well returns to the secret springs of the earth and out of darkness rises up through the mouth of the people."

It is with Martí's eyes that he sees Quevedo: "He penetrated so deeply into the future that we who live today speak with his tongue." Quevedo, "the greatest of the great," shows him the profundity of Spain, where Neruda had discovered half his roots, as "I became aware of an original part of my existence, a rock foundation where the blood's cradle is still trembling." It is an indispensable but not obvious recognition by him.

He does not criticize, but he points out certain memory lapses. Spain forgot her conquest of America, and America forgot her conquest by Spain, especially her cultural inheritance. Whereas Darío at the beginning of the twentieth century went to Spain by way of Paris to reestablish the broken link, Neruda is an American whose voyage of recognition takes him across an entire continent, his own forested world, in order to contemplate the visage of Quevedo, his "supreme father who beckons from Spain." He sees the early poet's discredited fate repeated in a very different kind of writer who is the personification of Mediterranean and Moorish charm, Federico García Lorca. Still and all, in Neruda's eyes, Lorca's death is a nightmare out of Quevedo, as were the deaths of Antonio Machado and Miguel Hernández.

His "Journey Along the World's Shores" is proof that the politically defined poet has not abandoned nor impoverished his soul. He travels in search of man, lands, and oceans. He descends into the sea on Captain Nemo's expeditions and other Jules Verne adventures, drawn to scenes of deep-sea fishing, with giant crabs and blind crustaceans.

Following his plunging pilgrimage to the Spanish Golden Age, he comes back to his native soil, the Arauco. He derives pride and sustenance from knowing that he comes from the land which was a long-ago national front against invaders, the scene of 300 years of Indian resistance to the Spanish. There the first settlers came to establish Temuco, and shortly afterward his family arrived. And there, somewhat later, his poetry began to emerge. He is proud to be of pioneer stock, saying "My parents saw the first locomotive, the first cattle, the first vegetables in that cold and stormy virgin land. I was born in 1904 and by 1914 had begun to write my first poems . . . "[47] Those dates are knot-holes in the southern tree that constitutes his existence.

"Journey Along the World's Shores" covers the Orient and a return to Spain. He notes something he said then to Colombians when he talked about America's darkened map and the military dictatorships that go about extinguishing lamps hither and yon. After those journeys over the face of the continent, he is convinced that beauty is not truth's enemy and that they must be spoken together in order to some day put an end to human suffering. He will speak on behalf of his fellow citizens in Chile and the other American nations, calling upon them "to fight with us and against the enemy," rejecting those who say to him, "Don't venture out of your house, nor your garden, nor your poetry." He is coming back as a man who has ventured out of his house and his garden so that his poetry may become an open house and garden.

The fourth journey, to the North, is an incursion into contrast. The boy from the forest, the child who picked up copihue nuts with hands wet from dew-covered ferns, now moves to a lunar-scaped world without vegetation, a strange planet on a strange earth. But he is struck more by its people, who are its undervalued mineral. He tours its sandpits with Elías Laferte, president of Chile's Communist Party, and both of them, according to Neruda, are "professional agitators." A Christian-Democratic congressman from the area, Radomiro Tomic, told him that "Capitalism is so very blind, to mistreat and kill the very instrument that gives it life." It was necessary to defend man, but the strangest thing was that man had to be protected from other men. All of this came to him in one of the most abandoned places on the globe, in the desert, where the sun-split salt deposits crackle in the night's endless solitude and he could hear deep voices dreamily singing of "that flower-edged field."

90. An Unusual Speech

The first English translation of his work, *Selected Poems* from the *Residence*, was published in the United States in a private edition in 1944, and almost simultaneously he is awarded tardy and limited recognition with Santiago's Municipal Prize for Poetry, which he accepts graciously, although he is probably aware that it will be a very small branch in a forest of laurels.

Neruda didn't all of a sudden come to political struggle, however indirect and filled with delays the road may have been. Once when he was taking stock, he recalled that at the age of fourteen he had become interested in the people's struggle, and "at fifteen I was *Claridad*'s correspondent and representative in the Temuco Lyceum. At sixteen and seventeen, I took part in the student movement of the period, and later was a staff member and occasional editorial writer for the day's most outspoken journal, *Claridad*. My entrance into the Communist Party was decided in Spain, where I realized that the most honorable and best organized of those fighting against fascism were the Communists."[48]

In his work with the Communists in Chile, the Party suggests that he be a candidate for senator from the first district, comprising the provinces of Tarapacá and Antofagasta, along with the Party president, Elías Laferte, a former nitrate laborer. Neruda's acceptance marks the beginning of a new phase, a direct social commitment which will signify his immersion in the people and daily awareness of their problems, an intimate grass roots contact with the country's harshest reality.

One question presented itself to him: As a senator, what will become of his poetry? Will he put it aside? Will it be silent during the eight years of his congressional term? Or will it become a poor relative to be remembered only in the few breaks left to him by the position's inevitable activity? He brings the matter up ahead of time to Party officials, and is relieved at their response. No, the point is not to convert the poet into a great or a bad senator. What is necessary is that the people be represented in congress by culture's highest expression, fusing an essential link to proclaim the joining of brawn and brain, as they put it in those days. What we want, they said, is for the poet Neruda to become one with Recabarren as a symbol of the unity between manual laborers and intellectuals. Time for poetry must be protected. In the Senate, you should give whatever speeches or make whatever comments you care to, they told him, but others can worry about contingencies. You should save yourself for the occasions you consider more in keeping with your concerns. The Communist

Party doesn't wish to be the poet's gravedigger; what it's interested in is that the poet increase in greatness and that the people see the most beautiful flags waving in his hands. This doesn't mean we want you as a decorative figure. By character and by nature you are known to be a man dedicated to struggles, and we are sure you will participate in all of them with the strength of your temperament and the power of your arguments.

Neruda asked something else: "How am I going to conduct my senatorial campaign? I have difficulty making political speeches. I don't know how to improvise, as others do. And a congressional campaign means making from three to ten speeches a day."

"Don't worry. If you want to, do it in verse. Others will give speeches in prose."

Neruda took to heart that tip about campaigning in verse, and his candidate speech was a long poem called "Greetings to the North."

In those days, we young intellectuals formed a committee in support of the poet's candidacy and witnessed one of his appearances, which was a unique experience. Everybody was gathered together in the terribly run-down, worn-out camp in the nitrate fields to hear Elías Laferte, their old friend, who talked to them in their own language and repeated their work chants, using the same pampean slang that he had spoken a thousand times because it was the slang of his childhood. Now he was back again as sometime labor leader and sometime politician. They called him "old Laferte," and he was indeed like a father to them. Elías was also quite an artist, having been a stage actor in his early days, in these very nitrate fields. He survived the 1907 massacre in Iquique's Santa María school, and he could talk openly to his people as their equal, but with a seriousness that he had learned from a master of ceremonies who was also his political teacher, Luis Emilio Recabarren. Elías was not exactly a theoretician, but purely and simply an evocative and lively speaker. Ending his speech, which was never long or flowery, he said, with a fond yet picaresque smile, "Now we're going to hear the most unusual speech that has ever been heard in the pampas. I present to you my esteemed fellow candidate, the poet Pablo Neruda."

The next speaker smiled, a bit disconcerted, and said a few prepared words: "You will pardon me, but since I'm not a speaker I have prepared a little something to read to you." His nasal voice got louder and the tone took on a certain sureness:

> North, I am finally here in your fierce
> mineral silence full of yesterday and today,

here in search of your voice and my own,
and I don't offer you an empty heart:
I offer you all that I am.

I looked at the crowd and saw on their faces a startled look. Some were perplexed, not quite knowing what that strange speaker was getting at with his twanging voice, which held a certain soothing musicality as he said things in a peculiar manner that astounded them.

He continued reading in a stronger tone in front of that gathering where there was no microphone or loudspeaker to amplify his voice. One old man recalled another poet who sang of the pampas at the beginning of the century, Carlos Pezoa Véliz, but he decided this man had something new to say:

I come to hear also the voice of pain,
the pampa's song that aches
like the heart of the pampa's people,
an old refrain that fills the throat
with a knot of tears that sings
of destiny's awful harshness.

This man was saying that he wanted to listen to them, to share even their sacrifice with them:

I will send my voice to the corners
of the pampa, to touch the earth
and write my song in nitrate,
then lift up again to drill the shaft,
and I want to be spattered with blood
when sorrow rains down on the pampa.

On the pampa, the only rainfall, besides blood, is sorrow. In those mixed rains is written the history of that land—the spilling of blood and tears, impotence and rage. That had been the region of Chile's worst massacres, there in the dark and miserable Sierra Overa nitrate field, which was still worked with the old Shanks system and was covered with "ashen dust by night, in the morning and all day." Neruda had been speaking for five minutes, and I saw that their facial expressions had changed from surprise to warmth. They felt he was one of them, and he was declaring his wish to be so:

I want to raise my song where long ago,
with his gray eyes and silvery hair,
our father Recabarren began his labor,
in every part of the desert,
carrying in my hands his banner,
for Recabarren has never perished.

He turned to his companion on the platform and said, "Laferte comes now / step by step, in battle, to interpret the dawn . . . "

The poem was a speech and the speech was a poem whose entire text reveals the movable limits of a poetry that goes from the whispered intimate secret to the great voice clamoring in the pampean desert. This time the desert heard what had rarely been heard in the world: a poet-candidate who used poetry as a weapon which convinced them with the "pure light" of language, because liberty had called out to them. Perhaps it was similar, though not precisely equal, to when Víctor Domingo Silva had recited "The New Marseillaise" to them thirty years earlier.

That was a political debut that gave Neruda new confidence in poetry's persuasive power over the masses, and at the same time revealed to the people that poetry was not an inaccessible, distant, elegant lady but rather a potential friend and companion.

Afterwards, there was a poor man's banquet, with the few provisions that could be had in that sandy desolation. The new experience left the poet overflowing with radiance.

He went from place to place, field to field, throughout that South American Sahara called the Tamarugal Pampa. Enveloped sometimes in the northern cold and sometimes in the thick white fog that shrouded his listeners' faces, and other times burned by the lunch-hour sun, he always made some opening remarks, progressively more extensive and touching on specific political problems, and then would go on to deliver the poem that after its publication in *El Siglo* on 27 February 1945 became a popular refrain, just as those spread through the pampa forty years earlier by Recabarren.

The poem used the technique of referring to several cities or nitrate fields by name or by the designations given them by the region's inhabitants. Thus, the María Elena fields became María *Polvillo* (Dust), where the poet described the landscape of labor as it passed before him: Chuquicamata's thunder, Iquique's blueness, Tocopilla's floridity (doubtless due to its boats, because vegetation is sparse). Antofagasta is "made of light," and Taltal is an "abandoned dove," Arica is a sandy rose that touches Peru with its pampean bud and "like an ocean firefly / leads the nation to its errant child." For him, Chile is a "flaming torch," with the South's green handle, the North's solid form, and Tarapacá's flame.

Laferte, as a youthful actor, had memorized long speeches in verse that he now recited during the endless drives through the pampa, much to the delight of Neruda. He also knew "Greetings to the North" from beginning to end, having heard it so often, and he could recite it perfectly, not with the air of a psalm that frequently took on a tone of imprecation or oath in Neruda's delivery, but with the slightly Castillian-accented inflection of his acting teacher Borrás.

The poem was the most efficient and moving of their speeches. It ushered in a new type of oratory, though naturally it wasn't to everybody's taste. Jenaro Prieto resorted to his usual guffaw in his article of 12 February 1945, "A Howling Candidate," in which he caustically speaks of the "respectable gentleman Don Neftalí Reyes Basoalto, former poet and current candidate for senator from Tarapacá and Antofagasta."

After ridiculing Neruda's poem-speech, Prieto returns to the attack, on 25 February, with a "Lyric Proclamation," "I Love the Love of Voters Who Vote and Go Away." Later, based on Neruda's "Song for Bolívar," the conservative satirist will compose his "Boli-Nerudian Ode."[49]

In the 4 March elections, both Elías Laferte and Pablo Neruda were elected by large majorities as Senators of the Republic.

91. Congressional Debut

That year of 1945, May didn't bring springtime to Neruda, in part because the southern hemisphere is in autumn that month, but it did bring him two attributes that he didn't consider mutually incongruent: one as a sitting senator and the other as winner of the National Prize for Literature, which Chile bestows not for any given book but for an entire collection of works. The prize, relatively new at that time, had been created partly through his efforts as president of the Alliance of Intellectuals. It had previously been awarded only to Augusto D'Halmar, Joaquín Edwards Bello, and Mariano Latorre, prose writers who were some twenty years older than Neruda. The honor carried a symbolic significance and a slight monetary compensation. The poet was not unappreciative of either.

Neruda was the first poet and the first writer of his generation to receive that prize. He was also an open and active Communist. And the award established official recognition of his position, considering the fact that it was conferred by a jury made up not only of writers but also of government and university representatives.

In that same month of May, the recently honored poet is sworn in as senator. On the twenty-first he is in the congressional hall of honor to hear President Juan Antonio Ríos deliver his state of the nation speech and to swear his own allegiance to the constitution. A few days later, he is elected to the foreign affairs commission. His congressional debut is not at all phlegmatic, rather it begins with stormy words. When the Senate president, Arturo Alessandri Palma (who had twice been president of the Republic) announced that the honorable Mr. Reyes, senator from Tarapacá and Antofagasta, had the floor, Pablo Neruda began by saying that "the ideological, moral, and legal responsibilities which all of us, or almost all of us, feel, are much greater in my case."

Not only were they greater because the poet rejected the fraud committed by the electoral certification court in overturning election results and depriving legitimately victorious candidates of their rightful seat in congress, but also because of more unique reasons that specifically concern him: the fact that as a writer he represents a profession that rarely has any influence in legislative decisions.

Therefore, as a writer he will speak about writers. "In reality," he declares, "writers whose statues, once they're dead, serve for such excellent inaugural speeches and for such happy pilgrimages, have lived and still live dark and difficult lives, in spite of illustrious positions and brilliant talents, simply because of their unorganized opposition to capitalism's unjust disorder. With the exception of a few examples inherited in Chile from Baldomero Lillo and Carlos Pezoa Véliz, whose work was identified with the sorrows and aspirations of their people, [writers] in general have had only an attitude of resigned poverty or undisciplined rebellion . . ."

Writers, who along with some sectors of salaried workers, sometimes experience long periods of unemployment, will be defined by Neruda at the outset as members of one segment of society which generally lives in misery, in contrast to the splendor in which the privileged minority exists, whose luxury, he will add, aspires to perpetuity and is partially achieved by virtue of the poverty of "the illustrious and heroic laborers in the pampa" whom he represents. "Those unknown, forgotten compatriots, hardened by suffering, poorly fed and badly clothed, sometimes gunned down, are the ones who have given me this award, which is the true National Prize, in my opinion . . ."

The comparison is revealing—the true National Prize. He is one step ahead of those who think he's a "rare bird" for the senate—a congressional poet who represents not only poets, who are too few in number to elect representatives, but also and above all represents workers from the nitrate fields, the copper and gold mines, and the coastal cities of the vast North . . . But he wants to show his constituents that he is proud to have earned their confidence. Perhaps the legislative responsibility he now assumes as a writer will serve his people. Maybe he can do something to contribute a tiny bit toward overcoming the backwardness in which they have lived ever since the days of Independence. Enough of fairy tales about the life of miners who "were living in beautiful little pink castles when a big bad wolf called 'agitator' came to distract them and lead them astray with his actions . . ."

His congressional debut is neither sweet to the taste nor smooth to the touch. Calling a spade a spade, he will offer some comparisons of tragedy as he declares that the thousand-year-old squalor he saw in India during his world travels was not as bad as the picture of Puchoco Rojas dwellings in Coronel, where the hovels are pitifully constructed of trash retrieved from the dump—cardboard boxes, pebbles, tin cans, barrel hoops. With these materials they build a room where fourteen people live one on top of the other, according to the longstanding custom of "bed warming," whereby the workers take turns sleeping as they emerge from the deep shafts, so that those straw mats never get cold in a whole year.

May God protect him if he's inventing things! He has seen it all with his own eyes and smelled it all with his own nostrils. In the North he has visited the sheds where the unmarried men live four together in a nine-square-foot space. All their lives, men, women, and children of the poor class suffer from the lack of water and electricity, which "has left an eternal bitter taste in my conscience." Those people are shriveling up, and the poet even supports his denunciation with revealing statistics on the dreadful standard of living and physical suffering.

He attempts to understand the reason for all that. It's not due to the bitter harvest of some perverse mentality, but rather to the vestiges of feudalism and a festering separation of classes. The people are derided and called *rotos* (broken-down bums). "At this stage of my life, in my first appearance before this honorable Senate, I am obliged by my conscience as a Chilean to wonder and to ask if such an unjust situation can continue."

The great absurdity in all this is that the one who creates things has none of them. The one who has them is the one who doesn't create them, and he denies those things to the very people who produce them. "Newspapers whose paper is manufactured by workers in Puente Alto, spew forth constant denigration of this active gigantic soul of our nation which provides life for all its citizens—denigration from these plunderers of civic trust, ensconced in comfortable houses that we would like to increase in number until they could shelter all Chileans, and which were built with cement mined by dint of laborers' hard work in El Melón. Inside those comfortable houses, the plunderers are surrounded by fixtures that were manufactured or installed by Chilean hands; they drink wine brought from the vineyards where even the crystal glasses are made by Yungay trade unionists, uncounted anonymous workers with our own ancestry, who also weave the cloth for our clothes, run our trains, man our ships, extract the coal and nitrate and metals, irrigate and harvest the fields in order to give us our daily bread after their hard nightly work. And from those newspapers whose linotype machines are operated by our laborers, denigration pours forth."[50]

Here the senator talks about the poet and the writer's responsibility. Nobody tells the doctor to walk away from sickness and not try to cure the patient, he says, but they tell the writer, "Don't concern yourself with your people. Don't come down from the clouds. Your kingdom is not of this world." Neruda rejects this appeal to not get involved in the problems of his people.

The biggest anti-Communist of those decades had just ended his orbit, and the poet refers to him as he ends his maiden speech in the senate, saying, "Until a few days ago, a madman existed who, under the banner of anticommunism, massacred and destroyed, defiled and blasphemed, invaded and murdered human beings, cities, fields and villages, peoples and cultures. This man gathered formidable forces which he guided into becoming the most immense torrent of hatred and violence that the history of mankind has ever seen. Today, next to the ruins of his nation, among millions of dead whom he dragged to the grave, he lies anonymously twisted like a piece of burnt, dried meat beneath the debris of his personal fortress, above which now flies a glorious red flag with a star and hammer and sickle. And this flag, along with the others symbolizing victory, means peace and reconstruction of our insulted human dignity."[51]

He pronounces these words on 30 May 1945, at a moment when recent world events encourage optimism. A few weeks earlier, Hitler had committed suicide in the chancellery bunker; the Red Army had entered Berlin; and in Potsdam the Third Reich had surrendered unconditionally. In the joint session of congress, President Ríos has just affirmed in his message that only a technicality kept Chile officially estranged from the Soviet Union, and Neruda, as a Chilean writer, wishes to pay tribute "To that great nation, in which the greatest strides in history have been made on behalf of cultural extension and diffusion, so that culture will not be, as it is with us, a privilege attained only with difficulty by the common people. I have just read in official statistics a fact that fills my writer's heart with a flood of invincible joy. The fact is this: 'During the war, one billion copies of 57,000 books in 100 different languages were published in the Soviet Union.'" He asks whether it isn't about time to put an end to calumny.

An apparent paradox exists in this outspoken orator, elected as a Communist senator but not yet a Party member, whose inaugural speech follows a line initiated by the Party's founder, Luis Emilio Recabarren. Communists, he adds, make no attempt to monopolize patriotic feelings, but rather to relieve them of "some of the rhetorical tone which has progressively weakened patriotic feelings, and to fill those feelings with solidarity and justice for our people." The accusation dates from long ago, as he recalls that when the fathers of all the American countries embraced ideas that came from a European revolution, they were called liberals and foreigners, when in reality they were echoing universal currents that were reaching our shores.

The speech enthused many and displeased others. Horacio Walker Larraín, spokesman for the Conservative Party, lamented that "The first words of the maiden speech by the inspired poet, who has come to represent Tarapacá and Antofagasta provinces, have been devoted to breaking a respected precedent of the honorable Senate," in his condemnation of the electoral court's certification ruling. In Walker's view, this represented a breach of respect for constitutional rule and the high court's good practices.

In effect, the poet had gone to congress not only to break precedents and to be disrespectful toward certain procedural norms, but also to cast doubt on the basic injustice of an entire system.

The moment arrived for him to assume completely the responsibilities dictated to him by the evolution of his political consciousness, without any subtlety or euphemism. Therefore, none of us among the 7,000 in attendance on 8 July 1945 in Santiago's Caupolicán arena were surprised as Pablo Neruda officially joined the Chilean Communist Party. He was not alone, for he was accompanied in that decision by a significant legion of the best known artists, intellectuals, and ranking names in various fields of creativity and knowledge, who on that day culminated an interior process of arriving at revolutionary convictions that life had taught them and were not totally removed from the influence exerted by Neruda, who was, in their eyes, an example of the intellectual who assumes political responsibility as a natural outgrowth of personal and professional development.

92. The Problem of Time

Will the poet, in this new phase of his life, be able to multiply time, as Christ did with the loaves and fishes? Or will the poet be silenced in the face of his senatorial work, trips to the provinces, visits to nitrate fields, needs of the voters, hundreds of requests for help in solving personal problems or simply asking for an autographed book? Has he gotten himself in too deep, because all these tasks seem to be deep water indeed!

Time, time! That's the crucial question. Can it be stretched like a rubber band? He will figure it out down the road and not get too exasperated for the moment. Besides, he has recourse to the Party's agreement to respect his creative time. It will depend on him to make it available, to limit demands on his public life.

However, he also knows he is an incorrigible traveler, with a need to move about and see new lands and new skies, and then to return, true enough. For now, he will head for America's broad green savanna, the country of fantastic flora and fauna and prodigious rivers, which he couldn't enter almost twenty years ago and hasn't seen since the day when the ship on which he made his first voyage into the world dropped anchor for one day in Santos port and a girl he still remembers, Marinech, came on board. This time he would take the plane to Rio, where he is received with warm solemnity by the Brazilian Academy on 30 July 1945. The poet Manuel Bandeira lauds him in terms that are not simply southern courtesy but real conviction about a great poet who is influencing not only literature written in Spanish but also that written in Portuguese.

Neruda is initially somewhat taken aback, but he soon begins to comprehend it all. Brazil not only borders geographically on all South America except for Chile, but also her language borders on our language, even though we go on being as ignorant of each other as if we lived on separate continents. In Brazil, Neruda senses a reencounter with unexpected likenesses and affinities. His poetry has traveled through all the language's basic meridians; he has personally witnessed its recognition in Spain, Mexico, Argentina, Colombia, and Peru, but now it's evident to him that his poetry also speaks to the sensibility of Brazilian readers, who accept it as if he were their own poet.

He is beginning to see that his work can send a message to all of

Ibero-America, maybe even farther. That evening in the academy opens a window to let in a warm breeze that seems familiar to him. The intellectual elite who vociferously welcome him in that auditorium are not known for being progressive, and their important elected members wear academic regalia that might have been created by a designer for Louis of France or an emperor from the House of Braganza. There the atmosphere is one of laboriously embossed letters, although a few voices can be heard from poets open to the avant-garde. Yet, Neruda doesn't feel like a fish out of water. He has an ability to adapt to the most diverse environments without giving up his own identity or hiding his literary and political opinions.

The following day he will go from the literary elite with their velvet costumes and gold-edged, three-cornered hats, to an immense mass of perspiring people in a Rio stadium. He had already experienced something similar in São Paulo, in Pacaembú Stadium packed with 100,000 fans paying homage to Luis Carlos Prestes, the poet who is received almost like the football heroes who will come later, like a Pelé or a Garrincha of poetry and struggle. Neruda's pulse beats with those people, for they smell of America and he knows that the people are the foundation of nations and of the continent. In addition, he feels pulled along by the tide of those demonstrations, which confirms to him his decidedly plebeian nature.

On the return trip, he gives lectures and readings in Montevideo and Buenos Aires, where he again notes a known fact—they consider him almost their own poet. He moves about absorbing America through his eyes and his pores, gathering it in, in order to take a leap which has been progressing within him in a kind of gestation process. He will give birth to an ambitious poem that will perhaps be the equal—he hopes—of the "Ode to Agriculture in the Torrid Zone" by his old master and founder of his university, Andrés Bello. But Neruda will write his poem 120 years after Bello and not in the classical form but true to his own vision and personality.

He has it all planned out. He will sleep his siesta in the afternoons, and in the evenings he'll invite friends in. At night, a large bottle of wine will be talked away, but in the mornings, fresh as a daisy, he will write this poem that seems to him a necessity which springs from deep within him. He said once that he used to write whether it was snowing or thundering, with inspiration or without it, because just as eating brings on an appetite, so too does work give birth to inspiration. He sits down at his desk at nine in the morning and in a large unlined notebook begins to write the long poem that he calls *Heights of Machu Picchu*. It's September, and spring is approaching. He feels as if that new climb to the lost city is like the explosion of a new springtime, which some said would never again flower, buried as it was under the ice of politics.

93. *The Honorable Mr. Reyes Praises Lucila Godoy Alcayaga*

Chilean poetry is a recognized springtime whose splendor is spread over more than one horizon. On Tuesday, 20 November 1945, the Senate president again recognizes the honorable Mr. Reyes, who will speak that afternoon not about politics but about poetry and a poet. He will talk about his little country, which he calls the first, and not the furthest, corner of the world, so far away from the center of the earth, it's true, but a country that has just pierced "the universal firmament of ideas with a royal purple arrow," leaving behind a brand new star.

He bows before Lucila Godoy Alcayaga, a leader who has emerged from the most profound essence of the people, with "Gabriela Mistral" as her pen name ("named for the archangel and with the wind for a patronym," as María Teresa León described her). She has just been awarded the first Nobel Prize for Literature ever given to a Latin American writer, and Neruda enjoys a collective victory, which he terms "an outstanding vindication of the common people" among our citizens. He thinks about all the young Gabrielas whose destinies are suffocated in the masses' deep mine pits.

The Senate listens quietly as Neruda talks about Mistral. This is not just an ordinary presentation, but one that involves the nation's two greatest poets. He views her from tip to toe, considering her as both a summit and a vein of hidden ore, for she has given voice to the anguish of many of her countrymen. Her poetry is not just the offspring of her own sensitivity; it has also been nourished by all her experiences, including the very bitter ones of her childhood. In that area, not exactly propitious for Orpheus, Neruda feels her work to be "saturated by an essential compassion that never reaches the point of becoming rebellion or doctrine but does go beyond the limits of charitable pity." He expresses his admiration and also delineates what separates him from her, for he has gone beyond that limitation. He doesn't look down on feelings of great pity for the people, like those expressed by such sympathetic greats as Dostoievsky and Gorky in their love for the humble and downtrodden. Many readers, he adds, get something more than pity out of reading compassionate writers. Gorky himself was a political man who helped establish "a human order and system of justice based on tenderness." He doesn't mention on this occasion that it had been Mistral who had loaned him books by those authors when he was a boy, but as he cites their names he is perfectly aware that she was his guiding light.

In another aspect, Neruda is like her. Perhaps that's why he emphasizes her quality as "a great lover of our geography and our collective life." This childless mother, he goes on, seems to be a mother to all Chileans. Her words sketch the inquiry into and praise of the country's character from top to bottom as she sings of its substance, its people and stones, its flowers and foods. Neruda looks at her as a person and returns to her work, convinced that Mistral is like a part of Chile's earth.

He will emphasize her rejection of aristocratic impulses and tendencies toward Europeanization. She will honor her country in its most profound and popular essence, turning her poetry and her message into an expression of the nation's values.

Neruda interprets her Nobel award as a call to protect all the country's seeds of knowledge, which can be achieved only by removing the neglect that surrounds the common people, that vein which produced the Mistralian ore, in order for all of Chile's young to develop their potentiality to the maximum. He closes with a kiss on "the beautiful high forehead, Araucanian and Spanish, of Gabriela Mistral."

The foundation of his speech is an intimately personal one. Although they were as different as night and day, Neruda like Mistral was also a child of the common people who could have been lost if it hadn't been for a personality and unconquerable vocation that linked them together, with all their differences and similarities.

In those days of national pride, there were those who concluded with finality that Neruda himself would never win the Nobel Prize, because he's a Communist and because it wouldn't be given twice to writers from a tiny marginal country.

94. Pro Memoria

The year 1946 begins as a busy but not stormy one. January brings with it a title from Mexico's government in the Order of the Aztec Eagle, which signals a succession of medals. This one, though, is very dear to him, for in some way Mexico has been in his heart for a long time.

That year's peaceful beginning is deceptive, soon to be closed into an acute angle by several events where death and treachery participate, as in a Shakespearean drama. President Juan Antonio Ríos has succumbed to cancer in his Paidahue villa, to be succeeded by his child's father-in-law, Vice President Alfredo Duhalde, a wealthy radical landowner from the South. An aging Don Juan with blue eyes and gray hair who spent many years as a senator, having been elected by virtue of a religious use of the bribes and voter roundups that were denounced by Neruda in his poem called "Elections in Chimbarongo," Duhalde believes just two things—that politics is an affair for gentlemen and that he holds unconditional authority that he can use as he pleases.

It is a period of rivalry between Communists and Socialists, aggravated after the breakup of the Popular Front. A group headed by Bernardo Ibáñez joins Duhalde's provisional government, proclaiming a so-called Third Front policy. In spite of his being general secretary of the Chilean Workers Confederation, Ibáñez's anti-union phobia grows stronger, especially when the workers elect Communist leaders.

Laferte and Neruda are mobilized in the northern pampa, where strikes have broken out in two nitrate fields, the Humberstone and the Mapocho. Neruda sets down a chronicle-style poetic report on the situation:

I was in the field, with hidden heroes,
with one who digs the fine fertilizing snow
on the planet's hard crust,
and proudly I shook his hands of dust.

They said to me, "Look,
my brother, see how we live,
here in Humberstone, here in Mapocho,
in Ricaventura, in Paloma,
in Pan de Azúcar, in Piojillo."

And they showed me their rations
of pitiful little food,
the dirt floors in their houses,
the sun, the dust, the bedbugs,
and the immense solitude.

I saw the work of the shovelers
who leave on the handle
of the wooden spade
the print of their own hands.

I listened to a voice that came
from the cramped depths of the shaft,
as from an infernal womb,
and then climbing upward
a creature without a face,
a dusty mask covered
with sweat, with blood, and with dust.

And he told me, "Wherever you go,
tell them about these torments,
tell them, brother, about your brother
who lives down below, in hell."[52]

The poet insists: I was . . . They told me . . . And they showed me . . .
I saw the work . . . I listened to a voice . . . And he told me, . . . thus
emphasizing his qualification as eyewitness to speak on their behalf and,
at their behest, to become their defender. And he complies.

He found himself there as a kind of shield, as Communist congressmen
were supposed to be. But above all he will also be the singer, the crier, the
herald, who denounces and reveals, acting as spokesman and recorder.

Some of us were in the square in front of La Moneda government
house one summer evening that January, near the equestrian statue of
General Bulnes, in the midst of a crowd that darkness was beginning to
swallow up. It was a demonstration of solidarity with the Humberstone
and Mapocho workers. Just when the people were ready to sing an old
tearful song, an unexpected rat-tat-tat of machine guns broke out. A
young girl whom I knew fell at my side, Ramona Parra, later called by
Neruda "the golden warrior," as he called out, one by one, the names of
those killed that summer evening: Manuel Antonio López, Lisboa Calderón, Alejandro Gutiérrez, César Tapia, Filomeno Chávez. After that episode, he writes "The Dead in the Square (28 January 1946 in Santiago)."

We in the information services labored to turn out a first edition of
this poem, illustrated by the painter José Venturelli. It deals with the massacres that have been the specialty of those who control Chile's guns—
murky killings later expunged "as if nobody died, nothing / as if they were
stones falling / on the ground, or water on water . . ." The poet demands
punishment and draws a line, with the people on one side and their enemies on the other. He doesn't want to see the guilty sent off as ambassadors, nor comfortably ensconced in their houses. He wants to see them
brought to trial in this same square. He will not permit the blood of the

fallen to disappear, and he hopes his poem will again call them to mind, because there's nothing worse than to forget the dead with that accursed administrative amnesia that makes martyrs disappear from memory.

In Chile, under Pinochet, they would later discover secret graveyards where they had surreptitiously buried peasants who had been done away with in the middle of the night. Some were buried in the underground vault of an abandoned cement mine. After the awful discovery of the Lonquén burial ground, the victims' survivors decided to engrave a marker with some words that would record the event and serve as an eternal memorial. They looked in the surest place for those words and chose these lines from Neruda's "The Dead in the Square":

A thousand dark-winged nights will fall
without destroying the day these dead await.
The day awaited throughout the world
by so many of us, suffering's last day.

A day of justice won in the struggle,
and you, fallen brothers, in silence,
will be with us on that long day
of the final struggle, on that immense day.[53]

95. *Strange Waltz*

In May he finishes writing his series of lectures with "Journey to the North of Chile," in which the man from the South will speak of that sorrowful region which leaves him as breathless as would a lunar crater.

He has earned a reputation as someone who touches the heart of crowds, which may be why presidential candidate Gabriel González Videla personally has him appointed national head of information services, where he will put his imagination to work and pay dearly for it.

He was supposed to popularize in every way possible the candidate's image as an unsophisticated standard bearer. His motto was to spread the image everywhere, "even into soup." He will resort to the press and the radio, television being still unavailable in Chile. He will cover the walls from Arica to Ultima Esperanza, and will spread the president's name with a catchy song. It is in regard to this ditty that he is led to ask advice of his Temuco acquaintance, the soprano Blanca Hauser, who comes to the appointment accompanied by her husband Armando Carvajal, at that time the director of the Chilean symphony orchestra, and by a singer friend of Blanca's. Something led Neruda to fix his eye on this friend, a delicate woman whose laughter struck an intimate chord in him. His friend Cotapos, in terms appropriate to a musician, once described her laughter as falling "like a falcon from a harsh tower." Neruda heard her sing and record the "Hymn of the Leftist Forces," whose music was not at all original but had been adapted from a popular song by the Andrews Sisters called "Rum and Coca-Cola." The poet decided to have a little fling with the laughing singer, which was of brief duration, for he was very busy and the woman whose laughter fell like a bird began to withdraw.

Afterwards, Neruda journeyed to the North, and his lady-friend, whose name he had trouble remembering, went off to Mexico, according to Blanca Hauser. All it had been was a lovely moment.

Somebody has said that his home in Los Guindos, which he calls "Michoacán," became one of the three most important residences in Latin America, along with literary centers in Victoria Ocampo's home in San Isidro, Argentina, and Guillermo Valencia's in Popayán, Colombia.

A writer described by Paul Valéry as "the most fundamentally American writer" arrives as a guest at "Michoacán." This giant among the continent's novelists is received as a beloved friend by Neruda, who opens his arms to "The Great Turkey-gobbler," Miguel Angel Asturias, whose *El Señor Presidente* brings artistic power to a renewal of the novelistic cycle about Latin American dictators, which had been initiated by Spain's Ramón del Valle-Inclán with *Tirano Banderas*.

Neruda is moving all about in this period. News comes that his work is spreading beyond its own language, as *Spain in My Heart* is published in Czechoslovakia, and *Residence on Earth* has editions in Denmark and the United States. He hears from São Paulo that the Portuguese-language edition of *Twenty Love Poems and a Song of Despair* is selling like hotcakes.

Nonetheless, as is well known, not everyone likes his poetry, and he has both rabid and sometimes furtive enemies. One of them is the Chilean president that he helped get elected. As national head of the information services, Neruda had written a poem that he himself read aloud in the packed National Stadium and would become almost a hit-parade chorus repeated in villages, cities and outlying settlements. Written for a specific occasion, the title of "The People Call Him Gabriel" doesn't refer to the archangel but to a Gabriel who knows as much about poetry as he does about Chinese and is annoyed by the poet's popularity. His typical greeting is "Give us a hug," and his smile shows all his thirty-two teeth, some of them false. In reality, he was elected thanks to enthusiastic Communist support, and he has uttered another well-known phrase in his falsetto voice and poor pronunciation that swallows the final letters of every word: "There will never be any human or divine force that can divide me from the Communist Party."

Upon being elected, he goes to a plenary meeting of the Central Committee, which, given the Cold War climate, was leaning toward the position of not participating in the government that the Party had decisively helped get elected. The man who was the subject of Neruda's poem asks to be heard at the meeting. In a tone which mixed entreaty with blackmail, he says, "You carry your Party membership in your pockets. I carry mine in my heart. If you don't participate with Communist ministers, I will resign the presidency." After this theatrical stroke, the plenum agrees to join the cabinet.

Meanwhile, Neruda has thoroughly fulfilled his responsibilities as senator. For almost two years he has been dedicating himself to his congressional tasks, and now he feels that someone within is calling to him. That someone is a jealous woman—Poetry doesn't like competitors, especially such absorbing ones as politics. She is claiming her rights of preference, if not exclusivity. The poet, aware that she is the most important creature in his life, listens to that insistent complaint, that claim which torments him, especially at night or in the Senate's tiresome sessions when he fights the tedium by watching some of his colleagues doze off like real camouflage artists, though they can't always stifle their snoring. He should be dozing in his own bed as God intended, and devoting his valuable time to writing poems that he would regret less than the wretched "The People Call Him Gabriel."

In addition, as an incurable traveler, he's a pendulum, always wanting to go away in order to come back. The time comes, after every return, when he gets an unbearable urge to weigh anchor again. The magnetic needle on his travel compass is pointing now to "The Country of Grape Clusters," which overflows with vineyards, like his native land. Isn't he being vociferously summoned by the country that is the home of good food, pure olive oil, and wine with the taste of a thousand years? There the gods and the greatest empire had reigned, but what he likes most are its people, who live their simple daily life among statues.

He comes to a decision and presents it straight out to the Party: he wants to be ambassador to Italy. The president of the Republic is consulted and agrees in principle. That way he would get Neruda out of the country, far away. But wouldn't that be too much of a golden exile? The president begins to weave an underhanded scheme to ensure failure of any appointment for Neruda, and has made a deal with the North American Admiral Leahy, Truman's emissary at the Chilean transfer of power, whereby the Communist Party will be declared illegal within a few months.

González Videla conspires in secret with the right wing, so that in the Senate, where ambassadorial appointments have to be confirmed, they will reject Neruda's nomination. As soon as the negative vote took place, aspirants for the post began to flutter around the Communist Party, among them a Mr. Angel Guarello, whose qualifications included two that ranked as valuable assets for President González Videla and the right wing: he had never written a single poem, and he had nothing to do with the Communists except for a request that they quietly approve his appointment as ambassador to Italy. The poet would have to wait twenty-five years to become Ambassador Neruda.

Serenity again rules. As of 28 December, he is guaranteed that in the Senate chambers he will no longer be recognized as the honorable "Mr. Ricardo Reyes" but rather as the honorable Mr. Pablo Neruda. It makes him want to laugh. There, one is "honorable" not because of his conduct in life but because of a rule that says so. In any case, on that Day of the Holy Innocents and Martyrs, he toasts a name that is definitely gone. With a glass of red Macul wine he bids farewell to the not-at-all angelical but certainly sacrificial name of Ricardo Eliecer Neftalí Reyes Basoalto, as it was inscribed in Parral's civil registry on 1 August 1904. From now on his legal name will be one he has used for many years, since that day when the boy decided to avoid the antipoetic ire of his father by adopting the pseudonym Pablo Neruda. In the future, he will use that name in all matters, including legal ones. He won't use a customary second family name. Peculiar? No, not at all. He had said farewell to "Reyes" and "Basoalto" long ago. In his mind, Reyes Basoalto was a child, "The Reed," that thin boy in Temuco who used to accompany the ballast-train conductor José del Carmen. When the train would make long stops for gathering stones to shore up the roadbed, that little boy who was named Ricardo Reyes would hunt partridge eggs, "snake mother" nests, *coihue* fruit, or he would pick some copihue flowers because he liked their bright blood-red color. All of that belonged to his prehistory, far away.

On New Year's Eve, among masks and songs, the man who has been an almost professional philanderer, wonders if he has remained faithful to the one he loves par excellence, to whom he truly gives his life—Dame, or Lady, Poetry, or simply poetry, whether naked or clothed. In the privacy of mornings, he continues his toil as a laborer, called to the task by an internal siren that sounds its whistle at seven. He is feeling very productive.

The *Third Residence* which appears in Buenos Aires is a book that gathers together remnants from his lonely past, his passionate furors and his dates with history, everything written in the ten years between 1935 and 1945, with a distinct change from beginning to end of the multiformed mosaic. He has experienced his extremely personal life in the same intimate way he has experienced political storms and the war and everything else, and the book is full of both night and day. The night contains "Girl Drowned in the Sky" ("Shattered at night among dead flowers: I pause and I suffer . . ."), "Alliance" ("Sonata. Nocturnal sugar, spirit of crowns . . ."). Sex is perhaps the longed-for lane of escape ("I'd like to remain, my love, with just one syllable / of mangled silver, with just one lip / of your snowy breast"). These are the final sparks from the Orient's verdant flash, or rather from the sun as it sinks into the ocean, which he often invited me to contemplate at Isla Negra when we closely watched the horizon in the moment of its final glory. The book is like the Marx brothers' house with two doors—if they opened one door they were faced with winter, and if they opened the other one they went out into springtime. Such is the strange "Waltz" of disconsolation ("There is no me, no reason to be, no one to know"). Such is the feeling in a ghostly city called Brussels, where in the midst of moons and knives he dies like a night person and declares that he is, by nature, alone. The climate is the same in "The Abandoned One." In "Furies and Sorrows" it's as if there were a buried seed wanting to emerge from the earth's surface but still maturing in darkness ("Like the labial heart of the cherry tree in June"). The sprout will push forth in "Reunion under New Flags," but only with *Spain in My Heart* and "Song to Stalingrad" will it leave the depths of earth to enter the world's piercing light of blood and flames.

The subterranean poet has come out into the light, but surrounded by torment and enveloped in thunder and lightning.

96. *The Great Somersault*

On the first Sunday in April 1947, municipal elections take place throughout the country, with results showing appreciable gains for the Communist Party. The next day, I went to La Moneda government house with General Secretary Ricardo Fonseca and another member of his political committee, Galo González, to speak with the president. We thought that he would probably start out with a few happy words about the previous day's victory, but he greeted us with his horns down and charged like an apparently blind bull. It could not be, he would not allow the Communists to become a great party by means of the elections. He used an expression that later became popular, asking us to "become a submarine" and telling us, "You have to submerge yourselves in darkness. Be like fish, make no noise, and stay where nobody will see you. That's the way to survive. Otherwise, you will perish."

Quite upset, we told him we had never heard such an antidemocratic proposal. After all, the people had given us their decision, and it must be respected. "You and we promised to carry out a program. We will attempt with all our strength to do so. What is that 'submarining' business? We have gone from town to town, from field to field, without hiding our faces, to make you president. And you never told us during the campaign 'to submarine.' We don't want anything that's not due us. We think our participation in the government is also a guarantee against deceiving a populace that wants changes."

He abruptly cut off the discussion, and we left the presidential palace with the feeling that we had witnessed the striptease act of a demagogue.

In his poetry and senate speeches, Neruda evoked the indescribable poverty of Puchoco Rojas, which was duplicated in Lota and the entire coal-mining region, along with the underwater tunnels where the miners have to travel for miles, lighting their way with little headlamps, in order to get to the work site. They will make it if a coal-gas explosion doesn't get them first. Those workers were on strike, and the poet-senator was with them.

I used to see him almost every day, and our conversations were mainly about what was happening in our country. Relations with the president had definitely been severed.

I had already noticed some disturbing signs in the latter's behavior, inasmuch as I was serving as the Communist Party's emissary to the chief executive's office. In this extra-official position, I was to talk with him once a week in order to exchange information and opinions and to suggest certain steps or strategies. One Monday in January 1947, President Gabriel González Videla arrived late for our meeting, explaining that a launch in which he had been traveling that weekend had capsized in Lake Pirihueico and everybody had been in danger of drowning, when they were saved by some field workers who were rowing nearby and were wearing sandals (González Videla included even this detail). When one of them learned that he had saved the president of the Republic, he was quite astounded. "I gave him fifty pesos," the president added.

We all offered him congratulations on his miraculous rescue, and when I added mine, he said as if in jest, "Maybe for you it would have been better if I had drowned. You would have been spared the hardest blow." He saw my puzzled expression and changed the subject, offering me some expert advice, "If you find yourself some time in a similar situation, the first thing to do is to take off your jacket and shoes. In the water they're as heavy as lead."

That scene seemed to be merely a tasteless joke, but later I realized that the man had long ago finalized his plans and just liked to play cat and mouse.

In August I was at the Bolivian embassy for that country's independence day celebration, when, suddenly, someone embraced me from behind. It was González Videla, who asked me with an innocent and sincere expression, "But why have you disappeared from La Moneda government house? Don't be such ingrates! Come see me tomorrow."

The next day, our same delegation met with him in the government house. He was alone in his office, and his tone was very different from the one he had used with me in the Bolivian embassy. He began by criticizing us for unfriendly demonstrations against him during his recent trip to Brazil, for which he blamed us. Then, as he drew lines on a piece of paper, without looking us in the eye, he proposed that we support him in dissolving the congress in a kind of self-inflicted coup d'état. It was a seditious proposal, but at the time just wildly preposterous. We didn't need to look at each other to realize that he was setting a trap for us. We rejected his invitation to a coup, and there were more threats. The meeting came to an abrupt end.

I related all this to Neruda, who knew the man better than we did, but not well enough. Obviously, none of us knew enough about what kind of man he was, but the poet had a gift for psychological penetration. "It's clear," he said, "we're heading for the worst."

He had known something about González Videla's conversation with Admiral Leahy, later confirmed in the *Mission to Chile* memoirs by the North American ambassador, Claude Bowers. Both González and Leahy had been diplomatic delegates to the Vichy government and were sympathizers of Marshall Pétain. The Chilean had been in Paris when Hitler's troops arrived, sparking his admiration for their shining boots and their martial confidence as they paraded near the Arch of Triumph. He said as much in some tongue-tied remarks in the Caupolicán Theater when he made a quick trip to Chile in response to the mortal illness of then President Ríos. The crow flew from France to swoop around the imminent demise, and then he returned to his nest. In October 1946, he would reassure his old acquaintance, the North American admiral, by explaining his plan to repay the Communists' support by keeping them in the government for six months and then ignominiously expelling them and declaring the Party illegal. As the poet somberly predicted, "The agreement with Truman's emissary is being carried out. We'll be pushed even further."

On 21 October, González Videla summons the Communist delegation to La Moneda. This time he is accompanied by Raúl Juliet, minister of foreign affairs, and several congressmen from the Radical Party, including Senator Ulises Correa. The president informs us that he has decided to ask the three Communist ministers to resign. We told him, "They will not resign, because that means a serious violation of their promise to those who elected you as president, and we won't allow anybody to get the impression that it's the Communists who are taking the initiative in reneging on their obligations to the people."

"Then I will remove them," threatened González Videla.

"You do whatever you want." This was like a spark that made him explode in a hundred low-caliber insults. Out of that swindler's mouth came the most indescribable crudities, as if he were having a hysterical fit. He presented a grotesque picture, pitiable in the eyes of those who believed in the formal dignity that should be demonstrated by a man who was president of the Republic. He finally went to the bathroom and came back in silence, with his head all wet.

We left La Moneda with the feeling that relations were definitively broken and proceeded to Central Committee headquarters to discuss the situation and agree on the course of action we should adopt. A few hours later, night by then, Representative Bernardo Araya arrived. As general secretary of the Chilean Confederation of Workers, he had gone to La Moneda because of the coal miners' strike. González Videla was in a council of ministers, but on learning that Bernardo Araya was in a waiting room, he came out to talk, telling him that he had declared war on the Communist Party, whereupon Araya told him, "I'm also included in that war." González Videla went on, "But before we go our separate ways, pal, give me a hug."

Bernardo Araya, whom Pinochet would send to join the "disappeared" twenty-six years later, came immediately to the Communist Party offices on the corner of Moneda and MacIver to tell us there was an order to throw all our officers into prison. We went off to our separate hiding places, in a state of illegality that would last several years.

Neruda, for the moment, didn't need to go into hiding, since, as a senator of the Republic, he was protected by congressional immunity. And as long as that wasn't stripped away, he could function legally.

97. *The Poet Accuses*

I usually would see him at night. Neruda decided on a nickname for González Videla —the Bluffer. He was concerned about my hiding places, and I told him we didn't have enough of them, for the persecution had taken us by surprise. He found me a safe house in the home of the Colombian poet Eduardo Carranza, who was cultural attaché in his country's embassy. A dedicated Hispanist, politically he had nothing in common with us, but poetry drew him to Neruda, and since I was Neruda's friend I should also be a friend of Carranza and his wife, whom Neruda once called "sweet Rosita Coronado." I can still see her carrying her newborn baby like a piece of fruit in a woven reed basket called a "Moses crib." In that house, where I could look through the windows toward Pedro de Valdivia square, I used to meet with the poet and learned that he was preparing a political document. It was later published in the Caracas newspaper *El Nacional* on 27 November 1947 under the title "A Personal Letter to Millions." In fact he conceived it as a political report that he was making to international public opinion on the situation in his country. For that reason, he originally called it "Chile's Democratic Crisis Is a Dramatic Warning for Our Continent." In it the poet expresses in completely frank language his belief that Chile will not be the only country in America to suffer the effects of a plan that comes from abroad. He stresses foreign pressure and outlines the relations between the Communist Party and González Videla. He refers to an interview that the latter gave on 18 June 1947 to an astonished woman correspondent from the London *News Chronicle,* in which the first paragraph reported precisely that "President González Videla believes that war between Russia and the United States will break out within three months, and Chile's current internal and external political situation is premised on this theory." It went on, "The president added that the imminence of war explains his present attitude toward Chilean Communists, against whom he has no particular objection." He assured that "Chile must cooperate with its powerful neighbor, the United

States, and when war begins, Chile will support the United States against Russia."[54]

One of the sections in Neruda's denunciation is emphatically titled "González Videla's Treachery," in which he alludes to his personal acquaintance with the man, whose whole ideal in life can be summed up in one sentence, "I want to be president." He recalled the subversive plan that González Videla had proposed in La Moneda to the Communist Party's central administration, "favoring the creation of a military government without the participation of any party." Under a law of extraordinary powers, which in practice makes him a dictator, he unleashed his persecution. The case is cited of Julieta Campusano, a Santiago councilwoman, who was dragged off to jail at four in the morning, in spite of being in advanced pregnancy. There, she gave premature birth because of the violence she suffered by order of the president whom she had accompanied throughout the country during the campaign. Neruda underlined a detail that was particularly odious for him, pointing out that González Videla, for years president of the Hispano-Chilean Anti-Franco Association, had attempted to deport the Spanish refugees who had arrived on the *Winnipeg*. He opened concentration camps in Pisagua and other locations, and he invented ferocious accusations in order to break off relations with Yugoslavia and then with the Soviet Union and Czechoslovakia. Neruda points out that González Videla was also honorary president of the Chilean-Soviet Cultural Institute.

In that document, written in the heat of battle and ending with a "Personal Message," there is an especially revealing paragraph in which he recognizes that his years as a congressman and errant writer have taught him a lot, for he has examined the life of the people. "But exactly two months ago, the Chilean Communist Party leadership called on me and requested that more time and attention be given to my poetic work. To that purpose, they offered me for one year the necessary isolation and solitude to move ahead with my *General Song*, in particular."

He emphasizes in this manner the respect for his work which was inherent in that request, which had allowed him to recharge his writing batteries and put his ear to the earth and listen to the sound of growing roots. That's when the president's treachery came to yank him out of his concentration, and he left his Isla Negra retreat to take up his battle post. He is determined to face up to his obligations as a writer and as a patriot, whatever the cost may be. He assumes personal risks, and he places direct and individual responsibility on González Videla for whatever action may be taken against him.

The response isn't long in coming. The next day, the president initiates the so-called political trial, an action in the courts asking for revocation of Pablo Neruda's senatorial status.

After Neruda was deposed, he immediately tried to leave the country and go to Mendoza in Argentina. He was being driven by Mexico's Ambassador Alba, but they were stopped by the border patrol, and he had to return.

We were together on New Year's Eve, along with a few friends, and we enjoyed ourselves, dressed up in costumes, but the midnight embraces to greet 1948 were not full of joy. Yet, Neruda will not be cowed. He was one of those people who believe in the ardor of the fray. On 2 January I watch him as he works on the speech he will deliver in the next senate session. He dictates the text to a friend, Faustino Jorge, a lawyer and Argentine exile. He gives it a Zola-like tone, titling it in his own handwriting, "I Accuse." He has read the *Dreyfus Case* many times.

In the senate chambers, suspense reigns as the poet begins to speak. He recalls that exactly seven years ago to the day, on 6 January 1941, Franklin Delano Roosevelt sent out his message proposing the world's four basic freedoms, in whose defense he would stand up to Hitler: freedom of speech and of religion, and the right to live free from poverty and from fear. In Chile, the poet said, one is persecuted because he speaks the truth, therefore there is no freedom of speech nor freedom from fear. This is an old American tragedy. Those who claim that to criticize the president is to turn against the nation have a sad idea about the nation. And he quoted some words spoken by González Videla himself in Constitución Square:

> This is what is desired by the hidden Fascists whom we all know in this country. And because I saw them acting in noble France, I fear the Left's treacherous Lavals much more than those on the right. The anti-Communist movement, in the end, is the persecution and liquidation of the working class. When Hitler's forces entered France and took Paris, the Nazi soldiers didn't go around asking workers if they were Communists; it was sufficient just to be in favor of a trade union or to belong to a labor organization, for them to be persecuted, jailed, and condemned to forced labor.[55]

It's a self-portrait by the Latin American Laval. The poet pronounces his sentence, listing thirteen charges, thirteen direct and specific accusations based on known facts. He charges that the previous night someone had tried to burn down his house, leaving part of the front door destroyed by flames. Since his telephone was tapped by the government, he wasn't able to call the police, which would have been completely futile.

Telling the truth doesn't do any harm, but the poet also reserves the right to pronounce a judgment that will pursue the guilty one unto eternity, through his literary work: "If I have to deal with his case in the long poem called *General Song of Chile,* which I'm writing now as a song of the land and events in our nation, I will do so with the same honor and sincerity that I have brought to my political activity."

The previous night he had heard the appellate court's sentence, which agreed to his dismissal from the Senate. He answers that "Nobody except the people can dismiss *me.*"

98. Clandestine Life

When the supreme court confirms the lower court finding, Neruda becomes liable to persecution. The hounds are lying in wait, and he must go into hiding. He plunges into clandestine life, together with Delia "The Ant" and they become "Uncle Pedro and Aunt Sara." Since there weren't many places of refuge, we used to meet or take turns in the hideouts. These were usually small apartments, which on one occasion provided a view of the enemy's headquarters where the roots of our persecution were housed—the United States embassy. That particular apartment, next to Forestal Park, was a match box. One night some friends of the house's owner unexpectedly came to visit her, and "Uncle Pedro and Aunt Sara" had to hide in a tiny closet, and just as in old cloak and dagger comedies, he got the urge to sneeze, but fortunately controlled it.

They decided to change hideouts, and at three in the morning they were taken to a parcel of land in Santa Ana de Chena. During the day, the poet was writing his book. He told me he was thinking of changing the title, or expanding it to "General Song of America," but later he simplified it. His *General Song* not only required inspiration, but the poetic effort also had to be fed by concrete information, for which he needed history and geography books. A historian friend who was in charge of their nighttime changes of hideout, managed to get reference material for him, and cosmetics, shampoo, and hair tint for "The Ant," who began to turn gray in front of their very eyes. By day, they remained shut up in the country house, and Pablo grew a heavy black beard. In the evening, they went out for long walks through the fruit trees, slipping along the path, usually accompanied by some friends—five cats, three dogs, and some horses that nuzzled their arms for ears of corn. The two strollers discovered there that dogs have their own biological clock and instinctively know what time it is, anxiously awaiting the walks that delight them so much.

The historian drives them around the city at night. Once, at a corner, they're stopped by a soldier, who gets in next to the driver and does nothing more than ask to be taken to a specific destination.

In one garden house, the children in charge of looking after "Uncle Pedro and Aunt Sara" saw them drawing flowers and birds, and they ask him to teach them how to draw. The "uncle" had the youngsters cut out big paper flowers and put a little vial of sugar water in the center. Then the children climbed a tree and left the flowers on a high branch. After a minute, the tree was full of hummingbirds, including one that had sort of a little cap on its head and didn't let any others come near. Neruda named it "Cone Head." Those youngsters who learned from the poet how to make paper flowers, were their best bodyguards, permitting nobody to enter their room and carefully keeping watch outside, so that nobody should see "Aunt Sara and Uncle Pedro."

Looking over some old newspapers and documents as I write these pages, I come across the first page of *El Imperial* dated 5 February 1948. The banner headline, in exceptionally large type, reads "NATIONWIDE SEARCH FOR NERUDA." In the middle of the page, a lead paragraph summarizes the report: "Numerous groups trying to locate the Communist congressman, who is a fugitive. Summary minister González Castillo signed an order to apprehend with armed force. An important effort in Isla Negra may provide clues as to Neruda's whereabouts." Then, in larger type, *"There will be a reward for the investigator who discovers his whereabouts."*

A supposedly playful advertisement for the magazine *Topaze* is at the top of the first page: "Chile begins the third world war with an atomic bomb in the Caupolicán Theater." The meaning of this "advertisement" is not fortuitous, for it refers to the atmosphere created by President González Videla as he emphatically stated that the third world war would break out within ninety days. The persecution of Communists and of the labor movement, as well as the hunt for Neruda, were the consequences of that presidential psychosis which, of course, was fed from Washington kitchens. It also served as a smoke screen for his own political treachery.

While Neruda, under cover of night, is going from hideout to hideout, the story of that safari with the poet as prey is circulating throughout the world. People everywhere, including artists and writers, are so disturbed that Pablo Picasso delivers the one and only speech of his life, at the July 1948 World Congress of Intellectuals in Wroclaw, Poland. Conceived in direct, personal terms, this unique presentation stated:

> I have a friend who should have been here, a friend who is one of the finest men I've ever known. He is not only the greatest poet in his country, Chile, but also the greatest poet in the Spanish language and one of the greatest poets in the world. He is Pablo Neruda.
>
> Pablo Neruda, my friend, is not only a great poet, but also a man who, like everyone here, has devoted himself to presenting good in the shape of beauty. He has always been on the side of the unfortunate, of those who ask for justice and fight for it. My friend Neruda is presently being stalked like a dog, and nobody even knows where he is.
>
> Our congress, in my view, must not accept such an injustice, which may be turned against all of us. If Pablo Neruda were not to recover his freedom, our congress would not be a congress of men who deserved freedom. I propose that the following resolution be approved and given the widest distribution:
>
>> The World Congress of Intellectuals, meeting in Wroclaw, send their expression of support, admiration, affection and solidarity to the great poet Pablo Neruda. The congress's 500 members, who represent 46 nations, denounce before all people the degradation of police procedures by Fascist governments who dare to attack one of the most eminent representatives of culture. The members urgently demand Pablo Neruda's right to express himself freely and to live freely wherever he pleases.

The Party leadership resolved to get Neruda out of the country so that he could carry out a campaign abroad which would expose what was happening in Chile, but several attempts failed. The many vicissitudes of that period found their way into his poetry, as can be seen in the tenth section of the *General Song,* titled "The Fugitive."

From a temporal point of view, Neruda writes two types of poetry: instantaneous chronicles, an interiorized history of what he has just seen and experienced; and retrospective poetry, with the perspective of years. The notion of immediacy corresponds to "The Fugitive" and to those parts of the *General Song* which include "The Land Is Called Juan," "Flowers of Punitaqui," and "New Year's Chorale for the Nation in Darkness." They are forged in red-hot steel just emerged from the furnace.

The poetic overlay doesn't hide daily existence. In "These Weary

Days" he moves by night as a fugitive from the police, going from city to city and from one friend to another, and in darkness he receives confirmation of a sense of brotherhood. Almost always he would be put up in the houses of strangers, where he would go to sleep wondering, "Where am I? Who are these people? Why are they protecting me today?"

That's how he remembers his arrival in autumn at the Santa Ana de Chena acreage. It was the grape season, and he delighted in listening to the owner, a tiny old man with spectacles who worked as an accountant but knew all the secrets of the earth and trees and had a surgeon's hand in grafting. That was where the poet talked to the horses as if they were children, and was followed about by the owner's five cats and three dogs, among the fruited peach trees.

That immersion in the depths was for the fugitive a contact with people who were risking everything out of solidarity with a man who was hunted because of his fidelity to values that they shared, a poet they knew because they had read a book or a verse by him, or simply because they knew his name and respected him. For others, he was just a decent man and the victim of an unjust pursuit.

Nocturnal transfers, for night meant travel. It was night when another new door opened to him, and he found the incompatible couple comprised by the golden writer and the Spanish engineer. They lived apart from each other, but they came together to receive the poet in their matchbox apartment. Her name was Marta Jara, but the christening poet gave her the name "Irene" for the sake of his clandestine life. The man, who has since gone back to Catalunya, was given the name "Andrés."

Many escape plans were studied. The poet was very well known, and the police were looking everywhere for him. At one point, a departure by sea was considered, and Neruda went to Valparaíso where he again breathed the smell of the Pacific and listened to the ocean. He took refuge in the home of two sailors, whose mother asked them, "What kind of accommodations can *we* give him?" Her sons answered, "He is one of us." When he arrived, he went to the window and watched a thousand blinking eyes of the city and its hills. After a while, he turned around and was struck with tenderness to see the table set with bread, wine, water, and folded napkin. He spent many hours at that window in Valparaíso, waiting. The sailors were searching for a boat to hire out on and slip the fugitive in as a stowaway. It was a period of promises that weren't fulfilled, first with the *Atomena* falling through and then the *Sultana*. The two sailors kept at the task, while the poet stayed alone during the day, contemplating Valparaíso and its poor houses with brightly painted doors, highwire dwellings miraculously clinging to the edge of the cliff. He anxiously watched the boats in the bay. This was his longest perusal to date of Valparaíso, and that secret stay led him to one day build his "La Sebastiana" house on the highest point of a hill in that port city, as the fugitive declared his love for Valparaíso: "I love everything you contain, Valparaíso, everything you exude, sweetheart of the ocean . . ." He would set up his desk in front of the window, to look at the city and write, "I'm the greatest sailor on paper . . . I declare to you my love, Valparaíso, / and I will again share your crusade, / when you and I are free / once more."[56]

One rule of clandestine life is that you can't remain for long in the same house. He had to move on, and he went from room to room, all of them humble, his secret protected by all of them. He lived in homes belonging to a little tinsmith, to the mother of some girls, to an awkward farmer, to a man who made soap, to "a young man impaled like an insect in a desolate office." He would enter unexpectedly, not knowing anyone, and he would be welcomed like a brother.

The backdoor poet gives thanks in that poem "The Fugitive" to all who hosted him. He presses their hands and is not alone. He is a part of an infinitude, because in the end those are his people and they have protected him.

99. Looking for a Way Out

When the plan to flee from Valparaíso by boat had completely come to naught, the poet returned chafing to Santiago.

From the moment in which Neruda was stripped of his senatorial status, we began to study how to prevent his capture, first of all, and then to get him safely out of the country. Many possibilities were analyzed, and some were set in motion only to end in frustration, like the Valparaíso initiative. Others were discarded out of hand.

Chile has two frontiers—the sea and the cordillera. The ocean was a closed door for him, so he would have to make his way across the Andes. The escape was organized by the Party in a multiphased plan. One night, we in the leadership bade him farewell with a few hours of fellowship. He was radiant, with a thick beard. In the wee hours of the morning, a car came for him, and he and I embraced each other. We wouldn't see him again for years.

More than half a year had already gone by since the beginning of his persecution when the Communist Party leadership made contact with

Jorge Bellet Bastías, a man who was a force of nature in the flesh, physically powerful, mentally alert, capable of any feat. He had held several positions in Chile and abroad, and had a personality that didn't run away from adventure, but at the same time he was cautious. Within a boxer's body lived a revolutionary's sense of responsibility and a businessman's practicality. In addition, he loved poetry and respected poets. That's why someone thought of him as the person who could see this complicated job through to completion. He was also selected because of another crucial fact; at the time, he was managing a logging estate in Valdivia province, adjacent to the cordillera, which is covered with dense forest in that area. When he was contacted, his eyes opened wide. The offspring of a French father and a Chilean mother, he had a brother in the film industry and a sister who was a delicate sculptress until her early death when the sea slammed her against a rock. Jorge had been involved in agriculture, industry, business, and later in the production of dried meat in Arica, but he was always interested in everything related to art and knowledge. In addition, he is a good friend to his friends. At one time he was a high-ranking official in the National Airline, and he likes to fly over great expanses, but he also knows how to move on land through thick forests and across the torrential rivers in the region that borders Neruda's childhood Temuco.

"Yes," was his immediate response, "but the operation should be carried out in full summer." He was asked to come to Santiago, where he talked with Ricardo Fonseca and Galo González. Several plans were discussed, with two hypotheses intersecting. One, have him journey from Santiago to Valdivia and from there to the Argentine border, escorted by a relatively hidden group of twenty experienced militants who would form a defensive screen around Neruda, to prevent the police from detaining him or shooting him, in case of discovery. This plan was discarded, for in spite of the assurances which were given, it carried many risks, including risks for the poet.

A more discreet alternative was chosen, with secrecy carried to the extreme. Aside from the most responsible nucleus of the Party leadership, only Neruda and Bellet would know what was involved.

The siege was becoming more and more restrictive, as the circle of pursuit was closing in. During that time, González Videla's police had been watching about 200 persons on the list of the poet's friends and acquaintances. Houses many miles away from Santiago were being raided at dawn. The poet was living hidden away in an apartment on Providencia Avenue near Pedro de Valdivia. The Party provided Bellet with a car and a driver-mechanic. In addition, we gave him a list of militants who lived in different towns along the highway that runs lengthwise toward the South, all of whom had been advised to stay alert, without telling them the reason.

At nine at night on escape day, another car stopped in front of the house where Neruda was staying. It belonged to Dr. Raúl Bulnes Cerdá, who was accompanied by Jorge Bellet. Dr. Bulnes and his wife Lala were Neruda's neighbors at Isla Negra, where the poet never could manage to have a coastal garden as beautiful as that of Dr. Bulnes, a laboratory researcher who spent all his weekends tending his flowers. A very close friendship had grown up between the poet and the gardening doctor, who was here now with his car to take Neruda by night to the town of Graneros, where he left him at the home of a Communist whose unofficial name was Andrés. In front, the Party's car was waiting, with the mechanic at the wheel.

The driver had difficulty recognizing his passenger, changed by the heavy beard and uncharacteristic clothing. He was informed of the traveler's identity—Antonio Ruiz, ornithologist. Even in his clandestine adventure, the poet enjoyed his little pleasures. He picked the first name of a poet, a last name that was common to several prose writers of different periods, and a profession he would have liked to have and in truth exercised, for he was an expert on the birds of Chile, and it wouldn't be long before he would write a book called *Art of Birds*. But it would have been tempting the devil to call himself an ornithologist on the identity card numbered 444,968, issued in Santiago on 1 April 1946 and due to expire in four years, according to the stamp of the Civil Registry General Office's Investigation Service. Such a strange occupation and such an unusual word would make a clerk look carefully from head to foot at that heavyset, round-faced gentleman of forty, whose full beard and mustache contrasted sharply with an almost bare skull where just a few recalcitrant hairs on top seemed to be the last wispy moss left over from a nearly vanished mane. Moved by the mysterious-looking "ornithologist," they might examine those small eyes set under heavy arching brows astride a harpoon nose, thus triggering a dangerous "he looks like . . ." kind of recognition by some inquisitive border patrolman. The choice of that profession had been his, to accompany the name Antonio Ruiz Lagorreta. His friends, acting as technical advisors, accepted all three names and, maybe because he looked older than he was, they suggested he add three years to his age with a birthdate of 14 February 1901. In addition, they urged him to give up Parral and Temuco in favor of a birthplace in gray Santiago, whose large-scale dimensions could easily keep the deception undiscovered. In that document, he also abandoned Delia del Carril, declaring himself a bachelor, which is a venal sin committed every day by more than one husband. He agreed to all of it, including the truth when he answered *yes* on the line which asked "Can you read?" Another solemn *yes* responds to the abbreviated inquiry "Writes?" which might suggest a profession but was simply an indication that he was not illiterate. Satisfied, he allowed them to invent a capital-city residence he had never set foot in but had seen many times, especially before his departure for the Orient, since it was just a few steps from the Alameda, at 49 Carmen Street. It was an insignificant detail that he had doubtless passed its door countless times without noticing it, for the important thing is that the house with that address did indeed exist. That was more than enough for their purposes. He insisted, though, on the profession whose designation he so much liked: "Put down 'ornithologist.' " He liked to teasingly call himself a big-bird poet or a poetic birdwatcher. But the experts were insistent that it be an unpoetic job, like "office worker." And so he became Ruiz, the office worker.

The document contained a solemn notation that it certified only his identity, not the quality of his background. What its owner wanted was not a certificate of good conduct, though, but only to become someone other than who he really was, in spite of the fact that any graphologist can see the unmistakable handwriting of a man named Pablo Neruda in the incomplete *Antonio* and the large *Z* of *Ruiz* on the signature line.

The journey was a long one, about 500 miles along the main highway, through many cities and towns, but it all worked out as planned, except that before reaching Valdivia they were stopped by the inevitable soldier who always turns up in these critical moments, but instead of demanding their papers he just asked for a ride to a town a few miles further south. He sat next to the bearded gentleman, who broke his silence to make some observations about the road and—the height of imprudence!—to slightly criticize the government.

100. *Preparations in the Forest*

The trip from the city of Valdivia to Futrono was more difficult. They were getting deep into marshy territory where they had to cross Lake Ranco, which he would evoke in his poetry, then through Lifén to Puerto de los Yoyos, before crossing another lake, the Maihue. Finally they reach Hueinahue, another indigenous name, where sawmills had been installed on the José Rodríguez estate. Years later, this entrepreneur would be chewed up by the banking system and would end up in jail, where he desperately would write to Neruda, by then back in Chile, who made great efforts to help free his old benefactor. In the Senate, I used to receive urgent notes from the poet asking me to do something on Rodríguez's behalf.

At that estate, Neruda had to climb back onto a horse for the first time since twenty-five years ago when he had spent his last summers in Temuco writing to Albertina from the countryside. He had forgotten how to ride and had to learn it all over again, for this might not be an adventure for a knight errant like Don Quixote but certainly it would require skill from a knightly ornithologist who had to escape on horseback. After his practice sessions, he would climb down all bruised and with his legs aching, but he knew he had to make that sacrifice. When he could finally walk on his own, he would chat a while with Juan, Jorge Bellet's eleven-year-old son, and then, immersed in the smell of freshly cut wood, he would write verses. Every day, he and Bellet would go over their situation. Preparations were coming along nicely.

Suddenly the devil stepped in with a gunfight between one of the region's indigenous chiefs and some estate workers. In this highly charged atmosphere, the chief appealed to the Lands Ministry in Santiago, which decided to send an official to investigate the complaint. Neruda grew pale—everything could fall apart and he would be discovered. It was quite unlikely that his presence would escape the inspector's notice. He didn't sleep for several nights.

When the inspector arrived, Neruda watched him from a window in his hiding place. His heart leaped—it wasn't Gogol's inspector, but Neruda's friend Víctor Bianchi Gundián, who was his same age, a man with a zest for life and many talents as an artist, a clever caricaturist, and a guitar-playing singer, who played above all to please the ladies. His brothers were variously Supreme Court justices or ambassadors, but he preferred being an inspector for National Lands, because it provided a chance to live in the forests and parks and to learn new secrets of nature, which for him was happiness. When the two of them embraced and Víctor learned what was going on, he became a collaborator in the adventure.

Many years later, on one of the inspector's many trips, he was killed by an automobile as he got out of his own car. When Neruda learned of it, he sat down at his desk and wrote some lines about the investigator who had gone to the Hueinahue estate to initiate an indictment and joined up with the group. The poet remembered that Víctor was never without his guitar, for he liked to hear music in the heart of the forest.

In those two pages, called "A Letter for Víctor Bianchi," the man is presented as "the active observer of feats and disasters, of exceptional events, of mysterious stirrings, of the most starry realm." An Andean climber like those in the Himalayas, he was one of the few survivors of a climb to the top of Aconcagua. He liked to row a *piragua* dugout through tropical rivers and explore salt mines and largely uncharted islands. He searched out volcanic vents in the desert and investigated mercury veins in Colombia. He was a small delicate man who had gone clear to Antarctica. "His guitar was adventurous," Neruda said. "Neither Jorge Bellet nor my anonymous companions on the trek were surprised when you lashed only a bedroll and your guitar to the saddle, to cross the Andes with me. And how that sonorous chamber did help us, how you sang and spread charm in San Martín de los Andes where we arrived like Chilean meteors all covered with Andean stardust. . . . What's to be done? Once more, my good companion Víctor Bianchi gives us a surprise. Once more he has gone away with his music, to a new territory."[57]

The crossing was so complicated that they even had to build a road to pass the border, but then the rain, Neruda's constant childhood companion, treacherously annulled the effort with a flood that wiped out the road. They couldn't wait for the earth to dry in order to reopen the trail, so they decided to risk crossing through the hazardous Smugglers Pass. Neruda agreed; the danger was great, but it was the only solution.

101. Toward the Ends of the Earth

On the appointed day, they set out early, accompanied by three boys whom Neruda called "the three Juans." They headed through the forest toward the pass, and when they reached open space they broke into a light trot.

"My speech," he says many years later, "will be about a long trek, my journey through distant and antipodal regions, not unlike the landscape and solitude of the North. I will talk about my country's extreme south . . ." That journey is the one we're talking about here, and the speech that evokes it is his address in Stockholm when he accepts the Nobel Prize for Literature. He delivers it twenty-two years after the time when he had had to cross the Andes in search of the difficult frontier. The faraway reminiscence sings of his country's forests, equally distant, which were like tunnels, where roads were non-existent and everything seemed inaccessible, but even worse than the lack of trails and paths was the fact that the riders had to make their way among trees that were like thick walls, across rivers that seemed unfordable, over rocks where they had to claw for a hold, for they were traveling in search of freedom. But more crucial than all of that, or graver if it should fail, was their sense of direction, for they had to guide themselves by signs cut into the bark of trees that pointed out the invisible route, through the green and silent realm of inhospitable virgin nature, where isolation joins forces with surprise and danger. Another opponent was the snow, which in some places never completely melts. They moved forward with slashing machetes, cutting branches in order to get themselves and their horses between the huge conifers, many of which served as gravemarkers for fallen travelers, whose passage was marked by fallen branches. That was also the domain of hazardous rivers, very different from European rivers, for in these regions the waters are born in Andean peaks and come hurtling down with insane speed, sweeping away everything in their swift current.

They looked for a fording place, and the horses entered the water, left their footing behind, and began to swim in search of the shore. Neruda felt his mount trapped by the river and realized that nothing was holding him up. He tried to grab the horse's mane, fearful that he would die there.

When they reached the other side, he learned that "the three Juans" had been behind him with their lassos ready, because in that very spot, one of them explained, his father had fallen off and was carried away by the current, and that wasn't going to happen to Neruda . . .

Then they entered a tunnel that hadn't been dug by human effort but by a seismic movement. Inside, the horses slipped and slid, striking sparks with their shoes. The poet fell several times, and his noble beast was bleeding from his legs and muzzle.

Suddenly, an almost bucolic valley appears on the side of the mountain, the very picture of peace. The Spanish Renaissance poet Garcilaso de la Vega would have been enchanted by so much crystalline water, the soft meadow, the riot of flowers sprinkled by no human hand, and the brilliant sky. In the center, like a god, there was an ox skull. The muleteers dropped some coins into the empty eyesockets, and like the ancient Indians, left some food in the hollows of the bones. The poet joined in the ceremony, in recognition of the divinity of men lost in the forest, and the muleteers took off their hats and began to dance on one leg.

They rode on for several hours and arrived tired and hungry at the

Chiu Chiu hot springs. Neruda, both in his *Memoirs* and in the Nobel speech, has recounted that journey and the sight of a twenty-foot-long fire burning in the room set aside for travelers of those lonely territories. Up above, they saw some wide planks, which held enormous cheeses. Over the fire, meat was roasting on an iron spit. As they entered, the smell of cheese and meat set their gastric juices in motion, promising full restoration of their strength. Rustic benches and boxes surrounded the gigantic fire. They took their fur saddle blankets to a corner and settled down.

When they had entered, they were blinded by the light from the blazing fire, and only when their eyes had become adjusted could they make out a man here and there, until they had counted more than twenty, most of them with intimidating faces reddened by the glow from the flames.

They were in the secret gathering place for smugglers, muleteers, people who lived outside the law, specialists in clandestine border crossings and in such activities as stealing cattle, all of them expert handlers of revolver and knife.

Without preamble, out of that darkness broken only by the flames, came forth what the poet described as a "song about love and distance, an amorous nostalgic lament against faraway springtime, against the cities we had come from, against the endless extension of life." He asked himself a question that was urgent in his situation, "Do they know who I am?" He never found out, but whether he was recognized or not, they all sang and ate together until they were stuffed.

For Neruda, that part of the journey was not only the road to freedom but also an image of life, an explication of the earth and a lesson in poetic art, for poetry's participants are the truths of consciousness and of dreams, of man and nature, of the apparently impenetrable forest, and the conclusion that "there is no impregnable solitude."

Neruda wasn't shy on that occasion. He bit off chunks of cheese, opined that the roasted meat was stupendous, took a sip of whiskey from his pocket flask, and proceeded to tell stories in his slow twang. A half-hour later, they realized that the smugglers' refuge had become a theater, with Neruda as narrator of astonishing adventures and more than twenty outlaws as his audience, who listened with rapt attention and delight to that man whom they had never seen before but who talked like nobody else they had ever heard. Among the enraptured listeners was the owner of that strange place, and when it came time to pay the bill, he refused to charge them. That was his way of compensating the stranger who had turned his hidden dining room into a stage occupied by an artist who neither sang nor acted, and without any guitar or horn had captivated the gathering with a special instrument that is rare in those out-of-the-way places—the spoken word.

And then they went off to a few unfurnished bedrooms, whose flooring was above some underground hot springs which warmed them with the heat from the cordillera's molten rock.

At dawn, they bathed in one of the springs that issued forth from that flow, as if they were trying to cleanse themselves for their meeting with freedom. They were so content that all began to sing as they mounted their horses, which also seemed happy to be moving forward through those heights.

VI.

The World Voyage

102. Saint Martin of Free Men

And then, behold the border! Neruda, remembering that he was a poet, spotted an abandoned railroad tie, which reminded him of his father's ballast train that used to carry timbers and rock to shore up the line. He sat down on the tie and broke off his lofty meditation to take up the weapon of a chastising poet as he wrote a bold verse of farewell:

How clean is this air
in the Pass of Lilpela
where there is no crap
from the traitor Videla.

They rode into the Argentine city of San Martín de los Andes, not exactly like Quixotes but like seekers of freedom, which for Neruda was like shedding a leaden weight. He wanted to let loose some intemperate shouts, but Bellet vehemently recommended caution, for they still hadn't come to where they could reveal their identity. The expedition's leader took command, as the third phase of the plan was put into operation. They were to present themselves as "rich *huaso* cowboys," Chilean ranchers with a lot of money who were coming to make some deals. Their first move would be to get lodging in the town's most luxurious hotel. Without much to choose from, they went to the Tourist Hotel where they were supposed to meet their Argentine contact within a few hours. They washed up and took some refreshment, but time passed and nobody came looking for them. They were to be recognized by Bellet's appearance: a heavyset man wearing a blue checkered shirt, with a pipe in his mouth or hand, and a riding cap. Bellet felt obliged to neither change his shirt nor remove his cap or pipe so long as the awaited saviour didn't appear.

Days went by with no sign of their contact, and these Chileans, who never left the hotel, were beginning to look a bit strange. They would have to do something to win the confidence of the town's authorities, so the three musketeers named Bellet, Bianchi and Ruiz, issued a dinner invitation to the police chief, the army commander and some officers, who were quite impressed by the very generous and personable Chileans.

Still their contact didn't show up. They became as tense as birds on a highwire, and after a while, trusting in the relationship he had established with the regimental colonel, Bellet decided to risk something that could very well prove to be a serious mistake. He told the officer that, for business reasons, he urgently needed to talk to a lawyer in Mendoza. The colonel asked for the individual's name, and Bellet answered, "Benito Marianetti." The officer gave a start, "But he's a Communist, man!" With a straight face, Bellet replied, "I don't believe it!"

The regimental commander gave him access to army radio, and Marianetti at first was taken aback by such an unexpected call. He didn't understand what it was all about and in his surprise, he almost gave it all away, but then he figured it out, with the result that the contact finally showed up at the hotel to take them to Buenos Aires.

In the Argentine capital, it was inevitable that Neruda would see some friends, and indeed he gets in touch with his old *confrère,* Rafael Alberti, who goes with him one day to Soviet Ambassador Serguiev's home to talk about Neruda's trip to Europe. The individual most taken by the Chilean poet is the ambassador's wife, the painter Tamara Alexieievna Siéverova, who does a portrait of him while the men are talking. The painting, which shows a young-looking Neruda, will later be given to Chilean exiles in Moscow, in 1980, after the artist's death. She had also sculpted a bust of the poet, which her husband donated to a museum in Volgograd, the city to which Neruda had dedicated several "Love Songs" under the name of "Stalingrad."

103. The Charge to Publish the General Song

He did depart from Chile, but first he had entrusted one task to his comrades—the clandestine edition of the *General Song*. The three initial members of the group in charge of the edition were: Américo Zorrilla, who had been director of the daily *El Siglo;* the painter José Venturelli; and another who shall remain nameless because he is still working inside Chile in opposition to the Pinochet dictatorship.

For a clandestine book, it had an unusually large and bulky format, difficult to hide. The publication was supervised by Guillermo Labaste, who had been a furniture maker, and Manuel Segundo Recabarren Rojas, a printer who would be detained on 30 April 1976 by agents of the DINA secret police (Department of National Intelligence), one day after the arrest of his sons, Manuel Guillermo and Luis Emilio Recabarren González, and his daughter-in-law, Nalvia Rosa Mena Alvarado. They all disappeared, and to this day their fate is unknown. Doubtless they were killed, like 2,500 other Chileans who also disappeared.

This team set about the task of publishing 5,000 copies of a 468-page book that measured nearly seven and one-half by eleven inches. The paper that went into it weighed a considerable four tons, and was of two types: rough pulp no. 264, rather coarse looking, and feather-weight tissue for 2,000 more expensive copies.

It was a time when the police were on the lookout for clandestine publications. They knew the location of all printing presses and could discover the origin of a text by means of its typography. The Communist Party dug out a collection of linotype matrices that had been kept aside for fifteen years, and the entire book was set by just one linotypist, the composition by just Comrade Osorio, and the printing by Manuel Recabarren. Each phase was done in a different location, and then the set-up type had to be transported to the composition point, and the page galleys finally taken to the press where the book was run off.

As invariably happens in these cases, agents arrived at that very printing press in search of illegal publications. They looked everywhere, while the officer in charge watched and gave orders from his perch on a rather high block of paper covered with several sections of an equestrian magazine. Underneath were the 22-by-31-inch uncut sheets of the *General Song*.

The problem of main headings was solved by loans from several presses. The plates for Venturelli's illustrations, separated out from the text, could be created without difficulty in a photo-engraving studio, but greater risk was involved in including photographs at the end and beginning of the book. The first one shows Neruda alone, and the second one, taken from behind, shows him strolling with Delia. It was necessary to glue them like laminated illustrations into each copy of the book after binding. The binding and handsewing were done by just one craftsman, who lived out in the countryside where he had a little tile-making factory.

In that lonely spot he devoted several months to assembling and binding each and every book. Proofs had been corrected by Joaquín Gutiérrez and by Luis Corvalán, who was then in charge of the Party's publicity campaigns.

Reservations were sold in advance for this book by Neruda, which was presented as "printed in Mexico" by the Juárez Press, with a false dust jacket which read *Risas y Lágrimas* (Laughter and Tears) by Benigno Espinosa.

104. Parisian Debut

Impudence and fantasy now make their appearance, as the two "turkey-gobblers," Asturias and Neruda, embrace each other in Argentina. A few years earlier, the author of *El Señor Presidente* had bewitched a Sunday morning audience in Santiago as he held them spellbound in Neruda's untamed garden where autumn leaves were raining down. He had recounted the miracles and prophecies of the Mayan chronicles of Chilam Balam and recited the songs of ancient indigenous rhapsodists, using a long school pointer to explain pre-Columbian drawings and hieroglyphics. But now these two heretics were concerned about such current and mundane items as the falsification of passports and identity cards. Since they physically resemble each other, they decide to take advantage of the similarity. Neruda was to travel from Buenos Aires to Paris with Miguel Angel Asturias's passport. Did the latter agree on condition that the passport be destroyed upon Neruda's entrance into France? Truth or legend? Maybe a true story that demonstrates the two poets' friendship? Or a fictional invention? *Se non vero e ben trovato.* If it's not true, it's nonetheless clever.

Toward the end of March or early April, in a Paris apartment a doorbell rings. The owner goes to open the door and finds a heavyset bearded stranger, wearing thick-rimmed glasses and a black Basque beret. The two stand there looking at each other. "Don't you recognize me?" the visitor asks. The surprised homeowner remains silent, trying in vain to identify him. The newcomer finally says, "I'm Pablo Neruda, come to ask you to take me in for a few days."

"Come in, Pablo. I'm glad you have come. Make yourself at home." The man who welcomes him, and later tells me about the encounter, is Luis Cardoza y Aragón, the Guatemalan writer we had met years ago in Neruda's Los Guindos house, when he had come to Chile as his country's ambassador.

After dinner, the poet's unexpected appearance was celebrated with champagne, and Neruda took out a notebook from his suitcase and read sections of the *General Song* until dawn.

The household staff called him "Don Antonio," but Neruda wasn't a man to live cooped up in hiding, much less in Paris. He used to go on automobile outings with Cardoza y Aragón's wife Lya. Like a dog restrained on a short leash, he went out to indulge pleasures long held in check—visits to secondhand bookstores and shops for naturalists and shell collectors. He was always looking for rare editions and shells.

He couldn't keep from playing jokes, even in the midst of his peculiar situation. He asked his host to arrange a café meeting with a friend, the Argentine writer Alfredo Varela, who was then an exuberant youth who would be very outspoken all his life. When Varela arrived at the café and Luis Cardoza y Aragón introduced him to "a Czechoslovakian professor who had legally left his country," Varela grew silent, refusing to open his mouth and just glancing quickly at the fellow who was with them there on the Café Marignan terrace on the Champs Elysée. Varela was afraid he might be one of those anti-Communist professionals, made for export, who was hoping to trap him in a cause that Varela had no interest in. At a certain moment, though, the Czech professor took off his hat and dark glasses, giving Varela a start, for the man was neither a professor nor a Czech. "Don't be silly," the fellow said, roaring with laughter and putting a finger to his lips. "I'm Neruda," he said, then warned the youth to keep it quiet because he was "clandestinely in Paris."

As we recall this episode, Alfredo Varela has just died in Mar del Plata in Argentina.

The poets' brotherhood sometimes operates as an international brigade. Jules Supervielle is Uruguayan, like the author of *Les Chants du Maldoror*. They both come from Montevideo, a century apart, but unlike Lautréamont, Supervielle is not an accursed poet, and some even consider him to be a pure poet, close to Paul Valéry. He comes from a prosperous family that has something to do with banks and also with the police. Supervielle asks a close relative in a high position to arrange legal status for Pablo Neruda's presence in France. Here is where not the brush but the hand of Pablo Picasso, a friend of Jules Supervielle, comes into play, as the one who delivers the results of that intercession. Alfredo Varela is waiting at a metro entrance when Picasso arrives by car at a prearranged hour to communicate the awaited news—Neruda can now appear in public. Just a few minutes later, he departs for the final session of the Peace Congress, which is being held in Pleyel Hall. There, Picasso himself announces that he has a surprise, whereupon Neruda dramatically appears on the platform, making his European debut.

On Monday, 25 April 1949, they adjourn the World Congress of Peace Supporters, which had begun five days earlier. Many of the world's most famous artists and writers, as well as political personalities, were in attendance. From France came Yves Fargue, Paul Eluard, Louis Aragon, Elsa Triolet, Eugénie Cotton, Jean Cassou, Aimé Césaire, Pierre Cot, Paul Rivet, Armand Salacrou, Frédéric and Irène Joliot-Curie, Pierre Seghers, and Pablo Picasso; from Italy, Pietro Nenni, Elio Vitorini, Italo Calvino, Renato Guttuso, Giulio Einaudi, and Emilio Sereni; from Germany, Anna Seghers and Arnold Zweig; from the United States, Howard Fast, Langston Hughes, Charlie Chaplin, Paul Robeson, Albert Kahn, and W. E. B. Du Bois; from the Soviet Union, Ilya Ehrenburg, Mikhail Sholokhov, Constantin Fedeiev, Wanda Wassilewska, and Dimitri Shostakovich; from Yugoslavia, Ivo Andrić; from Greece, Melpo Axioti; from China, Kuo Mo-Jo and Emi-Siao.

And from Latin America, there were two hundred delegates, including: Diego Rivera and Lázaro Cárdenas from Mexico; Antonio Berni, Luis Seoane, and Alfredo Varela from Argentina; Nicolás Guillén and Juan Marinello from Cuba; Jorge Amado and Caio Pedro from Brazil; Luis Cardoza y Aragón and José Manuel Fortunny from Guatemala; René Depestre from Haiti; Miguel Otero Silva and Héctor Poleo from Venezuela.

Yves Fargue presides over the final session, announcing in deliberate tones: "I will give the floor to the final speaker, who will close the general discussion. The man who will speak to you has only been in the hall for a few minutes. You have not yet seen him, for he is a hunted man. . . . He is Pablo Neruda."

Everyone rises to their feet. They weren't expecting this electrical shock in the theater. Neruda delivers a short speech, in which he seems to apologize for his tardiness. "Dear friends," he begins, "if I have arrived a bit late at your meeting, it is due to the difficulties I have had to overcome in order to get here. I bring to you the greetings of all the people in distant lands. The political persecution which exists in my country has allowed me to appreciate the fact that human solidarity is greater than all barriers, more fertile than all valleys . . ." Then he reads his "Song for Bolívar" out of the Chilean edition of the *General Song*. That very day he had received the first copy in Paris. He went to the congress carrying the thick tome with him and had presented it to Picasso, from whom he had to borrow it back again in order to read the poem. As soon as the meeting was over, giving no credence to the saying that "One who gives and then retracts will grow a hump upon his back," Neruda took the book away with him, explaining that it was the only copy he had.

Back in Chile, some kind of correction would be called for as a result of a wire story carried by Santiago newspapers the day after Neruda's appearance in Paris, which said verbatim: "Unexpectedly and without warning of any kind, the hunted Chilean Communist poet Pablo Neruda appeared today in Paris. He attended the morning session of the World Congress of Peace Supporters, which is being held here, and spoke from the platform. The deepest mystery surrounds the circumstances by which he managed to leave his country and make the journey."

One day before Neruda's public appearance in Paris, the Chilean chief of investigation and political police, Luis Brum D'Avoglio, had declared to the Santiago press that Neruda was on the point of falling into the hands of his men.

A journalist from France Press went to see Neruda to inform him that González Videla's government, upon hearing the news of the poet's appearance in France, had declared emphatically that the individual who was presenting himself as Pablo Neruda was an imposter. The journalist said he just wanted to take a look at the poet's twin.

105. Europe Makes a Discovery

A new period in his life was beginning with that exile. In 1949, critics considered Neruda to be the number one Latin American poet. At least within our own continent, that was the more-or-less prevailing opinion, but except for learned circles, he still had not been discovered by the great European public.

But the poet was a methodical conqueror of successive audiences. First, a provincial poet in Temuco, then the student generation's poet in Santiago of the 1920s, and later national poet of Chile and sort of jack-of-all-trades for lovers.

He had spent four years in Asia, where almost nobody realized that he was a poet, and those who did couldn't read him, since the Spanish language was inaccessible to readers in that part of the world.

His reputation gradually had begun to spread through personal contact, through physical and spiritual contact with the man himself and with his books, first in Argentina and then in Spain and Mexico, and ultimately in brief trips to almost all the Latin American countries. That was the extent of his fame in those days, the widest region where his name was known.

Nonetheless, his renown had not reached the vast North American or European readership. His exile and residence for several years in the Old World, along with a number of other reasons growing out of the social and political movement of the times, contributed to the discovery and acclaim for his poetry by readers in other languages and cultures.

He became recognized in a city that had seemed impossible to him twenty years earlier. Paris was well worth a thousand celebrations of the mass, which in his case were celebrations of friendship that transcended talent. In May, the foreign writers who attended the Peace Congress were honored by the National Committee of French Writers in the Maison de la Pensée. There, Neruda read his poem "The Fugitive," which asks:

> What can you do, Beast, against the wind? . . .
> How sad is your petty and fleeting
> victory! Whereas Aragon, Ehrenburg,
> Eluard, the poets
> of Paris, the valiant
> writers
> of Venezuela and more and more and more
> are with me,
> you, Beast,
> have Escanilla and Cuevas, Peluchoneaux and Poblete![58]

Louis Aragon accompanied his rendition with a French version by Alice Ahrweiler.

Neruda was always inclined to cordial fellowship, and in Paris old and new friends gathered around him: the old comrades from Spain, who during the civil war had opened up a Pyrenees path of communication for him; friends from Mexico; Ehrenburg, Aragon, Anna Seghers, Nicolás Guillén, Jorge Amado, and other Latin Americans. And now, deep new friendships were formed with Paul Eluard, Paul Robeson, Jean Marcenac, Pierre Courtade, and Renato Guttuso.

This man, whose recent isolation had limited his expansive and eloquent conversation to smugglers and horse thieves in faraway hideouts in the middle of the remote forest, was now the man of the hour in the center of the world, hungrily listening and talking, granting ten interviews a day.

But his nights were for his friends, and his Sunday mornings could hold no greater joy than to profitably waste time in the flea market, which compensated for the now out-of-reach Persian Market in Santiago. He had strategically planted his flag in Paris, and soon the compass needle was pointing toward a new irresistible city—Moscow.

106. The Wind of the Old New World

He had begun to write a new book, although he was still nagged by the *General Song*. He thought he had said good-bye to it with his "New Year's Chorale for the Nation in Darkness," in which he again wrote of persecution in a time when he carried in his fugitive's cloak just a freshly cut hawthorn branch and two books, a geography of his country and a book about the birds of Chile. In that New Year's greeting he had addressed "The Men of Pisagua," the prisoners who could easily have been his companions. He evoked Félix Morales and Angel Veas, dead in that concentration camp, and he once more cursed the "lying dog." In Europe he had one overriding preoccupation—that the voice of Chile should continue to be heard, and that his own voice should be heard in Chile. Neruda was always a poet who put real people into his works, calling heroes and anti-heroes by their names, including the "mice in the budget" and "mercenaries with outstretched hands." He vehemently declares vengeance:

> They will be named. You, my country, didn't give me
> just the sweet privilege of naming
> your gilly flowers and your sea foam,
> you, my country, didn't give me just words to call you
> by gilded names, full of pollen, full of fragrance,
> to sprinkle about like drops of dew
> that fall from your regal black mane:
> along with milk and meat you gave me words
> that will also name the pale worms
> who travel about in your belly,
> poisoning your blood and wasting your life away.[59]

"'They used to call him a Chilean,' these maggots say of me," he bitterly complains. He'll go even deeper. "Behind the traitors and gnawing rats, / there's an empire that sets the table, / that serves up food and bullets." He will not forgive; he will fight. "I'm no longer a citizen of my country: they tell me / that the uncouth clown who governs has erased / my name and thousands more / from the rolls that once were the Republic's law." In the last section of the *General Song,* the autobiographical note is so strong that he nakedly defines himself in "I Am." He is what he was, what he has always been: the frontier, the slingsman, his companions on the journey, the youth in love with the student from Santiago in the colonial territory of New Extremadura, the traveler in Burma, the critic in India, the man who strolled the streets of Saigon and Madras and watched the chalk-faced dancing girls of Bangkok. He is also Spain, which gave him love and war; Mexico, where he touched the earth of America; and always Chile. He will live another twenty-four years, but in that book he leaves two wills, indicating his wish to be buried at Isla Negra. The book is finished on 5 February 1949, a few months before his forty-fifth birthday, in Santa Ana de Chena, which he calls "Godomar de Chena."

The new book that he is beginning to work on every morning is sort of a collection of travels through Europe and Asia, which will be called *Las uvas y el viento* (Grapes and Wind). But first this peripatetic correspondent will have to experience new nations and their people. The New World must discover the Old World, though there are many things old in the New, and much that is new in the Old.

Whereas in many countries in Europe he is accepted with public acclaim, in several nations of his own continent he bears the mark of the heretic. There were times in Latin America, and there still are, when Neruda's poems and books constitute unlawful texts. César Godoy Urrutia recounts that, during the period of González Videla, he was subjected to a police search in Mendoza, and it was only by some miracle that they didn't find the original of Neruda's poem, "Let the Woodsman Awake."[60] In his exile, the author is free to stroll about in safer lands.

107. Farewell to the Senate

During this period, concerned about his Senate permission to remain out of the country, Neruda writes to me through intermediaries and couriers. My own clandestine situation isn't as severe as it was during the early persecution, when I wouldn't dare go out by car except at night to carry out my duties. Now, I am determined to carry out the mission requested by the poet, as a man waits for me in a house on Phillips Street, across from the Plaza de Armas in the heart of Santiago. I go up in the elevator, and when I ring the apartment doorbell, a girl answers.

"The gentleman is ill, but please come in," she tells me. I wait a few minutes until a tired voice calls me to a bedroom where a feverish man in pajamas is lying on the bed.

"Forgive me, Don Arturo. I didn't know you were ill," I explain. "They told me you would see me now."

"That's alright. It's just a bad flu. What did you wish to talk to me about?"

"I'd like to ask you, as president of the Senate, to renew for one year Neruda's permission to remain out of the country."

Without a word he gets out of bed, leaves the room and returns with a bundle of papers which he hands to me. "Read them," he says, I look at them and see that they're telegrams whose urgency has passed, dealing with things that happened more than a quarter of a century ago. I rapidly glance through them.

"You can see," he adds insistently, as if it were very important to him, "I had nothing to do with the deaths in La Coruña and San Gregorio." I don't agree with him, but now isn't the time to go into it. Subtly I come back to the reason for my visit.

"Don Arturo, I hope that you will give this extension to Neruda."

"I will do what I can," he answers. "Come back next week."

When I return for the next appointment, he again brings out the telegrams about the massacres in La Coruña and San Gregorio. I insist on an answer, and he replies in a paternal and soothing voice, "Don't worry, young man. We'll give it to him, we'll give it to him." He spoke about Neruda as a special kind of senator, and then Arturo Alessandri Palma recalled the speech Neruda had given in the Senate when Gabriela Mistral had been awarded the Nobel Prize for Literature. That type of oratory wasn't typical of that assembly. What Neruda had not said in that speech was that Gabriela Mistral, in accepting the prize, had said, "If the Stockholm Academy wanted to honor the poetry of Chile, the prize should have been given to Pablo Neruda, who is the greatest poet in my country."

In Arturo Alessandri's judgment, Neruda wasn't just a poet-senator in the Senate, for in fact he knew how to speak in prose about national and international politics, about the United Nations Charter that was then being ratified, and about the renegotiation of revenues for national education. He knew how to pay tribute to famous men who had died, whether it be the historian Domingo Amunátegui Solar or the president of the Soviet Union's Supreme Soviet, Mikhail Ivanovich Kalinin. He welcomed to Chile a cultural delegation from Uruguay, and he defended the Spanish poet Antonio Aparicio against political persecution. He analyzed the latest military coup in Bolivia, and he supported an agreement to facilitate the diffusion of books. He proposed the creation of a Gabriela Mistral incentive prize. He supported women's suffrage, and in an irony of history, he was interested in the renegotiation of salaries for the armed forces! He took part in debate about the situation in Nicaragua, which was then submerged under the apparently eternal dynasty of the Somozas, and he analyzed the recent overthrow of the Ecuadoran president, José María Velasco Ibarra.

He tried to conduct himself like a senator who was attentive to all the requirements and duties of the office, but he very quickly became convinced that even though he might be doing it very well, that job was not for him. He should be writing verses at Isla Negra, looking through the window toward the sea, talking with his male friends and bantering with his female friends, instead of listening to Ulises Correa, a senator who—to show the disparity between him and the poet who attacked González Videla in verse—claimed that Bernardo O'Higgins never wrote a word against the Spanish royalist governor Casimiro Marcó del Pont.

"Neruda isn't an orator," Alessandri told me, "but he is a writer."

"Which do you think is worth more?" I asked.

"In politics, being an orator is worth more. In life, a writer is worth more, a good writer. An orator doesn't last. A good writer remains."

The renewal of Neruda's absence permit was granted on a one-time basis. When the period came to an end, and the senator was still absent, his senatorial status was nullified.

108. Encounter with Pushkin

He will arrive in the Soviet Union for the first time in 1949, by way of poetry, having been invited to honor a fellow poet at the 150th anniversary of Pushkin's birth. Neruda's arrival is preceded by his poetry, for ten years earlier *Spain in My Heart* had been published in Moscow in Ilya Ehrenburg's Russian version. A year prior to that, in 1938, the first poems from this book were read in a translation by Fiodor Kelin. Neruda's recent odyssey sparked many articles in the Soviet press, especially in *New Times* and *The Literary Gazette*. The war in Spain had been the platform that launched awareness about the poet, and his name had appeared so frequently in wire stories that when he finally arrived in the Soviet Union he found that he was already well known. He was greeted by the VOPS tourist organization, which in those days handled relations with foreign visitors. His first interpreter and guide was Viera Kutieishikova, a young woman who would become a recognized authority among Soviet experts on Latin America. She had recently married Lev Ospovat, who was not only a scholar on the literary and cultural expression of our continent, but would also become a famous Russian translator of Neruda's poetry.

He visited Pushkin's house in Mikhailovskoie, and decades later, on the eightieth anniversary of Neruda's birth, Viera Kutieishikova turned her thoughts back to that visit to the town where the Pushkin family had a farm. They were there at an outdoor party in the midst of a crowd of country people, poets, and admirers who had made a pilgrimage to the locale. Suddenly, when a bolt of lightning struck almost at their side, and the skies unleashed a downpour, Neruda felt as if he were back in Temuco, under a cloudburst.

On 8 June, he arrived in Leningrad, in the season of "white nights," when the city is wrapped in a pale twilight for a half-hour, at most, before daylight returns. He cruises the Neva River by ship and travels through its canals. He is overwhelmed by the atmosphere, where it almost seems as if his friend, the long dead Russian poet, were still wandering along the bridges in his cape (which reminds Neruda of his own cape when he was a boy, the poet-son of a railroad man). He silently enters Pushkin's house and scrutinizes his books, discovering that many are also books that he owns. When he emerges, "close to Leningrad the fir trees / were dancing a slow waltz / on the watery horizon." He had come to see a man who had lain buried for more than a century with a bullet in his body. He had come to see the murdered Pushkin's blood and the healing of that wound.

He senses shadows in doorways and porticos, under the arches, near the Admiralty Spire, among the columns of St. Isaac—the shadows of Gogol and Dostoievski, and those of his poet-cousins, beginning with Maiakovski.

Not far from there, eighty years after Pushkin's death, "Lenin, with a signature affixed to hope, changed History . . ." At that point the ugly opening left by a murderous bullet was cauterized, and "Pushkin looked at his shirt. The people had expelled the bullies in gold tunics . . ." His friend, young Pushkin, didn't speak, thus it was necessary to read him, and he began to do so with a passion, because he knew that's how he would better understand Russia and the Soviet Union.

From an old Leningrad book dealer he bought several original editions of Pushkin and the first edition of his complete works in eleven volumes. Years later, when he donated his library to the University of Chile, including those books acquired near the Neva river, he explained that he had also bought an 1838 Gotha almanac, "because it contains a tiny notation in minuscule handwriting that says the following: 'On 12 February 1837, the Russian poet Aleksander Pushkin dies in a duel.' For me, this line," he went on, "is like a knife thrust. World poetry still bleeds from that wound." He has passed through the Pushkin door.

His first encounter with the country he would often return to found him still in the airport with his interpreter-guide as the homage to Pushkin was already beginning in the Bolshoi Theater. Thus it was that he arrived late at the solemn meeting, and when he sat down he felt a shiver of excitement. So many years had gone by since those days in Temuco when Gabriela Mistral and Professor Torrealba had loaned him the first books by Russian authors that he was to read, and now there he was, somehow recognizing familiar surroundings in a country that he had wanted to know since he was a boy. He was finally there.

A country is made up of people, nature, and friends. In a ceremony of tribute to Neruda on 27 June 1949, the great auditorium of the Moscow Conservatory was full. In the audience were several individuals who would become lifelong close friends: his translator Ovadi Savich, Martinov, Mikhailkov, Safronov.

Later he went to give a reading in the social center of one of Moscow's huge factories. An interpreter who accompanied him, Vladimir Kuzmichev, will never forget the impact on the Soviet workers when Neruda read the "Love Song for Stalingrad." He also recalls that the poet had a few customs which struck him as extravagant, such as going to the home of a Spanish seamstress whenever he was in Moscow, to order a dozen shirts. He was always particular about the shape of the collar. It was small details that led him to like something, and if he didn't find those details, he would order them. The interpreter was sometimes taken aback by Neruda's absent-minded expression of complete lack of interest in the place they were visiting, but later he would discover in his poetry that the most unexpected angles and shadings had been caught by that seemingly distant and drowsy glance, which interpreted reality in its own way through a very personal lens.

The reception for Neruda on 27 June in the conservatory was organized by the Writers' Union and presided over by Aleksander Fadieiev, author of *The Rout* and *The Young Guard*. Among the many poets present are Nikolai Tikhonov and the exuberant Simion Kirsanov, who will later make several trips to Chile and will become an enthusiastic friend of Neruda. Constantin Simonov is also there, with a face that makes Neruda sometimes think of the people of Chillán in Chile and sometimes of the Turkish people. He's a tall handsome youth, solidly built like most Soviets, marked forever by the smoke and gunpowder of the war from which he had emerged.

One of the speakers at the reception is Ilya Ehrenburg. He and Neruda are reciprocal translators and prologuists, with Ehrenburg having translated *Spain in My Heart* to Russian and Neruda having written the preface to the Spanish version of *Death to the Invader*, which used to appear almost daily in the Soviet press as Ehrenburg's cannonade against Hitler. In his speech that night he synthesized his personal view of Neruda's poetry from his prologue to a volume published a few days later by the State Literary Publishers. According to Lev Ospovat, "Ehrenburg's brilliant essay on 'The Poetry of Pablo Neruda,' published in 1949, is our country's first analysis of the Chilean's work."[61]

From then on, Neruda will be a constant subject for Soviet scholars in Latin American literature. Articles and essays about his work number in the hundreds, and almost all his books have been published in Russian as well as in several other languages of the Soviet Union.

The foreign writers invited to the reception were asked which part of the country they would like to visit, and Neruda answered without a moment's hesitation, "Stalingrad!" There he would bare his head in memory of Rubén Ruiz Ibárruri, the son of Dolores Ibárruri.

The gesture was not lost on that woman, "La Pasionaria," who says, "How can I express my sorrow, the deepest of all, the sorrow of a mother who loses her child. He was my only son. Now, out of the six children I brought into the world, only Amaya was left."[62] In her memoirs, Dolores Ibárruri maintains that Pablo Neruda, more than anybody, was able to meld Spain with Stalingrad, and as a lover of poetry she cites his exact lines:

And at the wall of executions
the Spaniard asks if Stalingrad survives:
and in prison a chain of dark eyes
bores your name into the walls
and Spain shudders with your blood and your dead,
because you, Stalingrad, stretched out your soul to her
when Spain was giving birth to heroes like your own.

On this first visit, he simply had to meet the city to which he had dedicated two "Love Songs" when the metropolis was still unknown to him. When he reached its shores, bathed by the Volga River, the sounds of war had been quiet for four years. It was summer, and everything was blossoming again, out of ruins. He couldn't help but dedicate a third poem to the city where normalcy had returned, symbolized by a dog crossing the street that dusty day and by a girl with a paper in her hand who runs up to convey a message. Before him the dark waters of the Mother River flow deep and slow. Women again give birth, children again go to school, and cherries once more ripen on branches that tremble in the wind. The city had died and come to life again. Her poet cuts an acacia branch and sniffs in the aroma of Stalingrad, which this time was smiling at him like a grateful woman, visibly scarred but shining with radiance and pride, who greets an old friend from past days of hardship as he comes to visit on a clear summer day.

In Moscow, Neruda preferred to stay at the National Hotel, and so much the better if they gave him the room where Lenin had lived for a while right after the capital was moved from Petrograd to Moscow. Sometimes, however, they put him up in the luxury of another epoch, in the Metropole Hotel, which in the czarist period had been frequented by nobles and wealthy businessmen. There he had an apartment, complete with a pair of grand pianos, enormous bathtubs decorated with purple flowers and huge emerald-green leaves. The rugs were of deep plush, made of pure wool and excellent conductors of electricity. Kuzmichev remembers that when visitors were announced they would have to wait a few minutes while Neruda walked about building up a charge, so that when the guest entered, the poet would touch his forehead or shake his hand to create an electrical spark. The astonished newcomer would feel the shock, and some even claimed that the Chilean poet's brain exerted an electrical force.

In later years, he regularly returned to Moscow. As a member of the International Lenin Peace Prize committee, he had to go there every year. Once, he went back to Chile telling how, on a visit to the Hermitage, he had discovered a portrait of Alonso de Ercilla y Zúñiga that some attributed to El Greco and others to an unknown artist. In Chile he raised a great fuss over that portrait, whose reproduction he took with him. He had been dumbfounded and incredulous when he had discovered it.

When the committee was considering a Lenin Peace Prize for Baldomero Sanin Cano, the Colombian writer and linguist proposed by Neruda, they sent the customary cable asking whether he would accept the honor. Pablo was responsible for drafting the inquiry, and afterwards he would show off the response with great delight, not only because the prizewinner said he was very pleased with the award, but especially because the famous grammarian had returned Neruda's cable with corrections of some mistakes. This eternal conflict between the poet and grammar always made the poet laugh.

Sometimes during the committee's deliberations, Neruda would write verses or sketch his guide, Ella Braguinskaia, with whom he talked about anything and everything. He always loved talking to women, and if they had a touch or two of the coquette, so much the better. On this occasion, he suddenly discovered that his neighbor, the Italian painter Renato Guttuso, was doing a portrait of the same woman, which plunged Neruda into an envious melancholy.

109. The Verse Underlined by a Young Suicide

During that trip to Europe, Neruda visited Poland and then Hungary, where he was invited to discover another brother in poetry, Sándor Petöfi, who had died a century earlier. Neruda had read that poet, who for Hungarians is like Pushkin for Russians, like Byron or Shelley for the English, like Victor Hugo for the French. But each poet writes, lives, and dies with his own profile, faithful to his own unmistakable makeup. From that period, when the great romantic poets usually die young, Petöfi, who was dead at twenty-six, is the most exalted public and intimate voice in Hungarian poetry. Neruda can't be indifferent to this bard of the 1848 revolution who used to recite impassioned verses to the multitudes, calling for independence from the Hapsburg monarchy.

Once more, a gathering of poets, which for Neruda is a table of fellowship. He embraces a dear friend whom he loved like a brother, Paul Eluard. Also in attendance was Eugene Jabeleanu, the Rumanian poet who had translated Neruda into his own language. They went from reading to reading, and after a visit to factories where Eluard read a Petöfi poem to the workers, they went to Budapest's Luna Park, the Vurstli, where they committed a serious breach of protocol, getting into a target-shooting match and, as if that weren't enough, sitting on a donkey for photographers.

The refined Hungarian poet György Somlyó had recently translated some of Neruda's newer poetry, which was published concurrently with his visit. The book included many photographs by Neruda's good friend Antonio Quintana, made available by another close acquaintance, the Hungarian Judith Weiner, who had returned to her country after living in Chile during the Fascist period in Hungary.

At this time, Neruda is asked to represent the World Council for Peace at the American Continental Peace Congress in September 1949 in Mexico, and he accepted with pleasure, for it was a cause that he embraced for many reasons, both intellectual and humane. The atomic bomb had just come onto the scene, and the Cold War was freezing international relations between the two systems. He would also recall that González Videla had recently predicted outbreak of a world war in three months' time, in order to justify unleashing his persecution against an entire people, a persecution in which Neruda was very personally ensnared. Fortunately, two years had passed and many more would go by without that war, and nobody with any sense, including the poet, could wish for that final conflict to ever explode. Yes, he would go to that country which was in great part his own. On a Sunday, 28 August, he arrived in Mexico City with Delia del Carril, Paul Eluard, and Roger Garaudy.

The following day, he acted as spokesman at a press conference, saying: "We have received support from the pride of our continent: Lázaro Cárdenas, Gabriela Mistral, Baldomero Sanin Cano, Joaquín García Monje, Henry Wallace, Thomas Mann, Alfonso Reyes, Paul Robeson, Diego Rivera, Enrique González Martínez . . . We are trained soldiers in a great civilian army which will prevent war . . . Whoever opposes peace, opposes life . . . "

The night of 5 August, the Mexican poet Enrique González Martínez opened the congress in the Coliseo Arena. The next day, the American delegation, headed by Professor Linus Pauling, and the Canadian contingent, led by Dr. J. G. Endicott, asked the United Nations to take control of all nuclear weapons. The Mexican labor leader Vicente Lombardo Toledano called on Latin American workers to organize peace movements in every nation, city, factory, and school. In addition to the great Mexican figures present, delegates from Cuba included Juan Marinello, Carlos Rafael Rodríguez, Nicolás Guillén, and Lázaro Peña; from Venezuela, Miguel Otero Silva; and from Chile, Salvador Ocampo.

On closing day, Neruda spoke. The New York reporter for *Masses and Mainstream* wrote that Neruda was "a key figure in the Congress, and his speech was the high point."

There was one empty delegate chair at the congress, that belonging to José Clemente Orozco, one of the three giants of Mexican painting. Neruda remarked on the living presence of that artist who had died three days earlier. His speech was a political-literary discourse with references to the obligations of the writer in the face of possible war. It was an anti-existentialist speech, a *No* to evasion and neurosis as aesthetic values. But he also assailed those values in his own work, repudiating those pages which "bore the bitter wrinkles of a dead period."

The literary world was shocked by the declarations of a poet who would erase his own poems and books. It was a very polemical question. He was denying a whole period of his own poetry, and explaining the action in accord with his feelings of the moment. In Hungary they had asked that he select the pages that should be included in an anthology to appear in Budapest, and to comply with that request from the translators, he began to reread the old books and felt that "they no longer were of use, they had aged." He had just received a tragic piece of news: in Santiago, next to a young suicide victim, a book by Neruda had been found, with some verses underlined by the victim before he shot himself. The book was *Residence on Earth* and the underlined verse read, "It so happens that I'm tired of being a man . . ." Neruda was stunned. The episode reminded him of his youthful reading of *Werther,* which had loosed an epidemic of suicides in its time. He felt responsible.

All of this made a terrible impression on him, and he publicly renounced those books, and especially *Residence on Earth,* though he didn't specifically single it out. He went on to explain, "I refused to allow old sorrows to bring despair to new lives. I refused to let the reflection of a system that had been capable of leading me into anguish, go on to bury swelling hope under the terrifying mud that our enemies used to darken my own youth." He went even further, to oppose reprinting of those books in America.

This gave rise to the unheard of phenomenon whereby many readers came forth in opposition to the author himself, to defend the condemned portions of his work.

Those were times when the poet was living in the eye of the storm. He had just ridden a horse out of a homeland turned into the tomb of his dreams, and for the first time he had seen a new kind of world which was emerging from ruins and the death of tens of millions of human beings. He believed he had a responsibility to his country and to humanity. He wanted to be of some use.

In retrospect, he was troubled by his youthful sadness, which had made him suffer within himself but which came from without. He yearned for his poetry to contribute to life's joy, to add something to human happiness. Was that indescribable innocence or unwarranted naiveté on the part of an intelligent man? Was it the impossible utopia of a relatively newborn Communist? A revolutionary fervor that deludes him into demanding the guillotine for portions of his own poetic work? Maybe. And perhaps much more than all that.

Deep down, it was the romantic impulse of a man who wished good for mankind, and whose spirit aspired for his poetry to be—if not the somber Beethoven's "Ode to Joy" or "Friend, I Love You"—at least an antidote for the corrosive poison of pessimism and loneliness, of poverty and emptiness, as laws of life. In this sense, Neruda was poles apart from the fashionable nausea of Paris, for he was a philosophically affirmative human being.

And he said so in an aggressive way, not limiting himself to joshing "The Celestial Poets" but also severely faulting them:

> What did you do, intellectualizing
> Gidists and Rilkists,
> mystifying false wizards
> of existentialism, surrealist
> poppies blooming
> in a tomb, Europeanized
> fashionable corpses,
> pale maggots in the cheese
> of capitalism, what did you do
> in the face of agony's reign,
> confronting this obscure human being,
> this form trampled in the dust,
> this head buried deep
> in manure, this essence
> of bitter trod-upon lives.[63]

He sat them in the chair of the accused, for having chosen to flee, to sell rubbish, to search for blue hair, to pursue "pure beauty" and "sorcery," all of which were forms of evasion, in his opinion.

The preceding diatribe was reserved for the cream of "our America's aristocratic fakes," while a subsequent one was dedicated to the exploiters and devourers of the continent. Both are poetry along the lines of Quevedo, with scorn for the vulgar, the favored, the advocates of the dollar, diplomats who are just decorated fools, whorehouse politicians; Standard Oil Company, Anaconda Mining, United Fruit, all those who manufacture beggars, kill Indians, buy judges, and set up dictatorships that fill the squares with corpses. The "celestial poets" were just the flower in the buttonhole of that ilk.

Out of my own experience, which is shared by nearly all his readers, I can simply say that I never stopped reading the poems he tried to erase. I think almost nobody paid any attention to the poet's directive. Young boys went on declaring their love with verses from *Twenty Love Poems,* and introverts went on exploring the secret waters of *Residence on Earth.* We did so without ever losing respect for the poet's noble motives, but his work no longer belonged to him. The reader was sovereign in deciding to read it or not, without any suggested prohibition, even if it came from the author himself.

A few years went by while Neruda silently reconsidered. His *Complete Works* do include the banned books, thank God! In 1951, Neruda authorized his Buenos Aires editor, Gonzalo Losada, to reissue *Twenty Love Poems,* which were enthusiastically received by readers. Shortly thereafter, that little book reached a distribution of more than a million copies in Spanish. And in time, *Residence on Earth* was published in the Soviet Union, along with almost all his works.

Later, he spoke more calmly about *Residence,* reading it as a distant work but one that belonged to him and had come out of his inner being. "The tone of that book," he explained, "was deliberately gloomy, though it came from a hopelessness that was quite real. Naturally, my own concept of poetry resides in the exaggeration therein, just as in other books I exaggerated the superabundant tone of joy. But joy doesn't kill anybody."

He was sure that joy wouldn't have killed that young man. "Apparently he was an intelligent boy, full of life. My book, soaked in that death, that calamity . . . that's a very serious matter. And it gave me a lot to think about. I've changed my attitude, but I still think a writer must be aware of his responsibility, not only in his life but also in his work."[64]

The years brought a reconciliation between Neruda and his poetry written prior to the war in Spain. On several occasions, at his readings, I saw him accede to requests from young audiences who frantically begged him to read Poem 20. Neruda would put his glasses on the end of his nose and begin to read with nostalgic pleasure, "I could write the saddest verses tonight . . ."

110. *Love and Phlebitis*

In Mexico, Neruda went to Orozco's funeral and began to feel ill with an attack of phlebitis. He braved it out and remained at the Congress of Intellectuals to the end, then took to his bed. As usual, friends came to visit, filling his room, as if it were a literary salon or a tavern at nightfall. And, naturally, women also came to visit. One face in particular, perhaps glimpsed before, a laugh like falling water, and skillful hands that begin to arrange the bedsheets, to adjust the pillow, to lift the patient's head and give him medicine. Where had he seen those Chilean eyes that said "We have met before." It seemed to him she had something to do with music heard under some trees once upon a time, but not all that many years ago. When she again lifted his head to give him the anti-phlebitis pill, he asked her straight out if they had met before. Yes, in an open-air concert in Forestal Park, they had been introduced by a couple who were mutual friends. On that occasion, Neruda had asked Blanca Hauser who her companion was. That was three years ago, but something more had transpired then, something that often flashes between a man and a woman, all in the clamorous midst of the 1946 presidential campaign. The adventure had sunk almost forgotten into the poet's subconscious. After leaving the Santiago Conservatory, she had had a recital tour through several Latin American countries and then settled down in Mexico where she founded a music school. Now the singer had willingly become a nurse who had never forgotten the fleeting romance in Forestal Park.

Matilde Urrutia and a phlebitic Neruda began a secret relationship that intensified his mania for fictitious names. He baptized his new love "Rosario," and even introduced this name into the *General Song* section called "Let the Woodsman Awake," where he asks for peace on behalf of his right hand, "which only wants to write 'Rosario.'" He would add other poems to the book he had left behind in Chile, but possibly he took his greatest pleasure in sprinkling that apparently innocent name among its pages.

All this took place in a rented apartment on the Reforma in Mexico City. The convalescence was lengthy, but that relationship which was definitively established in 1949 would last for twenty-four years, until the poet's death.

Yet it would be a mistake to think that Neruda was inactive in his sickbed. He would punctually begin to write every morning, and from under his covers he would devise a great variety of plans and undertakings for the outside world. He celebrated the Chilean national holiday on 18 September with a reception for 300 guests, including a who's who of Mexico, in addition to some foreigners he invited. The affair was unusual in one detail: the hosting poet was home in bed and followed all the happenings by telephoned remote control.

He was planning a magnificent edition of the *General Song*. Neruda was never one for half-way measures in these matters, and he created an editorial board which included María Asúnsolo, the engineer César Martino, the architect Carlos Obregón Santacilia, the Spaniard Wenceslao Roces, and the Chileans César Godoy Urrutia and Enrique de los Reyes. Typography would be under the direction of Miguel Prieto. The list combined figures with public prestige and with a capacity for generating financial backing. Neruda had wanted the three muralist giants to do end-paper illustrations for the book, but after Orozco's death, only Diego Rivera and David Alfaro Siqueiros were left to contribute two works which were on a par with the text.

Neruda added poems up until almost the last moment. Even though the *General Song* carries a termination date of 5 February 1949, in December of that year Neruda wrote an epilogue to the fifth part, "González Videla, Traitor of Chile," whose original typewritten copy, corrected by the author, was conserved by his friend, Luis Enrique Délano. Chapter XII, "The Rivers of Song," also includes a last-minute poem written in December, called "To Miguel Hernández, Assassinated in the Prisons of Spain." The two selections are quite different. The first is a biting imprecation; the second has a tone of lyric nobility, but it also curses and declares that the guilty will pay with their blood. The poet has the acrid taste of gunpowder in his mouth, surrounded by events that explain his state of mind.

One day he leaves his bed, the house and the city to make an exhausting trip to Veracruz, where he visits Gabriela Mistral. In August 1949, Luis Enrique Délano and César Godoy had gone to visit her in Xalapa to ask her support for the Peace Congress. Délano recounts that they spent twenty-four hours with her, twenty of them in conversation. She offered her support, which along with that of Neruda and Claudio Arrau, represented the three most universally known Chileans speaking out against the danger of war. A short time later, Gabriela Mistral published an article that would become famous, "The Accursed Word." For her, "peace" was a blessed word: "Let us say it every day, wherever we may be, wherever we may go, until it becomes flesh and creates a militancy for peace, which will fill the thick, dirty air and gradually purify it." Neruda hadn't seen her since Spain. After Lisbon, she served as consul in Santa Barbara, California, and later in Petropolis, Brazil. She and Pablo Neruda sponsored the entrance of Délano into the consular service. Gabriela had sent Luis Enrique a card telling him that she had been fired "like a servant" from *El Mercurio* after twenty-some years of service. All this she repeated to Neruda in Veracruz, and talked in passing about "that thing in Stockholm," which was how she referred to her Nobel Prize. She lingered a long time, weeping, as she talked of the death of her nephew, Yin Yin. She spoke of murder, but likely it was suicide in Brazil, as with her dear tormented Stefan Zweig, who had also taken his own life in those environs.

Neruda left Gabriela Mistral's house to go to the port, where he would board a ship that would take him back to Europe. He had come to Mexico for a few days and had remained for ten months. During that time he had met someone who would be a determining force throughout the rest of his life. With his love for the "wild Matildina" from Chillán, his "she bird," henceforth his own species, which he calls the "me bird" *Pablo Insulidae Nigra,* would sing in a new way, while she would give up singing to devote herself to that hidden relationship which would be nourished every day by secret messages. It wouldn't be long before she would also go to Europe to be near the poet, who was officially continuing to share his house with Delia, but would share his bed with the mysterious "Rosario de la Cerda" in a double life that he would maintain for seven years.

III. *Conversation with Exiles*

It's a time of journeys. He has again visited Guatemala, and for a while he lives near Jorge Amado outside Prague, in the Dobriss Castle, hosted by the Czech Writers' Union. The two friends discuss their exile. The Brazilian, whose novels are flavored with mulattas and his Bahía, shares this fervent period with Neruda, while they both keep their ears open for any tidbits that might come from across the ocean. Neruda receives the sad news of the death of Ricardo Fonseca, the Chilean Communist Party's general secretary, one of whose final acts was to plan the poet's flight across the cordillera. In reminiscence he writes:

> We both came from the forsaken
> lands of the frontier,
> and between squalls of the storm
> we shared the same roof
> next to the fire built by man
> out of his own heart.

In India, he meets with Nehru, and that same year of 1950 he attends the Second Congress of Peace Supporters in Warsaw, receives the Stalin Peace Prize, journeying throughout almost all of Europe before going to Asia.

He records it all like a traveling correspondent in his book, *Grapes and Wind,* which is not a tourist book in verse but the discovery of two continents as seen by a committed eye. The chronicler will proceed step by step in an ordered narration, beginning with the termination of the *General Song.* He begins this new cycle with his journey on horseback across the cordillera, treading on humus untouched for a thousand years, struggling to advance through the forest whose birds have never been seen by man, where the "electric-tailed foxes" run freely about. With axes the fugitives clear their way through the piercing thorns on this road to calvary. Every time he needed help, someone came forth to provide it so that he might go on. That's how he completed his journey, with someone giving him a hand.

And ultimately he reached the Old Palace in Florence, whose Arno River is contrasted with the Orinoco and the wild slopes of the Andes. In Rumania, it's the yellow Danube that he compares to his native currents. Back home, everything is so untamed, and here so refined, so layered with history, like the old Charles bridge near the Prague castle, where he chats with the radiant Julius Fučik.

Now that there's no need to keep his name secret and to hide from his friends, he almost skips through the streets. In Vallauris, he visits Picasso in his studio, where the painter sets small centaurs to gallop. Later, he goes to visit the hirsute Ehrenburg in his dacha and then tells me, "If you want to learn about jasmine, write him a letter."

The wandering Latin American talks to Europe and asks her not to close her doors to him, but one morning, very early, he departs for Asia, later to return to the Baltic. And he will plead for Spain, a country he can't enter but which he misses, a country that for him is "a profound visceral element."

He will sing of the broad Russian earth, the changing of history, the autumn adventure on the trans-Siberian express. He travels through Mongolia, which reminds him of Chile's Great North, and he thinks of his native sand hills, with the wind of the Gobi Desert in his face.

It's not that he's trying to name all the places of the map, but these are debts he owes to culture and freedom. Greece, the rose of Praxiteles, the acanthus leaves, where in remote times the blood of his people flowed.

One day he awoke and through the window saw Berlin, tortured in the mill of death. But he also saw the people who were emerging so soon from the hellish winter to lift their country anew from the ruins, as if spring would come again.

His poetry is polemical, clear, and with no beating about the bush.

In every city he visits he carries within him his own unshakable country. "Chile, When?" is his poem of identification with his homeland, where "if it rains in Lota / the rain falls on me . . . Cautín's dark wheat grows in me. / In Villarica I have an Araucan pine, / sand in the Great North is mine, / in the province I have a pale rose . . ."

These are the years of the Korean war, which he relates to other events. "Before, they leveled Nicaragua. They stole Texas. They humbled Valparaíso. They strangle Puerto Rico in their vile claw. They've gone to Korea . . ."

His outspoken alignment shouldn't be taken as ingenuous one-sidedness. He isn't fond of the British Empire's politics, yet he feels a kinship with some Englishmen who fathom secret meanings, like "Shelley who sings in the rain."

"Burned Light" is a rose for Vietnam, in which he asks for peace to come to that land of shattered heroes, where a wind perfumed with death stirs among the vines and thickets.

One other country that he loves is Portugal, where he can set foot only in secret. When he sees Lisbon from on board ship, "its port the color of the sky," he senses that death wardens prowl behind its windows, and the golden lyre of Camoens is forgotten. He'd like to ask the ordinary citizen if he knows the whereabouts of Alvaro Cunhal.

For Neruda there is "more than one France." This man who had fed on Rabelais "like on tomatoes" had been thrown out of the country by a policeman who very courteously offered him a cigarette. It made no difference that he honored the memory of Louis D'Orléans and had harbored Rimbaud in his home for many years, at least in book and spirit. They had thrown him out in spite of the decoration pinned on him by the Count of Dampierre. Such were the frigid delicacies of the Cold War.

He had known that his French friends Aragon and Eluard would suffer even more than he because of that rejection. The matchmaking Chilean, in a way, had had a hand in Eluard's discovery in Mexico of his last love, Dominique, and now with *Grapes and Wind* barely finished, he receives a telegram which adds to his sorrows about France: Paul Eluard has died. "How many things / on the face of the earth and time go into / making a man." Later he will say, "He was my daily friend, and I've lost his gentleness, which was part of my daily bread. Nobody will ever give me what he did, because his active brotherhood was one of the greatest gifts in my life."

This book, like others by Neruda, inevitably speaks of friendship, an experience he cultivated throughout his life. It was his friend Nazim Hikmet, the Turkish poet, who told me about Neruda's secret love for Matilde. Neruda had given me a letter for Hikmet, who was a truly marvelous figure. They had met when Nazim had just emerged from a long and terrible imprisonment in Turkey, and the first thing he did was to give Neruda his gold-embroidered shirt. How much that new friend had suffered! He came from a country that was "shaped like the head of a donkey / that comes galloping from far-off Asia / to bathe in the Mediterranean. / That country too is ours." Hikmet was born in Salonica in 1902, into an old family of Ottoman dignitaries. He began to write while still a boy, took part in the revolutionary movement, and in 1921 went to Moscow where he enrolled in the Asian People's University. When he returned to Turkey in 1928, he spent his life in hiding or in prison on account of his militant communism, and in 1951 went into exile. As Turkey's greatest poet and one of the most exalted of all in the twentieth century, Neruda wishes for his picture to never be forgotten: "He is tall / like a tower / erected in peaceful meadows / and at the top / two windows: / his eyes full of Turkey's light." In 1952, as Hikmet and I are in the Peking airport waiting for our luggage, he asks me about "Rosario," laughing at my puzzlement, with that laugh that Neruda said was like no other.

Neruda's book of his travels would be sealed only when his exile ended, with an epilogue written in Chile. He returns bearing new branches and driven by the wind, having seen the rubble left by war and the birthing of peace. He returns with the joy of a still-secret love. He returns happy.

112. *Italian Interlude*

Lacking the Appollonian majesty of Goethe, Neruda never wrote an "Italian Journey," nor was he ever a minister of state, a mine inspector, an irrigation project director, or designer of army uniforms, all activities of Johann Wolfgang von Goethe, the personification of European civilization, culture, and art, with a regal body and a gentleman's elegant bearing. Our traveler from the hinterlands, though he was a poet and sometime senator, ambassador and presidential candidate, was simply an unpolished New World commoner named Neftalí Ricardo Reyes Basoalto, who exuded something typically Latin American in his spirit and his dress. Yet the two men were similar in some aspects, both being poets and, in a way, politicians. And both believed in the power of men and of poets. First, man, then man the poet. Didn't the writer who revised the Faustian legend wonder who is the one who supports Olympus, who is the one who assembles the gods? Who but the power of man as revealed in the poet? Neruda also accepted the role of what Chilam Balam says is the voice that speaks on behalf of all.

Both poets went to Italy as mature men, Goethe at thirty-seven during a mid-life crisis. His trip is a disguised flight, not from the Dukedom of Weimar but from the empire of Charlotte von Stein. That crisis was historically minor compared to the greater one of the French Revolution a year afterwards.

Neruda would much later evoke his own journey to Italy with these words: "In this wandering about in all directions during exile, I came upon a country I wasn't yet acquainted with but learned to love deeply—Italy. Everything there seemed fabulous to me, especially Italian simplicity—the olive oil, the bread, the local wine."[65] He is forty-seven years old, and like Goethe, he also arrives at a time of changing emotions. To state it in broadest terms, it's the eye of a storm in terms of national and international crisis, and more trivially, in terms of a marriage crisis which would be triggered by a new love that had been kept under wraps but in Italy would unashamedly become less secretive.

The country appeals to both poets as somewhere they'd like to stay for a long time. Goethe calls himself "a fugitive from the north," but the fugitive from the south is truly a hounded man. He had escaped across the Andes on horseback, running from a Cold War hunt. He comes to Italy in search of refuge and an amorous hideout, but even here he runs smack into the Cold War.

Goethe will publish his experiences in his *Italian Journey* and in letters. Neruda will express his in his poetry, his correspondence, and, finally, in his memoirs, without dedicating a separate book to Italy. Whereas Goethe, while in Italy, will correct unfinished works and give final form to *Tasso, Egmont,* and *Iphigeneia,* Neruda will write two books there, *The Captain's Verses* and *Grapes and Wind.* His Italian pages are devoted to love, friendship, a bit of nature, and a lot of politics, as a cross-country personal experience. He customarily speaks of his run-ins with the police as adventures and looks back on them with a humorous eye. He savors the laughing gas that events give off, and he is capable of side-splitting guffaws. He enjoys ordinary people and the so-called Italian personality.

Goethe reminds us that "what glitters has been born only for the moment, and what is authentic remains intact for posterity," yet during the two years he spent in Italy he devoted barely three hours to Florence, choosing instead to gather botanical specimens and to discuss etymology. Neruda will observe the Mediterranean environment, comparing the seas of Naples and Chile as well as wines and onions, studying the female bust and ways of speech. Few museum visits are recorded in his memoirs. Once, in Milan, I accompanied him to an exhibition of modern Spanish painting, sumptuously displayed in the Royal Palace across from the hotel. His indifference to celebrated ruins often surprised me. In Italy he took greater pleasure in observing how daily life evolved so easily out of hundreds and thousands of years. With his poetic capacity for internal vision, he knew that everyone must live his own life in his own period, and he viewed everything in that way, selecting in accordance with a largely unconscious process. He admired monuments, but he says that what interests him most from the Middle Ages is the search for unicorns, "a mystic and aesthetic sport." The Renaissance expresses his own love for the body, but what most intrigued him was the passage of time and, within time, the passage of human beings and the weight of their passions. He was a great intruder, incorrigibly curious about what was going on in people's hearts. When he translates *Romeo and Juliet,* a feverish and sometimes chilling effort that leads him to confide afterwards that "I will never again try to translate Shakespeare," he doubtless does so because of the play's supreme art but especially to poke about in its emotional twists and turns. Shakespeare's sonnets were among his favorites, "carved in sorrow's opal, in love's ruby, in jealousy's emerald, in mourning's amethyst." On more than one occasion, I listened to him read several of them aloud.

On Capri, he memorialized several deceased friends in writing, Augusto D'Halmar, Gerardo Seguel, Muñoz Meany, and did the same for one still alive when he sent me his prologue for the second edition of my novel, *Hijo del Salitre* (Nitrate's Child), published by Austral in 1952. There he said that the two of us, alongside our people, "had shared magnificent and difficult times," which was to be true for as long as he remained in this world.

This glutton for secrets could steep himself in contemplation of the Temple of Minerva or Gothic architecture. A sensual pleasure in looking at things prevailed in him. It has often been said that he himself is without doubt an American baroque in spirit and in poetry, like a great part of our continent's literature. He was captivated by the black pottery of Quinchamalí, the textiles of village embroiderers, the native fig trees of Mexico, gargoyles and decorative details, stone rosettes. They're all in his poetry. Perhaps classical antiquity was alien to him because he was from a country without historical antiquity and from a continent that was anticlassical.

He enjoyed Italy, even in dangerous moments. Witness his amusing narrative about his escape in a Venetian gondola, when "the police wanted me to leave that city where Desdemona was born and suffered." Neruda's behavior isn't that of a casanova but of a big mischievous boy, delighting in the caper of cutting through the Grand Canal headed out to sea in the motorized gondola of the mayor's office while the police followed him in a conventional vessel with oars, one of those "painted black and gold, and used by Venice's lovers." This time the gondola of love, manned by Gasperi's forces, was just a duck hopelessly pursuing poetry's distant sea dolphin. The scene will be repeated on land with violent variations when he alights in Rome's train station, turned into a battlefield of Agramante for combat between literature, art, and politics. He liked to remember each individual at that stormy reception, Moravia, Guttuso, and Carlo Levi, who calmly handed him some roses and later painted him in his studio while "the Roman twilight slowly descended, and the colors faded out as if time were impatiently extinguishing them." For him, "Carlo Levi was an owl, with his searching night-bird eyes." But one image that would never be erased was that of Elsa Morante beating up on a too-diligent policeman with her umbrella.

He took real pleasure in Milan, Turin, and Genoa, the port of departure for several thousand emigrants to Chile, among them a lifelong friend, Solimano, who had introduced him to the delights of Italian cuisine. This strolling Chilean troubador always recited his verses in theaters, universities, and packed auditoriums, as he traveled the world. In Italy he improved his tone, diction, and melodic line. I once heard Neruda recite his verses in Milan, followed by a local actor's reading. Although Neruda liked to read his poetry aloud, unquestionably the poetry was worth more than his twangy recitation, which Chileans had nonetheless grown accustomed to and ended up accepting, perhaps out of admiration. He was very pleased to hear his poems read in Italy, where "someone at my side would repeat the stanza in divine Italian, and I would relish hearing the lines filled with the splendor of that magnificent language."

But his happiest days in Italy are spent in Naples and Capri, for very personal reasons and for the atmosphere. Under the cold lava of now silenced Vesuvius, he hears internal bells ringing once more. On the island, like a great stationary ship where he arrived one winter night with his beloved, the next morning the coast in the rising sun and later in the burning coals of sunset looks like a stained-glass window. That first encounter was evoked for me years later at Matilde's side, in the same spots where the events had taken place, around Naples and gazing on the landscape and rocks of Capri, where an inscription on a stone near the sea bears testimony of her return nearly thirty years later.

There, without Pablo but with Matilde, we stopped wide-eyed on the cliffs, in front of the white bungalow that Erwin Cerio had put at the disposition of the Capri lovers. In the poet's words, the gesture had represented "Italy's sweet generous heart." We could see the house only from outside, for its current occupants wanted nothing to do with emotional reminiscences or literary celebrations.

Neruda never viewed Italy as a collection of postcards or an operatic backdrop. Lounging in the keel of a boat where he was experiencing dream and creation, he discovered in Capri "her two delineated burnished countenances: one of poor people, coachmen, fishermen, sailors, grape workers, olive peddlers," and the other, supposedly decadent one, where "all the novelistic wickedness that you read about does happen." The latter was an ungraspable phantom for him. "I shared a happy life," he said, "either totally alone or among the happiest people in the world. An unforgettable time. I would work all morning, and in the afternoon Matilde would type my poems. There I wrote the greater part of one of my most ignored books," he emphasizes, with a bit of criticism for the critics, "*Grapes and Wind*." And there a visitor came with his Sarah from Naples, the fiery, eloquent, energetic Mario Alicata, to enter into a sustained duel with Neruda to see who could best cook onions. It's a homeric culinary clash between two cultures and civilizations, on the one hand Phoenician, Etruscan, Levantine, and Roman, and on the other the primitive sense of taste from the West Indies, neighbors of the wild south that borders the Antarctic. They engaged in the intellectual joy of cooking, which has with such epicurean delight attracted many men of letters since before Rabelais until after Günter Grass. Theirs was the pride of creating an edible masterpiece; nothing to do with Marinetti's "futurist cuisine" with dishes laboriously created by means of purposeful digression. Here reigns the physical and papillary sense of taste, with frantic sampling, poetic reading of nature's edible elements, all put together like a piece of light music sprinkled with accents that are smooth, sharp, stinging, voluptuous—all selected by a woman's hand or a poet's pithy imagination.

In Capri he wrote a book that was anonymously published in Naples, *The Captain's Verses*. It is neither a pure nor a celestial book, but rather a dramatic and sensual work in which pornography is carefully avoided. Nonetheless, sexuality and the smell of the sea float through its pages, woven with desires and hellish doubts, the devouring passion of his forties. It's all poured into the words of a self-denied text. The writing reveals no censorship, but the author hides his face behind a mask. On the book's dark cover is the word "anonymous," which converted it into a contradictory myth full of strong suspicions, because the hidden identity was given away by the cries of the flesh within. One critic, proud of his feline cleverness, announced that the driving force behind the book was Neruda, leading us to shiver with a sense of impending tragedy. The worst of it was that among the presumptuously erudite explorers who deciphered his poetic style, there were some terribly indiscreet individuals who proclaimed it in front of the woman who had been the cause of its anonymous publication.

I discovered that clandestine first edition one night in 1952, in the Prague home of Alfredo Varela. My host loaned me one of the privately published copies for bedtime reading—today it's a rare bibliographical jewel, with illustrations by Paolo Ricci, printed in Bodoni type with engravings of Pompeian vases. Varela handed it to me not as a soporific for an insomniac guest, but as a friend's invitation to enter a mysterious domain that hovers between heaven and earth, covered in light and shadow, where one could barely make out the profile of the portrait which had been hidden by the will of the poet. He didn't want to show his face, but he ingenuously reveals his soul, only fleetingly covered by an ephemeral disguise, which will soon disappear under the impact of sexuality and tenderness, under the avalanche of impetuous lines written by the hand of one unmistakable man. The reason for that impossible anonymity? One alone: his unwillingness to hurt Delia.

In her presence, one tropical evening in Goiânia, Brazil, near where the still unplanned dream of Oscar Niemeyer would later challenge the vast green spaces as Brasilia, I listened to the poet arguing violently with an individual who was boasting that "you can't fool me, you're the author," while Delia's expression of feigned indifference couldn't hide the image of a lonely crushed woman shrouded in tragic gloom. For me, that scene continues to symbolize Neruda's delicate wish to avoid torturing a woman twenty years his senior.

113. The Two-headed Woman

Those years of his double life were exhausting. Matilde had to make parallel trips with the Pablo-Delia couple in order to be with him in the shadows. That's how it was in Mexico and Bahía. Pablo was a lover who never forgot he was also a poet, and every day he would send her love poems, sometimes written on scraps of paper or on napkins that he would fill with quick verses while he dined with other people. The first place where they lived together was Capri. She kept the originals of *The Captain's Verses* in a wooden box decorated with mother-of-pearl. He hadn't written them at his desk, but during sessions of meetings he attended, on train trips, or at a café table in Paris.

They were times of pretense, when lies with the appearance of truth are spoken, but with deceptions and misleading geographical details which locate the birth of that love on the French-Spanish border.

Matilde had earlier made a film in Perú, which she laughs about to hide embarrassment. Then she became a radio singer in Buenos Aires and Mexico. In 1952, Diego Rivera painted her portrait as a woman with two heads, one full-face and the other in profile—Matilde Urrutia and "Rosario de la Cerda." (Her mother's maiden name was "de la Cerda.") When Neruda takes me to "La Chascona," the house he built for her at the foot of Santiago's San Cristóbal Hill, he shows me the portrait and asks, "What do you see?" I silently peer at it, and there concealed in her thick hair I make out the poet's sharp profile, her hidden lover.

From Capri, the couple go often to Naples, where a happy coincidence has Gabriela Mistral serving as Chile's consul. She welcomes them with open arms and offers them her home. In doing so, she is risking her position, because all the embassies and consulates have been ordered by the Ministry of Foreign Affairs to close their doors to the fugitive Pablo Neruda. A bit taken aback by the order, Gabriela laughs and writes to a friend: "They forbade me to receive Neruda, but they don't know me very well. It would have killed me to close the door of my home in the face of my friend, the greatest poet in Spanish and, in final analysis, a persecuted Chilean. I was once persecuted, and how! I was also thrown out of newspapers and magazines, just as many others will be. Never forget that one must give the fullness of one's soul and bravely say what comes from the heart."

Sometimes Neruda sowed confusion, hiding his whereabouts for weeks or months at a time and giving out false clues. In Chile we were worried about our illustrious fugitive, having received reports about his imminent return to his motherland. We were all committed to helping him avoid capture, and nothing could be better than protection by the masses, signaled by some graffiti warning "Don't touch Neruda!" written in white chalk and black paint on Santiago's walls and buildings. One Sunday morning, I am speaking in the city's enclosed Caupolicán Stadium, when a comrade comes up to have me insert a notice in my speech. Slowly I read it to the 7,000 people gathered there. "Pablo Neruda arrives today at 2 P.M. at Cerrillos airport, and you should all go to meet him in order to prevent police interference." The message is taken as a religious duty, which none will fail to fulfill. With nobody wanting to listen to speeches any longer, the meeting breaks up and the crowd heads enthusiastically for the airport.

But Neruda doesn't arrive! Has he been apprehended along the sinuous roads of a South American continent full of dictatorships? Or has he already reached Chile and been taken prisoner, in spite of more than three years of efforts to finally get the detention order lifted? We make a thousand inquiries, and finally go to the home of his friend Carlos Vasallo, who will later be ambassador to Italy in Salvador Allende's government. There we try to call Europe, not such a simple undertaking in those days when the miracle of direct dialing wasn't even dreamed of. Anxious waiting, but no, he isn't in Italy. Where is he? Unknown, but he was headed for Switzerland. Calls to Geneva, where we talk to the Spanish poet Herrera Petere. Yes, he was here, but he left for France. There we lost his trail, still unable to put aside our initial fears. Finally, we learned one day that he had stopped for a few days in Montevideo to visit his friends, the Mantaras. When he ultimately reached Santiago on 12 August, I didn't mention the strange delay to him, but later, as the years went by, I asked him several times, "What happened, Pablo?" He would assume an innocent, distracted expression. I told him in great detail what had happened, the whole escapade including the multitudinous farce in the packed stadium. He, who was so given to laughter, didn't even smile, but became serious. It was a while before I understood what had transpired. Didn't he have to keep the secret of the "Captain" who was traveling to South America on an Italian ship with "Rosario de la Cerda," therefore suggesting deceptive schedules worthy of an agency of amorous disinformation? I don't know whether the woman who was the target of this strategy believed him, but we certainly swallowed it, hook, line, and sinker. These tricks of the poet and his heart went along with his secrecy about the paternity of a book born during the Cold War out of burning passions, a book he would stop working on only in the afternoons when the heights of Anacapri were tinged with purple.

114. Polygamy and Disinformation

With very few exceptions, everybody had been hoping for Neruda's return, as testified to by a document that proclaimed his right to come

back home. Representing that immense majority were the following signators: the novelist Eduardo Barrios, the Christian Democratic leader
Eduardo Frei, the next president of the Republic Carlos Ibáñez, the Socialist professor and writer Eugenio González, Gabriela Mistral, the historian Francisco Encina, and the Radical politician Marcial Mora.

The official newspaper responded with righteous indignation that
González Videla had given orders to condemn without any hesitation that
petition. The author of the denunciation wasn't brave enough to sign his
name but hid behind the misleading pseudonym of "Historian." It was on
30 March that the government newspaper's editorial page carried that in-
vective article titled "The Case of Neruda," which nobody could call a
work of art. The author says he must force himself to write about such an
unpleasant matter as "the campaign unleashed in Chile by international
communism in regard to the return of that sect's leader, Pablo Neruda."
Heavens! Dealing with this subject is spiritually repellant to him because
"there exists an inherent justice, which never fails to punish someone who
has broken the law, someone who has done wrong, or someone who has
persistently spoken villainous slander." The Comintern, he says, has planned
this campaign and "has begun it with a proclamation signed by, among
others, Don Francisco Antonio Encina, a member of the Liberal Party,
former deputy in the 1800's and now a historian; Don Eduardo Barrios,
editor of *El Mercurio* and leader of Mr. Ibáñez del Campo's presidential
campaign; and Gabriela Mistral, female poet." There isn't exactly an
abundance of respect accorded to the signators, who want to convince the
country that "Mr. Neruda is a victim of political persecution, . . . and that
is false. Mr. Pablo Neruda was the subject of two legal actions, which had
been brought against him in court under the Chilean system of justice:
one charge of public wrongs and slanders, filed against him in accord with
legal decree 425 and the penal code, and another charge of bigamy . . ."
According to the self-styled "Historian," it wasn't the first charge that deeply worried Mr. Neruda, but the second one. Mr. Neruda had slipped
away in the face of bigamy accusations filed by his first wife, "a Dutch
citizen whom he abandoned in Java, and in Chile denied her the alimony
to which she had a right."

With public funds, González Videla personally had Maruja Agenaar,
that first wife, brought from Holland to Chile, where she entered a world
she really was not familiar with, the world of manipulation and promises
of fabulous sums of money. The president provided her with a lawyer,
who treated her as if she were an automaton. She felt trapped in the cogs

of a monstrous unknown machine, caught in a Kafkaesque snare, completely disoriented and beside herself. Coached like a zombie, she doesn't quite know what they're forcing her to do nor what she's getting into.

In addition, adds the "Historian," those who clamor for Neruda's return aren't asking for a pardon for him, but rather they're demanding "an apology." Incredible arrogance! Some statements by Neruda in Mexico and Paris pop up in the diatribe, and then, "If all this weren't harmful to the country which unfortunately witnessed his birth, it would be tremendously ridiculous and laughable, since everybody knows about the soft life of an Arab sheik that the poet-politician has always led in Chile and abroad, thanks to the increased dues lifted from the pockets of workers controlled by international Sovietism."

This very objective "Historian" has one other reason to be sad. He feels abandoned, for only one ultraconservative publication, *El Diario Ilustrado,* follows him in his crusade. And only one traditionalist politician, Deputy Luis Valdés, has threatened that when Neruda arrives in Chile he will ask the courts to condemn him for "wrongs to the motherland." That's the "Historian's" only consolation.

Neruda prepares his return and sends out preliminary messages. He travels leisurely by ship, accompanied by Matilde, which forces him to play his misleading game, announcing inexact routes so that nobody can know his whereabouts until he deems it necessary.

From "somewhere on the African coast," on 27 July 1952 he sends out a public message: "I am returning to my homeland in answer to a call from my people. I'll be in Chile in mid-August." It's also a political message, as he adds, "We Chileans have much to do." In veiled response to the aforementioned "Historian," he declares, "I have devoted my life to defending Chile's honor."

So the arrival I had announced in the stadium when I asked those present to go meet Neruda, was postponed until 12 August, when an aged workingwoman handed him a bouquet of withered flowers that had been fresh when she had gone to the airport the first time to meet him. On this Tuesday, he left the plane accompanied by Astolfo Tapia, Carlos Vicuña Fuentes, and Sergio Insunza, who had gone to Montevideo to meet him. The three were not only a committee to welcome him before he reached Chile, but also his body guards, for some kind of reprisal by the regime was feared. As he stepped out of the plane, the people began to sing the national anthem.

According to the legal system, Neruda could have been detained at the airport, since he had been declared guilty by default. But nothing happened, and the customs inspectors only perfunctorily opened the luggage. The next day *El Mercurio* finally stopped calling him Neftalí Reyes and accorded him his already legalized name of Pablo Neruda.

On a sunny day in that same year of 1952, I went to the telephone office in Quillota with Salvador Allende, who was then the presidential candidate of the People's Front, for which I was one of the general secretaries. First Allende and then I welcomed the poet. The following day there was a mass welcome for him in Santiago's Bulnes Square, where Neruda called on Chileans, divided by the upcoming elections, to work for world peace and national well-being. Afterwards, a joyful pilgrimage went to his Los Guindos home, where two soldiers had been assigned to take note of the license numbers of all cars that drove up.

Neruda told his good friend Lenka Franulic, who interviewed him for *Ercilla,* that the country's struggles shouldn't be seen as merely electoral. He would naturally support Allende, but that campaign was just one in a longer battle. "I am a professed Chilean Communist," he said. "I have come back without any conditions, because my return represents a triumphant struggle that began the minute I left. History is the science of the past, but politics is not history. It is the creation of new vital sources in order to ensure fulfillment of the people's aspirations. If we face backwards, we can't go forward. That doesn't mean that we should forget."

115. Welcome at Home

In August, when he entered his "Michoacán" house in Los Guindos, after four years of obligatory wanderings with Delia, who had returned a few months earlier, the happiest of all were his two dogs, Calbuco and Kuthaka. When they caught sight of this heavyset man wearing an overcoat and fashionable dark broad-brimmed hat, Calbuco embraced him by standing on his hind legs and putting his front paws on Neruda's shoulders, while little Kuthaka danced around him in circles before sniffing him to confirm the recognition. Once he was quite certain, he licked the poet's hand.

Neruda went into the house and out to the half-abandoned garden. The next day, unable to keep his feelings to himself, he wrote an article on "The Smell of Return," about the odors and tastes of that experience. In the untended garden veritable thickets had grown up, giving off unfamiliar fragrances. He had planted a young poplar which was now an adult. It took longer for the leafless chestnut trees to greet him, but finally one spring day a tender shoot, moved by the wind, waves to him from on high. In his library, where he was met by winter's aftertaste, he decides that that's where his absence was felt the most. Locked-up books, like buried bodies, give off a sensation of being forgotten. The volumes are out of order, and he finds Salgari's *La capitana del "Yucatán"* next to an eighteenth-century edition of Bacon. But his warmest reception comes from his seashells. The returnee also brings some new occupants to his home, including a woman called "María Celeste," a prow's head he bought in a Paris suburb. He had never bothered with roses, considering them excessively literary, but now they surround the house, spreading their pale perfume and brilliant flashes of color with a professional dedication that is exceeded only by an uncultivated provincial fragrance that seems to overpower everything and carry him back to his youth. That aroma of honeysuckle is the first secret kiss of a springtime that is waiting at the door.

He talked at length about those sensations of return, in his discussion with Lenka Franulic, who would see him often until she bade farewell forever nine years later, inspiring these lines from him:

> "I put on a black tie to say good-bye, Lenka."
> "How foolish—take it off."
> "We wept last night thinking of you, Lenka."
> "How silly. Think more about when we all laughed."
> "And what can I tell you, Lenka!"
> "Tell me a story, and then be still."

Their relationship was one of deep spiritual affinities, but in his reminiscence of her Neruda also recognized her great courage:

> "I remember when they were persecuting me and the people, and we lived in a carnival of masks, your pale face kept its purity while your golden head carried high the dignity of the written word. Some false journalistic lords followed my poetic tracks like bloodhounds to carry out their mission as clowns and informers, whereas you embodied the clarity of truth, your truth without illusions and without lies."

> "Pablo, I don't recognize you in this exaggerated praise."

> "Excuse me, Lenka, if I'm still so human. You're even more lovely now, a crystal leaf with blue eyes, exalted and resplendent, whose golden snowy froth may never again be seen on our poor sand."[66]

Once back in Chile, Neruda almost immediately joined Salvador Allende's presidential campaign at Playa Blanca among the pines. The campaign would take him back to Puerto Saavedra and again to Lota, to once more talk to miners, who searched as deeply as did he. The poet talked to them about his exile, saying "The sea is wide, and wide is the earth, but I have crossed it twice." Somehow he had thought he might never see those miners again, and he wanted to thank them. "I owe my return to my people, and not to any gratuitous governmental irregularity."

116. The Intellectuals Gather

Neruda could plan and carry out projects on a grand scale. He had an idea for a meeting of American intellectuals, so he contacted three cultural representatives of the continent who had the influence to call such a meeting: Gabriela Mistral, Baldomero Sanín Cano, and Joaquín García Monje. The invitation went out in July, brief and with a certain warning tone. Human consciousness was experiencing anxious and uneasy times, and everyone had a responsibility, including writers, artists, those in scientific and cultural spheres—in short, all intellectual workers. Why not get together in a meeting of men and women of all perspectives in order to create a point of contact for contributing to the best American causes? Let opinions and criteria be put on the table. Such a meeting would be useful not only to intellectuals but also to all people.

The invitation drew responses from Canada down to Argentina and Chile. In Brazil, for example, acceptances came from the architect Oscar Niemeyer, the painter Cándido Portinari, the poet Vinicius de Moraes, and the novelist Jorge Amado, who went to Santiago to help organize the meeting.

The Continental Cultural Congress was held in late March and early April of 1953, in spite of many roadblocks thrown up by the Carlos Ibáñez government, such as visa delays and threats to ban the meeting. The customary international machine gathered its cannons and fired off its classic artillery, as in the 26 April issue of the conservative *Diario Ilustrado,* which published a multicolumn caricature by the cartoonist Coke under the heading of "A Trap for Birdbrains," which showed a box labeled "Cultural Congress" and underneath a stocky Neruda calling the unsuspecting birds. It wasn't at all funny, but it showed the aversion to efforts of this kind.

Nonetheless, never had an intellectual gathering in Chile enjoyed such success or attracted so many celebrated figures in American culture.

It opened on a Sunday morning in Santiago's Municipal Theater. Since I was general secretary of the congress, I was well aware of the stage and sets on which it was conducted, as Santiago was turned into a kind of cultural zenith.

An old Tolstoian, the novelist Fernando Santiván, opened the meeting with the query, "Are the nations of America entirely free in an economic and spiritual way?" It was necessary to destroy the legend of intellectuals as incorrigible lone wolves far removed from their people's and their nation's needs. In his opinion, that meeting was establishing a principle of solidarity. For the first time, we were making contact with each other, not only among individuals but also among cultures that in their diversity have a basic unity. Latin America can't be a shapeless unstable conglomeration, for it is composed of nations which have moved along the path of their own historical formation as human unities whose characteristics are being interpreted in this meeting of intellectuals. Each delegation, he maintained, will convey the makeup of its people's cultural spirit, in a constructive coming-together without any secrets or closed doors. That congress is just a beginning.

In the Santiago Municipal Theater, which is an imitation of its illustrious European counterparts as the setting for operas and dramas in the midst of mink stoles, Caruso and Chaliapin had sung, Pavlova had danced, and Sarah Bernhardt had acted. Now the theater was packed for new voices. The most disconcerting and sensational was that of Diego Rivera, with his massively gigantic body and primitive countenance, as he traced an astonishing story of his murals and his dispute with Rockefeller when he had painted Lenin's face into the work commissioned by the New Yorker. There was one surprise after another for the audience, with the culmination coming as Rivera confided that he was Field Marshall Rommel's brother. He recounted that his father had had an affair with the wife of Germany's ambassador of the period to Mexico, and that's why Rommel was dark-skinned. Then, after talking about his own romance with famed actress María Félix, he added—as if emphasizing his passion—that he had eaten human flesh and found it very tasty. The audience, wrapped up in the hallucinatory atmosphere, took it for granted that this titanic painter was narrating his own truth, but in final analysis, his prodigious tales belonged to the witchcraft and delirium of our America and were a forerunner of what would later be called "magic realism."

In his appearance, Neruda began by quoting his bearded North American forefather, Walt Whitman, maintaining that "even though it may seem strange, the supreme test of a people is its poetry." Then he talked about the conditions under which his own *General Song* was born and described the struggle between obscurity and simplicity in his poetry. In his view, the poets of our lands write for a continent in which everything is still taking shape, and they want to give form to it all. Latin American people are just now learning professions, crafts, arts, and skills—rather, they are re-learning them, because the conquest exterminated all the old stonecutters and ceramists.

We have to begin all over again, above all in learning how to read. These are the people one writes for. He told how in one European country the translation of a line from "Let the Woodsman Awake" had created a feverish controversy. The line mentioned "the new-bought bells," which rang strangely to the European ear. He had had to explain that he was talking about the newly established southern towns where he had spent his childhood, where everything was new, including the bells. The translator had asked some Spanish acquaintances to decipher the enigma, but they were dubious, because in their country the bells had been bought centuries ago.

Neruda added that we write for people who are still buying bells in a land where there was poetry before the arrival of writing and the printing press. Poetry is like bread that both the literate and the illiterate eat. He recalled that a young Uruguayan critic had found a similarity between him and the Venezuelan poet Andrés Bello. Neruda gave a good-natured laugh, and later concluded that Andrés Bello had begun to write the *General Song* before he did.

Then he stated that one of the purposes of his poetry was an attempt to help discover America, and in discovering it, to reclaim it. In order to accomplish that task, he had to speak plainly. America must be clarity. That day, Neruda made a personal confession: it had been hard for him to move out of obscure expression into clarity, because obscureness in words has come to be a literary caste privilege, and class prejudices judge simple song and popular speech to be plebeian. Some people think that obscure speech is a sign of superiority, giving rise to the fetishism of cutting away roots and of unrealism, which Neruda called anti-motherland and a continuation of the separation between lordly splendor and serfly dark gray, projected into poetry.

Neruda's speech, which was a protest and a tribute to simpleness, was linked to a new poetic cycle he was beginning to write, the *Odas elementales* (Elemental Odes). He wasn't content with what he had already done along that line. "I intend to be more and more simple in my new songs." The poet's road is always paved with doubts, of course. Should he name the heroes and also the criminals and petty villains? He had decided to do so and to resolutely venture into the realm of the chronicle or journal, something that would have horrified him twenty years earlier. But now he undertakes it because he thinks it mandatory and is convinced that "there isn't anything that is antipoetic if it involves our own realities." It wasn't enough to sing of the flora, the rivers and the volcanoes. And it had to be done soon, because "we are the chroniclers of a delayed birth."

He also spoke about the book he had written after the *General Song* in which he talked about the new Europe. He wanted that book to be his contribution to peace, a gleaning of eastern and western Europe's best deeds. In that same sense, the meeting he was addressing was also a work of peace.

Neruda noted the absence of his silver-thatched friend Ilya Ehrenburg, who, along with other Soviets, hadn't been able to attend because the authorities denied them entry. Neruda maintained that without them a profoundly important element was missing from the congress. What he most admired about the Soviet land was its devotion to culture, and his dream for the future was to see in Latin America intellectuals from the Soviet Union and the United States, and he again recalled the words of his master, Walt Whitman, from 20 December 1881: "You Russians and we Americans, from such distant countries, with such diverse social and political situations . . . and nevertheless so like one another in some broad characteristics . . . You Russians and we Americans truly possess in common many undefined hazy things that still aren't permanently fixed but are similar in being the groundwork for an infinitely greater future."

Behind the footlights at that congress, there were also notable things happening. Diego Rivera went off to Mexico with a young Uruguayan newspaperwoman. Nicolás Guillén was the public king of Santiago, while Jorge Amado continued his backstage work in running the event. In his address to the congress he had said, "We are all different from each other in a thousand ways, and we are together." Famous as a novelist in Brazil, and recognized in Argentina, Amado was practically unknown in Chile. He hadn't yet written his "boom" book, *Doña Flor y sus dos maridos* (Doña Flor and Her Two Husbands). Neruda admired Amado's tireless dedication and wanted the intellectuals and the Chilean public to pay tribute to his great contribution. The opportunity came at the farewell for foreign delegates in the La Bahía restaurant. Amado's concise speech was respectfully applauded, and then Nicolás Guillén grandiosely announced that his sadness at leaving Chile was so great that he would need a green handkerchief with an area of four-million square miles to dry his tears. That handkerchief was Brazil, and he would go there the next day with Amado and his magnificent wife, Zelia Gattai. Once again, Guillén had stolen the limelight.

117. *Joy and Sadness of Sofré the Bird*

That Continental Cultural Congress in Santiago will spawn others throughout the continent. Shortly afterward, the Brazilians invite a Chilean delegation, headed by Neruda, to take part in their First Cultural Congress, to be held not in Rio de Janeiro or São Paulo but in Goiânia, spurred by the wish to spotlight the country's geographical center and put an end to Brazil's history as a coastal nation. It is that intention that leads one of the meeting's organizers, architect Oscar Niemeyer, to hatch plans for an outlandish dream, to build a new capital called Brasilia in the state of Goyaz.

Our trip was made in stages. In Rio we were welcomed by the tireless Jorge Amado. He took us to the most luxurious hotel in Copacabana, frequented by North American millionaires and Hollywood actresses. A horror! We spent all our time trying to avoid waiters afflicted with the vice of expecting a princely tip at every step. We quickly abandoned that problematic palace and proceeded to Goiânia in a journey that could be included in the adventurous annals of aviation's infancy, as we flew in a cargo plane whose passengers even included horses and landed at every town, flew at low altitudes, and had to traverse stormy skies.

At day's end, we came down with a sigh of relief from the perilous heavens to terra firma. Goiânia is a provincial city in the interior, with a certain flavor of Portuguese colonialism and a tropical feeling of freshness and calm. The Brazilian intellectuals of the period were there, including the film-maker Alberto Cavalcanti; the president of Brazil's Architectural Institute, Milton Roberto; the writer Orígenes Lessa, who had also been at the Santiago cultural meeting; the writer Alfonso Schmidt; the painter Werneck, the composer Edino Krieger, and many others.

Besides Pablo and Delia, the Chilean delegation included Baltazar Castro, politician and writer; Joaquín Gutiérrez, novelist born in Costa Rica; myself, and Margot Loyola, folklorist who created havoc with her flirting, her guitar and her singing, and drove the audience into frenzied excitement when she announced that she would perform a *cueca*, which for Brazilians is not the Chilean national dance but a woman's panties.

The girls flocked around the stars, especially Neruda, whom "The

Ant" never let out of her sight, though there was an unspoken sadness in her eyes.

Coming from the gloomy south, Neruda was attracted to the brilliance of the tropics and the flashing plumage of its birds. He decided to take back to Chile a pair of toucans, birds with a powerful hooked beak. In Rio, he put them in a cage in the apartment where he was staying, but that night, while everyone was asleep, the toucans escaped, pecked clear through the water pipes and managed to flood the apartment, necessitating a call to the fire department.

Another bird, Sofré, had been sent to him in Chile from Brazil. He admired its rapid pulse and its yellow bands of color. It would ride on his shoulder and perch on his open hand. Everything about it was a living sparkle. In its own country, the bird was like an eagle, a part of the windy heights of freedom. The fire went out of it in this cold country, where it missed its own surroundings and couldn't recognize this ashen light. It grew sad, yearning for its warm land and becoming more and more listless in its cage.

The day came when Neruda had to dig a tiny grave in the garden at Isla Negra, and there in the sandy depths he buried the lifeless body of what had been a bird of the sun. Remorseful for what he had wrought, he went to his room and recorded his sorrow in the "Ode to Sofré the Bird."

118. Tales and Tallies

In December 1953 we accompanied Neruda to the Second Soviet Writers Congress in the Kremlin. It had been more than twenty years since the first congress when Maxim Gorky was the central figure. In between those two meetings, a huge pool of blood had been spilled in what the Soviets call the Great War for the Motherland. Now, the corridors were filled with the repeated smacking of noisy kisses between writers who had fought together at the front and hadn't seen each other in all the intervening years. These were the ones who had won against death, but on the list of the fallen it could be seen that many fruitful branches had been cut from the tree of literature.

Neruda knew everybody and was the object of great attention. On behalf of the Chilean delegation, which included many participants from the Santiago meeting, he spoke about the writer's responsibility in those confused times so laden with gloomy omens. As usual, he acted as spokesman for his people.

Outside, everything was covered with snow. Neruda fell ill with fever, and the doctors prescribed antibiotics, yet he insisted on returning to Chile immediately, because he wanted to be in Santiago for Christmas. Delia's comment to me was bitter: "I don't know how he can make the trip in this condition. It's even dangerous. Why is he in such a hurry?" And she looked at me as if she were asking whether I knew something.

This took place in one of the sumptuous suites of the Metropole Hotel, furnished in turn-of-the-century luxury, where prerevolutionary Russian literature used to depict, with all its pathos, scenes of serious formality, decadent adventures, and pantagruelian feasts.

Neruda, sick but sitting up, told me insistently that he had to go back. Matilde "La Patoja" was expecting him, and he wanted to keep their rendezvous and see her. His temperature was above a hundred, but he would leave anyway.

That night he hosted his anticlassic farewell party. The huge dining room was filled with friends. The poet had no sense of the niceties of protocol, or if he was aware of them he ignored them, putting his closest friends in the seats of honor. He played the gallant with a beautiful Soviet tennis player who was married to one of his favorite poets, spinning tales to her about a fabulously poor and crazy land called South America. Thanks to Neruda's anarchistic antiprotocol, I had the good fortune to sit next to an enchanting young woman who was already a stunningly inspired Bolshoi ballerina by the name of Maia Plisetskaia.

Back in Santiago, we decided to give a public report on the Second Soviet Writers Congress, booking the Theater Eighteen for a Sunday morning. Neruda still wasn't well and was staying on the coast, but he was very eager to hear about the event. We communicated by letter, and one day in March 1954 I received this message from him:

Wednesday 21, Isla Negra

Dear Volodia, I'm very sorry but I can't come to see you tomorrow. I went out on Sunday to Villa Alemana for a peace event and while I was speaking I almost passed out on stage, just like at the ceremony for Stalin's death. However, I feel fine now and believe that the future will depend on the rest I'm getting. Jolting about in cars and meetings sets my heart racing.

In any case, I'm preparing the script, naturally just for the session on Russian poetry that would be included in the event. This is no quick task, since I'll have to translate Pushkin and Maiakovski from the English. It will be ready by the first. You'll have to talk to the actors—there should be six or seven to fill the stage. There should be uniformity in the men's and women's clothing, but without exaggeration—shawls of the same color (red?) for the women will produce sufficient effect. It doesn't necessarily have to be a shawl, just any cloth at all.

I'll come on Thursday the 29th and will bring the script. I'll come straight to your house.

I am writing every other day. I have to deliver a book to Losada in March, and the tally is three poems a week for the book to be finished.

It's cloudy here.

I send you a hug.

Pablo

He helped to make that event a small work of art and gave a speech called "The Lamps of Congress."

119. The Prize Adventure

Neruda goes in and out of the country, always in the nervecenter of disputes. Sometimes, when confronted by a farfetched enemy, he favors a provocative response, never shrinking from combat. With adversaries who tried to embarrass him he would always go on the offensive. He made no mystery of his political position, nor did he presume to keep it separate from his poetry. He authorizes Austral to publish his *Poesía Política* (Political Poetry) in two volumes. When he is awarded the Stalin Prize in 1953 (then called the Lenin Peace Prize), he is pleased, and he says why. Shortly before that, the Nobel Peace Prize had gone to General Marshall, a man of war. Neruda is pleased to accept this very different award in the good company of an Italian priest, a Swiss researcher, an Indian health technician, a North American writer, a Polish author, as well as the Belgian Socialist Isabel Blume, the French former minister Pierre Cot, and the British scientist Bernal.

On 18 September 1951, in Peking, Neruda had delivered this same prize to Madame Sun Yat-sen, wife of the Chinese Republic's founder. Now he greets the friend whose absence from the Santiago Cultural Congress he had noted, as Ilya Ehrenburg comes to Santiago to confer that award on him. Ehrenburg had had to traverse a mountain of difficulties almost as high as the Andes in order to deliver the prize.

Sherlock Holmes would have been delighted to tell of the various obstacles imposed by the secret police. At the airport they seized what they deemed to be encoded secret instructions, which turned out to be the puzzle he had done on the plane. In addition, they questioned this fervent amateur botanist about a list of *araucaria chilensis* seeds to take back from Chile, which was interpreted as a call for insurrection by the Araucanian Indians. Those expert sleuths also directed an ad hoc employee to uselessly translate from Russian some poems by Neruda that Ehrenburg himself had translated from Spanish into his own language. This Voltairean skeptic, like all good revolutionaries, detected certain romantic glimmers in the adventure, which again brought him into confrontation with the police, just as in czarist times when he was often imprisoned in Kiev's Lukiánova jail.

Government pressure made it impossible to book a theater for the Lenin Peace Prize ceremony, which finally took place in the Savoy Hotel on 10 August 1954. As a backdrop they hung a curtain on which Nemesio Antúñez had painted typical Chilean pottery motifs. Ehrenburg had made the trip with his wife Liuba and three eminent Chinese writers, Emi Siao, Ai Ching, and Chao I Ming. Presiding was Fernando Santiván, holder of the Chilean National Prize for Literature. The atmosphere was tense, due to the unconcealed police presence, which lent an air of defiance to the affair, turning it into a show of opposition. In his speech, Ehrenburg recalled his articles against Hitler, on the one hand, and on the other he offered a gentle appreciation of the man he had come so far to honor.

Neruda responded by drawing a contrast between his friend's journey and the frequent visits by protagonists of war and missionaries of atomic destruction, who are customarily received in our countries with official honors and without need to seize their papers, puzzles, and lists of scientific names of trees, and without need to retranslate poems to their original language.

He hosted the Ehrenburgs in his "Michoacán" house in Los Guindos, that freewheeling combination of stone and flaking wood where the cold from the nearby cordillera numbed their very bones. Ehrenburg, with a bittersweet smile and an ashy cigarette dangling from his lips, told us he had never in his life shivered so much, not even in Moscow or in Siberia. But every night the house would be heated by logs in the fireplace and most of all by wine and warm-hearted colleagues.

120. *Donations, Foundations, and Equivocations*

Neruda didn't celebrate any of his saint days, neither San Ricardo, nor San Eliecer, nor San Neftalí, nor even the apostolic San Pablo, but he did celebrate his birthdays, and how! For his fiftieth one, he turned the house upside down with a celebration that wasn't limited to the anniversary day or month but somehow extended throughout the year. After all, not every day or year does one's first half-century come to an end.

As a matter of fact, the jubilee started six months before his fiftieth birthday when Neruda donated what the *Ercilla* headline called his "Library Worth Fifteen Million Pesos" to the University of Chile. It was in the last days of December that he formally bequeathed the books from his house at 164 Lynch Street with a legal announcement in the notary office that the entire library, including maps, manuscripts and his seashell collection, would become the property of the university.

It wasn't an ordinary library. Along with 5,000 volumes, it included several rare manuscripts and first editions of Baudelaire's *Flowers of Evil*, a 1664 edition of Luis de Góngora's complete works, Victor Hugo's *Toilers of the Sea* with March 1886 annotations and corrections by the author, Marcel Proust's *The Guermantes Way* with a handwritten letter, others by Verlaine, Quevedo, the Count of Villamediana, Lope de Vega, and Aleksander Pushkin, as well as Dante Alighieri's *Prose and Lyric Poetry* especially published for Russian Empress Elizabeth Petrovna. He also donated manuscripts by Louis XIV, Victor Hugo, Louis D'Orléans, Gustave Flaubert, Paul Verlaine, Rimbaud, Leconte de Lisle, Rouget de Lisle, Francis James, and several by Marcel Proust.

In addition to his library, Neruda bequeathed his personal works in all editions and translations already published and those to come before and after his death.

It was very difficult at that time to estimate the value of the library, so rich in bibliographical rarities. What price could be put, for example, on two editions by Aldus, the printer who invented italics? Or on poems by Lorenzo de' Medici and by Victoria Colonna? What would be the value of a pre-1500 printing of Petrarch's poems, published six years before the discovery of America? What would that edition of *A Season in Hell* bring at auction? Or one of only eight existing copies of the deluxe edition of Tristán Corbière's *Yellow Loves*? Or a first edition of *Othello*? And the thirty documents about the poet Jean Arthur Rimbaud, including the two letters that his sister Isabelle wrote to their mother from Marseilles recounting the poet's death in a hospital there? For Neruda, the latter documents have an additional emotional value—they had been a gift from Paul Eluard.

The poet pondered for a long time before deciding which institution he would give his books to. At first he thought it should be the National Library, but he decided that his 5,000 volumes wouldn't even be noticed among that Library's millions of books. He chose the university in the belief that there they would be kept safe "for the new poets of America," as he says in the *General Song.*

The idea had come to him when he returned from exile and found his crated-up library almost dead from inactivity. He sensed that his poor beloved books had suffered hard times in his absence. He was also influenced by the euphoric university rector of those days, Juan Gómez Millas, who applauded the offering and characteristically began to envision projects that could develop out of the donation, including the creation of a University Center for Studies and Research on Ancient and Modern Chilean and Foreign Poetry, which would be devoted to expanding the Neruda collection with originals, biographies, and documentation about other poets.

A few months later in Los Guindos, the Pablo Neruda Foundation for the Study of Poetry was created in a ceremony where the poet publicly handed over his library to the university.

I remember clearly that afternoon on 20 June 1954 as we stood under the pale winter sun listening to the rector and then Neruda. The rector senses the poet's relationship to the people, and the poet was happy to recognize that link which, in the end, was his obligation. On that occasion he stated that "The poet isn't a rolling stone. He has two sacred obligations—to leave and to return."

He was one who left in order to collect books from all around the world and seashells from all the oceans, and then he returned laden down in order to give it all to the university, with the idea of repaying in some small way what he had received from his people. Those books contained not only their authors' lives but also their deaths, as in the case of his copy of the *Gypsy Ballads,* which had been dedicated to him by the assassinated poet, a book he held up as he spoke of Lorca that day.

He also recalled his minor disagreement from the past with Rafael Alberti [see Section 69] and their common praise for heavyset poets during their later years. Their motto was "heavy like Balzac, not thin like Bécquer." They measure their breadth in reflections from a bookstore window: "I extend clear to *Toilers of the Sea,*" said one, and the other, "I only go as far as *Notre Dame of Paris.*"

For Neruda, the bequest was a way of celebrating his fifty years by donating that half-century to the national heritage. He didn't come from "those families who preach their proud lineage to the four winds and then sell their past to the highest bidder."

He then made a retrospective comparison of himself and the young

Neruda. "My generation was anti-books and anti-literature, as a reaction against the decadent exquisiteness of those days. We were sworn enemies of vampirism, of nocturnal gloom, of spiritual alkaloids. We were the natural children of life."

Life made him understand many things that he hadn't grasped before. More than tomes about research and intellectual speculation, the books he bequeaths are mainly volumes about life and the pursuit of beauty. When he gives them to new readers, the books will "fulfill their mission to give and to receive light."[67]

Did Neruda make a mistake in doing what he did? In 1969, he recalled the deed with a bitter expression. "In order to preserve these collections from fickle fate, I made a decision to give them to one of our mighty universities. They were accepted as an overwhelming gift, with lovely words from a rector. I was complying with the duty to make my collections a part of our common patrimony. Fifteen years have passed since that day, and nobody has ever seen them since. Neither books nor seashells seem to exist, as if they had gone back into the bookstores or into the ocean. Some years ago when I asked about my donation, they told me, 'They're in a bunch of boxes somewhere.' Sometimes I wonder: Did I choose the wrong university? Did I choose the wrong country?"[68]

VII.

Narrator of Himself

121. Fifty Hurrahs and Two Condemnations

On the twelfth of July, at exactly 7 P.M., the birthday party began in the University of Chile's Hall of Honor. The actor Roberto Parada got it rolling with his bass-drum voice, like one of those announcers in some Golden Age dramas who declare the curtain opened. The occasion was the first of Neruda's five famous lectures, now incorporated into his books. The audience was mesmerized by the poet's clear narration of some essential elements in his own life.

He had once traveled inland from Lake Ranco, where he seemed to find the wellspring or forested cradle of his poetry, whose characteristic resides in the fact that it is both attacked and defended by all of nature. Poetry is not a placid undertaking, even if its face may sometimes seem quite lovely. It's the expression of contradictions, with a voice and with silence. Everything—the sky, the air, the tall tops of the cypress trees— seems motionless, but it's all just waiting for something, perhaps the wind, which will turn the whole forest into movement. Suddenly, everything begins to tremble, and birth is imminent.

In effect, the poet had seen the birth of a river whose waters at first were weak and silent, but which were searching for an outlet through enormous tumbled-down trunks and huge boulders. The fallen leaves of a millenium that covered the source had to be opened by the force of the current, but the water became impregnated by everything it passed through, as it found its way out. For the poet, the message became clear. That's also how poetry is born, secret and mysterious in its roots, solitary and fragrant. Like the river, it will take possession of all that its flow touches and will search out its path through the mountains. Moreover, "It will irrigate the fields and feed the hungry . . . It will sing out whenever men are at rest or whenever they struggle." It will sing in order to unite peoples. Poetry is useful, and it is also a means of conveying a message that human beings everywhere can take possession of.

He was once invited to a factory in Florence, where he read some poems to the workers and was seized by the shyness that easily comes over a poet from an untamed continent when he speaks in the capital of the Renaissance. Those workers gave him a 1500 edition of Petrarch. Poetry had moved about in Florence for centuries, and now the delicate Petrarch belonged to workers.

The celebration of one poet's fifty years is the celebration of poetry's 5,000 years. In the end, poetry is a victory of humanity. It's also a way of communication, which gives our America the feeling of one continent. Rubén Darío had come from tropical Central America to wintry Buenos Aires "to establish anew Spanish-language poetry." And now in 1954, Laura Rodig gives Neruda the correction-filled pencil drafts of Gabriela Mistral's *Sonnets of Death*, written forty years earlier.

In that lecture, Neruda recognized his debt to all of poetry's heavenly constellation, and to such other creditors as nature and geography. But his greatest teacher is Time, and on his fiftieth birthday he doesn't forget his hard beginnings, the beautiful and sad rain, and the poverty, abandonment, loneliness and frustration—not only his own but also his people's, to whom he proclaims his incalculable debt, as he says, "And all that I owe, I've tried to repay with my song."

He underlines one eternal obligation: "I'm indebted to love . . . My poetry has been totally occupied by love." And that occupant had no reason to be swept aside by the force of the wind that came into his poetry from the outside world. If at first he sang about a man's love for a woman, now he also sings of love for all humankind. It's all the same, all love.

His life had been a constant back-and-forth, coming and going, comparing nations and systems. And on that day of accounts and projections, he underscores what he is sure of: "I want the transformation of institutions and the rapid progress of my country."

At the end of his first half-century, he also wants his voice to go on carrying "love, peace, dignity, and joy" to his people and to other peoples.

Writers from many lands listened to him in silence. Among the score from Argentina were his old friends Oliverio Girondo and Norah Lange; his godson by marriage, Rodolfo Araoz Alfaro, and the Chilean writer Margarita Aguirre; his companion on Spanish excursions, the poet Raúl

González Tuñón; the writer María Rosa Oliver, in a wheelchair, and Pablo Rojas Paz. He regretted that Rafael Alberti and María Teresa León couldn't come, but because of document problems they had lived many long years virtually confined to the vast spaces of Argentina.

Nor could the Soviets come, due to entry difficulties, but the Czechs were there with the tumultuous president of their Writers Union, Jan Drda, author of *The Silent Barricade, The Little Town on the Hand-Palm* and *Living Water.* He was accompanied by the poet Jan Kostra and by Jaroslav Kuchvalek, Hispanist professor in Prague's Caroline University. These Czechs decided to experience the Pacific Ocean at Isla Negra and came face-to-face with its dangers in a midnight swimming contest that stood Neruda's hair on end.

The Bulgarian guests were calmer: the novelist Dimiter Dimov, author of *Lieutenant Benz, Condemned Souls,* and the famous *Tobacco;* and the poet Nicolás Furnandjiev, author of *Great Days.* The Czech and Bulgarian representatives had the distinction of a massive turnout of detectives at the airport and a meticulous baggage search for false linings full of poisonous Communist literature.

The celebration by Neruda had begun earlier with a banquet for 160 guests in La Bahía, where almost nobody failed to offer a toast and many expanded it with speeches both good and bad.

The week's festivities were supposed to begin on Sunday the eleventh, but it was postponed one day in order not to conflict with a gathering of parliamentarians and foreign dignitaries scheduled for the same day.

Nonetheless, not everyone was happy about the poet's birthday celebration. The opening event had been planned for the Municipal Theater, but the fiction-loving board of directors decided the authorization wouldn't be prudent, "since counterdemonstrations might take place." Therefore, the first meeting took place in the university's Hall of Honor and the remaining cultural events in the Law School Auditorium and in Valentín Letelier Hall. The bibliographical and documentary exhibit opened on the first day.

The week's events came to a close the following Sunday in the Caupolicán Stadium, with a program that matched the poet's philosophy: to gather together the nation's treasures, as sung by Margot Loyola and Violeta Parra, and as expressed in dances with native music and verses improvised for Neruda from the astonishing Valle Hermoso Dance Society of the Virgin of the Rosary in Ligua. The program also included the public unveiling of his first ode, the "Ode to the Wind," recited in duet by Roberto Parada and María Maluenda.

So much for the pleasant side, because not everyone applauded, as we were saying. The critic "Alone," who had once loaned money to a nineteen-year-old poet for publication of his first book, wrote an article for *Zig-Zag*, called "The Danger Represented by Pablo Neruda." At the book exhibit organized by the University of Chile, he had wanted to look at a particular little 1923 volume that he had helped finance, but his companion became lividly indignant: "How could you? Don't you know that this whole affair, the exhibit and these tributes, are a cover and sounding board for the Communist Party, which is sustained by Neruda's head and strummed on his belly? Do you really believe that they're ever going to be concerned in Chile with poetry and poets? Pedro Antonio González died in a hospital, Pezoa Véliz died in a hospital, and nobody knows whether Ernesto Guzmán and Max Jara are alive or dead. This is all a farce."[69]

Insulting verses were distributed in opposition to Neruda. In another literary chronicle in *El Mercurio* on 28 March that same year, "Alone" scolds the poet for writing songs for the masses and making his words so clear that they're understandable "by those who don't understand anything." He claims that someone (a terrible *deus ex machina* in the style of Orwell's *1984*) had criticized the poet's constant unjustified sadness and told him it was an insult to the new era. Actually, nobody had said such a thing, but in any case Neruda promised not to be sad any more.

As can be seen, Neruda's fifty years were heartily celebrated, attacked, and minimized.

122. Houses and Women

In one interview, Neruda says something that catches the attention. When he is asked what he had studied at the university, he answers, "In the beginning, architecture and French." Architecture? Maybe he attended a few classes and then dropped out of that school. A pity perhaps, because he had within him something of the born architect. I saw him always involved in building houses. They weren't whims, because except for the last one in the hills of Lo Curro, he finished them all and furnished them to his own personal taste. He was usually advised by new-wave architects, Spanish Republican Rodríguez Arias and Chileans Fernando Castillo Velasco, Carlos Martner, Ramiro Insunza, and Raúl Bulnes.

But the concept was almost always his own, and he usually relied only on one master craftsman, a humble inhabitant of Isla Negra who knew all the grains of woods and their veins, was familiar with the mysteries of stone, brick, and nails, and could resolve with his enormous practical knowledge the problems presented by the capricious construction envisioned by the poet. Much could be gained from watching and enjoying the relationship between the writer, with his large physique and riding cap and bulky sweater, in consultation with the short, thin foreman, leathery and trim and with a serious look on his clean-shaven face, as they discussed what was needed, showing mutual consideration and respect, for Pablo knew the worth of "Rafita," and Rafael Plaza admired his collaborator in the task of building rooms, equipping a garage, or installing a support for the heavy new prow's head that had just been off-loaded in Valparaíso.

Never a note of servitude in the carpentry artist, never a sign of bossy superiority in the poet. Reciprocal respect flowed from that relationship, with profound esteem for the craftsman's skill and his incomparable ability to understand everything about his work in just a few words. The Rafita-Neruda chapter shows them to be two masters who understood each other in their work and knew their craft very well.

The poet has three houses: one where "The Ant" has her sanctuary, in Los Guindos; another on Providencia, which serves as the secret nest of "Rosario"; and a third in Isla Negra, which he shares with one and later the other, but never simultaneously.

Delia, "The Ant," is accustomed to taking trips alone, and on those occasions Neruda settles in more comfortably in the clandestine nest. From there he writes me:

> Dear Balalaika, Your lack of a telephone is a bother. If you should need to see me, it would be possible today at 2457 Providencia, Apartment 514. Otherwise, I'll be at home tomorrow until 11:30, when I go to pick up Delia on the S.A.S. flight. It would be nice if you could come along. There's space, and I can come by to pick you up. Phone me. For your article, I recommend one by a Jesuit that appeared in Sunday's *Ilustrado* and a little critique in a letter from Schomlyo. I can give them both to you tomorrow.

As can be seen, in that period he is going from one house to another, from one woman to another, with perilous openness. His confidence may lead to catastrophe.

123. The Breakup

With the money from the Lenin Prize, Neruda starts to build a house on Márquez de la Plata, the little street at the foot of Santiago's San Cristóbal Hill, in an area where one can hear the animals in the nearby zoological park. The land had earlier been part of the old San Cristóbal mill, driven by the current from a canal. Neruda fell in love with the panorama and dreamed of a home on the tree-covered hill with the sound of water in back of the patio.

It turned out to be an eccentric construction, with a semi-Inca system of verandas on several levels. At street level, it's like a house in southern Spain, where you enter by a little door on the one-way lane. His neighbors are the sculptress Marta Colvin and his lifelong friend, the photographer Antonio Quintana and his Uruguayan wife, Queta. On the same level is the small dining room and some tiny rooms. Then there's a metal stairway with white-painted arabesques, like those I saw once in an Italian film of the 1950s. The stairway leads to a space where newsworthy events had taken place or will take place. There is the reception room, full of a Nerudian atmosphere and the portrait of the two-headed woman. This is the kingdom of the redheaded "Patoja," Matilde. Four or five inside steps lead to the bedroom, where the bed's wooden headboard has been branded with the intertwined initials *P* and *M*.

Later, the poet went on building up the hill and had a study constructed on a higher level, where he would close himself in to write. But that's a later story.

Meanwhile, Neruda continued to live in Los Guindos, where he would have friends in for lunch, but at the end of the second course, he would get sleepy and go off to have a nap, without giving any further explanation, of course. However, he didn't have his nap at home, but would go off to the "La Chascona" house, where the roar of the lions didn't at all disturb his sleep. In that period, he would unexpectedly go off without any warning whatsoever, every day. Everybody was aware of the drama, but nobody said anything, at least not in front of Delia.

Neruda became more and more careless. "The Ant" rarely went to Isla Negra. The one who would settle in there for long periods with the poet was "Rosario" (Matilde). The housekeeper didn't change, but had to serve two different women. Apparently without any advance agreement, Neruda trusted in her discretion.

One day, some domestic problem came up at Isla Negra, and the girl who worked there went to tell Delia everything. With her pride wounded, she broke with Neruda. Did she already know about that intimate friend-ship, which she had perhaps suspected but which had remained without the confirmation that had just been so cruelly given to her?

She was crushed, and in his own way, Neruda also suffered. He had decided from the outset of his relationship with Matilde, who was in agreement, that his marriage to Delia would continue. After all, by this time it was just a platonic marriage. Whereas Pablo was fifty years old, she was seventy, and a fact of life was simply imposing itself. Pablo would have his true love and at the same time would maintain his legal ties. He didn't want to hurt Delia. His motives for keeping up a lengthy fiction were not political, but rather his consideration and his need to avoid a break that would be painful for "The Ant."

With Matilde he had a lover's ties, and the two had no need to get married. Even the day-long waits, and (as she herself says) the frights they had were full of emotion. Furthermore, Matilde felt no jealousy toward Delia, and she says she couldn't be envious, for she was sure that Pablo belonged to her even when he was in the other house. The clandestine period of their love lasted for eight years.

On the day that Delia finds out the truth about the situation, Pablo calls me that same night to come see him at the house on Márquez de la Plata. He's alone, Matilde having gone out for a few hours so he can think matters out by himself. When I arrive, he says, "You have to do me a very big favor. See that a letter from me is delivered to Delia."

I have to wait, because the letter isn't ready. He sits down at an opened writing desk in the reception room, beneath a painting of a lonely landscape he had brought back from Italy, and for hours he writes in green ink his farewell letter to Delia. I pick up a book and begin to read while waiting. Then I pick up another, and another, because the farewell message is lengthy and, I imagine, difficult.

It's very late when I leave with the letter and go to deliver it to a friend of Delia's, Luis Cuevas Mackenna. I suppose that neither one of us ever knew what that letter said, nor did we have any right to know, but afterwards, "The Ant" behaved differently with me, and I with her, at least for a few years. Later our relationship tended to get back to normal.

At the time, Pablo would tell me, "She has a Basque pride." Without that pride, which he believed came from the shores of Cantabria, perhaps he could have gone on living with her and, despite the handicap of her age, she would have survived him by many years, as his wife.

News of the separation shocked the group and produced dissension among the close acquaintances of the Pablo-Delia couple. Lifelong friendships were ended, including his relationship with Tomás Lago, for example. Neruda's former loves took great offense, among them Albertina, who was a part of Neruda's close circle in her own right, and as one of Delia's predecessors, she didn't accept the devastating appearance on the scene of a younger woman and one she didn't even know.

124. *The Invisible Man Makes an Appearance*

Toward the end of 1954, the publication of *Elemental Odes* sparked a new storm, just as had happened with the appearance of *Grapes and Wind*. There were those who criticized him because the odes were primarily in short verses, and someone said that was how the poet tried to fill pages in a hurry.

A Catholic priest, Francisco Dussuel, attacked them in *El Diario Ilustrado* for being materialistic, Marxist, and anti-Christian. He found blasphemies in the book and disagreed with the poet for denying the "holiness" of poverty and not recognizing its role in the "eternal destiny of human beings."

Father Dussuel wasn't the only one of his faith to condemn the book. In Argentina, where Losada had published it, the Catholic journal *Criterio,* headed by Monsignor Franceschi, published an interpretation by Brother Verísimo who, while calling Neruda a "great poet," warns young Catholics against "the dangerous message" of the odes, but assures that in any case, Neruda will reach the "true motherland," heaven. The article doesn't contain open condemnation, but says that Neruda is authentic and it's the Nerudians who are false. According to Brother Verísimo, what is lacking is an intimate picture of the poet, "his moral and *theological* spectrum." In his view, Neruda enters into the metaphysical realm and in calling himself a "resident on earth" renounces any hope, any salvation, any light. Curiously enough, as an almost professional optimist in that period of his life, Neruda is presented by Brother Verísimo as an incurable pessimist who reaches the most supreme heights of desolation. "It chills the heart," he says, "to peek into the darkness of this astonishing soul, this creature voluntarily exiled from a heaven that seems to call to him from every form, from every word, from every pulsation of his very life." But, he affirms, perhaps within the poet some insights that will carry him to the light may be about to come forth.

In reality, the book represented a change in Neruda's poetry, not the one observed by the mistaken prophet Brother Verísimo, but a new stage in that leaping and shifting course. Great distance had been traveled, with respect to its other pole, the first volume of *Residence on Earth*—a difference in form, a diversity in content. When the poet was asked about the book, he said that in the odes he had wanted to create a very simple poetry about very simple things. The choice of themes was wide open, in a desire to break with the poet who is limited to a single range. Similarly, in the *General Song* he had attempted epic themes, which twentieth-century poetry had almost completely discarded. No material should be excluded, though today little is written about what was yesterday the subject of much poetry, for example, the moon. We must get back to the moon, the sun, the air; we must get back to all themes.

La Nación in Buenos Aires claimed that in the *Elemental Odes* Neruda tried to create an inventory of the world. The poet responded, "What's left out is immense . . . Like all poets, I still have the universe, and so many things to do."

In addition, the book was written because the author wanted to show young poets the underlying mass of beauty that exists in the simplest of objects and things.

The first poem, "The Invisible Man," embodies his theory of poetry at that time. He adores all poetry that's ever been written and its freshness, but he smiles at the excessive use of the first person, which makes it hard to see the rest of the pronouns, because he wants his words to be "the song of the invisible man / who sings along with all men." This song is as varied as an Oriental bazaar full of the world's elements, with odes to the air, the artichoke, joy, the Americas, love, the atom, the birds of Chile, eel stew, a chestnut on the ground, the onion, clarity, copper, criticism, Angel Cruchaga, a happy day, a building, energy, envy, hope, the earth's fertility, a blue flower, fire, Guatemala, thread, a simple man, intranquility, winter, a lab technician, Leningrad, a book, the rain, the tardy Malvenida, the sea, bird-watching, murmuring, the night, numbers, autumn, bread, folk poets, spring, a clock at night, Río de Janeiro, simplicity, solitude, the third day, time, the earth, the tomato, a storm, a suit, tranquility, sadness, Valparaíso, César Vallejo, summer, life, wine. The Spanish titles form an alphabetical index of eternal themes that might have been extracted from a dictionary, but they offer Olympian proof that all throb with latent poetry when touched by a poet's magical hands.

The index seems exhaustive, but the poet offers a smiling threat that "I'm writing another book that will be called *New Elemental Odes*," which is promptly published in 1955. The subjects are varied, some of them eternal poetic themes and others unconventional, in accord with contemporary precepts, like the odes to barbed wire, to socks, to an uneventful day, to the liver. Now, with this second volume, the poet called by one critic a "thing-ist" surely must have exhausted the supply of objects.

But no, many things still remained for him to convert into odes. With a mixture of challenge and mockery, he publishes his *Third Book of Odes,* which is the poetry of a persistent observer. Frequently when I go to visit him in Isla Negra, he invites me to stroll through the enigmatic Petras Forest, where we sit down among trunks that are centuries old, scarred and full of enormous spider webs. Everything seems quiet, like the petrified forest we saw once in the movies, but when I read his "Ode to the Petras Forest" I realized that the eye of the poet is blessed from birth to see what others look at without seeing.

Neruda uses his poetry to settle accounts, as in the 1956 "Ode to the Insulted Scoundrel," which he writes in response to some critics he considered obnoxious. The fact is that there's room in the odes for everything that belongs to the world, including the "Ode to the Waltz 'Over the Waves,'" the beloved waltz of his young heart that brings him forgotten perfumes, and "Ode to the Successful Voyage," sung by the poet throughout a trip around the world and upon his return to the wide-set eyes of his beloved.

125. The War of Less Than a Hundred Years

After his great personal Lutheran schism, the war didn't last a hundred years, although something had been shattered forever in the spirit of the long-lived "Ant." Yet the rancors and recriminations that circulated through the city and even reached friends scattered about the world, gradually began fading.

The woman who had been a retired painter during the twenty years she lived with Neruda returned to her pictures of immense disjointed horses. She changed the character and atmosphere of the "Michoacán" house, which she stopped calling by that name after the breakup, referring to it simply as "Los Guindos" or as "164 Lynch Street." She set up her studio where the former glass-paned dining room let the light in and offered a view on the park.

The house lost the bustling air it had had when the poet lived there. Gone was the always prepared table where once it had been customary for strangers to sit without being asked who they were nor why they were there, an occurrence so normal that one day as dessert was being served they realized that among the many guests was a tall Boris Karloff type who turned out to be Waldo Palma, general director of Criminal and Political Investigations in the government.

A calm was established and reigned over by Delia, abandoned but finally sovereign, queen of delicate conversation and manager of charm, who maneuvered like a swan in the lake of elevated ideas and discussed every event with adorable poise.

Pablo, who had moved to "La Chascona" to live with Matilde, was always concerned about "The Ant" and hopeful that she would revive from the depression of the abrupt separation. When he began to hear that a new literary-artistic circle was starting to meet in his former home in Los Guindos, which now belonged exclusively to Delia, he breathed a sigh of relief.

He himself was more at peace, now that his exhausting double life was over. He didn't have to leave home to have an afternoon nap in another house. He didn't have to pretend any longer, and could even recognize a literary offspring that had been wandering the world calling him its father despite his denial. That offspring was *The Captain's Verses.*

Pablo wanted to have children with Matilde, and so did she. "I lost three babies," she recalls, "the last one in the sixth month. I had stayed in bed almost the whole time in order to keep it. Afterward Pablo told me we wouldn't try again." He told her, "I would hate that child if anything happened to you."

The early period of their love had drawn to a close after a tentative beginning one day in 1946 and a later solidification in Mexico when Neruda was ill. From that point on they had found and lost each other in the airports of many nations, where they used the guise of foreign languages to pretend not to know each other. They would separate and always meet again in the streets of Paris or in Transylvania where Dracula's eyes gleam at night. The woman from Chillán was born of Ñuble's clay, but he had seen her in so many different places of the globe that she seemed to him not only like a dark pitcher from Quinchamalí village but also like an amphora from Pompeii, that city rescued after 2,000 years from its thick layer of lava, not far from the Capri house where they had first been able to peacefully share the same roof, back in the winter of 1951.

Now, secrecy was finished and they were sharing their life in "La Chascona" and in Isla Negra. They were contented. "Even if this is of no interest to anyone," the poet wrote me, "we are happy. We spend some of our time together in long stays on Chile's lonely coast. Not in summer, because then the sun-parched shore becomes yellow and desertlike, but in winter, when it's clothed by the rains and the cold in a strange florescence of green and yellow, blue and purple."

An active routine, full of trips, verses every day, and an occasional illness when even talking was forbidden, except by letter, like one he sends me from Isla Negra on 17 July 1958:

> Valentín, You already know that my doctor is prescribing silence for two months. Juvencio Valle would have been pleased. I was overjoyed, because something worse was suspected. I have a little book in which I write down my thoughts, like When do we eat? and What a dog! So much silence prevents a visit from you two, which we had looked forward to. Tell Correa [Corvalán] that perhaps it would be better toward the end of March. Will I have recovered my voice? Tello will examine me in another month. Love, P.

The order to be quiet doesn't keep him from writing, and on the official beginning of autumn, he writes again:

> Isla Negra, 21 March

> Dear Vol: My throat is a little bit better, thanks to some ointment wraps that "Patoja" applies. Ivette [Joie] is coming on Sunday from Valparaíso; it seems a pity that you don't see more of her. If you can, try to arrange a visit. We'll be here until after Holy Week. I'm finishing one of the books and am satisfied. This material has arrived from José [Venturelli]. Inform our friend, and give it to him on my behalf. I'll soon plan the publicity campaign. And that manifesto, too.
> There's nobody on the coast. It's all marvelous, somewhat gray and humid, which is captivating in a way that the sun can't match. No wish to return to civilization. Love, P.

Nonetheless, the world calls out to the hideaway in Isla Negra, but still only words on paper come forth. On 11 August, he sends me a couple of typewritten pages: "Dear Val: After several good days of work (only on correspondence), tomorrow I'll begin to write." He is worried and outraged by the constant intrigue against Cuba, the machinations of the Organization of American States, as he writes, "Letter to the O.A.S. Since Fidel didn't come, I'll stay here until the plenary session. But I've written this letter that I want you to show to Lucho [Luis Corvalán]. If he approves its publication, hopefully as a pamphlet, it should be sent to each delegation. The original that I've sent to you should be delivered to Secretary General Mora at the Hotel Carrera." The O.A.S. official, along with every one of the delegations, did receive Neruda's declaration in defense of Cuba.

126. Exchanging Titles

With the sun filtering through the foliage, we are chatting on the green second level of "La Chascona." We talk without haste, with the sensation of having lots of time. Neruda tells me, "I'm writing a different kind of book." I ask him if he has finished the odes cycle. "I think so . . . for now. This one is a philosophical book, full of questions. How many days fit into Monday? How much happens in one day? It's the book of Autumn's beginning, my Autumn . . ." He falls silent. "What's it called?" "It still doesn't have a title." "Do you have one in mind?" He shakes his head. "I just don't know, but it should have an unusual title. What would you recommend?" "Me? Maybe my taste is conservative. I'm very fond of the title *Crepusculario* (Book of Twilights)." "Crepusculario?" "Yes. The Crepusculario of an extravagant book."

Shortly thereafter *Estravagario* was published, forerunner of the *Libro de las preguntas* (Book of Questions): "How long does a man live, ultimately? / Does he live a thousand days or only one? / What does 'forever' mean?" The poet is contented, but he believes that "from time to time, you have to bathe in the tomb." He defines his ambivalent profession: "I'm a professor of life / and an idle student of death."

There's a perception of indelible images, like that of Berlin in winter, when "suddenly, led by a man, / ten horses appeared in the mist / Their color was of honey, amber, fire . . . / I've forgotten the winter of that dark Berlin. / I'll never forget the sheen of those horses."

Estravagario contains many surprises and wide variations. It's a book full of freely selected subjects, with a mixture of whole tones and semitones. It indicates displeasures and shows traces of the fray over his relationship with Matilde, as it bombards "enemy friends" who were just waiting their chance to drop him:

> But when I was tormented
> by the flames of a mysterious love,
> when out of love and compassion
> I suffered in sleep and awake,

the caravan disintegrated,
and with their camels they stole away.

The wound has still not healed, as he notes that they had joined together
to condemn him and find various ways to annihilate him. "They decided
on slander," he says.

This Neruda, now past fifty, doesn't forget anything, neither friends
nor adversaries. Naturally, he doesn't ignore the most obdurate of his enemies, the "lifelong Barrabas, / forever fervent and fermented . . . I'd like a
new book from him / with blasting arguments / that finally would finish
me off."

A book full of yes-no, as in "Contra-City" and "Contra-Santiago,"
the capital's two-sided coin which "the surly conquistadors . . . cut out of
sad adobe."

The poet-enthusiast dictates inheritance documents in case of his
death, closing the book with "Autumn's Last Will and Testament," osten-
sibly disposing of goods for all eternity, but still with the unavoidable
reflections and emotions of the present moment. Suggestively, he again
raises his fist against his enemies, demonstrating that when he wrote the
book he still felt the spiritual gnawing left over from the combat occasioned by the breakup of his marriage. "I've been cut to pieces / by angry
beasts / that seemed invincible." He answers those who ask him "why I
wrote so obscurely," and also that "cruel pair who attacked me for being
so simple." He's obviously responding to what still exists now or has
existed.

After replying to those "well-meaning" questions, he distributes his
sorrows, bequeaths his joys, and declares his opposition to hatred. The
codicils of his will culminate with words of "rapture for his beloved," to
whom he says, "You are red and spicy, / you are white and salty / like
marinated onion." In the fashion of *Don Quixote,* "The poet ends his book
addressing his various transformations and confirming his faith in poetry."

From time to time, he would return to our conversation about book
titles, and before long he spoke to me about a new book that would take
him back to the odes, but he said, "I don't want to call it a 'Fourth Book
of Odes.'" As usual, there would be something of everything in it, including trips, returns, and new returns. "Then call it *Navegaciones y regresos*
(Voyages and Returns)."

As for me, I told him I had just finished a novel about the concentration camp in Pisagua, and I asked him, "Give me a title, since you're such
a great titler."

"*La cárcel transparente* (The Invisible Prison)," he suggested on the spot.

"Prison? No," I told him, "it's too obvious." In time, I regretted it, and after several years I came to believe that his title would have been better than *La semilla en la arena* (Seed in the Sand).

We enjoyed playing the titles game, and some of them went into print, while others vanished like words offhandedly spoken in those chats we engaged in for the pure joy of communication, moved by our indescribable delight in the passion for words.

Although his proposed title wasn't accepted for my novel, he did write some generous lines about the book, which were never published in Spanish and appeared only as the prologue to a 1981 Portuguese edition.

127. *Neruda Yes, Neruda No*

It has been said that Neruda liked to create houses, books, and journals, like the 1955 *La Gaceta de Chile*, which he directed. He also enjoyed celebrating a work's appearance by gathering his friends together, whether to sign a collective dedication or to drink wine and eat pastries in the topping-off ceremony for a new house he was building. Even in exile, I still have a copy of *La Gaceta de Chile*, signed by Neruda, Matilde Urrutia, Blanca Hauser, Antonio Quintana (Toñita and Toñito), and other faded or illegible names which I can't make out.

There's a letter to the readers from the *Gaceta* editor, thanking them for their good wishes and announcing that Mariano Picón Salas and Miguel Angel Asturias, from Caracas and Buenos Aires, "are sending us magnificent prose pieces which we will publish later."

But the enemy can always be counted on to strike a blow. A little Nazi publication rails against the *Gaceta* and attacks Thomas Mann, in an article appropriately signed "Gestapo."

Along with the "Journal of Arts and Letters directed by Pablo Neruda" there is a supplement, *Rosa de Poesía,* printed on leaf-green paper. In it are the young poets of that time, including one page of powerful poetry by Spanish and Latin American women, among them his new friend from Valparaíso, Sara Vial, who many years later would write a luminous book about Neruda and the port city. Understandably, the journal's featured pages are dedicated to the centenary of *Leaves of Grass*. Not for nothing does Neruda have in his home a full-length portrait of Walt

Whitman, that young man with the thick, white beard whose "Salut au Monde!" antedated the Chilean poet by 100 years.

He experiences the joy of receiving translations of his books into inaccessible languages, and jokingly asks me, "Can you translate this poem from Persian for me?" Not from Persian, or Arabic, or Urdu, or Bengali, nor from so many other translations into unknown languages that are being sent to him.

As an inveterate addict of deluxe editions and collector of poems as concrete things, he's enchanted with the special reprint of his "Ode to Typography," and the Stockholm publication of "The Great Ocean." He is fascinated by the grace of whimsical characters and curved letters, and always would have liked to be a printer. Since early adolescence he has drawn bookcovers with a handsome masculine calligraphy for works of his own which were never published. That same fascination had taken him into the print shop where his first book was being composed, to discuss with the editor questions of format, cover, typeface, color, weight of the paper, bulk of the book, and attractiveness of the headings. He never lost his spontaneous passion for the implicit allure of the printed word.

Invitations are coming from everywhere, and he is captivated by travel. Trips are a part of his pleasure and his work, as seen in a prose book that has just come out, called simply *Viajes* (Travels). Throughout his life there will be new departures and returns. He goes to the Soviet Union and other Socialist countries, and with Matilde he goes to China, accompanied on the sea voyage by Jorge and Zelia Amado. He finds sadness among his Chinese poet-friends who see the approaching cultural revolution as a dark tide that may envelop everything in a long night.

Back in Uruguay, he writes me a letter on 7 November 1956: "I've had a lot of success in this country. Too many things to write here. I'm leaving on Wednesday for Rio. Jorge (Amado) has insisted and has arranged the trip. From there I'll go to Buenos Aires to give two readings, and I'll be back with you around the first of the month." The atmosphere he experiences during his trips always comes across in his correspondence. "Apparently the danger of war in the Suez has passed, and Hungary has recovered. Here, there's a climate of unceasing provocation, with 'anti' propaganda over loudspeakers and in airplane trailers."

Abroad he is treated well and, on occasion, badly. Anything can happen in one and the same city. In Buenos Aires, on 30 January 1957, Losada publishes his *Complete Works,* several thousand pages and poems, on Bible paper. We've reached a point where the exhaustive bibliographical material requires the supervision of his unforgettable and evanescent secretary,

Jorge Sanhueza, taken suddenly by death at an early age. His indispensable bibliographical study will be continued and updated by Hernán Loyola, with a wealth of information about editions, early versions, fragments, and publications about each and every book. By now Neruda is widely included in scholarly studies, dissected and minutely analyzed by exegetes who are sometimes cold-blooded rather than awed. They're also beginning to collect "Neruda Miscellanea," letters, prologues, speeches, articles, invitations.

It's very hard to find a critic or scholar on Chilean literature who hasn't written about Neruda. It would be impossible to offer a complete list here, because they are legion, both inside and outside Chile, but in addition to those already referred to in this book one must mention the very authoritative and copious work by Jaime Concha, including his book titled *Neruda,* and the scholarly doctoral thesis by Eugenia Neves, in addition to analyses by Juan Loveluck, Jaime Alazraki, Saúl Yurkievich, Alfonso Carrasco Vintimilla, Emilio Miró, Frank Riess, María Magdalena Solá, Carlos Santander, Jaime Giordano, and Luis Iñigo Madrigal.[70]

We have said that sometimes he was treated badly. Whereas in Italy and France they tried to detain and deport him, now, with Cold War delicacy, he is arrested on 11 April 1957 in Buenos Aires and held for a day and a half in the national penitentiary. In the center of the polemic, Neruda dishes out, takes, and dishes out again.

It's a point where Neruda moves into music, with his "Ballad of the Carreras" set to a melody by Vicente Bianchi, who also did the music for his "Song to Bernardo O'Higgins." His patriotic theme carries him into the barracks, where along with his "Tune for Manuel Rodríguez," the lyrics become army songs.

In 1957, Nascimento publishes a *New Anthology* by Pablo Neruda, which unleashes a chain of storms. In reality, it's a third edition of the *Anthology* selected by Arturo Aldunate Phillips, Margarita Aguirre, and Homero Arce, which includes poems from the three books of odes and a few later verses. The tempest is stirred up by politics.

"Alone" quotes a French scholar's mathematical conclusion that the poet will reach his peak and produce his masterpiece at the age of fifty-six (laudable precision). But "Alone" is not always enthusiastic, especially when he doesn't like the poet's "message."

A more direct reference to the heavy artillery directed at Neruda, even from Europe, comes in Germán Sepúlveda's review of that same anthology in *La Nación* on 23 February 1958. The journal *Cuadernos,* voice of the Congress for Cultural Freedom, specializes in gnawing anti-Neruda articles by Julián Gorkin, Javier Abril, and Ricardo Paseyro, whom he judges to be victims of what Max Scheler called "existential resentment" and the Spanish medievalist Ramón Menéndez Pidal referred to as "*Invidencia,* sorrow at another's well-being," or envy. He recalled that the essayist Mario Osses, speaking at the Writers Meeting in Concepción, had claimed that "Neruda's greatness lies in the fact that he can be slandered indefinitely."

But there was something more behind all that well-organized and exploitative vituperation—the poet's political activity.

The Congress for Cultural Freedom challenges him, and he returns the gauntlet without hesitation, refusing to give in to his enemies. "I will never stop being a Communist," he emphasizes in a lecture on Sunday, 15 June 1958, in the Municipal Theater. In March, he had spoken on behalf of Communist intellectuals at funeral services for Galo González, the Party's general secretary, and in May he had been elected president of the Chilean Writers Society. That same month, he sent a letter to President Ibáñez concerning the abnormal civil status of citizens who had been eliminated from the voter rolls, including himself. And on 3 August 1958, he will proclaim "Victory!" in an article in *El Siglo,* titled "These Are Glorious Days: The Accursed Law Has Expired."

128. Clear Days and Cloudy Ones

The poet has a combative spirit, yet nobody is more concerned than he about writers and about their extra-literary causes relative to the fate of a world at risk. He is a poet who fights for peace and also for poetry.

In the final issue of *Ercilla* in 1953, he had replied to Leopoldo Panero's *Canto Personal* (Personal Song), which was anti-Neruda in its title and its content, from beginning to end. In September 1954, from Isla Negra, he publishes his "Welcome to Gabriela Mistral" for the poet who was visiting Chile after many years of absence. In November 1955, he reads an emotional prose piece at the funeral of Mariano Latorre, father of the literary school called *Criollismo.*

Whenever he can, he takes refuge in Isla Negra, but even there the city's clamor follows him. "Valentín, stranger, unreachable and loony— why don't you come to the sea? We have to talk," he writes me on 17 January 1957, referring to "indecent and crude" allusions by a certain critic. He says he'll go on the attack. "Naturally, I'll do it in my own way, with odes that will sting for several years to come. To hell with [Chamberlain's] umbrella! Very shortly you'll see them wallowing in their own poison."

On 9 March, he repeats the invitation. "The days are transparent here. I'm writing several times a day. Don't be a lazybones—come on Saturday, and we'll go back together on Monday. For the sake of continuity in my work, I've decided to stay two weeks straight in Isla Negra and then two weeks in Santiago throughout the whole year. That way I can get my fill of meetings during the two-week periods in Santiago. I'll arrive at noon on Monday the 18th. I'd go to the Writers Society office if I could be sure ... Whenever we get together, ask me about Valparaíso."

I receive frequent letters from him postmarked in distant parts of the globe. One from Paris in September 1957: "Here we are, almost back home. I've a lot to say about Armenia, Ceylon, India, China, and Moscow, but it'll wait until we're in Isla *Noire* in front of the wide ocean." He remembers an awesome child, my son Claudio, whom he nicknames the "Screwdriver" because of his uncontrollable eagerness to discover the hidden secret of all things—by taking them apart.

Another letter from Stockholm on 10 November, where he says they'll sail "on the Johnson Line's *Bolivia*. This ship will reach Valparaíso in mid-December." The poet is known to love boats and long trips, ocean voyages that last for months, because he would always arrive with a book that he's written on board ship. "I'm laid up in one foot with some sort of painful rheumatism. Therefore, I'm writing this letter with Pat-hoja's hand ... I've a lot to talk about with you. I'll go straight to Isla Negra, where I'll be expecting you. Unless you surprise us by being there when we arrive. That wouldn't be a bad idea. Nobody is to know the date of our arrival except as absolutely necessary."

He will take part in Salvador Allende's second presidential campaign, when the candidate is cheered by a large group of intellectuals on 8 August 1958 in the Baquedano Theater. There Neruda declares that "with Allende we have the best of the past, the best of the present, and all of the future." He said it fifteen years before Allende's death and his own. In our judgment, he wasn't mistaken. Other speakers on that occasion were Benjamín Subercaseaux, a narcissistic and iconoclastic writer who was a great novelty, and I myself, who wasn't anything unusual.

One winter night, we departed for the coast, apparently headed for Isla Negra, but we stop a bit before there, in Cartagena. The car halts at a corner, and someone takes us through dark deserted streets where winter lends the beach resort a lonely feeling. We stealthily enter a big old wooden house, where I'm taken to a room with two beds. An hour later, the door opens and Neruda appears, wearing his heavy sweater and merchant seaman's cap. We burst out laughing, and he says, "We're living the clandestine life! You don't know who I am nor what my name is!" He'll have to share the sparsely furnished room with me.

The next day, in that same house, an illegal congress of the Chilean Communist Party begins. Neruda speaks about the need to unite the Party and culture, saying that the workers' Party must also become the intellectuals' Party. Some of this was accomplished, and ten years after the poet's death, Chilean Communists proudly designate their organization as the Party of Recabarren and Neruda.

Politics in his case does not interfere with matters of the heart. The more involved he is in public undertakings, the more he writes emotional verses. As if to deliver a slap to those who talk about the bad Communist crowd's having dried up his soul, he is in the midst of writing no less than *Cien sonetos de amor* (One Hundred Love Sonnets), directed to his very beloved companion, Matilde Urrutia. In a chivalric prologue dated October 1959, he offers her rhymes sounding not of "silver, crystal, or cannon," but rather "sonnets of wood, cut with ax, blade and penknife, little houses of fourteen planks, so that in them may dwell your eyes, which I adore and sing."

Already in his preceding book, *Voyages and Returns,* a seeming hodgepodge, he had traveled in all directions, including Venezuela, where several pages praise the country he had just sadly said good-bye to after a five-month visit.

In 1958, after recovering his voice, he returned to his home province for the thousandth time. From the window of the train that crosses Cautín province, he sees nobody in the wood-built towns, just as when he was a boy. The rain clings to the walls like ivy and fine moss. He no longer has any family here, and familiar persons and things have disappeared. He has the feeling that he is actually going away, for "going away means to return when only the rain, / only the rain awaits. / And no longer are there doors, no longer bread. There's no one."

He has gone all the way from the lakes of southern Chile to Lake Razliv. "I like to see Lenin fishing in the transparency / of Lake Razliv . . ." He imagines the Russian as somehow like himself, because Lenin also used to dream. Or he would have liked for there to be a similarity, but he asks that there be no mistake about Lenin: "Don't confuse him with a cold engineer, / don't confuse him with a fiery mystic. / His intelligence burned and never turned to ash, / death still hasn't chilled his fiery heart." [71]

In late 1959, a limited private edition of *One Hundred Love Sonnets* appears. In it the lover in his fifties discovers wisdom and the four seasons of life—morning, noon, evening, and night. "Harsh love, a violet ringed by thorns," because the relationship wasn't exempt from passionate rages and jealousies. They burned with a "painful fire." On occasion he seems to return to the flaming brilliance of *The Slingsman:* "I hunger for your mouth, your voice, your hair, . . . total woman, carnal apple, warm moon."

Matilde is not just a "Tenant," for she is expert in the ways of the heart and in the domestic arts. She is both queen bee and worker in their hive, and she's not one to kill the drone. In the cooking realm, she is the sauce maker, the seasoner, and the adjustor. In the house, nothing escapes her attention. "Your house sounds like a noonday train, / wasps are buzzing, saucepans humming . . ." is the picture he draws of what happens in their home every day of the week, among the sounds of the canal and the lions. Sometimes "Homero comes up in silent shoes," not the *Iliad's* blind poet but Homero Arce, Neruda's secretary.

The couple is also visited by attacks, but she is strong and apparently unaffected by them, although a few people still criticize their relationship. The sonnets echo some of those sharp cuts, but they also contain the poet's query, "Where are you, Matilde?," reflecting a need for her that is as great as his need for winter's heavy southern rain. He recalls when Diego Rivera painted her with "two flaming heads of a volcano," with the gaze of the poet hidden inside.

And again the night is associated with another of the sonnets' themes, death: "Whenever I die, I want your hands on my eyes."[72]

129. Sebastiana and Wine Pitchers

The topping-off celebration at the "La Sebastiana" house on the summit of Valparaíso's Florida Hill was a happy affair. The hosts were Neruda and Matilde, residents of the top floor, and Dr. Francisco Velasco and Mari Martner, who would occupy the lower level. It was an unusual building, invisible from the street and located behind the Mauri Theater (named after Mauricio, the owner's son). To reach the house, you had to go through the "Callejón de los Meados" (Urine Alley). Unlike the other seaside house, Isla Negra, here there was very little space, so expansion had to be gained by going upward with a winding stairway. Neruda began its construction in 1958, with its rhyme-scheme already fixed, because the foundation and frame were already in place. It had sat as an unfinished abandoned construction for ten years, inhabited by ghosts and bats, awaiting discovery by the eye of the poet who for so long had wanted a house in Valparaíso. He bought it from the estate of a Spanish builder and businessman, Sebastián Collados, whose hometown of Tamarit de Litera reminded Neruda of Lorca's *Diván del Tamarit*. The original owner had made a fortune and was also somewhat of a dreamer, for he wanted to dedicate one floor of the house to an aviary, and on top of the tower terrace, which also extended over the movie theater, rumor had it that he planned to install a small heliport, which was a rarity in those days. When Neruda heard these reports, he was entranced. He simply had to buy those ghostly ruins and pay honor to that lyrical Spaniard, dead for ten years, a kindred spirit who hadn't written verses but had picked the precise location from which to view all of Valparaíso.

In all truth, architecturally speaking, the house as planned was outrageous, as unfunctional as anyone could imagine: no real comfort, each level another hill climb, water problems, and besides, at the first earthquake it would all collapse. Maybe that's why it had sat there for ten years without interesting anyone.

The writer Sara Vial was a friend of Collados's daughter, an elegant blond with a Celtic air. Sara spoke to Neruda about that building shell that had no market value, and led him through the Camino de Cintura and Alemania Avenue to show him the house at night. In the darkness he could see the lighthouse at Angeles Point, near the Piedra Feliz where lovers customarily meet and where suicides leap to their death. He took it immediately.

In three years he finished the house, which turned out to be Isla Negra's vertical cousin, withdrawn and pinched, and also a sister to another vertical construction, "La Chascona." Upstairs, the library became home to his childhood wooden horse, saved from the fire in Temuco and restored by Julio Escámez. A small bedroom was on the fourth floor, and even closer to the sky was the terrace where we celebrated several New Year's Eves as we gazed at the lights in the spectacular bay.

The 1965 earthquake destroyed the tower and toppled the prow's head from Morgan's pirate ship, which used to preside over the dining room like an oceanic terror.

For Neruda, Valparaíso was one of the most sparkling places in the world. That night when he first went to see "La Sebastiana," the port was clearly visible, "bright and noisy, foamy and whoring." He was fascinated by the fate of that port, which had been plunged into decline by the opening of the Panama Canal. More than a historical city, Valparaíso was a port with many histories. Before, all the ships and frigates that had battled the storms and cyclones of Cape Horn used to pass through its bay. Those which cut through the Straits of Magellan regularly called there. "On one ship a grand piano arrived, on another Flora Tristán, Gauguin's Peruvian grandmother; on the *Wager* came Robinson Crusoe, the real one, recently revived by Juan Fernández."

Just as in *Spain in My Heart,* where he gives himself over to the sound of penisular placenames, here he takes pleasure in the names of hills in the port city, savoring the words: Happy Hill, Butterfly Hill, Wolf Pack Hill, and the Hills of Rigging, of Potters, of Pastries, of Porridge, of the Bushy Topped Tree, of Popcorn Stands, of Don Elías, of the Quince Tree, of the Ox, and finally, Florida Hill, where "my house is located," he says with gentle pride.

In that city of stairways, he says that "If we climb all the steps in Valparaíso, we'll have gone around the world."[73]

Valparaíso was a city he had often visited but never before lived in, so he had to quickly create his own circle of friends, as was his nature. Precisely on 3 June 1961, he organized the Wine Pitcher Club, in the Alemán Restaurant across from the little Aníbal Pinto Square, where the god Neptune stands, holding his trident, in the middle of the fountain. The poet took to the inauguration ceremony a huge ceramic wine pitcher with matching individual beakers, which he had brought from Mexico. They were seated in a private area, separated from other customers by wood partitions. The members of this *Bota* (Pitcher) Club were called the *botarates* (which also means "spendthrift"). Neruda brought a logbook where the board of directors was recorded as being constituted by the Unknown Soldier, the Mysterious Bomber, the Solitary Navigator, the Happy Hill Panther, and other equally well-known officers, including the couple comprised by Helen of Troy (Elena Gómez de la Serna, grandniece of the Spanish writer Ramón Gómez de la Serna) and Lorenzo the Magnificent (the painter Arturo Lorenzo), both of them having arrived as young Spanish Republicans on the *Winnipeg's* voyage from the Trompelout harbor near Bordeaux. It was on that voyage that the two future *botarates* met each other. Thus, Neruda had been the indirect matchmaker for Helen of Troy and Lorenzo the Magnificent.

130. *The Party Man*

He used to begin thinking well ahead of time about the parties he would give, even when he was far away. He would plan them down to the last detail. As a forerunner of his *Comiendo en Hungría* (Eating in Hungary), we used to receive inspired communications like the following:

> We wish to lunch with you in Isla Negra on 1 January 1958. Imaginary menu: Choice seed beans. Tamales and Untamales. Divine seaweed. Tomato halves. Creamed baby onions. At last, Fried eel. Varied pastries. Grilled meat (Hot Damn!). Chilean casserole. Pure Chilean chicken.
>
> Before and after the meal, several Sputnik drinks will be served.
>
> ———Pablo-Matilde

> Alta Mar, near Curaçao, 5 Dec. 1957

Not only was he a gourmet poet and a fine food correspondent, but when he wrote the "Ode to Eel Stew," which is a recipe raised to the higher power of poetry, this versifying Brillat-Savarin was talking about dishes that he knew how to prepare in real life. Naturally, he knows the Latin American and universal secrets of the onion, which is why he engages in an Italian-Chilean duel with famous European onion experts. This scholar in putting together edible materials—and almost everything in nature is edible—combines the southern hemisphere's occult sciences with the witchcraft that emanates from the stones and fire of a pit barbeque. One afternoon in Isla Negra, he invites us to the garden for a conversation. Between the beached anchor and boat and the locomotive and bell are some newly fished mussels. He goes to the pine trees and gets some of their green needles, which he spreads on top of the mussels, and then he lights a nervous spitting fire. Miraculously, the flaming fingers open the shells, in the southern way. They taste three times as good, as if their flavor were multiplied by the smell of the sea, the pines and the fire.

One day in our house, he praises a dish that, to his great surprise, he's never tasted before. He asks Eliana, my wife, what it's called. His theatrical euphoria is doubled when he hears a name he would have to appropriate for his poetry, for the dish is called "blue lamb."

131. Epistles

In the back of his mind for at least twenty years, he's been thinking about a work he will call *Las piedras de Chile* (The Stones of Chile). He was already involved in studying rock formations and looking at pictures by an outstanding photographer, Antonio Quintana, when he received a book from France just like the one he envisioned. It had been done by Pierre Seghers and Fina Gómez, a Venezuelan who photographed rocks on the Atlantic and Mediterranean coasts. He will sing about the stones of another coast, the wilder one of South America that for 3,000 abrupt miles borders his long cold country. The stones are the earth's bones. In the prologue he states that "My companion, Gabriela Mistral, said once that in Chile we see our skeleton quite readily, with all the rock we have in the mountains and the sand. As always, there's a lot of truth in what she said. I came to live in Isla Negra in 1939, and the coast was covered with impressive stone outcroppings that have spoken to me in a soggy, hoarse language, a mixture of sea cries and primordial warnings." That dialogue between the man and the rocky giants will constitute the backbone of his new work.

As a judge for the Lenin Prize he has to go to Europe every year, and in 1960 he again visits the Soviet Union. In Yalta, on 8 May, he makes a long-distance joke and he pulls my leg: "Your absence prevented another meeting of the Big Three, Don Valentín." Then on to Poland, Bulgaria, Rumania, Czechoslovakia.

He stays a few months in Paris, where Pablo Picasso is creating sixteen etchings to illustrate the French version of the "Toro" series from *Cantos ceremoniales* (Ceremonial Songs) ("Then the bull was sacrificed . . ."), translated by Neruda's great friend, the poet Jean Marcenac, who also translated *One Hundred Love Sonnets*. Marcenac accompanied Matilde when we attended the UNESCO posthumous homage to Neruda, and as I write these lines I feel the sorrow of knowing that "Jeannot" (as he was called by Neruda and all his friends) has also left us forever. Among the verses that Pablo dedicated to him, he said: "The knight of Marcenac / is asleep in Saint-Denis. / In his house silence has fallen / because his head is at rest." Jeannot was still living at that time, and now the poem is unfortunately truer than when it was written, with only one slight correction to be made, for the resident of Saint-Denis now sleeps his final rest in his Figeac birthplace. What remains are his poems and his memoirs, called *I've Not Wasted My Time,* whose title Neruda might have approved with a smile of complicity, for his own memoirs reflect the same idea, *I Confess To Having Lived.*

In Paris, Neruda talked with Jeannot almost every night, and he didn't fail to write me a long descriptive letter full of atmospheric color:

Paris, 8 September 1960

Dear Vol: The lady novelist, who has filled out, lives just a block from here, with her husband, a heroic figure out of Turgenev, a huntsman who mutters. Margarita (Aguirre) claims she's not working, because she's hounded by subjectivism's sin and realism's obligation. I told her: Work and then figure out what school you belong to. This left her a bit disappointed, because she loves the great spiritual debates, especially literary ones. In final analysis, she's a subterranean in a world that's pursuing astronautics.

Alvaro Jara lives further away, with his companion and little kids; and beyond, our friend Marta Colvin. If you and the Quintanas were here, we would bring Orlando and the mysterious captain Aguirre and go on eating blood pudding, which is called *boudin* here and is the high point of the *cuisine française*.

Since we're totally out of money, we're not going to Sweden, also because the Chilean exposition there has been indefinitely postponed. My trips are not just a whim. We're inclined to go to Cuba on 2 November and from there to I.N., and then I'll speak all along the coast about our future parliamentary representative. If we were to leave for Chile earlier, we'd miss Cuba, because the navigational lines wouldn't take us there. We won't be changing address here, and you know the one in Havana . . .

Aragon has just finished a new book of poetry that is apparently very good, and he's beginning a new one with a very unusual title, *Anthology of Elsa,* with a 70-page (!) prologue by her.

Alice is still Gascar, and Gascar writes and writes, better and better.

M. Otero is spending a few days here.

Paris is becoming bleak with its old smoke, its exploited Montmartre, its countless dog droppings, and its abstract painting which bit by bit takes on the appearance of those droppings; in other words, it's becoming realistic without knowing it.

I read all your news about the next election, and I see you as you are: a youngster, an example of the *nouvelle vague.* As soon as I get there, I'll go everywhere, but don't forget that my bones are older. This may be the last campaign. There'll always be representatives.

I'll be glad if my Caribbean verses are well received. The book will come out soon in Cuba, sort of a rhymed meteor.

This is the longest epistolary effort in my life, and it's a weak expression of thanks for the immense pleasure I got from your letter. We had to go to the Ville Hotel to get it, and even show them a birth certificate (don't ever send registered letters to France). As we walked through the

Marché des Fleurs, Patoja and I were trading off the two brief but delightful pages of your missive. Please amuse yourself and amuse us by writing, for you don't have two such readers in the whole world as Pablo and Matilde, who love you.

132. *A Forgotten Heroine*

For some time, he has been intrigued by a dead woman. "I'm writing lectures," he tells me in a handwritten letter from on board the *Italia,* near Bilbao, in January 1958. "Also a long poem about Manuelita Sáez, Bolívar's lover. She died at a very advanced age in Paita (Perú), home of the famed taffy candy. We went down to see her tomb. That's what my poem is about."

He offers her appropriate respect and admiration in *Ceremonial Songs,* a book he's been working on for some time. "Paita's Unburied Woman" begins like a travel log, "From Valparaíso by sea," as the ship approaches the Peruvian coast. Then "In Paita we asked / about her, the Deceased: / to visit the land of the lovely Entombed One. / They didn't know. They didn't know where / Manuelita had died, / nor which was her house, / nor where could be found / the dust of her bones." So they asked the sea, but even her lover is absent. They searched in vain for her, and the poet wants to rescue her from Paita's dust. He invokes her so that she may again be an ancient dead woman, a shining name, so that at least her bones have a name. In this way, "Her lover, in his sleep, will feel the bones calling to him." The poet then left Paita's rotting docks full of crates and cotton bales, and as the ship pulls away and night falls over the earth, he feels they're sailing toward oblivion.

133. *Earthquake in His Childhood Land*

He is in Paris when news comes of the cataclysmic 1960 earthquake which has desolated his southern lands, sweeping away Puerto Saavedra in an expression of volcanic rage and contentious geological plates. The sea, which devoured the breakwater, washed in through windows and tumbled towers and bells. The quaking nation will have to be rebuilt. Neruda sets himself to the task while still in Europe, enlisting poetry and painting to rebuild a wall, a door, a village fragment. He asks for news and offers some. On 6 August that year, he regrets that we've not seen each other in Europe:

Dear, dear Vol: I don't hear anything about you, except for your trip that I learned about when you'd already come and gone. I'm at a point of near return, winding down next to the Seine. We've bought books and two parrots that scream like freed Congolese. I never leave this house on Saint Louis Island, which you should also consider your house. I plan to return by way of Cuba toward the end of the year. Now I'm taking a break from traveling and am straightening out some ticklish publishing problems. Matilde cleans house, washes clothes, cooks, and from time to time buys the most ridiculous beach hats. It's summer in Paris, the ideal season, with half-empty movie houses, plenty of taxis, and space to sit down in cafés and bookstores, where I've bought sixty volumes of Eugène Sue with a deposit, and now they've closed for a month so I don't have to pay them . . . In Kafka's I saw (José Miguel) Varas and Don Luis . . . Parra's Swedish girlfriend, destroyer of *coeurs de poètes,* came through and stayed *chez nous.* A beautiful rare animal. My rheumatic attacks sent me off to Yalta. Generally speaking, my bones resent the immense number of minutes they've lived through since my skeleton was formed in Parral. . . . (I'm sending you a bit of my *Heroic Song*), the book about the Caribbean which I finished on the sea voyage here. If you give it to *Siglo,* that's fine. We'll possibly go to Sweden on 10 September to open the aid-for-Chile week.

In the meantime, a poem of mine will be published in Paris in a deluxe edition of 100 copies (with illustrations by Picasso, Dalí, Tamayo, Miró, Matta, Portinari, Siqueiros, Lam, Zañartu, Poleo, and a Spaniard I forget). The proceeds will go to our earthquake victims and for reconstruction. It'll probably amount to several million!

I'll stop now and await your reply. Phone Laurita and go spend a month in Isla Negra! Don't be a lazybones.

Meanwhile, Matilde and I send you a big loving hug full of all the homesickness that's beginning to gnaw at us.

Good-bye. P.

18 Quai de Bèthune, Paris IV

134. *History's Bearded Men*

After journeying through so many nations and finishing up several texts, he'll return slowly by ship. As he prepares to sail, he sends me a few lines from Marseilles:

11 November 1960. The If Chateau, among some antiliterary waves. Young poets of the port city, all in the family. The Old Port full of ropes and sails. A marvelous port, with Monte Cristo, history's first bearded man. We leave tomorrow for Cuba. I think that before 1961 we'll be talking nonstop with the candidate for parliamentary representative for Isla Negra. Hugs!

     P. and M.

In Havana the third of December. In Chile, I hope, we'll spend New Year's in "La Sebastiana"!

It was on 12 April 1960, on board the packet boat *Louis Lumière* from America to Europe, a little more than a year after the victorious Cuban Revolution, that Neruda had finished writing the *Heroic Song,* which he dedicated "To the liberators of Cuba: Fidel Castro, his companions and the Cuban people; to all those in Puerto Rico and the Caribbean who are struggling for freedom against the threat from the north." He repeats in the prologue that he proudly accepts his "public service obligations as a poet, that is to say, obligations as a pure poet." He wishes to offer something, for "Our peoples have suffered so much that we will have given them very little even if we give them everything."

He reads verses from this book in many parts of the continent, proud that it was the first book that any poet anywhere in the world had devoted to the Cuban Revolution, which he went on defending as long as he lived, despite some painful misunderstandings.[k]

The book opens with "Puerto Rico, Puerto Pobre" (Rich Port, Poor Port), suggested to him, according to his account in the first part, by a fact that had moved him long ago, before he had gone to the Orient as a young man. Puerto Rico is the unredeemed land. The third poem speaks of the maggots of a Nicaraguan dynasty that dishonors the blood of Sandino and the seed of Rubén Darío. Neruda didn't live long enough to see the triumph of the Nicaraguan Revolution, but he declared it in his call to "the raging sword's heirs," saying that "Sandino was a tower with flags, / Sandino was a rifle with hopes," and calling Somoza "the traitor, / the mercenary, the tyrant, the executioner . . ." Then the brave Rigoberto López came to cut off his life in one burst. Such are the sorrows and struggles of Central America—assassination in Guatemala, and "death in Salvador."

In the fourth poem, Cuba appears and Fidel lifts his hand. "Fidel Castro, with fifteen men / and with liberty, went down to the beach." The poet recalls the man he saw from afar and from near, in the flourishing eyes of Cuba, José Martí, and next to Martí, cutting through time and the jungle, he makes out the captain of the people.

Liberty came to Latin America by way of Cuba, in the eleven-syllable ballad lines that take on the resonance of Spanish poetry's preclassic heroic meters. He turns his eyes to "Poor Port," and speaks of Venezuela, of Caribbean birds, of dismal O.A.S. meetings, of the 1960 explosion of the French ship *La Coubre* in Havana. He looks then at Panama and the Canal, at the infamies of a free press which, on a day when "the Buenos Aires police dragged me out of bed and off to prison," was terribly concerned about the latest Hollywood divorce but ignored the detention of an insignificant poet. He will return to things of truth and decency "dancing with the blacks, with my black brothers in Havana."

He proposes "a moment of song for Sierra Maestra, a meditation on those mountains, looking toward the year 2000":

> showing in Cuba the common flag
> of the dark hemisphere that hoped
> for a true victory at last.

In his book, *Fin de mundo* (World's End), he returns to Cuba, paying tribute to the dawn's handful of disheveled heroes: "Tribute and drumroll and praise / for gunpowder's birds / and the insurgents' profile."

In regard to the perplexing letter signed some years later by Cuban writers, Neruda says in his *Memoirs* that "A blind spot, a tiny blind spot within an entire process is not very important within the context of a great cause. I have continued to sing about, to love and respect the Cuban Revolution, its people and its noble protagonists."[74]

135. *The Joking Bird*

The Neruda generator is working on *Plenos poderes* (Fully Empowered), which Losada will publish in September 1962. That book has much to do with Valparaíso, the ocean, and human speech sometimes forbidden to him by a throat infection that moves him to speak through the pen in graphic words, as he silently navigates through the rivers of his language. He lifts a toast to words.

And another to himself as builder of fanciful houses, including this one called "La Sebastiana," which he fashioned first out of the air and then of cement and steel. He gave it the least costly of doors. I went with him many times to establishments that feed on the scrap from razed buildings and live on dead houses, enriching themselves with demolitions. He proceeded to build his aviary with those castoff materials, until all that's missing, he says, is some blue, and the house will begin to bloom: "And that is work for springtime."

He likes to measure time and enjoy laughter without counting the hours, therefore he pays tribute to a Valparaíso watchmaker he has just met, Don Asterio Alarcón, who measures minutes as if he were the clock man par excellence.

Different, very different, is the "Ode to Acario Cotapos," the most formidable humorist among all the friends he ever had, the fat man of surrealistic comedy comparable only to Chaplin, even though they were as different as a violin and a lyre. Acario had written "The Joking Bird" about himself as a generous playful joker who had several abilities that belonged to him alone. He knew the secret telephone number of cats; he was shipping representative for Mississippi paddle boats; he would tell stories about Ivan the Terrible in ancient Russian without knowing a word of the language; and he sang the role of Boris Godunov, in his own fashion. He used to act out Hitler's arrival at Hindenburg's funeral, and he would announce the election of a new pope. He performed a spirited meeting of the French Chamber of Deputies as a comic opera, and mimed the flight of an attacking wart hog that swells up like a zeppelin and flies to Brazil where it lands on the Amazon. And all of this would be accompanied by a full orchestra in which he, all by himself, was piano and trombone, flute and cello, oboe and harp, as well as the "Acarín" bird. A matchless lunatic, he was the only one who would dare compete with Federico García Lorca, who used to yield to this magical clown who could imitate with absolute pitch all the Vatican's bells as they proclaimed the white smoke of a papal election. In Spain he used to be booked to play obese bishops in films, and he would hold out his right hand like nobody else so that the faithful could kiss his prelate's ring. One day in his cheap basement room in Paris, he's awakened by some antimusical jackhammers knocking down walls, as two helmeted workmen, covered with dust and singing the "Marseillaise," carry the French flag into his room. They were two laborers on the Metro construction who had just completed a subway tunnel, in Acario's room.

He was a unique character, whose enemies were germs. He used disinfected protective tissues in order to avoid touching paper money. He never shook hands with anybody, for hygenic reasons, much less with weak-looking people. One time, I went to visit him with Pablo, who wanted to take him a little joy, because this personification of joy for others had to spend his last years in a wheelchair, as a result of an automobile accident. In his ode, Neruda tells him "Teacher, companion . . . Now / I'm writing a book about what I am / and in this 'I am' you, Acario, are a part of me." He is also recalled as reliving the unequalled fables of "Mr. Puga Borne" and the parade of tiny Bolivians.

Among tributes to laughter, love and the world, the book also includes a key poem in which Neruda reveals the multiple character of which he is a part. The original version of "The People," dated in March 1962 at Isla Negra, was written for the Chilean Communist Party's twelfth congress. I think that rarely has something so profound been written for a political meeting. In my opinion, it should be considered a classic text, full of terrible and beautiful truths about unappreciated human beings. It should be read in all Communist congresses, and every revolutionary should read it at least once a year.

The poet is assuming full powers of speech, which he never tires of, perhaps because "others sing so that I may sing."

136. Outlines

Hear ye! Hear ye! Hypnotic attraction for those who are tempted by the chance to peer into the inner world of VIP's. Attention! From 16 January to 1 July 1962, Neruda lifts several corners of his seven veils of mystery, as he publishes ten contributions to the Brazilian journal *O Cruceiro Internacional* under the title "The Lives of the Poet."

In my discussion with him about these selections, he informs me that "They're only an outline. My idea is to write my memoirs, and this is just a small beginning." In any case, those autobiographical pages announce his intention to do in prose what he has always done in his poetry—tell his life story. The titles and the order of those ten pieces indicate that the poet has decided to narrate at length according to a chronological progression: 1) The Provincial Youth; 2) Lost in the City; 3) The World's Roads; 4) The Oriental Street; 5) Light in the Forest; 6) In Ceylon's Luminous Solitude; 7) Storm in Spain; 8) America's Innards; 9) Struggle and Exile; 10) Final Statements and Counterstatements. The selections constitute a primitive skeleton for his posthumous book, *Memoirs (I Confess to Having Lived)*.

137. *Airy and Earthly Poetry*

Being a twentieth-century poet, he acquires the habit of writing while in flight. On the plane between Iquique and Vallenar on 19 February 1961, at nearly 500 miles an hour, he scratched out a poem in memory of Elías Laferte, an oblique homage in the style of Rubén Darío: "Now that this golden man / finally goes to his rest / you'll understand that if I don't weep / it's because he taught me not to weep."[75] Laferte had the same dignity and grace of the common people that Neruda also had found in Modesto, a figure from the Spanish civil war with whom I used to watch him chatting for hours on end in a Prague beer hall. In that same locale, he would also write to another Spanish poet, Marcos Ana, who had been in prison for twenty-four years, since he was a boy. Neruda never avoided topics that came along by chance, for life has a lot of contingency and only a little of permanency.

Neruda the militant publishes "To the Chilean Communist Party on Its Fortieth Anniversary," in the January-February 1962 issue of *Principios*. In March, he delivers his address on "America's New Heroes" at the twelfth National Party Congress, a mixture of political reflection and literary meditation.

On 30 March, in a public ceremony in the University of Chile's Hall of Honor, the School of Philosophy and Education names him Academic Member "in recognition of the universal quality of his extensive poetic work." Nicanor Parra delivers the welcoming address, and in Neruda's acceptance speech on "Latorre, Prado, and My Own Shadow," he delves into the diverse currents of Chilean literary history and into a clarification of his own work.

Some years earlier, on 11 November 1955, he had bade farewell to Mariano Latorre in the General Cemetery. Many snobs had turned up their noses at this author who proposed to incorporate rural Chileans into the short story, situating himself in their world of submission to the will of the earth. Emphasizing that he had never had personal contact with Latorre, Neruda admits that it was through reason that he had come to appreciate his "qualities as a great writer . . . A truly national writer is an exceedingly pure hero that no citizenry can afford to ignore." Latorre was not only ignored but was also a victim "of critical malevolence, superficiality, or hostility." Neruda's perspective, both literary and social, is distinct from Latorre's, but the latter nonetheless had woven "the patrician reed into the cradle of the nation," and that was sufficient to guarantee him a place of honor.

Pedro Prado, another departed professor in the school, is quite different, in his opinion—an antiprovincial in the backward remote province that was Chile in the 1920s. Neruda, coming from a mute region where only monosyllables were necessary, suddenly finds himself in the capital, face-to-face with an overflowing talker who digresses at great length and whose discourse is in perpetual motion as it expresses ideas that frequently come from afar. Prado was a man who used to talk for the pure joy of displaying his high-voltage intelligence at every opportunity.

He was the first to write about Neruda's *Book of Twilights,* in a "calm masterful piece, full of sense and insight like an ocean sunrise." Yet his disagreements with Prado were significant. Neruda was more a man of the street and of nature. He couldn't stand endless disquisition about the mystery of existence without doing something on behalf of real life. In the midst of his poverty he rejected the concept of austerity, and he didn't go along with Prado's eternal metaphysical preoccupation. Pedro Prado was untouched by the waves of literary revolution, and even less by social revolution, whereas Neruda was so captivated by Apollinaire and, earlier, by Stéphane Mallarmé, that he published *Endeavor of the Infinite Man* without periods or commas. In addition, those are the days when he becomes interested in an even more dangerous individual, Lenin.

In reviewing his own literary roots, Neruda goes back a long way, to "our first Latin American novelist," who was paradoxically a poet, Alonso de Ercilla, but he can see something of Prado's gift for intellectual dissection in many of his friends, namely André Malraux, Louis Aragon, and Ilya Ehrenburg, though all were quite distinct in a hundred other ways.

138. Mysterious Simultaneity of Ideas

In the suggestive synchrony of widespread 1810 movements leading to the first declaration of independence among our Latin American nations, "shots resounded everywhere, from Texas and California to the mountain ranges of South America. New flags were hastily being sewn." That's his theme at the twelfth congress of the Chilean Communist Party in March 1962.

There's a campaign to convince the poet to renounce his political affiliation, but it is never successful.

In those days of independence movements, he adds, nobody could blame Marx, nor Lenin, nor the Soviet Union, nor Cuba. Nor the Nicaragua of today. At the heart of the matter, history was at work. And its agents were the French Revolution and Napoleon's invasion of Spain. Behind that not-so-enigmatic simultaneity, there were ideas to be found. "Ideas were flying about, just as pollen flies about, and as if the furrows were already prepared and lying open, the seeds of liberation and notions of a republic, transplanted from Europe, began to grow into healthy trees throughout all the lands of America . . . "

Referring to Bolívar, Neruda said, "He awakes every hundred years, when the People awake." He later explains that, "With this prophecy, I meant that a second independence would find its new fathers of the nation."

He recounted that two months earlier, he had been at a meeting of writers and academicians from the entire continent, sponsored by the University of Concepción. In that meeting, a North American professor who was associated with the State Department expounded on the idea that imperialism comes only from Europe: "Philip II and Napoleon were imperialists. We don't know imperialism, and to avoid its ever reaching our shores, we should unite in a federal system of government." A young Mexican writer, whom Neruda had never seen before, Carlos Fuentes, interrupted to ask, "Sir, what do you mean by 'federalism'? A federal republic of Latin American nations exclusively, or in conjunction with the United States?" The professor stammered out a response: "I'm talking about a federalism of the entire continent, including the United States." Neruda recalled that twenty hands shot up to request the floor. Those were the hands of our continent, and for two solid hours there was a parade of all the aggressions carried out by imperialism against our nations. Invariably, Washington's policy in our America has been to support tyrants, reactionaries, and executioners.

In the 1962 Party meeting, the poet told how three days earlier he had received a letter from that same Carlos Fuentes, which said, "Whatever I might tell you about the Punta del Este farce [where the O.A.S. adopted a resolution ostracizing Cuba] wouldn't be the half of it. Coercion, blackmail, and vote buying were carried out in broad daylight, accompanied by pounding fists and shouts from the North American senators, who were responsible for 'softening up' the Latin American ministers. What a tragicomedy! One didn't know whether to laugh or cry at this chorus of Guatemalans, Salvadorans, Nicaraguans, and Paraguayans, inebriates, illiterates, incoherent cowards hiding behind their sonorous tones: Providence, Divinity, Human Rights, Representative Democracy. As I listened to them, I recalled our meeting two months ago in Concepción and thought about the sad destiny that prevents our people from even speaking with their true voices and rents them out to the masquerade and to rank. Among the pygmies, how brilliant were the men from Cuba!"

139. Three-dimensional Man

A traveler of Earth! How good it is to depart, and how pleasant to return! The aforementioned flight to Europe, the Soviet Union, Bulgaria, Italy, France; jokes from 9,000 miles away, on the outskirts of Varna observing its golden sand: "13 May 1962. Here even these stones remember you. I'm in love with Bulgaria. In September we'll see you in Isla Negra, precursor of the Black Sea. Hugs—Pablo-Matilde."

His very intense life is divided between politics and literature. On 12 October, Santiago is covered with posters announcing that "Neruda Speaks Today." Off to the Caupolicán, where he delivers a lecture which will be published in a forty-two-page booklet: "With Catholics Toward Peace: Pablo Neruda Responds to the Bishops: Catholics and Non-Catholics, We Must Fight Against the Degradation that Poverty Imposes."

There's a torrent of research in several languages about the poet, and wire-services report that Neruda has a good chance of receiving the 1962 Nobel Prize. This rumor about the Nobel is repeated every October, and every year the poet's maniacal detractor, Ricardo Paseyro, travels to Stockholm. Now he publishes an "Open Letter to the Swedish Academy," while the newspapers claim that "Neruda, Sartre, and Beckett are candidates for the Nobel Prize for Literature." In an interview by Ligeia Balladares, Neruda declares, "I'm not obsessed by the Nobel Prize," yet those are critical days when he takes cover in Isla Negra, which is almost like a besieged fortress.

He's approaching sixty, and something has driven him to out-and-out reminiscence. He finishes his most extensive and complete book of autobiographical poetry, *Notes from Isla Negra,* his extra-biblical Pentateuch. Curiously enough, the first edition is published in Italy, by the skillful printshop run by Alberto and Bianca Tallone, the latter a woman Neruda is fond of and admires. From Alpignano, near Turin, he receives a sad letter from Bianca: "Our Alberto never managed to read your letter, nor to print your new book. Two months ago, he left us forever."[76] The Italian scholar Ignazio Delogu later has a long discussion with Bianca about those events. The Sardinian interviewer is a knowledgeable and inquisitive Hispanist and Latin Americanist, and now he pokes about and learns some secrets, revealing that in Neruda's most recent conversations with Bianca, the topic inexorably revolved around death.[77] He would have to begin preparing for it himself, and leave something concrete.

The careful edition of that first part of the book, *Donde nace la lluvia* (Where the Rain Is Born), isn't published under the generic title of *Notes from Isla Negra,* but under the title of *Sumario* (Summing Up).

From "La Sebastiana" in 1962, he will begin the accounting, the long retrospective journey, in order to confront death. He will spin the time machine around, pointing it toward the reconquest of the past. The unidentical poetic twin of *I Confess to Having Lived* will cover his journey until the age of fifty-eight, but he'll begin at the beginning, going in reverse back to his childhood. Even though he may have forgotten the way, he has left some signs, as the Indians did to show the path back through the forest. Many signs have faded, swallowed up by the mists. "My childhood as viewed from 1962 in Valparaíso, after such a long journey, is only rain and dense smoke."

Anyone who wants to learn something new about the poet should read *Notes from Isla Negra* with great care. It's a direct, transparent book. Almost everything he remembers is in it, except what he censors in himself.

He frequently returns to episodes already dealt with in his earlier work, but now the eyes are new, burdened by time, distance, recapitulation, and nostalgia.

He will reaffirm what he is. And to his enemies, "No, Sir"; we do not sell ourselves and I do not give up. He repeats his oath against the tyrants of America. This book comprises almost 200 pages of his *Complete Works,* but he hasn't finished yet. He still has twelve years left, though he doesn't know that, of course. What he does know is that "The Future Is Space." He looks forward and will live to the utmost whatever time is left to him. Mistakes? Yes, "I treasure the errors in my song." But he still wants to create the everyday ocean, and he has a flower garden that doesn't exist. He is decidedly three-dimensional.

140. *With the Turk and the Spaniard*

When *Notes from Isla Negra* is published shortly afterward (1964), he states that he wrote it, in part, to celebrate his sixty years. On his birthday, he added that the book is a willful return to the *Book of Twilights*, to "a poetry with an everyday feeling. Although there is a biographical thread in that long, five-part book, I didn't seek anything except the expression of everyday blessings or misfortunes."

The fourth part, *The Root Hunter,* is dedicated to the Spanish sculptor, Alberto Sánchez, whose name had been recently carved into the beams that support the roof of the Isla Negra bar, next to Hikmet's name. He was so different from Nazim, though both were tall. Hikmet had blue eyes and a large frame in which Europe and Asia were joined. Jovial by temperament, he was the personification of intelligence and goodness. Alberto's long lean figure, with his severe face, "was a natural monument of Castille." This sharp-boned man was like a tree on the Castillian plains. He had been a baker, and perhaps that's where he got his custom of giving things a shape never seen in sculpture museums, like his "Bird Invented by Me." Neruda says that since this dark-complexioned Castillian was like a Don Quixote carved from stone, "he just had to marry a clear Sancho-like woman," and that's why he married Clara Sancha.

In the early 1930s in Spain, his sculpture was not understood at all, for this man from the Toledo countryside was a completely original artist who went way beyond what was established. Along with Pablo Picasso and Joan Miró, he created works for the Spanish Republican exposition at the 1937 World's Fair in Paris. That's where Picasso's *Guernica* was unveiled, but according to Neruda what attracted open-mouthed attention was Sánchez's unusual kind of obelisk of a Don Quixote without arms and without eyes, the image of a Spain in mortal danger.

Alberto had to go into exile, and he went to the Soviet Union. In Moscow, he not only designed the scenery for the film of *Don Quixote,* but it's also his voice that is heard in the old songs on the soundtrack.

Whenever Neruda and I were in Moscow at the same time, we used to go visit Alberto in his studio near the university, and sometimes in his apartment. When the sad news of the sculptor's death came on 1 February 1964, the poet wrote two pages of restrained but deeply felt words about "this great Alberto Sánchez, thin and jagged, made of bone and flint."

Once when I went back to Toledo, I made the obligatory return visit to El Greco's house, where the view from the garden spans the unique hilled city in its entirety as well as the surrounding countryside. We stayed a while in the Church of Santo Tomé, contemplating *The Burial of Count Orgaz,* and then we went out to look for another of Toledo's museums, that of Alberto Sánchez, but that day at two in the afternoon we found only a locked door, sadly typical of a man who was always out of place and spent most of his life as a hard-to-find outcast. Yet today, Spain is rediscovering this born revolutionary, this mysterious and pure artist whose sculpture of *The Root Hunter* provided Neruda with the title of one section of *Notes from Isla Negra*.

141. Civil Registry Official

On that 26 April 1964 when the "Alberto Rojas Jiménez Tavern" was solemnly dedicated in Neruda's Isla Negra house, the poet had the names of old departed friends carved into the wooden beams.

But he didn't want the elegiac notion that life ends to be the only idea associated with that nook, which had been created for toasting friendship. The notion of birth also was to be emphasized, and that inaugural day coincided with the baptism of the son of Rubén Azócar and Práxedes Urrutia. Neruda, acting as John the Baptist, submerged the child not in the Jordan River but in the planet's largest baptismal font, the Pacific Ocean, where the baby received the blessing of the ocean's somewhat salty holy water. The poet, like a precise ancient scribe, had prepared the certificate which his secretary, Homero Arce, copied with the calligraphy appropriate to a church recorder, giving notice that the newborn male had been baptized. His parents wanted to name him Vicente, but the erudite indigenist Alejandro Lipschütz demanded that he also be given the name of an Indian chief, Lientur. Pablo, remembering his own *General Song*, agreed, and with a serious expression dictated the final words of the baptismal certificate "of the new aboriginal Lientur, son of Azócar and Urrutia, residents of La Reina in the lands of Chief Tobalaba. The salt of the Great Ocean will bring strength and beauty to young Lientur and will make him worthy of his brave father."

The poet was also known as a matrimonial agent, who would dispense romantic advice without the authorization of anyone. He was fond of poking about in the secrets of unmarried hearts, taking on the role of Cupid. He would bring couples together and was delighted whenever he could get them to marry. They were always guaranteed a free honeymoon in a noteworthy and unusual location—the lofty tower at Isla Negra. The newlyweds would begin their life together in that imitation of Middle Age construction, among sounds of the ocean and surrounded by a sense of adventure and pictures of boats and fishes, not to mention an abundance of inviting books, if by chance they had time for reading.

Sometimes, more often than not, the prospective sweethearts were unaware of what the poet was cooking up in his amorous-projects workshop. One friend, Sara Vial, in her *Neruda in Valparaíso,* a book replete with unexpected information, recounts that one day he suggested to her that she marry the author of this book you have in your hand. He gave her his reasons and proposed a plan of action. He truly wanted to see his friends happy, but apparently Sarita turned up her nose at the idea. I've only learned about it twenty years later as I was reading her very spontaneous and doubtless very reliable book.

On other occasions, he was successful in carrying forth to the wedding. Sometimes the marriages lasted, and other times they were dissolved before they got off the ground.

142. The Burden of Fame

Deaths, baptisms, marriages, illnesses. Illness for a celebrity is especially difficult. One afternoon when we're with Neruda in the "La Chascona" house, he's stretched out on the sofa, talking very little and barely able to open his eyes, due to a fever. But he doesn't want the few friends who are there to leave just yet. We had an unspoken agreement not to make too much noise, but we also wanted to stay, simply because he didn't want to be alone.

All of a sudden, a young couple arrives, Venezuelan poets, accompanied by the writer Vicente Gervasi, who was at the time cultural attaché in the Venezuelan embassy. The woman is an outstandingly statuesque beauty. They've made a special trip from their country just to meet Neruda, but their idol is sick and has to exert himself to open his eyelids and his mouth. The admiring lady sits down next to him and begins to tell him things she has probably been thinking about for a long time: her devotion to his poetry, her deep understanding of the poet's vision, her hope that some day he'll be so kind as to read her poetry and give her his opinion. As she fervently rattles on, her voice clearly reveals that this is an important moment in her life. I can still hear her impassioned monologue to the poet, who lies there like a buddha with his eyes closed, perhaps hearing her from afar but unable to react. The beauty continues her soliloquy, which becomes more and more desperate in the absence of any response.

We're all aware of his condition, and finally I decide to gently interrupt, whispering into her ear that Pablo is ill, and that I'm afraid she might get the impression that he's always like this, or that she might interpret his

cataleptic state as indifference or bad manners or displeasure at the unexpected arrival of unwelcome visitors.

She apparently doesn't listen to me, being interested only in Neruda,
and she goes on talking to him for a long while, telling him about the
impression she got from her first reading of his books, sort of like
St. Paul's blinding light on the road to Damascus. She spells out how she
has followed his entire career almost religiously, clipping his articles and
poems from the Caracas newspaper *El Nacional*. Maybe in that way she's
trying to break down his apparent diffidence and convince him that she's
a knowledgeable and faithful admirer of his work, which she begins to
recite from memory. But the poet remains mute and withdrawn. The situation is quite clear to all of us, and we go over to the lady's husband,
who seems a bit calmer, explaining to him that Neruda has a fever. He
speaks to his wife, who answers with infinite disenchantment, "I never
thought the poet would be like this." After that, the only thing she wants
to do is get out of there as quickly as possible.

We were befuddled. Neruda carried on his shoulders the heavy burden of fame, and a celebrity wasn't ever supposed to get sick, but should
always be "the gentleman without any defects," that legendary character
who was part of his comic view of life, though in this case there was little
cause for laughter.

Happy ending: Years later, a healthy and alert Neruda traveled to
Venezuela where he became a good friend of that poetic couple who had
once arrived unexpectedly at the house on Márquez de la Plata, from
which the lady had retreated in extreme disappointment. In Caracas, their
contacts became a chain of pleasant dialogues full of much merriment.

143. *Summing Up and Self-analysis*

Although Neruda from early on is the first to celebrate his birthdays,
when he turns sixty half of Chile takes notice, admittedly on a smaller scale
than the jubilant ceremony with the air of an international conclave that
characterized his half-century anniversary. This one was more mature and
more profound, in terms of the analysis of his work. Three journals came
out with special issues: *Mapocho*, *Aurora*, and *Alerce*. The 12 July 1964 issue
of *El Siglo* carried Neruda's response to twenty-three questions and his
statement to Raúl Mellado that "For me, writing poetry is like seeing or
hearing," as well as Hernán Loyola's commentary on *Notes from Isla Negra*

and a "Basic Bibliography of Works by and about Pablo Neruda," by the meticulous Jorge Sanhueza.

I was with Neruda at several sessions in the National Library devoted to examining his poetry, and I listened to him speak without any notes, as if he were communing with himself or chatting with just one person. I was afraid that nobody would be taking shorthand notes, but somebody did indeed preserve what might have seemed unimportant, for the poet had given him the summary of what he might say, in order to comply with a bothersome promise he had made. It was later published in *Mapocho* as "Some Improvised Reflections about My Works," a title that accurately describes the theme and tone of what he said on those occasions. It's a verbalized meditation which leads to a summing up, where life is conceived as a continual spiral whose points are all related to one another and to the whole. The poet at sixty recalls the poet of less than twenty. The book he had written at nineteen or younger "greatly resembles some of my more mature books," he says, returning to the cardinal idea of his poetry as a diary of everything that happens within and beyond himself, which comes to him with deep urgency. The difference between his early and later poetry is that there was no fixed purpose in his youthful work. Later, his goal became part of his poetry and shaped its direction.

As soon as he had finished the *Book of Twilights* he had felt a critical need to depart from its path. He wanted to be a cyclical poet who would delve into everything from a central core and express himself in ambitiously vast themes, which would somehow embrace his vision of the cosmos, even though that vision sprang from his fascination with sex, which he had just discovered in all its glory. In his own words, that first attempt to embrace life from the perspective of a primordial nucleus was also his first failure, called *The Ardent Slingsman*. And for that reason he had held back for ten years the publication of those poems, which had been written in a kind of trance.

I sensed a detectable shock in the audience when Neruda recalled that he had written *The Slingsman* on an unusually quiet night in Temuco, during the summer, at his parents' home, where "Almost the entire second floor was mine. Outside the window there was a river and a flood of stars that seemed to be moving. I wrote that poem in a delirious way, reaching the point of feeling myself totally possessed by a sort of cosmic inebriation, like very few times in my life. I thought I had achieved one of my first aims."[78]

The audience was quite moved by the tone of self-analysis as the mature man referred to himself when he was just seventeen or eighteen years old. He talks of how his boyish pretentiousness had deceived him during the exchange of correspondence with the Uruguayan poet Sabat Ercasty.

When the latter had answered that, in *The Slingsman,* he recognized his own influence, "The response was like a cosmic stone landing on my immense vanity . . . " He was thoroughly upset, because his inexpert youthfulness didn't understand that the most important thing is not originality but achieving one's own expression with the aid of diverse influences.

He will make use of that experience to return to an intimate expression which produces *Twenty Love Poems and a Song of Despair.* Statistically, this is the most popular and most widely circulated of Neruda's works, but its creator took less joy in it than his readers, because it didn't correspond to his tormenting idea of great poetry.

He will again attempt to realize his dream with *Endeavor of the Infinite Man,* his second failure in as many years. The title, which the unhappy author characterizes as presumptuous, reveals the magnitude of the attempt. Although the book could never be what he tried to make it, he judges it to be one of his least appreciated works and treats it with a benevolence not accorded the *Twenty Love Poems.* In his opinion, *Endeavor's* merit was in showing him more clearly the direction he wanted to take.

He recalled that he had just recently received the manuscript of a book that would later be published under the title *El viajero inmóvil* (The Stationary Wanderer), by the Uruguayan critic Emir Rodríguez Monegal. Neruda took that occasion to reject a notion cited in the book, whereby the Chilean writer Jorge Elliot had pointed out an influence of Vicente Huidobro's *Altazor* on Neruda. The latter, unacquainted with all of Huidobro's works at the time under discussion and unaware even of the existence of *Altazor,* couldn't have been influenced by him because, among other things, the two poets had such different personalities, and their ideas about poetry were poles apart. He was unable and unwilling to share Huidobro's notion of poetry as a game.

Heights of Machu Picchu represents a victory for persistence, his return to a cyclical conception of poetry, which will be more fully achieved in the *General Song,* where he decided to use all kinds of techniques, including one that horrifies some purists—the idea of the poet as narrator of his epoch. For some, this seems to smell of dusty old chronicles, but why be scandalized by the dust that is part of the earth and the atmosphere, just as rain is? He will tell what happens during man's days and will feel no shame in being man's reporter nor in occasionally resorting to direct poetry.

In his poetic career that now spans more than forty years, he has often run into caustic misperceptions. He was frequently bombarded by objections to the changes in his work. First, they sarcastically repudiated *Endeavor;* then they denounced *Residence* for being obscure and difficult; and then they immediately accused the *General Song* of being prosaic. Later they criticized *Grapes and Wind* not for its geographic vastness but for its political flavor, and he understands that its "inevitable political passion makes its acceptance difficult for many of my readers, but I myself was happy writing this book."[79]

And when he again broke his own mold, there were new misunderstandings and new condemnations.

Notes from Isla Negra is a return to sensory yet diverse poetry, a return that will never be the same as the period returned to, for time has no turning back and always moves in only one direction, toward the future. One can only return through memory and the heart, and that is what he does. Nonetheless, it is a re-creation and therefore somewhat different from the past. The man who marks his sixtieth year can recall the boy of eighteen, but he can never again be the youth of those days.

Can anyone reproach his Communist comrades who have the habit of almost religiously celebrating his birthdays? When he turned sixty, they honored him with a dinner at which General Secretary Luis Corvalán spoke, recalling in detail Neruda's membership on the Central Committee. He referred to his own experience when he attended the poet's public readings: "Every time I have heard him read his verses to the people, to the miners in Lota or the textile workers in Tomé, to the rural people in Ñuble or the Mapuche Indians in Ponotro and Trauco, and other reservations, I have seen the light of understanding and pleasure which his poetry produces even in people who haven't been able to receive a cultural education."[80] This kind of talk sounds like sacrilege to those who believe poetry is for the minority, whereas the lower classes have their own hopeless kind of antipoetry.

144. His Companion William Shakespeare

During that year of 1964, he will indulge himself in the translation of a poet he considers to be supreme. Before it was Neruda's year, 1964 was the year of Shakespeare, and in order to celebrate the four-hundredth birthday of one of his idols, he undertook the risky task of translating *Romeo and Juliet*. When the Experimental Theater proposed it to him, he was immediately intrigued. He says he accepted with humility, wanting to bow his head in reverence to his fellow writer. That attempt made him see stars, and he told me afterward, "I will never repeat such endeavors."

Working his way into the spaces between the words, he saw the unfortunate adolescents' love in a new light, but behind their overwhelming passion and their moving sacrifice, he glimpsed what was hidden beneath love's shining surface: "condemnation of futile hatred." That work is a damnation of war and an entreaty for peace. When Tybalt anwers Benvolio, "What, drawn, and talk of peace! I hate the word," Neruda associated the statement with what his friend Gabriela Mistral had said to him, "Peace, that accursed word."

Neruda opened Chile's Shakespeare Year by saying a few words before the curtain opened on the heart-rending story of Verona's lovers, and he greeted the actors and his fellow poet of four centuries ago with words of yesterday and today: "Greetings, Prince of Light! Welcome, strolling players. We have inherited your grand dreams, which we go on dreaming. Your word is the glory of all the earth." And in a whisper, he would also say, "Thank you, comrade."[81]

145. Feet Blue with Cold

When they reached the little town of Monte Grande, on 29 July 1964, there was great excitement at the news that the mortal remains of Gabriela Mistral would be transferred from her grave in Santiago to a new burial place in a children's playground. Neruda said on that occasion that her body had been brought back to her birthplace because she had wanted her final resting place to be there. In carrying out that wish, the Writers Society had been instrumental, with Neruda as its president. And the exact site was chosen because from there one can see the entire valley. The marker would be a simple stone with carved letters and a branch of jasmine. On that July day, Neruda recalled that everywhere he had seen her, she would talk about her hillside, its poplar trees and the streams that ran over the rocky length of those valleys. "And when she was silenced, we fulfilled our responsibility to bring her to the place where she began her long star-filled journey, where she spoke out about the bare feet of children who had no shoes and who are still without shoes."

Neruda said these words at a time when he was fully engulfed in the 1964 presidential campaign of Salvador Allende, who was being attacked with a venom previously unknown in Chile. It was later established that the attacks were part of an international plan, backed by a great deal of money. Neruda, in particular, pointed out the need for a new cultural policy, and he emphasized it when he and Allende went to the hamlet of Monte Grande to visit Gabriela's grave. They repeated that through her poetry she had asked that children be protected and given an education and well-being. And that their tiny feet, "blue with cold," be covered. Feet that are still turning blue.

146. The Book of the Bountiful Table

That year, he again goes to Europe, where he is a member of the jury that awards the Lenin Prize to poet Rafael Alberti. Neruda had earlier become the first South American to be given an honorary Doctor of Letters degree by Oxford University.

Later, in Budapest, he and Miguel Angel Asturias, having stored up previous tasty experiences, begin to write one of the most appetizing books ever composed by two literary greats, with a straight-forward title, *Eating in Hungary,* which will be published simultaneously in five languages by Corvina in Budapest. In the prologue, Iván Boldizsar recalls that they conceived the idea when they all went to eat in the Alabardero restaurant, a Gothic mansion on the Buda side of the river, in the castle area, where the food inspired them so much that Neruda thought about writing a poem and Asturias suggested repeating the feast. The next night, relaxing in a sailors' bar on the Danube's shores, Asturias tried to write some verses, and Neruda was moved to convey his experience in prose. Each night, they came to know Hungary by dining on it, going from surprise to discovery.

That's how the book of the bountiful table was born, with its vinicultural characters Monje Gris, Tokay, and Sangre de Toro. In that savory country where peppers and paprika come together, they conferred new fame on a hearty fish soup and appropriated scintillating dishes. They gave themselves over to the pleasures of the King Matthew tavern where they wrote the date with their forks, 17 August 1965. They climbed up to the Citadel and composed a little ballad as they left the Golden Hind restaurant. They lifted a toast in the Bridge wine bar, and in a dialogue not at all like the one he had carried on twenty-two years earlier with Lorca in

Buenos Aires, but now in a dialogue over scallops resting on a bed of rice filled with mushrooms, Neruda asks with a mixture of epicureanism and nostalgia, "This garden, this table beneath the walnut tree, and the déjà vu sound of 'Over the Waves'—doesn't it remind you of those old German beer gardens of our youth?" Asturias answers, "I don't know why, but with the atmosphere and the people, it all takes me back to my old Spanish-style neighborhood in a loyal and noble Ciudad de Caballeros, Guatemala City." They drink to life and to the day when there will be a place for all at the world's tables.

A heterodox book, it was written at a table and was born out of good food and friendship, out of conversations as pantagruelian as meals and wines, with gypsy violins in the background. It's a mixture of music and taste, ear and palate, spice and surprise, sight and smell, cooking and writing, literary experiment and culinary essay.

It's a significant recipe-book adventure in poetry and prose by two who would be Nobel Prize laureates, a sister composition to the "Ode to Eel Stew" or "To the Onion" by our culinary poet and lover of food and drink, who was also an enthusiastic cook for all tastes—lyric, romantic, gastronomic, materialistic, traditional, and modern—and an intellectual creator of main dishes and desserts, extolling both the ordinary and the exquisite, from goulash to his native stew, from paprika to green chili, from songs to Bacchus to reminiscences about the grapes of his childhood.

They drank the delicately perfumed traditional wines of greenish-yellow hue that newlyweds drink before their wedding night. They consumed everything that produces a favorable effect on the human organism, as recommended by physicians to combat fatigue and lack of appetite. They were fortified by Eger's Sangre de Toro wine and Badacsony's Tallo Azul, good for blood circulation.

They used to say they had written the book to the joy of their palate, their body and their spirit, while imagining cavalcades of Hussars, branches of muscat and burgundy vines in Hungary and central Chile, and perhaps for Miguel Angel, aromatic coffee plantations in Guatemala.

147. Kites

Neruda, eternally childlike, always liked to fly kites. On windy days at Isla Negra, his hands would control the flight of huge painted fabric kites in the form of soaring eagles. This was the principal morning activity on the 18 September national holidays.

But he also resorted to using kite paper in the Christmas season's electoral campaign, writing on it his "Christmas greeting for Chile's mothers from Pablo Neruda." Inside was a piece of colored gift paper with his own drawings of sublime candles, and his greeting, "Merry Christmas and a better 1965, but only with Volodia (Teitelboim) as senator." It was all like a game, perhaps not as much fun as flying kites. He was generously recommending his friend, whose campaign he was directing. And as if Pablo Neruda's name weren't known, beneath his signature he added titles that would lend some credence: Ex-senator of the Republic, National Prize for Literature, World Peace Prize.

He prepared many little pieces of paper, all alike but with different messages: "Please allow me a word, . . . " or "This is a letter for you from Pablo Neruda . . ."

I should say that when the Communist Party considered the senatorial candidate for Santiago, they unanimously agreed that it should be Pablo Neruda. When he heard the proposal, he broke out laughing. Not for anything in the world—once is enough—I won't ever do it again! Let Volodia do it! Once having launched his friend in the campaign, he happily contributed his support, sending out his messages printed on kite paper. But I'm one who believes that his game was a serious one.

148. The Impersonator

After a lifetime of buying useless things, his house has trunks full of enough odds and ends to costume a regiment or a whole masked ball. He opens them up at parties, where some guests arrive already dressed for the carnival, while others, more timid or serious-minded, ring the bell dressed impeccably in street clothing. He will soon take away their jackets and trousers, leaving them in shoes and underwear to transform themselves into Arab sheiks, American Indians, turn-of-the-century harlots, Tyrolean singers, Himalayan monks, or Parisian apache dancers.

For his fiftieth birthday, his friend Teresa Hamel enters the circle disguised as the Golden Rooster, whereupon an incredulous friend undertakes to pluck her brightest tailfeathers. The Brazilian Thiago de Melo takes delight in impersonating Aleksander Pushkin, among other poets, and is very proud of his new identity. Through some kind of lapse, it is not his wife who accompanies him to the dance, but the heroine of *War and Peace*, Natasha Rostova, played by Anamaría Vergara with scrupulous exactness. In addition, Count Dracula roams about searching for victims, while Superman and the pliant Dalia are there in the person of Carlos and Carmen Vasallo.

The host covers his own girth with a *bashlik,* the flowing cape and thick shoulder pads worn by horsemen in the Caucasus, and a sheepskin cap.

My wife and I are among the inhibited ones who arrive without a costume, but Pablo scratches about for a moment in his miraculous trunk and, like a magician, lifts out a false beard and turban for me, and a mask and *sahri* for Eliana. Neruda paints a red spot on her forehead, and she looks as if she had just arrived from the Punjab.

149. *Paparazzi Ire at the Nuptial Hour*

One day when spring is about to turn into summer, a group of friends gather in Isla Negra. The whole house seems to glitter. The wooden statue of the Virgin and Child is waiting in the dining room, where Morgan the pirate gazes at a cupboard full of colored glasses and prepares for the nuptial feast. The bride and groom are in the stone house; the candleholders are spotless; and the gleaming cowboy stirrups mix with Toconao figurines and African sculptures. We're all expectantly waiting near the little tables in the bar.

The fence around Isla Negra is closed against various intruders, including some with cameras, who are the most daring. They shout demands to be admitted inside to take pictures, but more than pictures of the house, which has always drawn photographers, what they want now, on 28 October 1966, is to film Matilde Urrutia and Pablo Neruda in their marriage ceremony.

The commotion outside grows, and what is now a large crowd roars at the arrival of the Civil Registry official, a young woman with black hair that curls down over her ears to form a question mark against her cheeks. The gathering becomes more and more threatening. Some have climbed over the railing, and others are beginning to make their way up through the lower part of that irregular construction whose various sections were built at different times. Now they begin to invade the house, entering by force. At Neruda's request I go talk to the interlopers.

"What do you want?" I ask them. "This is a private marriage ceremony for just an intimate few. Respect the couple's wishes."

"Let him respect the right of the press to report. Let him not infringe on the freedom and the sacred right of the whole world to see a wedding photograph of a public figure."

Some went even further, saying things like, "And to boot, he's a Communist" and "He can't hide the fact that he's a totalitarian poet," provoking some laughter.

I propose a deal: "What you all want is a picture taken at the instant when the marriage is pronounced. You shall have it. A good photographer will take it, and you will receive copies."

They seem to calm down, and I go back inside. At the moment when the civil official with the interrogative locks asks the couple if they will love each other as man and wife, they are captured on film by Manuel Solimano. Matilde is wearing a white suit, and Neruda a dark one, with a flower in his lapel and a folded white handkerchief in his breast pocket. On either side are two cupids who had introduced them to each other: Blanca Hauser, Pablo's old friend and Matilde's singing teacher, and Armando Carvajal, founder of the Chilean Symphony Orchestra. The instant is recorded, and the paparazzi will have their satisfaction.

150. *The Mythical Bandit*

Neruda launches into two new adventures. Throughout ten successive Sundays, he offers weekly radio broadcasts. In addition, apparently undaunted by the cold sweat induced by his efforts in translating *Romeo and Juliet*, he undertakes something even more daring, the creation of an original drama, *Fulgor y muerte de Joaquín Murieta* (Splendor and Death of Joaquín Murieta).

When he is asked in an interview if the rumor about a play is true, he answers affirmatively but also a bit defensively, recognizing that he was a bit embarrassed about admitting that he had written a play, because he doesn't like poets who do everything and toot their own horn, running the risk of not doing anything well. "The theater is foreign to me," he says, "and I'm sure I've written a dreadful play."

The journalist then spits out a natural counterquestion, "Dreadful? So why did you write it and what's it about?" Neruda answered, "Well, a few years ago, the great actor and director Jean Louis Barrault asked me to write something for him to stage. 'I'm only a poet,' I told him, 'and I'm only interested in writing my verses. Besides, I don't know how to write for the theater.' Barrault answered me, 'That's your mistake. You write your poetry, and I'll turn it into theater.'"

That Chilean southerner, who often liked to describe himself as a person with delayed reactions, woke up one day a few years later and asked himself, why not? And he began to write a poem about someone he considered to be a romantic bandit who became a popular myth. It had all happened during the California gold rush. Joaquín Murieta went there to look for gold, along with many other Chileans in the middle of the nineteenth century, but what he found was persecution and death.

As happens with other bandits of history, this outlaw is claimed by several countries, and even a Chilean historian, Eugenio Pereira, maintains that Murieta was Mexican. Neruda, even with his title as Knight of the Aztec Eagle, de-Mexicanizes Murieta, arguing that in 1849 the bread he ate in California was made with Chilean flour from Valparaíso. Three thousand of his countrymen went to San Francisco, and in that region one of the Chilean emigrants founded a city called Washington. The poet gathers background facts like a meticulous historian. Joaquín Murieta wants protection and respect for his people during a period of greed and racism, when Chileans and Mexicans are treated in the same way as blacks, and the lynch law is applied to all. The epilogue is that the decapitated head of Joaquín Murieta is displayed in an exhibition that opens on 12 August 1853 in a San Francisco carnival stall, at twenty-five cents a ticket.

Neruda advocates the Chilean origin of his characters, but more than that, he attempts to give poetic and dramatic form to the tragic myth of his "brave, unfortunate, and errant" countryman, who is presented as a fighter against injustice.

As always, it had been everyday events and even chance that moved Neruda to give concrete shape to his dramatic impulse. Back in the days when he was moving from one hiding place to another under the regime of Gabriel González, he had seen in the slick pages of *National Geographic* a reproduction of the poster announcing the carnival display of Joaquín Murieta's head, something he had been unaware of until then. Later, when he visited California, he retraced Murieta's footsteps, gathering materials.

Another factor which influenced in the dramatization was Matilde's exclamation as she was reading a poem about Murieta in Neruda's still unpublished book *Barcarola*, "But Pablo, this is theater." His response was, "Really? That's how it came out; it wasn't planned." So he decided to write it as a drama, resulting in that hybrid that some call a "cantata" or a "dramatic poem."

Shortly before, a North American movie had been shown in Santiago, whose original title, *Murieta*, had been changed to *La última venganza* (The Final Revenge). The film was advertised with sensational hair-raising trailers: "The man who plunged a whole town into a blood bath. . . . He carried in his soul a reason for killing in cold blood . . . They had raped and killed his wife! . . . Now he would destroy all of California!"

On the night of Saturday, 14 October 1967, all Santiago turned out for the world premier of Neruda's play. We were seated in the orchestra section of the Antonio Varas Theater, anxiously awaiting the performance by the University of Chile's Theater Institute, along with some who had traveled from abroad for the event: Gonzalo Losada, the author's Buenos Aires publisher; Leopoldo Torre Nilsson, the Argentine film director; the novelist Beatriz Guido; his ever faithful friend Margarita Aguirre; and the singer Leonardo Favio.

In the single intermission, Víctor Jara sang songs with lyrics by Neruda and music by Sergio Ortega; soprano Matilde Broders sang "Barcarola," an anonymous nineteenth century traditional song; and Kerry Keller presented a spiritual.

Director Pedro Orthous and set designer Guillermo Núñez did exactly what Jean Louis Barrault proposed. Orthous had to work harder on Neruda's play than he ever had on Lope de Vega's *Sheepwell*, Chekhov's *Uncle Vanya*, Shakespeare's *Midsummer Night's Dream*, Labiche's *Italian Straw Hat*, Ibsen's *An Enemy of the People*, or Shaw's *Saint Joan*, but he threw himself into the task of turning it into choral or collective theater, as he had already sought to do with *Sheepwell*. He integrated all forms of stagecraft—dance, theater, song, pantomime—finding in Neruda an author open to the introduction of any element that would make the work more theatrical, an author who both orally and in writing asked that the staging, more than anything, be imaginative. The director used elements of the Greek chorus, the music hall, and folk celebrations from La Tirana village in Iquique province.

The music for the Murieta play was by Sergio Ortega, composer of the two most popular anthems sung by the people of Chile in the second half of the twentieth century, "The People United Will Never Be Conquered" and "We Shall Prevail." For Neruda's work, he created a popular kind of music, including melodies based on folksongs from the North, as well as anecdotal and dramatic songs, all of them carefully emphasizing the poetic text. At the play's final curtain, the composer took a bow, wearing a violet artist's cape.

Patricio Bunster's choreography was marked by a series of disparate movements: female choruses with ancient Greek accents, contrasting violently with others from the North American racist sect "The Greyhounds," and cabaret music, folk tunes, and a special ballet theme.

The work was presented in many countries and in several languages. Neruda's eyes would sparkle as he told me about a version he saw in Poland. He was very pleased that his instructions were freely interpreted to allow the *metteurs en scène* all the freedom and authority they needed to underscore the basic idea with theatrical devices.

That freedom has been carried so far as to recreate extremely daring versions, converting the work into a rock opera or into a very peculiar film by an authoritative Russian translator of Neruda, Pavel Grushko, who adds to the title his recognition of the film's innovative liberties, "based on a theme of Pablo Neruda."

The original creator would have doubtless liked that film, for he himself says of his play, "This is a tragic work, but it's also written partly in fun. It tries to be a melodrama, an opera, a pantomime. I say this to directors so that they may invent situations and objects that come to mind, costumes and set decorations."

And so the much discussed ghost of Joaquín Murieta still haunts California and unlikely locales with his many faces and in freehanded interpretations that would fill the author with satisfaction, if he could see them.

151. Jorge Sanhueza

There is one unobtrusive presence who slips in and out of Neruda's surroundings, who comes and goes pronouncing cryptic phrases and then almost dissolves into the sensation of absence, which was one of his character traits. Small of stature and dark blond, he had blue eyes that always looked either shy or questioning as he would vanish to carry out known or unknown duties. Among the known ones was that of acting as Neruda's secretary, a task he had accepted out of love for literature, devotion to the poet, and the wish to give a certain order to the poet's papers and books. When the Pablo Neruda Foundation for the Study of Poetry was created, he was in the background taking care of things, compiling lists of pre-1501 incunabular books, chronological notes on the poet's life, bibliographical catalogs, and compendia of references to citations in newspapers and journals. He was often imperceptible, and one suspects that he used to spend hours in the library dreaming with his eyes wide open. He used to fall in love with beautiful unattainable women, faithfully accompanying them when they were at their husband's side. He was concerned about the attempt to buy Latin American intellectuals through a plan forged in a city beside the Potomac River, and he would send me long, documented reports about the web that was being spun.

He wanted to write a book about the poet, possibly having in mind Eckermann's recollections of his daily work in Weimar with another poet (*Conversations With Goethe*), but almost without anyone noticing, Jorge Sanhueza died on 17 July 1968 in a hospital room at the age of forty-three. Neruda considered him so discreet in his way of living and dying that he thought it would be excessive to use his full name in the title of the poem he dedicated to his secretary, so he called it simply by his initials, "J. S.," writing that "Jorge Sanhueza died from distraction . . . His absence was his truth." He was an enigmatic man, and "Whether he's hidden in a door frame / under night's half-moon, or / he's behind a dark window / making us think he's no more, / I don't know, you don't know, and so / we'll go on playing we don't know."[82]

152. *Real Birds and Riddle Birds*

In his spare time, the poet writes books about flying objects, not saucers or planes or space ships, but avian birds: albatross, eagle, pelican, ibis, kestrel, swan, quail, condor, cormorant, wren, yellow finch, parakeet, dinca finch, sparrow. When he was a child in the land of the blooming double ulmo tree, he used to have visions of pink angels. It was the flamingo. He was also attracted by the egret that slept with its eyes open, and later by the swallow that would bring him airmail messages as it returned to Isla Negra in the spring. And his eternal secretaries, the gulls, were always in sight.

The boy loved the black-chinned siskin and the red-breasted meadowlark. He recalled that when he was a youth in Temuco, they called him "The Vulture," whose black cape opens and closes like an umbrella. The poet was always fascinated by the laborious *toc toc toc* of the woodpecker, the distinctive flight patterns of the streaking Chilean tinamon, and the hawk's suspended flutter as it prepares to plunge like a stone. His favorites were the green-backed firecrown, the Chilean lapwing, the long-tailed mockingbird, and the red-footed ring dove that he had adored since childhood.

But he's also interested in human birds with hieroglyphic names, like the "dodo-bird," the "she-bird" or *Silvestre Matildina,* the "me-bird" or *Pablo Insulidae Nigra*. He's a people's poet, a provincial bird watcher who travels the world on the wings of his soul and is immune to immobility, for he has spent an entire life watching the birds and still contemplates them for hours from his window at Isla Negra.

153. *The House with the Blue Flag*

He has seen so much in Isla Negra that he simply must devote at least one book to it, so he writes *Una casa en la arena* (A House on the Sand), 80 or 90 percent of it in prose. Only "Tooth of a Sperm Whale" and "Love for This Book" are in verse.

He still remembers the store in Temuco, "The Key," where an immense key guided the Indians to its doors. Things get lost, and although he had made off with that key, the ocean in turn had snatched it from him. Yet the ocean also returns things to him, his house key and his sand-filled hat. In that house on the sand, he took refuge from the Nobel Prizes that didn't come, and when one finally came he was living in a house that wasn't even his, the dark Chilean embassy in France.

He recalls the first time he saw the house at Isla Negra. They were riding along the lonely beach on horseback, Don Eladio Sobrino in front as they forded the Córdoba inlet. It was mid-afternoon. Later, the house will grow there, and when Don Eladio dies the poet will write his name above the stone fireplace. The house's architect was the Spanish Republican Germán Rodríguez, and the building foreman was Alejandro García. Rafita was the project's poet of carpentry, who followed Neruda's handwriting with his awl to carve the names of deceased friends into the beechwood beams.

The house was the destination of medusas who arrived as carved prow-heads from dismantled boats. One reminded him of Gabriela Mistral in Temuco, with its wind-blown tunic and majestic bearing. He found another one, the "Siren of Glasgow," in the far south, hanging from a soot-covered boat that had left the shipyard in 1866 and ended up carrying coal in the south of Chile.

"María Celeste," a weeping wooden lady, was salvaged from the flea market. "The Bride" is also there, with her face all wrinkled from so much salt spray, and "The Cymbelina" who had been buried in a sandy grave. And "The Beauty," too, "with her serene face and doll-like features and empty heart." Earlier, in 1964, the corpulent "Micaela" had arrived.

The poet feels like something more than a ship's captain. When he's at Isla Negra the house is like a government palace when the king or president is in residence. The flag waves on its pole, as Neruda's presence at

Isla Negra is announced by a blue banner with a horizontal fish enclosed in two contiguous circles.

There's an anchor from Antofagasta on the patio, where instead of resting in the sea or the desert, it leans on the broad expanse of Isla Negra, carried there by four oxen.

And near it stands the steam engine from the south, where it once roared like a locomotive and worked in the grasslands he used to contemplate in stupefaction as he traveled on his father's train. Once it was used to thresh grain and cut forests as it smoked along spitting fire. Neruda says he loves the steam engine "because it looks like Walt Whitman."

The fence that now the newshounds want to penetrate was originally erected so that the poet's two dogs, Panda and Yufú, couldn't get out to sacrilegiously eat the lambs in the nearby seminary at Punta de Tralca. That fence is obviously not a medieval castle wall, but nonetheless the dogs might be anticlerical.

154. *The Lilt of the Barcarole*

He publishes *La Barcarola* with a dedication to Matilde, "the fragrant woman from Chillán." It opens on an amorous note as he recalls the days when the "captain" who was writing his verses had to hide behind a black mask. He evokes the lovers of Capri, their dreams, the homesickness of exile, the return, and Alberto and Olga Mantaras, the Uruguayan couple who took them into their home on the Atlantic coast.

Then come poems stirred by the news in a cable, "Earthquake in Chile," when he went out into the pocket-sized Rue de la Huchette in order to shake off his demons.

Another notice comes, just as bad as that of the earthquake. Rubén Azócar has died. Neruda writes "A Wreath of the Archipelago" for him, expressing tenderness for his spiritual brother who was the blood brother of the aloof Albertina, as well as bitterness for that charlatan of long ago who had left Rubén "in hock in a dumpy hotel, with no money and no clothes, for the glory of literature." (See Section 37.)

Neruda, like other poets I've known, didn't listen to much music, so I was astonished one day when I caught him listening to both sides of a long-playing record. It wasn't an orchestra, nor the voice of Caruso or María Callas, but the solemn Rostov carillons. He had received the recording from far away. The next day he wrote his poem, "The Bells of Russia," about war bells, peace bells, and wedding bells. Their pealing tones moved him deeply. "Let's weep like bells, let's dance like bells, let's sing like bells / for eternal love, for the sun and moon and sea and earth and mankind."

Then the book sings in praise of Lord Cochrane, Chile's first naval admiral, and the Uruguayan Artigas, who had described exile more than a century before with a sorrowful phrase that Neruda loved, "A bitter task, exile."

And then he'll leap from the dawn of the last century to the dawn of the future, with a segment called "The Astronaut."

155. *The Mapuche* Trutruca *Horn and the Troubadour*

The new poetic year begins early, on the tenth of January, with a star-studded gathering in Santiago's Nataniel Stadium. The heat is suffocating as José Miguel Varas takes the microphone and asks for silence. The poets are all in their places, with glasses of water and lamps. Neruda addresses the guest of honor: "Eugenio, I haven't asked you here for a javelin tournament, but simply so that I can be your shield bearer, the interpreter of your poetry." Yevtushenko first reads his poem "The Sea," as translated by Neruda. The Russian poet is an actor-reciter-mime who presents a total theatrical spectacle all by himself, which we aren't accustomed to and which drives the audience crazy. Nothing could be further from Neruda's style of reading his poetry, which inscribes the words in a slow droning curve, like the sound of the Mapuche reed horn, the *trutruca*, of which he said, "You come from the poor south, where my soul is from . . . "

Yevtushenko, on the other hand, is like a troubadour or a juggler, but everything in his poetry makes sense. He recites "There Are No Uninteresing Men," "Tenderness," "Babi Yar," "Simbirsk Festival" (about Lenin's native city), and others, closing with "Sleet in Jarkov."

The majority of the poems had been translated by Neruda, based on versions by Yevtushenko himself, who speaks quite a bit of Spanish. Neruda had a passion for translation, which he normally did from French and English. He had undertaken translations ever since his youth, producing Spanish versions of Rainer Maria Rilke, James Joyce, William Blake, Walt Whitman, and later, of his friends Nazim Hikmet, Stephan Hermlin, Walter Lowenfels, Thiago de Melo, and more of the classics, whether Adam Mickiewicz or Charles Baudelaire.

He plans a publishing house that manages to publish *J. M. C., The Unfortunate Hussar,* a book of poems and songs about the life and death of Don José Miguel Carrera, with a remembrance by Manuel A. Pueyrredón. His idea had been to publish at least twenty rare and forgotten books related to Chile, the continent, and poetry.

156. *The Shell Collector*

The renown of Neruda is not limited to a literary elite, and as his appeal to the masses grows and spreads, he becomes almost a legend. When he makes a return visit to Colombia in 1968, a journalist recalls something said about Victor Hugo, whose word is something more than just a grunt of humanity, but is something that "expands our capacity to sense the secrets of the past and the enigmas of the future."

Newpapers headline an "Apotheosis at a Neruda Reading." In Manizales, the multitude that hadn't been able to get into the Los Fundadores Theater begins to surge about him in such a way that he has to seek safety behind a truck. The crowd rushes forward and breaks the glass doors of the theater, leaving an employee and several spectators injured by broken glass. In the reading, he recited first "A Man Is Walking beneath the Moon" and ended with "My Bad Manners."

That year, on 8 April, he receives the Joliot-Curie Medal in the Santiago Municipal Theater and delivers his address titled "The Name of This Medal Is Greater Than My Chest."

In *Ercilla*, he writes an article called "Meanderings on Beetles," about the fruits of some of his explorations at Isla Negra. He had an eye that could look into the microscope and discover what is most humble among nature's secrets. He liked to do research, especially among living things. His eagerness as a collector didn't come from any desire to hoard nor from any sense of private property, as demonstrated by his donating his collections to institutions he considered as serving the public need.

I had seen this scientific talent in Neruda most clearly years before, when he was visited one night at his "Michoacán" house by the English scientist, Julian Huxley, then secretary general of UNESCO. As he entered, I saw that the visitor was taller than his brother Aldous, with that coolness and dominating manner that is characteristic of some British intellectuals. With precision, as if studying that strange human animal who welcomed him to such a peculiar house, he told his host frankly at the outset, "I'm more interested in you as a shell collector than as a poet." Neruda took him to see his shells and also his spectacular butterflies. I heard an unexpected dialogue, which was a conversation between two scientists who knew everything about those creatures from the sea and the air. They used Latin nomenclature with the greatest of ease, and I began to discover an erudition in Neruda that I hadn't suspected. I concluded that his books about birds, his familiarity with the fauna of the earth and the ocean, his wisdom about plants, were not pure poetic invention but were founded on serious study that came from impassioned observation and endless reading.

This same year, he reaches a total reconciliation, *in absentia,* with Vicente Huidobro. Although they were poles apart as men and poets, Neruda takes off his hat to the writer who opened up Chilean poetry to favorable winds. He states it in an article in *Ercilla* on 7 February 1968, and even more definitively in the prologue he writes for an anthology of Huidobro's poetry that was to be published in Belgium but won't appear until after Neruda's death.

157. A Bit of Philosophy

Between departures and returns, this poet who writes handmade poetry in cars and trains and planes, at his desk and out behind the house and in bed, turns out a new book, *Las manos del día* (Everyday Hands), in which he blames himself for never having made a broom with the hands that God gave him. Because he wants to do everything, he regrets not having helped to make the sea, and he's dedicated to a life where places have been made for all to rightfully claim. He finds that there are negative hands, those which have never made anything. Even the cold makes things, for it is the father of fire. But he especially admires the makers of bells, of flags, iron spatulas, barrel hoops. He's preoccupied with making good use of the days, the body, and also the word, because—Good Lord!—the world is full of hacks. And there are so many portraits of dead people—better to use hands to make things, to make wine, to make songs.

His passion is to be socially useful. When a journalist asks him, "Among all your many enthusiasms, which do you enjoy most?" he answers, "Building." "How would you like to spend your future?" "Just as before and always, writing my poetry." "If you had to give the world one gift, what would it be?" "The best gift would be the restoration of a true democracy in the United States. In other words, the elimination of regressive forces in that country who spill blood in faraway lands. A great country like the United States, divested of its political and economic arrogance, would be a grand gift for the world."[83]

Any pretext serves him well for a celebration, including his half-decades. On the occasion of his sixty-fifth year, he will publish new books, and the Chilean Academy of the Language rather belatedly names him an honorary member. The delay was due to political prejudices, and although he had never shown any interest in belonging, now that a truce had been declared in that silent war, he will try to give "polish and splendor" to the language. His comment was accompanied by a corresponding half-smile.

Neruda, contrary to many writers and like very few, thought that talking about his literary projects would bring on the evil eye to curse them. On one occasion, though, he broke with that belief in sorcery, and despite Matilde's warning protest that "Pablo, one thing you've never done is talk about what you're going to write," he continued without paying heed. "When I finish the book that will come out on my birthday, I will immediately begin a new one, in a poetic-historical vein. I'll deal with an uprising of slaves that happened in eighteenth-century Chile." That book never appeared. He had put the evil eye on it forever. It would have been a counterpart to Herman Melville's *Benito Cereno,* which was inspired by the same events.

At this stage, the poet has been translated into fifty languages, and studies written about him number in the thousands. He's a living classic, who is asked a series of questions on his sixty-fifth birthday:

> "What mistakes that you've made do you regret?"
>
> "I've written some foolish things. When I'm criticized, I justify them, but I laugh."
>
> "The poems written to a president you elected, who later declared the Communist Party illegal?"
>
> "Those, too. Nobody's infallible."
>
> "What has been your greatest satisfaction or happiness?"
>
> "My campaign and my election as senator for the North."
>
> "Nothing literary or emotional?"
>
> "No. That was a unique experience in my life. I'm not built to be a senator, but I'm a man from the South and when I discovered the dry, dead pampa, with its people and their suffering, I felt something I will never forget. I don't know whether any more forsaken human beings have ever existed in this world. They would sing while they buried their dead, walking to and fro over the dead land. Nothing will ever match the happiness, and the sorrow, of this discovery."

The journalist asks him how he would define his philosophy of life. "You cannot be happy if you don't fight for the happiness of others. You can never lose the sense of guilt at having something if others don't have it also. Man cannot be a happy island. This isn't my entire philosophy, of course, but it's the most important part of it."[84]

A few days prior to that birthday, on 30 June 1969, he is interviewed on television's Channel Nine by four journalists: Julio Lanzarotti, Augusto Olivares, Emilio Filippi, and Carlos Jorquera. He tells them that the book he will give as his birthday present is *World's End*. When they ask about his method of working, he answers, "I would say that my work plan is white paper and green ink. More seriously, I work only in the mornings. It's impossible for me after noon, but I work every morning, or almost every morning, because I've forced myself into a habit or a discipline, whatever you want to call it."

He states that he had decided to live for poetry because he wouldn't know how to do anything else. So far as making a living from poetry, that's a fortuitous happenstance, but in no case have sales of his works been comparable to the sales of a successful novel.

When the inevitable question comes about whether his political militancy has limited him or clipped his wings or channeled him in any direction, Neruda answers, "My Party has never come to me to censure me for anything, nor to ask me to write in any certain way. Anything of this sort is just a legend."

Responding to those who accuse him of being a bourgeois who lives very comfortably, calling into question his militant position, Neruda asks whether it isn't obvious that a committed poet like himself "has had to confront many attempts at seduction and corruption from those in the other camp. Where is there any sign of my backing down?"[85]

158. Standard Bearer

Politics would soon snatch him away from Isla Negra. In 1969, Chile was already experiencing a preelection climate. Commitment to change had spread, but the forces in favor of it were seriously divided. On the left at that moment there was no common consensus for proposing one single candidate for president of the Republic. Several suggestions had already surfaced. Some didn't discard the idea of courting the votes of the Communist Party, which thought that unity would be achieved in a second phase that would join together all the progressive sectors around a single standard bearer. In those circumstances, consideration was given to the

tactical advantage of proposing a provisional candidate who would provide cohesion and open the way for the one definitive candidate.

In the political commission's internal analysis, several members
thought of me as the Party's probable candidate for president, which
seemed to me a mistake, for several reasons. There were more suitable
comrades with better qualifications, but above all, there was one who
couldn't be matched in this situation, one who would be the "deluxe"
candidate, the most exalted expression of a national symbol—Pablo Neruda. We proposed that somebody talk to him. It wouldn't be easy to get
him to accept. I myself was charged with sounding him out, so I went to
Isla Negra to get an idea of his reaction, prepared to give him the picture
just as it was: a candidacy that wouldn't reach the finals but only the semi-
finals. We understood that it would drag him away from his work and
throw him into the eye of the storm. But he accepted immediately, with
the eagerness of a child who is invited to assume a heavy responsibility as
if it were an irresistible adventure.

A few days later, we went back to Isla Negra with Luis Corvalán.

By unanimous acclamation of the Central Committee's sixty-five
members, Pablo Neruda was designated the Communist Party's presidential candidate. The plenum had begun on Tuesday, 30 September, at five
o'clock, and Oscar Astudillo, the general undersecretary, made the nomination on behalf of the political commission and the national commission
for candidate slates. He invited anyone having comments or objections to
present them. At 6:30, I gave the news to the numerous reporters from
radio, press, and television, and to the foreign correspondents who were
waiting in the Central Committee meeting room, next to the auditorium
where the plenum was taking place.

Outside in the streets, a crowd was packed from one side to the
other, extending several blocks. They began to wave flags, banners, colored plumes, and handkerchiefs, while balloons and fireworks exploded
and torches flared. Víctor Jara sang the "Pledge to a Laborer" and Patricio
Manns "The Final Hour." Other performers included Rolando Alarcón
and Héctor Pavez, the Aparcoa and Millaray groups, with Gabriela
Pizarro.

When the news reached Valparaíso, Concepción, and Temuco, there
were parades and chants of "Neruda, Neruda, the people salute you." The
same thing happened in numerous towns and cities throughout Chile.

Not all the reactions were cheers. A National Party official, with an
attempt at prophecy, expressed sympathy for the nominee, "Either we devote ourselves to politics or to literature." Adolfo Ballas added, "I truly

believe that this country has just lost its best chance to have a Nobel Prize. I personally believe that Pablo Neruda should receive it." The newspaper *La Nación* spoke of "Pablo Neruda's reappearance in society . . . his groomed, elegant and bourgeois demeanor," playing up "the fragrant cloud of smoke left behind by the candidate's pipe," and assuring readers that Neruda had a "gringo-ized" voice.

Toward the end of September, the Party's general secretary announced in a speech from the second floor of 416 Teatinos that "The Central Committee has unanimously decided to name a first class fighter as candidate . . . As a great personality, Neruda is a candidate in a great undertaking, that of embodying the desire for a revolutionary change in Chilean society. . . . We are not saying 'Pablo Neruda or nobody.' . . . We are inviting the other leftist parties and the other four candidates named by the rest of the popular forces to come together with us in the same endeavor."

When Neruda spoke, he described himself as a member of a working-class family, "and as a Chilean, not only by birth but out of love and duty . . . That's why I accept this candidacy. . . . That's why this candidacy won't be hidden away like a jewel in a crystal box, but will be eminently active, moving out to the whole country and becoming a mandate when the people take hold of it and endorse Popular Unity in every province, in every village, mine, or field."

One Christian Democratic senator referred to Neruda's nomination with these words: "As things stand in terms of presidential possibilities, I think my candidate won't be Radomiro Tomic but rather Claudio Arrau, who has *real* talent." Neruda laughed at the joke, but said that an even funnier comment was one in *El Siglo:* "It's about time that La Moneda government house had some poetry, because the previous governments have been nothing but song and dance."

He fields a related question: "Doesn't it strike you as absurd that in times like these, when it's not a simple matter to govern, a poet has been nominated for president of a country that seeks to be modern?"

"I've been a political man since my youth," Neruda responds. "I've never stopped being one, nor have I been out of politics, as some claim. I was only pretending."

He reassures the anxious reporter who fears that his political work will diminish the quantity and quality of his poetry. "Poetry will survive all the efforts and tasks I will have to undertake. It's like a living part of me, which I can't do without. It's impossible to know today whether the poetry of tomorrow will be worse or better, but I'm sure that I'll write it."

"Don't you think that this presidential campaign may be an insur-
mountable obstacle to attaining the Nobel Prize?"

"I don't know whether that's attainable. I am absolutely ignorant of
the workings of that prize."

"Are you prepared to give up your daily nap from two to five in the
afternoon, which has been a sacred custom for decades?"

"My nap is not negotiable. If I don't sleep, I'm sick for the rest of
the day. It's likely that if you dig into the history of Chile, you'll probably
discover that one can be president and have an afternoon nap. At least
Barros Luco managed it."

"Does this mean that in terms of napping, you are describing yourself as a conservative and a traditionalist?"

"Hmmmm—that's possible."[86]

159. An Unusual Campaign

The next day, the Central Committee named the campaign committee, designating me as its president. The idea was to open branch headquarters in every region.

A few days later, a small group left on our first northern trip, heading toward Arica, where the entire town turned out on 14 October, anxious to listen to Neruda but also eager for unity. In Iquique, on Thursday
the 16th, the euphoric scene was repeated. When we reached the hotel in
Antofagasta, on the 19th, we received the bad news that General Roberto
Viaux, commander of a military division, had declared open rebellion
against the government of Eduardo Frei, the Christian Democratic president. Viaux had been confined to quarters and was formulating demands
that constituted an ultimatum for the government. There was not the least
shadow of a doubt on our part, for although we were in the opposition,
we would defend the constitutional government. An alarmed Christian
Democratic senator asked to talk with me. He was so apprehensive that he
proposed an extremely secret meeting place, the back room of a neighborhood café. I went to meet him and tell him that we were supporting the
lawful regime. He was trembling with fear and saying dreadful things
about the military. That nervous senator, whose name was Juan de Dios
Carmona, would later be an instigator of the coup d'état against the constitutional President Salvador Allende and would serve as an agent of the
Pinochet dictatorship.

In the town the atmosphere was tense, but it was more necessary than ever to carry on with the rally, with crowds filling several blocks of Latorre Street in downtown Antofagasta. Neruda read a poem and above all called on everybody to defend the legal government against a rebellious mutiny. He recalled his experience in Spain, comparing Franco's uprising in Africa with the perilous insurrection by an insubordinate officer that very day in Antofagasta. It was a warning.

It was very late when, all keyed up, we returned to the hotel. Ligeia Balladares, a reporter from *El Siglo* who was traveling with us, had audaciously gone that afternoon to interview the rebellious general for herself. He told her many things that portended rough seas ahead. Neruda was writing something on a napkin as he listened to her, inventing all the variations on the name "Ligeia" that he could think of, maybe to vent his poetic feelings. It became a poem which shows the liberating force of words and sounds in a kind of free association. The fantasy of letters was another form of relaxation for him, the warrior's brief rest after a day of exhausting battles. In this sonnet to equivocations, Ligeia has many names: Ligenturia, Ligentina . . . Licosigla, Ligenta, Liprofesa, Lichuga, Litemuca, Lilinares . . .

Neruda covered the major part of the country with various and sundry comrades. I accompanied him to the central part, where we returned to Parral and Chillán, the neighboring birthplaces of Pablo and Matilde. The longest trip we made was to Punta Arenas on 18 October. There, everything is different, like being dropped into a Norwegian port or into Murmansk, on the way to the Antarctic Circle. It was springtime, and there was no snow, but inside the theater the public's acclamation was accompanied by a special orchestra outside—a tremendous storm—and a pianist well known to the poet, the rain, which was coming down in bucketfuls. It was beating on the roof with an energetic resonance that drowned out the speaker's voice inside the auditorium. He gallantly paused and remained silent for a few moments, yielding the floor to the grandame of the family, the great contralto from his childhood whose watery voice was falling from the heavens.

On our return flight, he made himself comfortable next to the window, and when we ran into some turbulence and he saw me stiffen and clench my fists, he recommended, "You have to do just the opposite—relax," as if he were an old hand at flying. Then he sank into contemplation of the immense and lonely Patagonian landscape, which looked like a land where man had never set foot, cut by fjords and inlets, hidden lakes and thousands of islands, dark valleys where one could take refuge in case of a worldwide cataclysm and found a new civilization. He talked to me about all this, and I listened as if it were the grandiose wild-eyed rambling of a dreamer. I was mistaken. He was looking at that mysterious virgin land not as an excuse for an insignificant chat, but because he was working on a poetic utopia that some deeply felt concern was dictating to him. He was plotting out a book and looking down at the earth not as a geographer but rather as a dramatist who resorts to being a geographer because he needs to carefully locate his characters.

There had never been a presidential candidate in Chile as special as this one. The nation deserved a commander-in-chief who had revealed to the country its true essence and more than anyone had helped create a worldwide image of its noble people, where man's great dreams could take shape. With his poetry, Neruda had created a Nerudian Chile, though that country still belonged to the future. The candidate was ahead of his time. It was not his moment to be president, and though he well deserved it, he would never achieve it. Besides, from the outset he had known that he was participating in the first lap of a great relay race. He was willing to pass the baton to the single candidate whenever all the aspirants on the track came to unanimous agreement to support the candidacy of a unified Left. When this laborious process came to a close, Neruda happily handed over his torch to Salvador Allende, yet he didn't retire to his home like a man who has completed his task, but instead he worked zealously for the triumph of their single standard bearer.

160. A Deaf Old Man with an Accordion

Time for recalling family roots, though Neruda wants to live for many years more:

My grandfather Don José Angel Reyes lived
a hundred and two years between Parral and death.
He was a great country gentleman
with little land and too many sons.
I see him now at one hundred:
a snowy old man with an ancient blue beard
who was still riding trains to see me grow up,
coming third class from Cauquenes to the South.
Faithful old Don José Angel was coming
to have a drink with me, the final one:
his hundred-year-old hand lifted high

the wine that trembled like a butterfly.

This poem is part of a new book, titled *Aún* (Still). Why *Still?* Because it's a response to those everlasting good souls who moan about the poet's decline, calling him a washed-up writer who no longer has anything new to say. *Still* he will go on annoying them, *Still* he will go on writing, *Still* he will go on discovering. He would like to live as long as his grandfather José Angel, in order to go on doing his work.

The book's first poem is called "1971," and it begins with a return to his childhood Araucanía. He will always go on pestering. If there is a stone worn by the wind, he's a part of it, and

> If you find on some road
> a little boy
> stealing apples
> and a deaf old man
> with an accordion,
> remember that I am
> the little boy, the apples, and the aged man.

He's a man who sees old age beckoning, but he wishes to pay "honor to the new day, / to dewy youth, / and to the world's dawning."

161. *The Poet and His Century*

His verses are in no danger. He has just completed a new book, and is now engaged in other intricate maneuvers, struggling with dark shadows and with himself. The 180-page *World's End* had required a great effort, for in it he talks with the twentieth century. "Where will it end up?" In the idolized revolution? It's the century of the Bomb ("incinerated humans, fishes, insects"). A century full of wars and disappearances. But this is the century he was born to, and he has been its citizen and has seen everything that has happened. It has given him joy and suffering, including his sorrow at the death of Ché. The poet had traveled his century's path and had known its solitude, its winds, its metamorphosis. And as a man of his century, his profession was to aim for the stars. When he was a child, he learned how to look for broken bottles and collect twisted nails, for he wished to bring to life the phosphorescent glass and the frenzied metal. And his greatest pleasure of all had been the bright-tailed kites, comets wed to the sky. He calls himself a carpenter poet who searches for roses in the garden, is fascinated by living creatures and fond of dogs and horses. His twentieth century is one of rampant revolutions, including one of rampant sex.

He talks about the writers he admires: "Cortázar chants his novena / as an imposing Argentine shadow / in his exile's church." There are verses for Juan Rulfo from Anáhuac, Carlos Fuentes from Morelia, Miguel Otero from Orinoco; for Ernesto Sábato, clear and subterranean; Juan Carlos Onetti, bathed by the moon; Augusto Roa Bastos from Paraguay; and, of course, Gabriel García Márquez, a volcano exploding with dreams just as mountains explode with fire.

It's also the terribly sad century of exiles and expatriates, yet he would like to live a hundred years and go on singing of his century.

162. Interdisciplinary Madmen

Neruda loved Roberto Matta, and Matta loved Neruda. In *Nicaragua violentamente dulce* (Violently Tender Nicaragua), Julio Cortázar tells of how Matta, when he saw Cortázar approaching a group, exclaimed in a loud voice for all to hear, "Here comes the idiot." Julio couldn't hide his astonishment, and Matta irreverently repeats, "Yes, the idiot. Dostoievski's idiot, Prince Mishkin, the simple man with the most profound sense of reason." Matta insults in order to praise, or rather in order to reveal a great truth.

Neruda used to follow that same course, calling him "Matto (Madman) Matta." Roberto Sebastián Matta spoke a hybrid combination of Chilean, French, and Italian, and he considered it a high honor that Neruda would use an Italian word to call him a madman.

Although Neruda was always pleased to have Matta's illustrations, the latter would complain to him, "You don't like my painting," and then he'd begin to clown around. He used to invite us all to Doña Blanca's restaurant in Isla Negra. His lovely wife Germana would take Polaroid photos, and the occasion would turn into a banquet of shellfish, acorn barnacles from the sea eaten by nuts from the earth in an orgy of wordplay. They would devise surrealistic jokes, cosmogonies, and gibberish. And something practical would emerge from all that, for both the poet and the painter were expert in going from dreams to deeds.

The poet had always had an interdisciplinary passion. He would create verses around singers, painters, people from the theater, movies, ballet, as well as musicians, reporters, and television personalities. A good friend is Mario Carreño, and the painter Julio Escámez is a longtime guest at Isla Negra, where he talks about his dreams, which are more fantastic than anybody's. One Christmas Eve, he vividly recounts in a blurry noc- turnal voice tales of terror and hallucination, silent movie serials from his childhood, with a final scene where the walls cave in to squash the drea- mer—all of it described with such an oneiric feeling that it's hard to be- lieve that such a lifelike dream could be just one of his literary inventions. He's at Isla Negra to sketch birds for the poet's book. He studies them in the trees where they live and also in the engravings of huge volumes belonging to Neruda the ornithologist. Angel Parra puts it all to music and sings to the birds.

Mario Toral illustrates an edition of *Twenty Love Poems*, with water- colors printed in six-color offset on 180-gram glazed paper. Neruda has requested Eusebius type for the text, with ornamental letters in Vulcan, taken from J. B. Silvestre's alphabet album. The typography is by Mauricio Amster with design by Mario Toral. The poet also likes leather binding with gold lettering. He was sometimes criticized for that passion for unique editions in enormous dimensions, preferably square. He had spent a long time looking at medieval illuminated Books of Hours. There was no reason for the delicate work of those monks to die out or to be forgot- ten. It was with good reason that the poet wrote his "Ode to Typography." Although it was the law of the publishing marketplace that determined the format of most of his books, he also felt obliged to balance a deluxe edition of any given book with a concurrent inexpensive edition.

163. The City of the Caesars

One night Neruda invites his friends to "La Chascona" for an unex- pected kind of gathering, an evening of poetry with three performers: María Maluenda, Roberto Parada, and himself. With a few intermissions, they read an entire book, *La espada encendida* (The Flaming Sword).

Listening to the recital, I immediately realize why he had been so attentively contemplating Patagonia during our return flight from Maga- llanes. Neruda reworks the myth of the City of the Caesars, a mythological city of gold, silver, and precious stones, located in the south of Chile in an imprecise point of the Andean cordillera. The myth tells of the Sun City of Campanella, the chosen people's utopia, a kind of primitive commun- ism where life is exempt from the problems of usual societies. It's a bit like the return to the "noble savage" idea. Many sixteenth-century conquistadors had set out to find it, and some didn't return, while others came back claiming to have seen it. New expeditions in search of the City of the Caesars were organized in the seventeenth and eighteenth centuries, and someone even attempted it in the nineteenth century.

The poet will make a twentieth-century contribution to the legend, but with variations which show the influence of his own biography. He begins with a quote from Genesis: "And God then cast out man and put cherubims in front of the Garden of Eden and a flaming sword that turned in all directions to protect the path to the Tree of Life." This twentieth-century man called Pablo Neruda, whose age has seen the dropping of the atomic bomb and lives with the danger of more such explosions, also weaves his poetic fable around "the story of a fugitive from the great devastations that destroyed humanity." Founder of a kingdom located in the lonely Magellanic vastness, he decides to live as the world's last inhabitant, until a maiden appears who has fled the golden City of the Caesars.

The same destiny that brought the couple together now threatens them with the ancient flaming sword in this new wild and lonely Eden. Rhodo and Rosía are the heroes of this recreation of mankind. Rhodo was an old man of 130 and Rosía an ageless precious stone. The dialogue about the millenary Rhodo's last love, in the midst of volcanoes and darkness, is a kind of final desperate love poem, encompassing some enigma in the poet's life, doubtless a hidden love for a young woman who is the model for the figure of Rosía. But the poet who finds the woman from the City of the Caesars will be able to recreate the world only through poetry.

164. Stones, Wait for Me!

Neruda is working in Allende's presidential campaign, accompanying him in his concerns and sharing that whole turbid atmosphere with its noxious plots and intrigues orchestrated from afar. During the afternoons, Neruda can usually be found speaking at some rally in the capital or the province.

He writes during the mornings, moving from *The Stones of Chile* to *Sky Stones,* which in reality are all earth stones that sometimes grow wings and fly as if launched, and sometimes fall like meteorites or aerolites. Some are special stones, like one of Colombia's superb emeralds that had been cut for him only to fly off through the air like a butterfly from Muzo province. There's no doubt that, for him, the sky stones include the marine agate and the golden topaz, but also the stone where lichen grows as it tumbles down from the cordillera or is carried along by streams. But where is there more stone than in the Andean chain? Near his home is the rocky Trasmanán labyrinth, between the Tralca crag and the first houses of the southern Quisco. He pays particular attention to the diamond's watery lines and the amethyst's splendor, and also to the block of salt. Someday he expects to become a stone, "I'm coming, I'm coming, stones; wait for me."

Contrary to the man in the street's prognostications that the poet would be silenced by his political activity, he often writes several poems in one day while talking with reality and his memory, with the things of this world and the spiritual realm of his *Geografía infructuosa* (Fruitless Geography). He talks with Valparaíso's sunshine, and in sustained soliloquies the word "farewell" slips out, though he never wishes to take leave of himself. Although he no longer can visit Federico García Lorca and Miguel Hernández and Alberto Sánchez, he wonders why he can't see José Caballero, who is still in Spain painting his white rose now stained with blood.

He travels many roads in praise of his friend who is the Popular Unity candidate. One day he sees a truck loaded with trees felled in Lonquimay and feels sadness for the dying forests that were the cold foliage of his childhood. An election campaign in Chile entails much travel, and he is "always on the road." One cloudy day between Metrenco and Villarica, he arises with a heavy heart and decides to take a trip to the distant islands where some statues had been fashioned by night, long ago. He invites me to go with him to Easter Island, but I tell him I can't, so he goes off and returns with *La rosa separada* (The Amputated Rose). The Chilean and Polynesian sections of his *Fruitless Geography* come to a close, and the book is interrupted for a time while he prepares once again to change his residence on earth.

165. Midnight Speech and Morning Conversation

The midnight speech of 4 September 1970 is delivered by Salvador Allende from the balcony of the Student Federation, before a crowd that fills the Alameda from the Plaza Italia to the University of Chile. He has just been elected president, and we are radiant, though others are furious, so irate that Chile will experience sixty days of the most unusual events, characterized by a murderous abnormality which was manipulated down to the second from outside and from within the country.

That division commander who had rebelled against the civilian government on the day that we had gone to Antofagasta where Neruda defended that civilian government, later had been transferred to the capital where he repeated the rebellion on a larger scale with the Tacna regiment, against that same President Frei. Once again the workers, the Communists and, of course, Neruda went into the streets to defend the government, which they hadn't elected but which carried with it undeniable legality. The poet's ever-present obsession with Spain's experience leads him to ask me, almost as if talking to himself, "Is Viaux another Sanjurjo or another Franco?"[1]

We didn't know then that the general would soon play a leading role in even more terrible actions by directing the abduction that resulted in the death of the Army commander-in-chief, General René Schneider. At the time of that assault by the plotters, including several youths from good families in Santiago's upper-class neighborhoods, the poet told me, "There's something fishy here."

Later, one thing became depressingly clear: it was all part of a bloody orchestration in which the baton was wielded by the venerable Central Intelligence Agency in order to prevent at all cost the full congressional ratification of Salvador Allende's election as constitutional president. Eventually, the whole twisted scheme was officially exposed in the United States Senate by the Church Committee. Nonetheless, on 3 November, Salvador Allende was proclaimed president of the Republic of Chile and entered La Moneda government house with a democratic and legitimate clear title. Neruda was present, knowing that he and his colleagues had contributed to that victory, but also aware that the most difficult part lay ahead. He wanted to collaborate in whatever would be the most useful way.

The following Sunday, I go to "La Sebastiana" to see him. Matilde is chiding him in a half-joking, half-serious way, laughingly calling him a dirty old man. It all seems lighthearted, and when his publisher, Gonzalo Losada, arrives, Neruda proposes that we all go over to Viña del Mar, as we had agreed the previous day. When we get to Viña's plaza, we observe the typical Sunday-morning scene—people going to eleven o'clock mass while some old horses harnessed to carriages are waiting for tourist couples to promenade through the city. Neruda tells Matilde, "You talk with Gonzalo. I have to discuss something with Volodia." As usual, he will get straight to the point.

"I have to get away, leave the country for a while, but in the service of the government. I think I should be ambassador to France. Talk it over with our colleagues, and if they're in agreement, have them suggest it to Salvador."

And so it was done. Allende thought that Chile couldn't have any better ambassador to France than Pablo Neruda, and the nomination was immediately sent forward. Clodomiro Almeyda, the minister of foreign affairs, presented it to the Senate, where it was approved without any problem, in contrast to what had happened years earlier. Eager to depart, he left within a few days.

A man carries a bit of the night with him even during the daylight hours, especially when he has a keen ear for hearing the thunder even before he sees the lightning. As if he had a covenant with something still hidden, Neruda didn't seem happy when we saw him off at the airport, even though things had been going well up to then. There was a certain anxiety in his expression, faint worry lines. Since emotional displays always bothered him, he wouldn't be dramatic, but he was tense as he went off, leaving behind a hint of crisis. He didn't claim to be any divine seer, but no man's power would be sufficient to save the Republic. He didn't want to give advice, but what was being prepared far away could be averted only if there were widespread unity, and only if we knew who we were up against and kept our heads. He spoke figuratively on that occasion, but the metaphors he used were apocryphal. The flattering stereotype of "the American Switzerland" would be replaced by the more accurate platitude of Chile as a country of earthquakes and volcanic eruptions. This time it wouldn't be the continental plates that would shift, nor would the trembling take place in the Andes nor in the realm of poetry and language. But a political earthquake could occur which would kill more people than any shudder in the bowels of the earth. It would be provoked by one system's implacable will to dominate, which he would denounce in his *Incitación al Nixoncidio* (Incitement to Nixoncide). They would resort to any means in order to pulverize that unpublished essay whose first words were written with Salvador Allende's arrival at La Moneda, that attempt to change the fate of the oppressed with more democracy and more freedom, an attempt that was as clean as fresh well water from deep within the earth. This was what Neruda said in a subdued voice at a farewell that couldn't be joyful. His barometer was forecasting a storm on the horizon, and skies that boded no stars. He was leaving without any elation but ready to throw himself totally into his new responsibility. He was confident that his health, which had begun to show signs of decline, would improve so that he could devote all his energy to securing friends for Chile's effort to make way for the new society he dreamed of.

Postscript (For the English-language Edition)

(Several years after the death of Matilde, I am free to add the following details, knowing that this recollection can no longer grieve her. On the other hand, it may provide one more trait for the psychological portrait of Neruda. His marriage with Matilde included passion, crisis, and struggle, all of them inherent in any couple who respect each other. As for the poet's image, the facts below emphasize the incorrigible need for love that was with him throughout his life.)

That tempestuous Sunday morning scene at "La Sebastiana," which resulted in Neruda's ambassadorship, took place in my presence. The three of us were standing as Matilde admonished her husband with agitated laughter and strong words. I had barely entered when she began to reproach him as he stood there looking like a child caught with his hand in the cookie jar.

"I can tell you," she said to me, "your friend is no little saint. He's a pig. He's been with some contaminated women and now he's sick in the obvious place. And he's not getting well. Every sin brings its punishment with it."

Pablo tried to calm her down. "Don't exaggerate, Patoja. Don't talk that way . . . "

"I'm telling the truth," she went on scolding him, but never losing control. Pablo, on the other hand, was visibly disturbed. In order to get out of the touchy situation and put a halt to the harsh denunciation, the best thing he could think of was to insist on that trip over to Viña del Mar that had been agreed to the day before.

"It's getting late, let's go," he urged with a clap of his hands and a glance that made an attempt at being natural and unconcerned.

What was it that had happened? Well, one day Matilde had discovered a scene which wasn't exactly a still life, but was extremely alive, a nude episode similar to the one which contributed to the breakup of the Neruda–"Little Ant" marriage, but this time involving someone new. Now the roles were reversed, and it wasn't Matilde who was in the bed wearing nothing but bare skin, but a young woman she had brought to Isla Negra, to live there as a companion who would help her with the heavy housework and be someone to share confidential conversation.

Pablo took a liking to that second woman, who used to move quietly about the isolated seaside house. It seemed to be a fatherly affection, and he acted as a bit of a grandfather, too, for she had also brought along her daughter, a little redhead who attended the local elementary school. In the poet's opinion, the child could draw so well that he decided to use one of her childlike sketches on the rather garish cover of a voluminous anthology of his poetry which, about that time, Nascimento had got special permission to publish, despite Neruda's exclusive Spanish-language arrangement with Seix Barral and Losada.

As his friend García Márquez says, one shouldn't ever confuse faithfulness with loyalty. Neruda was always loyal to Matilde, but he wasn't always faithful. He had been governed by that distinction in all his marriages.

In the version of this affair in *The Flaming Sword*, he again repeats the name twists he had used in *The Captain's Verses*, but without going to the extreme of hiding the identity of the book's creator, because the books are quite different. In that earlier extramarital episode which reached its culmination on Capri, he gave himself away, and it was evident from a mile away that the poems were brazenly autobiographical. So, too, are the later poems, but here the author assumes a grandiose disguise, frequently repeating the Genesis theme and humbly mixing it with the Apocalypse. To throw readers off the track, he coyly doubled his own age. With each new love, he would invent a new woman, not at all esoteric, as a way of creating another poetic motif which would enable him to marvel at life and would serve as the kindling necessary for nourishing and regenerating not only the fire in his blood but also the fire in his works. Where others would see nothing special in an ordinary woman, except perhaps a moment's throbbing sex, he transformed her into an intimate and at the same time exuberant theme, proclaiming her to be the new fountainhead of humankind. Probably nowhere in his poetry, so generous in its celebration of feminine charms, does he so totally bestow on any woman the role of Eve, mother of all humanity, as he did with this seemingly simple, quiet and, in his view, undoubtedly warm woman, who was in her thirties, a little less than half the age of the poet, who was more ready than ever to play the role of Adam to the hilt.

"Rhodo, stony patriarch, saw her without seeing her, / she was / Rosía, daughter of Caesars, a worker. / Ample of breast, small of mouth and eyes," (a faithful description, by the way, of the original model) "/ she'd go out for water and was a pitcher, / she'd go out to wash clothing and was pure. / Rhodo consigned her unknowingly to silence." Again a hidden love, as he turns his own situation into metaphor where everything is a personal key—visible writing, an invisible woman, and a profound adventure described in sympathetic tones. Throughout, there is his need to flee from catastrophe and find refuge in some inaccessible place: "It was nature's glacial circle / from Aysén to southern Patagonia." Rhodo senses that his "seventy wives had turned into salt," which isn't just a random image but one that corresponds to a round number taken from his own experience. Those women disappeared from his life, one by one, but they became a part of his memory. Were they turned to statues there? Not at all, for even though several have died, they still live within his active memory, just as they were in life, whether sweet or sour. In accord with his custom of playing with secret codes, composing cryptic dictionaries and apocryphal nomenclatures, he gave them new names, even those he had earlier identified under different labels. He would rebaptize them, so that they would continue to serve as inspiration in the new-found dawn: the red Niobe, "the delicate Rama" (was she the same Rama who, clinging to the storm, used to steal fruit?); Beatriz, of the endless tresses; and Abigail, Teresara, Dafna, Leona, Cascabela, Cristina, Delgadina, Granada, Petronila, Doralisa, Dorada, Dorotea—nocturnal reminiscences of the man alone in his bed who recalls them and playfully fantasizes names for them. But now he feels the ardor of this moment's passion, which disturbs him as he writes. And then Rosía appeared, and "she opened up so that Rhodo could enter her / and the earth gave forth / a gasp or a roar . . . " This is one of Neruda's books where sensuality rages like wild fire (see the poem "The Beasts," whose violent eroticism is no less than in some pages of *The Ardent Slingsman*).

Then, more than any sense of guilt, came sanction for transgressing tribal law, and again punishment by God (who isn't exactly Jehovah but has a woman's countenance). Having surprised the king in his nakedness, they wish to transform him into a beggar, but the poet uses his voice not only to defend himself but also to intercede before the tribunal of poetry on the younger woman's behalf, recreating her and speaking in her name to impart a sensation of birth and rediscovery: "And I became woman when you touched me / and made me grow as if you had given me birth . . . " He writes these words at the approach of the "Great Winter," his own final season. Rosía will suffer the punishment, expelled from paradise to become a fugitive, and he also, as the First or perhaps the Last Father. For an instant, he is tormented by the futility of new beginnings, "Why found humanity all over again?" But his duty to save the world prevails, and the road to salvation takes him on a long voyage: "Rhodo lifts an invisible hand. / 'The ship called to me, / the voyage will be a rite of hot coals.'" So much, so many things have been reduced to ashes. (It is that voyage, which in some ways is an escape, that he discusses with me, with no ambiguity and no poetry, on that Sunday morning in Viña's plaza.)

In the book, he artfully uses subterfuge and circumspection. She will be a "shadowy maiden," and he will submerge "the key to my love . . . beneath the waves," where his passion would have to stifle the cries and moans, to be consumed only in whispers, in the underwater realm of secrecy. The Caesar's granddaughter, who had fled the enchanted city, "felt even in her bones the planet's shudder. / Like a lonely leaf / the world trembled," with the crack of thunder and the shock of lightning, which also signified the rage of the offended institution. Exile followed (the young woman was summarily thrown out of the Isla Negra "paradise"). And the poet asks, Is life "a lost garden?" And the time of the expulsion, "Was it the orange-hued / time / of incineration and punishment?" Or possibly the time of sorrow's purple: "Why must I die if I have been born just now?" is the question asked by the lover who has been caught *inflagrante*. He will set his imagination to work and search for a reply worthy of the Old Testament, transforming himself into Noah and creating the ship, his own ark. He fills it with all the living creatures, but he won't make for Mount Ararat, for he belongs to another hemisphere. His ship from the south crosses in winter, pursued by the enraged volcano and the blazing curse—the river of sulphur holds fire and lava. It's the time of his domestic catastrophe, and the poet associates it with the fate of humanity. "Paradise will burn you, / hell will pursue you. / Depart, good sir, the kingdom is in flames. / Great love is paid for / with flesh and soul, / with fire." And so he talks to me about the need to get away for a while, and the idea of the embassy in France is born.

As is customary in his poetry, but here is profoundly accentuated, the autobiographical situation is preferably hidden in an encoded system of language. But at the same time, the hounded man will reject any insignificance and discard the spicy anecdote, to recast his personal problem into sorrow at the supreme cataclysm, putting it on a par with the flood of forty days and forty nights, and with the time of nuclear catastrophe. By means of emotion, he will survive it all. His response also reveals one more element: the power of poetry and of love will return to populate the world. Thanks to the condemned couple, Humanity will be saved, and

Time will go on, and the Future will be guaranteed: "You are the start of infinity. / Just you, abandoned herb of the field, you awakened me, / and I awakened you, when the roar / of the volcano decided to warn us / that the time limit was nearly up."

It's apparent that he wasn't a pessimist nor a minor-key poet. He took the ship, an airborne one, journeying to Paris with the volcano at his side, now quite pacified, for Matilde believed in the medicinal herb called "out of sight, out of mind." But without admitting it to anyone, Rosía was still in his heart. As he journeyed at 30,000 feet above the ocean, he was already thinking about how to send secret messages to her. And an occasional gift. He could no longer explore her "with his lips and his soul," but from France he would send back, with traveling friends, some mysterious suitcases full of presents from Rhodo, to show Rosía, expelled from Paradise, that in Paris he felt alone, "more alone than the snow."

In addition, he was feeling ill. Matilde's clinical eye had been mistaken that Sunday morning when she accused him in my presence of having been with some contaminated woman. Her blind anger led her to a false diagnosis. No, it had nothing to do with the symptoms of some venereal disease. Those were the first signs of a still undetected prostate cancer.

But he was also tormented by another kind of anguish, that of his political concerns.

VIII.

The Song of the Ancient Mariner

166. Upsetting News

He arrives in France as Chile's ambassador in the middle of winter, November 1970. He is wearing formal garb as the embassy car enters the government palace's gravel-covered patio along Faubourg Saint-Honoré. (The gravel reminds him of his father's ballast train.) With a serious expression, he emerges to present his credentials to President Georges Pompidou. There are the obligatory photographs, one of which he sends to me. Politically, he and Pompidou are far apart, but the latter has published an anthology of French poetry, and Neruda observes him carefully in an attempt to discover his poetic side, apparently in vain. He is once more back in the big old house full of ghosts and tales of suicide, which serves as Chile's embassy in Paris. The heavy, gloomy building on La Motte-Picquet, near Les Invalides, doesn't go well with his own architectural preferences nor with his need for light, and he immediately feels like a prisoner in a dark cell.

He has to attend important but unintelligible meetings which revive his childhood horror at mathematics. In a meeting of bankers and economists called the Paris Club, creditors to whom Chile owes dizzying sums are gathered together. Neruda, as ambassador, heads the Chilean delegation which is attempting to renegotiate the external debt run up by previous governments. No way to avoid mathematics!

Not everything is numbers, but nonetheless he has days when he can't write. His health is getting worse, and he finally prescribes a poetic treatment to change the air, taking up again the unfinished *Fruitless Geography*. At the end he publishes an explanatory note:

The year of 1971 was very disruptive for me. For that reason, and not to seem unduly enigmatic, I call attention to transfers, illnesses, joys and sorrows, different climates and regions, all of which alternate in this book. Some of it was written between Isla Negra and Valparaíso and on other Chilean roads, almost always in a car, taking in the changing landscape. Many other poems were written, again in a car, during autumn and winter along the roads of Normandy in France.[87]

Some months later, disturbing news comes about his health, when I receive a letter from Paris, dated 11 July 1971, in which he tells me about some illnesses:

> After having fed me and lifted me out of bed, for the first time in four days, to go to the bathroom (ten minutes to walk thirty feet), Matilde—brimming with good health—also permits me to finish dictating this letter. I've been down with some vague illness for several days and taking penicillin, which may get me back to the office, the next floor up, one of the most enchanting places in this city full of enchantment. I have a fever, which doesn't matter, except that tomorrow is my birthday, which also doesn't matter . . .

He goes on to tell me about difficulties with the trade section and the abysmal secretarial salaries. He draws a sad, self-mocking picture of his existence at that time:

> Here everything is the same in these catacombs; I don't see museums or friends; from time to time we go to the movies, with great exertion, as if we were going from Isla Negra to Valparaíso. I don't even say anything to you about my poetry, because I haven't got back to it . . . If I go on dictating to Matilde, I'll give her my fever. Love to you three from the two of us. By the way, I've never seen so many Chilean travelers in Europe; we courteously assist them, but the extraordinary increase in tourism can't help but worry us. On the other hand, I have asked that Graham Greene be invited to Chile, and after a thousand reminders they still don't answer. He will go in any case, and it's even possible that he might turn down reimbursement for the ticket, but I wanted us to have the satisfaction of spending a small amount on such a great man. If you can help, there's still time, because he wants to be there during the last two weeks of September. Now I'm going to take my temperature. So long.

I receive a joking message from him dated three days later, on 14 July, which eases our apprehension: "Dressed in tails, coming back from the Elysée, hugs for you both + the mariner" [my daughter Marina]. "Pablo, Matilde, Laura Reyes, Enrique Bello."

Then new fears, as he sends me a letter on 30 September along with some photographs taken on the 18 September national Chilean holiday, "which for the first time in this embassy had a popular flavor. Almost a thousand Chileans came with guests. This wasn't an official celebration, since the government forbade that, due to the earthquake, so there was no diplomatic reception, just a party for the Chileans, organized in great part and with lots of enthusiasm by the younger members of the community." The worrisome part follows:

> I'm writing you from the hospital, where I'm still undergoing tests that leave me weak and depressed—I need a nice letter from you to cheer me up.
>
> In mid-October, Dr. Raúl Bulnes is returning to Chile. I have asked him to explain to our friends about my present ailments and the medical and surgical prognosis. He will call you or leave a message for you when he gets there.
>
> I hug you both and also Marina, to whom I send a completely sterilized hospital kiss. To your health. Pablo Neruda.

When Dr. Bulnes returned, I talked at length with him. He had been present as one of the doctors when the poet had surgery at Paris's Cochin Hospital. This Raúl, who had also been present with Eladio Sobrino and Pablo Neruda when the Isla Negra house was built, is an immensely discreet person. He tells me just about everything, but he never tells me the exact nature of Pablo's illness. Perhaps he's a believer in the refrain, "A word to the wise is sufficient," but since I'm not wise, I go on harboring some hope.

I convey the gist of our conversation, and it's decided that I should go see Pablo, but before I leave we have to find out whether he is going to come to Chile, which is what everyone is hoping for, since he has just been given the Nobel Prize.

167. *The Swedish Decision*

The announcement by the Swedish Academy, meeting in Stockholm's Old Stock Exchange, began with a few light remarks by secretary

Karl Ragnar Hierow, who recalled that a few nights earlier, in a televised discussion, Premier Olof Palme had told him that it would be best to give all the prizes to ambassadors so there wouldn't be any problem about the laureates being present to accept. The remark was unexpected, but the fact is that in the recent past the academy has awarded the Nobel Prize to four diplomats: St. John Perse in 1960, Ivo Andrić from Yugoslavia in 1962, George Seferis from Greece in 1964, and Miguel Angel Asturias from Guatemala in 1967.

In response to the reporters' confused expressions, the secretary of the Swedish Academy smiled and said that they had decided to follow Olof Palme's suggestion, adding that "Ambassador Neftalí Ricardo Reyes Basoalto has been named winner." After a pause he went on, "Better known under the pseudonym of Pablo Neruda."

The text of the official announcement begins in a somewhat immoderate fashion: "This year's Nobel Prize for Literature has been awarded to a contentious author who is not only debated but for many is also debatable. This debate has been going on for the past forty years, which demonstrates that his contribution is unquestionable." The text also emphasizes judgments that are both sweet and sour. Next to García Lorca's celebrated words of a long-ago introduction, "More akin to death than to philosophy," are their opposite, expressed by another Spanish-language poet and also a Nobel laureate, who had said that Neruda was a "great bad poet."

The Swedish Academy documents the fact that Neruda's poetry is overwhelming in its quantity, adding that it is legitimate to wonder whether there is anything like it in the history of poetry. Statistics indicate that in 1962 he had already written 2,000 pages of poetry, and two years later he publishes five new volumes of poems under the title of *Notes from Isla Negra*. The academician uses very freewheeling expressions to refer to the immensity of Neruda's production.

> For us to try to present one poem or one collection out of this infinite world would be ridiculous, like trying to compress a shipment of 50,000 tons into a teaspoon. We cannot synthesize Pablo Neruda's work; he himself has not been able to do so.
>
> It would be simply inconceivable for all this gigantic literary production to be of one and the same quality. Whoever wishes to find the weak side of Neruda's poetry doesn't have to search far. Whoever wishes to find the strong side doesn't have to search at all. From his first literary triumph and even in his latest work, we might say that his strength can be

found in an inexhaustible richness. Certainly what is most outstanding is that evidently his inspiration has increased with the years. It is like one of those rivers on Neruda's continent, a current whose shores can't be seen, growing wider and more powerful as it approaches its outlet.

The statement points out that this long march has been carried out under the sign of a continual stylistic transformation, with an incessant renewal of motifs, metamorphosis of ideas, and shift in emotions.

This academy document occasionally resembles a European professor's criticism of a marginal pupil's lack of precision, whose abrupt piling on of metaphors reminds him of a hasty student who has learned about Europe's surrealist poetry from manuals and manifestos. Then the document opines that perhaps such an impression is due to the fact that the poet's imagination reacts differently than a European's would, "in immediate and mysterious relationship to the creation of language itself and of figurative expression."

The analysis by the Swedish Academy can't ignore the poet who also formulates a dazzling dream of the future while remaining a revolutionary of the present. To back up the assertion, it quotes Neruda: "And then I stopped being a child, because I realized that my people weren't allowed any kind of life, and they were denied even the grave." One can't fail to point out this moment in his life and his description of his country as "raped and oppressed since the days of the conquistadors." Though he himself was expelled and pursued time and time again, he never gave up. The community of the oppressed is found everywhere, and he has increasingly searched it out, "becoming the poet of violated humanity."

The discourse, which was later broadcast on the radio, demonstrates an expert hand in Neruda studies, belonging to the poet's sword-wielding academy angel, a famous Swedish writer who as a contemporary of Neruda had also been influenced by the same aesthetic revolution, and in addition was a specialist in Latin American literature. For twenty years, Artur Lundkvist had campaigned for Neruda in the Nobel competition. I met him in May 1964 when he was in Chile, during the last rainy days of autumn. In his book, *Elegy for Pablo Neruda,* he recalls how he had to step from stone to stone to reach the Isla Negra house. Later I visited him in Santiago's Crillón Hotel. He had made an earlier trip to Chile in 1957, when he saw all of Neruda's various collections, but it seemed to him that the objects collected by the poet symbolized the experiences and people and human destinies that he gathered to himself from throughout the world.

It was this man's long years of work in the eighteen-member conservative academy that culminated in the prize for a friend he considered the best poet of all.

168. Flashbulb Time

The telephone was ringing in the Motte-Picquet house. It was the Swedish ambassador asking for an appointment for nine in the morning. A horde of reporters entered the reception room, on the prowl for statements and reactions from Neruda, who was nowhere in evidence. They waited two hours, insisting on a statement. The invariable reply was, "The ambassador is awaiting official confirmation before talking with you." When he finally appeared, he was accompanied by Matilde and the French poet Louis Aragon. The room sparkled with exploding flashbulbs as a crossfire of questions filled the air, and reporters jockeyed for position. The poet managed to find his way to an armchair and slowly settled down in it. His wife was at his side, dressed in a blue tailored suit. The wave of queries swelled about them while Aragon, dressed in black with a red necktie, chatted with the Chilean poet in the midst of the bombardment. The artillery ceased for a moment when an official loudly announced, "President Allende is on the phone asking for you."

The majority of other writers who were interviewed said that he deserved the prize, though a few almost had a coronary. Aragon stated that Neruda was one of his most admired poets and the one he prefers among all those living today. In Vallauris, Pablo Picasso pointed out the coincidence between his ninetieth birthday and the awarding of the Nobel for literature to his friend and namesake.

A quick survey was taken in Spain, where Vicente Aleixandre, who would also receive the Nobel a few years later as the most important surviving poet, along with Rafael Alberti, from the Generation of 1927–1928, issued the generous-hearted statement that, "As a writer in the Spanish language, I take great pleasure in the awarding of the extremely deserved Nobel to Pablo Neruda, and as an old friend of this extraordinary poet, I join in the general satisfaction that will prevail in the realm of Hispanic literatures."

A dear friend, the novelist Anna Seghers, sent Neruda a very personal message from the German Democratic Republic. She tries to express "what you represent," remembering how they once sat around a table with Jorge Amado, Louis Aragon, and Ilya Ehrenburg, talking about one of literature's most enigmatic figures—Bruno Traven. Only two of them knew his true identity, and they kept the secret forever. They had said then that the presence of writers in the peace movement morally requires that every proclamation should be "a small work of art." Anna Seghers also recalls the wartime atmosphere in Spain when she first met Neruda, when the Chilean consulate had remained open during the bombing of Madrid. She remembers how Neruda and his poetry helped many people get their bearings at that time, "for it's a great thing to draw someone out of his loneliness, a loneliness that can be like confinement in a cell . . ."

He had struggled since childhood in order not to be alone, and now he senses that he has many companions.

169. Jubilation at Home

On Thursday, 21 October, I'm on my way to the Senate when I hear the news on the car radio: "Stockholm. Chilean poet Pablo Neruda today was awarded the Nobel Prize for Literature." Afterwards we learned that the winner confided to reporters that "Poets believe in miracles, and this time the miracle came to pass." The report explained that the Swedish Academy had awarded the prize for "poetry which like a force of nature gives new life to the destiny and dreams of an entire continent." The announcement was extensive and didn't withhold the amount of the prize, 450,000 Swedish crowns, equivalent to 88,000 dollars. It added that the winner, currently his country's ambassador to France, was the second Chilean to be awarded the prize, following the poet Gabriela Mistral in 1945. Another Latin American writer, it went on, the Guatemalan Miguel Angel Asturias, had received similar recognition a few years previously. The story indicated that the prize would be given to the laureate in person by King Gustaf Adolph VI on 10 December in a ceremony in Stockholm's Philadelphia Church, since the traditional location, the Music Palace, was closed for renovations.

I change direction and head for Party headquarters. Reactions are coming in from far and wide. The entire country is electrified. Allende delivers a network statement about the event, saying that "This prize, which bestows immortality on our countryman, is a triumph for Chile and its people, and also for Latin America."

The Communist Party's Central Committee holds a special meeting and sends congratulations to Neruda: "All the militants of the Party of Recabarren and Laferte, who have been praised by the poet along with his national heroes Lautaro, Caupolicán, Bernardo O'Higgins, Carrera, Manuel Rodríguez, and Balmaceda, take pride in this decision by the Swedish Academy."

There are celebrations in the shantytowns. In one of them, called "Pablo Neruda," whose unpaved streets are named after the poet's books, all the houses display the Chilean flag.

At four in the afternoon, television carried a telephone conversation between reporter Augusto Olivares and Neruda, in which the latter says, "I've been happy all day, but then when I found out that Isla Negra is full of flags, I was overcome with such joy that I'm beside myself."

Luis Corvalán published an article in *El Siglo* titled "Pablo's Example," where he says, "We all know that he has sung in praise of everything—love, birds, stones, southern rains, the rough Pacific Ocean, the Araucan pine, cactus, spoons, onions, salmon-bellied eels, everything he ever saw and touched with his poet's eyes and feelings. And also human beings, our national heroes and our Araucanian forefathers, the miner, the railroader, the baker, workers of all kinds, the great epics of our time. He has written moving verses for his Party, poetry of love for his people, and poetry of fire against the enemy."[88]

170. Red Corpuscles

On 6 November 1971, I receive a letter from Matilde in which she tells me that she's a bit terrified by the projected month-long visit to Chile. Pablo would probably have to spend several days in a hotel in Santiago, but now with the Nobel it would be impossible, for he would be accessible to the whole world. "I believe," she explains, "that we have to protect him a little. Pablo is still very weak, and his recovery is slow. With this Nobel earthquake, he has a lot of work. He wants very much to go to Chile, but I wonder whether it's wise."

Finally Neruda is convinced that he shouldn't travel for the time being, as he tells me in a letter on 20 December: "Dear faraway Vol, It's useless to write you, you're worse than I am in answering. I received Lucho's telegram in Stockholm [Luis Corvalán]. I'm happy to avoid that journey, after the exhausting events with the 'Price' [*sic*]. But I want to know more about the situation. Maybe you could send me some information with somebody or other among the many who come over here; the Bernsteins, for example, are notorious globetrotters."

After the Nobel, a flood of unauthorized editions of his work was unleashed. "And this," he tells me, "interferes with Losada's affairs, after he has been so fine and generous with me. He's getting requests for rights from everywhere . . . In short, I've been very upset at the increase in pirated editions of my books. You probably have a lot to say, and a lot for me to listen to, about your journeys and tours. I wish you could come over here to relax. What should I do with what I'm keeping for the family? Should I send it or hold on to it? I'm annoyed with you because of your silence. There must be some explanation. Meanwhile, we send hugs to Eliana and Marina. And for you my love and wish to see you. P."

He's miserable in "the old mausoleum," as he calls the embassy building on La Motte-Picquet. The first thing he intends to do with the prize money is buy himself a house in the country, get out of the city and go back to nature. He has made a thorough search and has finally found the place, a house in Normandy, which he'll buy "with the Prize, even though it will take almost all of it, because everything is expensive in this sweet France. In any case, I'll bring back something for our mutual clan. The house is an hour-and-a-half from Paris, with streams and woods. Tomorrow we'll sleep there for the first time, and we haven't yet paid a cent (the Prize makes anything possible). The house is lovely, just a dream, but it doesn't have a name yet. I hope you can come some day, with your offspring, and take a break from forums and elections." Then he comes back to the idea of traveling to Chile.

> I'd like to spend January in Chile with Patoja and a minimum of public appearances. How can I manage it? Maybe just one large public meeting. But you can decide for yourselves. Between you and me, I've been very weak and I need some transfusions. Red corpuscles, only three million. And my heart is beginning to slow down, so I've had to see a cardiologist and take some medications. They tell me to rest, but how? When?
>
> I was very pleased to receive the Prize, for myself, of course, but also for our beloved Party. Picquet told me it was the first time that it had been given to a Central Committee member from any country. I'm happy to make so many petty people swallow their anticommunism with this beautiful red pill! (A telegram and congratulations from the North American embassy in Paris(!) among other things), so it was all worth while, though an effort.

He insists that his poetry should be made available to all in a large-run inexpensive edition.

Losada suggests a small anthology (without any profit for him nor royalties for me) geared to students or labor unions, in other words, for free distribution. If it's okay with our comrades, it could be coordinated with my arrival, with a broad distribution of a million or so copies, but donated by the Party to the Ministry of Education, for example. Loyola for the anthologist? In any case, if anything is done, it should be for free, a stipulation that takes precedence over all the commercial requests that are driving Losada to distraction.

I can't think of anything else to say, except to send my embrace to all the comrades on the Central Committee, to Lucho, Lili [Corvalán], and for Eliana and Marina and you, this (worn out?) heart of your old brother.—Pablo. I don't ever remember writing such a long letter!

171. Revelation

After several delays, due to the difficult political situation, I'm finally able to make the trip. I find Pablo carrying out his normal responsibilities, though his face looks puffy, doubtless from the cortisone. We don't talk about illnesses. He is still feeling the euphoria of the Nobel, and he tells me that four days before the announcement, Artur Lundkvist had stayed overnight in the Chilean embassy during a trip he was making from Stockholm to the Balearic Islands. The two old friends had talked at length about everything except the prize, although Neruda thought he could detect a few cryptic hints in the other's words. He had just left the debates in the Swedish Academy where they had decided to award the prize to Neruda, but he really played dumb.[m] And Neruda was left with the feeling that he wouldn't win it that year either.

I'm staying in the embassy's Moorish bedroom. Across the corridor, the novelist José Donoso and his wife are guests for a few days. Lunchtime visitors usually include Miguel Angel Asturias and his wife, Blanca de Mora y Araujo. For the moment, everything seems fine. One night, Pablo and Matilde and I go to the movies, and at noon the next day we go to visit art galleries. Neruda wants to organize an exposition of esteemed artists who are affiliated with the Chilean government. In the evening we stroll a bit along the Seine. He walks slowly, but he wants to look around in some secondhand book stores. His conversation revolves around what is happening in our country. That night, some friends come to the embassy, including Louis Aragon, Jean Marcenac, Jacques Duclos, and other important officials of the French Communist Party. Neruda explains to them that in Chile there's a kind of silent Vietnam at work, and he asks for support.

The next afternoon, I get another kind of invitation as Matilde whispers in my ear that she wants me to go to a café with her to talk. We go to a place several blocks from the embassy, and when she is seated she blurts it all out: "Pablo has cancer. He has had surgery, but it's come back. The doctors say he can live for several years, provided nothing serious happens. I can't talk to anybody about it, but you should be aware of it so that whoever needs to know can be told. Pablo doesn't know, and I have to play the role of the happy wife all day long."

"And he doesn't suspect anything?"

"I don't know. He hasn't said anything to me, and I can't ask him."

172. *A Castle in the Air*

A black bell tower in a church tiny enough "for a dove to pray." On the trip from Paris to his Normandy house, Neruda stops the car along the road to show me the Authenay bell tower, which gives him both delight and a bit of chagrin that it wasn't he who had built that tower with its rooster weather-vane.

We proceed toward Condé-sur-Iton, with Matilde at the wheel. At her side, Neruda is writing, "I'm living in a country as silky / as the skin of grapes in the fall . . ." Knowing the poet isn't well, from the back seat I can detect more and more signs of the truth. The car's back window is covered with frost.

We get out of the car to go see the Duke of Rohan's castle, which the Chilean right wing and an international press network have falsely claimed is Neruda's property. There's still a midday haze as we walk across the damp earth, surrounded by a picture-book landscape. Slow-tolling bells are heard in the distance, and suddenly through the bare trees the castle with its high tower appears before our eyes. We cross the moat and see some workers who are restoring the castle, at the expense of its true owner, a North American multimillionaire who would like to be the Duchess of Rohan.

"Now you can report to the Senate that you've seen the castle with your own eyes, and that I have not been greeted with trumpets as the new castle owner. The castle prefers multimillionaires with dollars."

The house which is really his is located nearby. It's a former out-building of the castle, and had first been a combination storehouse and workshop where the Duke's serfs made slate tiles. Later it had served as stables. "But what can I do," Neruda exclaimed, "if some Chileans still think it's extravagant for me to have what was once used for a count's horses." Senator Bulnes used to speak very tastelessly about Neruda's "château," and when Pablo heard about it he said, "I tried to buy the Versailles Palace, but they refused to sell it to me." But they're upset by those stables?

"Alone" also put his oar into that question of the "château." Three days after the Nobel announcement, he had published an article in *El Mercurio* where he claimed that for the poet there's one thing better than beauty, and that's change. Four months later, "Alone" published another column, which demonstrates that he, too, practices the unavoidable principle of change, for now he signs himself not with the pseudonym by which everybody knows him, but with the two initials H. D., which only the initiated recognize as those of Hernán Díaz, his real name. He runs through all the speculations about how the prize money will be spent, wondering, for example, whether it will go into the Party's coffers in order to increase their anticapitalism propaganda. Apparently not, he says, for "The news that Pablo Neruda had bought a castle in France was a real bombshell." The information (disinformation, rather) was distributed throughout the world, and H. D. explains why. "The fact is that this is not just any castle, but that belonging to the Dukes of Rohan, one of the upper aristocracy's most novelistic families. A principal member of that historical family had been a prince and a cardinal to boot, who had tried to win the favor of Marie Antoinette by giving her a diamond necklace, as Alexandre Dumas tells it." Those holdings carried with them the noble title, therefore Neruda would become Duke of Rohan, if not a prince or cardinal. Nor could he pay court to Marie Antoinette, according to the article. But one small detail was overlooked—the French Revolution had not only guillotined the queen but had also abolished feudal property rights.

And so in plebeian Chile's frontier land, Pablo Neruda's castle in the air danced in the minds of his enemies, no less than in his beloved Dumas novels, *The Queen's Necklace* and *Viscount Bragelonne*. Poets obviously have a secret pact with fables.

The castle soon toppled and returned to being distinguished old stables, as the malicious enchantment fabricated in the Senate came to an end. The whole cheap fiction had originated when a bill was proposed to authorize purchase of the simple run-down family home in Parral where the poet had been born, in order to convert it into a museum.

H. D. lamented the unhappy ending devoid of prodigious castles. Stables make for ugly prose, but he could be sure that the Neruda castle would go on floating in the air as a legend, in spite of all the gray empirical evidence to the contrary.

And that's just what happened, but as slander rather than legend. When I returned from Europe, in every South American city where the plane made a stop, I read in the newspapers the same story, fabricated by the same press agency, about the Red poet who had bought himself the Duke of Rohan's castle in France.

In the Senate, I set about offering my eyewitness explanation of the castle, or rather the stables. An architect had redesigned them as a country house, and that's how the medieval tile factory was converted into a hangar without a plane, so to speak. In one corner, Neruda installed a carved bookcase and a desk, and a bit beyond it a cozy little dining table. The ground level was spacious enough to walk about inside the house. Then an imaginatively curved stairway led up to the second floor, where there was the master bedroom and a small guest room. The property was nestled in the bend of the Iton river, and from the window I could see robust Normandy women beating their laundry in its waters, in a scene straight out of a seventeenth-century painting. In the afternoon we went out with Pablo to take a walk in the nearby forest, which was wrapped in a fog that gave it a ghostly aspect. It was a literary landscape, worthy of cloak-and-dagger encounters and quite reminiscent of such adventures in some Alexandre Dumas novels. But we were not musketeers, and Neruda's steps seemed uncertain, but in spite of it all, he was content to be able to walk about and breathe the pure cold air, in whose curative power he had faith.

When we returned, we discovered a very tall couple who had just emerged from a little Citröen and were ringing the doorbell. It was the Argentine novelist Julio Cortázar and Ugné Karvellis, who joined us for a lively evening of affectionate and pleasant conversation. They hadn't come to talk about anything controversial, but just to visit a sick friend whose illness mustn't be mentioned. Later, when I went out into the dark night to point them in the direction of the village, Cortázar quietly asked me, "How is his health?"

A little later, I learned that Neruda had secretly traveled to Moscow for a medical examination. The diagnosis was the same; there wasn't any other treatment than the one already prescribed. He was accompanied on the trip by Ella Braguinskaia as interpreter, and he had some nostalgic reunions with friends, some of whom have since departed this earth. He writes a book for them, with the provisional title *Elegía de Moscú* (Elegy in Moscow). Premonitions.

173. *Futurism's Sister*

During our stay in Paris, Neruda and I had agreed to meet in Milan in March 1972. We had both been invited to attend the thirteenth congress of the Italian Communist Party. I arrive from London at Linate airport a little bit ahead of him. In my pocket I have his telegram informing me of his arrival with Matilde three hours later, so there's time to go to the Chilean consulate to pick up an official to greet the Ambassador to France. When the official informs the airport police that he's waiting for Pablo Neruda, he spontaneously exclaims, "The D'Annunzio of our time!" When Neruda hears about the official's appraisal, he doesn't get upset, though he knows how different he is from the great egomaniac from Pescara who was of some influence on him in his youth.

Having settled into a hotel that faces the Duomo, Neruda studies the magnificent cathedral, admiring its rock gardens. We walk slowly (by this time he has difficulty in moving about) and find a table in a nearby café, in the center of the Galleria. Next door, in the academy's bookstore windows, there are large photographs of the poet, advertising simultaneous Italian publications of his work: *Neruda, Le Grandi Opere, Tre Residenze sulla Terra, Canto General,* and *Fine del Mondo.*

At seven in the evening, the academy hall is full of Milan fans of Neruda, including "groupies" of several generations, who ask for his autograph as if he were king of the Beatles.

Afterward there's a reception in his honor at a restaurant where he sees his friend Guttuso, the painter, and a woman he doesn't know but listens to in fascination. She talks to Neruda about her father, the caffeine-poet who tried to wake up Europe with calls to do away with literary romanticism, proclaiming the reign of velocity, and praising war as the world's cleanser. Poor Papa! sighs that doe-eyed Italian, "He died a victim of the war and of his own words." She is Futurism's sister, daughter of the extravagant poet Marinetti.

174. *The Albatross Country*

A monster presents itself, threatening him with a modern garrote—the "standby," that radio term used to describe North America's hovering "protectiveness" toward Latin America. In April 1972 he's invited to give a speech about Walt Whitman at the New York PEN Club's fiftieth-anniversary meeting. His surprising contribution calls the meeting "the most mysterious assembly of all those I have ever had to witness and participate in." He was in the debtors' dock, surrounded by the world's great creditors, who were owed a great quantity of money by his country. Tightening around his throat he can feel the sharp-clawed hand of the International Monetary Fund.

He explains to the North American writers, "In this gathering, it's important to know what we owe each other. We writers, from every land, have to perpetually renegotiate our internal debt. We all owe something to our own intellectual tradition and to what we have spent out of the entire world's treasury."

Making good on his payment, he points out that he is almost seventy years old, but when he was barely fifteen he had discovered his greatest creditor, Walt Whitman. He also emphasized that Chile was in the midst of a revolutionary transformation and that many people felt insulted by that.

In his meeting with the creditors, he quoted the "Rime of the Ancient Mariner," written by Samuel Taylor Coleridge with reference to an episode in Shelvocke's memoirs of a voyage to the extreme south of Chile. Neruda's country is shaped like a slender albatross, and the creditors of an external debt that is so usurious and astronomical that Latin America can't repay it should remember that, in the "Rime of the Ancient Mariner," the story of the slain albatross ends with the navigator's perpetual condemnation to carry around his neck the dead corpse of the bird of storms.

His illness again rears its head. On 27 June 1972 he writes me that "I'm in the dungeon. Tomorrow they'll cauterize me. I send hugs to all. Pablo." Then he adds a grieved note, "We're saddened by the death of Chico," referring to our mutual friend Antonio Quintana, the photographer for Neruda's *The Stones of Chile*.

175. Projects and Relapses

After a few months, another traveler goes off to see him. This time it's Sergio Insunza, Salvador Allende's minister of justice. We've heard about a relapse. On 5 August 1972, the poet writes me from "La Manquel," his controversial Normandy house with the Araucanian name. "Sergio will tell you about my convalescence in 'La Manquel.' It has been so pleasant to have him here, and also very helpful. He'll tell you later about my thoughts and decisions. I'm sending you my latest book, which is quite melancholy, as a result of sicknesses and exiles. I'd like for a page to come out with some of these verses that nobody knows." He's referring to *Fruitless Geography,* where the sick man asks the winter cold to give him back his cup of energy, calling himself the survivor who talks to the birds. In the letter he again talks of the difficulties and hesitations about returning to Chile. "Sergio will tell you how impossible it is to plan our trip for any earlier than November, what with my uncertain health, which must be stabilized in order to hold up for the arrival and then the campaign tour. For now, the rest here in 'La Manquel' has done me a lot of good, but several times I've felt well only to have a setback." He has one consolation: "Homero [Arce], like a carrier pigeon, has landed in 'La Manquel.' We're working on the Memoirs every day. It's just a matter of finishing the text of the *Voyage* in order for it to be a substantial book. Homero and I are having quite a good time, and we enjoy each other immensely."

A few weeks later, Neruda and Matilde fix their return date. As usual, he sends me a letter explaining it all in detail. A Spanish poet once recalled that he had shown some verses to both García Lorca and Neruda around the same time. The former had given him a structural appraisal of form and content. Neruda, on the other hand, paid attention to specific words, especially adjectives, suggesting the elimination of those that seemed to him not sufficiently expressive, in accord with Rubén Darío's belief that when an adjective doesn't add life, it kills. Neruda's letters were always like that—concrete and extremely detailed. I think he did well on this occasion. He didn't trust our lack of organization, so he wrote like Sensible Sam:

> TRIP. Matilde and I have decided on the date for our trip, and you're the first person to know it. We'll leave on 31 October on the Italian steamship the *Eugenio C.* This ship arrives on 12 November in Buenos Aires, where we could stay two or three days. The date of our arrival in Chile can be decided by you folks and communicated to me at Margarita's address [Aguirre]. I think the arrival and what I'm supposed to do should be considered and communicated to me in plenty of time so we can prepare for it. As you and I already discussed, we've fixed these dates in order to help in the electoral campaign. My role should be given careful thought, so that it will be effective and not tire me too much. I'd like to take advantage of the campaign tour to the South in order to spend about ten days in some rus-

tic spot where I could get back in touch with the earth. You folks should also take care of my return, but I think it should be before the election.

I have turned down all the international invitations. The truth is that I'm not strong enough for exhibits and commotion. Nonetheless, I think the campaign can be helped by my tour, and I'm very worried about the outcome of the election. I hope you'll write me about this matter, which I don't have a very clear picture of.

Matilde and I send you a hug, also to Eliana and Marina. This hug is also for Lucho and family, including the comrades in the office. So long. P.

He adds even more concrete details about the passage, and then something more important: he wants to get together with Salvador Allende, without fail. He needs to talk with him in person, thus it is with certain alarm that he writes me on 15 August 1972 about the worrisome possibility of their missing each other:

Here it has come out in a newspaper that Salvador Allende will travel abroad toward the end of October. As you know, we'll be returning to Chile about that time, arriving in Buenos Aires approximately 12 November. On the one hand, it seems to me I should arrive in Chile when the president is not away on a trip, and on the other hand, I'd like to know if he'll be coming through Paris, in which case I should host him in the embassy.

I want you to do me the favor of finding out about it and sending me an answer, if possible by telegram through the ministry of foreign affairs, or else by the very earliest air mail.

He is continuing with the dictation of his Memoirs.

Another letter comes, dated 7 September 1972, with a copy of a message he is sending to Allende, whom he addresses as "My beloved President Salvador." In it he suggests that the government publish an inexpensive edition of a million copies of an anthology of his poetry, indicating that both Losada (owner of the copyright) and the poet will forego all profit and royalties, provided the edition in its entire run be given to schools, labor unions, and (such irony!) the armed forces. He asks the president to write a prologue, and if that isn't possible, the book should include the message that Allende had sent him on the occasion of the Nobel Prize. In his letter to me, he refers to the same question, but in addition he suggests another inexpensive anthology to be sold for a "kiosk price." He states that he has turned down invitations from Germany, Belgium, Yugoslavia, and other countries, and will go only to Oxford, where his friend, Professor Pring-Mill, a Neruda enthusiast and meticulous scholar, has prepared some new surprises for him. Then he encloses a third letter, directed to the president's advisor Antonio Benedicto, which reveals an almost Anglo-Saxon precision in the poet's passion for detail. He reiterates precise directions which should be followed in putting the anthology together. He asks that his recommendations be followed to the letter, especially in regard to punctuation. "I am insisting on this because I know from experience how stubborn proofreaders can be. The covers shouldn't have any photographs or drawings. The only thing I want is clear and elegant typography."

But now there's another fly in the ointment. On 18 October 1972, I receive a letter indicating a change of date:

Along with the apprehension we're feeling about the Chilean situation and the copper boycott, I also have to give you another piece of bad news. I've had a strong recurrence of the same illness, and am again subjected to many days of probing and injections and antibiotics. According to the doctor, they have to do another so-called "cleaning out," which in reality is an operation with total anesthesia.

In addition, the doctor thinks a sea voyage is dangerous, in case a difficult situation should arise, and he advises me to fly.

Nor can I go into hospital immediately, because I have to drag myself to some meetings about the copper mess and to the UNESCO conference where I'm to speak on Thursday 19 October.

On the 26th of this month, I'll be received by Pompidou to present our position in the copper boycott.

Tomorrow afternoon I have to drag myself off to the courts, because the allegations are to begin.

Therefore, I have picked the 27th, after the Pompidou interview, as the day to check into the hospital and go to the operating room.

This morning I sent you a telegram requesting that the meeting in the stadium be postponed until 2 December. This will give me time for some postoperative recovery, then I can take a plane and have a two-day rest in Buenos Aires.

Assuming that all of this will come about, I beg you also to keep in mind that I want to go directly from Pudahuel airport to Isla Negra, in order to prepare my speech with the help of Homero, who will be traveling with me. Naturally, it's important that nothing be known about my illness. A very strict silence should be maintained for now.

Don't say anything, but I deceived you when I said that I wouldn't resign. The press here told me that in Chile they assumed I would resign, without telling me the original source. This story, at this time, was diminishing my authority in complex day-to-day negotiations, even within the embassy. I don't want to prolong this letter, which is only intended to tell you what's going on. They say the hospitalization period will last a week. An embrace. Pablo.

176. Araucanian Stone

He hobbles out of the airplane, and reporters rush to ask him what's wrong. "It's the gout, the malady of English noblemen," he answers, trying to joke. Many people are there to greet him, even though his arrival hasn't been publicized. But he is the sacred monster who is returning after receiving worldwide recognition. The poet is not in a festive mood, and a car is waiting to take him directly to Isla Negra, without going through Santiago, which is an appalling city in these circumstances. The welcome has had an undeniable feeling of veiled sadness.

We go to visit him at the Isla. From the bed he is dictating the speech he's supposed to deliver in the National Stadium at a public reception for him. Allende is traveling abroad, so Neruda will be welcomed by the vice-president and Army commander-in-chief, General Carlos Prats, on behalf of the government and the nation.

The country is experiencing the triumphant development of the destabilization campaign, the black market, the flight of capital, and the psychological war. The right wing is confident that in the parliamentary elections scheduled for the first Sunday in March 1973, the opposition will win the two-thirds necessary to constitutionally unseat the president of the Republic. This is the "clean coup" envisioned as a checkmate move by the White House chess players, where President Richard Nixon, in the oval office with Henry Kissinger, has given CIA director Richard Helms the order to bring down Allende by any means. Many millions of dollars are provided to buy off newspapers, congressmen, generals. They have already had considerable success in the effort to spread confusion, under a motto which the Edwards newspaper chain repeats on a daily basis, "Amass Hate!"

That climate is reflected in the welcome for Neruda in the National

Stadium, where the expected 100,000 do not show up, and empty spaces can be seen in the stands. The National Police equestrian team performs, followed by the appearance on the field of police dogs, an ominous portent, for within a year that stadium will be converted into a concentration camp.

The vice-president contributes a speech that reveals both familiarity with the poet and his work and respect for a man who has enriched as few others the country's cultural and national treasury.

Pablo Neruda reads a text whose original manuscript I have had in my possession since it was saved from the conflagration of September 1973. It is a warning call. He had lived through the Spanish tragedy, and he doesn't wish any Francoism for Chile. On his return, he has breathed the dangerous atmosphere that hovers over the country, but there are still some purer climes, such as the roar of the sea that had awakened him that morning at Isla Negra. "In this ceremony, with its pipes and drums, I seem to have once again married my homeland. And you mustn't think that this may be a marriage of convenience. This is simply a question of love, the great love of my life."

That event left us all with sort of an icy feeling. The poet was ill, and the country had been made ill by injections of deadly tons of rancor from afar.

Feeling anguished by the situation, Neruda goes to Isla Negra to work. He will resort to poetry as a weapon.

Toward the end of the year, he sends me a card bearing his *ex libris*, the fish inside two interlocking circles, and the customary declaration: "On the last day of 1972 we will wait together for the first day of 1973 in 'La Sebastiana,' Valparaíso." That midnight when the years change and the whistles of the port begin to sound, we're again among old friends, including two from Venezuela, María Teresa Castillo and Miguel Otero Silva, there on the broad terrace that Sebastián Collados had once dreamed of turning into a landing pad for helicopters. Our thoughts don't fly so high, but are concentrated on wondering what will happen in 1973.

When the new year dawns, Neruda gives me a prologue he has just written for my book *El Oficio Ciudadano* (Civic Responsibility). The piece reflects his state of mind, using as a point of departure an article signed by E. B. in the Sunday, 17 December 1972 issue of *El Mercurio*. The poet begins by quoting a paragraph which reveals the mentality that was at work to turn back the country's history: "It was in the years of the 'handle-bar' Fords, of gentlemen with canes and spats, and ladies with feathered hats. With the flames of a war they thought would be the 'war to end all wars' extinguished, people took a deep breath, full of hope, without realizing that the newborn peace was deformed by the bolshevik cancer which would infect the idlers, the slackers, the incompetents, the loafers, the hoodlums, the cynics, the failures, the envious, and the violent. The deadwood negative minority of the human species would rise up with the monstrous pretension of running the world."

Neruda answered very directly: "Among these defectives, slackers, hoodlums, incompetents, and failures, who were or are Communists, are men like Maxim Gorky, supermen like Gagarin and the first cosmonauts, airplane builders like Tupolev, scientists like Joliot-Curie, painters like Pablo Picasso, Henri Matisse, and Fernand Léger, tapestry designers like (Jean) Lurçat, stunning artists like Paul Robeson, writers like Anatole France, Henri Barbusse, Vladimir Maiakovski, Louis Aragon, Paul Eluard, Bertolt Brecht, (José Carlos) Mariátegui, and César Vallejo, politicians like Lenin, Jorge Dimitrov, Antonio Gramsci, Ho Chi Minh, and Luis Emilio Recabarren. I humbly count myself among those defectives mentioned by the mercurial columnist."

A few days later, at about eleven one morning, along with Luis Corvalán, we're waiting at a field in Isla Negra where children and local people customarily play football. A whir comes down from the sky; the helicopter's thumping roar ceases as it glides and settles smoothly to earth like someone gently sitting down. The president emerges, and we go off to Neruda's house. After a laughing conversation and a few informal photographs, the poet goes to a little table and begins the strangest reading in his life, before an unusual audience of only three persons, beginning with Salvador Allende. He reads to this president a call for another president's death, savoring every word in the long title, *Incitement to Nixoncide and Praise for the Chilean Revolution*.

His voice matches the subject, sounding resolute and measured: "This is an incitement to an action never seen: a book whose purpose is for all ancient and modern poets, not to mention those present, to put a hysterical, cold, genocidal killer up against the wall of history."

It's immediately apparent to the mesmerized trio of listeners that this work, as Neruda explains, "shows no concern for nor attempt at delicacy of expression, nor does it exhibit the nuptial hermeticism of some of my metaphysical books." In that regard it is like the *Heroic Song*, which he had emphasized was the first poetic book in Spanish dedicated to the Cuban Revolution. He calls himself a man who, from time to time, has to "act like a brakeman, head shepherd, mason, laborer, plumber, or a simple regimental scoundrel, capable of getting into a bare-knuckled brawl or breathing fire even from his ears." In other words, he will behave like a "public utility" bard. He can't do otherwise, and against his people's enemies he will launch his song, "as injurious and hard as an Araucanian stone . . . Now, attention, for I'm ready to fire." He asks old Walt Whitman for support, as he brings judgment against the White House killer.

In this case, the poet is not an oracle; he's just a bard and a bit of a prophet. He foretells what will happen: the impeachment and the very first resignation of a United States president, named Richard Nixon, who had directed not only the Watergate conspiracy but also the conspiracy against Chile. One might say that Neruda's *Incitement to Nixoncide* was heard, taken to heart, and in some ways put into practice by the North Americans themselves, with or without the secret complicity of old Whitman. Nixon wasn't killed, but he was relieved of his office.

In those pages, Neruda charges Nixon with all the pending counts: the copper boycott, Vietnam, the CIA plot and its agents' well-organized chaos within Chile. "A Sordid Story" gives him the chance to recall the actions of their man Viaux, and of those who, behind the scenes, are preparing the coup of 11 September.

Cuba all over again! He says a farewell to the assassinated General Schneider, reproducing with his voice the sense of emergency that weighs on the air like molten lead.

Whereas he began by invoking his old brother Whitman, he will now end with a noble comrade, Don Alonso de Ercilla, because "the same magnificent struggle of old / comes from the heart of Araucanía . . . Chile, distinguished province of fertility, in the famed Antarctic land, . . . never submitted to foreign domination."

When he finishes the reading, we remain speechless, astounded by the passion of this wounded battler. Allende is first to break the silence: "Pablo, the poem is gripping. It says what we feel, it speaks or sings for millions of Chileans." After a pause, he adds, "But I'd like to ask you something."

"What is it, Mr. President?"

"Do you think, Pablo, that after publishing this book, you can go on being ambassador?"

"Exactly, Salvador, I wanted to talk to you about that. I'm asking that you relieve me of my office. I want and need to be in Chile."

At the request of *The New York Times*, on 28 June 1973 in Isla Negra, he writes an article called "Watergate: Which Scandal Do They Mean?" In it, he says, "It's not that I wish on the North Americans 365 Watergates a year. But if they insist, they'll have them."

Under the Reagan presidency, there has been a lot of talk about "Debate-gate" and numerous scandals have come to light, or to semilight. The Watergate for Chile, that is to say the *non sancta* responsibility of the honorable president of the United States in the violation of human rights in Chile, came to pass in Neruda's lifetime and still continues to be repeated over and over, through the years.

177. The Cantalao Dream

Neruda writes fighting poetry, but also intimate poetry. In the midst of ravaging winds, he goes on creating books, making plans, beginning new constructions. He decides that he should combine the sea air with the mountain atmosphere and begins the construction of a new house at the east of Santiago, in Lo Curro to be exact, which a dictator with a Hitler-complex will later choose as the location of his own palatial bunker. Neruda will breathe the pure air of the heights, but he'll abandon the aviary-like houses which can be reached only by exhausting climbs. This will be a spacious house on only one level. At night he'll be able to observe the clearly visible constellations in the heavens, where he knows every last star. Down below, he'll also see the Babylonian city lights, which he's ambivalent about but needs, because his doctors are there, for one reason.

He will build that house mostly for himself, but he will also create a town for poets, which he names Cantalao, from his *The Inhabitant and His Hope*. He buys the land, not far from Isla Negra, where he will establish that village for artists who are poor in money but rich in dreams. As professional designer and planner for the project, he selects an outstanding architect and a noble gentleman in every respect, Fernando Castillo Velasco, rector of Santiago's Catholic University.

One morning the three of us set out for the site, crossing hills whose coastal edges plunge vertically down to the sea, beyond Punta de Tralca. We stop on a grassy plateau where Neruda had had a small preliminary wooden structure built to store construction materials. We discover that in the midst of that lonely place, the structure has been destroyed by vandals who don't want any towns for poets and hate the poet who wants to build them. Back home, Neruda writes a poem which doesn't hide his sorrow.

The villainy directed at his dreams for Cantalao grieved him, but more than just discouraging him, it was a signal of bad times. After all, who could be hurt by that project? He just wanted his fellow writers to be able to have what he had achieved, a place to live and work near the sea. Years before, he had begun to harbor the utopian notion of founding a unique little settlement, and in 1970 he had finished paying for the property where it would be built, on the rocky heights of Punta de Tralca, an Araucanian name that means "thunder point," because at that spot on the coast the breaking waves reach a height of 300 feet. He himself used to go there for long hours of work or to relax in the cabin he had built as a rustic preview. He had written an entire book there. Once, some thieves had gone in and stolen a torn hammock, two glasses, and three books, one of them a collection of English poetry. On its first page he had written a poem that "now only thieves will read," as he ruefully said.

But that theft of beloved books and old objects didn't sadden him at all in comparison to his distress at the destruction in that remote area by political looters who broke windows and left the floor covered with pieces of blue, green, and red glass. It was like a small-scale version of what they would later do to his "La Chascona" house on the day he died.

Did that dream of the Cantalao writers' colony disappear forever with Neruda into the land of bliss? For now, under a regime which has confiscated Isla Negra as a danger to the state, the poet's idea remains filed away. Maybe some day it will come to fruition.

But meanwhile the incorrigible citizen-poet was working simultaneously on another task—transforming Isla Negra by creating a park and a square for it, the same way he would create a child or poems. The park will be graced by agates, the smooth colored stones discovered by Neruda and Mari Martner. A commission is established, headed by Sergio Insunza and composed of Carlos Matus, Flavián Levine, Gonzalo Martner, and architects Fernando Castillo Velasco, Miguel Lawner, Federico Wong, Sergio González, Carlos Martner, and Raúl Bulnes Cerdá. In one session, they agree to accept the Contemporary Art Society's offer to donate a sculpture by Marta Colvin for the square. Neruda is involved in the organization's financial and administrative aspects. He's like a twenty-year-old who dreams out loud, and he performs like an efficient forty-year-old upscale executive, without ever losing his joking informality.

178. Tapestries of the Poor

He obtains an agreement from Salvador Allende's government to build the Isla Negra Cultural Center, where there will be a permanent exposition of works by the weavers that together we went to see in the Quisco

Municipality, which holds jurisdiction over his property. He wanted those displays of humble burlap textiles to be shown around the world. Their touch gave him pleasure, for they were not confected of fine pale silk but of the light shed by a country lantern. They were the untutored creation of poverty, wherein the needy wove dreams and desires, in other words, what they could never achieve. After the coup, that art of the persecuted spread far and wide in not only rural but urban centers of poverty. In the teeming Babel of the shantytowns they could no longer paint the old popular frescos; the murals of the Ramona Parra Brigade were banned; but in the dark cloud left behind by the bloodletting, behind the closed doors of secrecy, there were hands, especially of women, which took up again those scraps of frayed cloth and enriched them, putting down on torn remnants their nostalgia for lost freedom and the story of their tragic experience. This craft is one which springs up from violence and is devoid of any sense of the bucolic. These are the textiles of the night, which resort to colors soaked in blood, because it flows all around. In the cloth they tell it all, hardships and needs, and they remember Allende in some and Neruda in others. On the intricate map of the marginal city, with its hundreds of rebellious and martyred shantytowns, somehow the poet's dream has taken root and come forth, for these textiles are reaching the far corners of the earth, like messages sent out so that the world will know.

Spreading beyond the deaths and the hunger, they multiplied like living documents to denounce the terrible period. They don't imitate the luxurious tapestries of old palaces, but are made by hand and spring from a sorrowful heart that wishes to leave a record and bear witness, by weaving the used threads of an old woolen vest, eaten away by time and discarded. And so they reproduce that pinched expression of unrelieved misfortune. In the suburbs, the modest rectangles, dominated by a vivid representation of horror, are often accompanied by a verse from the poet who always helps them lift their banner and express dissatisfaction with a world gone to pieces. Neruda's old dream of showing those textiles to the world is being fulfilled in an unexpected way, spreading out to become a mass movement in which combative poetry, painting, plebeian tapestry, and impoverished yet noble textiles all come together.

179. Revised Dedications

Neruda went often to Santiago, principally for medical checkups. On such occasions, before leaving Isla Negra he would make it known that he would have lunch that day in the house of one or another of his friends, and then would have his afternoon nap there. From time to time he would come to my house. He needed that rest, now more than ever, to counter his exhaustion and to prolong the night, which for him was always a time for delightful conversations, although now they were dampened by a misty sadness, which nonetheless didn't preclude his Chaplinesque little laughs.

García Márquez recalls that in his Barcelona house he had offered Neruda the master bedroom for his nap, and he still has a book by the Chilean with some revised dedications. The first one says, "To Merceditas, from her bed." His friend "Gabo" adds that after it was written, Pablo had said, "No, this isn't right." So he added, "To Merceditas and Gabo in their bed." After reflecting a moment, he decided that the addition made it worse, so he again adjusted it, "To Merceditas and Gabo in their bed, fraternally."

180. On Alert

What is unique about the conspiracy is that it was being carried out not only in the shadows but also in the light of day. Neruda attempts to give a warning. A poster by him, three feet high, is plastered on the walls of Chile, dated 20 May 1973 in Isla Negra, with a big red heading that says, "TO ARTISTS AND INTELLECTUALS." In a penultimate appeal to become conscious of the drama that's at the door, he proposes an action plan, asking that intellectuals, especially poets, go into the provinces and small towns, to industries, businesses, schools, shantytowns, to explain to all what is being plotted in darkness. He urges all to put their work in the service of saving the country from catastrophe, calling out to authors and artists of the theater, interpreters and composers of ballet and popular song, painters and engravers and sculptors, professionals and craftsmen. He appeals to his friends among the creative artists and intellectuals in Latin America, the United States and Canada, and the countries of Europe, Asia, Africa, and Oceania, that they might lend us their help, their voice, their feelings of brotherhood.

Obviously, the poet was neither tranquil nor immobilized. In spite of his suffering, he was moving about like a demon to avoid the worst.

The result of parliamentary elections on 4 March 1973 wrecked the "clean coup," for Popular Unity came out stronger than had been expected. The plotters have to bid farewell to their plan to unseat the president of the Republic, and since they see their legal opening sealed off, they opt for armed sedition. Everything must be carried out in function of this objective; generals are contacted, and the mechanism for a coup is articulated in the political and economic arenas and in the mass media. They will be implacable, stopping at nothing. They will not vacillate in bringing about a bloodbath, torture, disappearances, and exile for a million Chileans. The plan is in motion, and Neruda senses it more clearly than others, because he possesses antennae that frequently help him grasp invisible things that float on the air or take place in society's back rooms.

He doesn't hide from anyone his vision of the dangers, and his house is besieged by reporters who come from around the world to interview him.

One day when I'm in a radio station recording a program, the Spanish-Mexican reporter Luis Suárez comes to ask me to intercede on his behalf so that Neruda will talk to him. I shouldn't do it, but I realize that it's a worthy proposition, so I ring up the poet. A couple hours later Luis Suárez is clanging the bell that hangs from a beam above the log door at Neruda's home. He finds the poet seated in an armchair in the library, with his feet on a hassock. A fire is burning on the hearth. Neruda, wearing a gray sweater, is writing poems in a notebook when the journalist enters. Nearby, a carpenter is doing some repairs. The reporter wants to talk about the Nobel Prize, but Neruda wants to talk about Chile. The carpenter is making so much noise that the visitor can't hear well, so he moves closer.

Neruda refers to his *Incitement to Nixoncide:* "That is a poetic and pamphleteering book that spells out many things . . . All my life I have been the least sectarian of persons, and I am antidogmatic par excellence. I believe in realism and in irrealism, and these two laws are fundamental in artistic creation. Anyone who suppresses realism leaves life behind and becomes a floating specter, and the artist who denies dreams and mystery will capsize in the middle of the street."

181. The Overcoat

On 12 July 1973, together with congressional deputies Gladys Marín and Rosendo Huenumán, we go to Isla Negra to wish Neruda a happy sixty-ninth birthday. Before, on that date, the house used to be alive with the happiest of parties, with costumes and irresistible bursts of humor. Now, everything is just the opposite. The organizer of earlier festivities is in bed. We give him the Party's gift, and he immediately begins to talk about what is obsessing him—the political situation. Then he talks at great length with Huenumán, a Mapuche poet. Neruda has an idea for an institution that he believes should be one of the great works undertaken by the people's government, creation of an Araucanian University, where instruction would be in the native language and written form would be given to Mapuche literature and culture. The indigenous people are entitled to be respected as a nationality with their own rights. The topic enthuses him, and I'm marveled by the fire that is brought to this new project by the man who is lying there sick. A little later, Gonzalo Losada, Jr. comes in carrying a large package which he carefully unwraps. It's an impressive Argentine overcoat, lined with Patagonian lambskin.

"My father sends it to you, Pablo, because he doesn't want you to be cold this winter." Young Losada opens it out in all its magnificence, and Pablo responds, "Thank you, it's a marvelous gift." He has a smile that is both tender and sad.

Within a week, Neruda's car unexpectedly pulls up in front of my house at 394 Matta Oriente in Santiago. From my desk I'm surprised to see Manuel Araya, the driver, emerge with a package in his arms. He gives me a letter, which I read with bated breath:

18 July 1973

Dear Valentín: I think this overcoat (of Losadesque origin) would fit you very well, and it's more youthful than your dark cassock. Many thanks if you accept it; I'll be in bed in the winter, and it doesn't belong between sheets.

I hug you. Come out here and visit. P.

One didn't have to be wise to understand those few words. It wasn't Gogol's *Overcoat* but the gift did contain a metaphor, the metaphor of his farewell. It was a dying bequest, in advance and outside the will. He never talked to me specifically about death, because this good man, mistakenly considered by some to be weak, was in life a strong man, and when death began to hover over him, he faced it with a tough and creative stoicism that I had never before seen. I say this because in that scene where Gonzalo Losada, Jr. had delivered the magnificent overcoat, the poet had immediately responded with another gift, maybe a gift to himself, for Matilde came back at once with several portfolios which contained eight unpublished books. In our presence, Neruda formally handed them over to the publisher, who asked, "Are they for immediate publication?"

"No," Pablo answered, "they are presents that I'm giving myself for my seventieth birthday. They should come out in the first half of 1974."

That was another response to the death that was beckoning from behind the door and through the picture window that looked onto the sea, from the room where his wish to hear the song of birds had led him to install a huge birdcage with greenish-gold singing canaries.

182. Posthumous Work

Those unpublished books would appear as posthumous works that would sing forever of their author's indomitable love of life.

When Matilde and I saw each other in Europe in August 1974, she gave me copies of those books, recently published and with her personal dedications, which the bedridden Neruda had given to the junior Losada that birthday afternoon on 12 July 1973, in our presence. I take them in my hands and am moved by the willpower of the man who had written them while flat on his back, as death kept watch and told him every night that it was expecting him.

The books are a fountain of recollections. That trip to Easter Island, to which he had invited me in a January long past when I couldn't accompany him, is both a return to the theme of the unknown origins of ancient Rapa Nui and a philosophical meditation, a counterpoint between men as awkward transients and the little island forged in the middle of an immense ocean by the winds of Melanesia. The poet is searching for the faces of eternity, and he thinks he finds them there in those stolid masks carved in the heart of silence.

In contrast to the purity of the statues of *The Amputated Rose*, washed by light and salt spray, whenever people return to the continent they go back to old arguments, wars, assailing music, and false smiles.

The situation in Chile reaches him through all the walls of his house and enters into the pores of the supine man. "These months carry the stridency / of an undeclared civil war." The wolf's howling is heard near the garden, which is his life in *Jardín de invierno* (Winter Garden), where past seasons and women and passions file through his memory. It makes him think about Quevedo, for there is no springtime in the room, only illness. Springtime is outside, and must not torment him by reminding him of so many springtimes now reduced to ashes.

He has the sea before him, yet this summer he won't go out to the sea. "I'm interned, interred, and along the tunnel that holds me captive I hear a remote green thunder." It is the ocean that awaits him.

Around that time, two very different men die on the same day, two very different writers but both winners of the National Prize for Literature: Manuel Rojas and Benjamín Subercaseaux. Neruda is bedfast when he gets the news, which strikes him as two bugle calls that are speaking privately to him. "They died just hours apart: / one shrouded in Santiago, the other in Tacna: / both unique, alike only / now, just once, because they have died." We went one March morning, along with Salvador Allende, to see the one who had died in Santiago, Manuel Rojas. Just as Pablo envisioned as he himself was preparing to follow him, there was Rojas "obstinate and haughty, / severe and in wrinkled vestment, / quite given to silence." The other man, Benjamín, was far away, "a focused flame that flashes intermittently its magnificent beam." But both would silently become accustomed to the realm of darkness, and he didn't know when he would do the same.

He records in his heart every acquaintance's death, as if he were counting each beat of the metronome belonging to Asterio Alarcón, that old watchmaker in Valparaíso to whom he had dedicated a poem in *Fully Empowered*. In reality, he had dedicated it to Time, which is Life, but— Dear God!—is also Death, which comes to you in person when it calls the names of Manuel and Benjamín.

The book *2000* is an attempt to survive until the page is turned on the century and the millennium, and it's a vote in favor of survival for "this old excrement-colored earth" and "the accursed progeny who create the light of the world." His inquiry is very frank:

And we the dead, distributed in time,
scattered in utilitarian and proud cemeteries,
or tossed into bone pits for poor Bolivians,
we the dead of 1925, 26,
33, 1940, 1918, nineteen hundred and five,
nineteen hundred and a thousand, in short, we
who have expired prior to this stupid numeral
when we're no longer alive, what becomes of us?

In any case, we know what happens with him, something he had predicted in a verse: "It so happens that I'm bound to live on."

He speaks openly about his dead bones and the year that took him away, "leaving instead of song or testimony / an obstinate skeleton of words." But skeletons are solid, resistant to time, even surviving for thousands of years.

El corazón amarillo (The Yellow Heart) is one of his most surrealistically oriented books, wherein the man resists dying, though he knows that some consider him a corpse. "Journalists pointed / their extravagant machinery / at my eyes and my navel / asking me to say things / as if I had already died . . ."

It is not autumn that characterizes the unconventional humor of this poetry. "In my childhood I discovered / my depraved heart / that made me fall into the sea / and get used to being submarine." The fantasy is fresh, and more than being related to a yellowed heart, it's akin to the Beatles' yellow submarine.

This Galileo Galilei, who has retracted nothing, insists that "In spite of it all, I keep moving." One should read this book, worthy of the Marx brothers, with the penultimate laugh of a man who is looking at the world and his life with an outlandish eye, knowing that he hasn't much time left.

It's the farewell from "all of us, heroes and poor devils, / weaklings, braggarts, unsure / and capable of every impossibility, . . ." to the point that "they were robbed of their laurels, their medals, their titles, their names," as would happen to such a man as he was, as soon as he closed his eyes in a nation where anything could happen.

In the *Book of Questions,* the man who waits for death lies there on his mattress working like a poetry factory to turn out a work comprised of nothing but questions, each one two verses long. The questions come from the boy and the man, from the poet and the citizen. "Tell me, is the rose unclothed / or is it only dressed like that? . . . Why couldn't Christopher Columbus / have discovered only Spain? . . . That solemn-faced senator / who assigned me a castle / did he share with his nephew/ the fruits of assassination? . . . Is there anything sillier in life / than to be named Pablo Neruda? . . . Won't death finally be / an interminable cuisine? . . . Which hard labor / is Hitler's in hell? / Painting walls or cadavers? / Smelling the gas from his victims?"

There's another book whose original Neruda had given me so I could assess it for him. What judgment could I give him? It was a beautiful and somber book. My secretary rescued it from the repeated break-ins at my house and the confiscation of my library. Somewhere among the numerous way stations through which my correspondence had to be routed, avoiding all direct mention of my name, someone made a copy of that book, and it soon appeared in a pirated edition, which upset Matilde. The book is *Elegy,* in honor of his friends who had preceded him in death, but it also preludes a self-elegy. When he recalls Nazim Hikmet and his translator Ovadi Savich; Ilya Grigoriovich Ehrenburg, wearing wrinkled suits and flowing with uncomfortable opinions; when he sheds a tear for Sioma Kirsanov, he is also shedding it for their friend, for Pablo Neruda, for that Pablo who had dearly loved Alberto Sánchez, the Toledo spinner of tales, mythological baker, creator of forms, who never managed to return to Spain. The poet is preparing himself for death, where he will join Pushkin, whose monument is a forum for squabbling and melancholy pecking doves. He will join his colleague Maiakovski, another fan of poetry readings. The book bids farewell to the Arbat neighborhood in Moscow, the Aragbi restaurant, the National Hotel, for he knows he'll never see them again. It's a "Hail to Moscow among the cities," and an elegy for those who have departed and for the man who will go away one night in September, but who will return every time he's needed.

In *El mar y las campanas* (Sea and Bells), he is situated between the Isla Negra bell that announces visitors, along with all the other bells he has ever heard, and the sea outside his window, which he observes from his bed. Are the sea and the bells contradictory elements? The bells represent an image of life. Does the sea in this case represent death? From his bed he writes, "I have nothing but the sea's harsh noon, and a bell." But he wishes to see both elements as representations of life: "And the sea lives. The bells exist." He feels that many deaths are poised in profile to seek him out, but they still haven't found him, perhaps because he still makes bells sound and continues to travel the sea. A Soviet ship crosses the world's waters under the name of *Pablo Neruda.* The old ocean-going traveler goes on sailing away and returning.

Sometimes his tone becomes legalistic. "I declare four dogs: / one is already buried in the garden, / two others still surprise me, / and an unkempt bitch / far off." Then he alludes to the broken bell that still wants to sing. He is that bell. From afar he hears the sound of a country in turmoil, and he urges, "Yes, comrade, it's the time of gardens, / and the time of battles . . ."

He also wants once more to leave evidence of his loving gratitude to Matilde, "It has been so lovely to live when you were living."

The book *Defectos escogidos* (Selected Faults) is a kind of self-irony, which recalls that scoffing portrait the poet had offered of himself:

> As for me, I am—or think I am—hard-nosed, small-eyed, sparse of hair, swollen in the abdomen, long-legged, broad-footed, yellow-complexioned, generous in love, impossible at figures, confused by words, tender-handed, slow-walking, pure-hearted, fond of stars and tides and swells, an admirer of beetles, a walker of sands, institutionally dull, perpetually Chilean, friend to my friends, silent to my enemies, meddlesome among birds, bad-mannered at home, timid in gatherings, daring in solitude, repentant without reason, a horrendous manager, a sailor by speech, an herbalist in ink, discreet among animals, lucky with storm clouds, a researcher in marketplaces, gloomy in libraries, melancholy in the mountains, tireless in forests, very slow in answering, witty years later, common the year round, brilliant with my notebook, gigantic of appetite, a tiger for sleeping, calm in joy, an inspector of nocturnal skies, an invisible worker, persistently in disorder, brave out of necessity, a coward without guilt, lazy by vocation, lovable to women, congenitally active, a poet by curse, and a first-rate fool. [89]

183. *Memoirs and Manuscripts*

After the poet's death had interrupted final editing, his *Memoirs* were published in March 1974. *I Confess to Having Lived* immediately enjoyed wide popularity, with several reprintings and foreign language editions. Then, in 1977, *Para nacer he nacido* (I Was Born to Be Born) gathered together prose texts compiled from seven notebooks under the headings: It's Too Early, Travel Image, Flame of Friendship, Navigating in Smoke, Reflections from Isla Negra, Struggle for Justice, and Pablo Neruda Speaks.

Later, on a plane trip, Matilde tells me about a new book, comprised of unpublished poems and articles from his adolescence and early adulthood, which contribute to an awareness of Neruda's first literary efforts. They are included in *El fin del viaje* (Journey's End), which appears in October 1982 as a posthumous work, a collection of important texts on miscellaneous topics, gathered together from various periods and publications. There's a dialogue between Pablo Neruda and Herman Melville, which was the beginning of a film script that was never completed. The Chilean argues with the North American writer about *Benito Cereno*. The title of the unfinished dialogue is indicated as *Comienzo para un rebelde* (A

Beginning for a Rebel) and belongs to the script for a film called *Babo*. "Who is Babo? . . . Babo died a century ago. They hanged him in Concepción, Chile."

There's an "Elegy in Song" for the singer named in its lines:

> When you were born you were baptized
> as Violeta Parra:
> the priest elevated grapes
> over your life and said:
> "You are Parra [arbor] and you shall turn into wine.
> Into happy wine, into playful joy,
> into the people's earth, into simple song."
> Santa Violeta, you turned into
> a guitar with leaves that shine
> by the light of the moon,
> into a wild plum
> transformed,
> into a true people,
> into a dove in the field, into alms for the poor.

On 3 May 1963 in "La Sebastiana," for her birthday Neruda had written "A Balloon for Matilde": "One more year, chopped into weeks / by God, the Cardinal and Company, / one more year, sovereign Patoja, for your faulty orthography . . . You are one year younger, dear heart."

The slender volume includes a precious jewel in the publication of a long-ago text, unpublished until now, "The Dove Within." As we have said, its special value derives from the fact that the creator of the verses is Pablo Neruda and the creator of the drawings is Federico García Lorca. The sole copy, belonging to the fair Sara Tornú de Rojas Paz, is published for the first time here, in 1982.

Matilde tells me that there are still materials by Neruda that haven't been gathered into books, and I myself have evidence of several.

184. Farewell

Neruda often asked me to come visit him, and I did so every chance I got. The last time was on 30 July 1973. The next day I was to leave for Europe on a trip that had been postponed many times. President Allende was sending me abroad to explain the situation in Chile and to request all possible assistance for his government in avoiding the breakdown of democratic institutions and a sea of blood.

Neruda, whose life more and more was submerged in his concern about the collapse he saw coming very shortly, insisted that I should return soon, hastening back as quickly as I could, because he had to talk with me. In his eyes I read his fear that he wouldn't be here when I returned. I told him yes, that I had a lot to do in Europe but that I would be back as soon as possible. He repeated his demand. There was an unspoken language in our conversation, but his eyes and the writing between the lines expressed by his words said it all, his worry not only about his health but also his anguish because he discerned a great sickness that was threatening the whole country.

I embraced him, not knowing that it was the last time I would see him.

Luis Corvalán and his wife visit him eleven or twelve days before the coup. His preoccupation is with what he sees coming, including his belief that if the plotters triumph they will carry their violence to Isla Negra. Corvalán tries to calm him. "Yes," he says, "there may be a coup, but they can't touch *you*, Pablo. You're such a great man that they wouldn't dare."

His reply was calm, sure of what he was saying: "You're wrong. García Lorca was the prince of gypsies, and you well know what they did with him." [90]

185. Death in the Midst of Death

The coup of 11 September 1973 takes place while I am flying from Rome to Moscow. That very night I'm supposed to go on to Santiago to resume my duties within Chile, where I plan to go visit Pablo in Isla Negra the day after my arrival. As I enter the hotel to spend a few hours before taking the plane for Santiago, a Cuban companion, Blas Roca, asks me if I've heard the latest news from Chile. "There's a military uprising, and Valparaíso has been taken. Allende has gone to La Moneda government house . . ."

"Valparaíso has been taken." Neruda's death throes really began on 11 September when he tuned in the radio on the nightstand next to his bed and discovered that only Radio Magallanes was transmitting. With clenched fists he listened to Salvador Allende's last message from amidst the falling bombs: "I shall pay with my life for my loyalty to the people . . ." Then, deep silence.

Neruda desperately turns the dial, searching for a voice. He tunes to the short wave frequency from Mendoza, which is reporting the tragedy.

Matilde tries to calm him, but it's impossible. He will not turn loose of the radio. He wants to hear it all, to know it all, even though he is dying. Matilde telephones Dr. Vargas Salazar, who tells her, "Get rid of the radio, the televison—disconnect them. If he finds out what is happening, it will be his death."

"But Doctor, how can I get rid of the television and the radio, when Pablo is like a madman trying to find out what is going on?" (In the European summer of 1974, I spend two weeks with Matilde at the sea. She is in need of a rest after so many ordeals. For me, it's a grand reunion. During our two weeks, she tells me step by step what happened in that period.)

When he heard Allende's final speech, Neruda realized that all was lost. To soothe him, Matilde said, "Maybe it won't be so horrible." Pablo answered, "Not so, it's fascism." That night, his fever went up. On television he had seen the attack on La Moneda six times, and on radio broadcasts from Mendoza he listened to news of Allende's death.

The doctor recommended that he be taken to Santiago, because with the curfew neither the physician nor the nurse, who lived in San Antonio, could move. "Take him by ambulance to a private hospital." Along the road they were accosted twice by soldiers, who stood the stretcher bed up on end. For the first time, Matilde saw him weep, and he asked her, "Wipe my face, Patoja." It wouldn't help at all for Matilde to say, "This is Pablo Neruda," and it doubtless would have made things worse. She knew that, because earlier they had invaded the house in Isla Negra, looking for weapons, they said. Neruda had no weapons, but in the moment the troops arrived at the house he was dictating to Matilde the last pages of his Memoirs, which he considered to be indispensable in order to leave them behind as a record and an accusation:

> I am writing these hurried lines for my Memoirs only three days after the indescribable actions which led to the death of my great comrade, President Salvador Allende. His assassination was kept secret, and he was buried secretly; only his widow was permitted to accompany those immortal remains. The aggressors' version is that they found his lifeless body showing visible signs of suicide. A different version has been published abroad. Immediately after the aerial bombardment, tanks, many tanks, were mobilized to fight against one man, the president of the Republic of Chile, Salvador

Allende, who was waiting for them in his office, accompanied only by his great heart, shrouded in smoke and flames.

They had to take advantage of such a ripe opportunity. It was necessary to machine-gun him because he would never give up his post. That body was secretly buried in whatever niche was available. That corpse which went to its grave accompanied by a solitary woman bearing all the sorrow in the world, that glorious dead figure was riddled and torn apart by machine-gun bullets from Chile's soldiers, who had once again betrayed Chile.

Could he envision that scant weeks later he himself would be buried in some obscure niche? In the death of his friend the president, he foresaw a part of his own fate. It carried a premonition for him.

The president of Mexico, Luis Echeverría, sent a special plane to take Neruda to that country. The invitation was extended to him in the Santa María Clinic by Ambassador Martínez Corbalá. Neruda, thanking him, rejected the offer. Soon the ambassador would take up the cause again, when Matilde told how they had just broken into and ransacked "La Chascona," diverting the canal and flooding the house. The ambassador insisted, "You'll have better medical attention up there than here. You'll get well." Neruda resigned himself to leaving. He thought it was very important to get the Memoirs out of danger, especially on account of the final pages. They were taken out of Chile in a diplomatic pouch, after he had personally closed them with his words about Allende and the plotters' responsibility.

Matilde went to Isla Negra to pick up some clothing for the trip and a few books that he kept locked up. When she returned, she found him very upset. During the night, in his delirium, he kept repeating, "They're shooting them." Next day, some friends came to see him, leaving early in order to get home before curfew. At night, in fitful dreams, he again repeated, "They're shooting them, they're killing them." The poet was isolated in his clinic room, listening to the nightly helicopter flights. He knew what was happening. Between the day of the coup and Neruda's death, Pinochet's people murdered tens of thousands of Chileans. The poet felt every one of those deaths. Matilde was holding his hand when she felt a sudden shudder. His broken heart had stopped. The nurse came and tried to massage his chest, but the doctor entered and told her, "Don't go on, leave him in peace."

It was 10:30 at night on 23 September 1973

186. The Errant Coffin

Matilde opened the suitcase she had packed for the trip to Mexico and took out his favorite checked jacket, a plaid shirt and a red silk scarf that she tied around his neck. The doctor had said he might live five or six more years if nothing unforeseen happened. Teresa Hamel helped her dress him from head to toe, for this was a man who had died with his boots on. The two women went out to telephone the news of his death, and when they returned, Pablo was no longer there. They ran down to the ground floor to search for him, but they didn't find him there either. They went to the basement, where they saw a sign that read "Chapel." Inside, it was dark and deserted. Moments later, they saw him being wheeled along the passageway to the sound of squeaking metal. Matilde entered the chapel, but a male nurse told her, "Madame, it is forbidden to stay here." She screamed at them, "You can get out. You have no business here." Then she leaned her head against Pablo's, as someone entered on tiptoes. It was his sister Laurita. They held his vigil not in a room, but in a dark corridor.

Around midnight, a radio announcer had broadcast that "The poet Pablo Neruda is on the verge of death, and it is anticipated that he will not live through the night. It is absolutely forbidden to visit him in the Santa María Clinic where he is hospitalized."

The next day, when the curfew was lifted and reporters and photographers began to arrive, the clinic administrators decided to remove the deceased from the passageway and put him in a vestibule. He was a VIP.

A swarm of photographers clicked their shutters until Matilde told them, "Please, no more pictures." Among the friends who came were Homero Arce, Graciela Alvarez, Juvencio Valle, Francisco Coloane, Aída Figueroa, Enrique Bello, Juan Gómez Millas, and others.

Neruda was laid out on a table, wrapped in a white shroud, with his face uncovered. He was smiling, which is hard to imagine, considering the time of jackals that prevailed in the country at the moment of his death. When the casket arrived, the sheets were removed and he was placed inside. Coloane finished buttoning his shirt, then they closed and sealed the casket and left for "La Chascona." When they got there, they couldn't enter. The steps leading up to the house were inundated, covered with mud and water and blocked by debris. The casket couldn't enter. The junta people had done their job. So the members of the cortege decided to go around the block and go in through the back entrance that faced the hill. There, a handful of youths gathered next to the coffin and, raising their fists in the air, broke the silence to respond to a spokesman who resonantly called out the poet's name:

Comrade Pablo Neruda!
Present!
Now—
And forever!
Now—
And forever!

Those suicidal shouts were the first rebellious expressions to be heard in the two weeks since the beginning of a slaughter which would continue to be carried out, with thousands of victims up to now.

They spent some time trying to enter through the back door, but that was also impossible. Emissaries of the junta had diverted the canal that ran up above on the hillside, unleashing a flood of water which isolated that part of the house. In addition, it had rained, and the place was like a swamp. They put the casket down for a few minutes while they rested and discussed what to do. Someone raised his voice to propose that Neruda be taken to the house belonging to the Chilean Writers Society.

Matilde tersely replied, "Pablo wanted to be taken to his home. We will not take him anywhere else."

Aída Figueroa quietly suggested another solution, "Why don't we take him to my house?" Matilde answered her, "Don't you think that the worse off the house is, the better off Pablo will be in it?"

At one side, behind an open barrier, there were some building materials—planks and posts. Someone spotted them and called for building a bridge in order to get through. Enrique Bello picked up a plank, and the others did likewise. Within a few minutes there was a bridge. They took up the casket and began the climb up the steep incline. As they advanced, they saw signs of destruction all around. Their shoes made crackling noises on the broken glass that covered the path. They saw the piles of ashes to which Pablo's collections had been reduced. They could make out paintings, half-burned books, broken fans, brilliant feathers tossed into the mud. It was a freezing spring day, and on all levels of the house they saw the window frames without glass. The dining room looked as if it had been bombed. On the walls, here and there a torn painting hung askew. On the floor, bits of lamps.

When they reached the living room, they discovered boot prints.

Some of the mourners began to pick up the broken glass with their bare hands, but Matilde intervened, "No, Pablo would have wanted you to leave it all just as the intruders left it."

They set the casket in its place, and Matilde put a bouquet of red carnations on top. Later, Ambassador Harald Edelstam appeared with a grand wreath and placed it at the foot of the casket. Across it was a long blue and yellow moire ribbon with the message, "To the great poet Pablo Neruda, Nobel Prize. Gustaf Adolf, King of Sweden."

The house at Isla Negra wasn't sacked, but the one in Valparaíso, "La Sebastiana," was, by Navy sailors.

Enrique Bello went to get the permits for the death certificate and cemetery pass. The Civil Registry wasn't functioning, and the officials had closed the books. In those days so many people were dying that there wasn't room in the books for them. When they found out who the deceased was, the two clerks silently expressed their solidarity, for without saying a word, they reopened the books and asked where the burial would take place.

"In the tomb of Carlos Ditborn, Central O'Higgins Street between Limay and Los Tilos, at the General Cemetery," Bello detailed.

Since Neruda couldn't be buried at Isla Negra, as he had repeatedly requested, Adriana Ditborn offered her family's tomb to Matilde.

Several young Communists who worked in the Quimantú publishing house, where troops were then slashing millions of books, came to the house with a request: "Please don't take any pictures, because we want to pay homage to Neruda with an honor guard." While the ceremony took place, nobody took photographs, but when it was over, the Swedish ambassador openly urged the photographers to "Take pictures, pictures, and more pictures of all this destruction, so that the world may know."

At the entrance of Márquez de la Plata Street, a busload of national police *carabineros* had been stationed. Headquarters was rung up and Matilde was told, "Madame, it's only to give you and Mr. Neruda protection."

187. Unwelcome Visitors

People continued to arrive. The ambassadors of France and Mexico were seen hopping over mud and water, avoiding obstacles, in order to form part of the strange picture of that sacked room where they were keeping vigil over the poet's remains. It was like a scene from a war movie. Suddenly someone spied an old withered man, twisted and thin as a vine, hidden behind dark glasses and dressed in black, who was looking furtively about as if he didn't understand anything that was happening. This was the man who had loaned money to a nineteen-year-old Neruda to publish his first book, and in his articles had called for the fall of Allende because he hated anything that smelled of "communism." But "Alone," in that moment, watched with confusion what was occurring. Maybe it wasn't the triumph he was hoping for.

Aída Figueroa spotted the singer-writer Patricio Manns and asked him why he was there endangering himself, in view of what had happened to Víctor Jara, murdered just a few days before. It was a time of widespread death, and those who hadn't succumbed had to go into hiding.

Others who arrive leaping over puddles are Radomiro Tomic, Máximo Pacheco, and Flavián Levine.

Virginia Vidal, who had been present in Stockholm as a journalist when the Nobel Prize was conferred, contemplates Neruda through the glass casket-cover. His eyes are closed but she detects the smile on his full lips, and she recalls the reporters' questions when he had descended from the plane in Stockholm. "What is your favorite possession?" "Old shoes." "What is your favorite word?" "The word 'love.'" Now he lies there, surrounded by ruin and by people who are risking their lives to keep him company. The *Tree of Life,* his marvelous piece of Mexican folk art, has been smashed to bits. Virginia salvages a small clay figure of the Virgin from it. The canvases by primitive Chilean painters have disappeared from the dining room walls. Later they will find them in the canal, rotted away by the water.

The alien visitors had also gone into the bedroom, where the only thing exempt from destruction is the fireplace with its bronze bell and the carving of the linked letters *P* and *M*. The bed is broken, and the gutted mattress shows the muddy traces of military galoshes.

On the third floor, in the library and Neruda's workroom, shaded by foliage, everything smells of burned paper. Roberto Parada picks up a charred title page, torn from its covers, and reads the caption: Miguel de Unamuno's *The Tragic Sense of Life.* He smoothes the paper with his hand as tears come to his eyes, and then he puts it in his pocket. The clock, as tall as a person on its antique pedestal, has also suffered damage. Its pendulum and weights have been yanked out, and it has no hands.

The cold comes in through the broken-out windows. The neighbor, Queta Quintana, suggests that Matilde go home with her to eat something hot, but no, she will remain there, that is her place. That September afternoon is frigid. Suddenly, Matilde says, "There they come. I will not greet them," and she goes upstairs to her bedroom and slams the door, first telling Aída Figueroa, "You talk to them." Though the terrain isn't conducive to military parades or goose-steps, the group comes pressing forward, civilians in addition to men in uniform, both military personnel and national police *carabineros*. They don't remove either helmets or berets. Some are wearing camouflage field uniforms, pants and jackets with painted splotches, which the Cubans metaphorically called caterpillar clothes. One of them introduces himself as General Pinochet's aide-de-camp, "I wish to speak with the widow and family members of the great poet Pablo Neruda, glory of the nation's literature, in order to express the condolences . . ." He cuts off the sentence, then asks, "Where is the widow? Where is some Neruda family member?"

The response comes in the impetuous voice of Chela·Alvarez: "Every one of us here are Neruda's family. We demand respect for our grief!"

The aide-de-camp repeats almost verbatim the words he spoke earlier. He asks to speak with the widow.

Aída Figueroa answers him, "The widow is resting and will not see you." She asks them to go into the dining room, and they follow her, stumbling in the midst of destroyed books, paintings, knickknacks, hand organs. The man who is acting as leader again says, "We have come to pay condolences to the widow."

The military spokesman is confused: "We have not done all this."

Aída replies, "It's strange, but nothing has been stolen." Then she takes them to Neruda's desk and shows them the eviscerated clock with its cabinetry riddled with holes, its broken chains and detached pendulum. The aged lady in one of the paintings has the mark of a knife plunged into one eye and a long slash. Afterwards, they are shown some of the things salvaged from the canal, which were beginning to form a small mountain. The official again goes back to his refrain, "We wish to offer condolences . . ."

Chela Alvarez tells them, "In these ruins left by you, we are holding a vigil for Neruda. We wish, first, for respect and tranquility in order to pay him our last homage, and, second, for a guarantee that tonight we can be left alone."

The official maintains that "The Army of Chile is respectful of national glories." More and more things are being taken out of the canal—trays, ceramics, torn paintings, broken dishes.

The official announces that the government will decree three days of official mourning for the poet, to take effect on the day of his death. The official announcement is made on the day of his funeral. In effect, they are decreeing a retroactive mourning period of three days which comes to an end a couple hours after the official communique. Nobody laughs, nobody shouts, nobody weeps. Everybody looks at them with a stony expression, and they go away like whipped dogs.

More or less simultaneously with the decree of official mourning, an official report is disseminated saying that a gang of children led by a ten-year-old boy is to blame for the destruction at the house belonging to the poet Pablo Neruda.

188. The Cortege

Curfew is approaching, and people have to leave. Only nine persons remain at the vigil: Matilde, Laura Reyes, a couple named Cárcamo who are relatives of Matilde, Aída Figueroa, Elena Nascimento, Juanita Flores, Queta Quintana, and Hernán Loyola, who had gone home to get some blankets and returned before the eight o'clock curfew. There was nothing in the house to keep warm with. It truly seemed a house of death, but everything also exuded a strong feeling of dignity.

Matilde tries to sleep a bit, but within two hours she's up again, to spend the rest of the night next to Neruda, watching over him.

The next morning, when the curfew is lifted, a string of visitors begins to arrive—writers, professors, workers, humbly dressed women—all with expressions of tragedy.

It's time to go to the cemetery, and again there's the problem of how to take the casket out. They manage it through the carriage entryway, with a maneuver that demands great effort and skill. When they appear on Márquez de la Plata Street, the day's first shouts greet them, as one voice exclaims "Comrade Pablo Neruda!" and all the rest answer in chorus "Present!"

The shouts come from workers and students, but there are other people there who hide their perverse faces behind dark glasses. As the cortege flowed into the little square at the foot of San Cristóbal Hill, about 150 feet from Neruda's house, a handful of people was waiting to join them.

At that moment the funeral march became an unusual procession, because all those people were confronting death all around them, death that was watching from trucks full of soldiers with machine guns at the ready. Nobody in the procession glanced to either side; they just looked straight ahead. At the corner they met a woman who was crying. She covered her head with a black scarf and joined the line. The police were moving about in all directions, disoriented perhaps because the crowd had dared to march in a column. The motorcycle police maneuvered as if to drive over the cortege, speeding away and then coming back again. When the crowd passed in front of a power station, they were met point blank by a company of "black berets" who directed their rifles at that funeral procession, which by now was a huge multitude.

At some point, the marchers began to look to the side, beyond the cars full of soldiers with their readied weapons. They looked toward windows where astonished eyes were staring out at them. Even those fixed gazes were a sign of bravery and a way of being present. The same could be said of a moving window curtain that revealed the presence of someone contemplating the cortege. In other windows on Purísima Street or Perú Avenue, some revealed themselves more openly with a waving hand or kerchief, some with a small gesture. When the crowd began to file along Santos Dumont, the procession was swelled by people who got out of their cars to join in. Someone opened one of Neruda's books, like a priest who opens the Bible at mass, and began to read aloud: "Generals / traitors. / Look at my house, murdered, / look at Spain, torn apart . . . Jackals that the jackal would reject . . ." It was the Quimantú labor union president reading *Spain in My Heart*. Others didn't need to refer to books, for they knew his poems by heart and began to recite them.

As they reach La Paz Avenue, someone suddenly begins a timid rendition of the first notes of the forbidden song, "Arise, ye prisoners of starvation, / Arise, ye wretched of the earth." Another voice joins in, then falls silent. But the song begins to sound again at several points in the crowd, then everybody seems to be singing it almost in a murmur, and a crippled youth suddenly launches into a loud recital of verses by Neruda. The funeral procession had definitely become a throng. Many women were carrying flowers. When they passed in front of the morgue, which was filled to capacity with "No Name" corpses, even more people were waiting to join in.

In the procession there was a tall chestnut-haired woman with blue eyes and a pale countenance, leaning unsteadily on two friends. One of them called out at the top of her lungs with a voice that came from the depths of horror:

Comrade Víctor Jara!
Present!

Comrade Víctor Jara!
Present!
Now—
And forever!

The woman they are assisting remains silent. She is the ballerina Joan Turner de Jara, Víctor's widow who had personally retrieved his body from that same morgue they're passing in front of.

Surrounding the small square of the General Cemetery are armored cars and jeeps full of soldiers. As the cortege enters the graveyard, they put the coffin down on a rolling platform. "The Internationale" is now being sung by all in a great sobbing lament. One man who opposes such plaintiveness opens a book by Neruda to defiantly insist, "Here you have / my heart / like a mountain of swords / ready for battle."

When they pass through the wide gates of the cemetery, someone shouts an expected motto, one name: "Salvador Allende!" All reply in chorus, "Present!" The voices reverberate on the cupola and echo back, "Present!"

The people again sang "The Internationale," with fists raised, caution to the wind. They all sang it, even those who had never sung it, and those who didn't know the words and just hummed along. Rarely had that hymn resounded with such tremulous intensity as there in the midst of the death they were both accompanying and surrounded by. It was a hymn to life and a hymn of protest against everything that was happening.

The soldiers looked on, stupefied and confused. They couldn't believe their ears. In the crowd many believed that without warning there would be shots.

Again the voice, "Comrade Pablo Neruda" and the reply "Present!" But the cry spontaneously changed again to "Comrade Víctor Jara!" with the universal response, "Present!" After a silence, the spokesman proclaimed in stentorian tones, "Comrade Salvador Allende!"

He was answered collectively by almost a war cry, a "Present!" which contained all their support for the fallen president, all their rage against the assassins, all their yearning for justice, all the unrest of the moment, all their sorrow for Pablo and for so many dead, all their fear that they themselves might fall. It was the very moment when panic must be routed and fear set aside, so they again sang and sobbed "The Internationale." They may have felt vaguely protected by the presence of several ambassadors and foreign journalists.

189. Until We Meet Again!

Once inside the cemetery, the procession had to stop while formalities were discussed. Then they again took up the march through internal streets bordered by trees and tombs. The journalist Luis Alberto Mansilla ran into Professor Alejandro Lipschütz, whom Pablo had once called "Chile's most important man." The wise old man had just turned ninety, and he was there to say good-bye to his friend with whom he used to exchange flowers and poems, and to whom he used to send his translations of Ovid from the Latin. Quietly he confided to Mansilla, "Last night I had unexpected visitors."

They had broken into his house on Hamburgo Street and kept him locked up all night in one room, along with his wife Rita, who was older than her husband, as he liked to mention on his birthdays. The house was turned inside out as they searched for weapons and more especially for Luis Corvalán. The professor had a garden almost as large as that of his near neighbor Pablo Neruda, when he was living in Los Guindos, but Lipschütz's was much better cared for by a skillful gardener, Doña Margarita. The invaders dug it all up with shovels and picks, and then they went upstairs to the library, one of the finest in Chile, where they destroyed papers and stole relics.

Professor Lipschütz had the appearance of a medieval wizard, and like someone who had accumulated all the world's experience and was very attentive to the lessons of history, he told Mansilla, "This bunch isn't eternal . . . I've seen a lot. Fascism did the same thing in Europe, and you see how it ended."

The cortege suddenly broke into a run, becoming a multitude without order as everybody tried to position themselves close to the tomb in order to see the burial with their own eyes. And thus, almost without realizing it, all of them pushed forward, even Matilde. Even those who were carrying the casket quickened their pace. Everyone felt an attack of haste.

There was nothing programmed in that final farewell ceremony. Someone read some verses from the *General Song*, and a working-class youth read a poem he had doubtless written just the night before, using images that desperately tried to express what not only he was feeling but also all those present and absent. Chela Alvarez, a former actress, again brought forth her voice to recite verses she had spoken during the life of the poet, sometimes in his presence.

In front of the crowd there was a towering mausoleum, as big as a house, and on the roof numerous photographers recorded the image of every one present. They all sensed that they were being documented by the unavoidable eye of the police.

The final "Internationale" is sung as the casket is placed in the mausoleum. This time it's a calmer hymn, one that has the sound of farewell or until we meet again.

Now they had to consider how to leave the cemetery, which could present a trap. The rumor was that "Outside they're picking up people," and the advice was "Go out the back way, on the side of Recoleta Street, quickly, without stopping at the door." The foreign correspondents said they would go out first, to see if anyone was being arrested. For the first time since the coup two weeks before, small protection teams quickly came forth to act as security guards for the individuals most sought after.

In the rotunda outside the cemetery, there were cars full of soldiers, pointing their machine guns and observing the crowd's departure, but they didn't make a move.

That funeral was the first demonstration to take place in Chile against those who struck down the government on 11 September 1973. One more virtue of the poet—he went on fighting even after he had died.

190. *It So Happens I Will Live On*

Neruda didn't remain long in the Ditborn family mausoleum. There were threats and pressures from the regime, and with him was repeated the story he had recounted in "The Cup of Blood" about having to move his father to another burial place in Temuco's cemetery. This time they had to remove the son's coffin, where mushrooms were beginning to creep in, though it didn't pour forth the liters of rainwater that fell from his father's coffin (if not from his corpse) when his final resting place was changed. Matilde and a few friends took care of this transfer, whereby Neruda went to his rest in a modest niche hollowed into the wall of those who had died that September. When all is said and done, it was appropriate for him to be there with his companions, both known by name and anonymous, all fallen in the same month and for the same cause.

The junta promulgated a resolution declaring Isla Negra a danger to national security, and decreed its confiscation. In the face of protests from 100 countries throughout the world and some from within Chile, a sentence was added, declaring that the property would pass into the government's hands, but for as long as Matilde Urrutia should live, she could retain her rights as usufructuary. No mention was made of complying with the wish of the poet to be buried at Isla Negra, as he had expressed in several bequests disposing of his books.

Matilde Urrutia took into her hands the Nerudian banner, as she determined to live her life according to one supreme law: to be faithful to the spirit of that man, to imagine in each situation what he would have done if he were alive, and to participate to the fullest in the causes that had been her husband's. She has done so with great courage and with keen intelligence. In Chile she is the symbol of a feeling shared by millions, because in the end, Neruda isn't just Neruda. He is all that for which he resolutely fought until the last day of his existence.

Matilde, the aunt of some disappeared ones, stands in line at the iron gates of the National Congress, along with others who are looking for family members and asking their whereabouts. After being detained for hours in depressing police stations and in spite of her failing health, she is present at all the ceremonies which take place, she works in the Mapocho Cultural Center, and she sponsors the creation of the Popular Democratic Movement.

She has invitations from many parts of the world, but there are two sacrosanct dates when she prefers not to be out of the country: 12 July and 23 September, anniversaries of Pablo's birth and death.

Caravans of young people and the not-so-young appear at Isla Negra. On the poet's birthdays, the wooden fences along the street and the road are covered with inscriptions which convey messages and greetings and observations for the poet. Isla Negra becomes a site of constant pilgrimages.

The General Cemetery is filled with people and carnations on every 23 September, and with policemen who charge with loaded weapons trying to disperse the crowds. Matilde is always there, acting as a link with the poet's eternal vitality.

Theaters are consistently denied for memorial ceremonies. Nonetheless, on 22 October 1983, with the National Protest Meetings having staked out a great step forward in the struggle for freedom and democracy, there was a three-part homage to Neruda in the Caupolicán Theater to commemorate the tenth anniversary of his death, under the title "Chile Salutes Her Poet." All of the nation's cultural figures participated, as well as the Chilean people. Massive expressions of support from abroad came from Swedish Cultural Minister Bengt Goeransson, and from Claudio Arrau, Rafael Alberti, Gabriel García Márquez, Ernesto Sábato, Alberto Moravia, Mario Benedetti, Juliette Greco, Bernardo Bertolucci, Federico

Fellini, Renzo Rossellini, Ettore Scola, Gian María Volonté, Mónica Vitti, Vittorio Gassman, Claudia Cardinale, Hortensia de Allende, José Venturelli, Gustavo Becerra, Harald Edelstam, Mikis Theodorakis, Melina Mercouri, Paco Ibáñez, Pierre Galand, Roberto Matta, Miguel Orozco.

Collaborators included the Chilean Human Rights Commission, the Chilean Writers Society, the Chilean Cultural Coordinator. The acclaim was magnified when the eightieth anniversary of the poet's birth was mentioned in that same ceremony.

We joined with Matilde when she went back to Capri, where the sub rosa *Captain's Verses* had been born. I heard her speak in Naples at the commemoration of Neruda's seventy-fifth birthday, where she had been invited by the mayor, Maurizio Valenzi. Matilde evoked those happy days, when he had just begun to write *Grapes and Wind* and the first Ode, "The Invisible Man," which is recited now by all Chilean poets, understandably so, as she says.

We saw her again in a meeting of exiled writers in Frankfurt-am-Main, and from there we took the plane together for Stockholm, where the tenth anniversary of Neruda's Nobel Prize for Literature was being commemorated in the Dramat Teatr. In that workplace of Ibsen and Ingmar Bergman, Matilde moved the audience with her personal reminiscences about those days so long ago, so lovely, and so different from the tragedy that one year later would close in on the poet and all his people. I was called on to say some well-deserved words about that woman who was keeping the banner with Neruda's fish symbol waving, even in the dark of night.

In 1983, in the UNESCO theater, this foremost cultural organization paid tribute to the character and the poetry of Pablo Neruda. The universal mime, Marcel Marceau, who by principle and profession never uses speech in his performances, broke his silence that night to say some words that moved the UNESCO representative to whisper in my ear, "This is a world event. Marcel Marceau has never spoken from a stage." The mime said only a few words: "Several years ago, I performed in Chile in the presence of Neruda. Now I do so in front of his widow. I wish to present a work which, at this time, has a certain significance for the country of Neruda and Matilde, 'The Cage.'" In that performance, without opening his mouth, he said everything that an imprisoned man must do to escape his incarceration.

Matilde was spotlighted on the stage, inside a darkened theater. She recounted new things that were happening in Chile and talked of how Neruda and poetry were shining weapons in the hands of ever-greater multitudes. Then a giant of a man, who was seated at our side, slowly drew his tall body to its full height and climbed the steps that led to the stage, to talk about "that smiling warrior." It was the poet's friend who had asked me during a visit to "La Manquel" in Normandy, "How is Pablo's health?" I hadn't asked the six-foot writer with the face of a good-natured child how was his own health. After my turn at saying a few words, I returned to my seat and later, with a fond embrace, I said good-bye to the gangling man with blue eyes and taut skin, not knowing then that it would be the last time I would see the splendid and generous Julio Cortázar.

The next day, French President and Madame Mitterand receive Matilde in the Elysée Palace. They ask her to bring along four friends, and since she includes me on the list, I have the chance to see our hosts' extraordinary interest as they listen to how one poet lives on, and then hear what is happening in Chile, the good and the bad, and how the resistance is growing.

Matilde returns to Chile, where she faithfully carries out her task of keeping Neruda's legacy alive, translating it into new reality with every passing day.

191. Postscript of 12 July 1984

Hernán Loyola dedicated his long article on "Pablo Neruda, the Founding Space" [91] to the memory of Laura Reyes, the sister who had preserved from his childhood the poet's school notebooks, and who always had been with him, from the rainy province to his final second, when he said, "I'm going, I'm going." She didn't survive him by much, having lost her reason for being.

The one who long outlives him is Delia del Carril. When Neruda's eightieth birthday was commemorated, she turned 100. She continued to move about the Los Guindos house in her wheelchair, among her paintings of gigantic disproportionate horses, between wanderings and gaps in her memory, submerged in the realm of arteriosclerotic haziness and a senility which doesn't preclude lucid periods and happy moments when she thinks that Pablo is alive and at her side. In some ways, she may be right.[n]

As for me, with that Nerudian overcoat I have now confronted sixteen successive versions of the harsh drawn-out Russian winter. The long *dublionka,* lined in Patagonian lambskin, goes on being of service, rejecting retirement in spite of its age. Like the man who gave it to me as his farewell, it refuses to become a museum piece.

Neruda will continue to live as long as his poetry is alive. But to judge by what is known, by all the odyssey and trajectory described here, it is no exaggeration to conclude that he didn't need to "confess to having lived," because that was a very well-known secret.

192. Six Months Later

Books have their own destiny and sometimes their own adventures. In spite of the prohibition against this book's entering Chile, it nonetheless had to make its own Ulyssean journey and return to Santiago, because it had an appointment with a dying woman.

As soon as the first edition came out, in November 1984, I sent off three copies from Madrid for Matilde Urrutia. They were supposed to be smuggled in to her, through personal, secret and separate messengers, in a race against death, for I knew she was incurably ill.

In this regard, an obscure law of the bonds of love comes into play. Just as with Pablo, cancer was rapidly eating away at Matilde. I wanted to hopefully give her a last bit of happiness with this book about the poet, a book which also belonged profoundly to her.

Every day that passed without receiving news of Matilde, who was declining more than 9,000 miles away, I tried to find out about her condition and wondered if those forbidden volumes had reached their destination. And if so, the next question was whether her very advanced illness would permit her to read the book or at least glance through it.

I received the news of her death the same day it happened, through a telephone call relayed through a European capital city. With her departure, another circle of Nerudian lives comes to a close.

A week earlier, Matilde had sent a call to the actress and ex-ambassador to Vietnam, María Maluenda, and to her friend Quena Horwitz. Quena and her husband had accompanied her when she was admitted to Paris's Cochin Hospital. Now she was nothing but eyes, the rest of her having been reduced to skin and bones. What did she want to tell them? She went straight to the point. She wanted to die like Pablo and have a simple funeral. She emphasized the word "we."

María tried to change the subject, and asked her if she knew the book *Neruda*. Determined to talk about anything but death, she told Matilde she had read it in an incomplete copy that had some blank pages. (It belonged to my son Claudio, who on a sunny morning in early winter had traveled with me and the publishers in a little car from Madrid to the town of Fuenlabrada where the printshop is located. When we arrived, the presses were turning out the book while two craftsmen in coveralls pored over the precise shading for the mixture of colors on the cover. In the rush of the moment, an incomplete copy was put together, without gloss on the cover and with the glue still fresh, because Claudio didn't want to leave Spain that afternoon without taking the book with him. In Chile, that copy reached the hands of María Maluenda and Roberto Parada, who walk through its pages as if it were their home.)

Matilde answered with a nod of her head. "I have a complete copy here." She loaned it to María as a password, saying, "Come see me again. And use this book as a passkey. Show it to them downstairs and they'll know you can come in without asking."

A few nights later, Matilde's young secretary, the poet Gustavo Becerra, went in great distress to the house of María and Roberto. "She's dying," he murmured. Quena Horwitz proposed going to "La Chascona" immediately, for the curfew would soon begin.

"Let's wait for morning," said María. When they got there, they didn't need to show the book as a passkey. Matilde was already gone. She had died at daybreak. Her sister Angela was there, and a niece, and the household staff. María telephoned Radio Chilena, which was grateful for the exclusive. It was ten in the morning.

Three days later, a mutual friend called me from Paris. He had seen Matilde on her last Wednesday, and she had told him that she had received the three copies of the book in separate deliveries. I think it was the last book she read. Then she had added, "I would have told Valentín many more things . . ." Nonetheless, she didn't carry her secrets to the grave, for in her dying days she found the strength born of desperation to write her memoirs, which above all else tell the personal story of a great love.

Those memoirs, *Mi vida junto a Pablo Neruda* (My Life with Pablo Neruda), which were published by Seix Barral in November 1986, begin at the end, with the coup of September 1973 and the poet's death and funeral, utilized later as the literary point of departure and contextual frame for José Donoso's novel *La desesperanza* (Despair). In the memoirs, there is Matilde's lonely anguished return to Isla Negra, and from there the time machine takes her back to their first encounters, to their life stories, the cities of their love, their secret return trips, her days as a woman alone, their world travels and their homecomings at Isla Negra. In her 250 pages, she tells some of what is known and much of what is not known about their relationship. But it also returns to post mortem responsibilities, when she assumes command in her own right, in the chapter on the "kidnapped and disappeared" victims of the dictatorship, including one of her own nephews. She still carries Pablo within, but what was Pablo really like? "Pablo was not at all secretive, . . ." Matilde's explanation begins, and it ends with the words, "That day of 11 September 1973 began peacefully . . ." That day that hastened the arrival of death for him, for her, for so many . . .

She received from the poet one nickname that predominated over all others—Patoja, despite the fact that she was an appropriately sized human and not the large clumsy duck-waddler suggested by the name, and she was also refined and with no sign of crooked legs. Once Neruda wrote these lines for his Patoja: "Two happy lovers form one loaf, / one moon drop on the grass, / they leave behind two shadows joined in one, / a single empty sun in one bed."

And so, on Saturday the fifth of January in 1985, at three in the morning in "La Chascona," the poet's "little horse of black clay" broke apart, his "evening bird" flew away down a one-way street, his "penny bank full of tears" shattered and spread weeping over the world. And she went to her final sleep in a niche close to his, in number 44 of the Mexico Patio of Santiago's General Cemetery. His beloved Matilde Patoja took leave of us all, except for him, perhaps. Hadn't Neruda written that "two happy lovers have no end nor death, . . . they have the eternity of nature."

1987

Notes

Author's Note: Due to the fact that this book has been written for a very general audience, the author has chosen to specify the source of quotations only when it seemed indispensable.

Translator's notes are indicated in the text with superscripted lowercase letters.

1. *El río invisible* (Barcelona: Seix Barral Editores, 1980), 91.

2. *El Siglo,* Santiago, 3 December 1967.

a. The pun of the Spanish expression, "*dos estaciones,*" is lost, since unlike the Spanish language, which uses the same word for the seasons of the year and for the railroad station, English offers no such word play.

3. *Obras completas,* 3 vols. (Buenos Aires: Editorial Losada, 1957), II: "Memorial de Isla Negra." [Subsequent references to these volumes will be indicated as *OO.CC.*]

4. *OO.CC.,* II: "Memorial de Isla Negra."

5. *Aurora,* Santiago, Segunda Epoca, 3–4 (July–December 1964).

6. *El río invisible.*

b. Neruda in *Confieso que he vivido* recounts the earlier meeting between this strange man and the then healthy Rojas Giménez. Apparently, the stranger found the youth fascinating enough to add to the list of interesting people he had met in his life, to whom he paid homage by jumping over them after they had died—his only hobby, he said. The idea pleased Rojas Giménez, and he gave his permission for such a leap. Neruda, *Confieso que he vivido: Memorias* (Barcelona: Editorial Seix Barral, 1983), 59–60.

c. The reference is to a tyrannical schoolmaster in the seventeenth-century Spanish picaresque novel *El Buscón,* by Francisco de Quevedo.

7. *Ercilla,* Santiago, 2 February 1954.

8. *El río invisible.*

9. *Ercilla,* Santiago, 2 February 1954.

10. Ibid.

11. *Para nacer he nacido* (Barcelona: Seix Barral Editores, 1978), 65. Subsequent author's notes will refer to this edition.

d. The book referred to, *Cartas de amor de Pablo Neruda,* was also published in 1975 in Argentina, by Editorial Tucumán, Buenos Aires.

e. Thirty-four letters from the collection were published by the Banco Exterior de España in 1983, in a deluxe, boxed edition of 3,000 copies, which includes the faithful reproduction of Neruda's manuscripts, down to the color of ink and quality and shape of the paper on which they were written. The edition was not sold commercially, but was made available to scholars and collectors.

f. The Banco Exterior's edition refers specifically to III letters to Albertina plus three to her husband, Angel Cruchaga.

12. *OO.CC.,* II: 1116.

13. *Cartas de amor de Pablo Neruda,* ed. Sergio Fernández Larraín (Madrid: Ediciones Rodas, 1974).

g. Presumably from the village of Roma, in the region of San Fernando, province of Colchagua.

h. Raúl Silva Castro in *Panorama literario de Chile* (Santiago: Editorial Universitaria, 1961), 105, says he was imprisoned for a crime he didn't commit. He was born in 1900 and died in Argentina in 1929.

14. *El Siglo,* Santiago, 11 July 1954.

i. Actually, he was married on 6 December 1930, as he would more accurately inform his father.

15. *Cartas a Laura,* compiled and annotated by Hugo Montes (Madrid: Ediciones Cultura Hispánica del Centro Iberoamericano de Cooperación, 1978). Subsequent quotations are taken from this edition.

16. *OO.CC.,* II: "Memorial de Isla Negra," 543.

17. Ibid., 545.

18. Margarita Aguirre, "Cartas a Eandi," in *Genio y figura de Pablo Neruda* (Buenos Aires: Editorial Universitaria de Buenos Aires, 1964), 110–118.

19. *La Nación,* Santiago, 7 February 1929,"Oriente y Oriente."

20. *Para nacer he nacido,* 227–229.

21. *OO.CC.,* I: "Residencia en la tierra," 180.

22. Ibid., 223.

23. *El libro de las preguntas* (Buenos Aires: Editorial Losada, 1974).

24. Pablo Neruda, *Selección* (Santiago: Editorial Nascimento, 1943), 305–306.

25. "Pablo Neruda," *El Sol,* Madrid, 2 January 1936.

26. Statements by Neruda to Alfredo Cardona Peña.

27. *Pablo Neruda,* ed. E. Rodríguez Monegal and Enrico Mario Santí (Madrid: Editorial Taurus, 1986), 176–177.

28. *OO.CC.,* III: 640–641.

29. *OO.CC.,* II: "Federico García Lorca," 1048.

30. *OO.CC.,* I: "Vals," 255.

31. Ibid., "Las furias y las penas," 264.

32. Anne Chisholm, *Nancy Cunard* (Paris: Oliver Orban, 1980).

33. *OO.CC.,* III: "Copa de sangre," 651.

34. Ibid.

j. The reference is to Matthew 25: 1–14, which has as its moral the injunction to be prepared for any eventuality.

35. *Para nacer he nacido.*

36. *OO.CC.,* II: 1053.

37. Ibid.

38. Luis Enrique Délano, *Lenin y otros escritos* (Mexico City: Universidad Obrera, 1975).

39. "Discurso," in *Tierra Nueva, Revista de Letras Universitarias,* nos. 9 and 10 (1941).

40. *El Nacional,* Mexico City, 24 August 1940.

41. Ibid., 22 August 1943.

42. *Gaceta de Cuba,* no. 180, Havana 1979.

43. *Excelsior,* Mexico City, 1 June 1943. (Luis Carlos Prestes, often called the "knight of hope," died at 92 in March 1990 and was given a state funeral in Brazil—Translator's Note.)

44. Edmond Cross in *Anales de la Universidad de Chile,* January–December (1971): 178.

45. *Vistazo,* Santiago, 14 July 1952.

46. *El Siglo,* Santiago, 12 July 1964.

47. *OO.CC.,* II: 34.

48. *Enfoque Internacional,* no. 31, July 1969.

49. *Humo de pipa* (Santiago: Editorial del Pacífico, 1955).

50. Chilean Senate, third session, Santiago, 30 May 1945.

51. Ibid.

52. *OO.CC.,* I: 501–502.

53. Ibid., 505.

54. *Para nacer he nacido,* 289.

55. Ibid., 326–327.

56. *OO.CC.,* I: 600–601.

57. *Para nacer he nacido,* 205.

58. *OO.CC.,* I: 603–604.

59. Ibid., 647.

60. *Vida de un agitador* (Mexico: Universidad Autónoma de Sinaloa, 1982), 148.

61. "Un poeta querido por millones de hombres," in *Literatura Soviética*, Moscow, July 1964.

62. Dolores Ibárruri, *Memorias de Pasionaria, 1939 1977* (Barcelona: Editorial Planeta, 1984), 68. (La Pasionaria died in 1989, at the age of 93, in Madrid. She had returned to Spain in 1977 after 38 years in exile—Translator's Note.)

63. *OO.CC.*, I: "Los poetas celestes," 479.

64. *Hoy*, Santiago, November 1979.

65. *Confieso que he vivido*, 6th ed. (Buenos Aires: Editorial Losada, 1978), 289.

66. *Para nacer he nacido*, 109.

67. *OO.CC.*, II, 674.

68. *Ercilla*, Santiago, May 1969: 50.

69. *Zig-Zag*, Santiago, 24 July 1954: 29.

70. A partial inventory of just those in Chile who have written about Neruda, gleaned from nine special issues dedicated to the man and his work by Chilean journals, reveals 125 authors between 1952 and 1984.

71. *OO.CC.*, II: 237.

72. Ibid., 309, 335.

73. Ibid., 1135, 1143.

k. In the sixties, Neruda was harshly criticized by the Cuban intelligentsia, and in 1966 an open letter from Cuban writers accused him of counter-revolutionary activities for having attended the New York meeting of the PEN International Congress. He refers extensively to the letter in Chapter 11 of his *Memoirs*.

74. *Confieso que he vivido*, 438.

75. *OO.CC.*, II: 1089.

76. *Para nacer he nacido*, 219.

77. Ignazio Delogu, "Pablo Neruda en Italia."

78. *OO.CC.*, II: 1116–1117.

79. Ibid., 1120.

80. *Aurora*, Santiago, 3–4, July–December 1964.

81. *Para nacer he nacido*, 180.

82. *OO.CC.*, II: 319.

83. *Enfoque Internacional*, no. 31, July 1969.

84. *El Mercurio*, Santiago, 20 April 1969.

85. *El Siglo*, Santiago, 13 July 1969.

86. *La Segunda*, Santiago, 3 October 1969.

l. General José Sanjurjo, leader of a premature coup against the Spanish Republic in 1932, and senior collaborator in the successful coup of 1936 which brought General Francisco Franco to power as military dictator instead of Sanjurjo, was killed in a plane crash in July 1936.

87. *OO.CC.*, III: 603.

88. *El Siglo*, Santiago, 23 October 1971.

m. Again, the author's pun is lost in English: *hacerse el sueco*, literally "to play the Swede" means "to play dumb."

89. *Panorama.*

90. *Santiago-Moscú-Santiago* (Madrid: Editorial Coirón, 1983), 55.

91. *Araucaria de Chile,* no. 3 (Madrid 1978), 61–82.

n. Delia del Carril died in 1989 in Santiago, at the age of 105. Neruda's early love, Albertina Azócar, died in November of that same year at the age of 86.

Index of Names

Abril, Javier, 372

Aeschylus, 251

Agenaar, María Antonieta (Maruca, Maruja), 75, 148, 154–155, 160, 168, 170, 175, 339

Aguirre, Margarita, 159, 251, 356, 371, 380, 406, 448, 488

Aguirre, Sócrates, 159

Aguirre Cerda, Pedro, 83, 221, 230, 238, 240, 245

Ahrweiler, Alice, 312

Ai Ching, 351

Alarcón, Asterio, 385

Alarcón, Rolando, 416

Alazraki, Jaime, 371

Alba, —— (ambassador), 291

Albert, Tótila, 103

Alberti, Rafael, 92, 136, 159, 163–165, 172–174, 177–178, 181, 183, 186, 188, 197–199, 205, 207 208, 211, 235–236, 241, 306, 353, 357, 400, 438, 480

Aldunate, Roberto, 220

Aldunate Phillips, Arturo, 371

Aldus. See Manutius, Aldus

Aleixandre, Vicente, 178, 181–182, 186, 211, 241, 438

Alessandri Palma, Arturo, 37, 43, 51–52, 210, 230, 237, 271, 315–316

Alicata, Mario, 335

Alicata, Sara, 335

Alighieri, Dante, 11, 251, 352

Allende, Hortensia. See Bussi de Allende, Hortensia

Allende, Salvador, 48, 52, 73, 338, 341, 343, 373, 400, 418, 420, 424–428, 438–439, 447–449, 451, 453–454, 456–457, 462, 466–469, 473, 477

Almagro, Diego de, 19

Almeyda, Clodomiro, 427

"Alone." See Díaz Arrieta, Hernán

Alonso, Amado, 242

Alonso, Dámaso, 186

Altolaguirre, Manuel, 180–181, 207

Alvarez, Graciela (Chela), 470, 474

Alvear, Elvira de, 144, 164

Alviso Escalona, Amalia, 64, 145, 159

Amado, Jorge, 310, 312, 328, 343, 346–347, 370, 438

Amado, Zelia Gattai de, 347, 370

Amarasingan, S. P., 152

Amster, Mauricio, 423

Amunátegui, Gabriel, 220

Amunátegui Solar, Domingo, 315
Ana, Marcos, 387
Andersen, Hans Christian, 251
Andrei, Stefan, 12
Andreiev, Leonidas, 40
Andrews Sisters, 282
Andrić, Ivo, 310, 436
Anguita, Eduardo, 191, 193–194, 218
"Ant." *See* Carril, Delia del
Antúnez, Nemesio, 114
Aparcoa (group), 416
Aparicio, Antonio, 315
Apollinaire, Guillaume, 50, 90, 195, 217, 388
Aracena, Alberto, 25
Aragon, Louis, 174, 177, 206, 211–213, 215–216, 238, 310, 312, 330, 380, 388, 438, 422, 453
Araoz Alfaro, Rodolfo, 251, 346
Araya, Bernardo, 288
Araya, Juan Lenín, 150
Araya, Manuel, 460
Arce, Homero, 54, 104–105, 126, 371, 375, 393, 448, 450, 470
Arellano Marín, Manuel, 236–239
Arenal, Angélica (Siqueiros), 245
Arguijo, Juan, 162
Argensola, Bartolomé and Lupercio, 162
Arrau, Claudio, 166, 327, 417, 480
Arrué, Laura, 104
Artigas, José M., 411
Astorga, Enrique, 11–12
Astudillo, Oscar, 416
Asturias, Miguel Angel, 253, 282, 308, 369, 400–401, 436, 439, 442
Asúnsolo, María, 248, 327
Avila Camacho, Manuel, 247
Axioti, Melpo, 310
Azócar, Lientur, 393
Azócar, Rubén, 42, 54, 77, 81, 84–85, 94, 97, 101–103, 107, 110–112, 119, 220, 393, 410
Azócar Peña, Ambrosio, 85
Azócar Soto, Adelina, 85

Azócar Soto, Albertina Rosa, 64, 75–107, 111, 116–121, 140, 148, 155, 300, 362, 488, 491. *See also* "Marisombra," "Netocha," "Rosaura"
Azócar Soto, Augusto, 85
Azócar Soto, Etelvina, 85
Azócar Soto, Víctor, 85
Azorín, 38

Balladares, Ligeia, 390, 419
Ballas, Adolfo, 416
Balmaceda, José Manuel, 440
Balzac, Honoré de, 353
Bandeira, Manuel, 275
Barberis, Víctor, 51, 104
Barbusse, Henri, 453
Baroja, Pío, 37
Barrault, Jean Louis, 404, 406
Barrios, Eduardo, 107, 339
Barros Luco, Ramón, 418
Basoalto, Beatriz, 9
Basoalto, Buenaventura, 6
Basoalto, Manuel Ijidio, 9, 147
Basoalto, Rosa Neftalí, 3–6, 9, 34
Batori, Madame, 174
Baudelaire, Charles, 29, 50, 212, 352, 411
Baudrillart (Cardinal), 241
Becerra, Gustavo, 481
Beckett, Samuel, 215, 390
Bécquer, Gustavo Adolfo, 353
Beecham, Sir Thomas, 213
Bellet Bastías, Jorge, 297–298, 300–301, 305–306
Bello, Andrés, 122, 276, 345
Bello, Enrique, 435, 470–472
Benavides, Julio, 104
Benedetti, Mario, 480
Benedicto, Antonio, 450
Benítez, Fernando, 248
Bergamín, José, 144, 184, 198, 245, 249
Bergerac, Cyrano de, 62
Bernal, John, 350
Bernardin de Saint-Pierre, Jacques Henri, 28
Bernhardt, Sarah, 344

Berni, Antonio, 310
Bernstein (family), 440
Bertolucci, Bernardo, 480
Bianchi, Vicente, 371
Bianchi Gundián, Víctor, 54, 300–301,
    306
Bingham, Hiram, 258
Blake, William, 198, 411
Bliss, Josie (Maligna), 128, 132, 141–
    142, 151
Blum, Leon, 233
Blume, Isabel, 350
Boldizsar, Iván, 400
Bolívar, Simón, 258, 381, 389
Bombal, Loreto, 64, 160
Bombal, María Luisa, 64, 160
Borges, Jorge Luis, 137, 160
Borges, Leonor de, 160
Borrás, Eduardo, 270
Bowers, Claude, 287
Braguinskaia, Ella, 321, 445
Brampy (servant), 153
Brecht, Bertolt, 453
Broders, Matilde, 406
Brown, Lloyd L., 322
Browning, Elizabeth Barrett, 251
Brum D'Avoglio, Luis, 311
Buddha, 127
Buffalo Bill, 28
Bulnes, Francisco, 444
Bulnes, Lala, 298
Bulnes Cerdá, Raúl, 298, 358, 435, 456
Bunster, Patricio, 406
Burke, Maud Alice, 212
Burkhardt, Charles, 214
Bussi de Allende, Hortensia, 481
Bustamante, Abelardo (Paschin), 54,
    57–58

Cabada, Juan de la, 248–249
Caballero Bonald, José, 425
Cabezón, Isaías, 54
Calvino, Italo, 310
Campanella, Tomás, 423
Campíns, —— (General), 200

Camprubí, Zenobia, 185
Campusano, Julieta, 290
Candia Marverde, Micaela, 14
Candia Marverde, Trinidad
    ("Momother"), 14, 18–19, 21,
    64, 146, 235
Candia Quevedo, Ramón, 122
Cantón, Wilberto, 251
Capdevilla, Arturo, 161
Carabantes, Raúl, 245
Cárcamo (couple), 475
Cárdenas, Lázaro, 246, 310, 322
Cardinale, Claudia, 481
Cardona Peña, Alfredo, 488
Cardoza y Aragón, Luis, 245, 308–310
Cardoza y Aragón, Lya, 309
Carlota (cousin), 99
Carmona, Darío, 239
Carmona, Juan de Dios, 418
Caro, Rodrigo, 162
Carpentier, Alejo, 164
Carranza, Eduardo, 257, 289
Carrasco Vintimilla, Alfonso, 371
Carreño, Mario, 423
Carrera (brothers), 80
Carrera, José Miguel, 411, 440
Carril, Adelina del, 174
Carril, Delia del ("Ant"), 53, 76, 114,
    172–177, 219, 232, 235, 246, 249,
    258, 292–293, 299, 307, 322, 328,
    336, 341, 347–349, 359–363, 364–
    365, 428, 482, 491
Caruso, Enrico, 344, 410
Carvajal, Armando, 281, 404
Casanueva, Carlos, 236
Cassou, Jean, 310
Castillo, María Teresa, 452
Castillo Armas, Carlos, 80
Castillo Velasco, Fernando, 358, 455
Castro, Baltazar, 347
Castro, Fidel, 383
Castro, Oscar, 220
Castro Leal, Antonio, 246
Caupolicán, 15, 44, 440
Cavalcanti, Alberto, 347

Cela, Camilo José, 53
Cerda, Rosario de la. *See* Urrutia,
    Matilde
Cerio, Erwin, 335
Cernuda, Luis, 181, 185
Césaire, Aimé, 310
Chacón y Calvo, José María, 253
Chaliapin, Fedor, 344
Chao I Ming, 351
Chaplin, Charles, 310
Charry Lara, Fernando, 257
Chávez, Filomeno, 280
Chávez, Manuel, 108
Chekhov, Anton, 32, 95, 406
Chisholm, Anne, 489
Cid, Vicente, 25
Cifuentes Sepúlveda, Joaquín, 51, 105–
    107, 109–111, 192
Cochrane, Lord, 411
"Coke." *See* Délano, Jorge
Coleridge, Samuel Taylor, 447
Collados, Sebastián, 376, 452
Coloane, Francisco, 12, 220, 470
Colonna, Victoria, 352
Columbus, Christopher, 463
Colvin, Marta, 360, 380, 456
Companys, Luis, 253
Concha, Jaime, 371
Concha Riffo, Gilberto. *See* Valle,
    Juvencio
Condon, Alfredo, 163
Conrad, Joseph, 48
"Coper, Diego," 91
Corbière, Tristán, 352
Coronado, Rosita, 289
Correa, Ulises, 288, 316
Cortázar, Julio, 422, 445, 482
Corvalán, Lili de, 442
Corvalán, Luis (Lucho), 308, 366, 382,
    398, 416, 440, 442, 449, 453, 478
Cosette (*Les Misérables*), 28
Cot, Pierre, 310, 350
Cotapos, Acario, 198, 220, 282, 385–386
Cotton, Eugénie, 310

Courtade, Pierre, 312
Cross, Edmond, 489
Cruchaga Santa María, Angel, 54, 77–
    79, 81–82, 119–120, 194, 220, 363,
    488
Crusoe, Robinson, 377
Cruz Ocampo, Luis David, 220
Cuevas, Luis Alberto, 312
Cuevas Mackenna, Luis, 361
Cunard, Sir Bache, 212
Cunard, Nancy, 212–216
Cunhal, Alvaro, 330

Dalí, Salvador, 382
Dampierre, Count of, 330
D'Annunzio, Gabriele, 65–66, 446
Dante. *See* Alighieri, Dante
Darío, Rubén, 157, 161–162, 181, 189,
    256, 264, 356, 383, 448
Decroly, —— (professor), 117
Deglané, Bobby, 200
Délano, Jorge ("Coke"), 343
Délano, Luis Enrique, 114, 168, 170,
    211, 244–245, 251, 327, 488
Délano, Poli, 246
Delmira, Doña, 48
Delogu, Ignazio, 390
Depestre, René, 310
D'Halmar, Augusto, 270, 333
Diaghilev, Sergei, 212
Díaz Arrieta, Hernán ("Alone"), 193–
    194, 358, 371, 444–445, 472–473
Díaz Casanueva, Humberto, 220
Díaz del Castillo, Bernal, 251
Dickens, Charles, 28
Diderot, Denis, 28
Diego, Gerardo, 165–166, 178, 181, 186
Díez Pastor, Fulgencio, 199
Dimitrov, Georgi, 453
Dimov, Dimiter, 357
Ditborn, Adriana, 472
Ditborn, Carlos, 472
Ditborn (family), 479
Donoso, José, 442, 484

D'Orléans, Louis, 330, 352
Dostoievski, Fëdor, 32, 95, 251, 277, 317, 422
Dracula, Count, 403
Drda, Jan, 357
Dreyfus (case), 291
Du Bois, W. E. B., 310
Duclos, Jacques, 442
Duhalde, Alfredo, 279
Dumas, Alexandre, 444
Dussuel, Francisco, 362

Eandi, Héctor, 129–130, 132–137, 144–145, 159, 163–164, 488
Echeverría, Luis, 247, 469
Eckermann, Johann Peter, 408
Edelstam, Harald, 472, 481
Edward VIII, 213
Edwards Bello, Joaquín, 154, 270
Edwards MacClure, Agustín, 211
Egaña, Juan, 80
Ehrenburg, Ilya, 216, 247, 310–312, 316, 319, 329, 346, 350–351, 388, 438, 464
Einaudi, Giulio, 310
Einstein, Albert, 253
Eliot, T. S., 138, 159, 190, 212
Elizabeth Petrovna, Empress, 352
Elliot, Jorge, 397
Eluard, Dominique, 330
Eluard, Paul, 310, 312, 321–322, 330, 352, 453
Emi-Siao, 310, 351
Encina, Francisco Antonio, 339
Endicott, J. G., 322
Engels, Friedrich, 195
Epstein, Sir Jacob, 212
Ercilla, Alonso de, 16, 251, 320, 388, 454
Errázuriz, Ladislao, 43–44
Escámez, Julio, 376, 423
Escanilla, 312
Escobar, Zoilo, 57
Espinel, Vicente, 16
Espinosa, —— (Colonel), 202
Espinosa, Benigno, 308

Fadieiev, Alexander, 318
Falcón, Lola, 216
Falla, Manuel de, 166, 201
Fargue, Yves, 310
Farías, Eliana (Teitelboim), 403, 441–442, 449
Favio, Leonardo, 406
Fedeiev, Constantin, 310
Felipe, León, 176, 181, 245, 249
Félix, María, 344
Felizardo de Prestes, Leocadia, 254
Fellini, Federico, 65, 481
Fernández Larraín, Sergio, 79–86
Fernández Montesinos, Manuel (Doctor), 201
Fernández Ordóñez, Francisco, 84
Fernando VII, 80
Figueroa, Aída, 470–475
Filippi, Emilio, 415
Flaubert, Gustave, 352
Florescu, Mijail, 12
Fokine, Michel, 212
Fonseca, Ricardo, 285, 297, 328
Fort, Paul, 29
Fortunny, José Manuel, 310
France, Anatole, 453
Franceschi (Monsignor), 362
Francke, Guillermo, 230
Franco, Francisco, 83, 178, 183, 199, 202, 209, 217, 219, 419, 426, 490
Frank, Waldo, 216
Franulic, Lenka, 341–343
Frei, Eduardo, 339, 418, 426
Fučik, Julius, 329
Fuentes, Carlos, 389, 422
Furnandjiev, Nicolás, 357

Gagarin, Yuri, 453
Galand, Pierre, 481
Gandhi, Mahatma, 28, 149
Gandulfo, Juan, 42–44
Garaudy, Roger, 322
García, Alejandro, 409
García Lorca, Federico, 44, 135, 160–

164, 166, 169, 178–181, 183, 186,
    193, 198–203, 206–207, 211, 219,
    232, 241, 264, 353, 376, 385, 400,
    425, 436, 448, 466
García Lorca, Francisco, 201
García Márquez, Gabriel, 422, 429,
    458, 480
García Márquez, Mercedes, 458
García Monje, Joaquín, 322, 343
Garcilaso de la Vega, El Inca, 261
Garfias, Pedro, 244
Garro, Elena, 248
Gascar, Alice, 380
Gascar, Pierre, 380
Gassman, Vittorio, 481
Gatica Martínez, Tomás, 154
Gauguin, Paul, 377
Gervasi, Vicente, 394
Giordano, Jaime, 371
Girondo, Oliverio, 160, 356
Goded, Angel, 213
Godet, —— (General), 199
Godoy Alcayaga, Lucila. See Mistral,
    Gabriela
Godoy Urrutia, César, 314, 327
Goeransson, Bengt, 480
Goethe, Johann Wolfgang von, 251,
    263, 331–332
Gogol, Nikolai, 317
Gómez, Fina, 379
Gómez, Laureano, 257
Gómez de la Serna, Elena, 377
Gómez de la Serna, Ramón, 161, 377
Gómez Millas, Juan, 353, 470
Gómez Rojas, José Domingo, 42, 44–
    45
Góngora, Luis de, 196, 352
González, Galo, 286, 297, 372
González, Pedro Antonio, 358
González, Sergio, 456
González Castillo, —— (court minis-
    ter), 293
González Martínez, Enrique, 245, 250,
    322
González Rojas, Eugenio, 42, 339

González Tuñón, Raúl, 160, 182, 211,
    219, 357
González Vera, José Santos, 26, 31, 41–
    42, 44
González Videla, Gabriel, 26, 54, 236,
    281–284, 286–291, 293, 305, 311,
    314, 316, 322, 327, 339, 405
González von Marées, Jorge, 219
Gorkin, Julián, 372
Gorky, Maxim, 28, 47, 277, 348, 453
Goya, Francisco de, 162
Gramsci, Antonio, 453
Grass, Günter, 335
Grave, Jean, 31
Greco, El, 320
Greco, Juliette, 480
Greene, Graham, 137, 434
Greiff, León de, 257
Grez, Alfonso, 237
Gris, Juan, 174
Grushko, Pavel, 407
Guarello, Angel, 284
Guerrero, Juan, 181
Guerrero, Xavier, 245
Guevara, Ernesto "Ché," 253, 421
Guido, Beatriz, 406
Guillén, Jorge, 178, 181, 186
Guillén, Nicolás, 211, 216, 249, 310, 312,
    322, 346–347
Güiraldes, Ricardo, 174
Gullón, Ricardo, 184
Gustaf Adolph VI, 439, 472
Gutiérrez, Alejandro, 280
Gutiérrez, Joaquín, 308, 347
Guttuso, Renato, 310, 312, 321, 334, 446
Guzmán, Ernesto, 358
Guzmán, Juan de, 16
Guzmán, Mónica, 82
Guzmán Araujo, Roberto, 247
Guzmán Cruchaga, Juan, 257

Hamel, Teresa, 402, 470
Hauser, Blanca, 121, 174, 281–282, 369,
    404
Heine, Heinrich, 252

Helfmann, Federico, 194
Helms, Richard, 451
Hemingway, Ernest, 216
Henestroza, Andrés, 251
Henestroza, Cibeles, 251
Henríquez, Camilo, 80
Heredia Spínola (Marquis), 205
Hermlin, Stephan, 411
Hernández, Miguel, 178, 181–184, 188–
     189, 241, 264, 327, 425
Herrera, Ariosto, 83
Herrera Petere, José, 164, 244, 338
Herrera y Reissig, Julio, 186, 249
Hidalgo de Cisneros, Ignacio, 245
Hierow, Karl Ragnar, 436
Hikmet, Nazim, 330–331, 392, 411, 464
Hinojosa, Alvaro, 113–115, 126
Hitler, Adolf, 80, 200, 205, 233, 244,
     246, 252, 273, 287, 291, 319, 351,
     455, 463
Ho Chi Minh, 453
Howard, Brian, 211
Huenumán, Rosendo, 459
Huerta, Efraín, 192
Hughes, Langston, 211, 310
Hugo, Victor, 122, 352, 412
Huidobro, Vicente, 22, 58, 77, 82, 109,
     186, 190–196, 216–219, 397, 413
Humboldt, Alexander, 258
Huxley, Aldous, 212, 412
Huxley, Julian, 412

Ibáñez, Bernardo, 279
Ibáñez, Paco, 481
Ibáñez del Campo, Carlos, 148, 152,
     339, 343, 372
Ibar, Eusebio, 51
Ibarbourou, Juana de, 94
Ibárruri, Dolores (La Pasionaria), 319,
     490
Ibsen, Henrik, 406
Iñigo Madrigal, Luis, 371
Insunza, Ramiro, 358
"Irene," 91
Iturriaga, José, 251

Jabeleanu, Eugene, 321
Jacob, Max, 195
James, Francis, 352
Jara, Alvaro, 380
Jara, Aníbal, 36
Jara, Heriberto, 245
Jara, Marta, 295
Jara, Max, 358
Jara, Víctor, 406, 416, 473, 476–477
Jiménez, Juan Ramón, 162, 178, 184–
     190, 436
Joie, Ivette, 366
Joliot-Curie, Frédéric, 310, 453
Joliot-Curie, Irène, 310
Jorge, Faustino, 291
Jorquera, Carlos, 415
Joyce, James, 55, 144
Juliet, Raúl, 288

Kafka, Franz, 49
Kahn, Albert, 310
Kalinin, Mikhail Ivanovich, 315
Karvellis, Ugné, 445
Kelin, Fiodor, 316
Keller, Kerry, 406
Khrushchev, Nikita, 214
Kid Azteca, 245
Kindermann, Francisco, 15
Kirsanov, Simion (Sioma), 318, 464
Kisch, Erwin, 49
Kissinger, Henry, 451
Kostra, Jan, 357
Kozintsev, Grigorii, 198
Krieger, Edino, 347
Krishnamurti, 131
Kuchvalek, Jaroslav, 357
Kuo Mo-Jo, 310
Kutieishikova, Viera, 317–318
Kuzmichev, Vladimir, 318, 320

Labarca, Guillermo, 220
Labarca, Santiago, 42, 44
Labaste, Guillermo, 307
Labiche, Georges, 406

Laferte, Elías, 265–266, 270, 279, 387, 439

Lago, Tomás, 48, 53–55, 57, 59, 82, 108, 192, 362

Lam, Wilfredo, 382

Lamabadusuriya, Alex S., 150

Lange, Norah, 160, 356

Lanzarotti, Julio, 415

Larraín (Marquis), 80

Larraín, Fernández, 80

Larraín, Sergio, 220

Larrea, Juan, 165, 186, 221

Lastra, Fernando de la, 81

Latorre, Mariano, 270, 372, 387

Lautaro, ——, 15, 440

Lautréaumont, Count of, 191, 195, 309

Lawner, Miguel, 456

Lawrence, D. H., 138, 212

Leahy, William (Admiral), 284, 287

Leconte de Lisle, Charles Marie, 352

Léger, Fernand, 173, 453

Leighton, Bernardo, 220

Leiva, María Luisa, 7

Lenin, V. I., 317, 344, 374, 388, 453

León, Estanislao, 7

León, Fray Luis de, 181

León, María Teresa, 165, 199, 235, 277, 357

León Bettiens, Teresa. See "Marisol"; "Terusa"

León Muller, Rosa, 74

Lessa, Orígenes, 347

Letelier, Marco Aurelio, 54

Levi, Carlo, 334

Levine, Flavián, 456, 473

Lillo, Baldomero, 84, 271

Lipschütz, Alejandro, 393, 478

Lipschütz, Margarita de (Rita), 478

Lira, Armando, 54

Lisboa, Calderón, 280

Lombardo Toledano, Vicente, 322

Lope de Vega Carpio, Félix, 15, 196, 352

López, Alfonso, 257

López, Manuel Antonio, 280

López, Rigoberto, 383

López Portillo, José, 247

López Velarde, Ramón, 245

Lorca. See García Lorca, Federico

Lorenzo, Arturo, 377

Losada, Gonzalo, 325, 362, 384, 391, 406, 426, 429, 441, 449

Losada, Gonzalo, Jr., 460–461

Loti, Pierre, 125

Louis XIV, 352

Loveluck, Juan, 371

Lowenfels, Walter, 215, 411

Loyola, Hernán, 371, 395, 442, 475, 482

Loyola, Margot, 347, 357

Lugones, Leopoldo, 135, 190

Lundkvist, Artur, 437, 442

Lurçat, Jean, 453

Machado, Antonio, 162, 178, 190, 217, 233–234, 264

Machado, Gerardo, 248

Magallanes Moure, Manuel, 84

Maiakovski, Vladimir, 317, 349, 453, 464

"Mairena, Juan de," 234

Malatesta, Paolo, 66

Maligna. See Bliss, Josie

Mallarmé, Stéphane, 50, 90, 93, 217, 388

Malraux, André, 145, 217, 388

Maluenda, María, 13, 123, 357, 423, 483–484

Mancisidor, José, 245

Mann, Thomas, 322, 369

Manns, Patricio, 416, 473

Manrique, Jorge, 233

Mansilla, Luis Alberto, 478

Mantaras, Alberto and Olga, 338, 410

Manutius, Aldus (printer), 352

Maples Arce, Manuel, 249

Marceau, Marcel, 481

Marcenac, Jean, 312, 379, 442

Marcó del Pont, Casimiro, 316

Marianetti, Benito, 306

Mariátegui, José Carlos, 453

Marín, Gladys, 459

Marinech, 124, 275

Marinello, Juan, 216, 310, 322

Marinetti, Filippo Tommaso, 191, 446

"Marisol," 67–68, 76–77, 86, 100, 140.
See also "Terusa"
"Marisombra," 67, 75–79, 86. See also
Azócar Soto, Albertina Rosa;
"Netocha"; "Rosaura"
Marshall, George C. (General), 350
Martí, José, 131, 264, 384
Martín, Carlos, 257
Martínez, José Luis, 255
Martínez Corbalá, ——— (Ambassador),
469
Martino, César, 327
Martinov, ———, 318
Martner, Carlos, 358, 456
Martner, Mari, 375, 456
Marx, Karl, 358, 456
Masson, Carlos, 14
Masson, Orlando, 22, 27–28, 36, 38, 52
Masson Candia (family), 17–18
Matisse, Henri, 453
Matta, Germana de, 422
Matta, Roberto Sebastián, 382, 422, 481
Matta Figueroa, Enrique, 148
Matus, Carlos, 456
Medici, Lorenzo de', 352
Melfi, Domingo, 36
Mella, Julio Antonio, 248
Mellado, Raúl, 395
Melo, Thiago de, 402, 411
Melville, Herman, 414, 465
Mena Alvarado, Nalvia Rosa, 307
Mendelssohn, Moses, 253
Méndez Bravo, Alberto, 36
Menéndez Pidal, Ramón, 372
Mercouri, Melina, 481
Meredith, George, 212
Mery, Juan Luis, 195
Meza Fuentes, Roberto, 42, 49
Michelet, Jules, 215
Mickiewicz, Adam, 411
Mikhailkov, ———, 318
Millaray (group), 416
Milocz, ———, 251
Miró, Emilio, 371
Miró, Joan, 382, 392
Mirto, Fernando, 107

Mistral, Frédéric, 66
Mistral, Gabriela (Lucila Godoy Alca-
yaga), 29–32, 46, 66, 84, 107,
110, 134–135, 166–168, 173, 190,
193, 227–229, 234, 243, 277–278,
315, 318, 322, 327–328, 337, 339,
343, 356, 379, 399–400, 409, 439
Mitterand, François, 482
Mitterand, Michele, 482
Modesto, ———, 387
Modotti, Tina, 248
Molina, Enrique, 117
Molina, Tirso de, 198
Molina Ventura, Eduardo, 191
Mon, Amparo, 160, 219
Monestier, Renato, 55
Monje (railroader), 21, 32
Montagnana, Mario, 248
Montale, Eugenio, 190
Monte Cristo, Count of, 383
Montes, Hugo, 488
Mora, ——— (OAS secretary), 367
Mora, Constancia de la, 245
Mora, Marcial, 339
Mora, Matilde, 10
Mora y Araujo, Blanca de, 442
Moraes, Vinicius de, 343
Morales, Félix, 313
Morales Hermosilla, Natalia, 7
Morante, Elsa, 334
Moravia, Alberto, 334, 480
Moreno Villa, José, 245
Morgan, Henry (pirate), 376, 403
Morla, Bebé, 198
Morla Lynch, Carlos, 163, 166, 173, 198,
201
Mujaes, Jaled, 251
Muñoz, Diego, 25–26, 55, 60, 192
Muñoz Meany, Enrique, 333
Muñoz Rojas, José A., 181
Murga, Romeo, 51, 104
Murieta, Joaquín, 404–407
Mussolini, Benito, 65, 199–200, 205

Napoleon I, 389
Naranjo, Vicente, 158

Nascimento, Carlos George, 107, 159, 429
Nascimento, Elena, 475
Negri, Pola, 95
Negrín, Juan, 235
Nehru, Jawaharlal, 149
Nenni, Pietro, 310
Neruda, Jan, 49–50
Neruda, Malva Marina, 169–172
Neruda, Matilde. See Urrutia, Matilde
"Netocha," 95–98, 119. See also Azócar Soto, Albertina Rosa; "Marisombra"; "Rosaura"
Neves, Eugenia, 371
Niemeyer, Oscar, 336, 343, 347
Nixon, Richard, 451, 453–455
Novoa (journalist), 57
Núñez, Guillermo, 406
Núñez de Balboa, Vasco, 256
Núñez Morgado, Aurelio, 210

Obregón Santacilia, Carlos, 327
Ocampo, Salvador, 322
Ocampo, Victoria, 172–173, 282
O'Higgins, Bernardo, 80, 316, 440
Ojeda (hairdresser), 112
Olivares, Augusto, 415, 440
Oliver, María Rosa, 357
Onetti, Juan Carlos, 422
Opazo, Tomasa, 6
Orélie-Antoine I, 15
Orozco, José Clemente, 29, 322, 325, 327
Orozco, Miguel, 481
Ortega, Abraham, 234, 240
Ortega, José, 172
Ortega, José Manuel, 9
Ortega, Sergio, 406
Ortega Masson, Rudecindo, 37, 59, 123, 147
Ortega y Gasset, José, 161, 164
Orthous, Pedro, 406
Ortiz de Zárate, Julio, 54
Orwell, George, 213
Ospovat, Lev, 317, 319
Osses, Mario, 372
Ossorio, Fernando, 37

Otero Silva, Miguel, 13, 310, 322, 380, 422, 452
Ovid, 478
Oyarzún, Aliro, 56, 108
Oyarzún Garcés, Orlando, 47, 48, 54, 56–59

Pacheco, Máximo, 473
Palacios, Enrique, 201
Palma, Waldo, 365
Palme, Olaf, 436
Panero, Juan, 181
Panero, Leopoldo, 181, 372
Parada, Encarnación, 7
Parada, Roberto, 355, 357, 423, 473, 484
Parodi, María, 64
Parra, Angel, 423
Parra, Nicanor, 382, 387
Parra, Ramona, 280, 457
Parra, Violeta, 357, 466
Parra del Riego, Juan, 186
Paschin. See Bustamante, Abelardo
Paseyro, Ricardo, 372, 390
Pasionaria, La. See Ibárruri, Dolores
"Patoja." See Urrutia, Matilde
Pauling, Linus, 322
Pavez, Héctor, 416
Pavlova, Anna, 344
Paz, Octavio, 216, 245, 248, 249, 255
Pedro, Caio, 310
Pellicer, Carlos, 245
Peluchoneaux, Oscar, 312
Peña, Lázaro, 322
Pereira, Eugenio, 405
Pereira, Jimena, 11
Pérez, Onías, 193
Pérez Rosales, Vicente, 15
Perse, St. John, 436
Pétain, Henri (Marshall), 287
Petöfi, Sándor, 321
Petrarch, 352, 356
Pezoa Véliz, Carlos, 268, 271, 358
Philip II, 389
Picasso, Pablo, 174, 293, 309–310, 329, 379, 382, 392, 438, 453
Picón Salas, Mariano, 369

Pieres, Boya, 150–151

Pineda y Bascuñán, ——, 26

Pinilla, Norberto, 26

Pino, Yolando, 103

Pinochet, Augusto, 281, 288, 307, 418, 469, 474

Pizarro, Gabriela, 416

Plato, 251

Plaza, Rafael (Rafita), 359, 409

Plisetskaia, Maia, 349

Poblete, Dario, 312

Pola, Erika, 126

"Polentani, Francesca de," 66

Poleo, Héctor, 310, 382

Pompidou, Georges, 433, 450

Porset, Clara, 246

Portales, Manuelita, 77

Portinari, Cándido, 343, 382

Posada, Jaime, 257

Pound, Ezra, 190

Prado, Pedro, 387–388

Prats, Carlos, 451

Presa, Fernando de la, 166

Prestes, Luis Carlos, 254, 276, 489

Prieto, Jenaro, 193, 270

Prieto, Julio, 251

Prieto, Miguel, 244, 327

Pring-Mill, Robert, 450

Proudhon, Pierre, 41

Proust, Marcel, 55, 352

Pueyrredón, Manuel A., 411

Pushkin, Aleksander, 316–318, 349, 352, 402, 464

Queiroz, Eça de, 47

Quevedo y Villegas, Francisco Gómez de, 162, 193, 196, 198, 208, 253, 263–264, 352, 462, 487

Quintana, Antonio, 220, 321, 360, 369, 379

Quintana, Queta, 360, 473, 475

Quixote, Don, 28, 59, 300, 368, 392

Rafita. *See* Plaza, Rafael

Rapún, Rafael Rodríguez, 198

Ratnaigh, 137

Reagan, Ronald, 455

Recabarren, Luis Emilio, 52, 229, 266–267, 269, 274, 374, 439, 453

Recabarren González, Luis Emilio, 307

Recabarren González, Manuel Guillermo, 307

Recabarren Rojas, Manuel Segundo, 307–308

Rejano, Juan, 244, 251

Renn, Ludwig, 244

Revueltas, José, 251

Revueltas, Rosario, 248

Revueltas, Silvestre, 248

Reyes, Abdías, 7, 28

Reyes, Alfonso, 245, 322

Reyes, Amós, 7, 28, 147

Reyes, Enrique de los, 327

Reyes, Joel, 7, 28

Reyes, Oseas, 7, 28, 147

Reyes, Raúl (Raulillo), 145

Reyes, Rodolfo, 34–35, 122, 145, 154

Reyes, Salvador, 107

Reyes, Teresa de, 145

Reyes Candia, Laura, 25–27, 34–35, 38, 49, 58, 63, 122–124, 144–146, 149, 154, 163, 201, 382, 435, 475, 482

Reyes Hermosilla, José Angel, 6, 147

Reyes Morales, José del Carmen, 6, 7–10, 14, 17–18, 19–20, 54, 111, 170, 221–223, 284

Reyes Parada, José Angel, 10, 420

Reyes Toledo, Raúl, 14, 163

"Rhodo," 424, 429–432

Ribalkin, Igor, 12

Ricci, Paolo, 336

Riess, Frank, 371

Rilke, Rainer Maria, 108, 190, 251, 411

Rimbaud, Arthur, 29, 50, 125, 217, 330, 352

Rimbaud, Isabelle, 352

Ríos, Juan Antonio, 245, 271, 273, 278

"Rivas, Florencio," 91

"Rivas, Lorenzo," 40

Rivera, Diego, 29, 190, 310, 322, 327, 337, 344, 346, 375

Rivet, Paul, 310
Roa, Israel, 54
Roa Bastos, Augusto, 422
Roberto, Milton, 347
Robeson, Paul, 310, 312, 322, 453
Roca, Blas, 467
Rocco del Campo, Antonio, 55, 192
Roces, Wenceslao, 245, 246, 327
Rockefeller, John D., 344
Rodig, Laura, 29–30, 356
Rodríguez, Carlos Rafael, 322
Rodríguez, Germán, 409
Rodríguez, José, 300
Rodríguez, Manuel, 80, 371, 440
Rodríguez Arias, ——, 358
Rodríguez Monegal, Emir, 86, 397
Rohan, Duke of, 443–445
Rojas, Jorge, 257
Rojas, Manuel, 43, 107, 462
Rojas Giménez, Alberto, 53, 54, 55–58,
     105, 110, 487
Rojas Paz, Pablo, 160, 161, 357
Rokha, Pablo de, 58–62, 98, 101, 109,
     190, 193–196, 243
Rokha, Winett de, 194
Romero, Alberto, 216, 220
Rommel, Erwin (Field Marshall), 344
Roosevelt, Franklin D., 247, 291
Rosales (family), 201
Rosales, Luis, 181
"Rosaura," 120–121. See also Azócar
     Soto, Albertina Rosa; "Mari-
     sombra"; "Netocha"
"Rosía," 424, 429–432
Rossellini, Renzo (Roberto), 481
Ross Santa María, Gustavo, 230
Rostova, Natasha, 402
Rouget de Lisle, Claude Joseph, 352
Rubio, Alberto, 13
Ruiz, Eduardo, 52
Ruiz Alonso, Ramón, 201–202
Ruiz Ibárruri, Amaya and Rubén, 319
"Ruiz Lagorreta, Antonio," 298–299,
     306
Rulfo, Juan, 422

Saavedra Rodríguez, Cornelio, 15
Sabat Ercasty, Carlos, 36, 107, 186, 397
Sábato, Ernesto, 480
Sabella, Andrés, 30
Sadoul, Georges, 215, 216
Sáenz, Luis, 198
Sáez, Manuela, 381
Safronov, ——, 318
Salacrou, Armand, 310
Salas Viú, Vicente, 241
Salgari, Emilio, 28, 342
Salinas, Pedro, 164, 178, 181, 186
Samper, Darío, 257
Sancha, Clara, 392
Sánchez, Alberto (Cuban captain), 253
Sánchez, Alberto (Spanish sculptor),
     198, 392–393
Sánchez, Clara. See Sancha, Clara
Sánchez Vásquez, Adolfo, 245
Sandino, Augusto César, 383
Sanfuentes, Juan Luis, 44
Sanhueza, Jorge, 371, 396, 407–408
Sanin Cano, Baldomero, 320, 343
Sanjurjo, José (General), 426, 490
San Martín (priest), 9
Santaella Blanco, Antonio, 115
Santander, Carlos, 371
Santa Teresa, 167, 251
Santiván, Fernando, 344, 351
Sartre, Jean-Paul, 390
Savich, Ovadi, 318, 464
Scheler, Max, 372
Schmidt, Alfonso, 347
Schmidt, Johann Lorenz (Laszlo Rad-
     vanyi), 244
Schnake, Oscar, 42
Schneider, René, 426, 454
Schweitzer, Daniel, 42
Schwob, Marcel, 108
Scola, Ettore, 481
Scorza, Manuel, 462
Seferis, George (Giorgos Seferiades),
     436
Seghers, Anna, 244, 245–246, 310, 312,
     439

Seghers, Pierre, 310, 379
Seguel, Gerardo, 26, 54, 108, 333
Seoane, Luis, 310
Sepúlveda, Germán, 371
Serani, Alejandro (Sacha), 25, 53–54
Sereni, Emilio, 310
Serguiev, —— (Ambassador), 306
Serrano Plaja, Arturo, 164, 181, 241
Sforza, Count, 232
Shakespeare, William, 333, 399, 406
Shaw, George Bernard, 212, 406
Sheeko, Georgui, 12
Shelvocke, ——, 447
Shelley, Percy Bysshe, 330
Sholokhov, Mikhail, 310
Shostakovich, Dimitri, 310
Sicard, Alain, 156
Siéverova, Tamara Alexeievna, 306
Sijé, Ramón, 181, 183
Silva, Víctor Domingo, 269
Silva Castro, Raúl, 37, 488
Silvestre, J. B., 423
Simonov, Constantin, 318
Simpson, Wallis, 213
Siqueiros, Angélica. *See* Arenal,
    Angélica
Siqueiros, David Alfaro, 29, 245, 327,
    382
Sobrino, Eladio, 232, 409, 435
Solá, María Magdalena, 371
Solimano, Delia, 81–82
Solimano, Manuel, 81–82, 334, 404
Somlyó, György, 321
Somoza (dynasty), 316
Somoza, Anastasio, 383
Soto Rodríguez, Juana, 85
Stalin, Joseph, 349
Stevenson, Robert L., 138
Storni, Alfonsina, 160
Stravinsky, Igor, 212
Strindberg, August, 28
Suárez, Luis, 459
Subercaseaux, Benjamín, 373, 462
Sue, Eugène, 382
Sully-Prudhomme, René, 29

Sun Yat-sen, Madame, 350
Supervielle, Jules, 309

Tagore, Rabindranath, 185, 192–193, 251
Tallone, Alberto and Bianca, 390
Tamayo, Rufino, 382
Tapia, Astolfo, 340
Tapia, César, 280
Tchernigov, Anatoli, 12
Teitelboim, Claudio, 373, 484
Teitelboim, Eliana. *See* Farías, Eliana
Teitelboim, Marina, 435, 441, 442, 449
"Terusa" (Teresa), 64–75, 88, 192. *See*
    also "Marisol"
Thaelmann, Ernst, 253
Thayer, Silvia, 113, 115
Theodorakis, Mikis, 481
Thirion, André, 213
Tikhonov, Nicolai, 318
Togliatti, Palmiro, 248
Tolstoy, Leo, 32
Tomic, Radomiro, 265, 417, 473
Toral, Mario, 423
Tornú de Rojas Paz, Sara, 162, 466
Torrealba, Ernesto, 28, 32
Torre Nilsson, Leopoldo, 406
Torres Rioseco, Arturo, 108
Traven, Bruno, 439
Trigo, Felipe, 28
Triolet, Elsa, 177, 236, 238, 239, 310,
    380
Tristán, Flora, 377
Truman, Harry S, 284, 288
Tupolev, Andrei, 453
Turner de Jara, Joan, 476–477
Tzara, Tristan, 211

Ugalde, Pedro León, 42, 148
Ugarte, Eduardo, 244
Uhse, Bobo, 244
Umaña Bernal, José, 257
Unamuno, Miguel de, 44–45, 57, 83,
    178, 190, 198, 473
Ungaretti, Giuseppe, 190
Uribe, Armando, 58

Uribe, María de la Luz, 58
Urrutia, Matilde (Neruda), 4–6, 11,
    64, 120, 152, 175, 326, 328, 331,
    334–341, 349, 360–362, 365–366,
    369–370, 373–375, 379–383, 390,
    403–405, 410, 414, 419, 426–
    427, 428, 429, 432, 434, 438,
    440–443, 446, 448–449, 461,
    464–466, 468–475, 478–485
Urrutia, Práxedes, 393

Valdivia, Pedro de, 44
Valencia, Gerardo, 257
Valencia, Guillermo, 282
Valente, Julio, 44
Valenzi, Maurizio, 481
Valéry, Paul, 282
Valin, Ninon, 174
Valle, Juvencio (Concha Riffo, Gil-
    berto), 20–23, 28, 220, 366, 470
Valle, Rosamel del, 54, 194
Valle-Inclán, Ramón del, 162, 282
Vallejo, César, 144, 165, 208, 216, 221,
    251, 363, 453
Varas, José Miguel, 382, 411
Varela, Alfredo, 309–310, 336
Varela, Lorenzo, 244
Vargas, Getúlio, 254
Vargas Salazar, —— (Dr.), 468
Vargas Vila, José María, 28
Vasallo, Carlos, 338, 403
Vasallo, Carmen, 403
Vasconcelos, José, 110
Vásquez, Teresa. See "Marisol";
    "Terusa"
Veas, Angel, 313
Velasco, Francisco, 375
Velasco Ibarra, José María, 316
Venturelli, José, 280, 307, 311, 481
Vergara, Anamaría, 402
Verísimo (Brother), 362
Verlaine, Paul, 29, 257, 352
Verne, Jules, 28
Vial, Sara, 369, 376, 394
Viaux, Roberto, 418, 426, 454
Victoria (Queen), 141

Vicuña Fuentes, Carlos, 108, 148, 152,
    220, 340
Vidal, Virginia, 473
Vidali, Vittorio (Commander Carlos),
    248
Videla Pineda, Alfredo, 84
Vilarín, Cástor, 152
Villamediana, Count of (Juan de Tar-
    sis), 198, 253, 352
Vitorini, Elio, 310
Vitti, Mónica, 481
Vivanco, Luis Felipe, 164, 181
Volonté, Gian María, 481

Walker Larraín, Horacio, 274
Wallace, Henry, 322
Wassilewska, Wanda, 310
Waugh, Evelyn, 212
Weiner, Judith, 220, 321
Wells, H. G., 202
Wendt, Leonel, 138
Werneck, —— (painter), 347
Whitman, Walt, 108, 139, 251, 344–346,
    369, 410, 411, 447, 454
Wilde, Oscar, 212
Wilson, Blanca, 62
Winter, Augusto, 86, 102, 199
Wong, Federico, 456

Xirau, Joaquín, 250
Xirgu, Margarita, 199

Yáñez, Alvaro (Juan Emar), 148–149
Yáñez, Eliodoro, 149
Yeats, William Butler, 190
"Yegulev, Sachka," 40, 49, 97
Yevtushenko, Eugenio, 411
Yin Yin, 328
Yurkievich, Saúl, 371

Zalamea, Jorge, 257
Zañartu, Enrique, 382
Zola, Emile, 291
Zorrilla, Américo, 306–307
Zweig, Arnold, 310
Zweig, Stefan, 328